ARCHITECTURAL DIAGRAMS

ARCHITECTURAL 1
DIAGRAMS
346 PROJECTS OF 83 DESIGN TEAMS

The *Deutsche Nationalbibliothek* lists this publication in the *Deutsche Nationalbibliografie*; detailed bibliographic data are available in the Internet at http://dnb.d-nb.de.

ISBN 978-3-86922-148-9 (2 vol.)

© 2010 by DAMDI Publishing Co., Seoul/Korea
© 2011 by DOM publishers, Berlin/Germany
www.dom-publishers.com

This work is subject to copyright. All rights reserved. No part of this publication may be reproduced, stored in a retrieval system, or transferred, in any form or by any means, electronic, mechanical, photocopying, recording, or otherwise, without the prior written permission of the publishers. Sources and owners of rights are stated to the best of our knowledge; please signal any we might have omitted.

Editor	Miyoung Pyo
Design	Minjung Bang
Assistant	Sueun Bae, Kyungyoung Roh, Jieun Lee

ARCHITECTURAL DIAGRAMS

ESSAY
■
PUBLIC SPACE
■
LANDSCAPE
■
URBAN DESIGN

DOM publishers

CONTENTS

ARCHITECTURAL DIAGRAMS vol.1

ESSAY

010 **Jungwoo Ji**   Partner, eu concept / New York Partner, BAU Architects

PUBLIC SPACE

018 **AALBORG HARBOUR BATH**   JDS Architects
020 **A BUILDING FOR BOOKS**   Z-A Studio & Studio ST
022 **ALTIENS BATHHOUSE**   JDS Architects
024 **ARNHEM CENTRAL**   UNStudio
026 **BARCELONA ENCANTS**   JDS Architects
028 **BELGIAN PAVILION SHANGHAI**   JDS Architects
030 **BICYCLE STORAGE**   VMX Architects
032 **BULLFIGHTER'S COSTUME**   nodo17 Architects
034 **BUTCHER'S BRIDGE**   SADAR VUGA ARHITEKTI
036 **CWBG**   NL Architects
038 **DUBLIN DOCKLANDS OPEN AIR BATH**   JDS Architects
040 **DUNE TERRACE**   nARCHITECTS
042 **DUSTY RELIEF / B-MU**   R&Sie architects
044 **ENTERTAINMENT COMPLEX**   MANUELLE GAUTRAND ARCHITECTURE
046 **EXTENSION OF THE LILLE MODERN ART MUSEUM**   MANUELLE GAUTRAND ARCHITECTURE
048 **FILMMUSEUM**   NL Architects
050 **FLOATING ISLANDS**   Vincent Callebaut Architectrue
052 **GENERAL AVIATION TERMINAL**   VMX Architects
054 **GRAND EGYPTIAN MUSEUM**   JDS Architects
056 **GRONINGER FORUM**   NL Architects
058 **GROUNDNOISE SCHIPHOL**   NL Architects
060 **GUBEN GUBIN**   J. MAYER H. ARCHITECTS
062 **GUIYANG HUAXI URBAN CENTRE**   Serie Architects
064 **HEALTH SCIENCES CAMPUS**   Serie Architects
066 **HELSINGOR PSYCHIATRIC HOSPITAL**   JDS Architects
068 **HIGH SQUARE**   JDS Architects
070 **HIGHWAY...ING**   SMAQ
072 **HUA_CULTURAL & SHOPPING CENTER**   JDS Architects
074 **INCOGNITO**   AA+U partnership for Architecture, art and urbanism

076	**LAVA LAND**	NL Architects
078	**LES HALLES**	PERIQHERIQUES architects
080	**LIBRARY**	ma0
082	**LIGHT HOUSE**	Re_Load
084	**LINDESNES CULTURE SQUARE**	JDS Architects
086	**LJUBLJANA PASSENGER STATION**	SADAR VUGA ARHITEKTI
088	**LK 0**	AMID [cero9]
090	**LOW ENERGY HOUSING**	JDS Architects
092	**MARITIME YOUTH HOUSE**	JDS Architects
094	**MARKET IN SANCHINARRO**	Leon11 ARCHITECTS
096	**MENSA KARLSRUHE**	J. MAYER H. ARCHITECTS
098	**METRO D**	IaN+
100	**MM**	AMID [cero9]
102	**MUSEUM NEUHAUS LIAUNIG COLLECTION**	SADAR VUGA ARHITEKTI
104	**MUZIEKPALEIS**	NL Architects
106	**MY SCHOOL IS A FLOWER**	IaN+
108	**NEURONAL ALIEN**	Vincent Callebaut Architectrue
110	**NEW TERAMO THEATRE COMPLEX**	IaN+
112	**NURSERY SCHOOL**	mxg architects
114	**PADUA AUDITORIUM**	kadawittfeldarchitektur
116	**PINAUL FOUNDATION FOR CENTEMPORARY ART**	MANUELLE GAUTRAND ARCHITECTURE
118	**PONTE PARODI**	UNStudio
120	**PROSTNESET TERMINAL**	SPACEGROUP
122	**RED BAOBAB**	Vincent Callebaut Architectrue
124	**REEFMOD**	servo
126	**ROLLING AQUA CENTER**	JDS Architects
128	**SALZBURG CENTRAL STATION**	kadawittfeldarchitektur
130	**SAMI CULTURAL CENTRE**	Galvez + Wieczorek
132	**SCHOOL IN ROME**	ma0
134	**SCOOP**	SMAQ
136	**SHENZHEN INTERNATIONAL AIRPORT - TERMINAL 3**	Reiser + Umemoto RUR Architecture PC
138	**SJAKKET**	JDS Architects
140	**SPINDERIHALLERNE**	JDS Architects
142	**SPORT PARK**	nodo17 Architects
144	**STAVANGER CONCERT HALL**	JDS Architects
146	**STOCKHOLM'S GARDEN LIBRARY**	JDS Architects

148	**STRIJP S**	NL Architects
150	**TAIPEI PERFORMING ARTS CENTER**	NL Architects
152	**TAIPEI PERFORMING ARTS CENTER**	Serie Architects
154	**TALLINN TOWN HALL**	BIG
156	**THEATRE AGORA**	UNStudio
158	**THUNNUS THYNNUS**	nodo17 Architects
160	**TITTOT GLASS MUSEUM**	IaN+
162	**TREVISO CULTURAL CENTRE**	Re_Load
164	**WELZIJNSCLUSTER ZOETERMEER**	SeARCH
166	**WROCŁAW 2012**	Guallart Architects
168	**X SITE**	NL Architects
170	**ZWALUWEN UTRECHT 1911**	NL Architects

LANDSCAPE

174	**A 10 HOGHWAY**	kadawittfeldarchitektur
176	**A8ERNA**	NL Architects
178	**BATOUTZ PORT AND OCEAN PLAZA**	Guallart Architects
180	**BAYWATCH**	PEG office of landscape + architecture
182	**BIOBOX**	servo
184	**BONN SQUARE**	CJ Lim | Studio 8 Architects
186	**COMPOSER TUBIN MONUMENT**	Zizi&Yoyo
188	**ELEFTHERIA SQUARE**	AA+U partnership for Architecture, art and urbanism
190	**ESA STAHLHOF**	plattformberlin
192	**FREGENE SEASIDE**	2TR ARCHITETTURA
194	**FROM FLOWER TO FLOWER**	nodo17 Architects
196	**FUGEE PORT**	Guallart Architects
198	**GARDEN IN BARI**	ma0
200	**GUANGMING SUSTAINABLE PARK**	CJ Lim | Studio 8 Architects
202	**HAG ST. JOSEPH**	plattformberlin
204	**HEART OF MAGOK IS NATURE OF LIVING WATER**	Samoo Architects & Engineers
206	**INDRE SOGN ARTS CENTRE**	IaN+
208	**ISOLE D'ACQUA**	NL Architects
210	**JOIE DE VIE(W)**	PEG office of landscape + architecture
212	**KALEIDOSCOPE STREET**	Re_Load

214 **KEELUNG**   Guallart Architects

216 **LA JOLIETTE**   plattformberlin

218 **LINEAR PARK**   Galvez + Wieczorek

220 **MASDAR PLAZA, OASIS OF THE FUTURE**   LAVA

222 **MIES VAN DER ROHE PLAZA**   PEG office of landscape + architecture

224 **NANYU SHOPPING PARK**   CJ Lim | Studio 8 Architects

226 **ON CANAL STREET**   beva

228 **OPATIJA NEW SQUARE**   PSA

230 **PLANKEN MANNHEIM**   plattformberlin

232 **PLAYA LAVA**   J. MAYER H. ARCHITECTS

234 **P.O.R.T**   nARCHITECTS

236 **PUBLIC GRADATION ON GREEN ARMED PLAZA**   Jungwoo Ji

238 **ROZZOL MELARA**   ma0

240 **SCHOOLS**   ONE ARCHITECTURE

242 **SENSATIONAL PARK**   NABITO ARQUITECTURA

244 **SQUARE IN COPENHAGUEN**   Leon11 ARCHITECTS

246 **THE NEW ENTRANCE TO TJÖRN**   gunnarsson pettersson

248 **TRONDHEIM FJORDPARK**   JDS Architects

250 **UPGRADE PILONI**   NABITO ARQUITECTURA S.C.P

252 **URBAN STUDY**   beva

254 **VINARÒS PROJECT**   Guallart Architects

256 **VOSSELVELD**   ONE ARCHITECTURE

258 **WATERCOURSE**   PEG office of landscape + architecture

260 **WATER PARK**   Ecosistema Urbano + TECTUM

URBAN DESIGN

264 **ALMERE HOUT**   ma0

266 **BADAJOZ CH 852**   Leon 11 ARCHITECTS

268 **BRUSSELS ADMINISTRATIVE CITY**   JDS Architects

270 **BRUXELLES LANDSFLOW**   Actar Arquitectura

272 **CAMPUS BORDEAUX**   Tania Conko Architects

274 **CARLSBERG VORES BY**   Leon 11 ARCHITECTS

276 **CBO COTTBUS**   plattformberlin

278 **CIPPS**   2TR ARCHITETTURA

280	**CONTEMPORARY RAUMPLAN**	EBPC
282	**CUMULUS**	SMAQ
284	**CRYSTAL PALACE**	mxg architects
286	**DOTSANDLOOPS**	SMAQ
288	**DUTCH MOUNTAINS**	ONE ARCHITECTURE
290	**ECO VILLAGE RIGA**	Iotti+Pavarani Architetti
292	**FBM PERUGIA**	EBPC
294	**FILIPSTAD**	SPACEGROUP
296	**FOSHAN SANSUI URBAN PLAN**	Reiser+Umemoto RUR Architecture PC
298	**GPRU PORTE DE MONTREUIL**	ONE ARCHITECTURE
300	**HICAT: NEW PORT, NEW CITY**	Willy Müller Architects
302	**IFCCA 42ND-23RD STREET**	UNStudio
304	**KLM**	BIG
306	**L.A.R.S**	SMAQ
308	**LA PIROTTERIE**	PERIQHERIQUES architects
310	**LACTARIUS**	nodo17 Architects
312	**LES HALLES**	ONE ARCHITECTURE
314	**LJ:SONIC POLDER**	Bernd Kniess Architects Urban Planners
316	**MAPPING:PLAY**	Bernd Kniess Architects Urban Planners
318	**MARITIME FRONT OF ALMERIA**	Willy Müller Architects
320	**MAYDAY**	data architects
322	**NETWORKING FOR THE MULTI-FUNCTIONAL ADMINISTRATIVE CITY**	Jungwoo Ji
324	**NEW TAINAN TAIWAN BY DESIGN**	Willy Müller Architects
326	**NOUVEAU BASSIN**	ECDM
328	**OSAKA CENTRAL STATION AREA**	IaN+
330	**PANIC&PLANTING**	Bernd Kniess Architects Urban Planners
332	**PERFUMED JUNGLE**	Vincent Callebaut Architectrue
334	**REFILLING GREEN**	Re_Road
336	**SEEDS AND VECTOR**	Enrique Arenas Laorga & Luis Basabe Montalvo
338	**SLOW TOWN VEMA**	Iotti + Pavarani Architetti
340	**STEPSCAPE – GREENSCAPE - WATERSCAPE**	Florian Krieger
342	**STU CAMPUS**	CJ Lim | Studio 8 Architects
344	**SUBURBAN FRAMES**	Florian Krieger
346	**SUN-FIELDS**	Florian Krieger
348	**THE URBAN CORSET, A HYBRID INTERMEDIARY**	Vincent Callebaut Architectrue

350	**TOUCHING WATER**	b4architects
352	**URBAN LIVING ROOMS**	Iotti+Pavarani Architetti
354	**URBAN VOIDS**	Ecosistema Urbano + TECTUM
356	**VELIKA PLAZA**	SPACEGROUP & JDS Architects
358	**VEMA**	ma0
360	**VORESBY CARLSBERG**	ECDM
362	**WEST SIDE CONVERGENCE**	Reiser+Umemoto RUR Architecture PC
364	**WID**	Bernd Kniess Architects Urban Planners
366	**WIESENFELD**	Florian Krieger
368	**WORLD VILLAGE OF WOMEN SPORTS**	BIG
370	**XERITOWN**	SMAQ & X Architects
372	**ZAKUSALA RIGA**	SPACEGROUP
374	**ZIRA ISLAND MASTERPLAN**	BIG
376	**ZOETERMEER AFRIKAWEG**	ONE ARCHITECTURE
378	**3X2 - ELEMENTS FOR THE URBAN LANDSCAPE**	Florian Krieger
380	**16 DWELLINGS CHERLEVILLE-MÉZIÈRES**	mxg architects
382	**288 DWELLINGS**	mxg architects

ARCHITECTURAL DIAGRAMS vol.2

394 ARCHITECTURE

548 INTERIOR DESIGN

628 INSTALLATION

726 PROFILE & INDEX

Jungwoo Ji
(Partner, eu concept /
New York Partner, BAU Architects)

Diagram as Design Tool

`Diagram` is one of the most used words in architecture and urban design. There's always the thought, "We need some diagrams to explain the idea."
As one usually says, "If we draw the parti-diagram, we can show it as these two parts.", diagram is seen as a tool to deliver an idea. However, it is more than simply showing the client, the public, or the boss to help them understand the idPea. It is an element of design in itself.

Depending on the well-ness of the organization of the diagrams, they can become the ideas that perfectly visualize the context of the site. For example, Rem Koolhaas' Seattle Library's massing was the product of the program diagram derived from the reinterpretation of change in program due to change in time. We can also often see the diagram being the initial concept as well as the final product like Zainie Zainul's winning proposal of Shinkenchiku Residential Competition: Another Glass House in 1991 where Tadao Ando was the judge.

Although there are moments of unclear boundaries with a sketch or a concept model, I think a diagram is more of an intended expression coming from the head than a result that is created by new ideas coming from experiments that happen within unconsciousness of the fingertips. Although there are various ways to express ideas, such as physical model, sketch, cartoon, computer model, or photography, a diagram takes the initial step to become a design tool by its ability to deliver the idea very clearly and precisely in minimal form. Therefore, like the final design product, architect's unique style of creativity is an important factor in the diagram as well.

The finished form of architecture is a space that is felt and remembered without any special descriptions or diagrams, and some that leaves behind sentimentality is impossible to be explained by diagrams. Also, there is no guarantee that people will read and remember the architecture by the exact intentions expressed by the diagrams. The so-called 'master of architecture' architects may not need diagrams to create their masterpiece - they have their recipes and senses. However, the society is becoming more complex. There is an increase in information and desires of the city, where architecture is the design subject. With broad issues including material, environment, ecology, and behavior, clear diagram becomes more important within today. This applies especially to the young architects yet to be stable, and I, as well, have my architectural mind into diagrammatic form in order to communicate more clearly within the design process and also to develop the design itself.

ESSAY

"THE SOCIETY MORE COMP INCREASE IN AND DESIRES BROAD ISSUES TERIAL, ENVIRO OGY, AND BE DIAGRAM BE IMPORTANT

S BECOMING
X. THERE IS AN
IFORMATION
 THE CITY. WITH
ICLUDING MA-
IMENT, ECOL-
AVIOR, CLEAR
OMES MORE
THIN TODAY."

Many things said by diagrams
These are some of the diagrams from the projects I, alone or in a team, participated in the last few years.

(Urban Territory, 1995)
In creating a diagram, architects occasionally use hands as well. It can bee seen in Le Corbusier's hands depicting the plug-in units of Unite d'Habitation or Coop Himmelblau's two hands in action to describe the concept. The concept of a pulley was thought for the height difference of the opposite rooms within one residential unit and the change in view of the skyline outside when looking out from one point of view inside.

(Contemporary Narratives, 1996)
'In the competition where the topic was 'Korean Aesthetic', I approached it differently than the other projects. Whereas the others created architectural form and space by it representing traditional symbols, I created Seoul itself as the icon of 'Korea Aesthetic' because it holds the trace of everyday lives that make up the city today. It was the idea as well as the final product.

(Earthing System, 1997)
This diagram expresses that the influential circulation system of the elements that make up residence, such as the roof, human, skin, earth, is the residence itself. The one that influences and communicates with each other is the 'technology', and is the developed form of fire found by human.

(Seoul City Hall Plaza Pavilion, 2003)
The hand-drawn drawing illustrates the structure, and two different images are expressed to show the options that different situations are possible. It is a key diagram to illustrate the concept of flexibility within public space; there's a screen to be seen from inside the pavilion, and a bigger screen to be seen from the outer plaza.

(Chicago Water Taxi Stop, 2004)
The main design concept was to express the water movement created by a moving water taxi on the platform as an oversized illustration. There are times where the situation at the end of the sequential diagram is portrayed.

(Fligh 93 Memorial, 2004)
A dark tube is created to depict the place of plane crash caused by terrorists, and glass blocks are placed at the top of the roof to resemble the victims. During the day, the light from the sky will be filled into the tube, and during the night, the tube will spill out light unto the sky. On the memorial day of the victims, the one day of the year, the light that will penetrate through the tube and onto the ground is shown in concise arrows.

(MPPAT, 2007)
A cartoon diagram illustrating the various use of the exterior space because of the form of the ground plane, and that the exterior space connects different government offices.

(Blogram, 2007)
Creation of a new concept, 'Blogram= Blog + Diagram'. 2D and 3D diagrammatic illustrations of everyday positings of a blog and its responses were created to experiment the possibility of creating an architectural form through simple data. I also thought that there might be a meaning to simply visualize writings and communication into diagrammatic form.

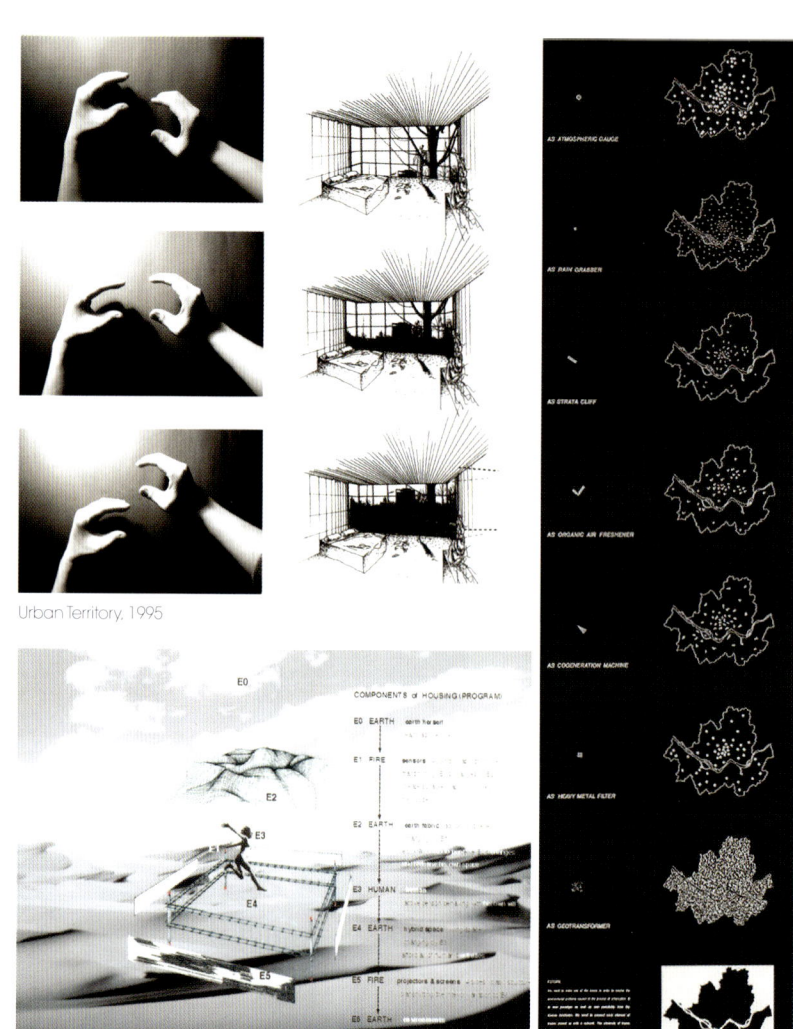

Urban Territory, 1995

Earthing System, 1997

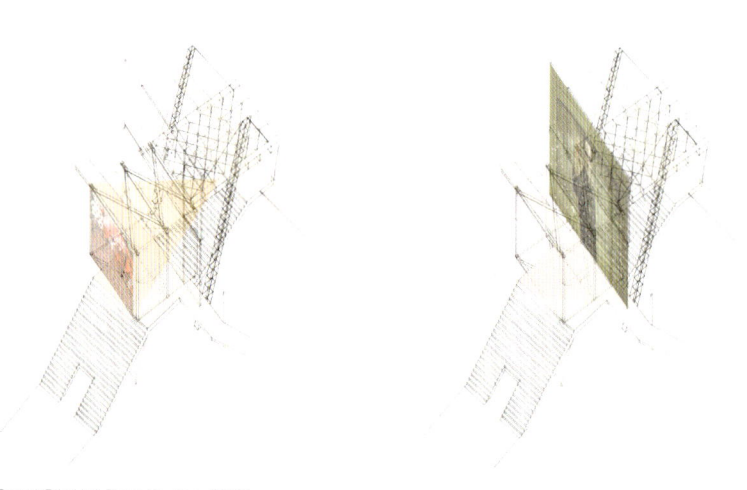

Contemporary Narratives, 1996

(Seoul City Hall Plaza Pavilion, 2003)

LIGHTING SITUATION : DAYTIME
SKY -> MEMORIAL

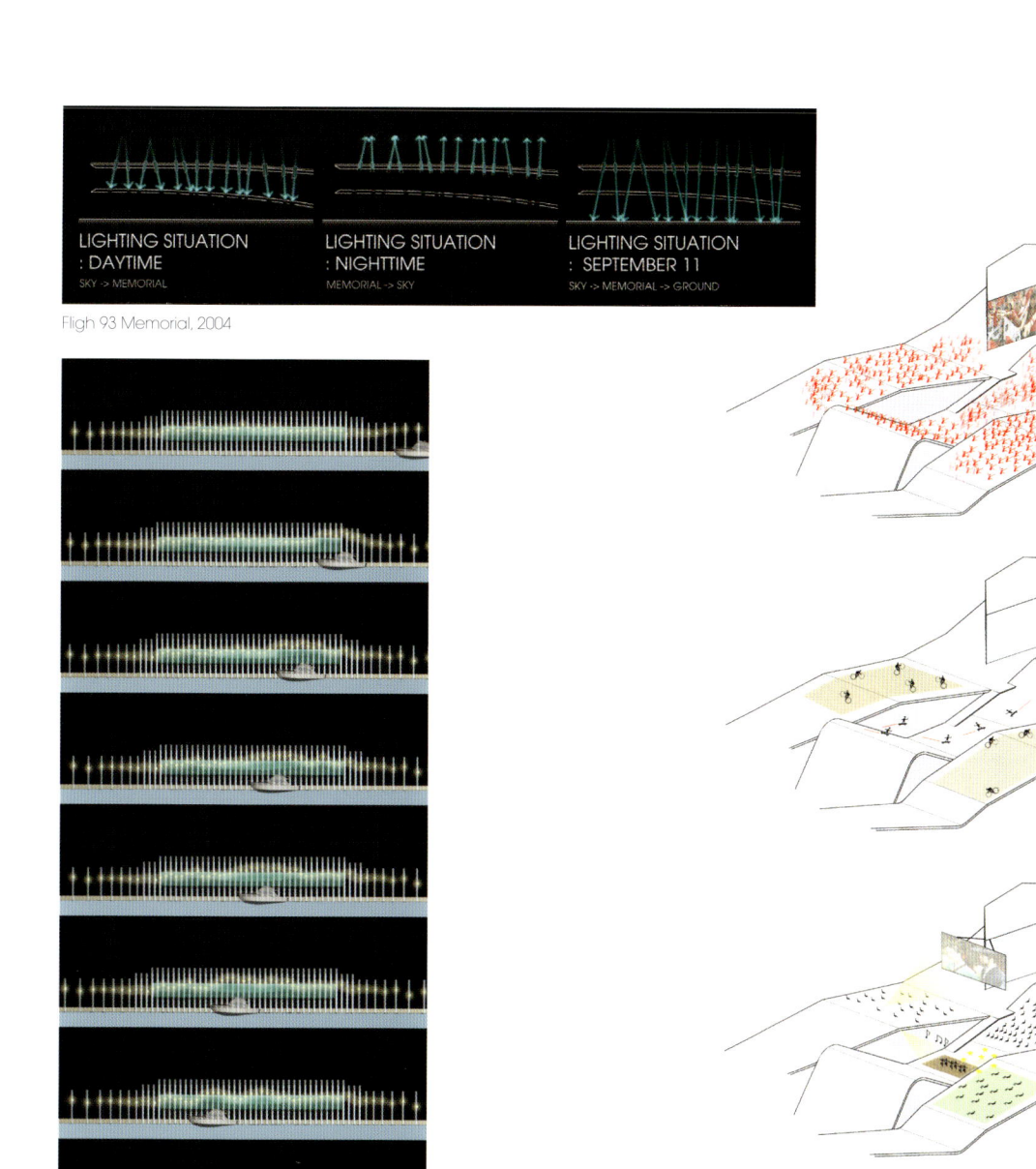

LIGHTING SITUATION : NIGHTTIME
MEMORIAL -> SKY

LIGHTING SITUATION : SEPTEMBER 11
SKY -> MEMORIAL -> GROUND

Fligh 93 Memorial, 2004

Chicago Water Taxi Stop, 2004

Blogram, 2007

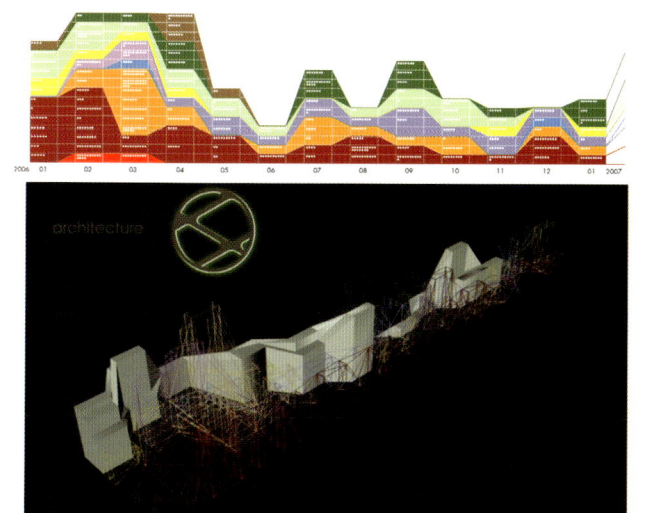

MPPAT, 2007

ARCHITECTURAL DIAGRAMS 013

(ooZoo, 2007)
It is a proposal of a new type of a zoo, where an animal does or does not have to look like he is trapped in, and be physically visited by a person. It is an idea where a person is able to 'commune with the animal' without actually facing him, or have 'awareness of the animal' in everyday life. At the bus stops of the city, there is a device that connects with one where the animals live and play. Through this device, person and animal is able to be aware of each other's change through subtle signals.

(City Tower, 2008)
This diagram is an illustration of a very simple cylindrical tower being used as the city's canvas, and how the experience is not vertical but rotational. Through this, the user will experience the city 360 degrees, and it becomes a place where only sky can be viewed.

(Seoul Bench, 2008)
Although it's a bench where people can sit on, it's also a frame where plants can grow on. The design intent was to have it become a part of nature and a part of landscape as time pass by.

(Green Armed Plaza, 2008)
When one layer is added to the plaza, the units forming the layer gradually changes, and then is followed by the vegetation and activity, which is shown in 3D model and image.

(Grand Narratives, 2009)
Get help from the artists living around the area. This diagram illustrates how those do not own a home in the area, but live in the area can become the owners of the streets by making fabric circular tubes with their pictures and artworks on them and hanging them at the streets. These will gather rain water for the plants below and create scenery of a wave by the wind.

(North Bund Landscape, 2008)
It is a parti-diagram expressing the concept of securing diverse direction of view within the overall flow of riverside landscape.

(A-co Landscape, 2009)
As the boundary between city, architecture, and machine disappears these days, it is important to show the operating principles of that machine in one sight. The pressure created by human activity changes into electricity that operates a machine that purifies water and turn on lights and night. It is the illustration of the paradoxical situation where, the more human activity, the more improvement in natural environment.

(Korea Tourism & Culture Center in New York, 2009)
Although it does not look like this in the actual architecture, the building was unfolded and the circulation path was drawn from the ground to the top floor to illustrate continuous path of circulation. It can be seen very easily how the city skyline is experienced through the composition of each space according to its landscape.

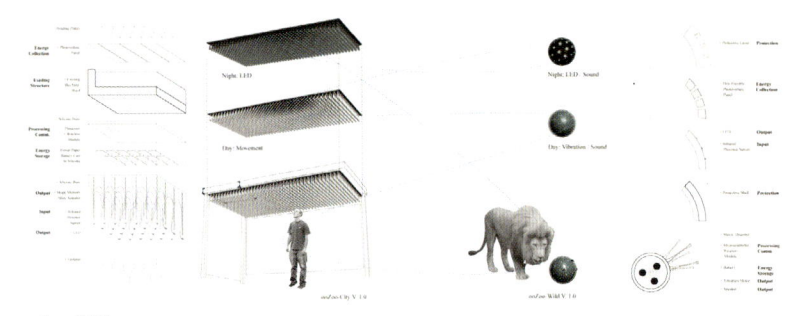

ooZoo, 2007

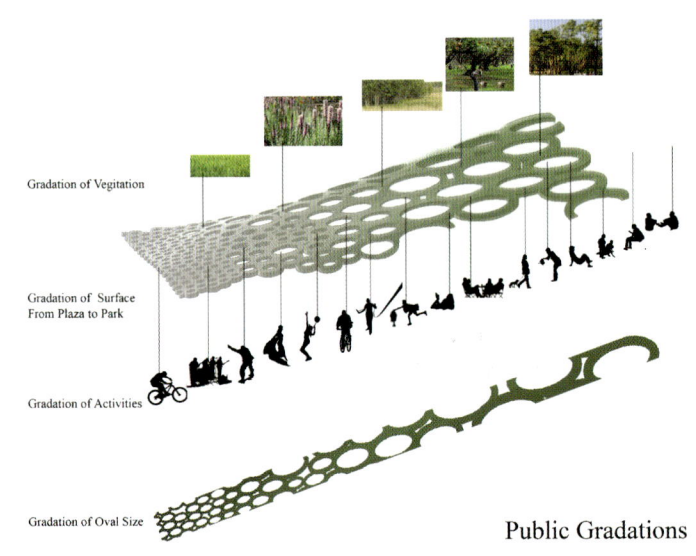

City Tower, 2008

Seoul Bench, 2008

Green Armed Plaza, 2008

Public Gradations

PHOTO BY LOCAL PHOTOGRAPHERS

PRINT ON TRANSLUCENT BANNER FABRIC

PRINT ART WORK

NEEDLEWORK

TWINKLE UNDER THE SUN

WAVE BY WIND

RAINDROP TO LANDSCAPE

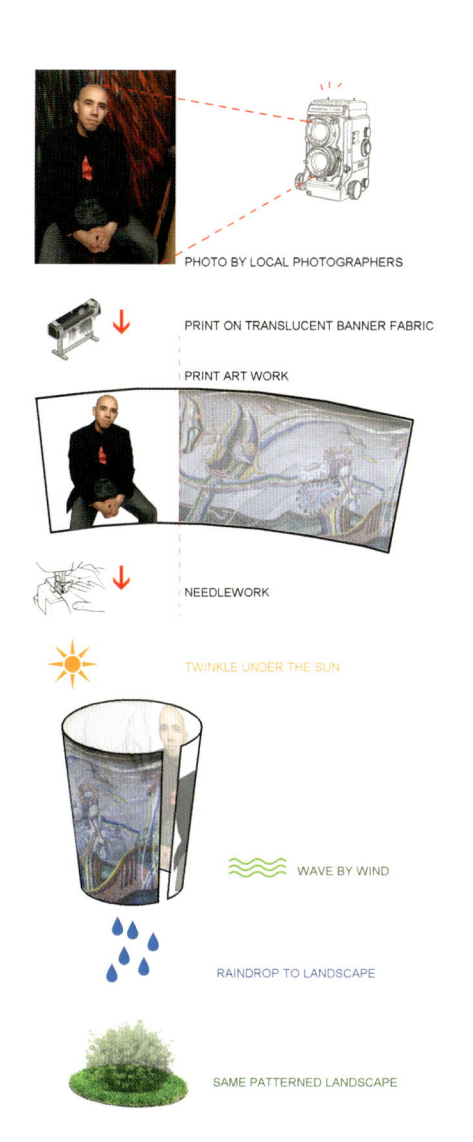

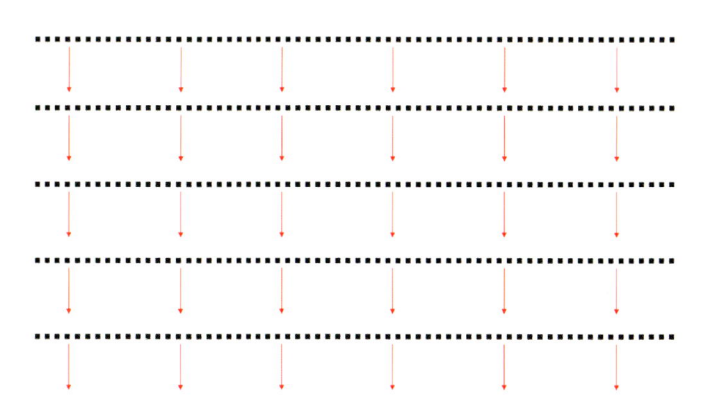

SAME PATTERNED LANDSCAPE

Grand Narratives, 2009

ONE DIRECTION

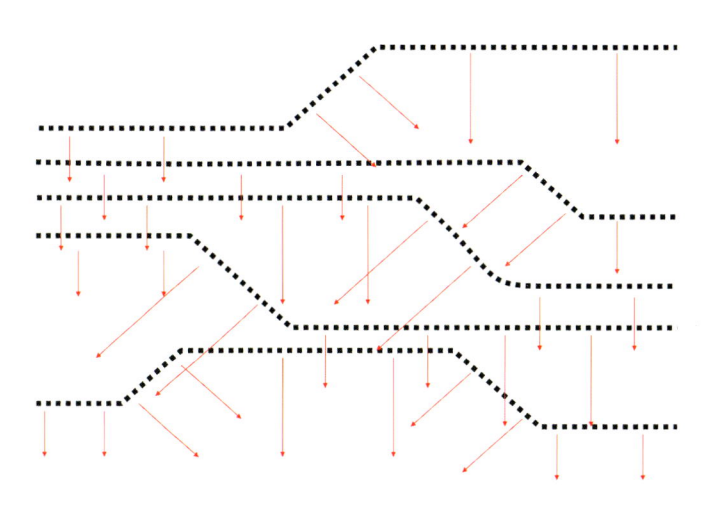

VARIOUS DIRECTIONS

North Bund Landscape, 2008

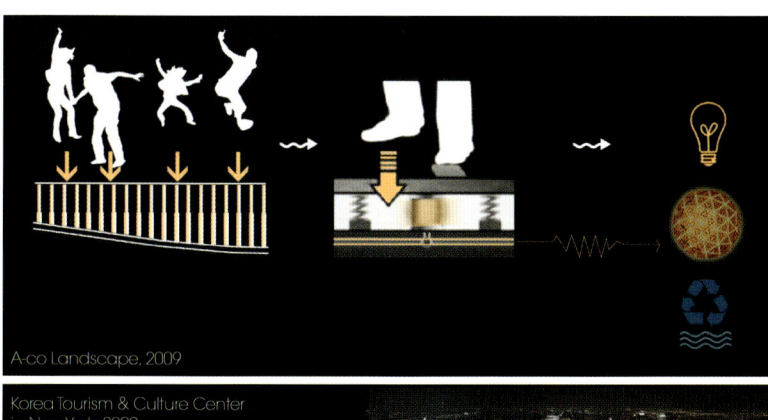

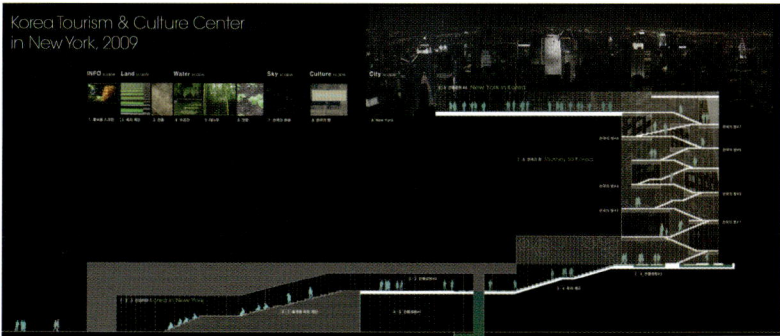

A-co Landscape, 2009

Korea Tourism & Culture Center in New York, 2009

ARCHITECTURAL DIAGRAMS 015

PUBLIC SPACE

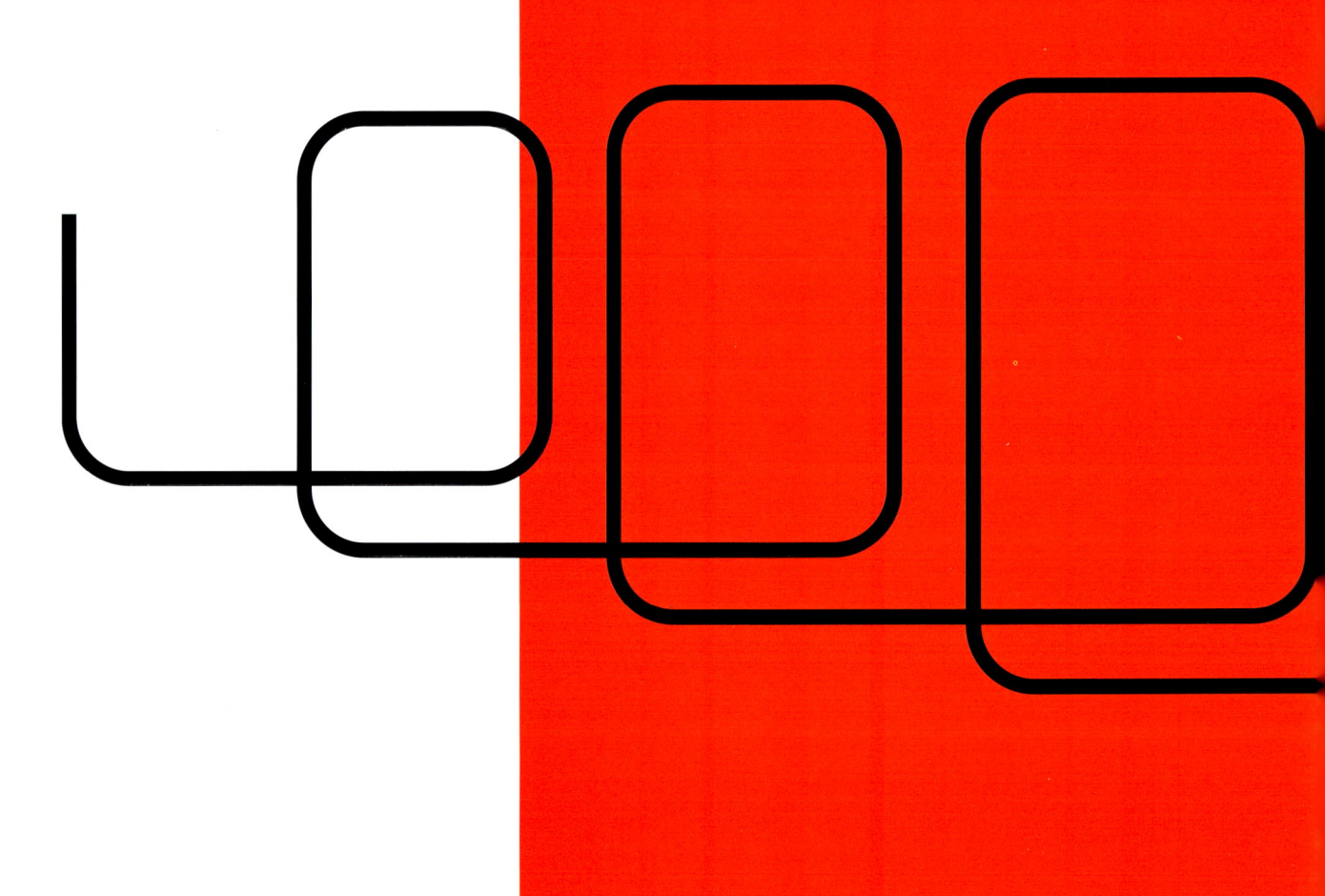

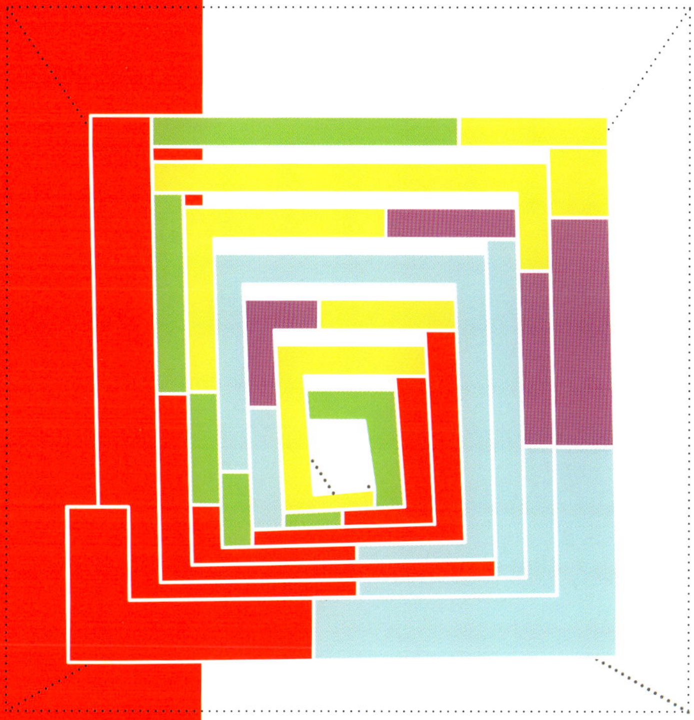

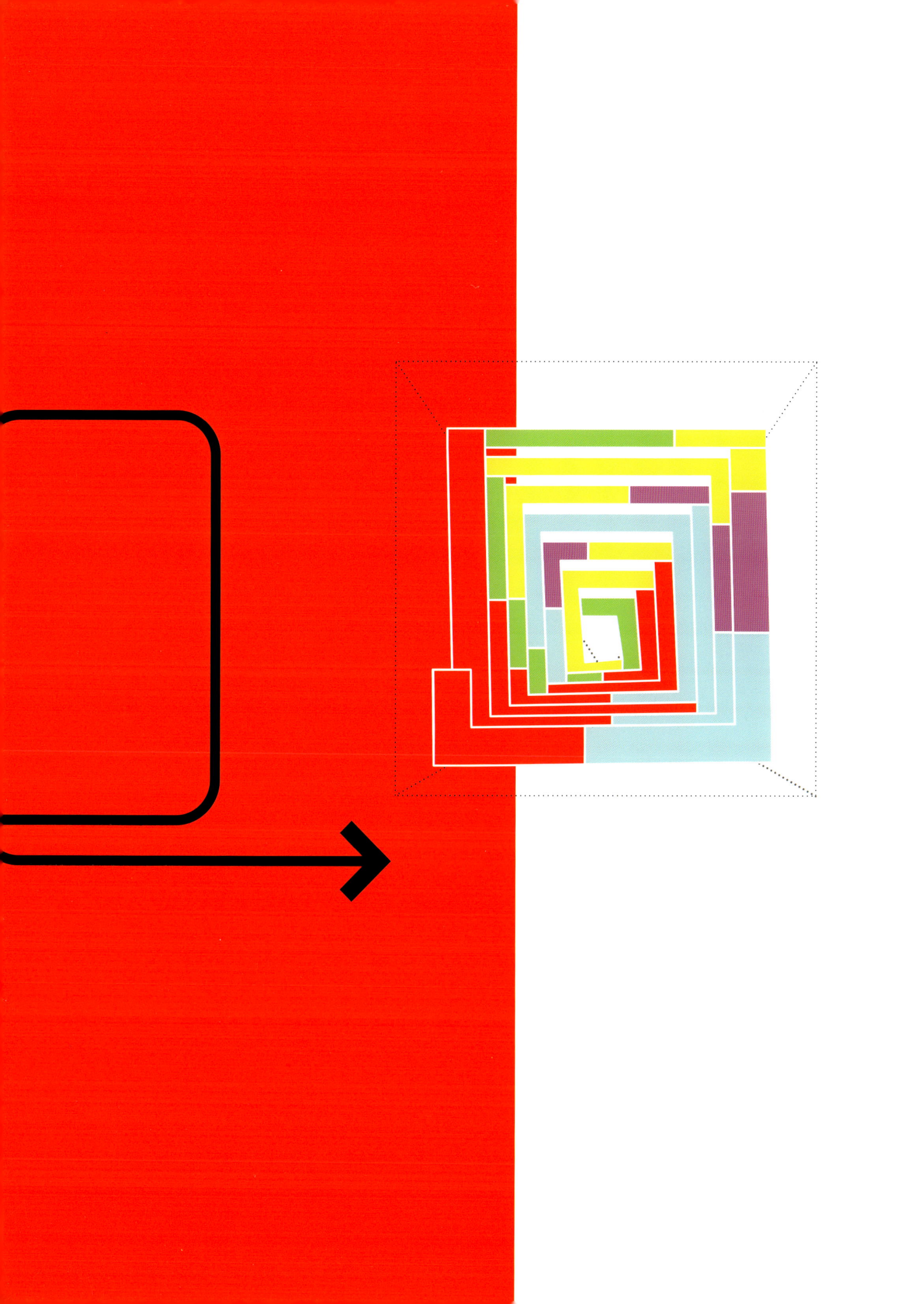

AALBORG HARBOUR
BATH JDS Architects

"ITS VISUAL AND PHYSICAL CONNECTIONS WITH THE SURROUNDING CONTEXT HAVE BEEN IMPORTANT IN THE DESIGN PROCESS."

Context

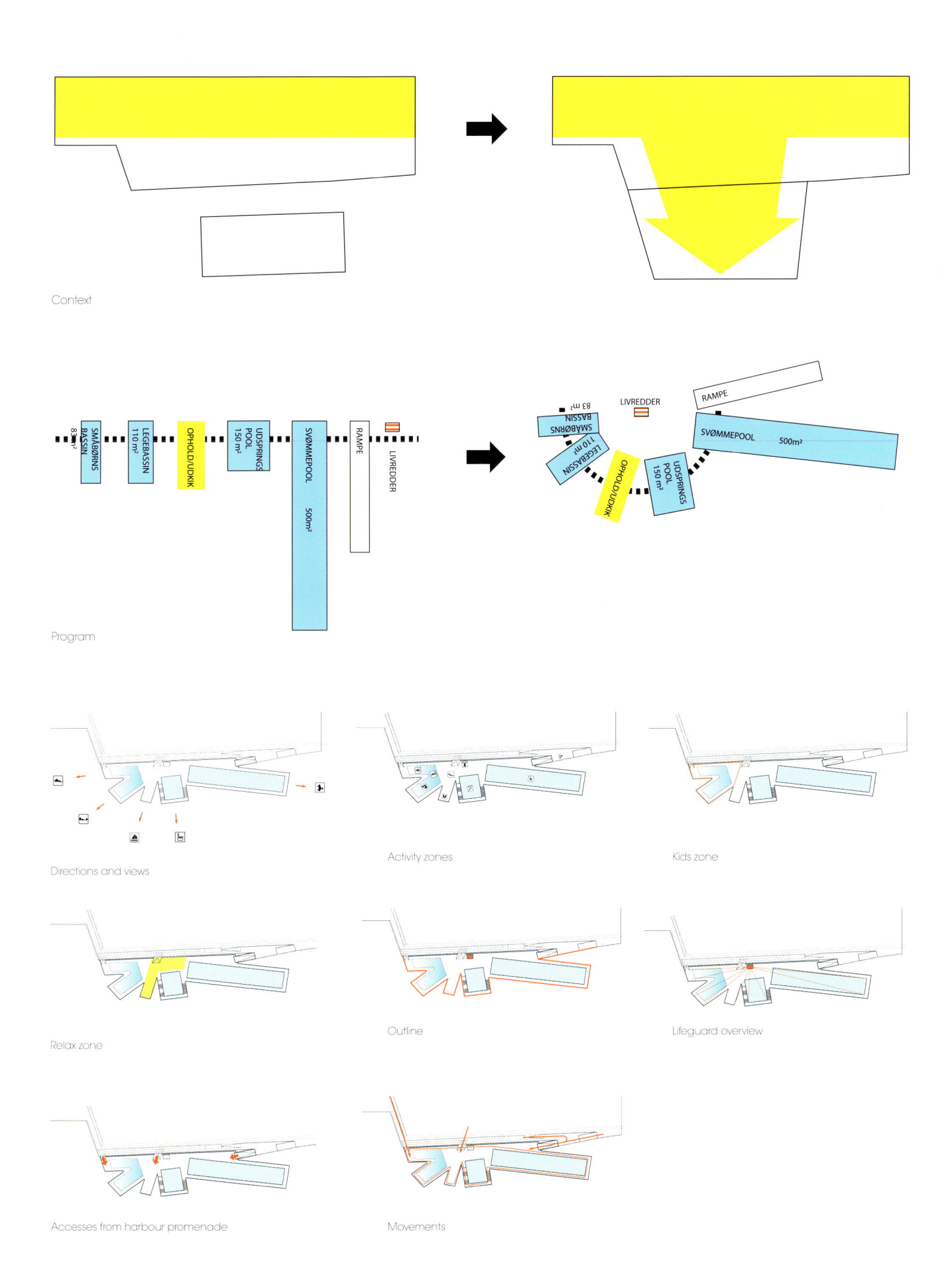

Program

Directions and views

Activity zones

Kids zone

Relax zone

Outline

Lifeguard overview

Accesses from harbour promenade

Movements

ARCHITECTURAL DIAGRAMS 019

A BUILDING FOR BOOKS
Z-A studio & Studio ST

"THE STRUCTURAL COLUMN GRID SUPPORTS BOTH THE BOOKSHELVES AND THE BUILDING AS A WHOLE."

Sections

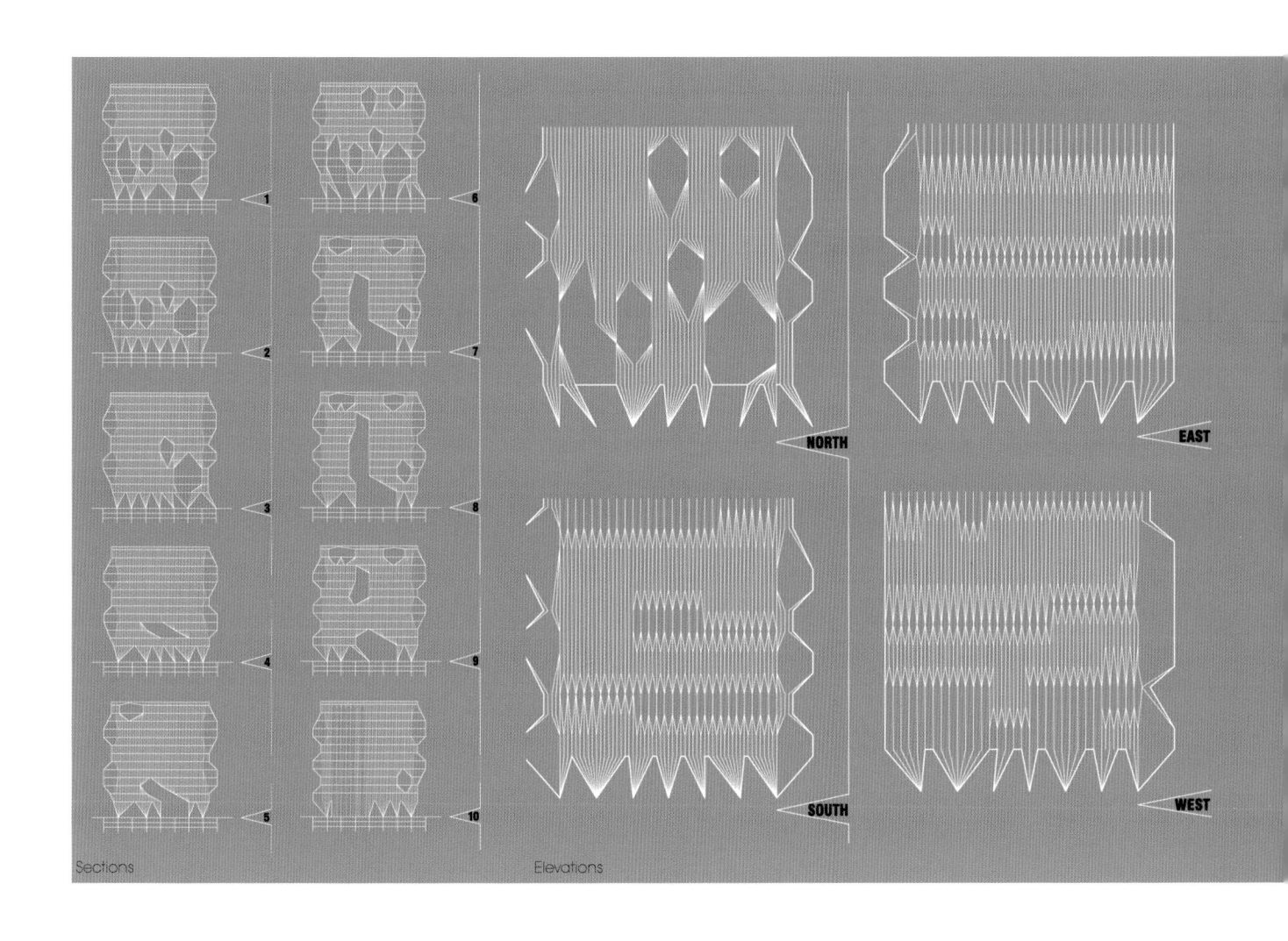

Elevations

NORTH

EAST

SOUTH

WEST

ARCHITECTURAL DIAGRAMS 021

ALTIENS BATHHOUSE
JDS Architects

"BY PROPOSING A STAR-SHAPED FIGURE, WHERE EACH ARM CONTAINS A POOL, ALL POOLS ARE SURROUNDED BY NATURE ON 3 SIDES."

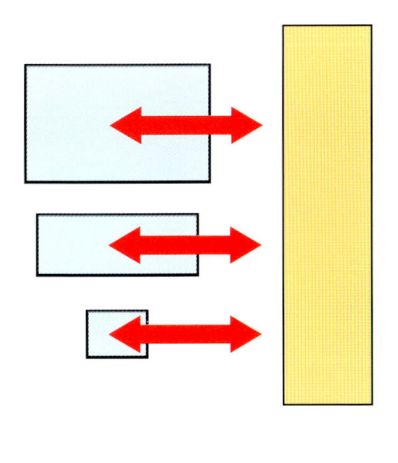

Pools   Services 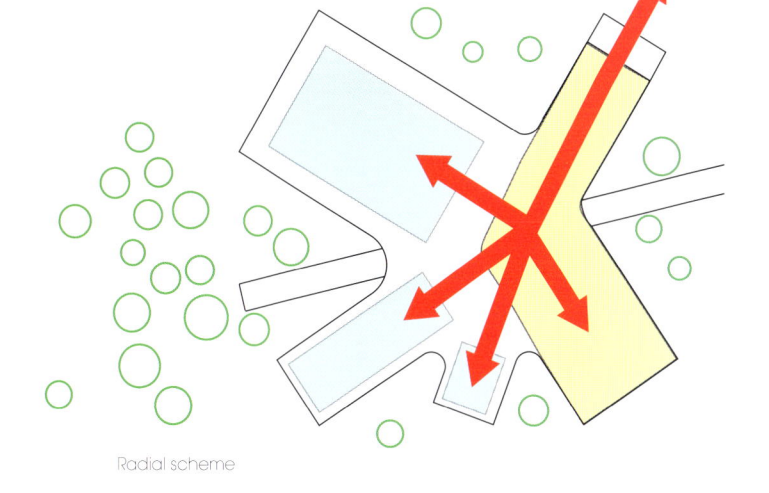   Radial scheme

Programs 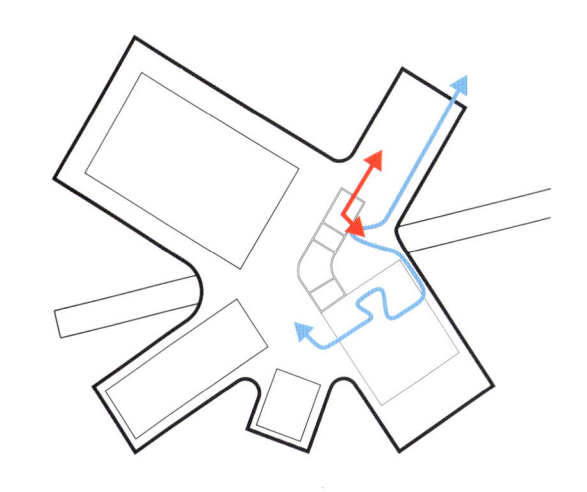   Dry/Wet zone

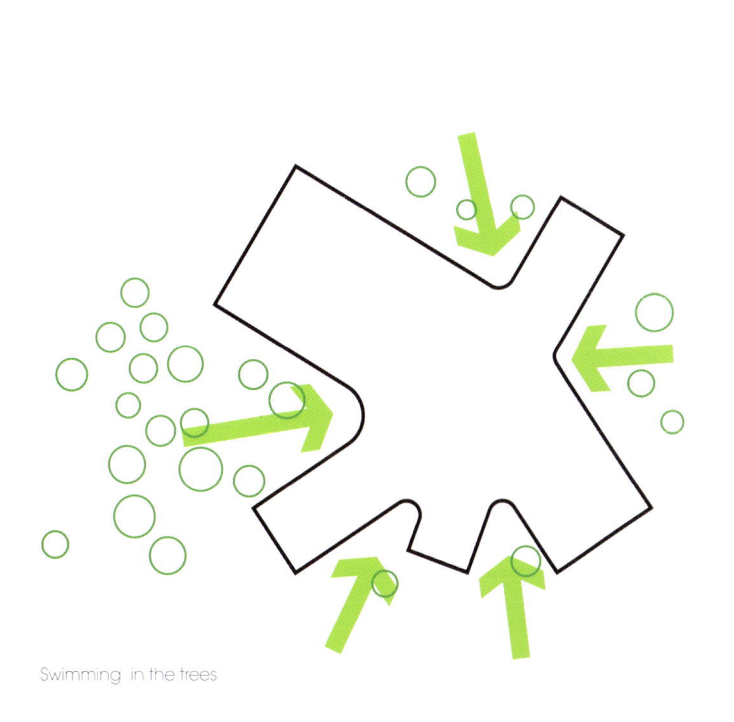

Swimming in the trees 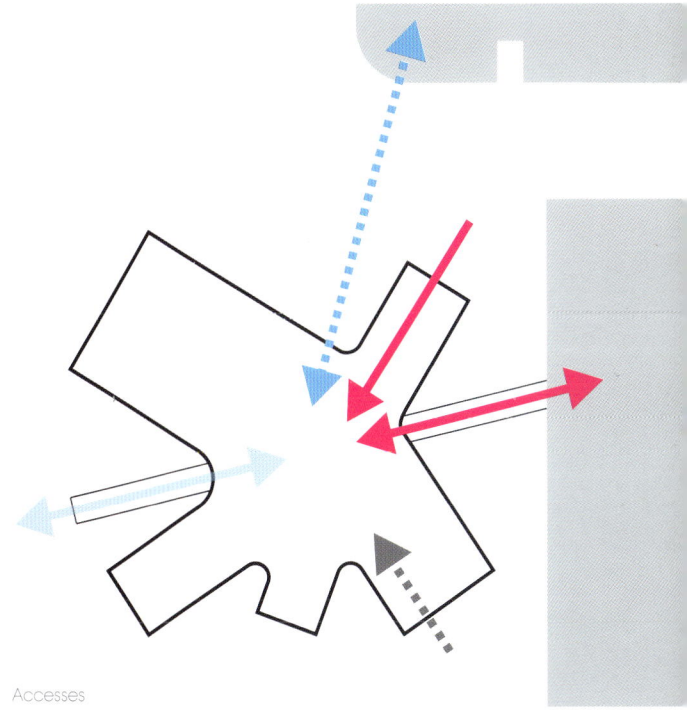   Accesses

ARCHITECTURAL DIAGRAMS 023

ARNHEM CENTRAL
UNStudio

"BUS TERMINAL AND TRAIN STATION ARE COMBINED INTO A NEW TYPE OF COMPLEX - AN INTEGRATED PUBLIC TRANSPORTATION AREA."

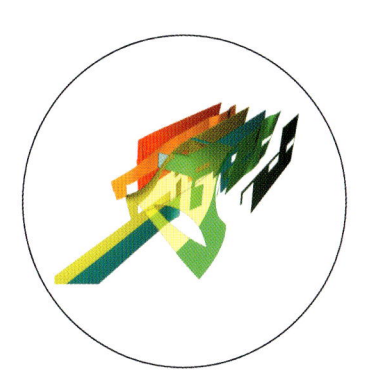

v-walls

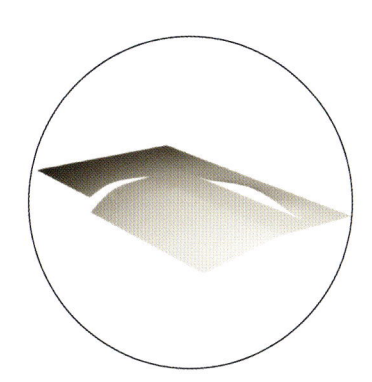

cuts

kleinbottle

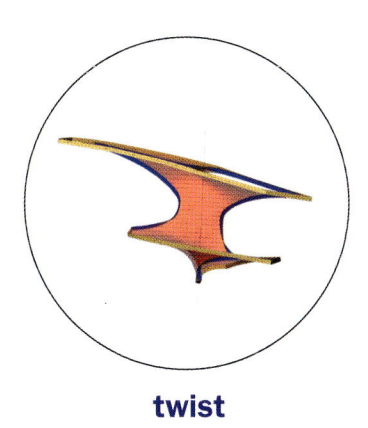

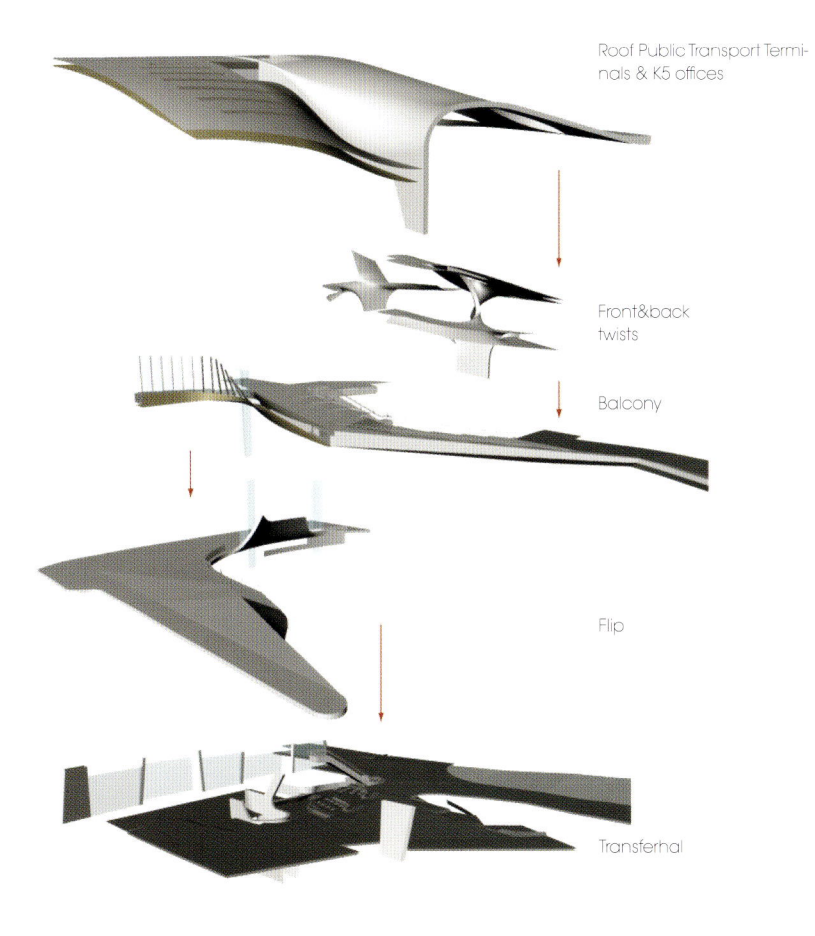

twist

Roof Public Transport Terminals & K5 offices

Front&back twists

Balcony

Flip

Transferhal

Exploded view main constructive elements

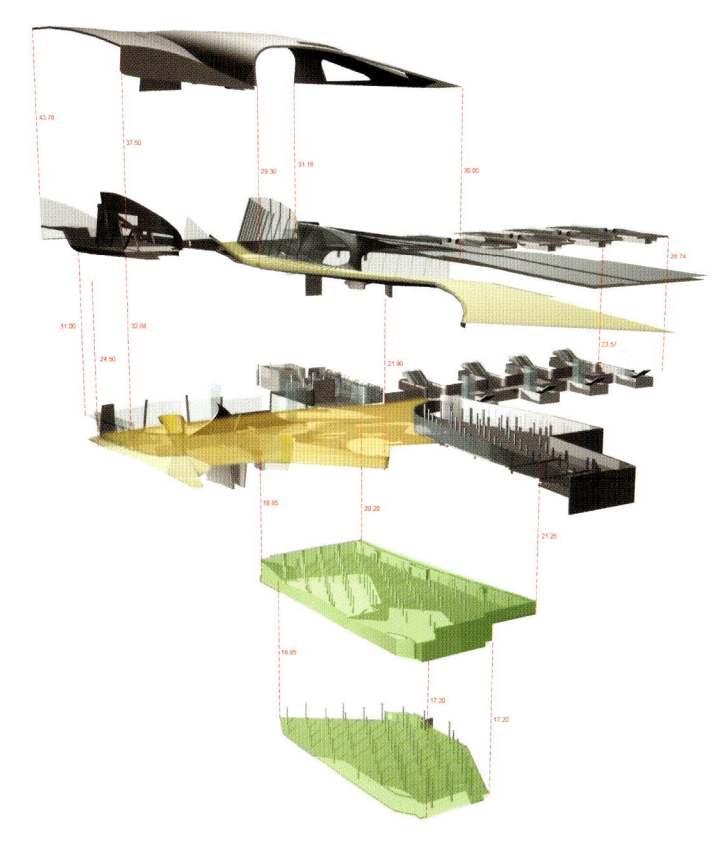

3D plan

ARCHITECTURAL DIAGRAMS 025

BARCELONA ENCANTS
JDS Architects

" THE ENCANTS MARKET IS THOUGHT AS A PLACE FOR PEOPLE… AN OPEN PLACE."

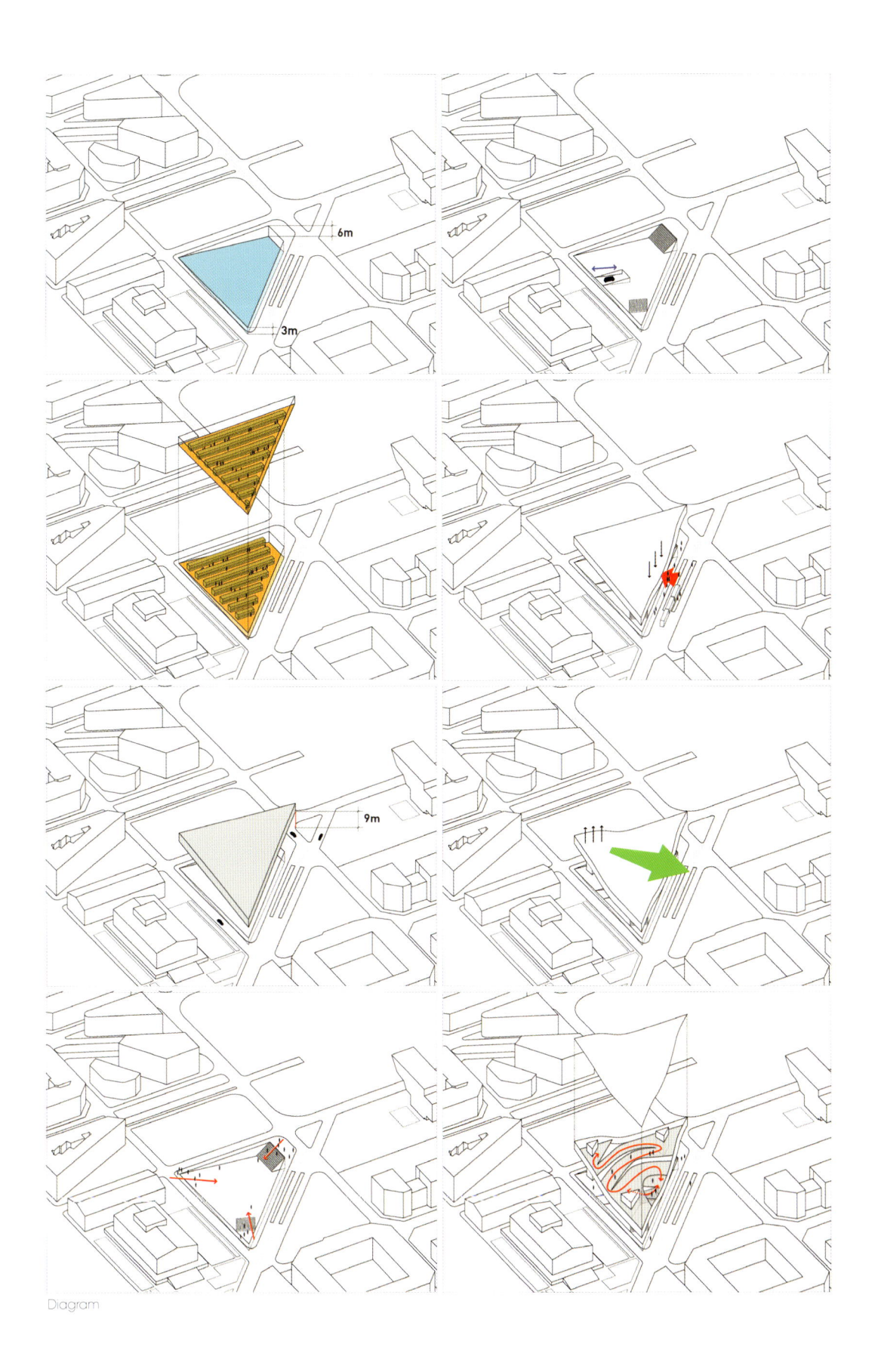

Diagram

ARCHITECTURAL DIAGRAMS 027

BELGIAN PAVILION
SHANGHAI JDS Architects

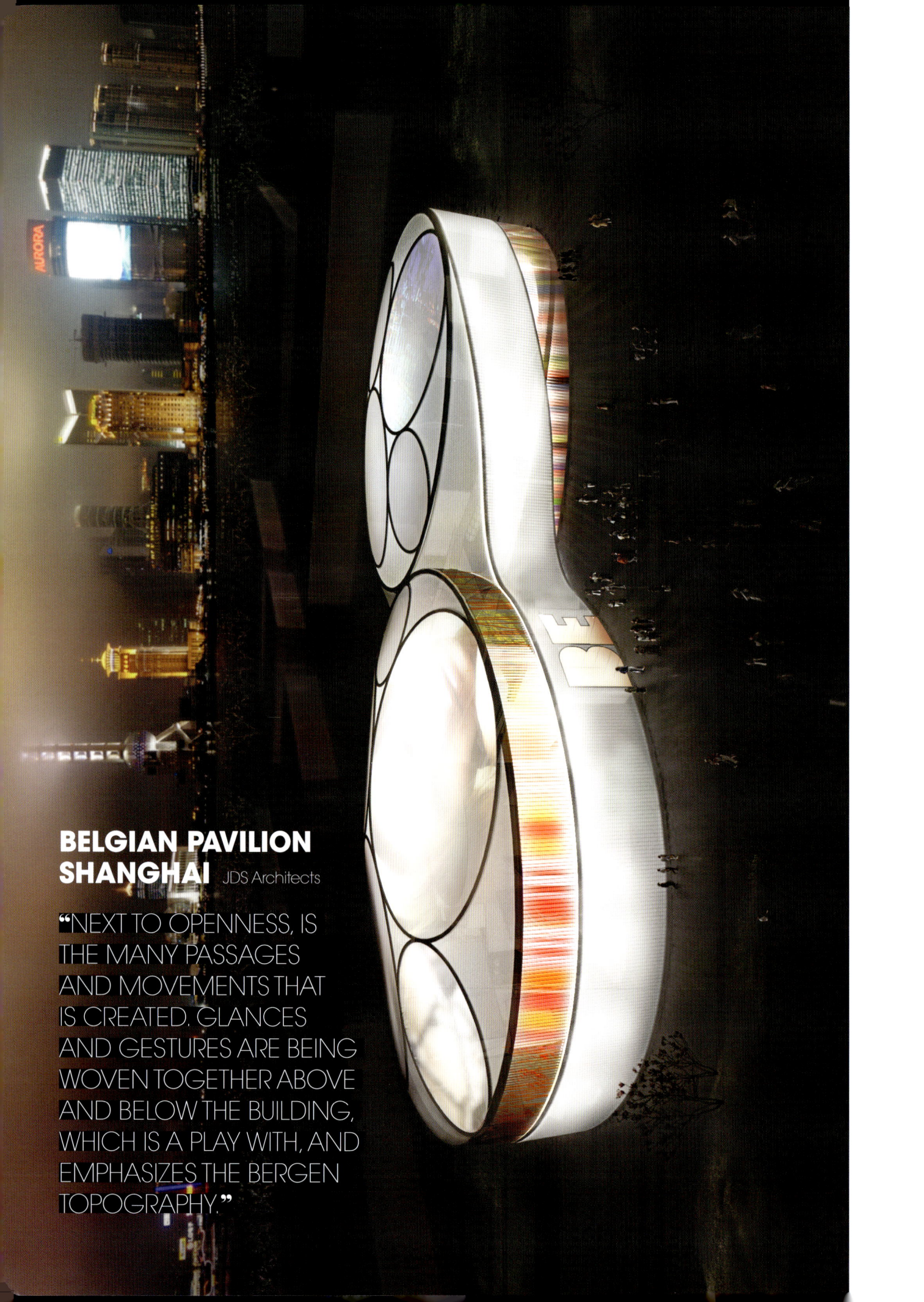

"NEXT TO OPENNESS, IS THE MANY PASSAGES AND MOVEMENTS THAT IS CREATED. GLANCES AND GESTURES ARE BEING WOVEN TOGETHER ABOVE AND BELOW THE BUILDING, WHICH IS A PLAY WITH, AND EMPHASIZES THE BERGEN TOPOGRAPHY."

EXPO BELGIUM · VIP BUSINESS · TECH STORAGE · EXPO EU

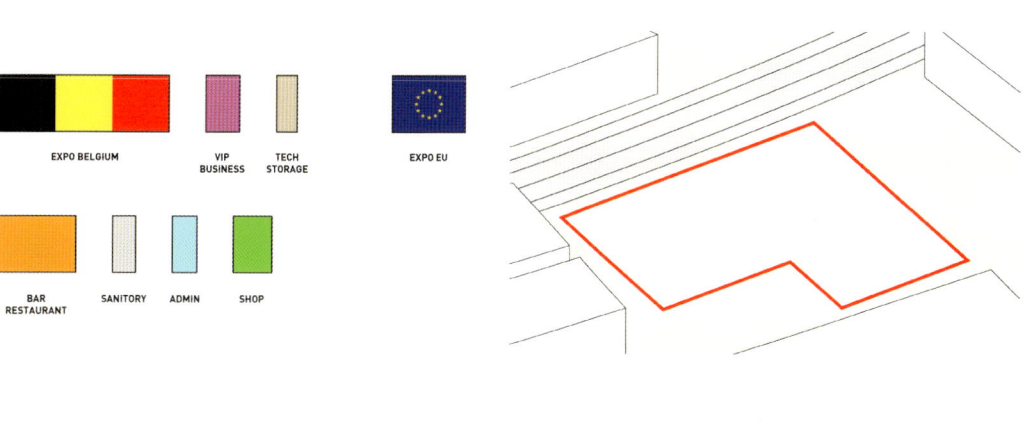

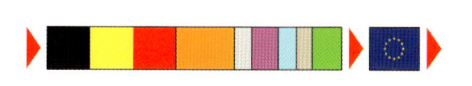

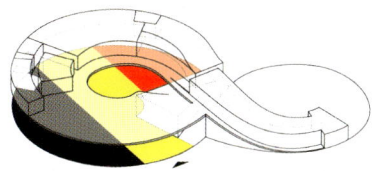

BAR RESTAURANT · SANITORY · ADMIN · SHOP

EXPO BELGIUM

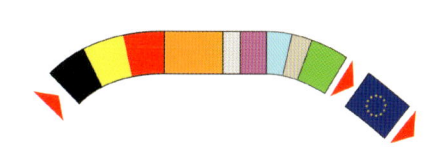

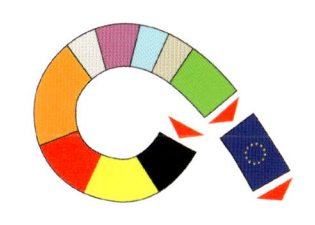

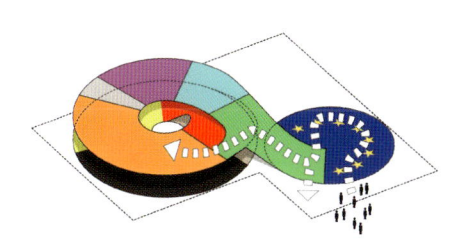

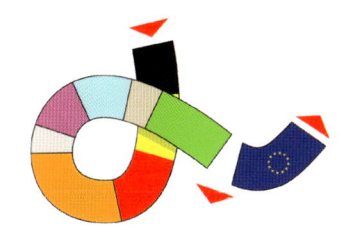

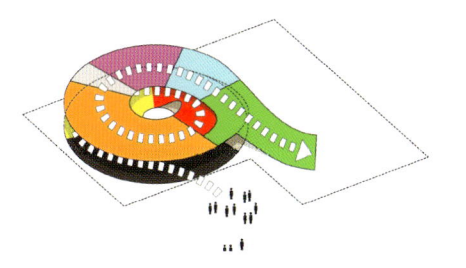

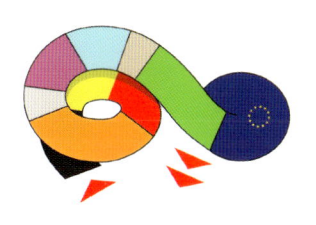

ARCHITECTURAL DIAGRAMS 029

BICYCLE STORAGE
VMX Architects

"THE DESIGN IS BASED ON A VERY FUNCTIONAL 1960'S CAR PARK. RED ASPHALT IS AS USED THROUGHOUT THE CITY ON BICYCLE PATHS."

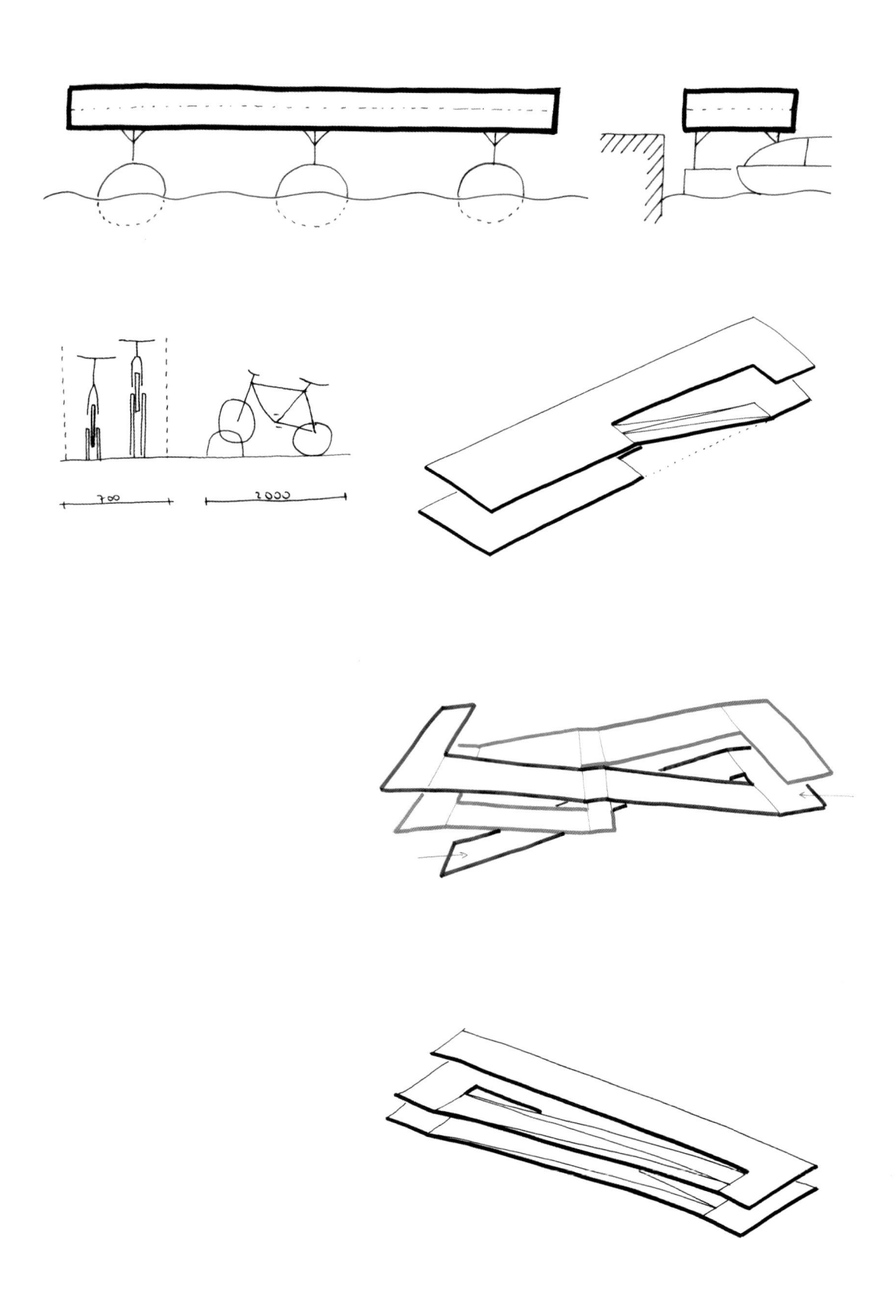

ARCHITECTURAL DIAGRAMS 031

BULLFIGHTER'S COSTUME nodo17 architects

"BULLRING IS THE MOST HYBRID BUILDING IN EXISTENCE IN RELATION TO THE VARIETY OF PROGRAMS."

Pattern extraction

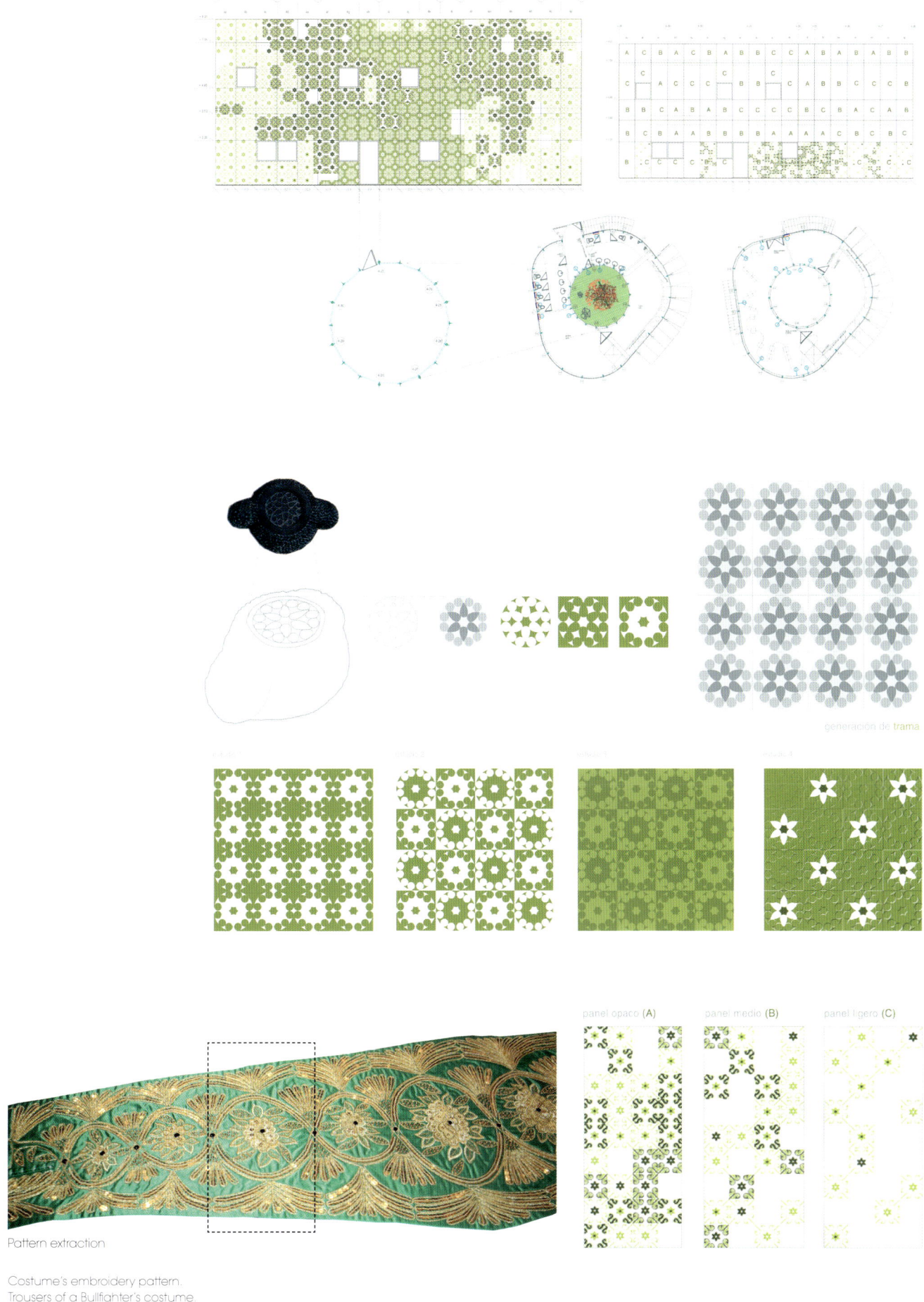

Costume's embroidery pattern.
Trousers of a Bullfighter's costume.
Design: Enrique Vera. Tailorshop Naty

ARCHITECTURAL DIAGRAMS 033

BUTCHER'S BRIDGE
SADAR VUGA ARHITEKTI

"THE PROPOSAL ENVISAGES A 'HOUSE-BRIDGE' WITH THREE HORIZONTAL PLATFORMS."

Concept

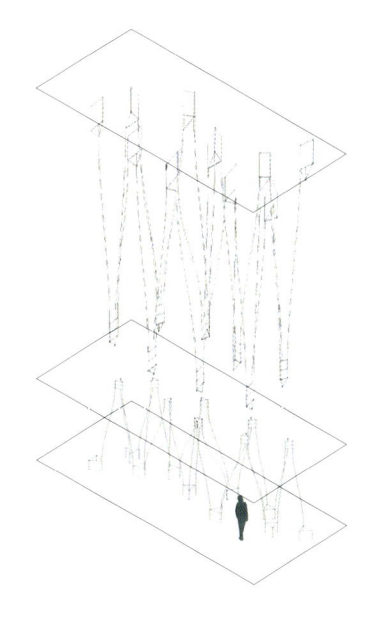

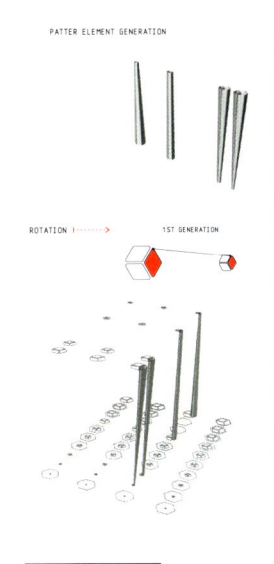

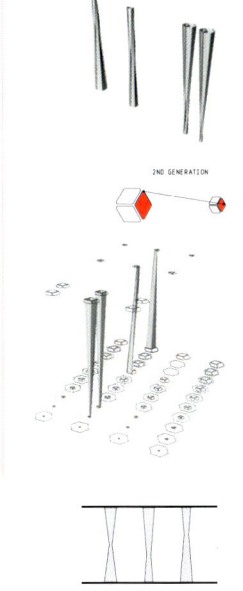

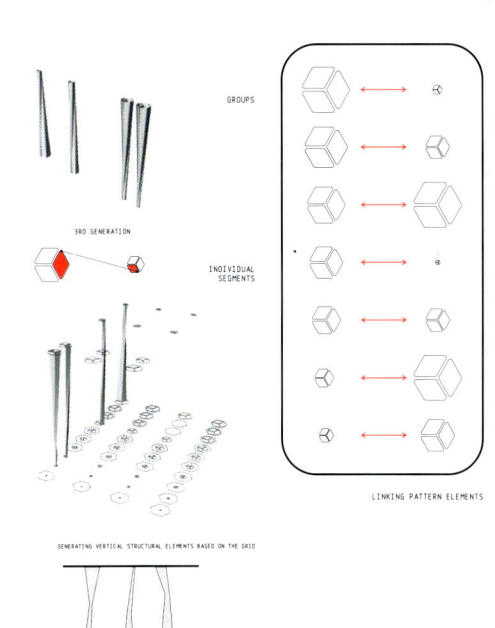

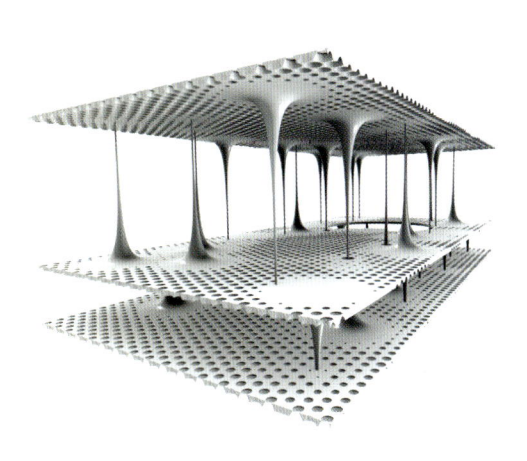

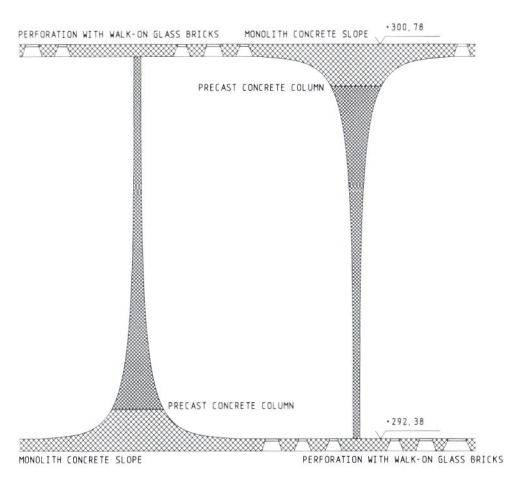

PATTER ELEMENT GENERATION

ROTATION 1ST GENERATION 2ND GENERATION 3RD GENERATION

GROUPS

INDIVIDUAL SEGMENTS

LINKING PATTERN ELEMENTS

GENERATING VERTICAL STRUCTURAL ELEMENTS BASED ON THE GRID

PROGRESSION OF ASYMMETRY

Prototype development

PERFORATION WITH WALK-ON GLASS BRICKS   MONOLITH CONCRETE SLOPE   +300,78

PRECAST CONCRETE COLUMN

PRECAST CONCRETE COLUMN

MONOLITH CONCRETE SLOPE   PERFORATION WITH WALK-ON GLASS BRICKS   +292,38

SCALE 1:100

ARCHITECTURAL DIAGRAMS 035

CWBG NL Architects

"ONE SIDE IS SKEWED IN ORDER TO ALLOW THE OLD TREE IN A FORMER COURTYARD TO SURVIVE THE OTHER SIDE IS CUT OFF."

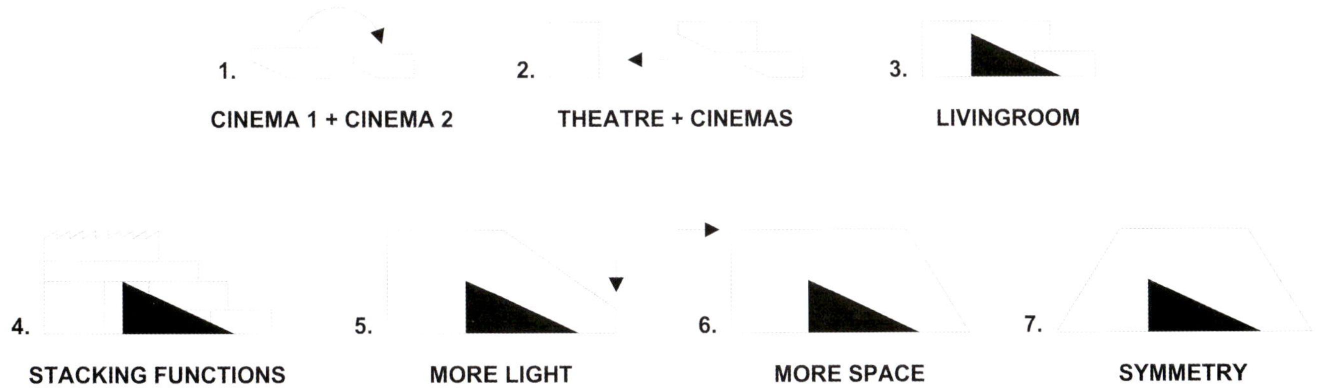

1. **CINEMA 1 + CINEMA 2**
2. **THEATRE + CINEMAS**
3. **LIVINGROOM**
4. **STACKING FUNCTIONS**
5. **MORE LIGHT**
6. **MORE SPACE**
7. **SYMMETRY**

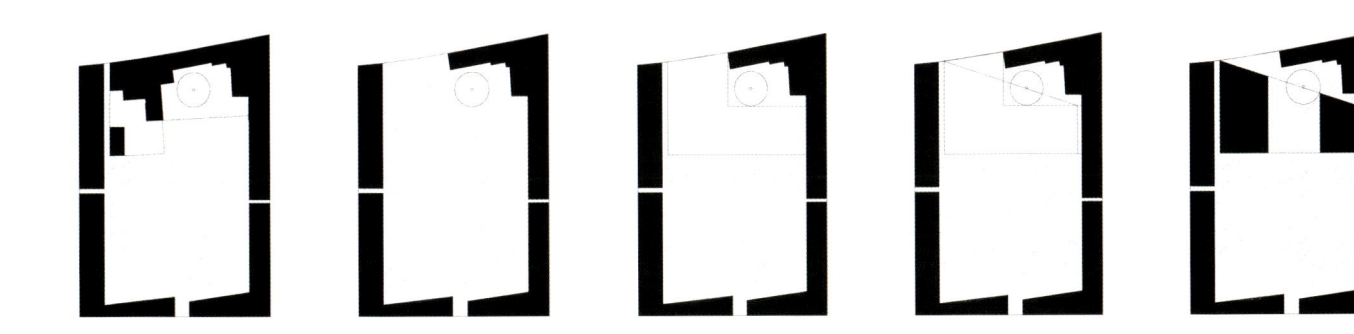

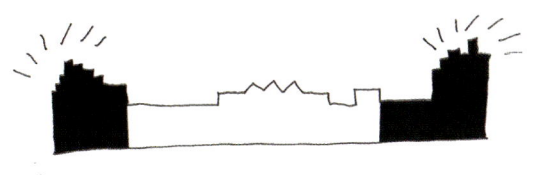

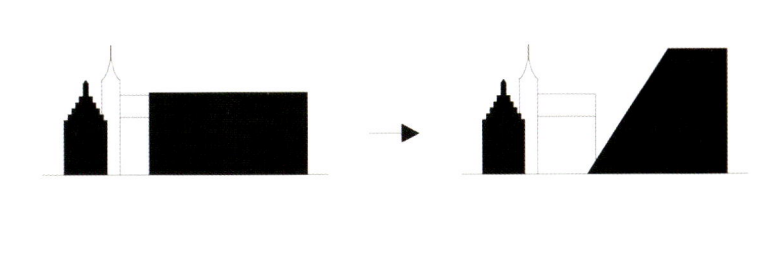

ARCHITECTURAL DIAGRAMS

DUBLIN DOCKLANDS OPEN AIR BATH

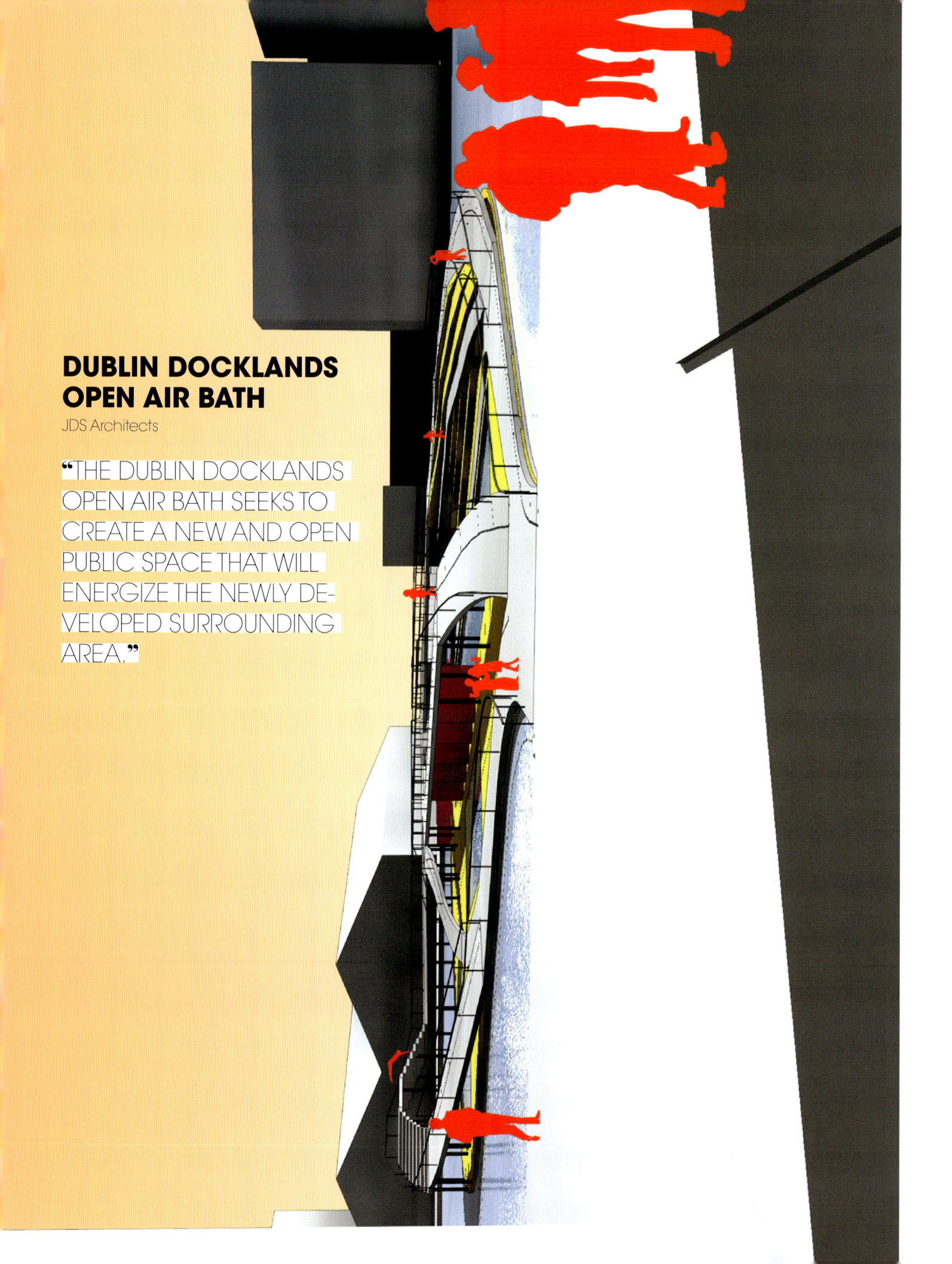

JDS Architects

"THE DUBLIN DOCKLANDS OPEN AIR BATH SEEKS TO CREATE A NEW AND OPEN PUBLIC SPACE THAT WILL ENERGIZE THE NEWLY DEVELOPED SURROUNDING AREA."

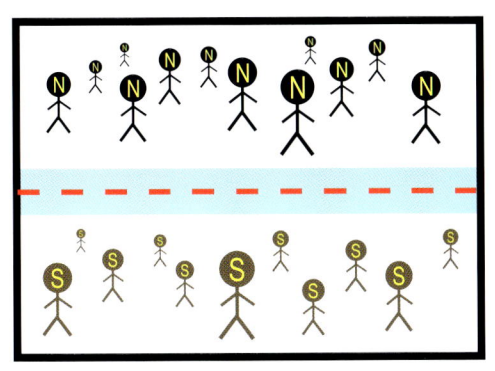

- Then, how should we do it?
- Community members (families, children, young people etc.) stay around their zones and develop their own activities there.

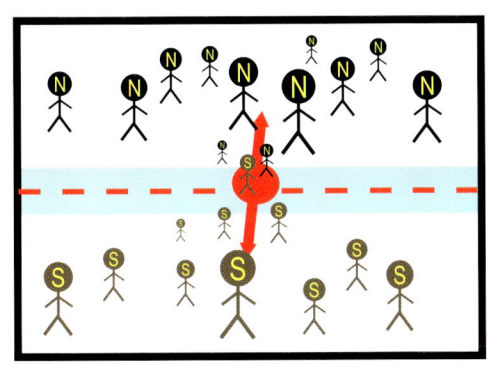

- We need a neutral platform to generate an open public space for everyone
- We need an island in the liffey
- Then, the tensions will start to decrease with the new shared space

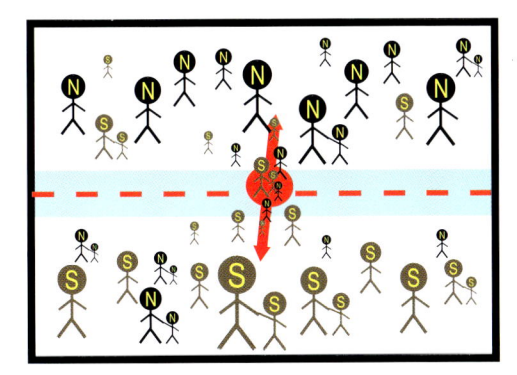

- Eventually, the whole community should feel identified with their private space and share different activities
- Swimming pools and other complimentary programmes will be essential.

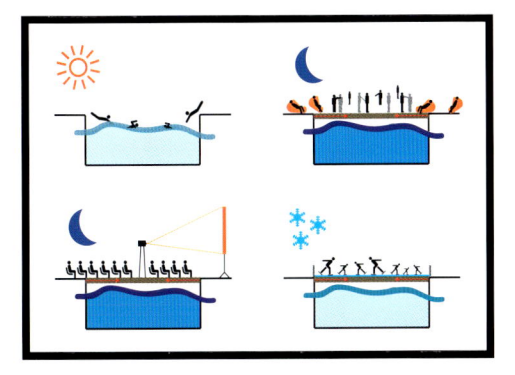

- If we develop a way to cover the swimming pools easily enough, we could enjoy the big areas for community activities...
- Parties, expositions, open cinemas
- Winter activities: ice skating, etc.

ARCHITECTURAL DIAGRAMS 039

DUNE TERRACE
nARCHITECTS

"THE AIRPORT MODEL OFFERS A RICH AND CUSTOMIZABLE MUSEUM EXPERIENCE THAT CAN VARY WITH EACH TRIP."

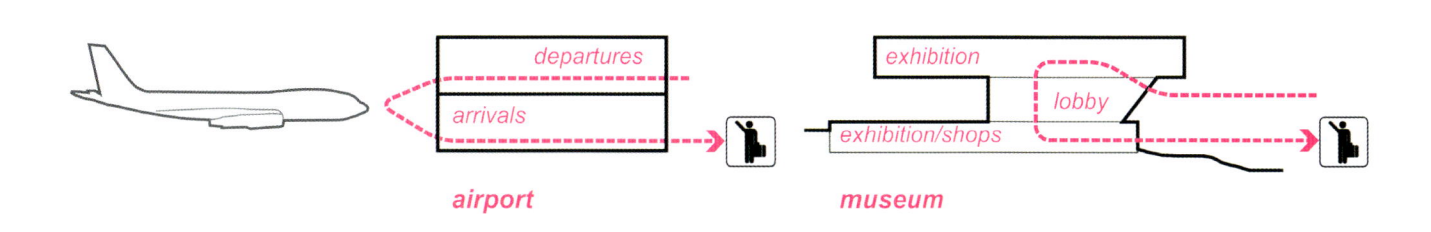

departures
arrivals

airport

exhibition
lobby
exhibition/shops

museum

Typical museum

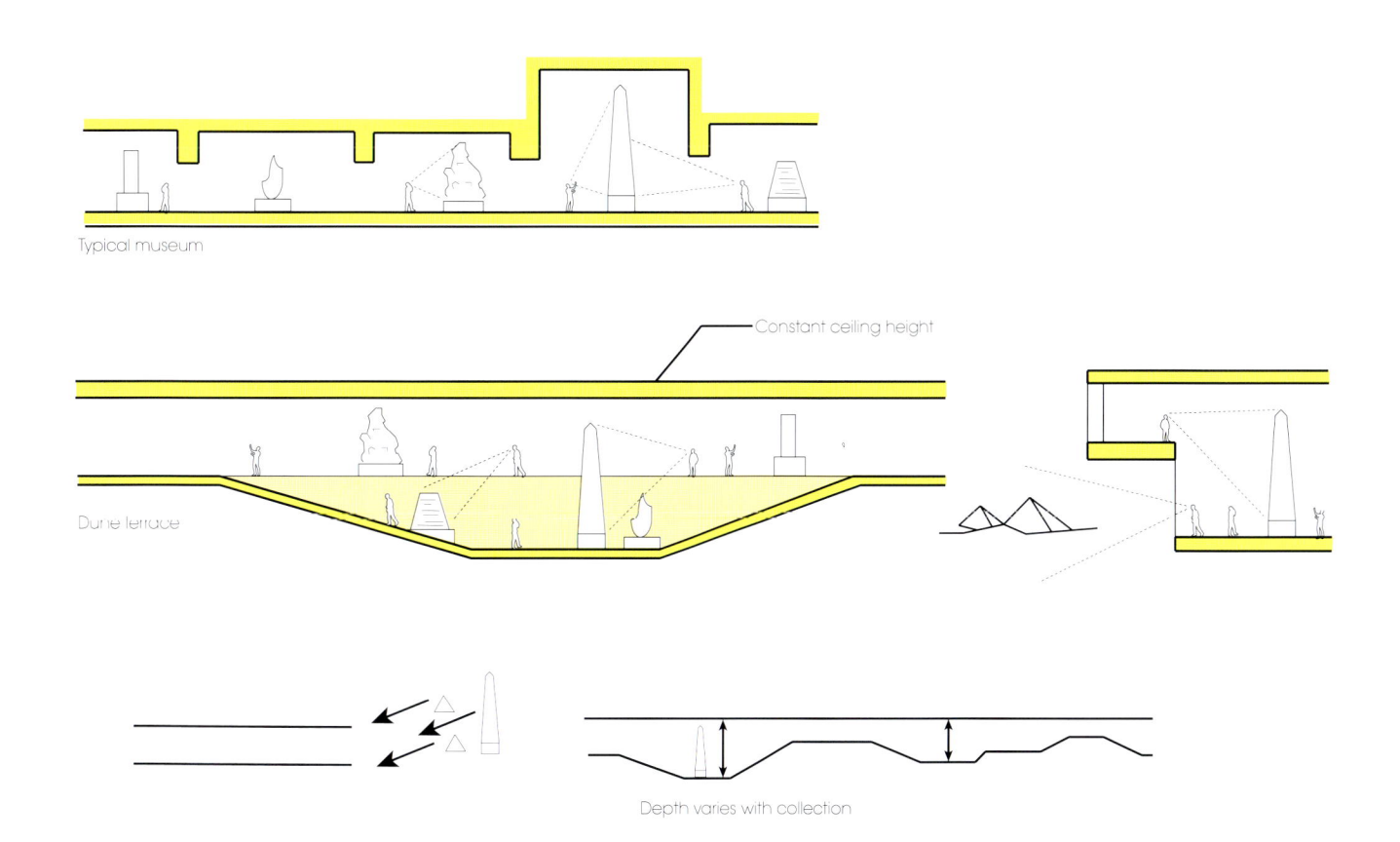

Constant ceiling height

Dune terrace

Depth varies with collection

ARCHITECTURAL DIAGRAMS 041

DUSTY RELIEF / B-MU
R&Sie architects

"EUCLIDIAN, GLOBALIZATION INCASED, WHERE CULTURAL MERCHANDISES ARE CIRCULATED IN AN ASEPTIC AND DETERITORIALIZED UNIVERSE."

Epiphyte and gray plants

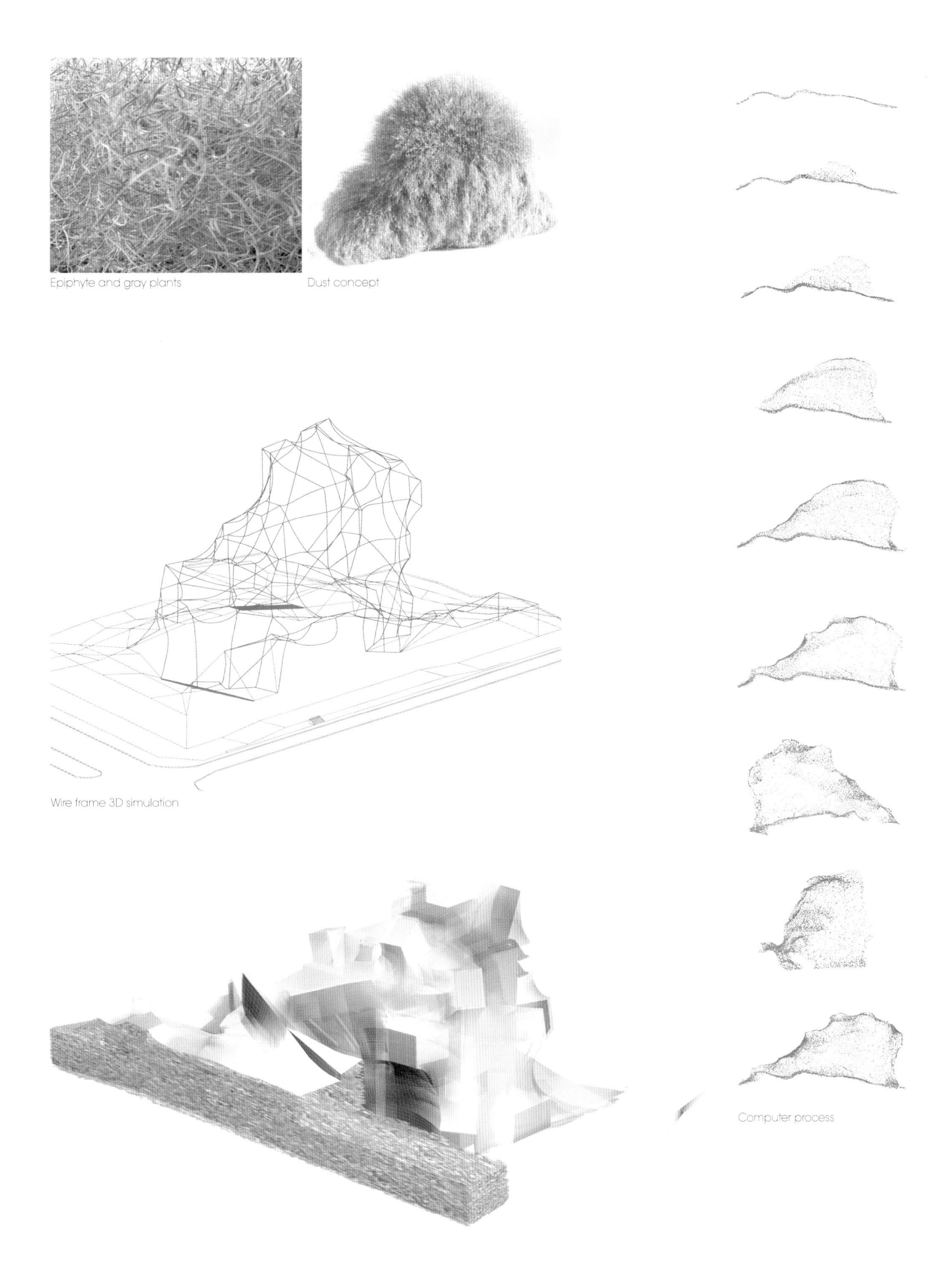

Dust concept

Wire frame 3D simulation

Mesh and concrete for a ghost appearance

Computer process

ARCHITECTURAL DIAGRAMS 043

ENTERTAINMENT COM-PLEX
MANUELLE GAUTRAND ARCHITECTURE

"THE FOUR STUDIOS ARE ENVELOPED IN A SHIMMERING SILKEN SHEATH FORMED OF STAINLESS STEEL DISCS OF DIFFERENT SIZES."

Integration of motif in the project

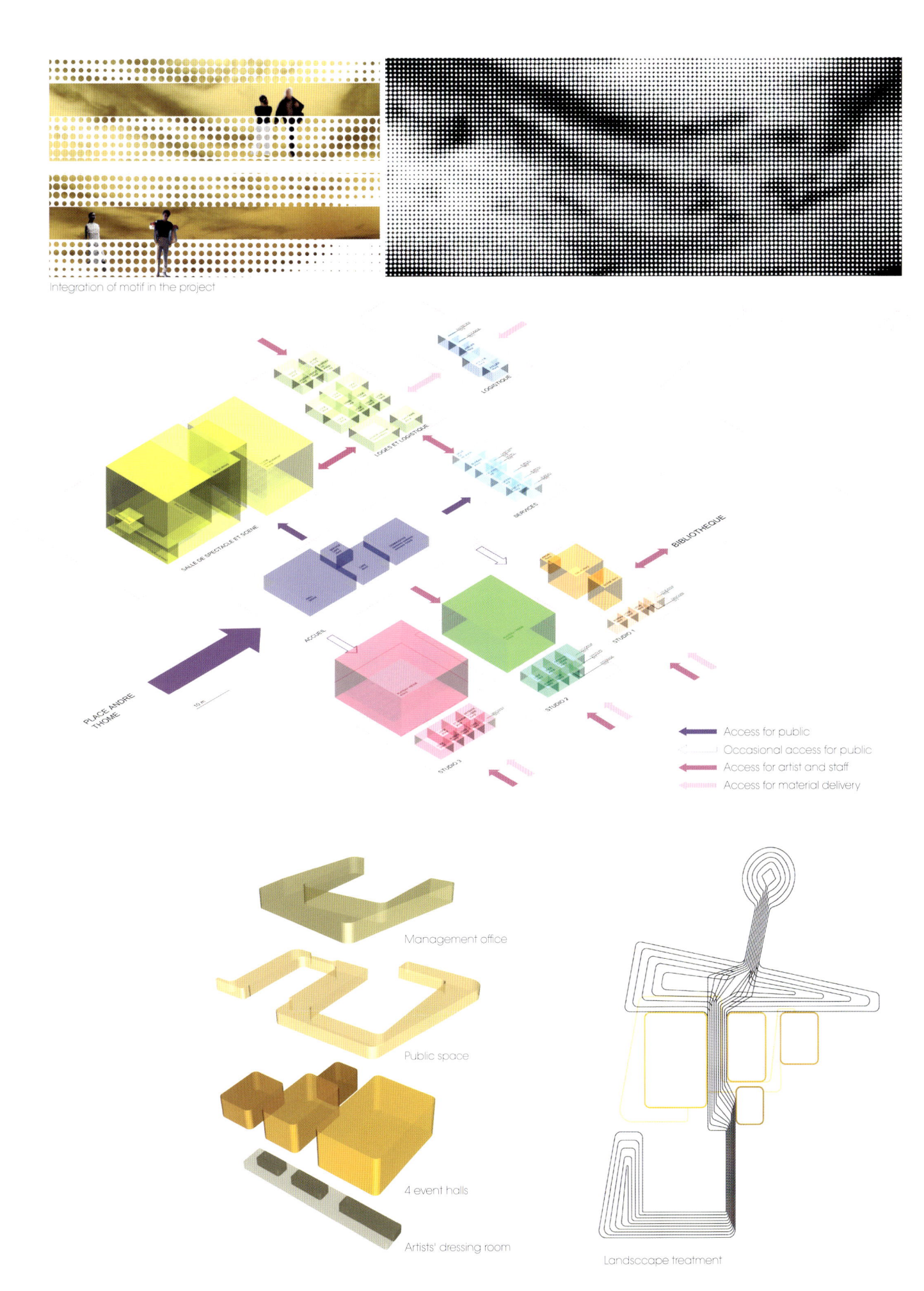

- Access for public
- Occasional access for public
- Access for artist and staff
- Access for material delivery

Management office

Public space

4 event halls

Artists' dressing room

Landscape treatment

ARCHITECTURAL DIAGRAMS 045

EXTENSION OF THE LILLE MODERN ART MUSEUM

MANUELLE GAUTRAND ARCHITECTURE

"THE ART BRUT ROOMS ARE DESIGNED AS AN ATYPICAL RECEPTACLE"

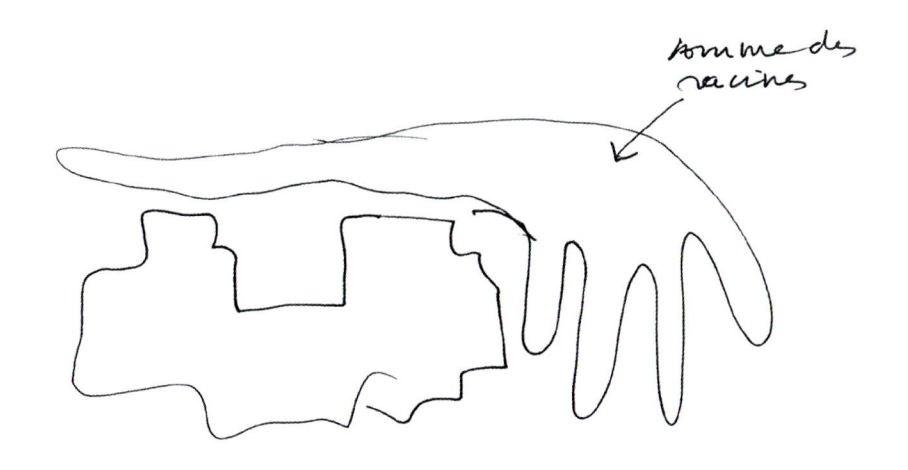

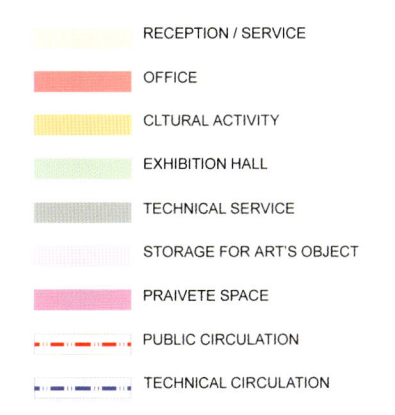

ARCHITECTURAL DIAGRAMS 047

FILMMUSEUM
NL Architects

"THE MAIN INVENTION IS THE BOWL WITH THE HALLS A KIND OF BOWL."

hight limit

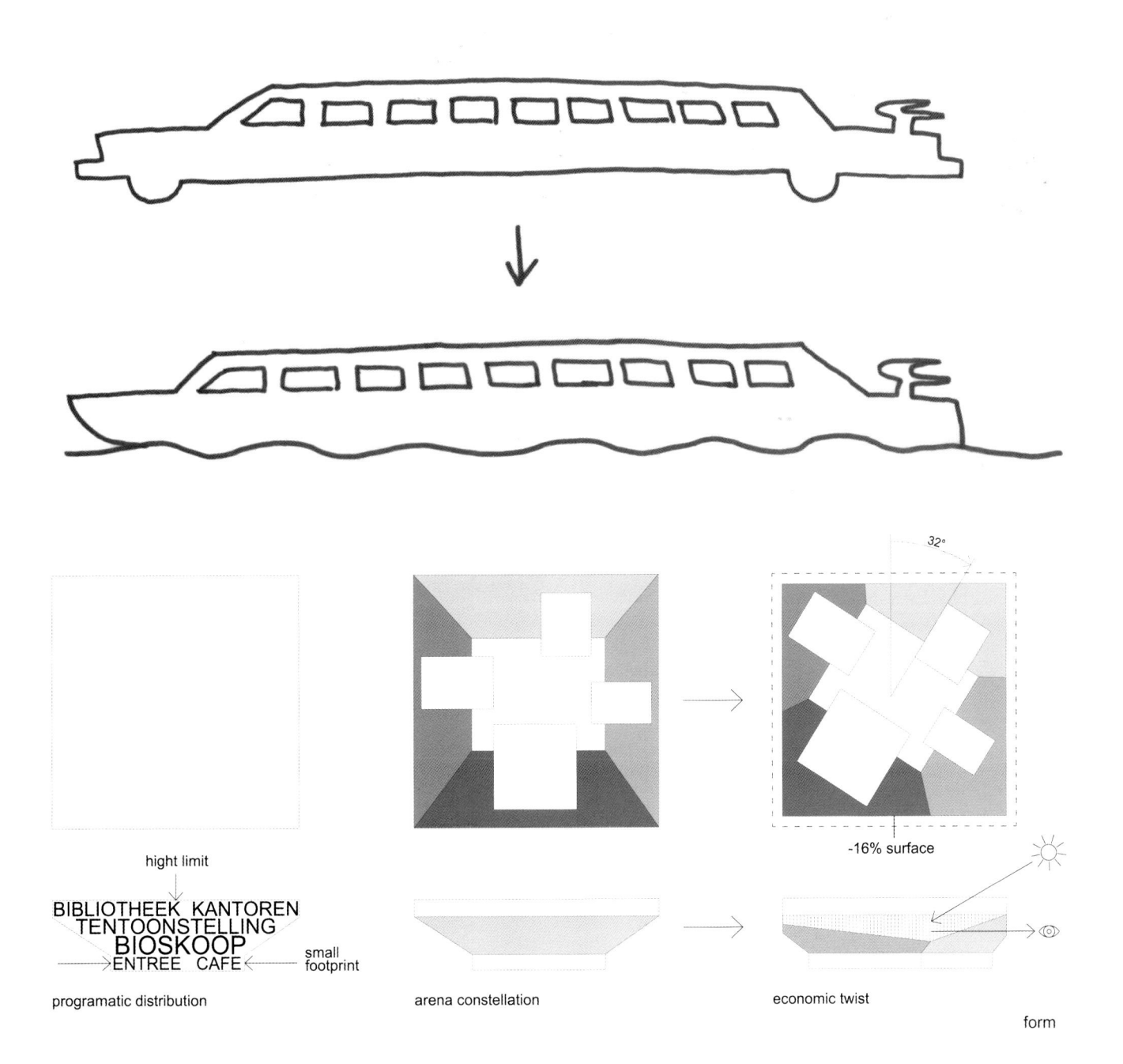

BIBLIOTHEEK KANTOREN
TENTOONSTELLING
BIOSKOOP
ENTREE CAFE — small footprint

programatic distribution

arena constellation

−16% surface

economic twist

form

ARCHITECTURAL DIAGRAMS 049

FLOATING ISLANDS

Vincent Parreira Architectures

"THE OBJECTIVE IS THUS TO DEVELOP A NEW IMAGE OF THE SITE BY THE CONSTRUCTION OF A PROGRAMMATIC GEOGRAPHY."

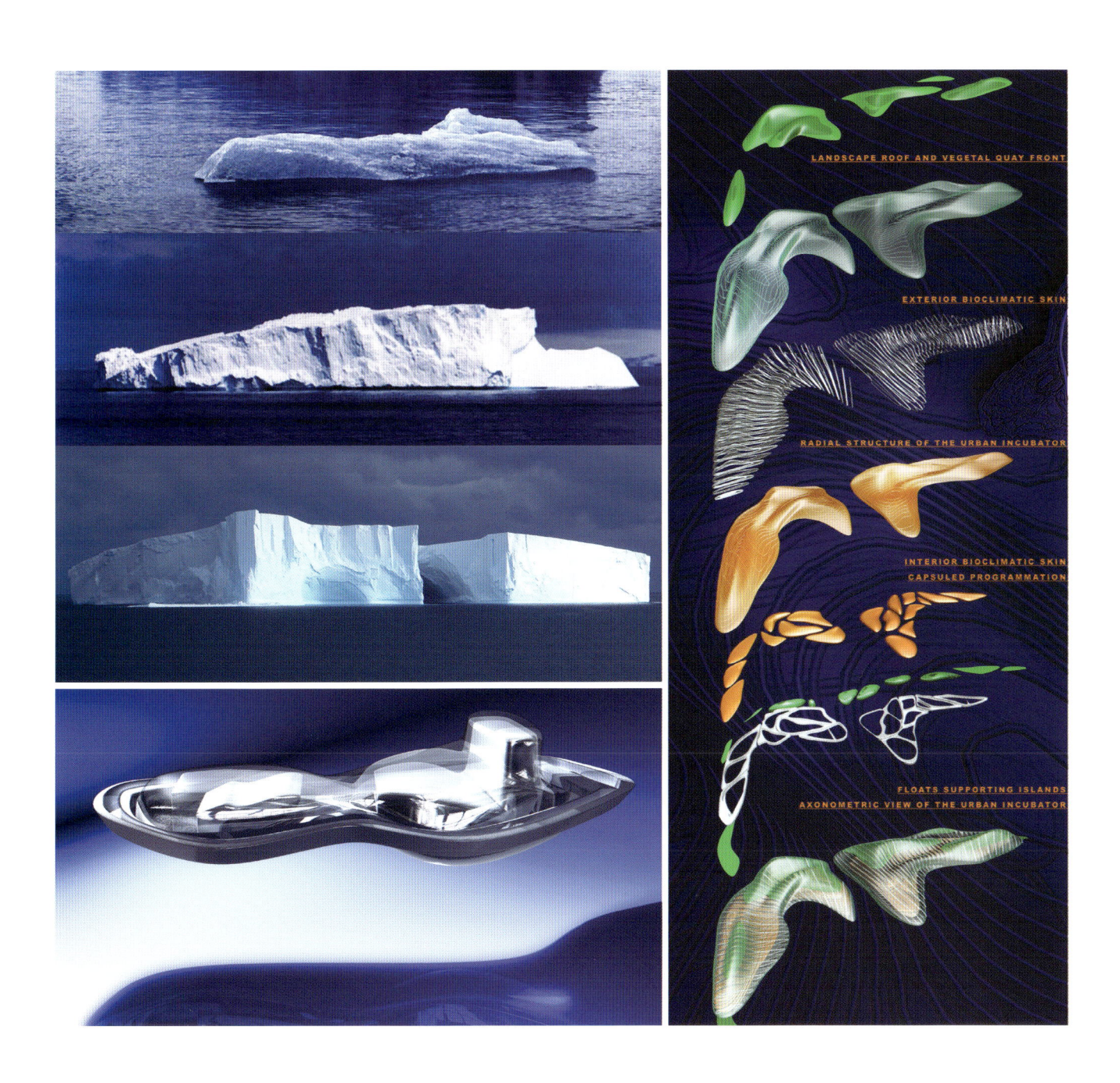

LANDSCAPE ROOF AND VEGETAL QUAY FRONT

EXTERIOR BIOCLIMATIC SKIN

RADIAL STRUCTURE OF THE URBAN INCUBATOR

INTERIOR BIOCLIMATIC SKIN
CAPSULED PROGRAMMATION

FLOATS SUPPORTING ISLANDS
AXONOMETRIC VIEW OF THE URBAN INCUBATOR

ARCHITECTURAL DIAGRAMS   051

GENERAL AVIATION TERMINAL VMX Architects

"THE TERMINAL DESIGN EXPRESSES ITS FUNCTION OF PRIVATE TERMINAL AND THE NEED FOR PRIVACY IN AN INNOVATIVE WAY."

AIRSIDE   **LANDSIDE**

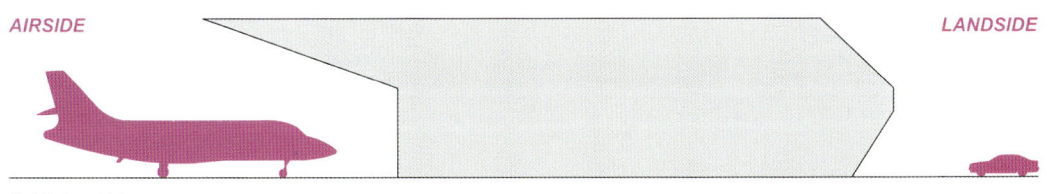

Airside landside

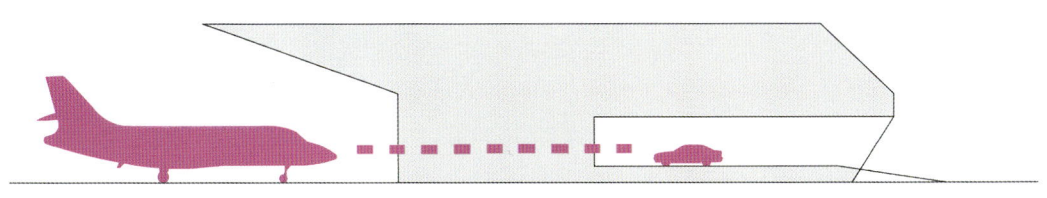

Limited distance

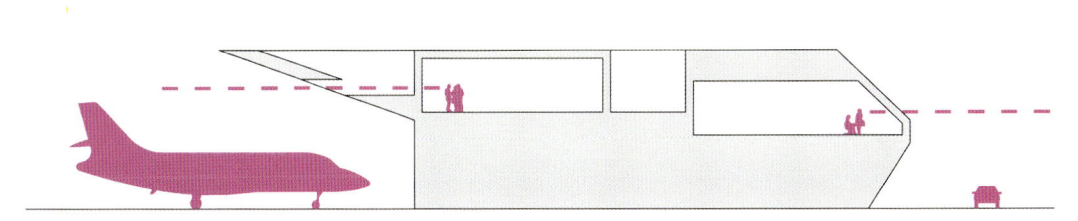

Limited view on platform and drop-off

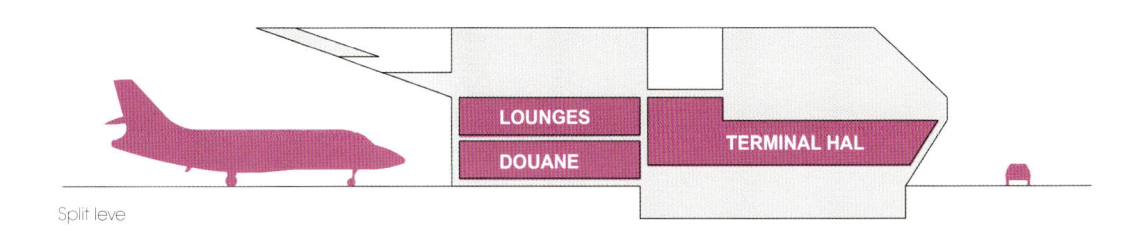

LOUNGES
DOUANE
TERMINAL HAL

Split leve

ARCHITECTURAL DIAGRAMS 053

GRAND EGYPTIAN MUSEUM JDS Architects

"WE DECIDED TO ORGAN-
IZE THE SIMPLE TIMELINE
AS A LONG TRACK WHERE
EACH THEME WOULD REAP-
PEAR IN EACH PERIOD IN
TIME."

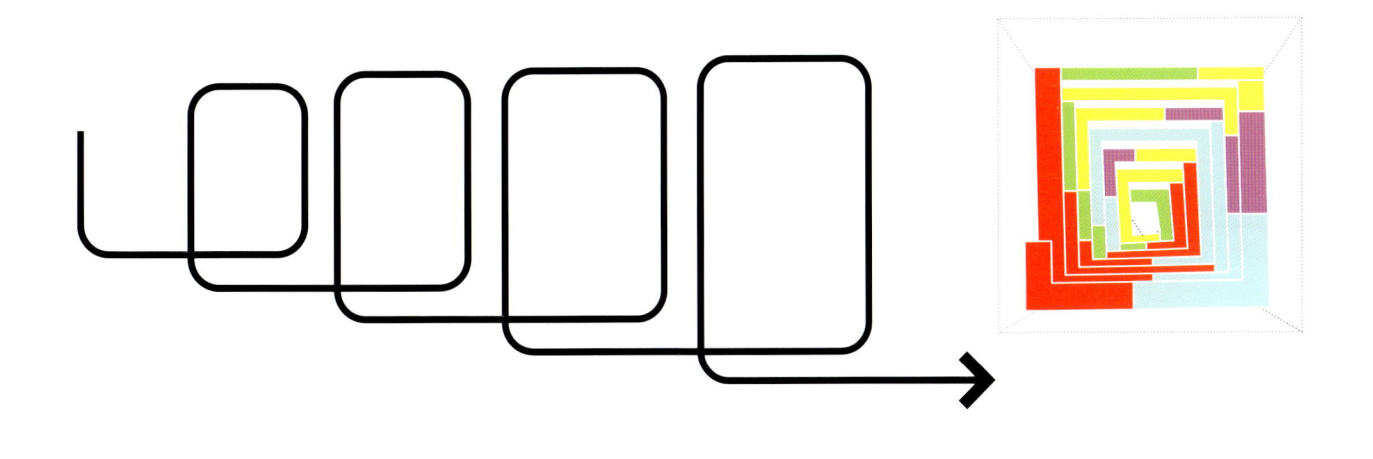

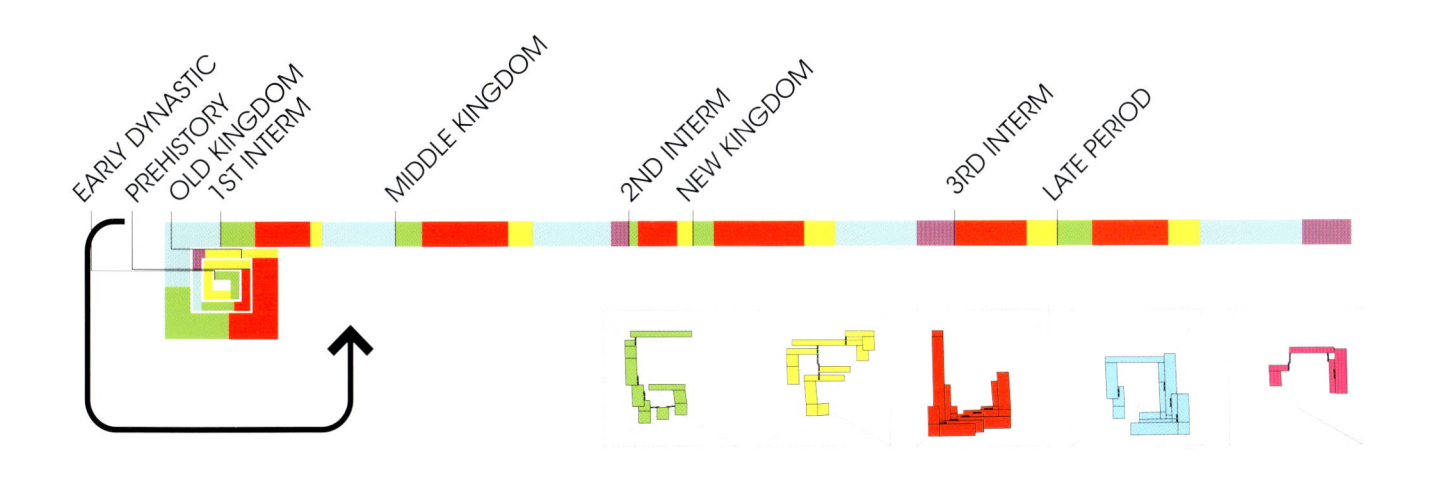

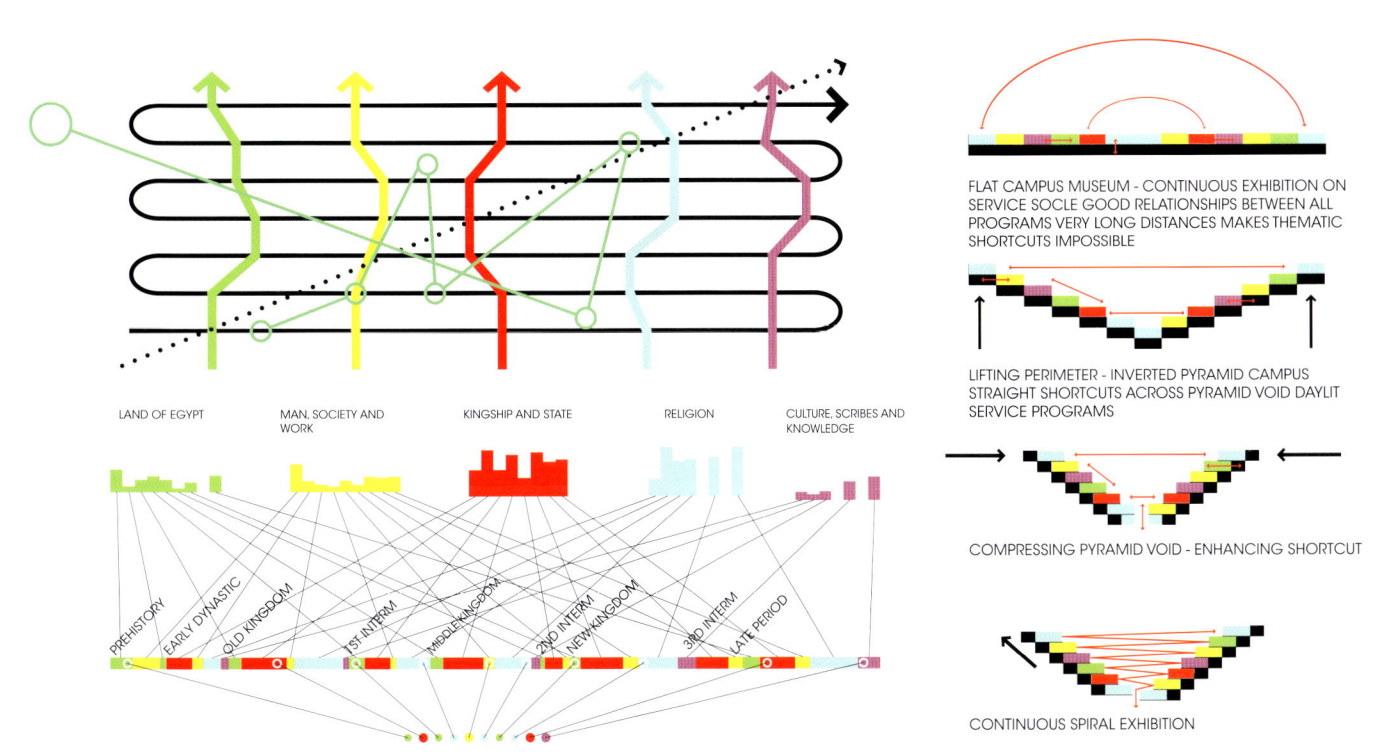

EARLY DYNASTIC
PREHISTORY
OLD KINGDOM
1ST INTERM
MIDDLE KINGDOM
2ND INTERM
NEW KINGDOM
3RD INTERM
LATE PERIOD

LAND OF EGYPT
MAN, SOCIETY AND WORK
KINGSHIP AND STATE
RELIGION
CULTURE, SCRIBES AND KNOWLEDGE

PREHISTORY
EARLY DYNASTIC
OLD KINGDOM
1ST INTERM
MIDDLE KINGDOM
2ND INTERM
NEW KINGDOM
3RD INTERM
LATE PERIOD

FLAT CAMPUS MUSEUM - CONTINUOUS EXHIBITION ON SERVICE SOCLE GOOD RELATIONSHIPS BETWEEN ALL PROGRAMS VERY LONG DISTANCES MAKES THEMATIC SHORTCUTS IMPOSSIBLE

LIFTING PERIMETER - INVERTED PYRAMID CAMPUS STRAIGHT SHORTCUTS ACROSS PYRAMID VOID DAYLIT SERVICE PROGRAMS

COMPRESSING PYRAMID VOID - ENHANCING SHORTCUT

CONTINUOUS SPIRAL EXHIBITION

ARCHITECTURAL DIAGRAMS

GRONINGER FORUM
NL Architects

"THE BUILDING IS DESIGNED AS ONE CLEAR VOLUME TO EXPRESS THE COLLECTIVE AMBITION OF COMBINING DIFFERENT FACILITIES INTO ONE NEW COMPLEX."

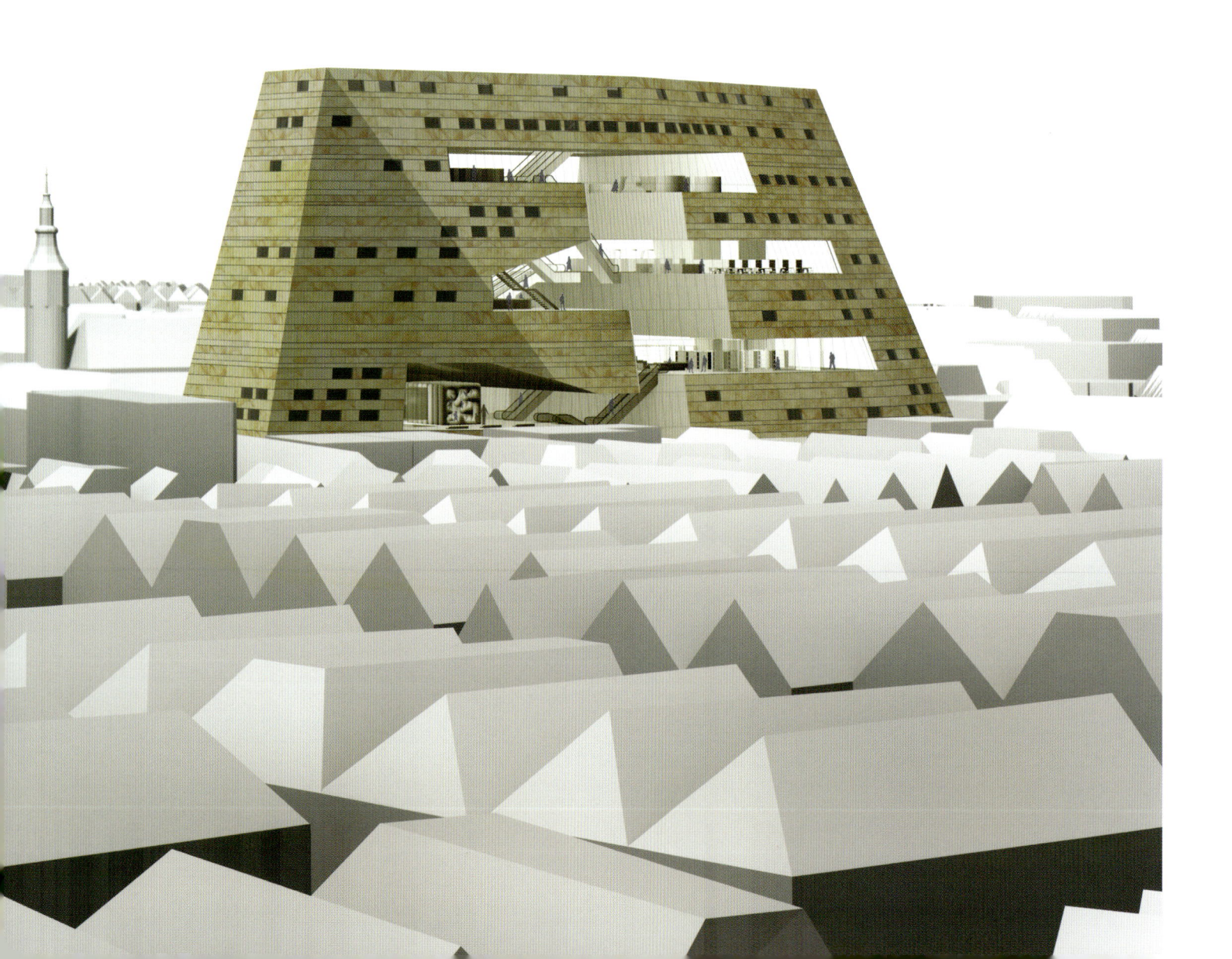

Plot

Envelope

Tapered

Entrances

Thinner silhouet

Extrusion

ARCHITECTURAL DIAGRAMS 057

GROUNDNOISE SCHIPHOL
NL Architects

"SCHIPHOL WOULD LIKE TO PROPOSE AN INNOVATIVE WALL THAT CAN HAVE A FLEXIBLE POSITION TO THE LANDING STRIP"

Flat roofs = No sound distortion

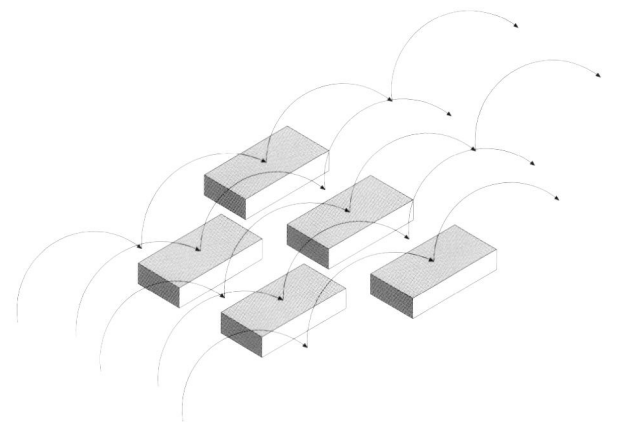

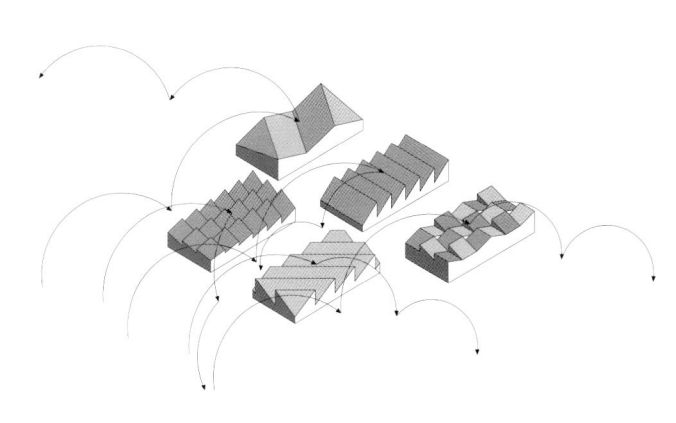

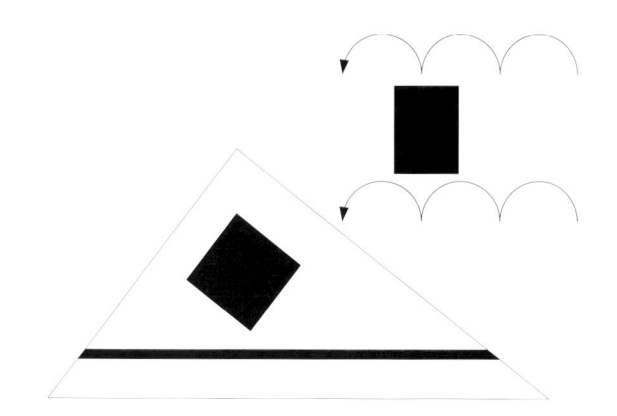

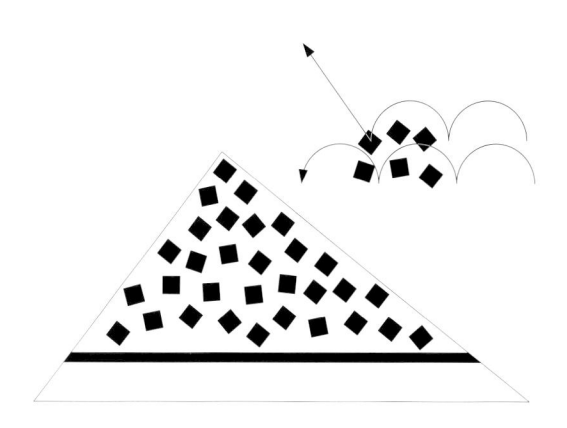

Oblique roofs = Sound distortion!

1. Dillema: Program not big enough to cover the plot

2. Low rise sprawl to create bigger coverage

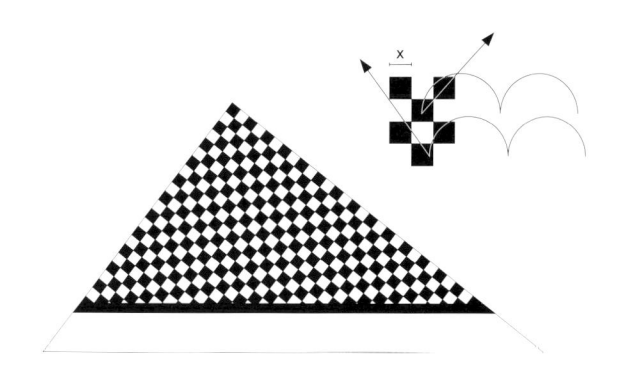

3. Checker board structure provides the biggest sprawl and coverage possible

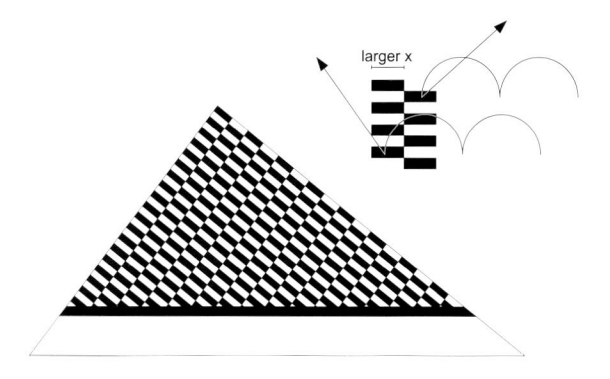

4. Strechted plots to increase possibility of sound reflection

ARCHITECTURAL DIAGRAMS 059

GUBEN GUBIN
J. MAYER H. ARCHITECTS

"THEY ECHO THIS UNCERTAINTY AND SEARCH FOR AN ARTICULATION OF SUCH A COMPLEX PLACE."

ARCHITECTURAL DIAGRAMS 061

GUIYANG HUAXI URBAN CENTRE
Serie Architects

"FROM THE PUBLIC GROUND TO THE SHARED COURTYARDS TO THE DOUBLE FACADES OF THE ROOMS."

Landscape Massing Strategy

An interweaving of programme and floor plates produces a landscape in which the SOHO component of the project is concentrated in 3 "peaks", opening up their plan to give them access to daylighting and views, while seeding the "valley" ground as a public terrain.

Tulou/hakka House: Differentiated Courtyards

The four minor courtyards are set within smaller clusters for different families, separated from public zones, allowing light and private outdoor spaces.

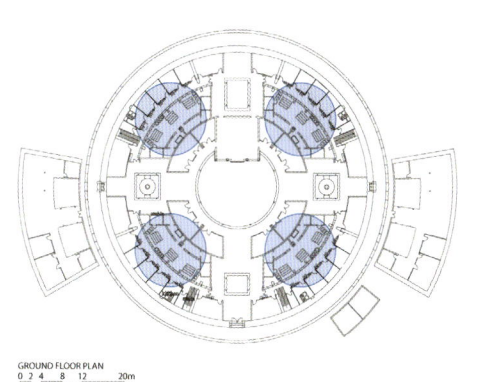

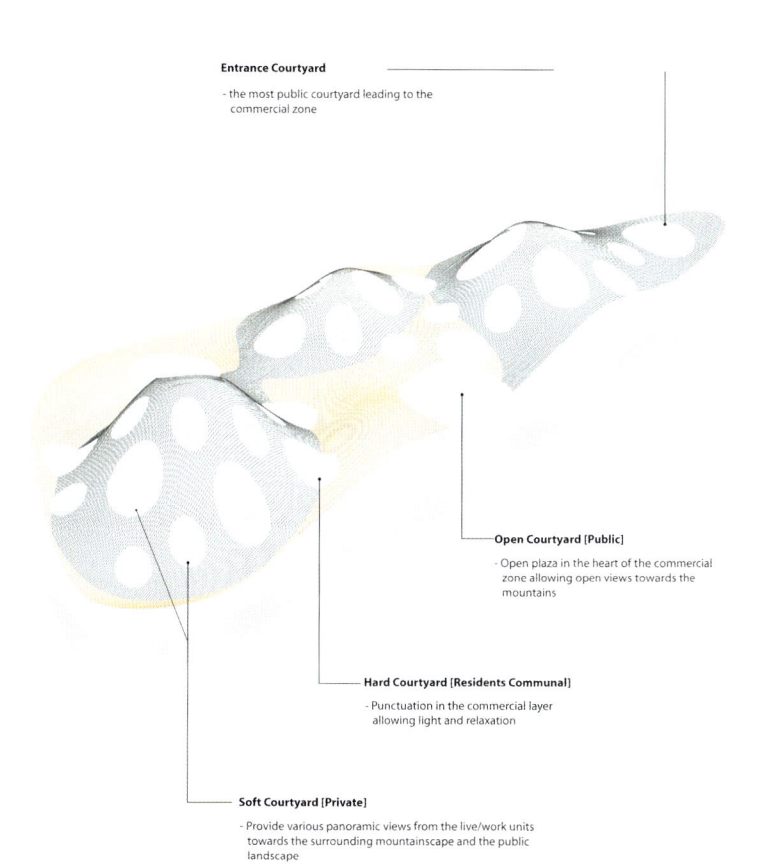

GROUND FLOOR PLAN
0 2 4 8 12 20m

Entrance Courtyard
- the most public courtyard leading to the commercial zone

Open Courtyard [Public]
- Open plaza in the heart of the commercial zone allowing open views towards the mountains

Hard Courtyard [Residents Communal]
- Punctuation in the commercial layer allowing light and relaxation

Soft Courtyard [Private]
- Provide various panoramic views from the live/work units towards the surrounding mountainscape and the public landscape

Proposal : Landscape of Differentiated Courtyards

ARCHITECTURAL DIAGRAMS 063

HEALTH SCIENCES CAMPUS Serie Architects

"THIS IS ACHIEVED BY RE-DEFINING THE TRADITIONAL COURTYARD BLOCKS AS AGGREGATED INTER-LINKED CELLS."

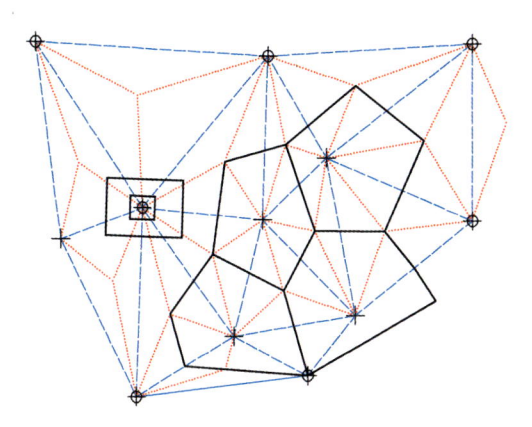

Nodes for potential courtyards, open spaces and existing building. Delauney triangulation to create Vorenoi diagram of cellular faculty buildings with compact massing

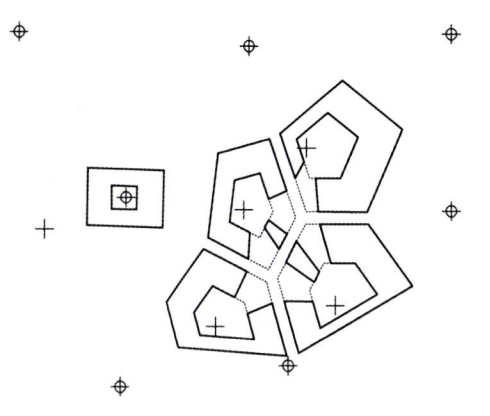

Inter-linked cellular courtyards created within compact faculty buildings that are consistent in massing and differentiated

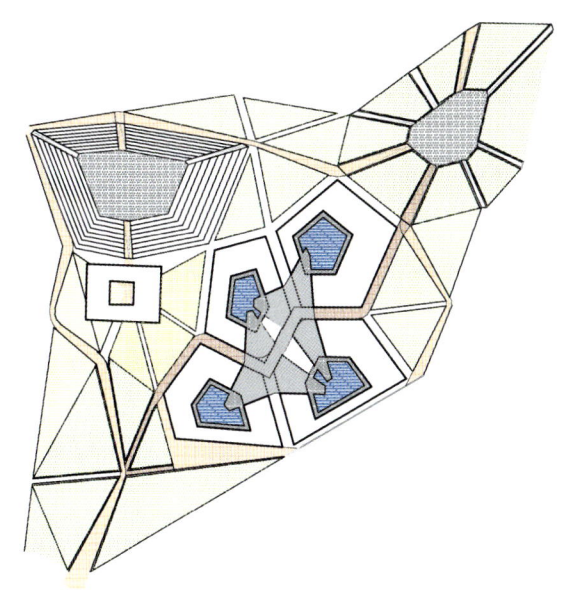

Triangultion lines further create paths and differentiated landscape. The compact massing and courtyards allows for shaded open spaces and pedestrian paths

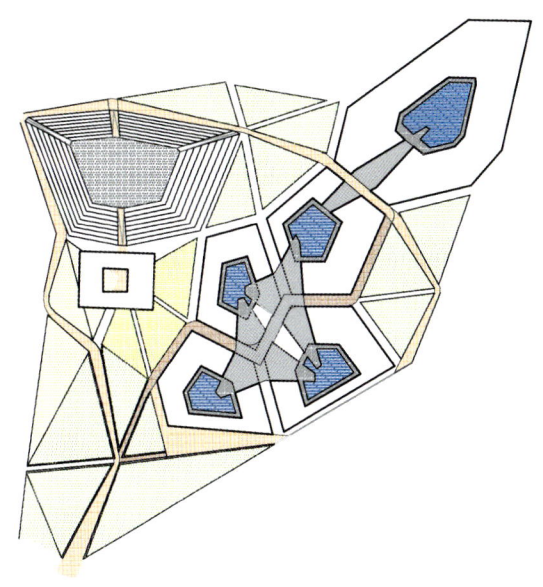

Cellular organization allows further growth and expansion of faculties whilst maintaining coherence of overall urban form

HELSINGØR PSYCHIATRIC HOSPITAL JDS Architects

"IT NEEDS TO ALLOW CONTROL AND PROTECTION WHILE MAINTAINING A FREE AND OPEN ATMOSPHERE."

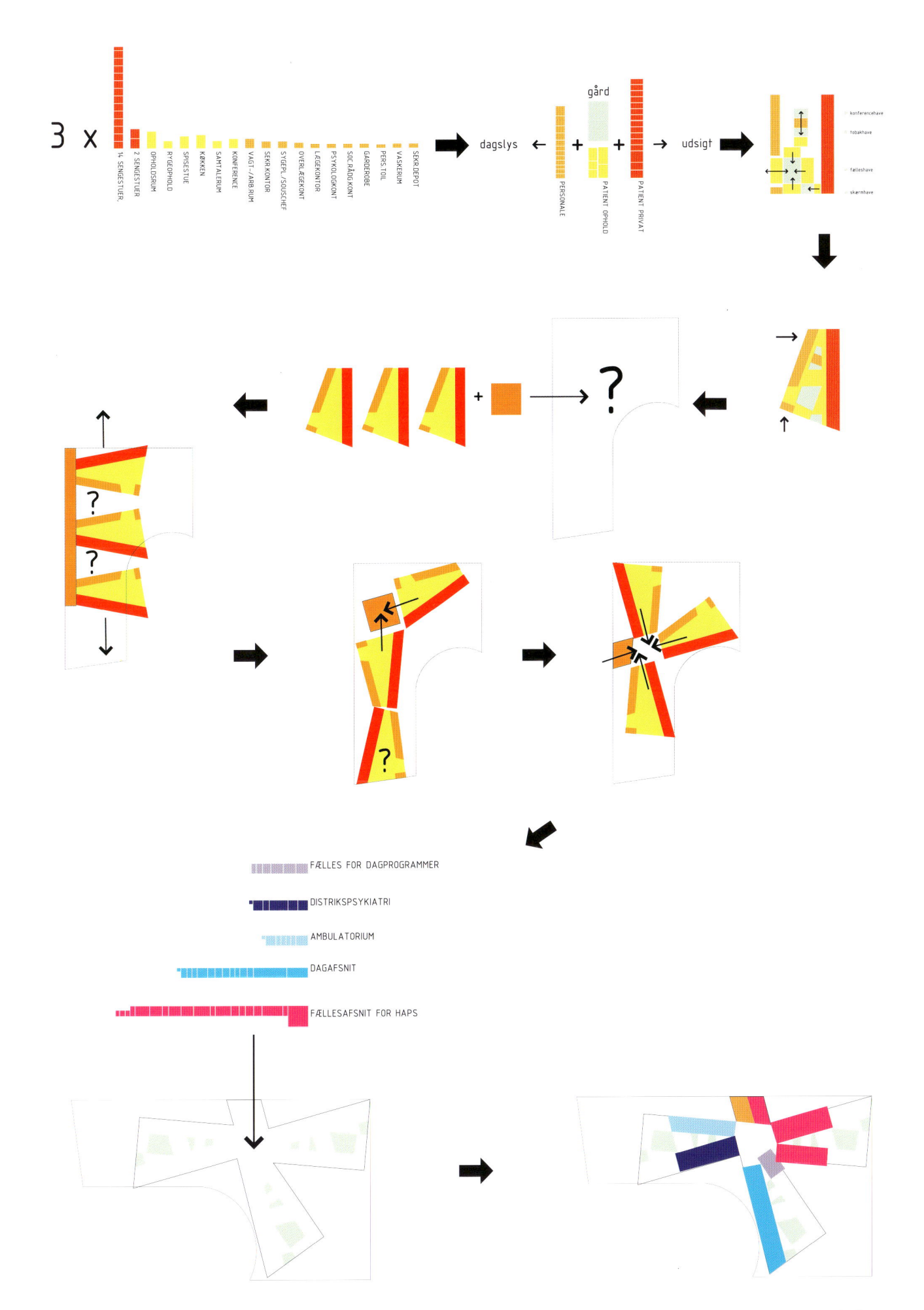

ARCHITECTURAL DIAGRAMS 067

HIGH SQUARE JDS Architects

"FOLLOWING THE OPENING OF ITS NEW SUBWAY, COPENHAGEN WILL RECEIVE A NEW BREED OF PUBLIC SPACE."

Concept　　　　　　　　　　　Context　　　　　　　　　　　High square

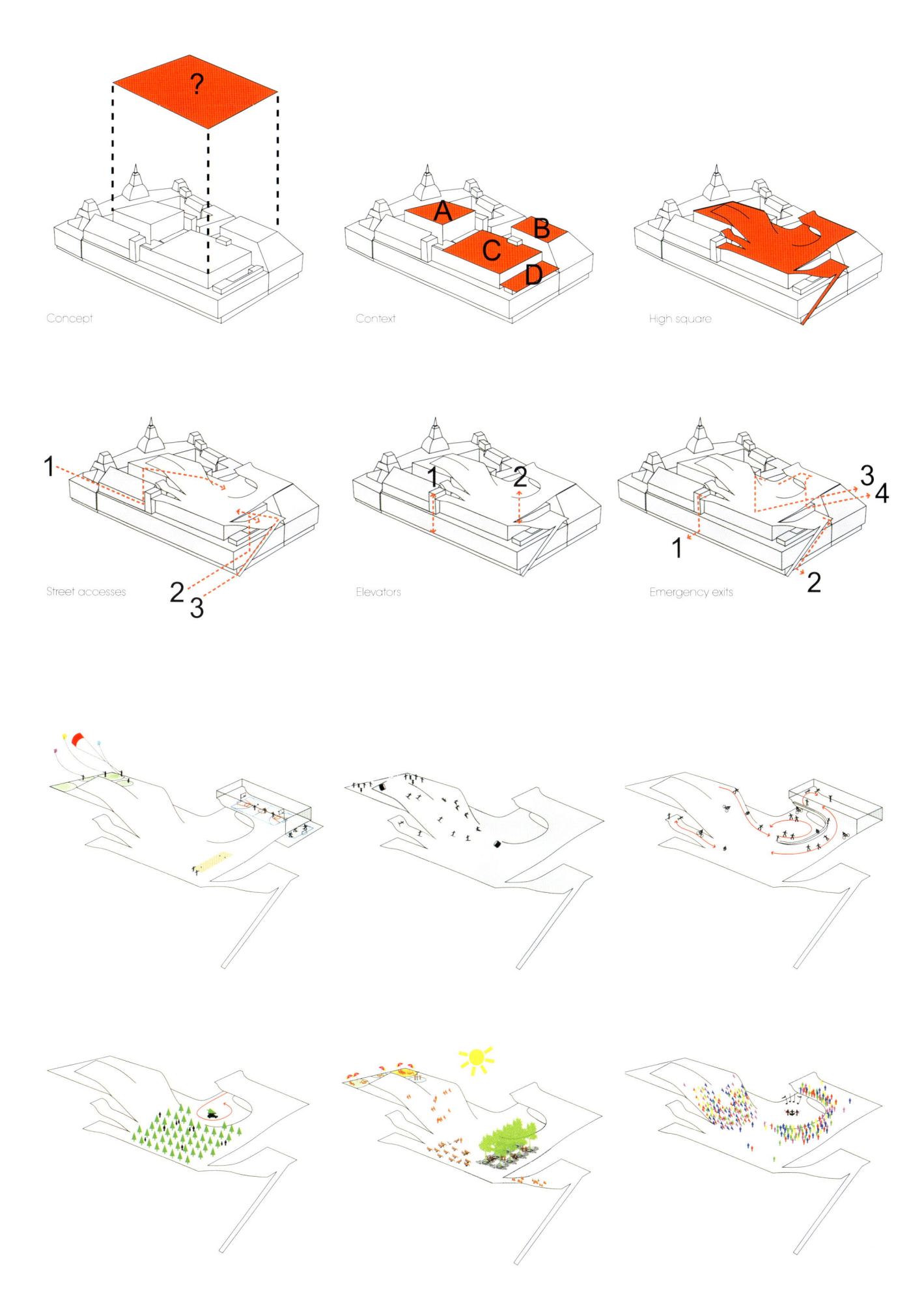

Street accesses　　　　　　Elevators　　　　　　　　　　Emergency exits

ARCHITECTURAL DIAGRAMS 069

HIGHWAY…ING
SMAQ

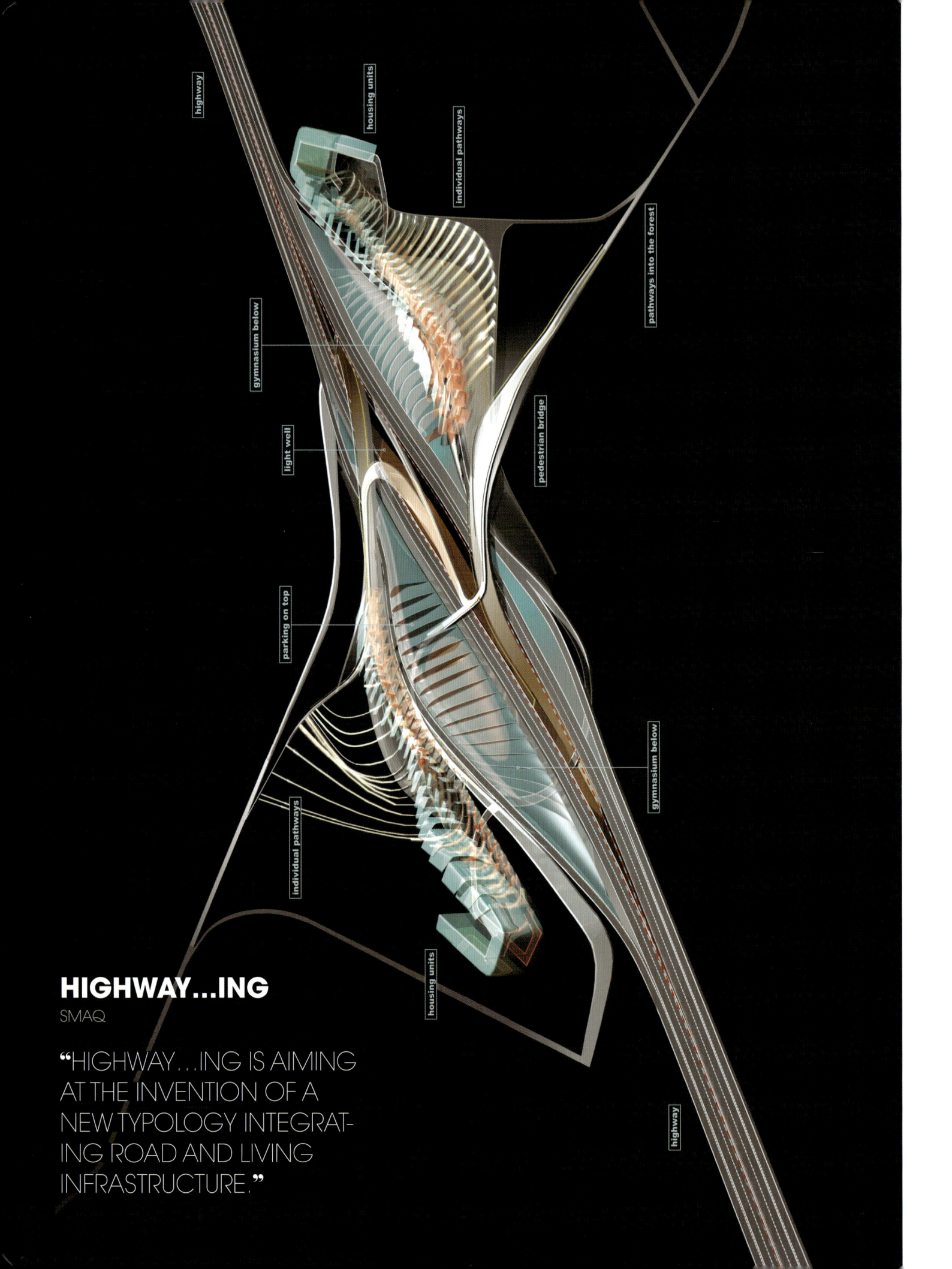

"HIGHWAY…ING IS AIMING AT THE INVENTION OF A NEW TYPOLOGY INTEGRATING ROAD AND LIVING INFRASTRUCTURE."

incompatibility of elements ☐ ☐ integration of programs

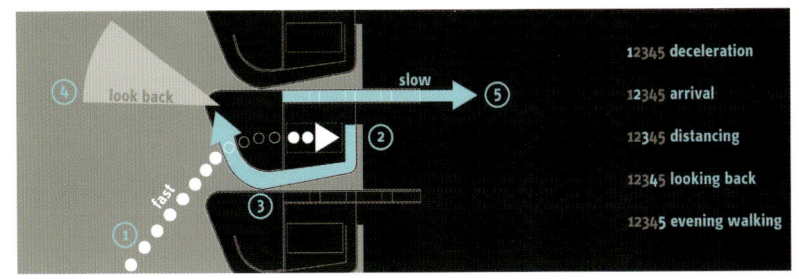

12345 deceleration
look back   slow
12345 arrival
fast
12345 distancing
12345 looking back
12345 evening walking

Plan of a single house

01 02 03 04
05 06 07
Top view

08 09 10 11
12 13 14
Road view

ARCHITECTURAL DIAGRAMS 071

HUA_CULTURAL & SHOPPING CENTER
JDS Architects

"AS A THEMATIC FOR THE SHOPPING CENTRE AS EXTERIOR AND CONTEXTUAL HABITAT AS WELL AS A LARGE SCALE SHOPPING MALL."

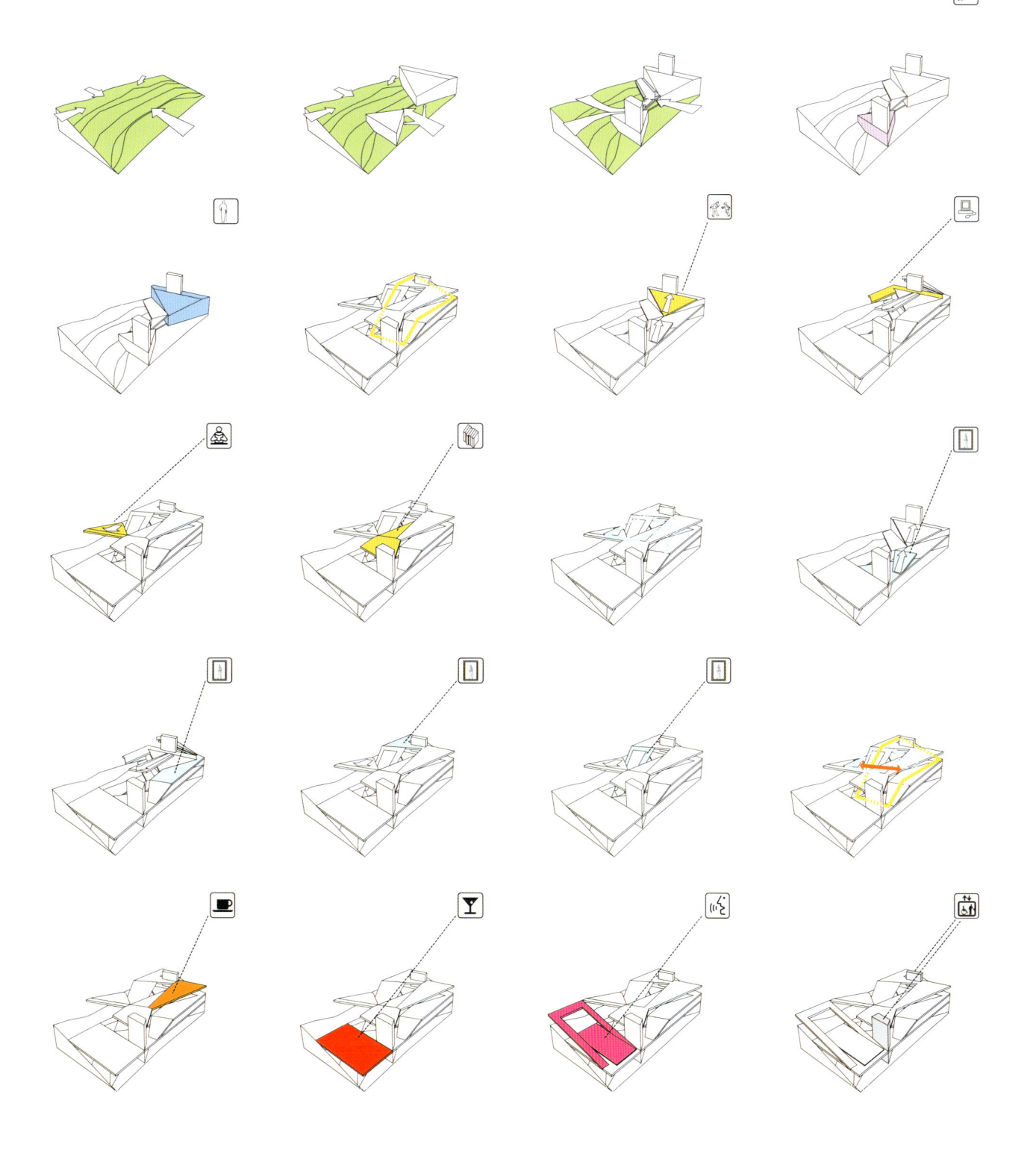

ARCHITECTURAL DIAGRAMS 073

INCOGNITO

AA + U partnership for Architecture, art and urbanism

"THE VISITORS' ACTIVITIES ARE CONTAINED INTO THE COURTYARD AND IT GIVES THE POSSIBILITY TO A VERY SMALL BUILDING TO HOUSE LARGER SCALE ACTIVITIES."

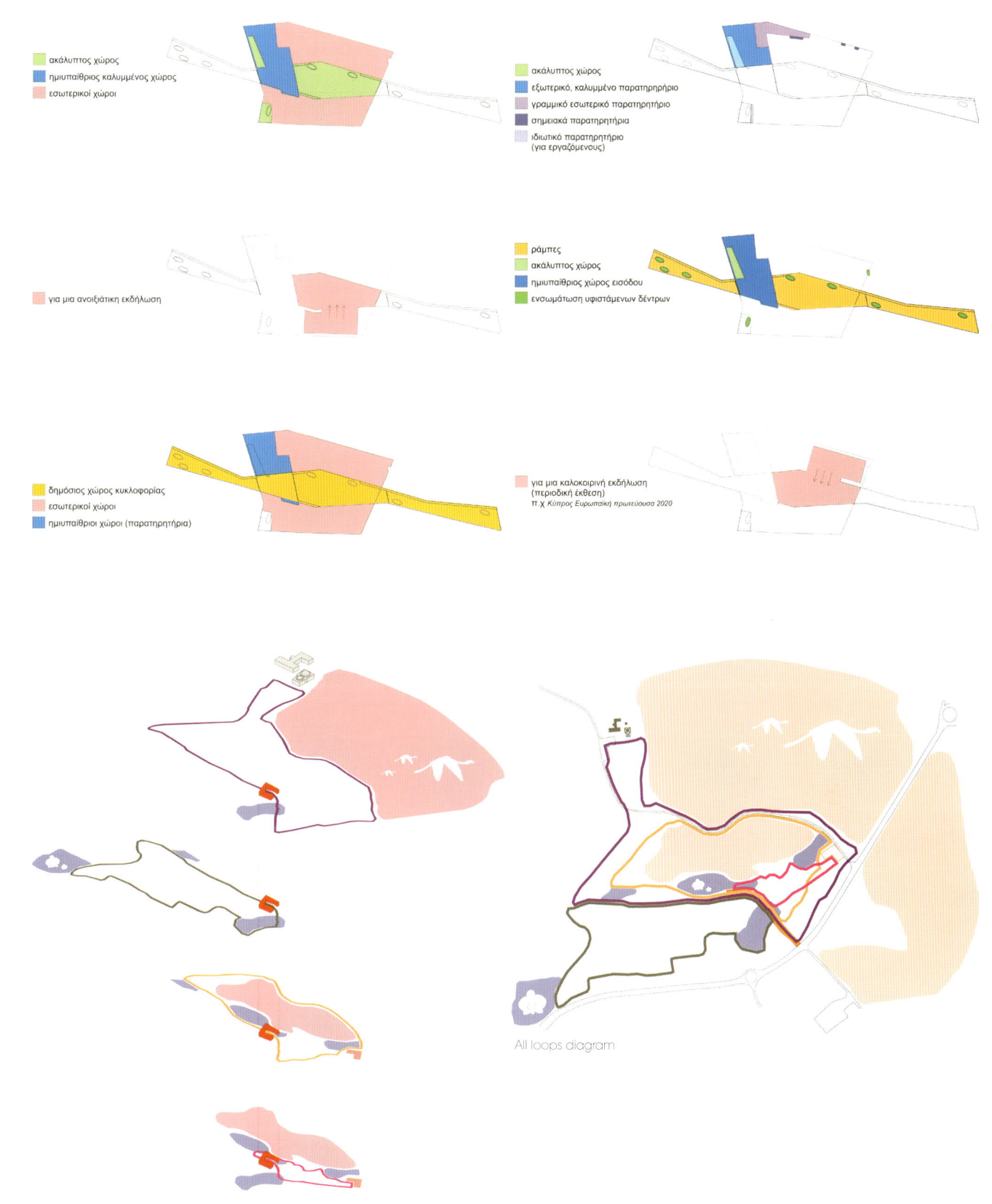

Legend 1
- ακάλυπτος χώρος
- ημιυπαίθριος καλυμμένος χώρος
- εσωτερικοί χώροι

Legend 2
- ακάλυπτος χώρος
- εξωτερικό, καλυμμένο παρατηρητήριο
- γραμμικό εσωτερικό παρατηρητήριο
- σημειακά παρατηρητήρια
- ιδιωτικό παρατηρητήριο (για εργαζόμενους)

Legend 3
- για μια ανοιξιάτικη εκδήλωση

Legend 4
- ράμπες
- ακάλυπτος χώρος
- ημιυπαίθριος χώρος εισόδου
- ενσωμάτωση υφιστάμενων δέντρων

Legend 5
- δημόσιος χώρος κυκλοφορίας
- εσωτερικοί χώροι
- ημιυπαίθριοι χώροι (παρατηρητήρια)

Legend 6
- για μια καλοκαιρινή εκδήλωση (περιοδική έκθεση)
  π.χ *Κύπρος Ευρωπαϊκή πρωτεύουσα 2020*

Loops_explosion diagram

All loops diagram

ARCHITECTURAL DIAGRAMS 075

LAVA LAND NL Architects

"LAVA LAND SUGGESTS CREATING A SMALL SQUARE THAT CAN ACCOMMODATE MANY DIFFERENT OUTDOOR ACTIVITIES."

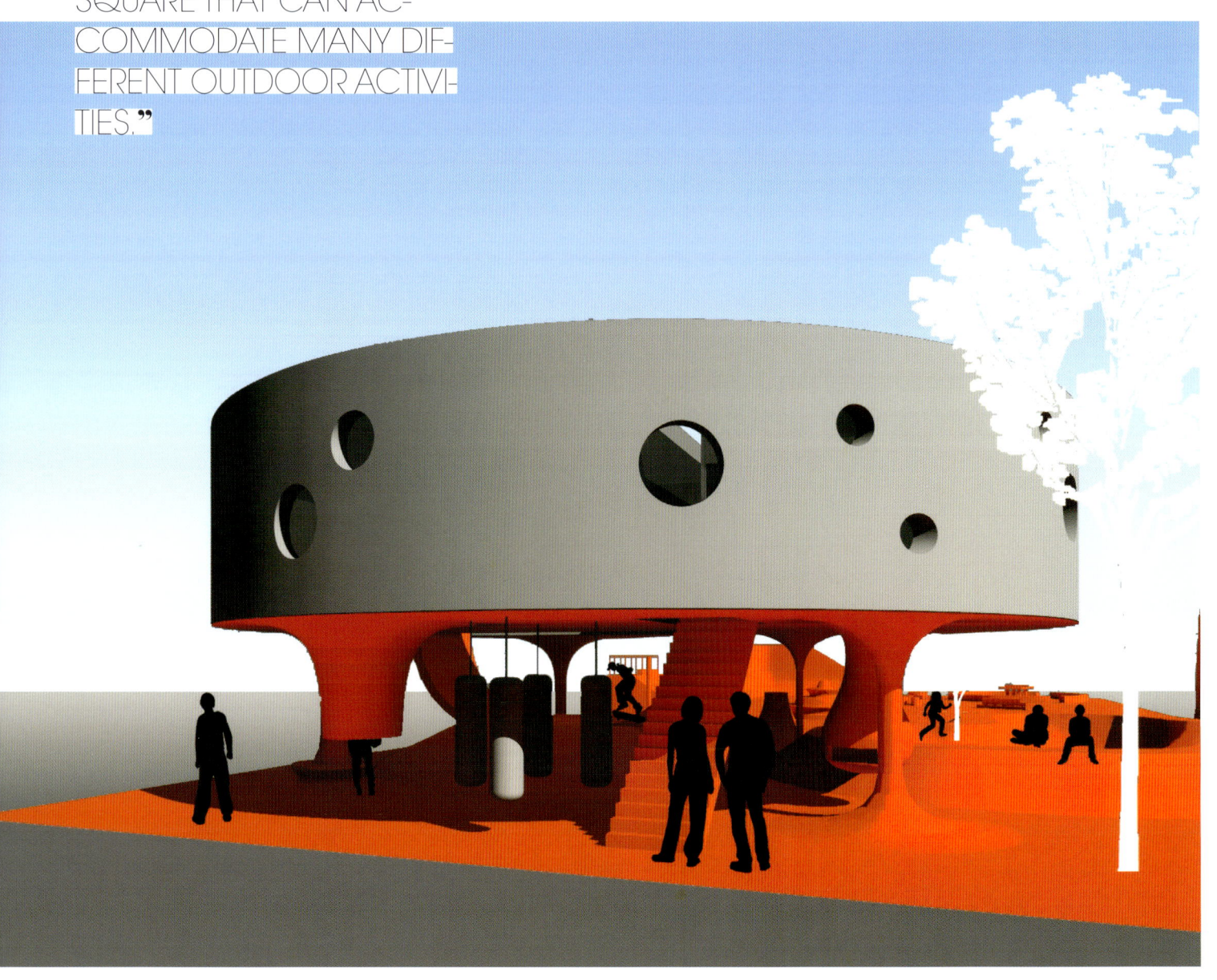

Axonometry

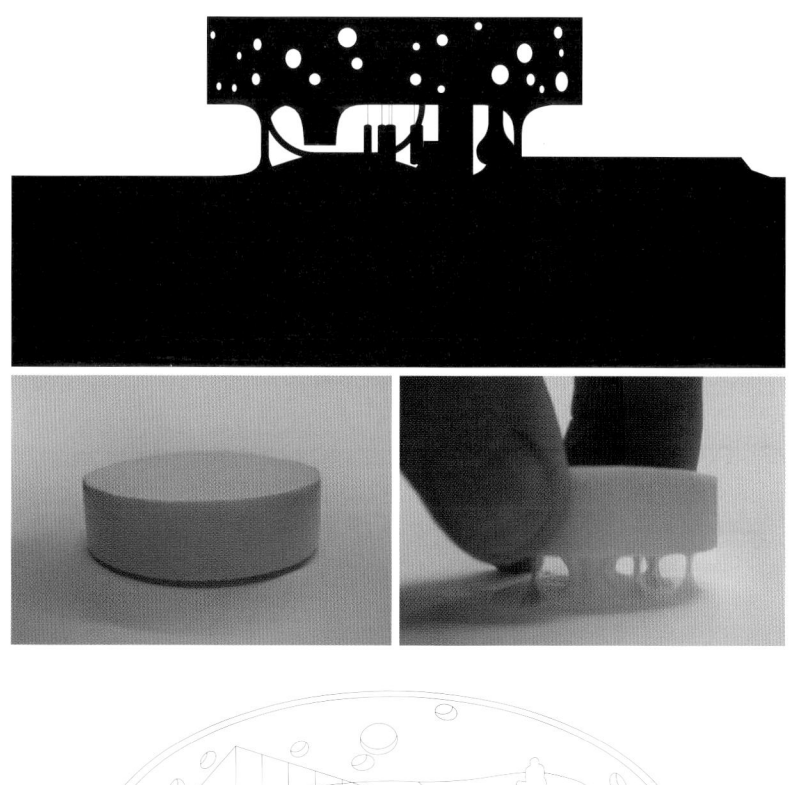

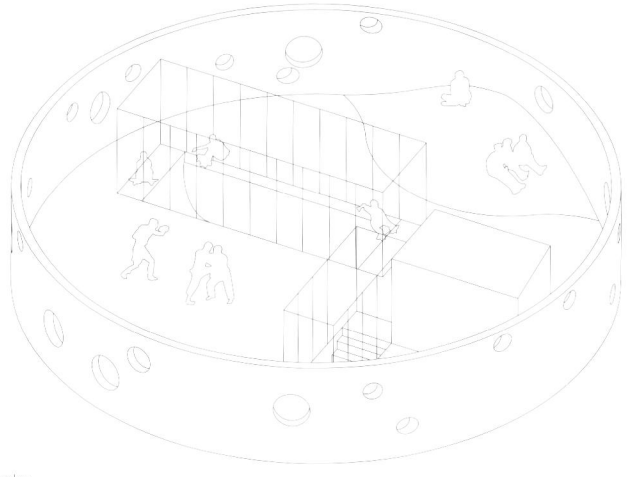

ARCHITECTURAL DIAGRAMS 077

LES HALLES
PERIPHERIQUES architects

La Seine

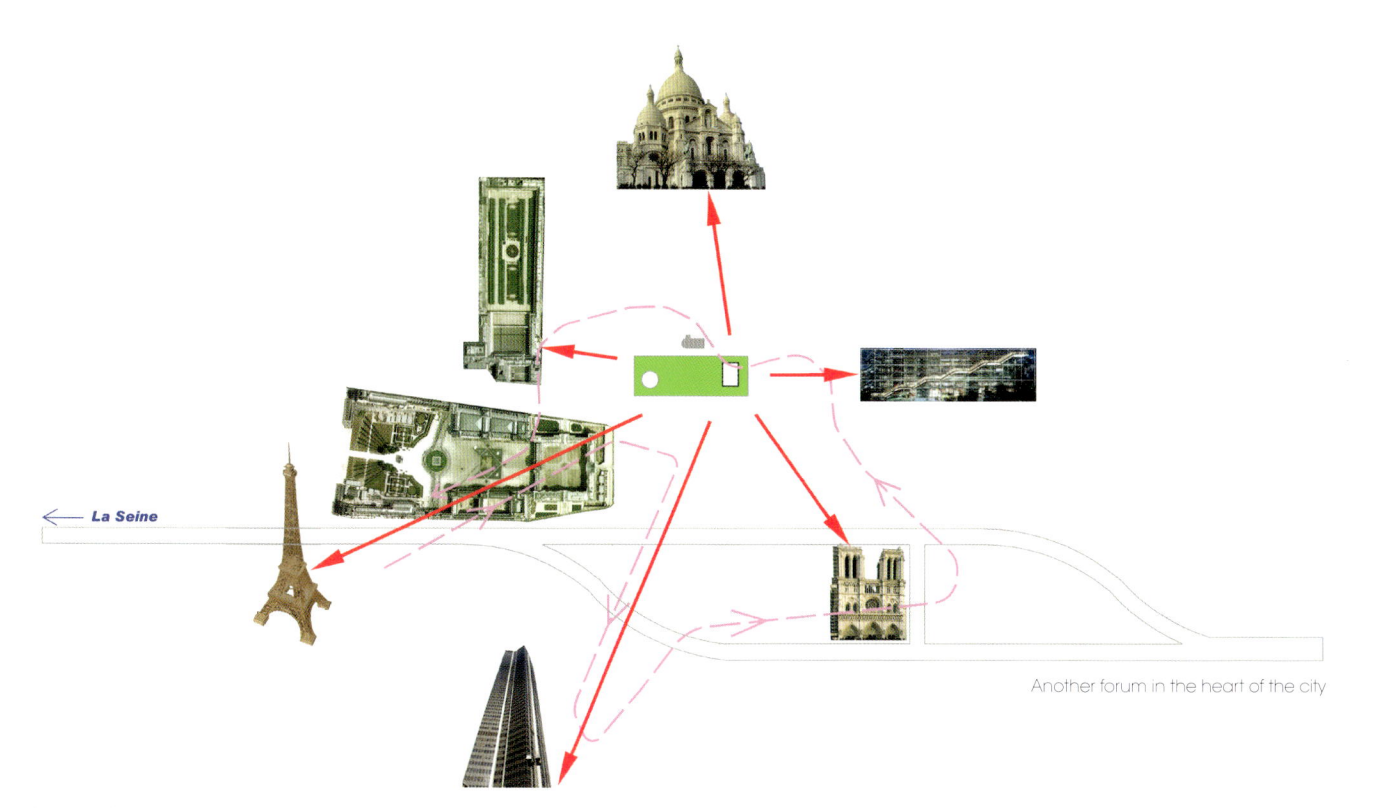

Another forum in the heart of the city

Issues and urban landscape

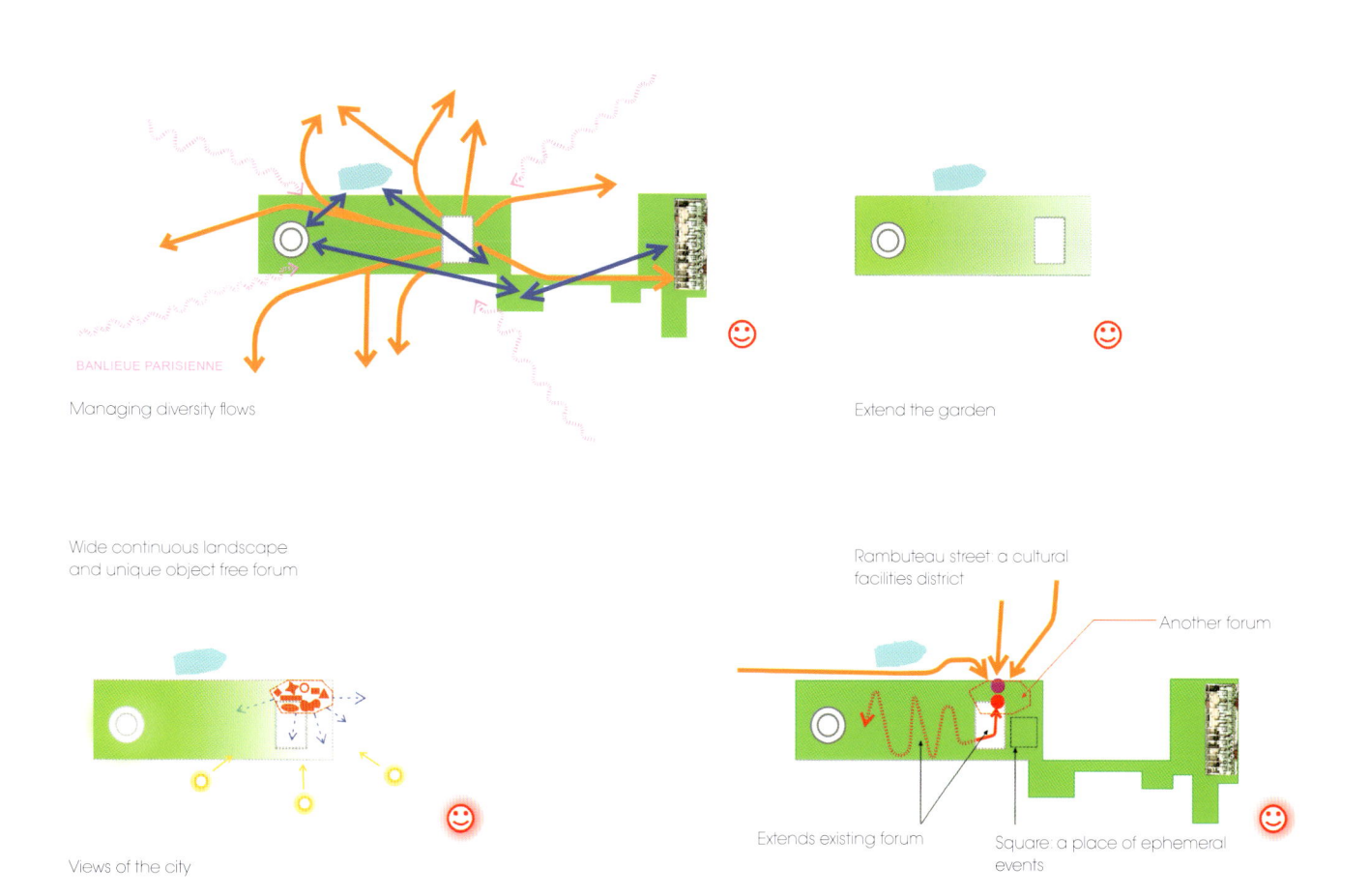

BANLIEUE PARISIENNE

Managing diversity flows

Extend the garden

Wide continuous landscape and unique object free forum

Views of the city

Rambuteau street: a cultural facilities district

Another forum

Extends existing forum

Square: a place of ephemeral events

ARCHITECTURAL DIAGRAMS 079

LIBRARY ma0

"THE COLLAGE OF STU-
DENT PORTRAITS WAS
CHOSEN AS THE IMAGE
THAT BEST PORTRAYED THE
VITALITY."

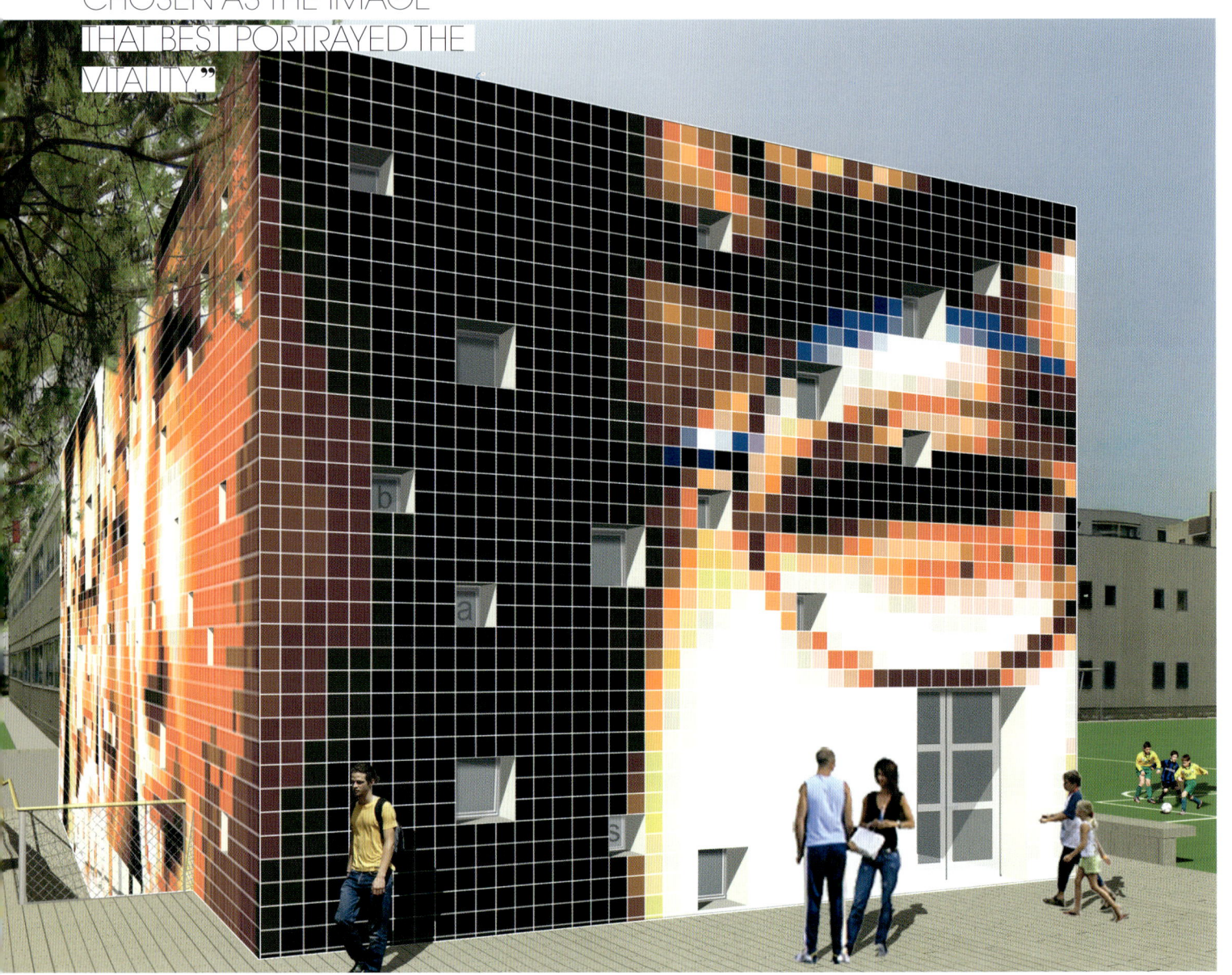

Concept 01 / every book is a window on the world

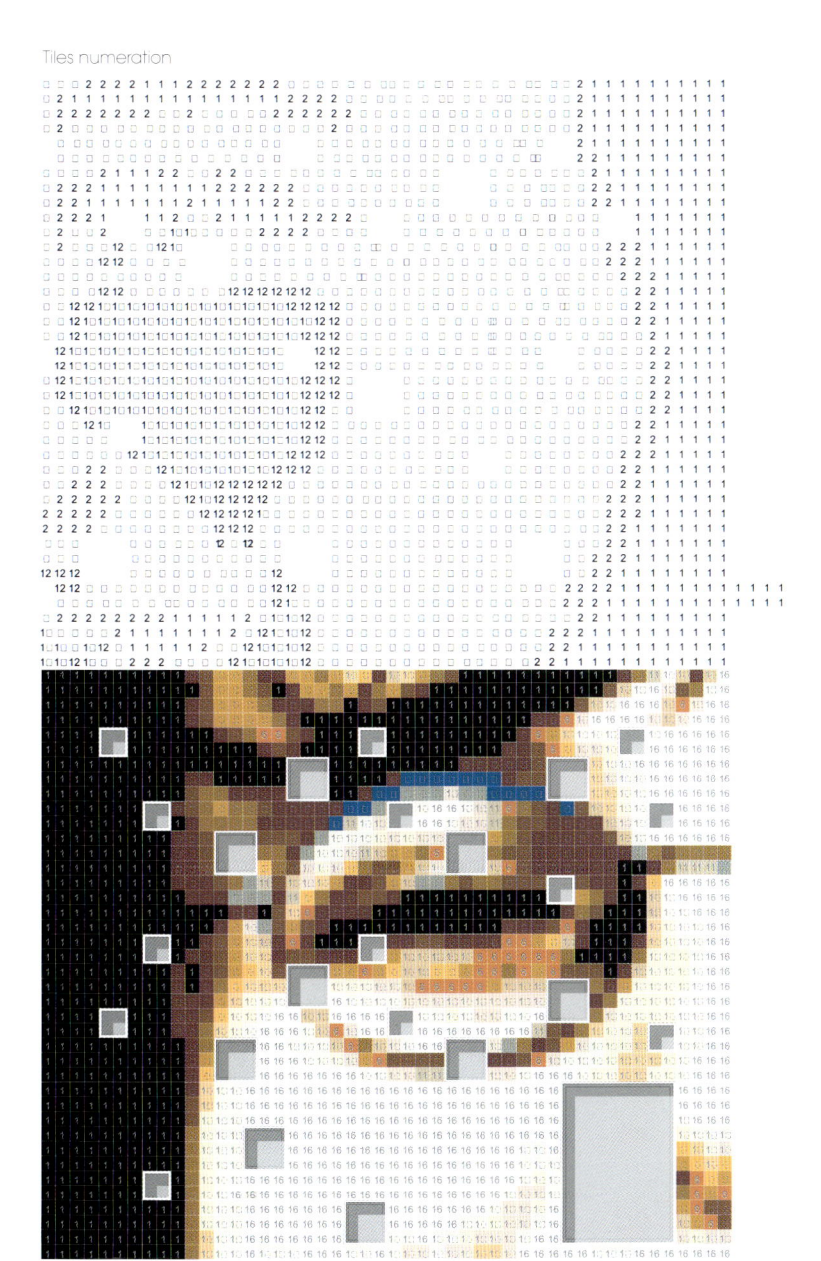

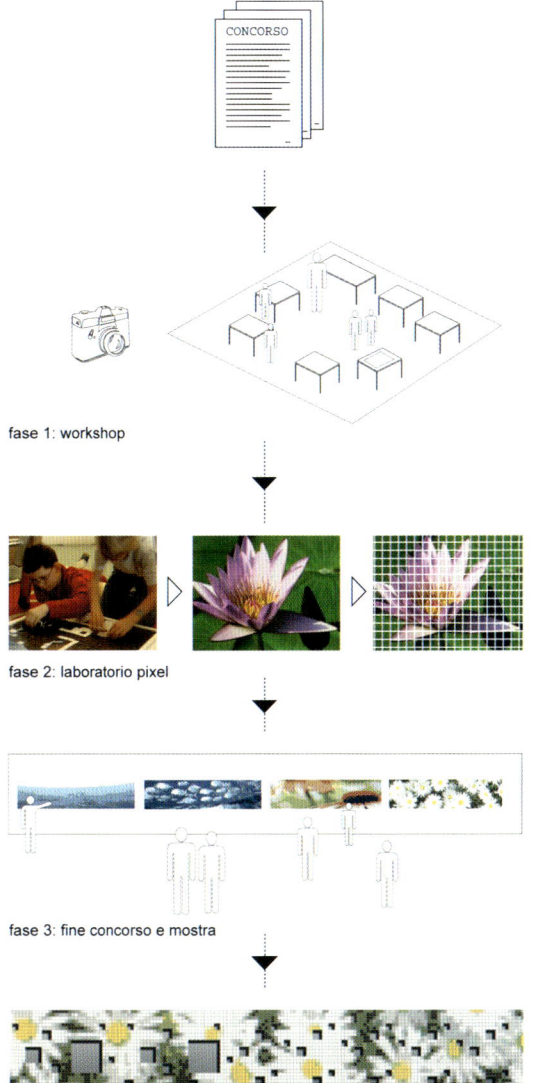

Concept 02 / creativity comes from knowledge

Tiles numeration

The participative process

fase 1: workshop

fase 2: laboratorio pixel

fase 3: fine concorso e mostra

fase 4: costruzione

ARCHITECTURAL DIAGRAMS 081

LIGHT HOUSE Re_Load

"THE PLAN SHAPE IS CHARACTERIZED BY THE COMPOSITION OF THREE VOLUMES."

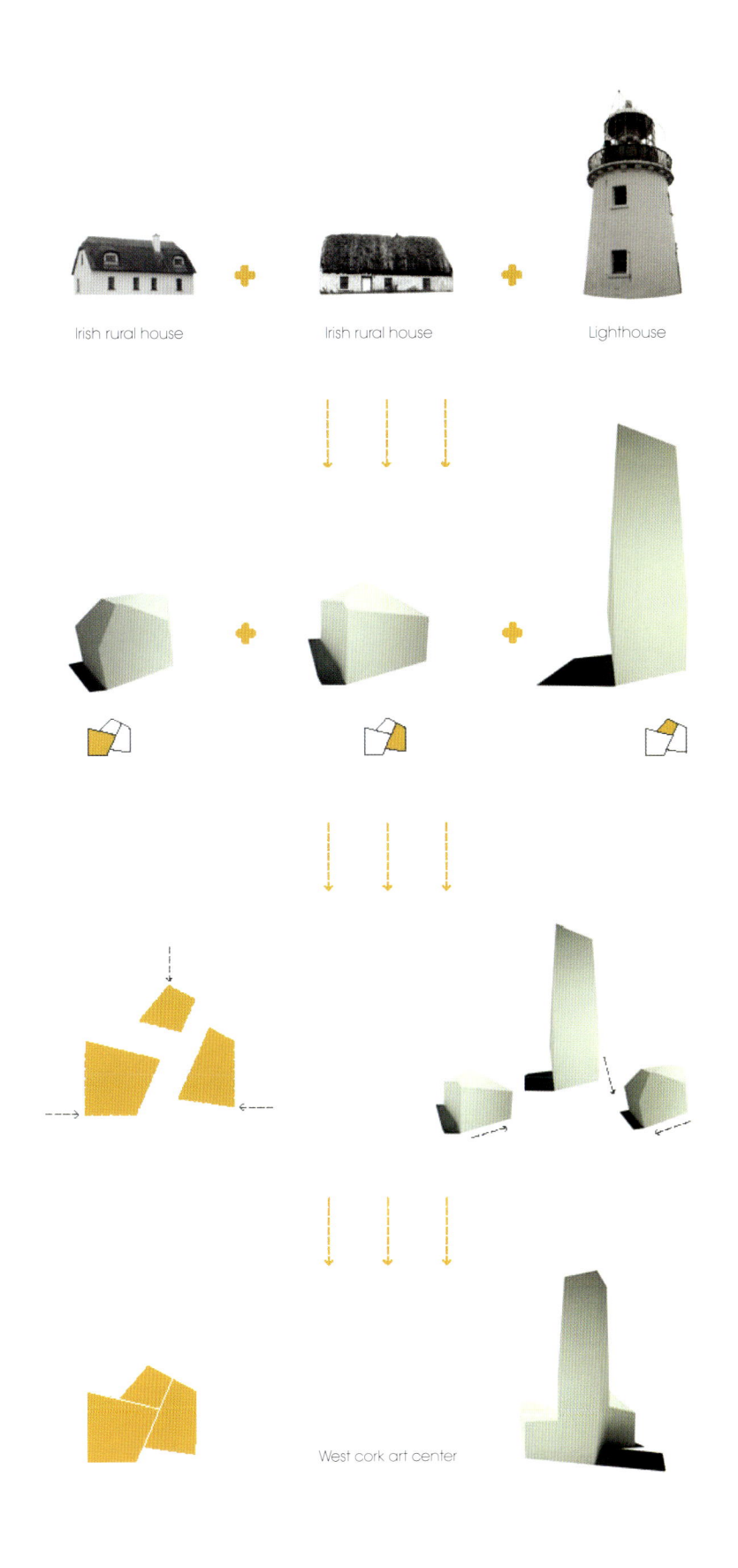

Irish rural house + Irish rural house + Lighthouse

West cork art center

ARCHITECTURAL DIAGRAMS 083

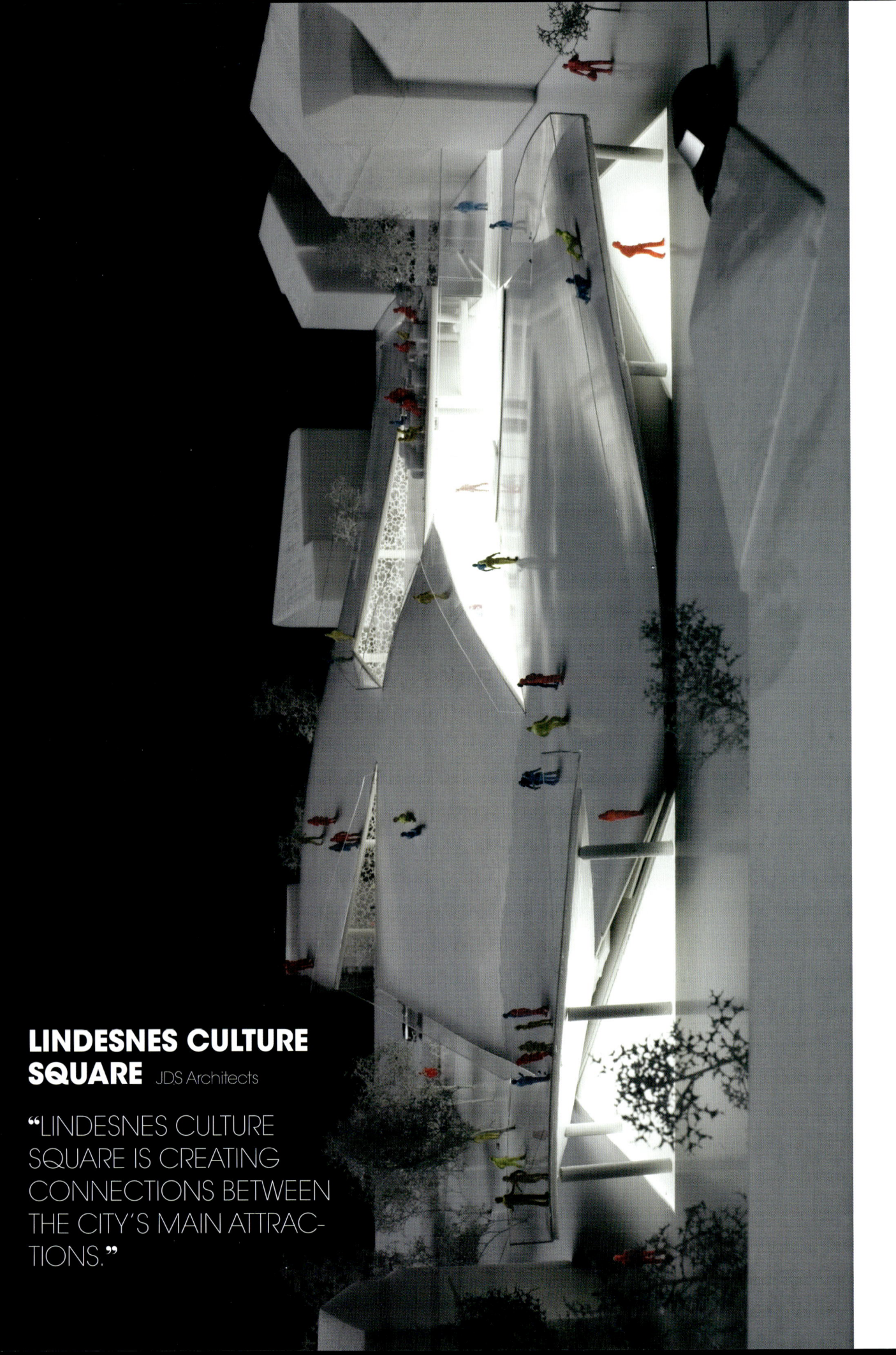

LINDESNES CULTURE SQUARE JDS Architects

"LINDESNES CULTURE SQUARE IS CREATING CONNECTIONS BETWEEN THE CITY'S MAIN ATTRACTIONS."

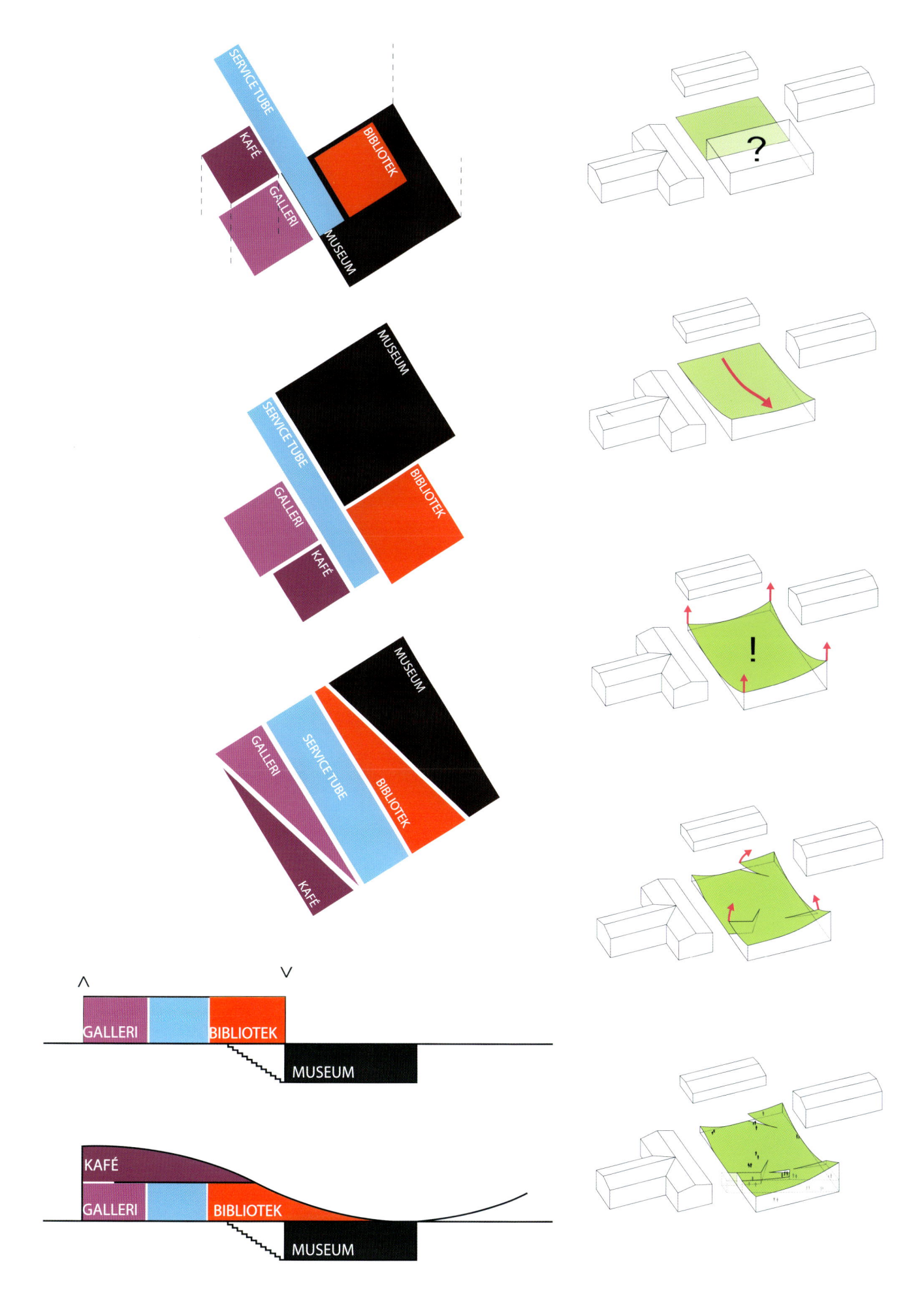

ARCHITECTURAL DIAGRAMS 085

LJUBLJANA PASSENGER STATION
SADAR VUGA ARHITEKTI

"THE BRIDGING STRUCTURE IS A SPATIAL TRUSS THAT SPREADS RADIALLY FROM THE CENTRE TOWARDS THE PERIMETER."

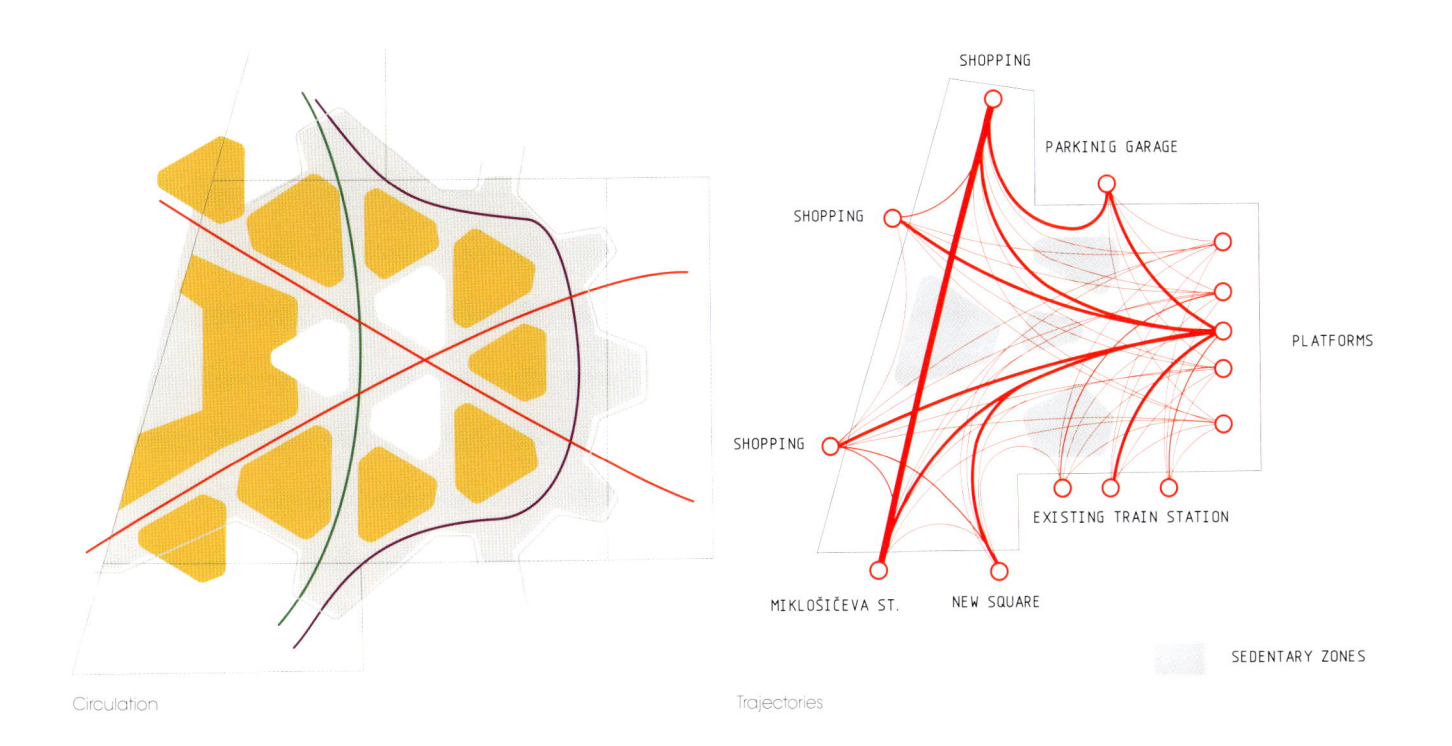

SHOPPING
PARKINIG GARAGE
SHOPPING
PLATFORMS
SHOPPING
EXISTING TRAIN STATION
MIKLOŠIČEVA ST.   NEW SQUARE
SEDENTARY ZONES

Circulation

Trajectories

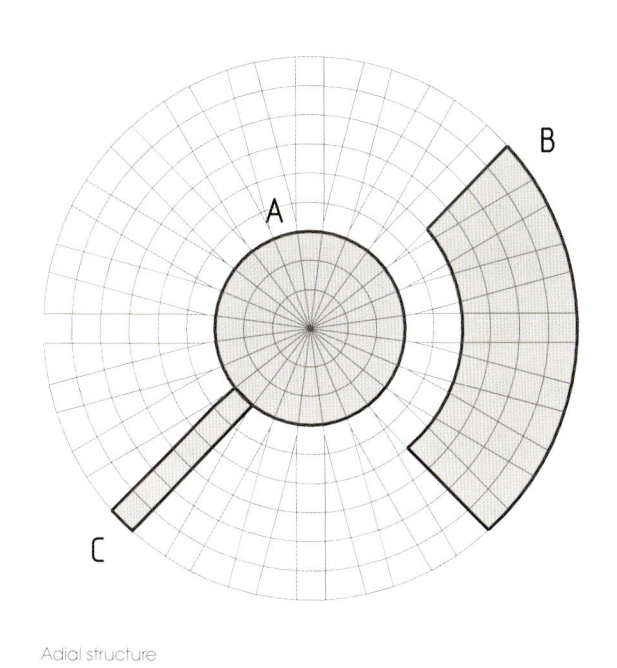

Adial structure

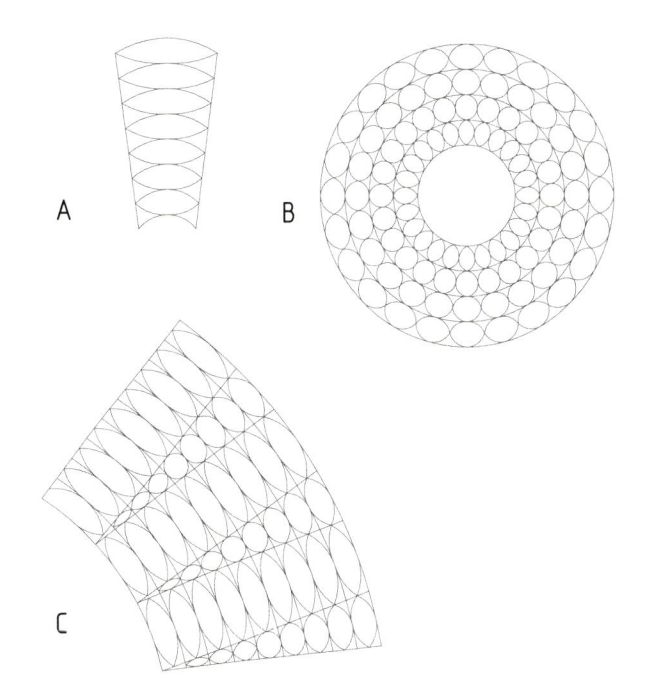

ARCHITECTURAL DIAGRAMS 087

LK 0 AMID [cero9]

"WITH WHICH MATERIAL, IDEAS, TOOLS AND SCALE WE CAN WORK TO PRODUCE CIVIL CONTEMPORARY ARCHITECTURE?"

1 EDIFICIO = 4 EDIFICIOS

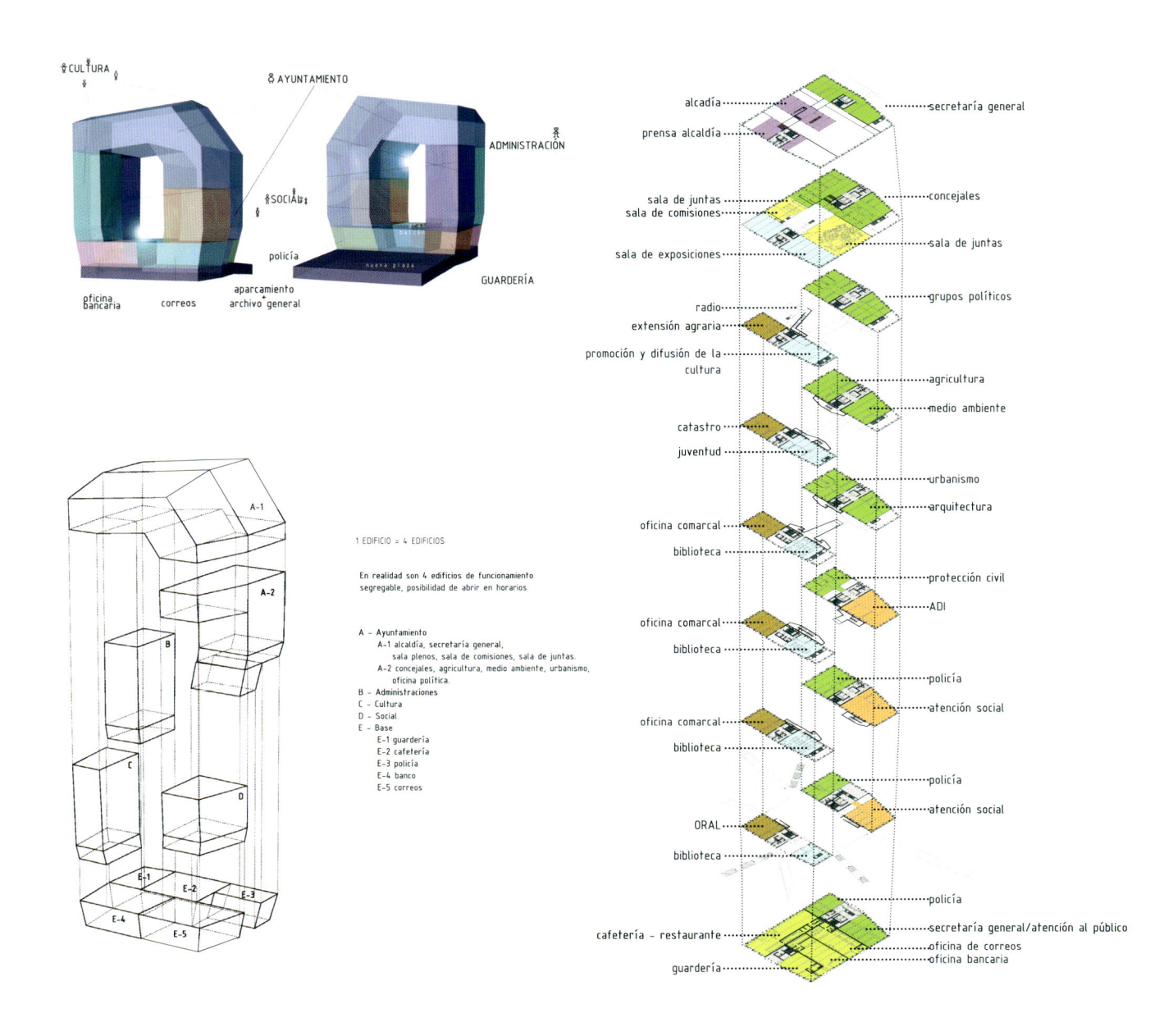

En realidad son 4 edificios de funcionamiento segregable, posibilidad de abrir en horarios

A – Ayuntamiento
  A-1 alcaldía, secretaría general,
    sala plenos, sala de comisiones, sala de juntas.
  A-2 concejales, agricultura, medio ambiente, urbanismo,
    oficina política.
B – Administraciones
C – Cultura
D – Social
E – Base
  E-1 guardería
  E-2 cafetería
  E-3 policía
  E-4 banco
  E-5 correos

ARCHITECTURAL DIAGRAMS 089

LOW ENERGY HOUSING
JDS Architects

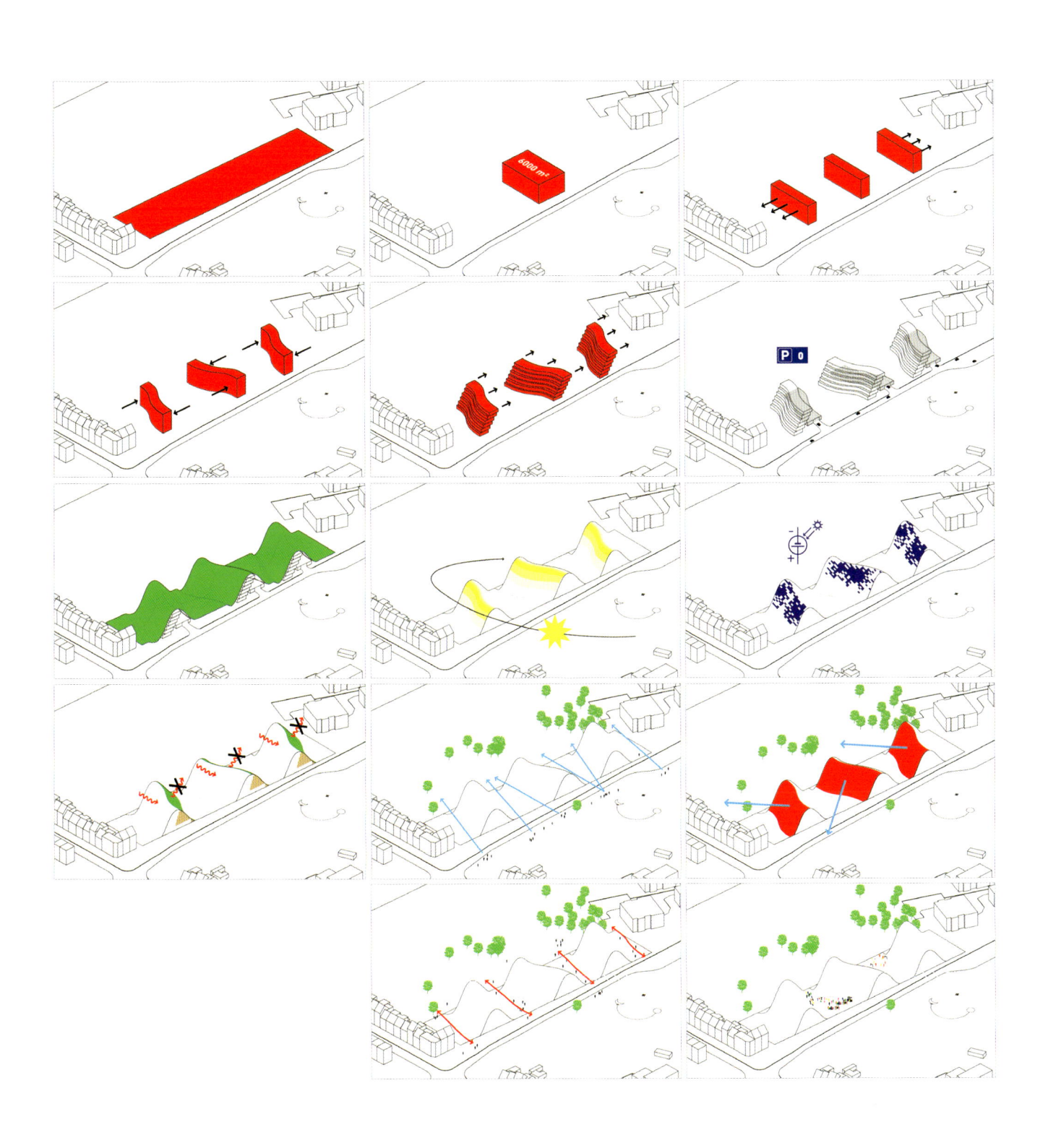

ARCHITECTURAL DIAGRAMS 091

MARITIME YOUTH HOUSE
JDS Architects

"BUILDINGS AND BOAT STORAGE UNDER THE DECK, LEAVING ITS UPPER SIDE FREE FOR RECREATION AND EDUCATION."

Polluted soil - 2500m²

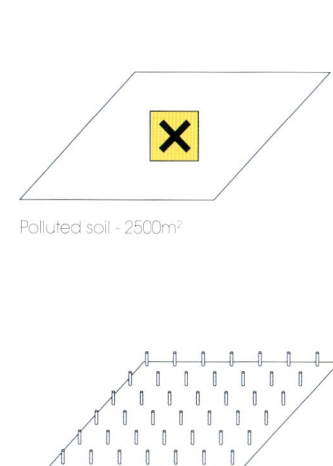

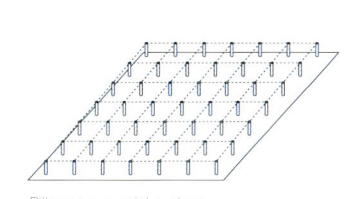

Placement of a raised platform - 2500m²

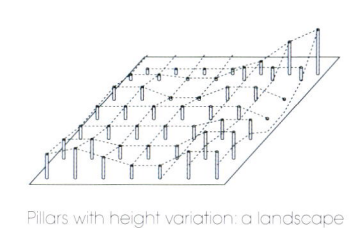

Application of building and landscape 375m² in / 2000m² out

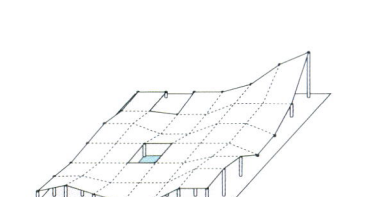

Pillars on the ground

Pillars on a grid system

Pillars with height variation: a landscape of opportunities

Dips and holes for activities: fishing pond / bonfire

Integrated spaces

A new natural environment

Amphitheater

Sets out the cookr

Beach

Boat ramp

Storage under deck

Campfire

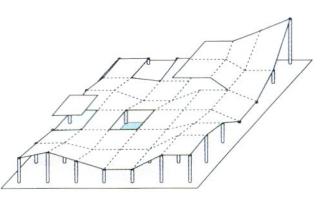

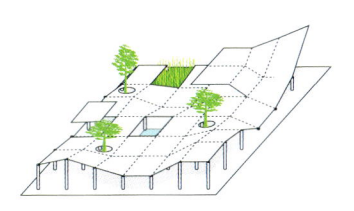

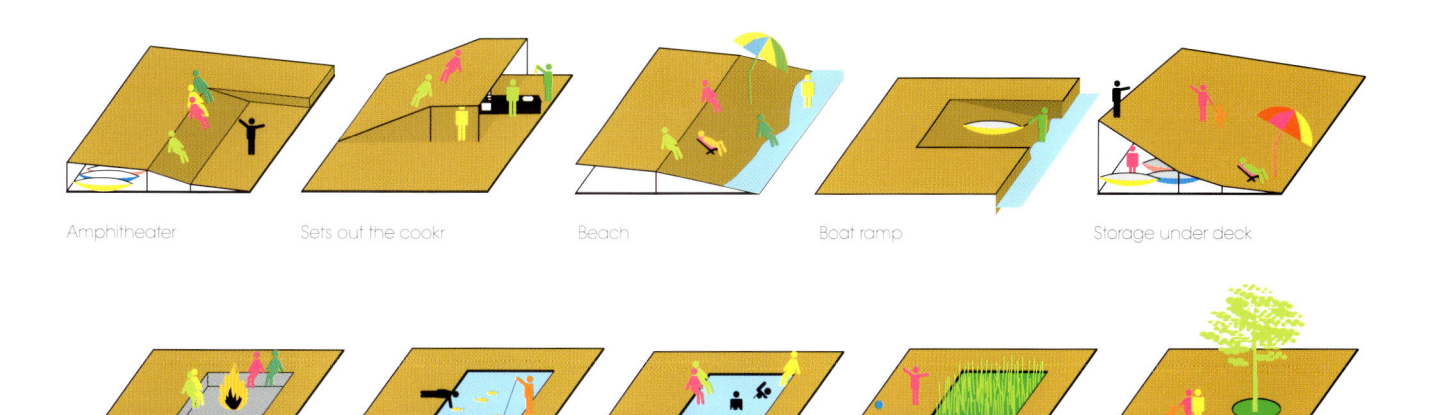

Fishpond

Swimming pool

Arrows have

Existing tree

ARCHITECTURAL DIAGRAMS 093

MARKET IN SANCHI-NARRO LEON 11 ARCHITECTS

"THE FLOWS BETWEEN ONE AND OTHER ONE CAN BE ALTERED BY SMALL INTERVENTIONS THAT IT INTRODUCES NEW SERVICES IN A PERIPHERY PRACTICALLY BARREN."

Market adds contemporary market
Market classes = Ways to consume

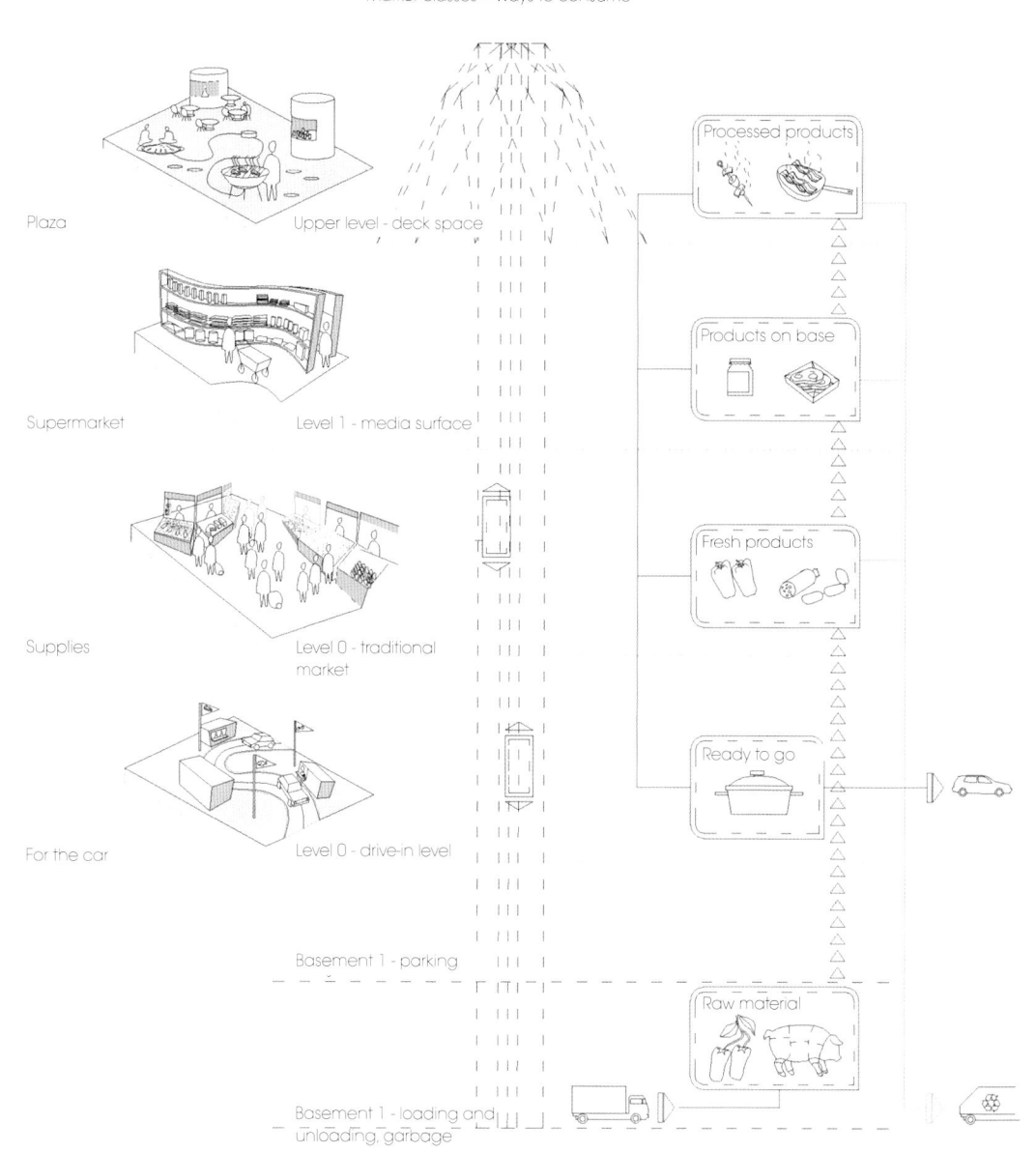

Plaza — Upper level - deck space

Supermarket — Level 1 - media surface

Supplies — Level 0 - traditional market

For the car — Level 0 - drive-in level

Basement 1 - parking

Basement 1 - loading and unloading, garbage

Kind of market

Processed products
Products on base
Fresh products
Ready to go
Raw material

ARCHITECTURAL DIAGRAMS 095

MENSA KARLSRUHE
J. MAYER H. ARCHITECTS

"THE BUILDING REACTS TO THIS SECIAL CONDITION WITH DIFFERENT STAGES OF POROSITY."

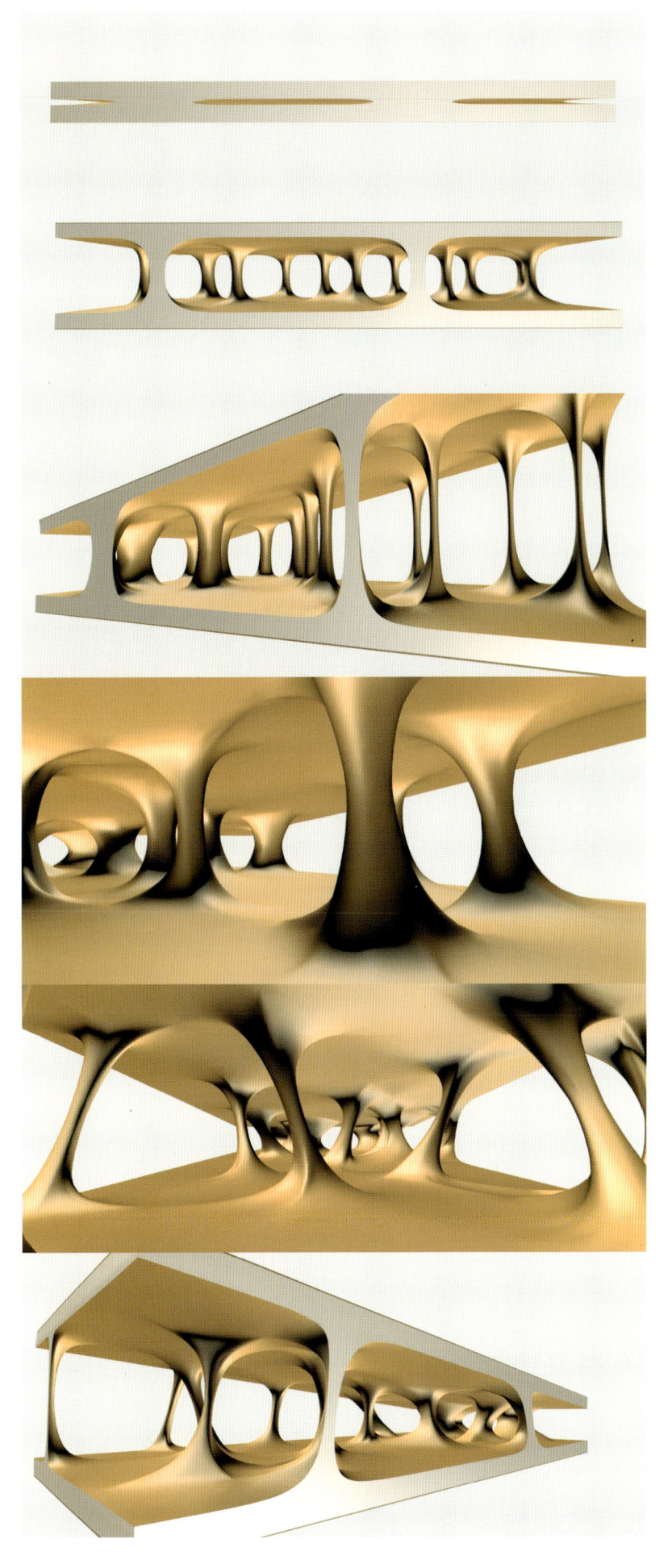

ARCHITECTURAL DIAGRAMS 097

METRO D IaN+

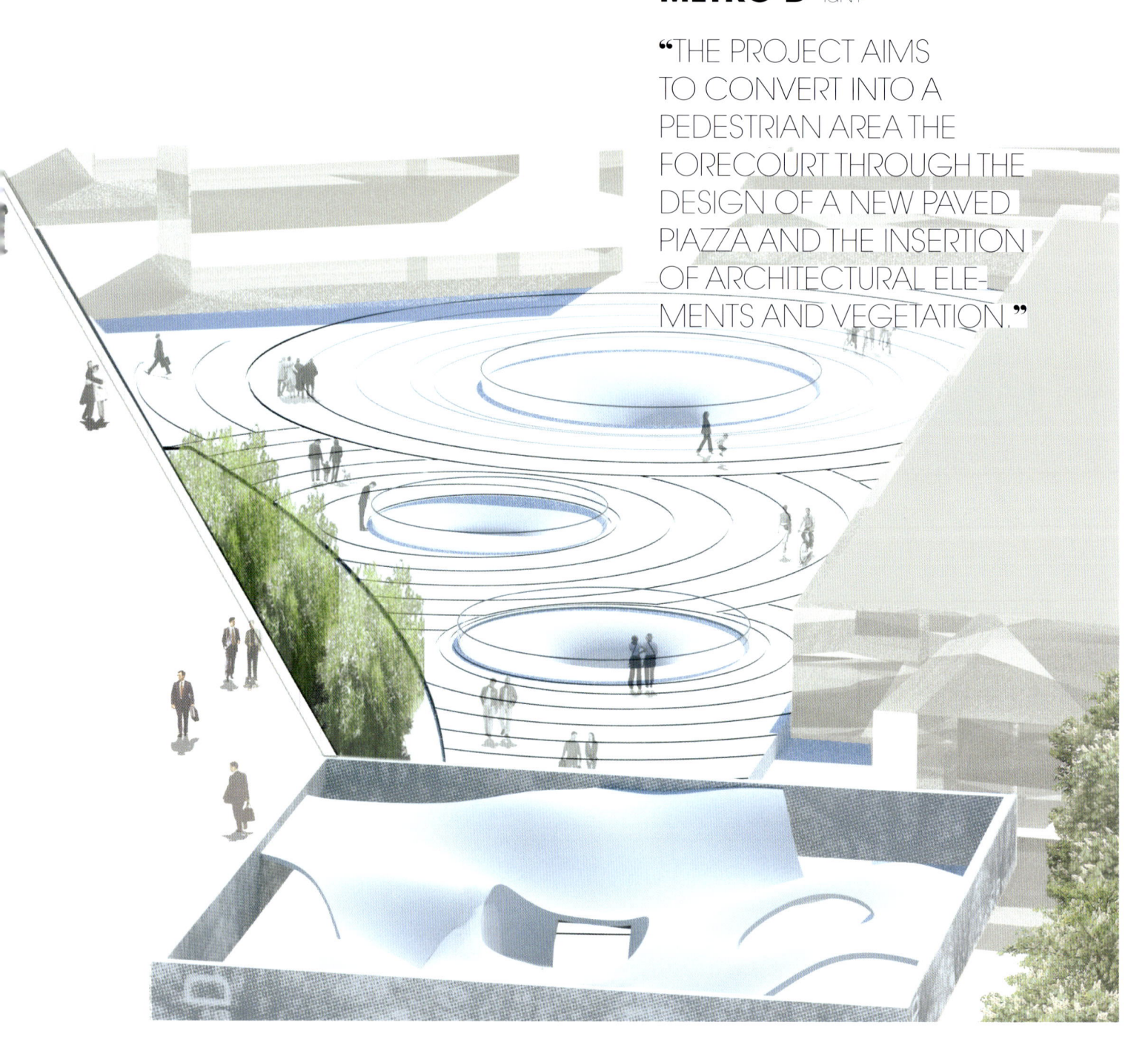

"THE PROJECT AIMS TO CONVERT INTO A PEDESTRIAN AREA THE FORECOURT THROUGH THE DESIGN OF A NEW PAVED PIAZZA AND THE INSERTION OF ARCHITECTURAL ELEMENTS AND VEGETATION."

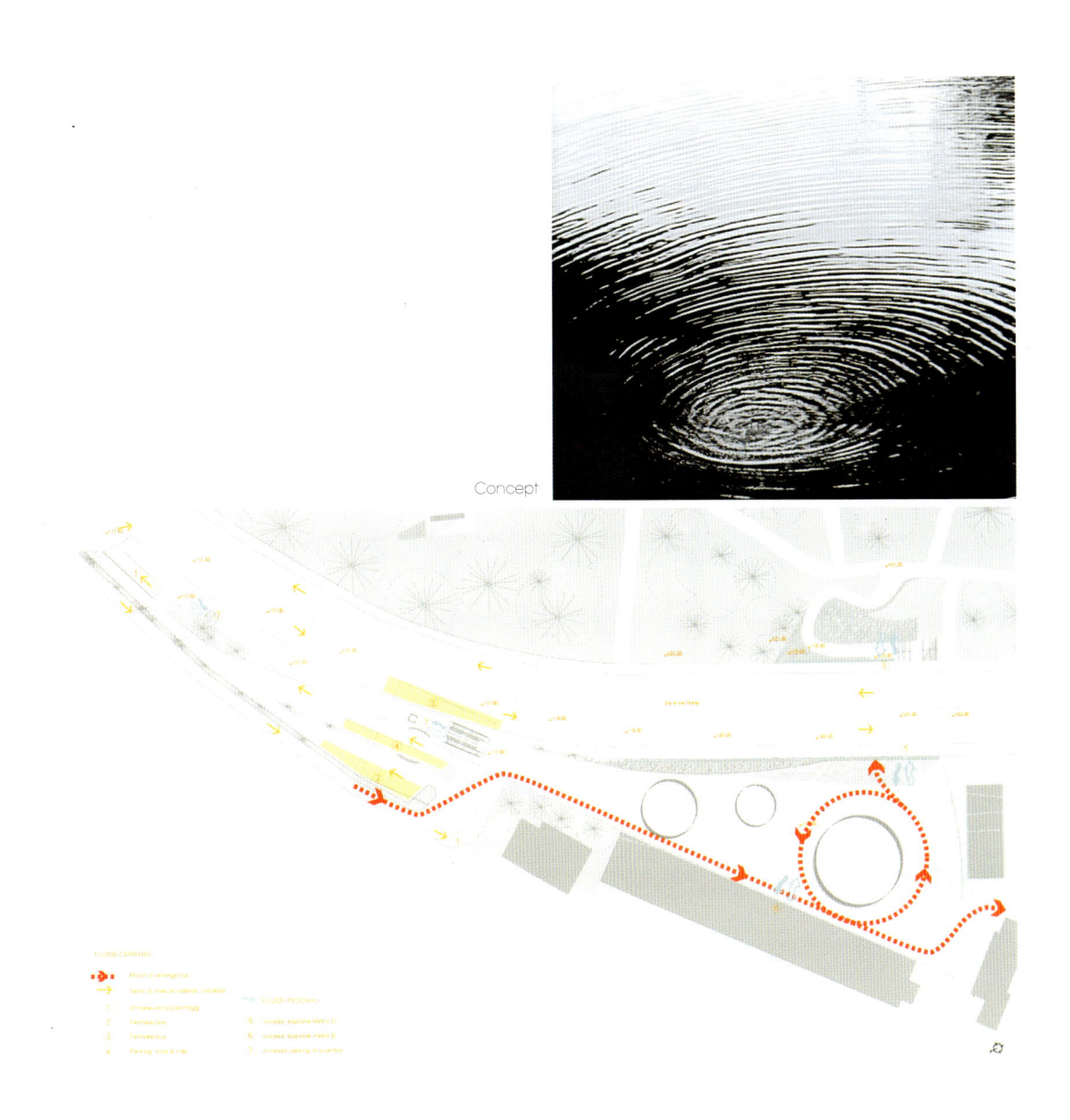

Concept

ARCHITECTURAL DIAGRAMS 099

MM AMID [cero9]

"A NATURAL MONUMENT THAT IS GENERATED ARTIFICIALLY."

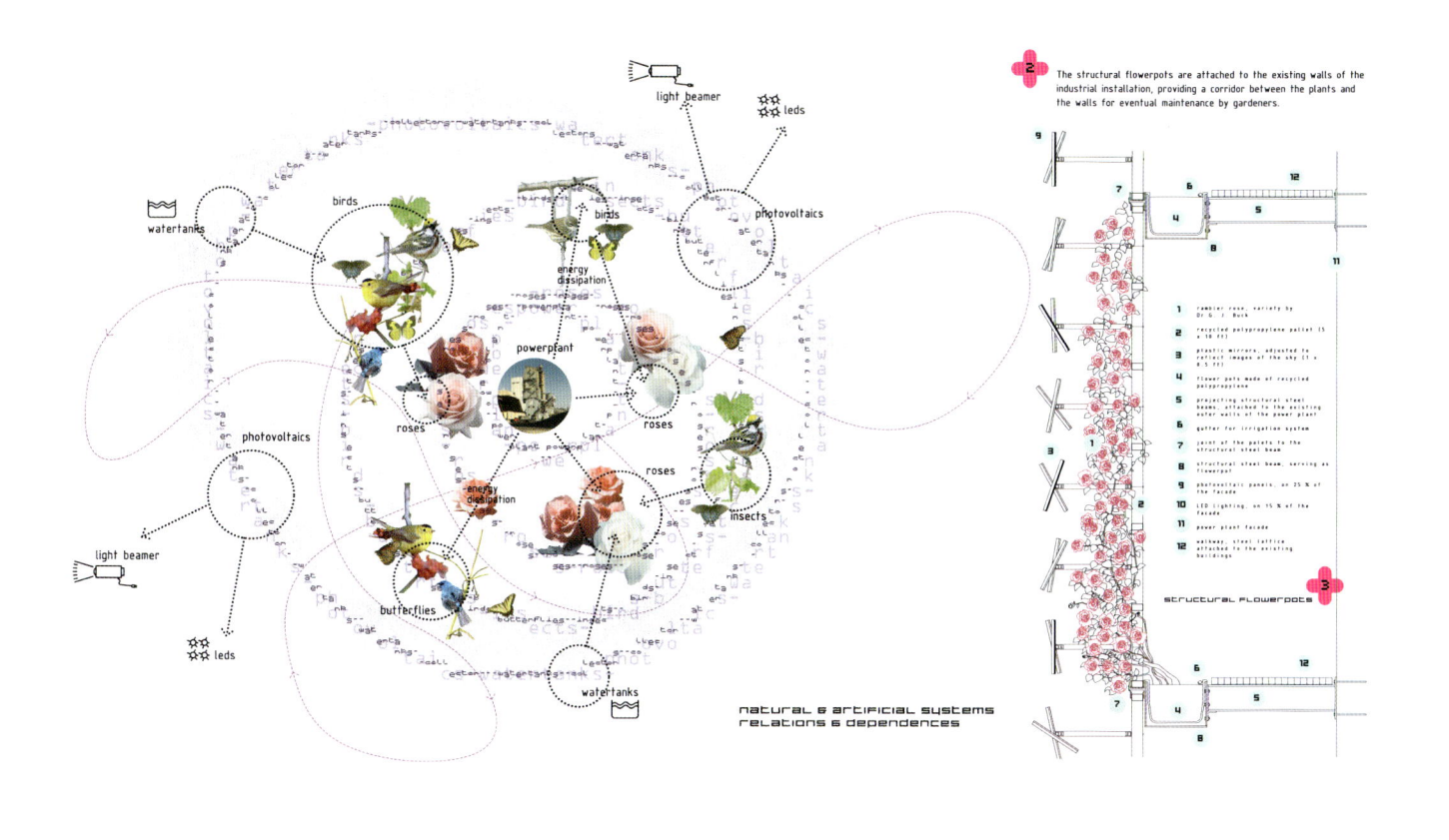

2 The structural flowerpots are attached to the existing walls of the industrial installation, providing a corridor between the plants and the walls for eventual maintenance by gardeners.

natural & artificial systems
relations & dependences

structural flowerpots

color to roses

living panels: roses and leds

pattern of the living wall

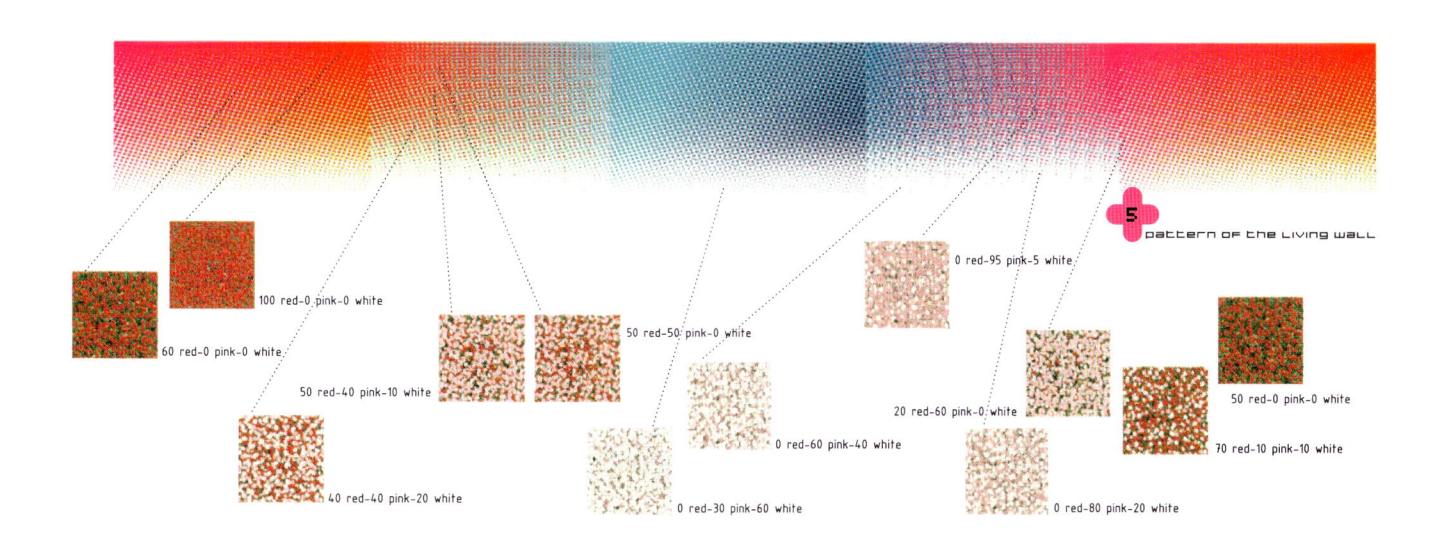

100 red-0 pink-0 white
60 red-0 pink-0 white
50 red-40 pink-10 white
40 red-40 pink-20 white
50 red-50 pink-0 white
0 red-60 pink-40 white
0 red-30 pink-60 white
0 red-95 pink-5 white
20 red-60 pink-0 white
0 red-80 pink-20 white
50 red-0 pink-0 white
70 red-10 pink-10 white

ARCHITECTURAL DIAGRAMS 101

MUSEUM NEUHAUS
LIAUNIG COLLECTION
SADAR VUGA ARHITEKTI

"THE CORE AND THE SHELL. THE CORE IS PROTECTED BY THE SHELL. IT IS MASSIVE AND HEAVY. IT IS STABLE."

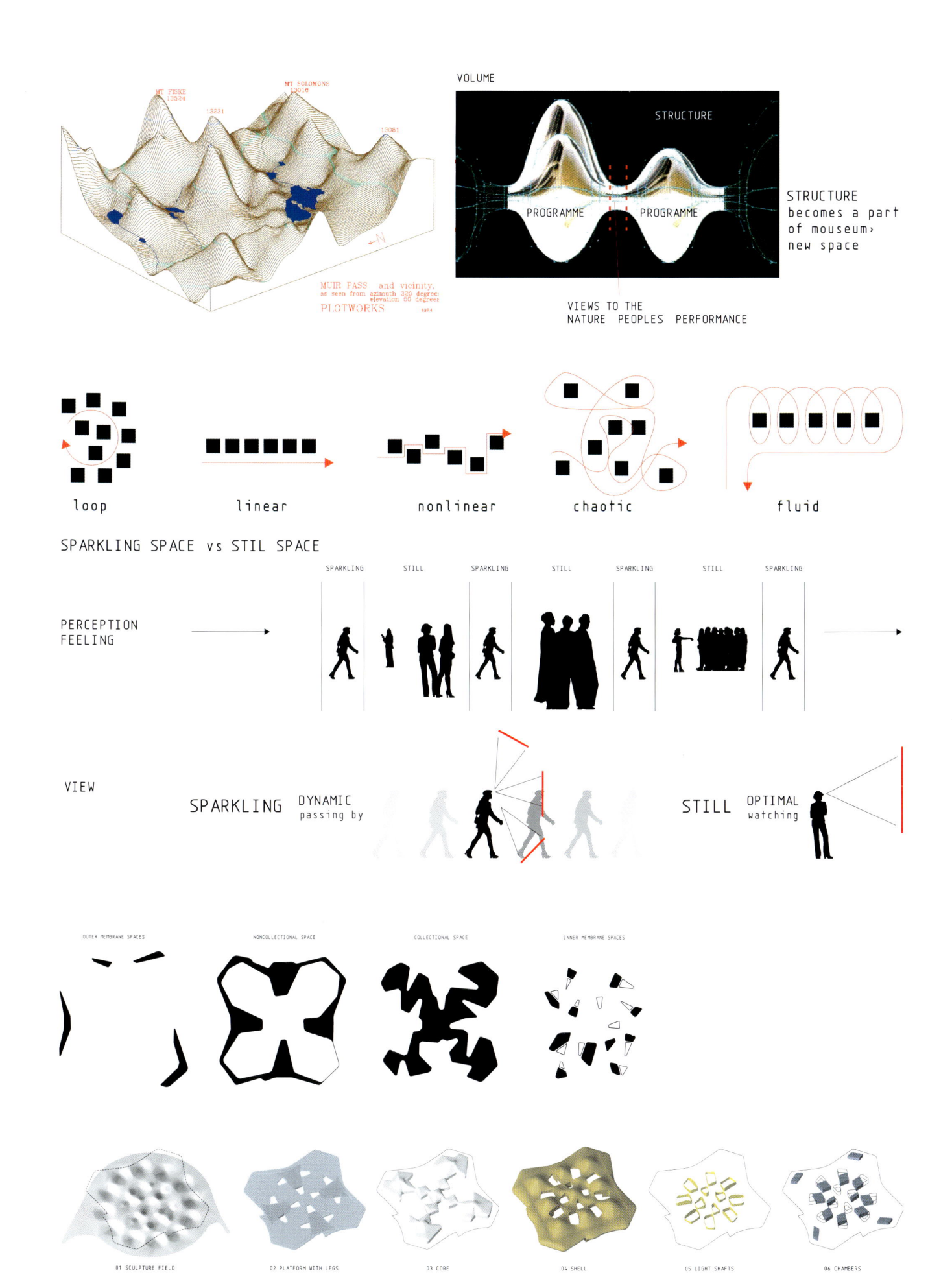

MUIR PASS and vicinity,
as seen from azimuth 320 degrees;
elevation 60 degrees
PLOTWORKS

VOLUME
STRUCTURE
PROGRAMME PROGRAMME

STRUCTURE becomes a part of mouseum› new space

VIEWS TO THE NATURE PEOPLES PERFORMANCE

loop   linear   nonlinear   chaotic   fluid

SPARKLING SPACE vs STIL SPACE

SPARKLING STILL SPARKLING STILL SPARKLING STILL SPARKLING

PERCEPTION
FEELING

VIEW   SPARKLING DYNAMIC passing by   STILL OPTIMAL watching

OUTER MEMBRANE SPACES   NONCOLLECTIONAL SPACE   COLLECTIONAL SPACE   INNER MEMBRANE SPACES

01 SCULPTURE FIELD   02 PLATFORM WITH LEGS   03 CORE   04 SHELL   05 LIGHT SHAFTS   06 CHAMBERS

ARCHITECTURAL DIAGRAMS 103

MUZIEKPALEIS NL Architects

Sole jazz

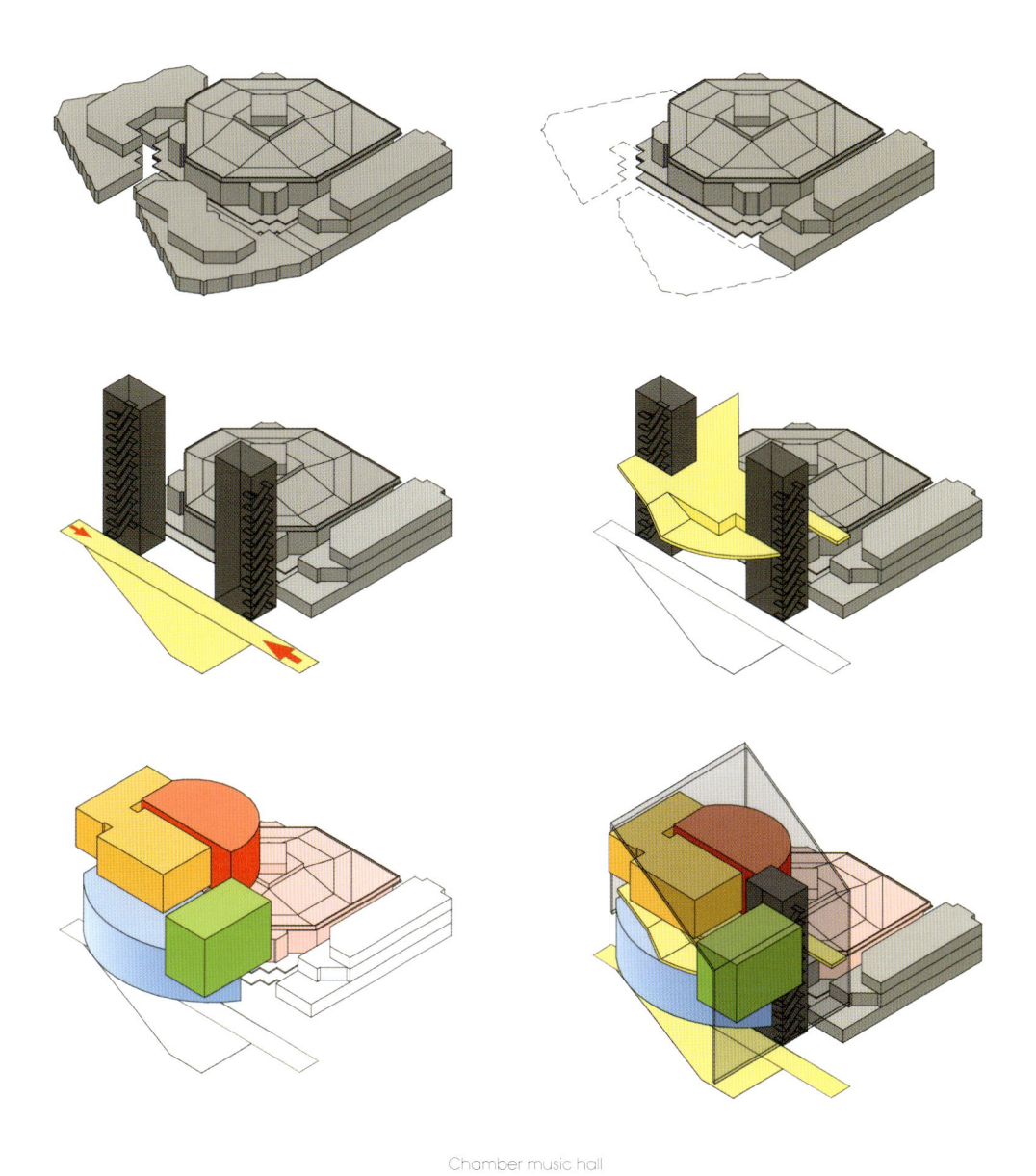

Chamber music hall

Crossover room

Pop rock hall

Symphony Hall

ARCHITECTURAL DIAGRAMS 105

MY SCHOOL IS A FLOWER IaN+

"A FLOWER, WHICH COMES TO REPRESENT THE ASPIRATION TO EMBRACE THE IDENTITY OF THE NEIGHBORHOOD WHERE DIFFERENT ELEMENTS CO-HABIT."

Educational facilities access

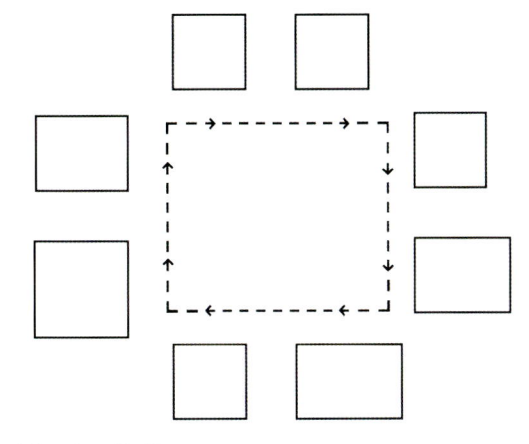

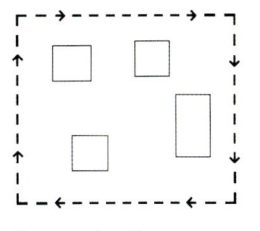

Common facilities access

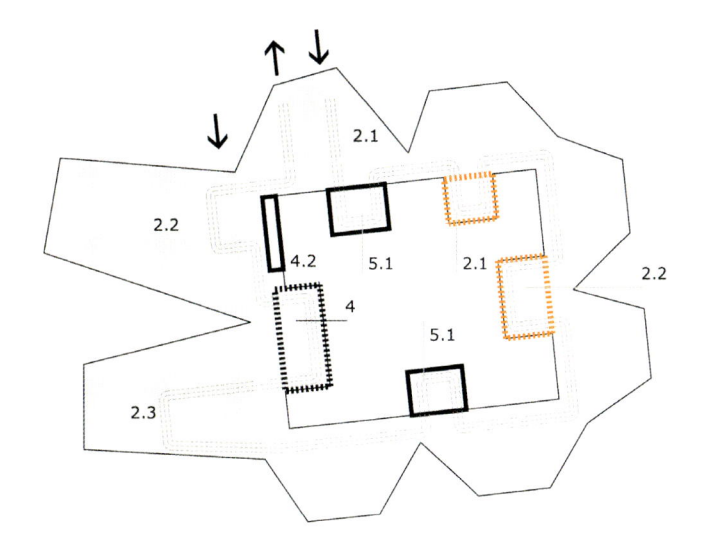

ARCHITECTURAL DIAGRAMS 107

NEURONAL ALIEN
Vincent Callebaut Architectures

"THE NEURONAL ALIEN EXTENDS ITSELF BETWEEN THE FAUNA AND THE LOCAL FLORA TO REBUILD A NEW MULTI-BIOTOPE."

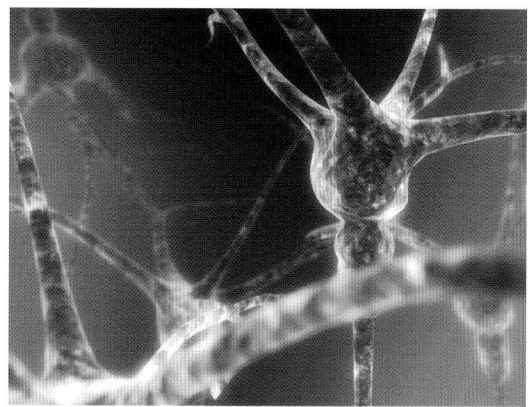

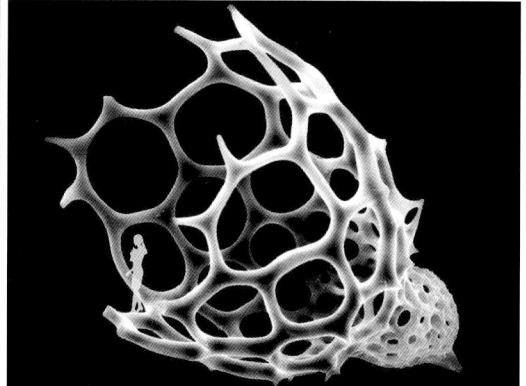

Concept

Radiolar structure

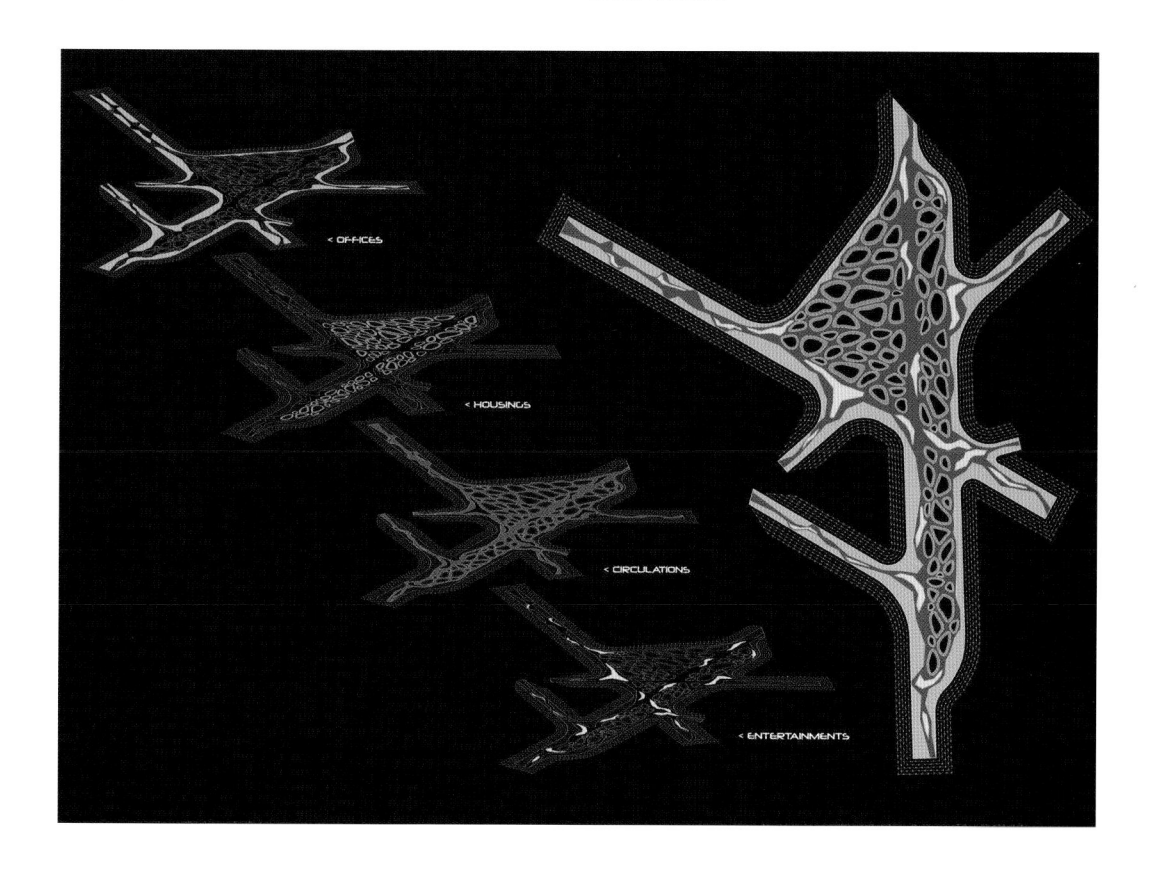

< OFFICES

< HOUSINGS

< CIRCULATIONS

< ENTERTAINMENTS

ARCHITECTURAL DIAGRAMS 109

NEW TERAMO THEATRE COMPLEX IaN+

"OUR DESIGN WANTS TO DIALOGUE WITH ALL THE SURROUNDINGS, WITH THE CITY, WITH THE LANDSCAPE."

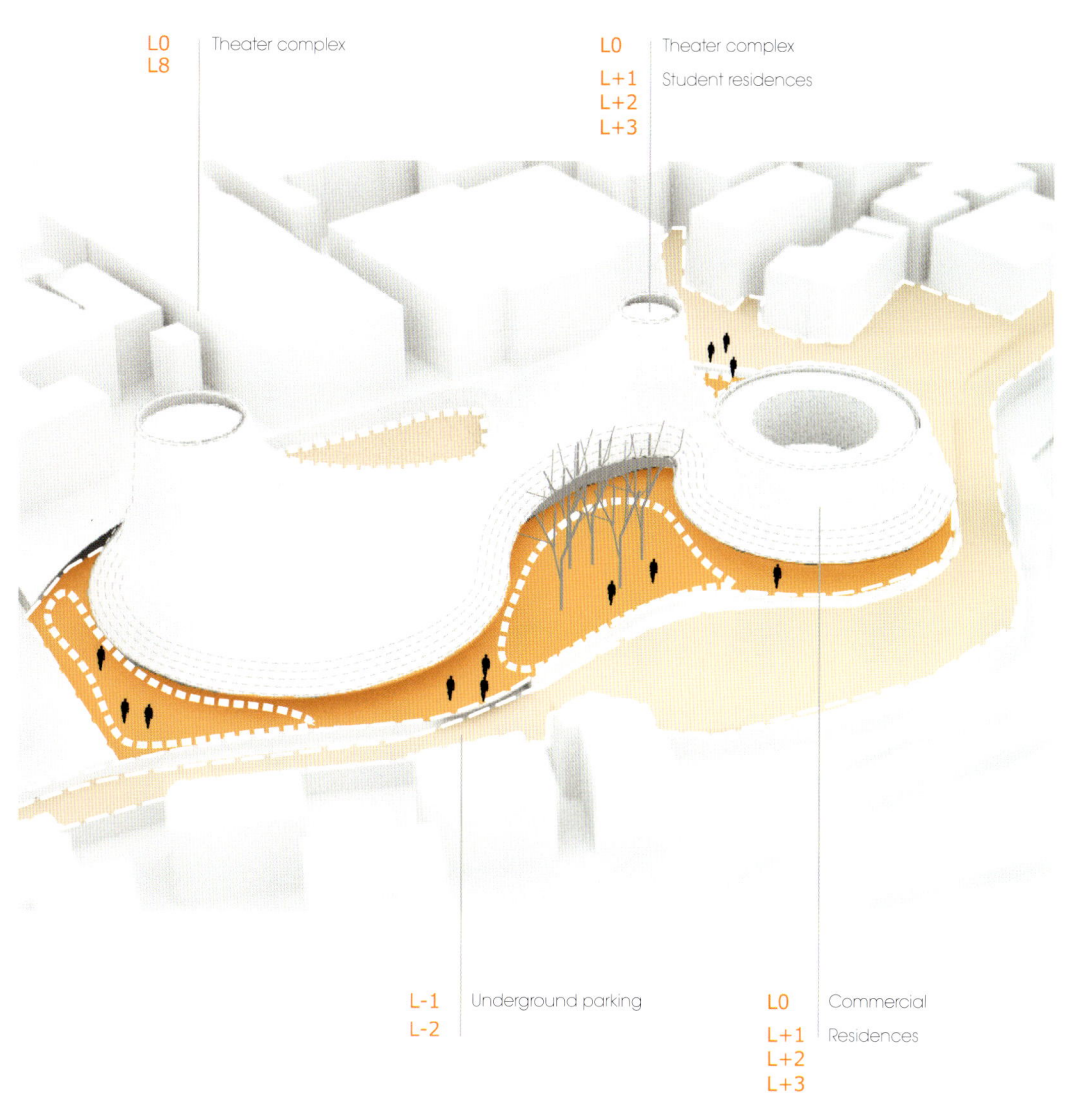

| L0 | Theater complex
| L8 |

| L0 | Theater complex
| L+1 | Student residences
| L+2 |
| L+3 |

| L-1 | Underground parking
| L-2 |

| L0 | Commercial
| L+1 | Residences
| L+2 |
| L+3 |

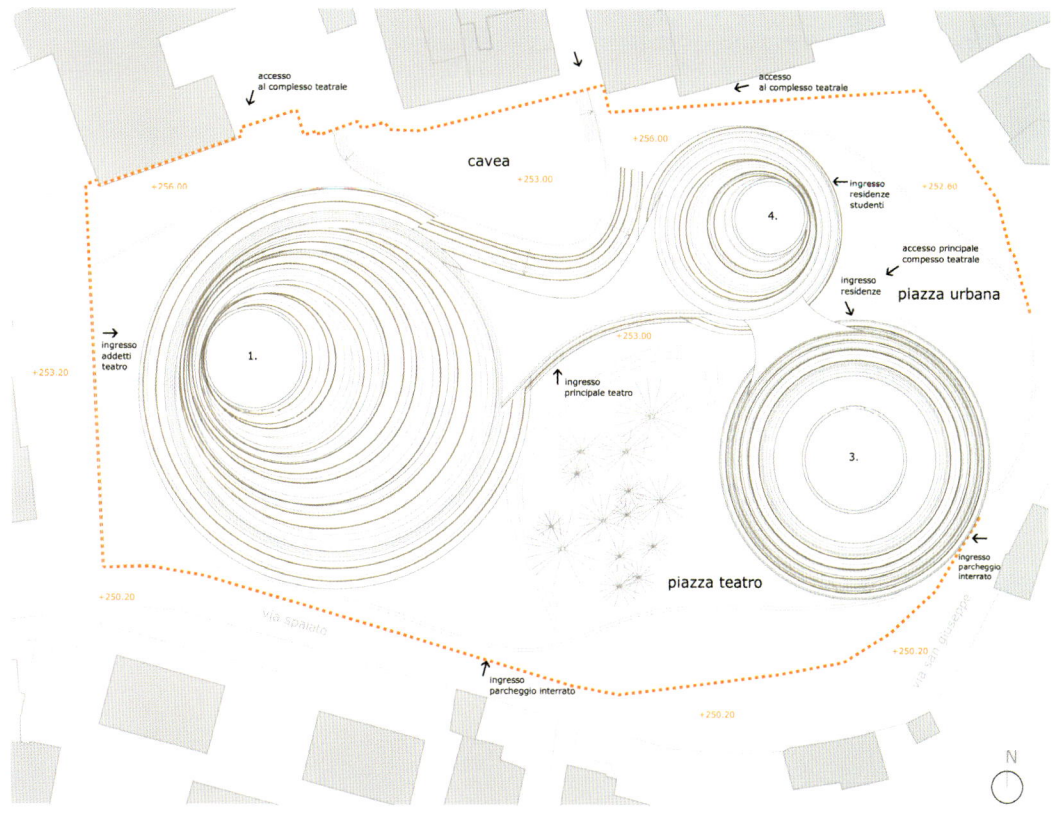

accesso al complesso teatrale

accesso al complesso teatrale

cavea

+256.00

+253.00

ingresso residenze studenti

+252.60

accesso principale compesso teatrale

ingresso residenze

piazza urbana

ingresso addetti teatro

+253.20

+253.00

ingresso principale teatro

ingresso parcheggio interrato

piazza teatro

+250.20

+250.20

via spalato

ingresso parcheggio interrato

N

ARCHITECTURAL DIAGRAMS 111

NURSERY SCHOOL
mxc architects

Plan

Phasage 1 + 2 with possibility of extension | Existing trees | Growth ceiling and elimination | Insertion vegetation

Stratification | Visibility | Summer | Winter | Cycle | Temperate area

References

Playground + Mens / game + Administration + Lighting

ARCHITECTURAL DIAGRAMS 113

PADUA AUDITORIUM
kadawittfeldarchitektur

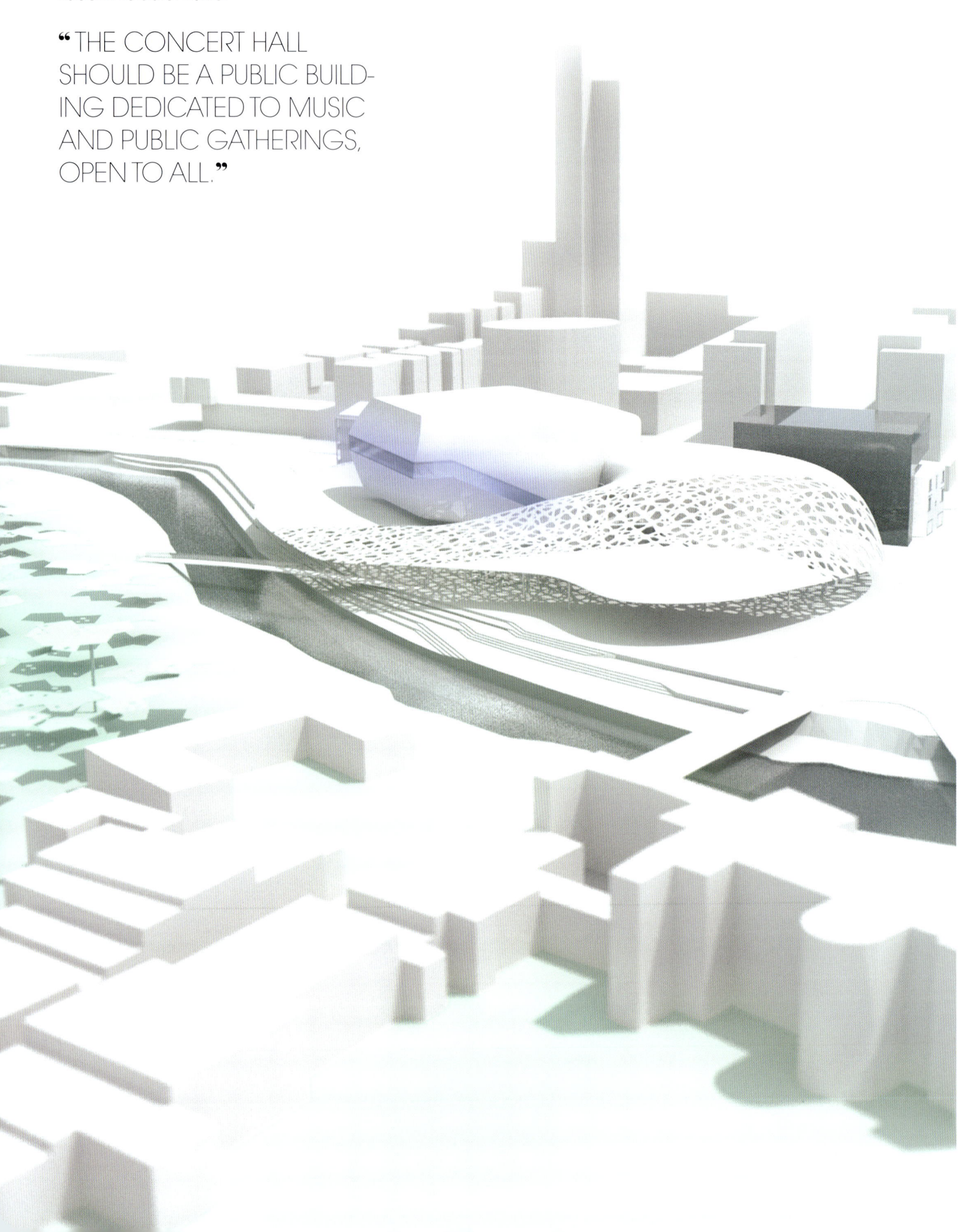

"THE CONCERT HALL SHOULD BE A PUBLIC BUILDING DEDICATED TO MUSIC AND PUBLIC GATHERINGS, OPEN TO ALL."

First sketches

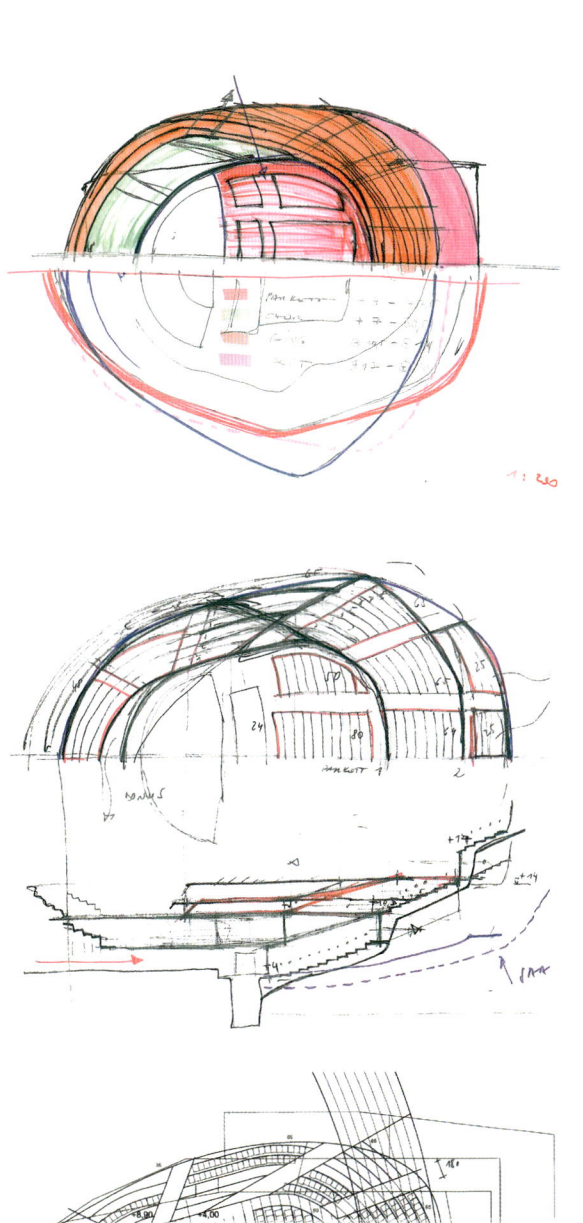

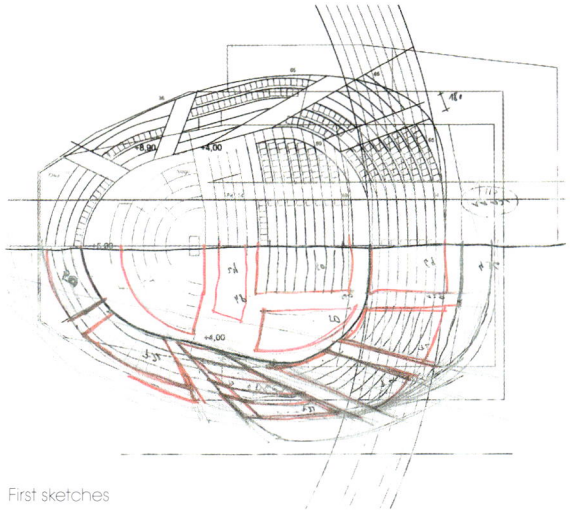

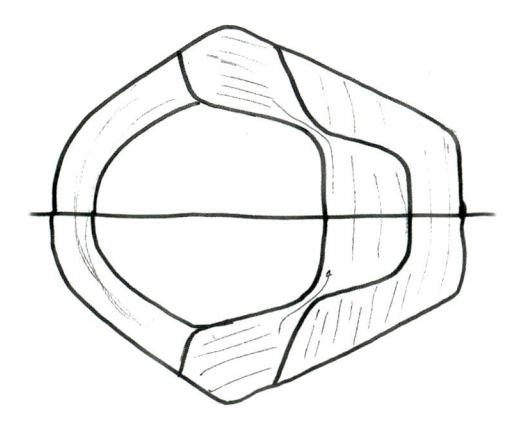

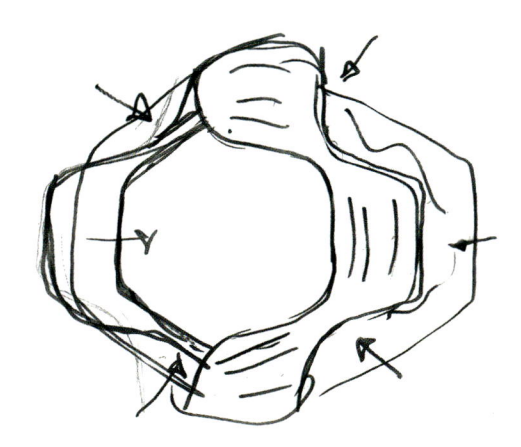

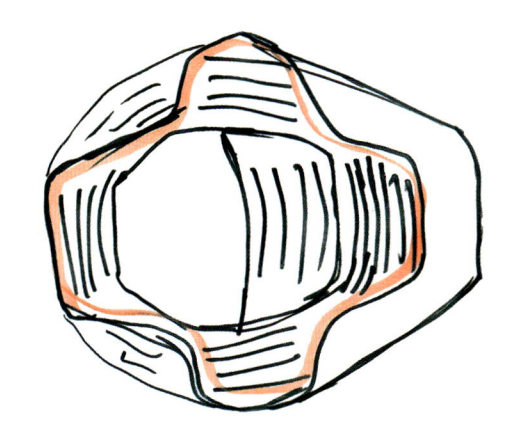

From shoebox to "quadrifoglio" concept
(cloverleaf concept)

ARCHITECTURAL DIAGRAMS 115

PINAULT FOUNDATION FOR CONTEMPORARY ART
MANUELLE GAUTRAND ARCHITECTURE

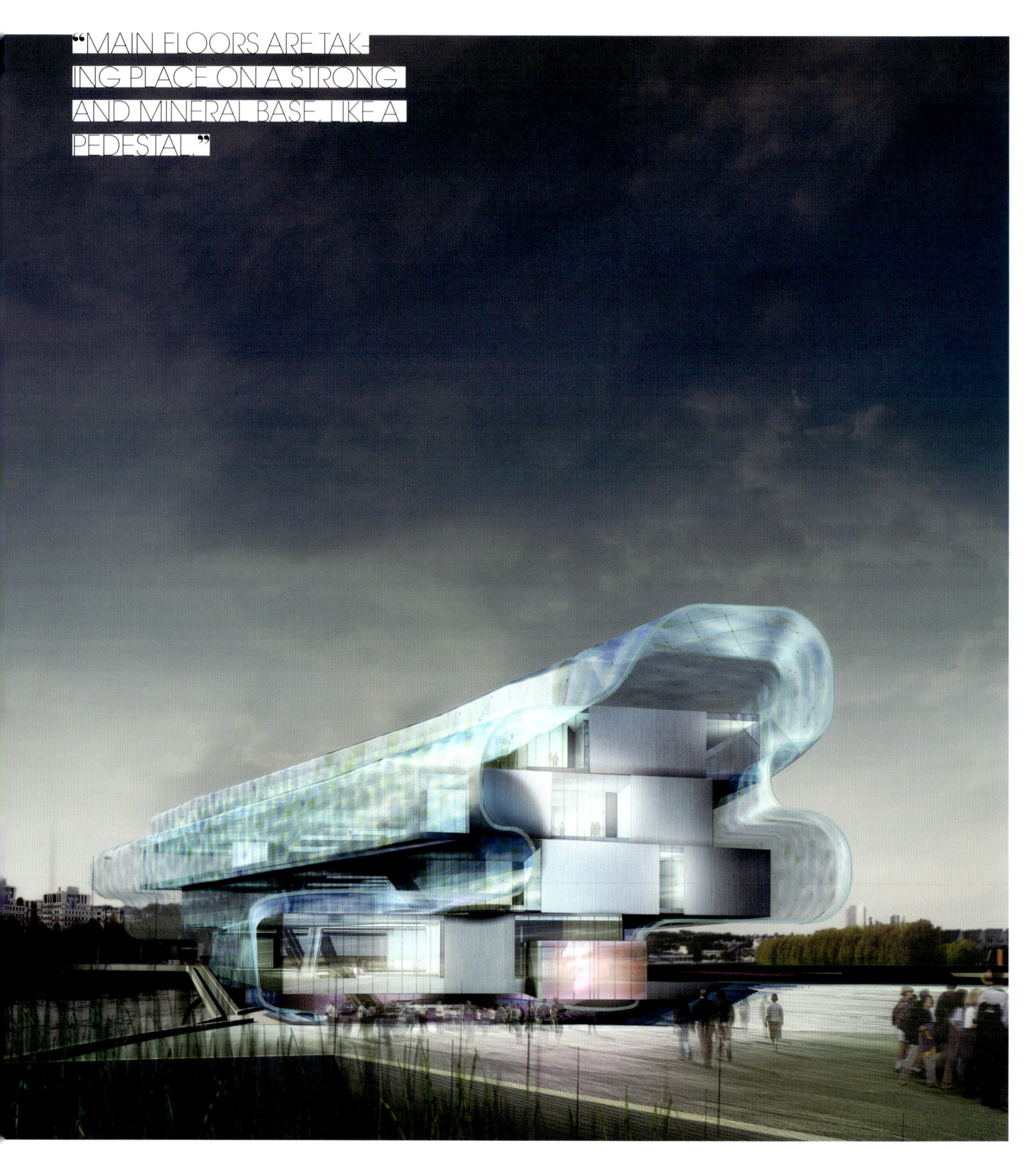

"MAIN FLOORS ARE TAKING PLACE ON A STRONG AND MINERAL BASE, LIKE A PEDESTAL."

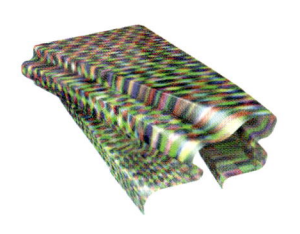

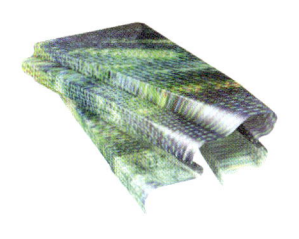

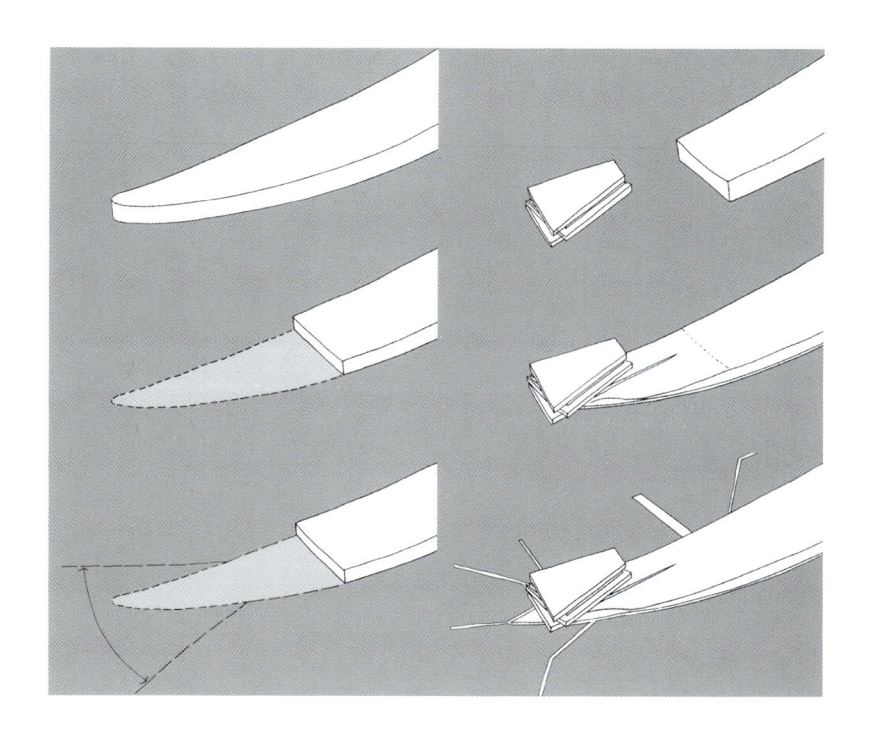

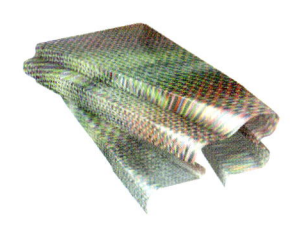

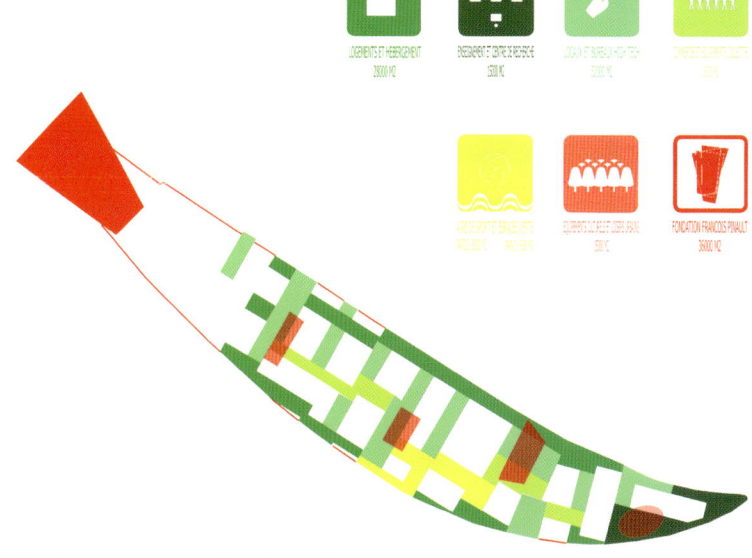

<ICON> for reconstruction of Seguin Island

ARCHITECTURAL DIAGRAMS 117

PONTE PARODI UNStudio

"THE PROGRAMMES ON THE PIAZZA ARE ORGANIZED AROUND CLOCKWISE ACTIVITIES."

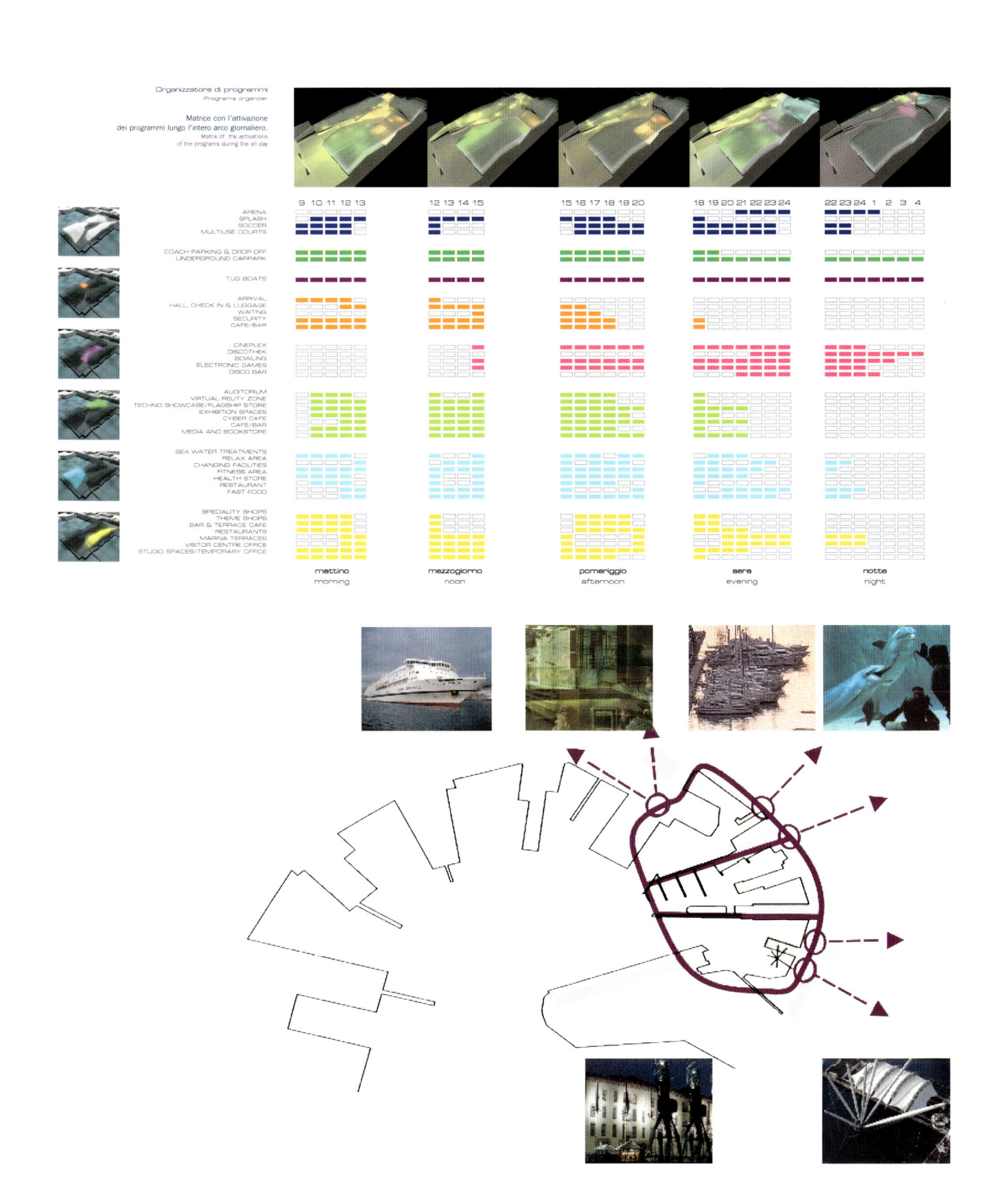

Organizzatore di programmi
Programs organizer

Matrice con l'attivazione
dei programmi lungo l'intero arco giornaliero.
Matrix of the activations
of the programs during the all day

	9 10 11 12 13	12 13 14 15	15 16 17 18 19 20	18 19 20 21 22 23 24	22 23 24 1 2 3 4
ARENA / SPLASH / SOCCER / MULTIUSE COURTS					
COACH PARKING & DROP OFF / UNDERGROUND CARPARK					
TUG BOATS					
ARRIVAL / HALL, CHECK IN & LUGGAGE / WAITING / SECURITY / CAFE/BAR					
CINEPLEX / DISCOTHEK / BOWLING / ELECTRONIC GAMES / DISCO BAR					
AUDITORIUM / VIRTUAL REUTY ZONE / TECHNO SHOWCASE/FLAGSHIP STORE / EXHIBITION SPACES / CYBER CAFE / CAFE/BAR / MEDIA AND BOOKSTORE					
SEA WATER TREATMENTS / RELAX AREA / CHANGING FACILITIES / FITNESS AREA / HEALTH STORE / RESTAURANT / FAST FOOD					
SPECIALITY SHOPS / THEME SHOPS / BAR & TERRACE CAFE / RESTAURANTS / MARINA TERRACES / VISITOR CENTRE OFFICE / STUDIO SPACES/TEMPORARY OFFICE					
	mattino / morning	mezzogiorno / noon	pomeriggio / afternoon	sera / evening	notte / night

ARCHITECTURAL DIAGRAMS 119

PROSTNESET TERMINAL
SPACEGROUP

"WE PROPOSE A NEW LANDFILL THAT WRAPS THE EXISTING COASTLINE ESTABLISHING THE CLEAREST RELATIONSHIPS."

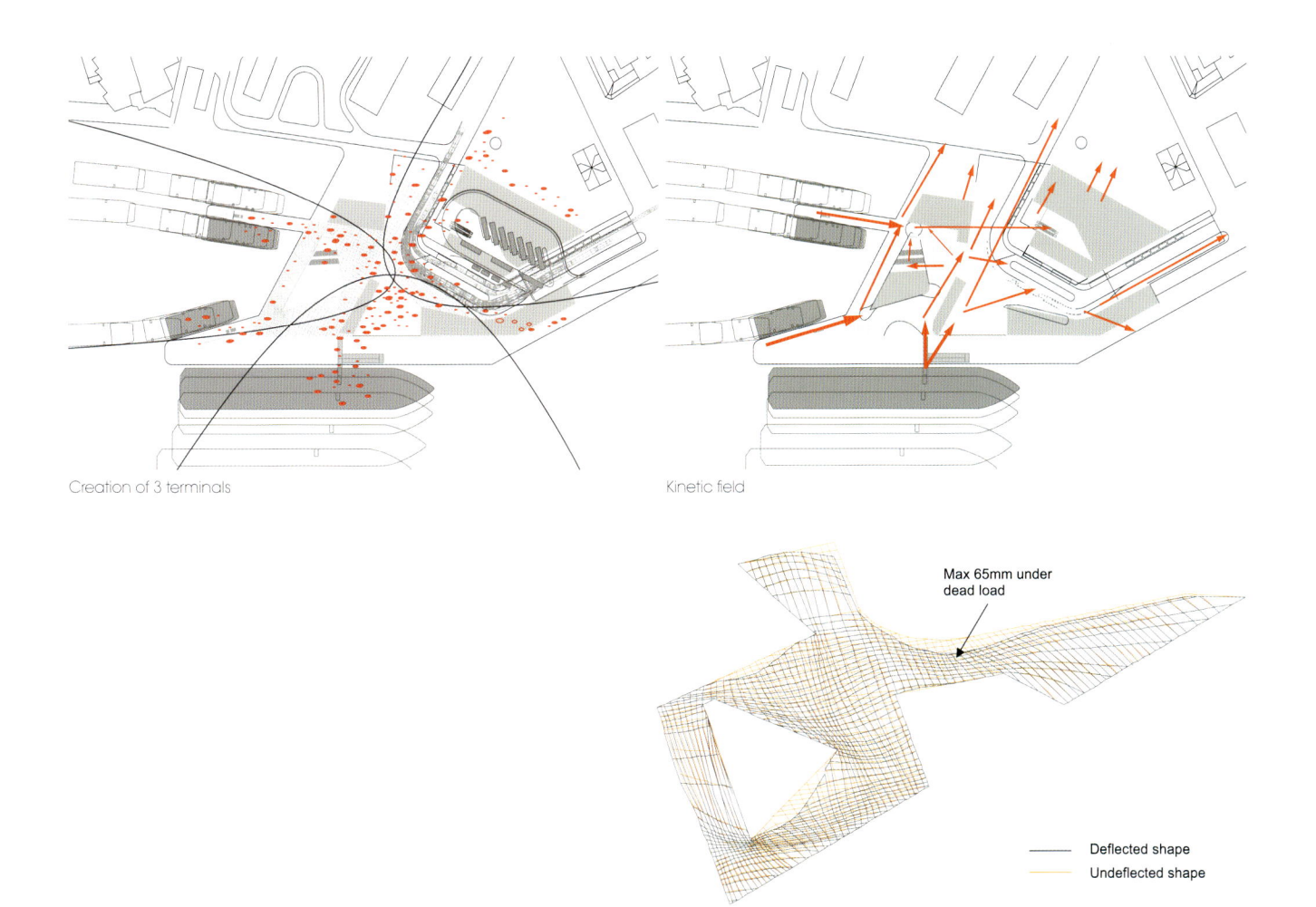

Creation of 3 terminals

Kinetic field

Max 65mm under dead load

Deflected shape
Undeflected shape

Exaggerated deflection of roof

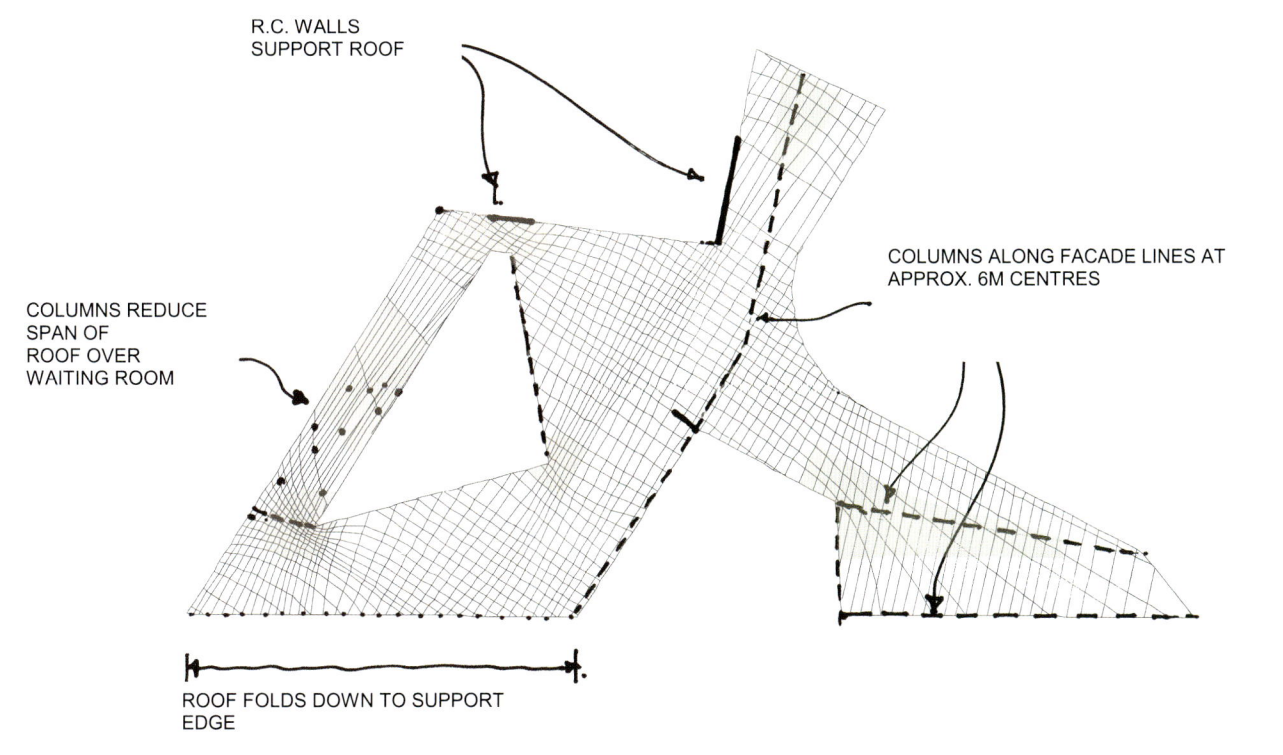

SHADED AREAS INDICATE
CRITICAL STRESS ZONES
WHERE THE CONSTRUCTION
IS REINFORCED BY STEEL PLATES

R.C. WALLS
SUPPORT ROOF

COLUMNS ALONG FACADE LINES AT
APPROX. 6M CENTRES

COLUMNS REDUCE
SPAN OF
ROOF OVER
WAITING ROOM

ROOF FOLDS DOWN TO SUPPORT
EDGE

Roof: Critical points of stress in steel web

ARCHITECTURAL DIAGRAMS

RED BAOBAB
Vincent Callebaut Architectures

"THE BAOBAB LINKS UP WITH FLUIDITY THE DIFFERENT LEVELS OF ACCESS AND SAFETY NECESSARY TO THE GOOD FUNCTIONING OF THE PROJECT."

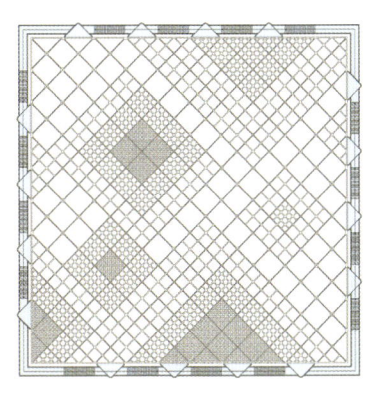

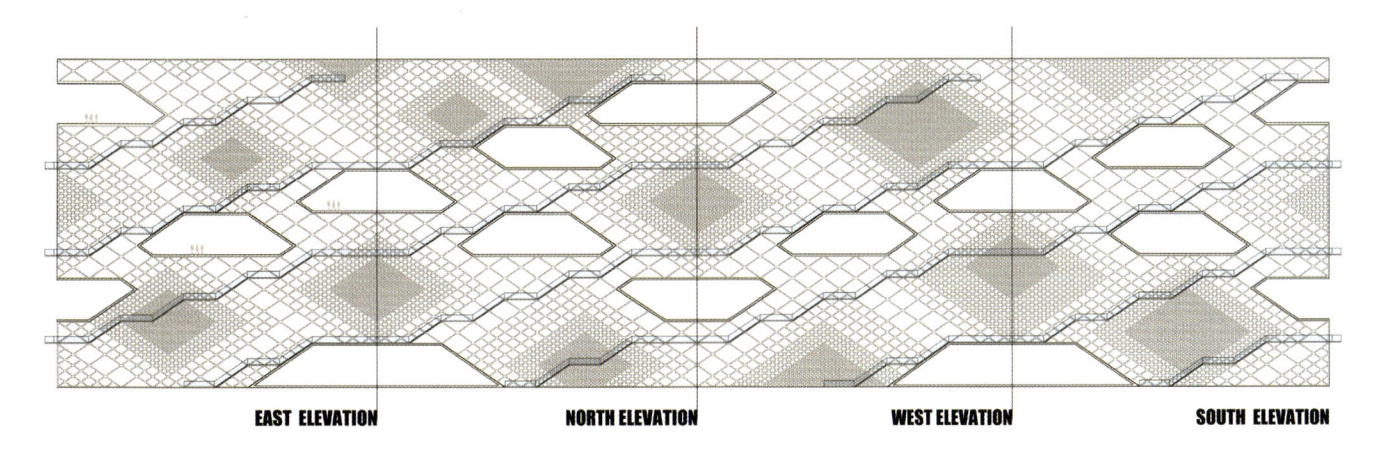

EAST ELEVATION   **NORTH ELEVATION**   **WEST ELEVATION**   **SOUTH ELEVATION**

ARCHITECTURAL DIAGRAMS 123

REEFMOD servo

"DUE TO ITS CELLULAR QUALITIES THE REEFMOD HAS BOTH PARASITICAL AND STAND-ALONE CAPABILITIES."

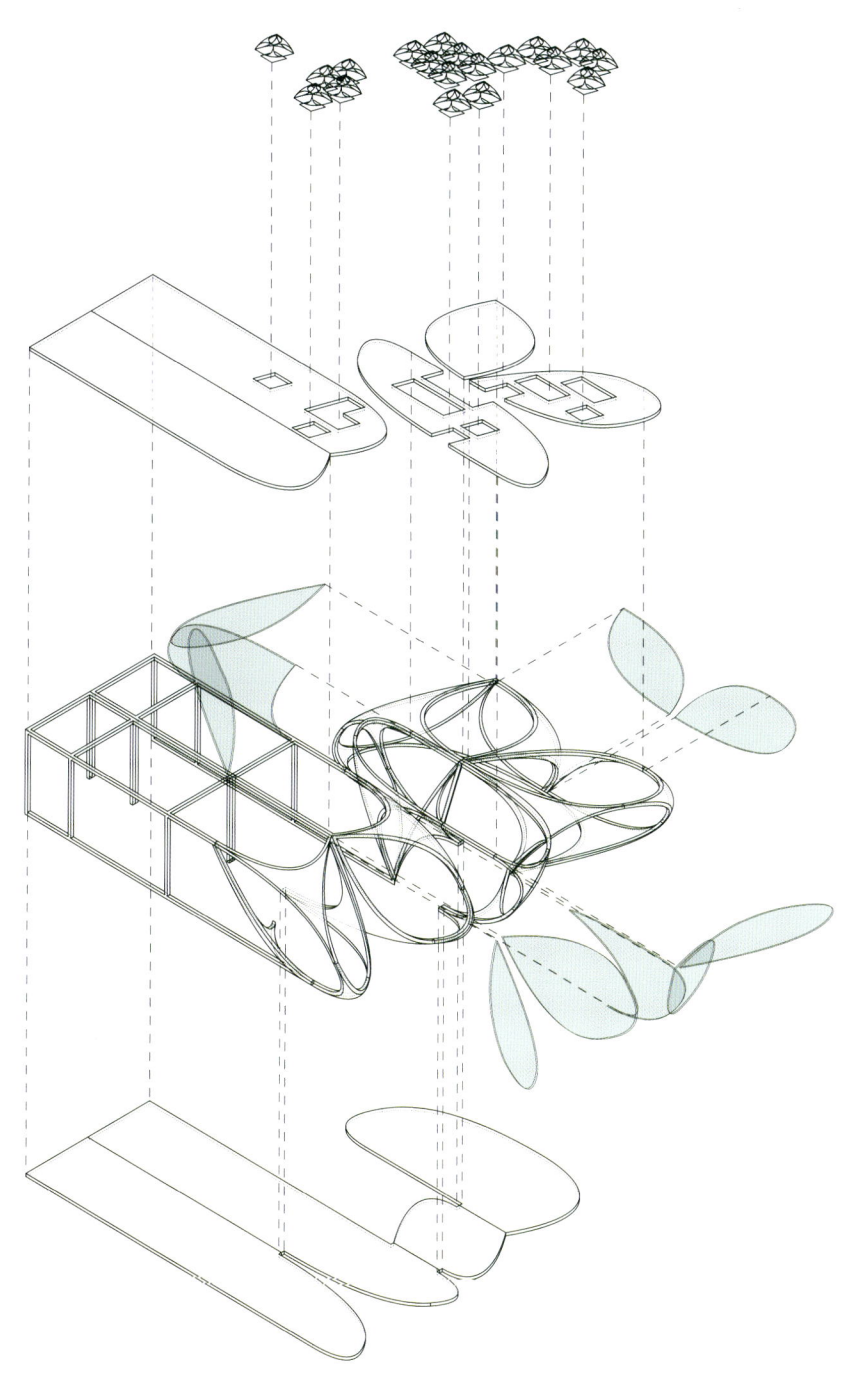

Exploded axonometric of reefMod systems: Primary structural latticework, secondary latticework fenestration, and building skin system.

Coexistence of systems

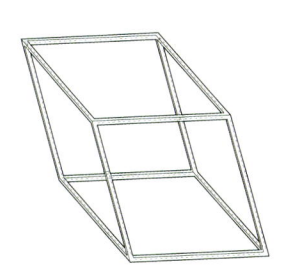

Generic space frame

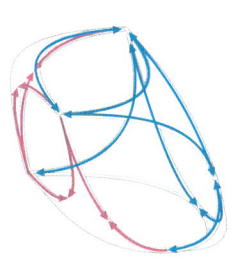

Force distribution diagram

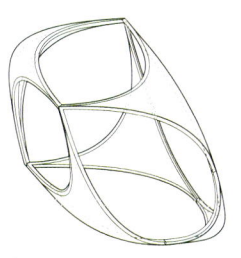

Cellular structural system

ARCHITECTURAL DIAGRAMS 125

ROLLING AQUA CENTER
JDS Architects

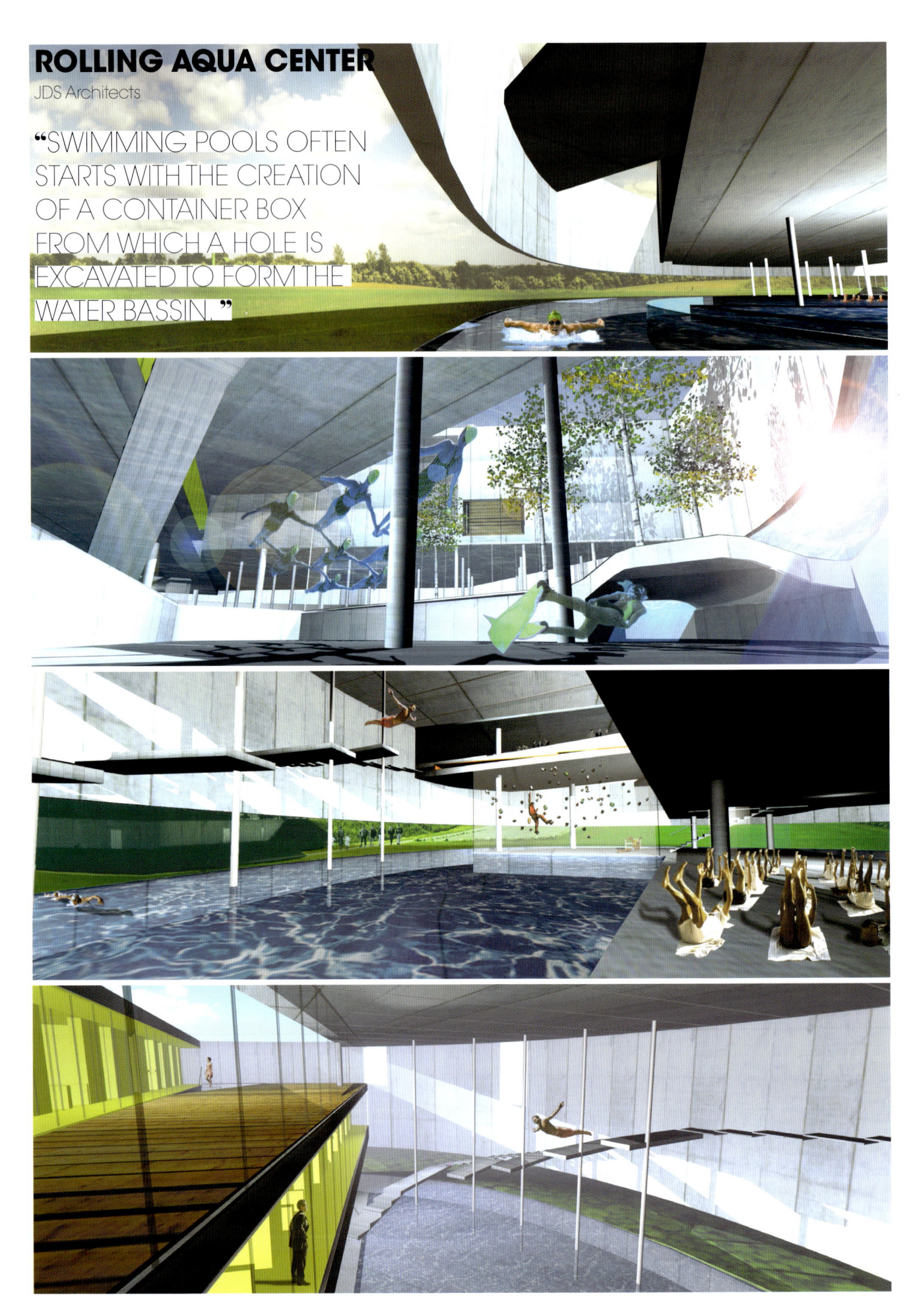

"SWIMMING POOLS OFTEN STARTS WITH THE CREATION OF A CONTAINER BOX FROM WHICH A HOLE IS EXCAVATED TO FORM THE WATER BASSIN."

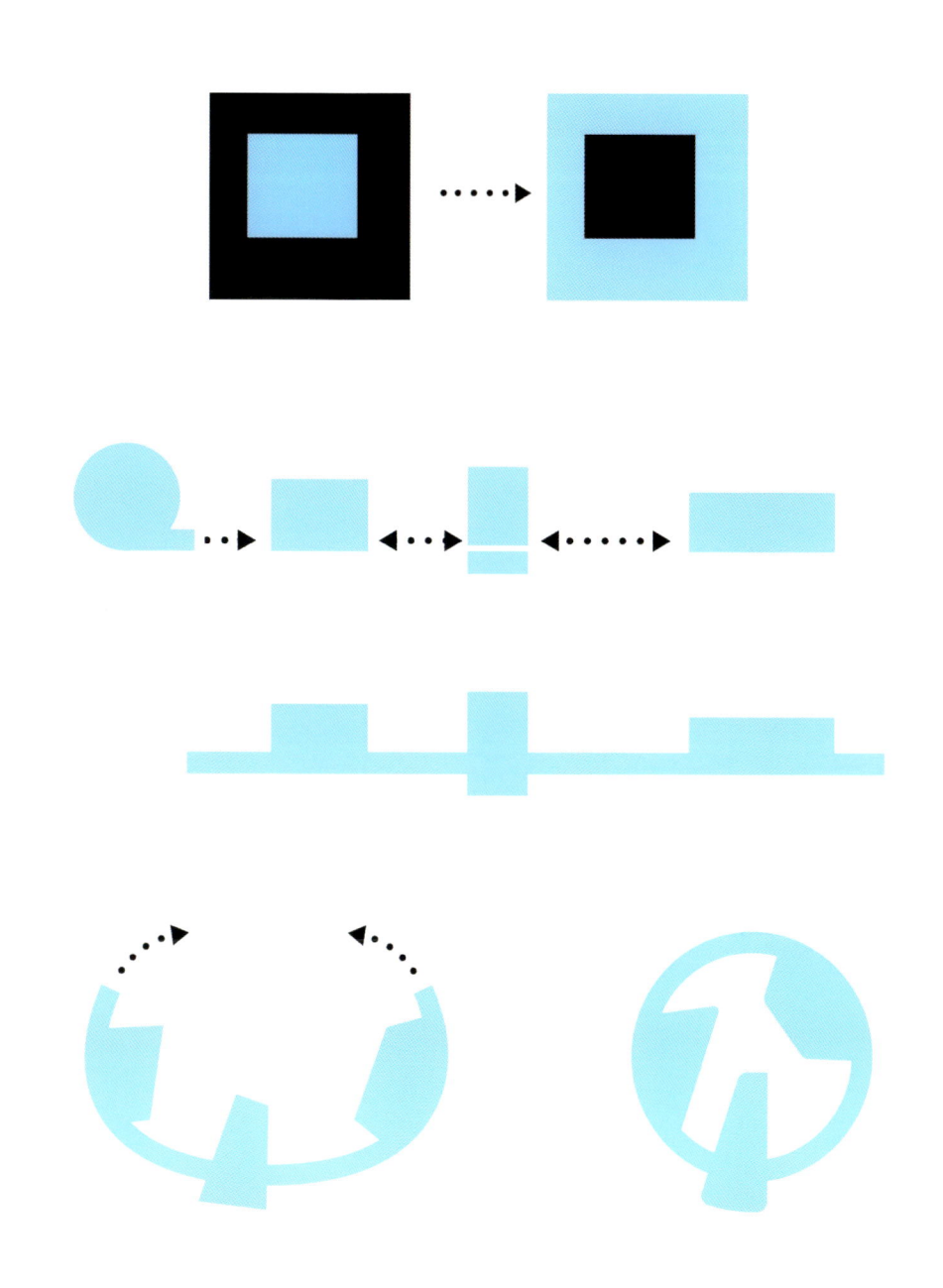

ARCHITECTURAL DIAGRAMS 127

# SALZBURG CENTRAL STATION kadawittfeldarchitektur

"COMFORT AND SERVICE UNDERSCORE THE CONCEPTUAL VISION OF SALZBURG'S FUTURE RAILWAY STATION."

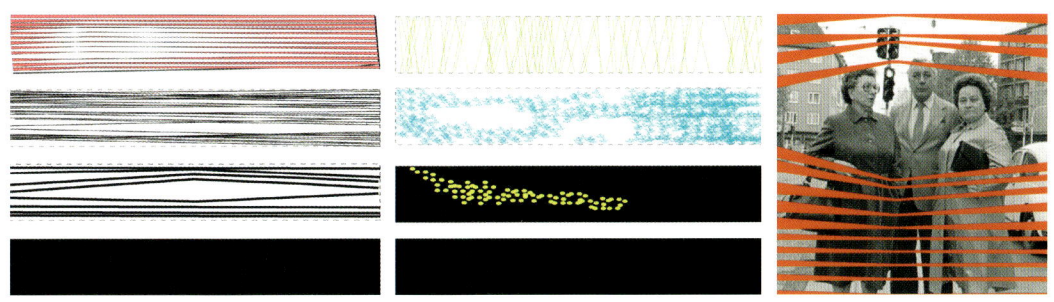

Studies, noise protection wall

The louvers are tilted in certain areas, helping the passengers to orientate themselves below, visualization noise protection wall

ARCHITECTURAL DIAGRAMS 129

SAMI CULTURAL CENTRE
Galvez+Wieczorek

"THE MAIN GOAL OF THE PROPOSAL IS TO ADJUST THE BUILDING TO THE SPATIAL PERCEPTION OF THE SAMI AND ITS LANDSCAPE."

Conceptual explanation

1. Piece of landscape and large piece of program

FOCO POSIBLE

2. Ring delimiting the focus program

NUEVO FOCO!

3. Possible flows around the outbreak

4. Around the focus of the program possible

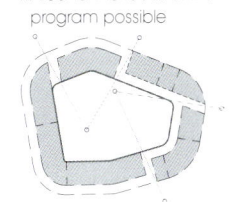

5. Links between outbreaks / lobby branched

Visual connections between spaces

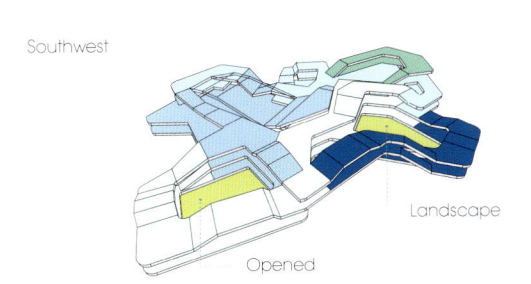

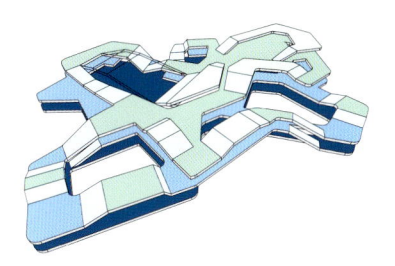

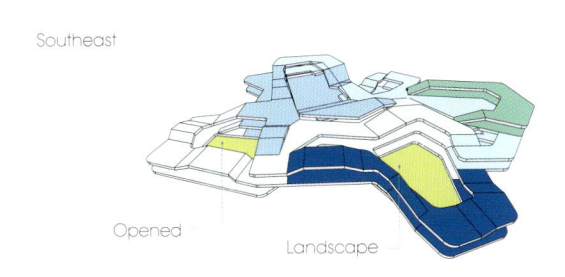

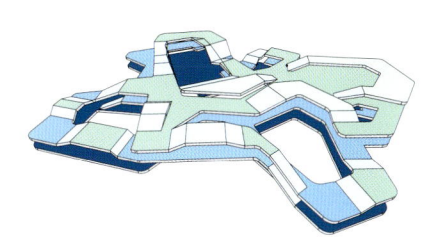

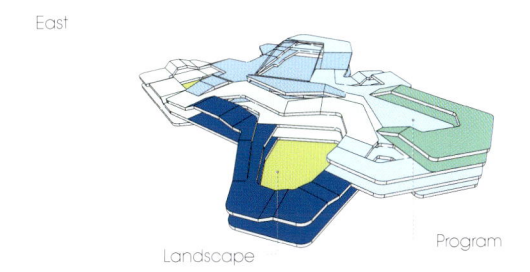

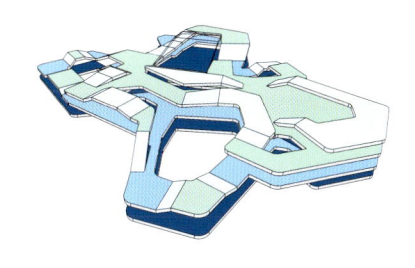

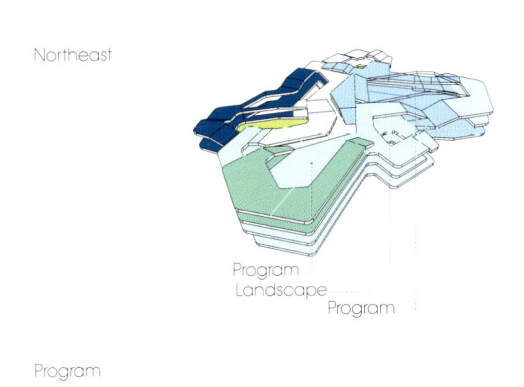

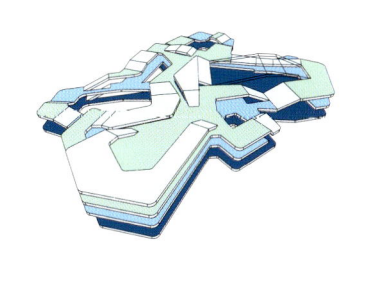

Southwest

Opened Landscape

Southeast

Opened Landscape

East

Landscape Program

Northeast

Program
Landscape
Program

Program
- Sami parliament + foyer
- Sami association
- Education and research
- Common areas and lobby
- Library
- Existing Forest

Sequence levels
- Level 1
- Level 2
- Level 3
- Level 4
- Level 5

ARCHITECTURAL DIAGRAMS 131

SCHOOL IN ROME mao

"THIS IS WHERE ONE EXPERIENTIALLY MEASURES DIRECT RELATIONS WITH INDIVIDUAL FREEDOM AND SPATIAL SHARING, RULES, AND VALUES."

Diagrams / the school

Diagrams / the park

ARCHITECTURAL DIAGRAMS 133

SCOOP SMAQ

"THE ARCTIC CULTURE CENTRE IS AN EXTROVERTED, CLIMATICALLY ACTIVE AND USER-INTERACTIVE BOW."

No sunrise 22 Nov - 25 Jan

- beach
- new pier
- boardwalk connecting the city centre and the beach
- research centre
- hotel / congress centre
- arctic culture centre
- town square

Sun response

Triple orientation / connections

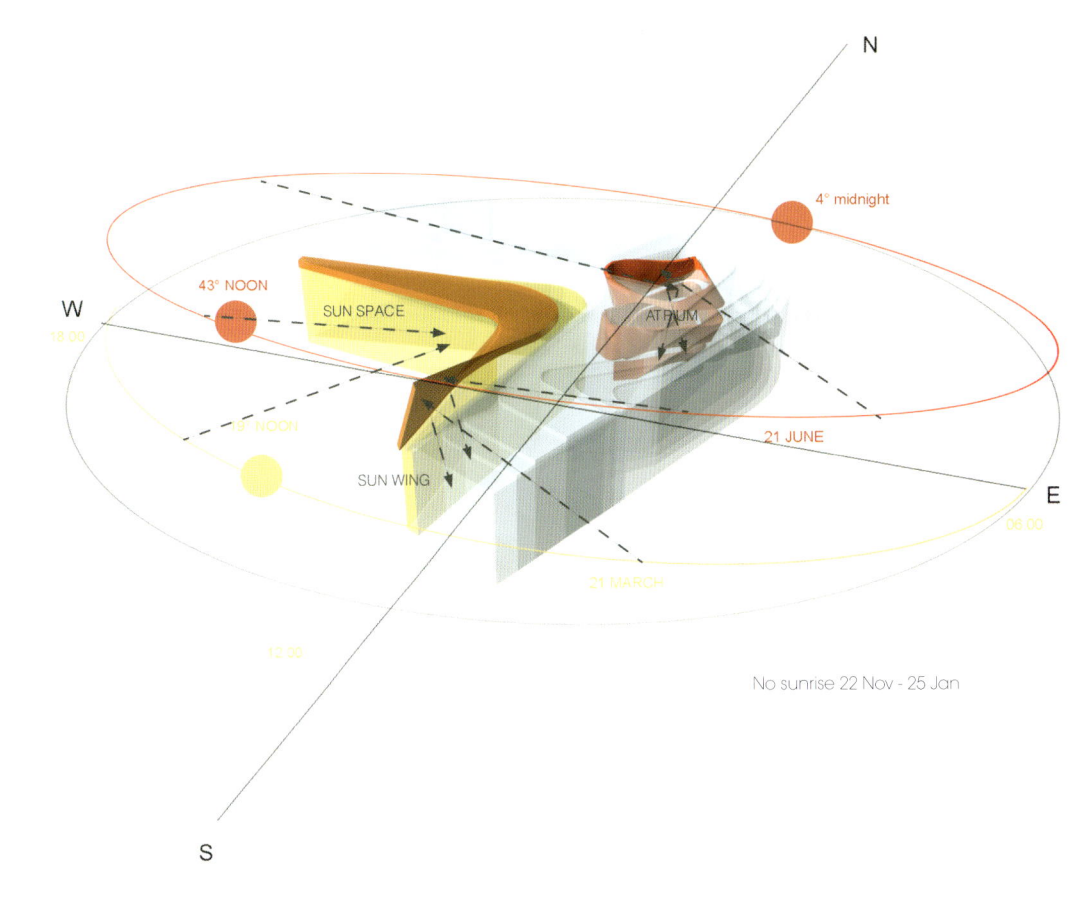

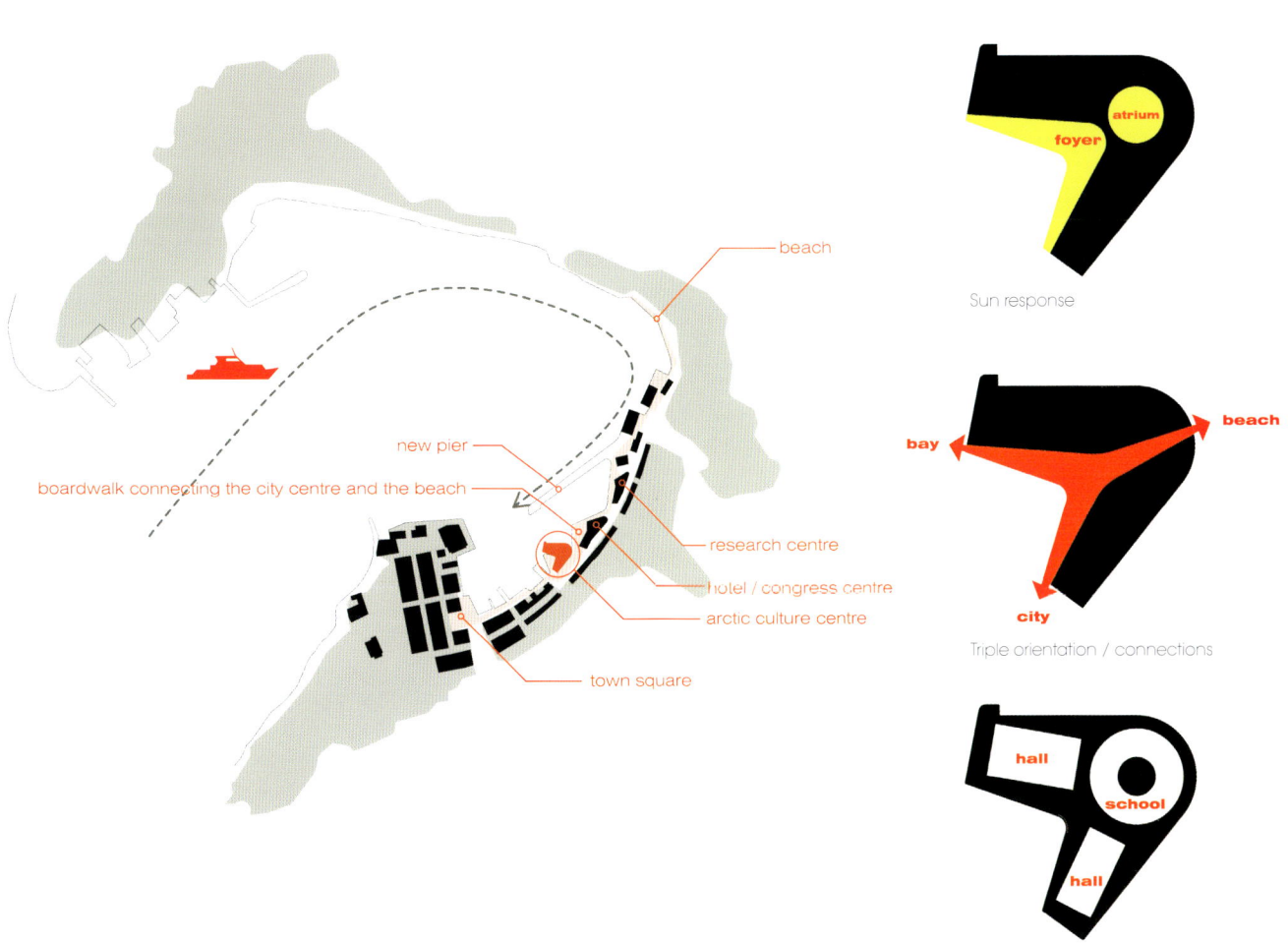

Programs distribution

ARCHITECTURAL DIAGRAMS 135

SHENZHEN INTERNATIONAL AIRPORT - TERMINAL 3

Reiser + Umemoto RUR Architecture PC

"THIS SYSTEMATIC FLEXIBILITY ALLOWS US TO MODULATE THE CROWN OF THE VAULT WITH A CLOUD DAPPLE PATTERN."

AREA M²	PEAK POWER GENERATED (KW)	ANNUAL ENERGY SAVED (MWH/YR)	GHG EMMISIONS AVOIDED (TONNES/YR)
70,000	9,900	10,400	4,900
52,000	7,425	7,800	3,785
35,000	4,950	5,200	2,456
17,000	2,430	2,560	1,205

fig. 6. Water Collection diagram

fig. 4. fritting detail

A grid of solar collectors on the terminal roof will provide enough electrical energy to make T3 self-sufficient.

Axonometric

Buildability Sequence

ARCHITECTURAL DIAGRAMS 137

SJAKKET JDS Architects

"THE CANYON BETWEEN THE TWO VAULTED ROOFS BECOMES THE SECRET OASIS OF THE KIDS."

Mezzanine

Beams

Outdoor area

Storage

Atrium

Ramps

Vertical / horizontal

Program wall

Greenhouse

Ground level

Soundroom

Elevated house

Sliding walls

Barcode

Crevasse

ARCHITECTURAL DIAGRAMS 139

SPINDERIHALLERNE
JDS Architects

"SPINDERIHALLERNE IS A COMPLEX OF ADJACENT BUILDINGS ENTWINED IN A COMPLICATED ROAD SYSTEM."

THE SAND BOX
Basically purpouse as a parking area for the day to day users of the komplex. It is also possible to implicate for special events.

CONCRETE DESERT
The biggest of the two southward squares. Coated with concrete elements primaraly for the purpose of bike and car parking.

VIRGIN FOREST
The area round building F, G and H is cleared of any hard pavement. The area will overgrow with lawn and willow foreland. The willow is a eficiant plant, it helps purifying any polution of land.

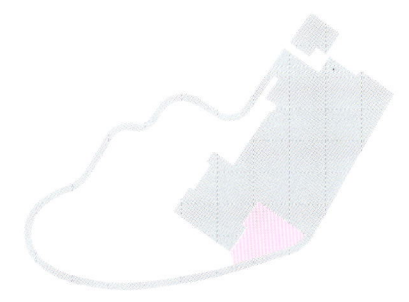

THE WIND PORCH
The southern arrivals area. Main arrivals for the museum and BIZ-Art. Like the concrete desert this square is also covered with perfabricated concrete elements.

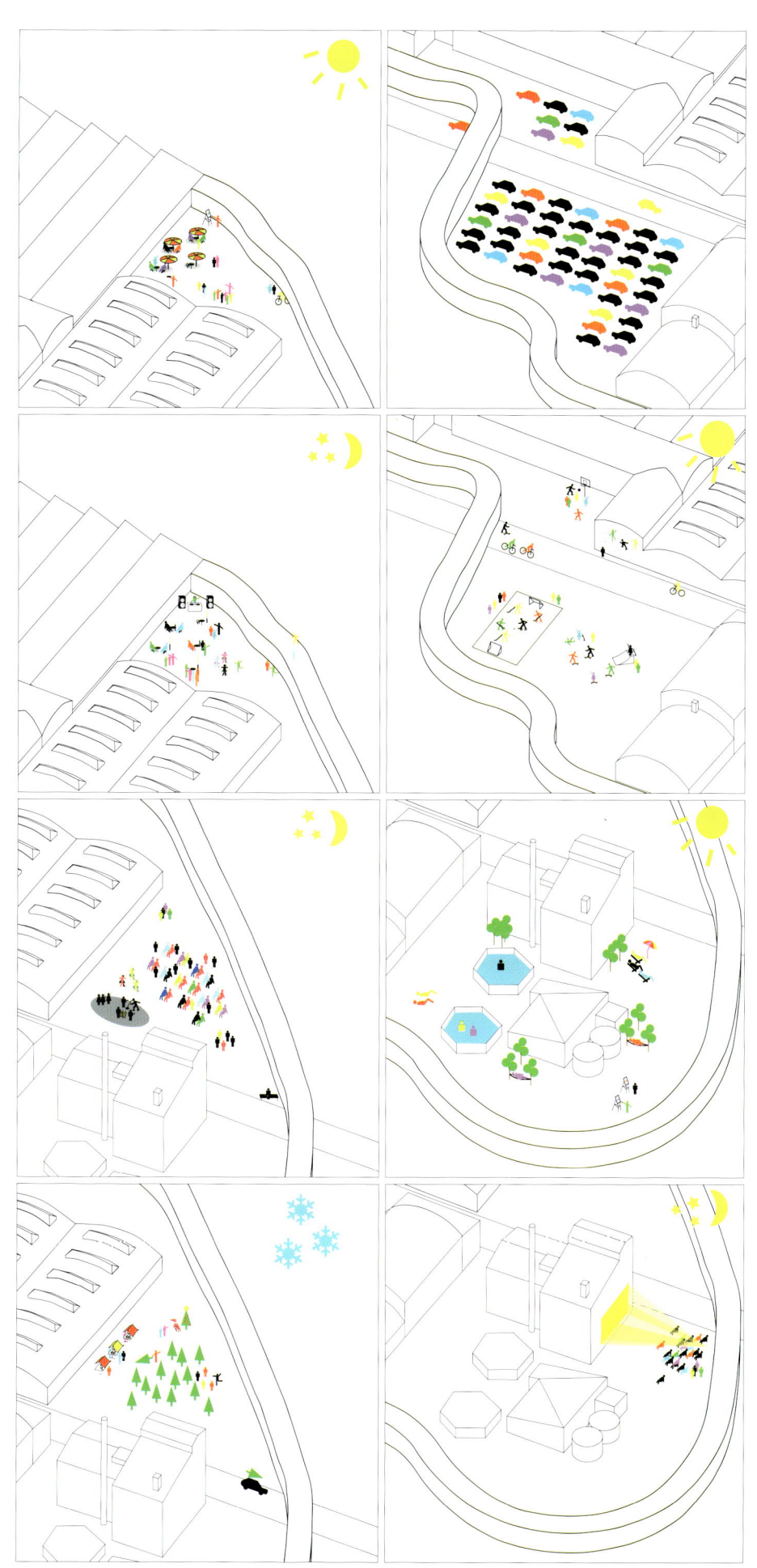

ARCHITECTURAL DIAGRAMS 141

SPORT PARK *nodo17 architects*

"A SPORTS PAVILION THAT IS CAPABLE OF MIXING WITH THE PARK, WHICH IS NOT LIMITED TO THE TRADITIONAL SHAPE."

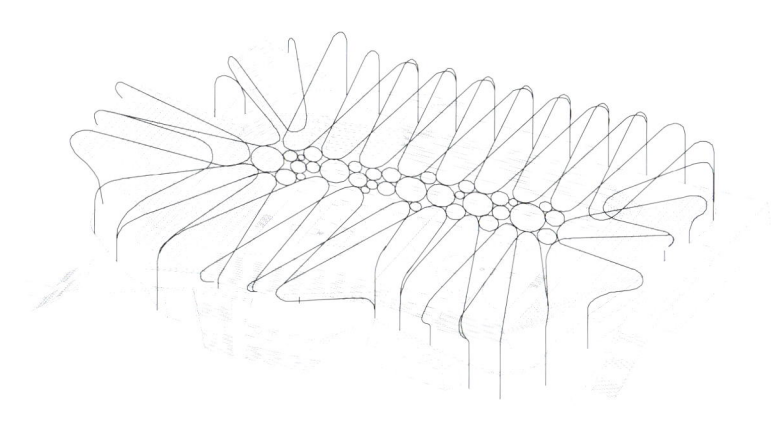

Cover level
Structure

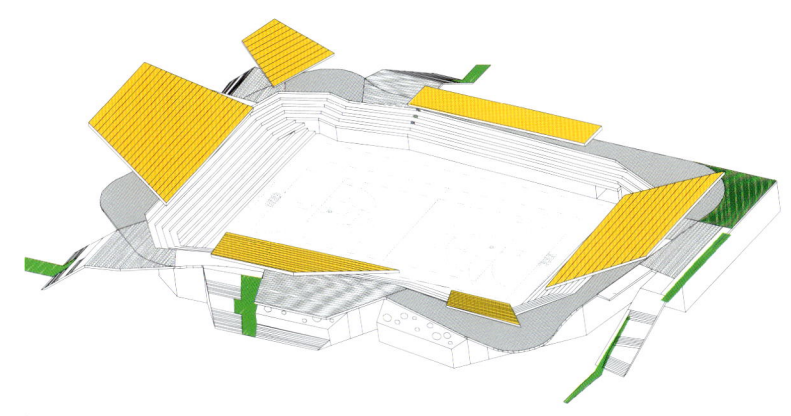

Stands level
Access to stands from deambulatorio

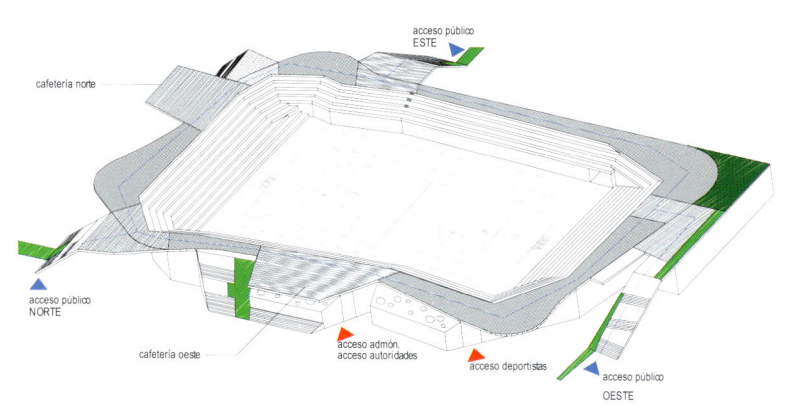

Nivel deambulatorio level

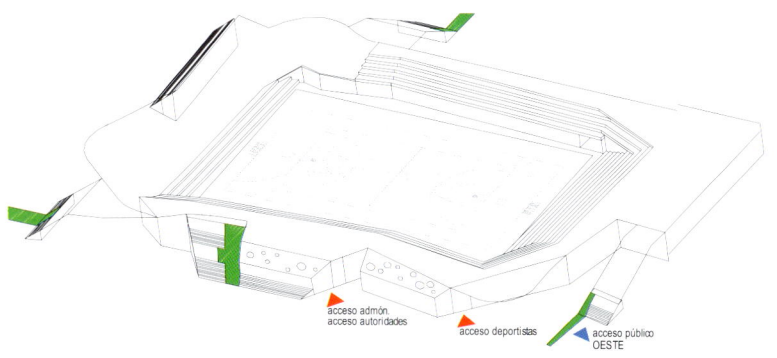

Access level

ARCHITECTURAL DIAGRAMS 143

STAVANGER CONCERT HALL JDS Architects

"THE NEW CONCERT HOUSE PLAYS A FUNDA-MENTAL ROLE IN THE LONG-TERM STRATEGY FOR POSITIONING STAVANGER."

+ 30.00
+ 14.00

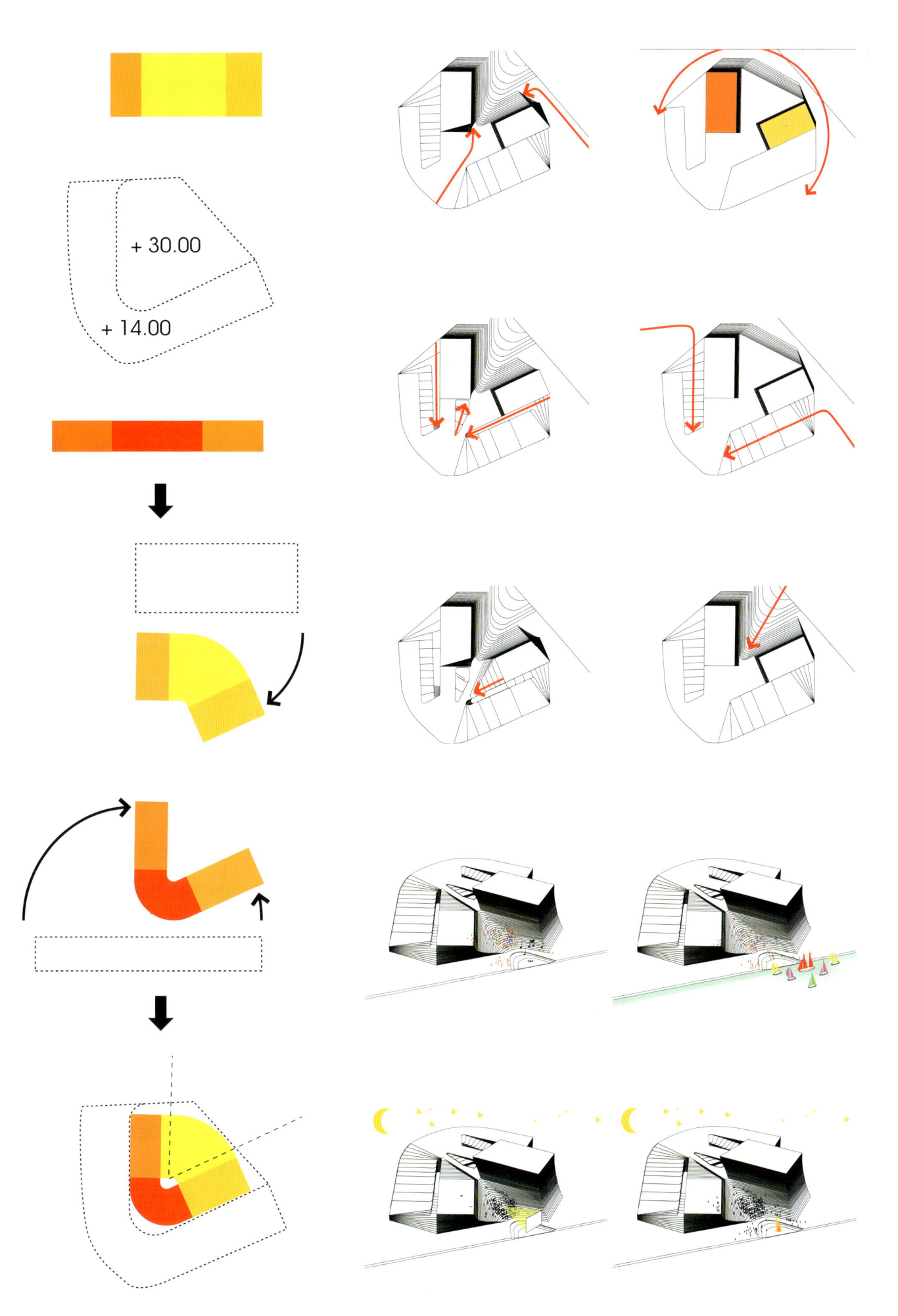

ARCHITECTURAL DIAGRAMS 145

STOCKHOLM'S GARDEN LIBRARY JDS Architects

"WE SUGGEST UNIFYING THE NEW FACILITY WITH THE STREET ON ONE SIDE AND THE OBSERVATORY PLATEAU ON THE OTHER."

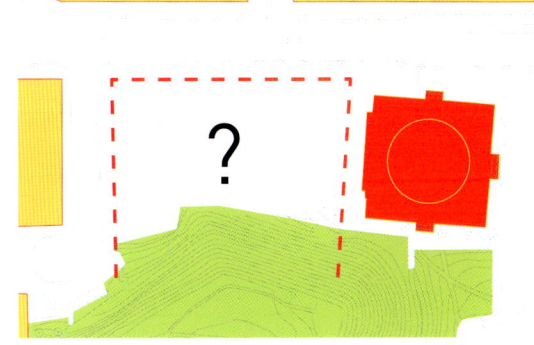

How should we address a site entangled in urbanity, nature and facing an icon?

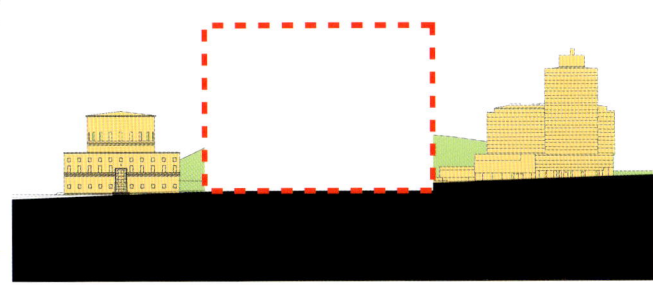

Building limits in elevation.

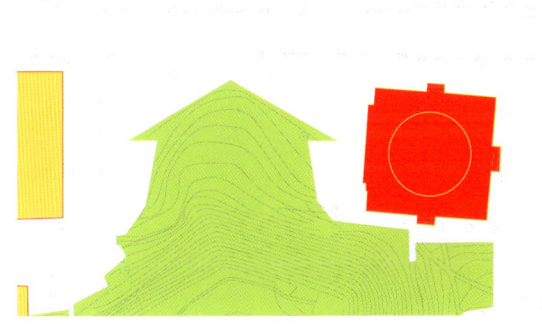

Until now the observatory hill had only one face towards the city. We suggest to turn the library's extension into a garden library, unifying the new facility with the street on one side and the observatory plateau on the other.

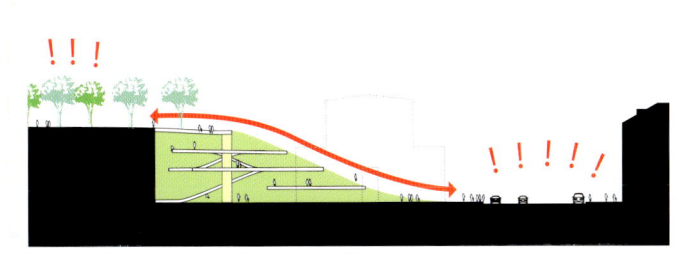

From street to observatory, the garden of the library.

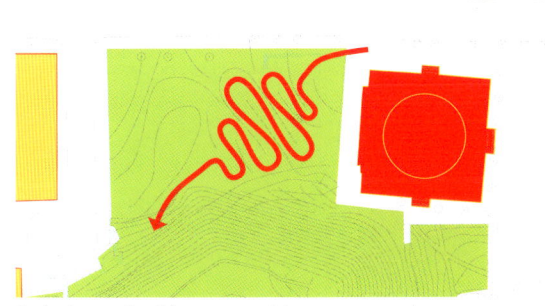

A winding path will form new outdoor spaces and open a connection from street level to the hilltop.

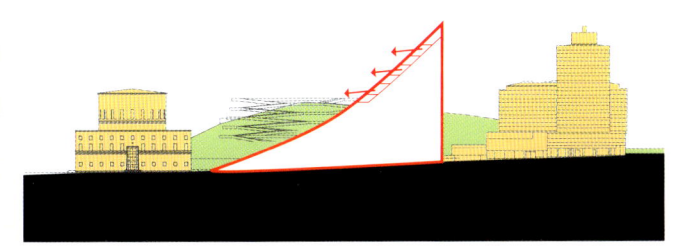

The new elevation stays within the envelope of the neighbouring buildings and gives hommage to asplund's library offering it as a spectacle to the study rooms.

ARCHITECTURAL DIAGRAMS 147

STRIJP S NL Architects

"THE VEEMGEBOUW, A FORMER WAREHOUSE, WILL BE TRANSFORMED INTO THE SO-CALLED STIJLFAB-RIEK."

Concept

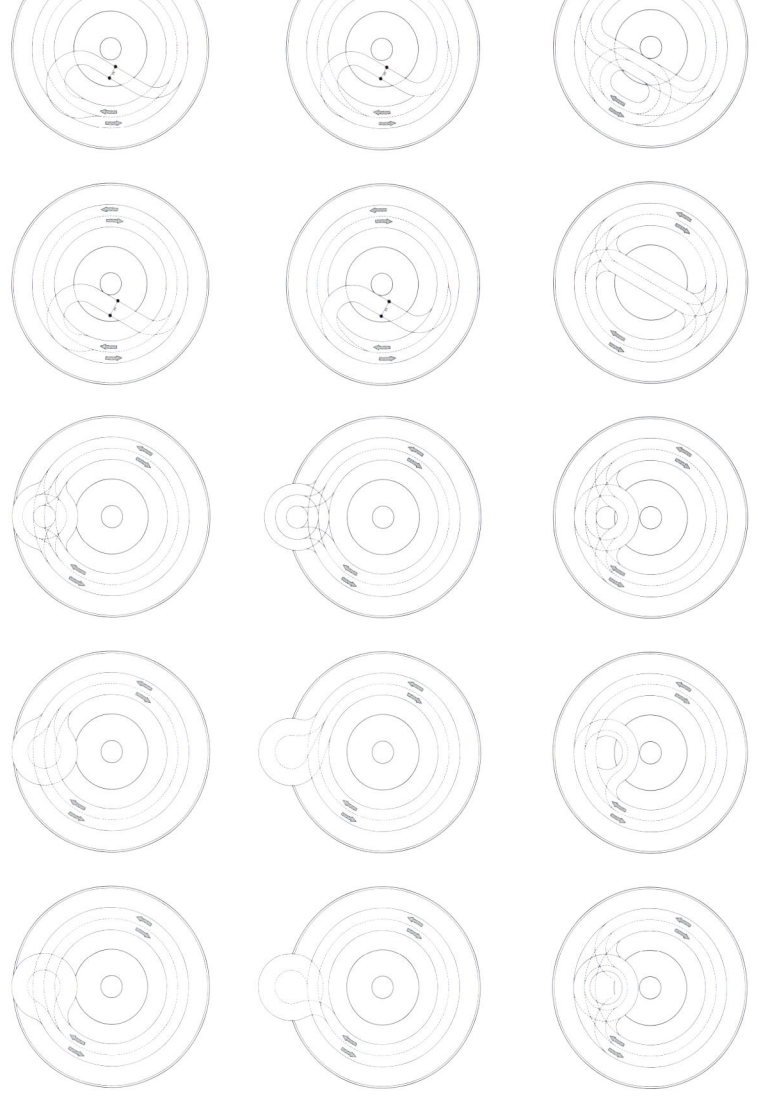

Road system

ARCHITECTURAL DIAGRAMS 149

TAIPEI PERFORMING ARTS CENTER NL Architects

"THE TAIPEI PERFORMING ARTS CENTER ASPIRES TO BECOME ACCESSIBLE FOR EVERYBODY."

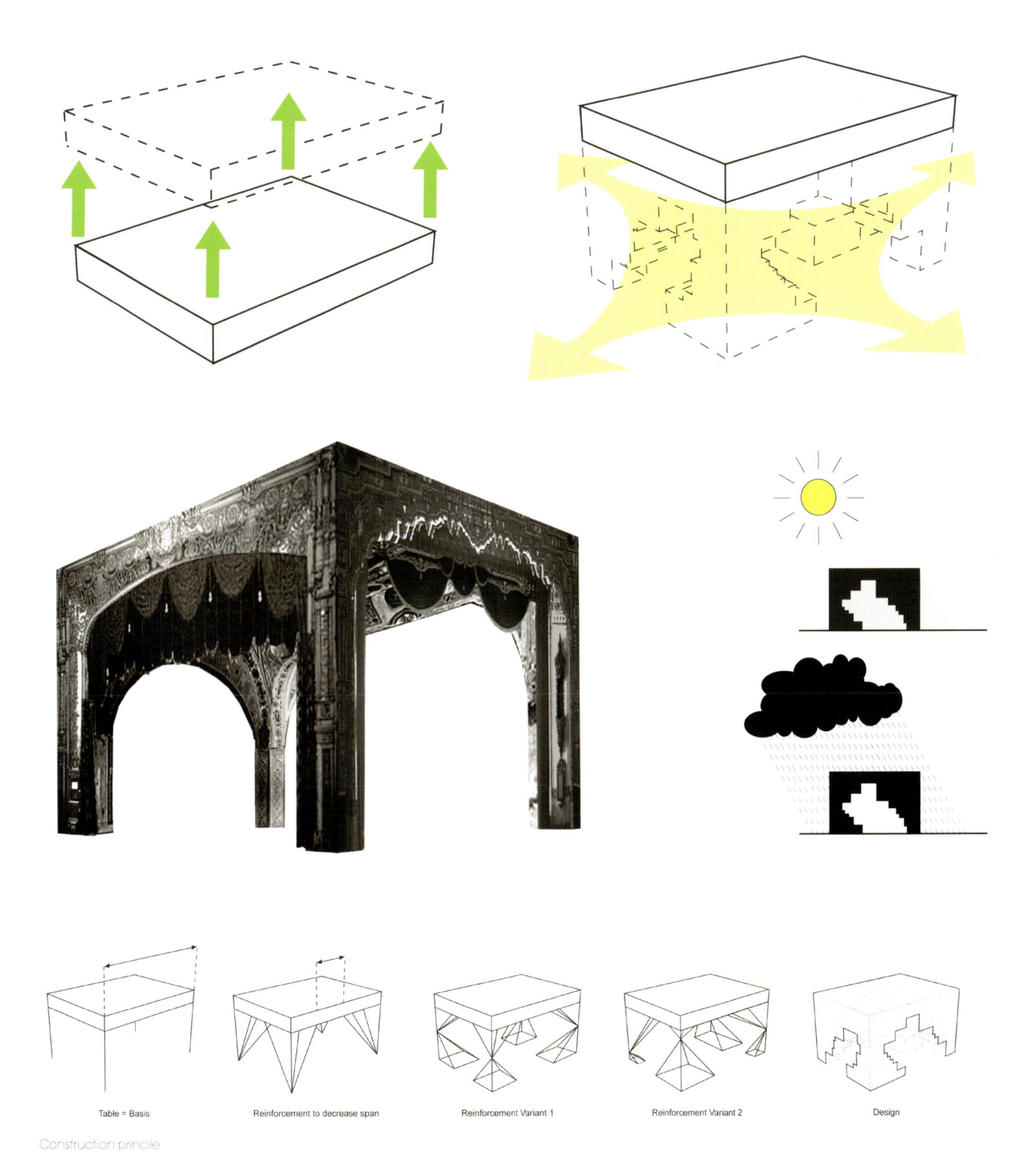

| Table = Basis | Reinforcement to decrease span | Reinforcement Variant 1 | Reinforcement Variant 2 | Design |

Construction princile

ARCHITECTURAL DIAGRAMS 151

TAIPEI PERFORMING ARTS CENTER Serie Architects

"WE PROPOSE A MATTED PLINTH THAT ACTS LIKE A SINGLE LAYER OF CITY FABRIC THAT DRAWS THE CITY INTO THE BUILDING."

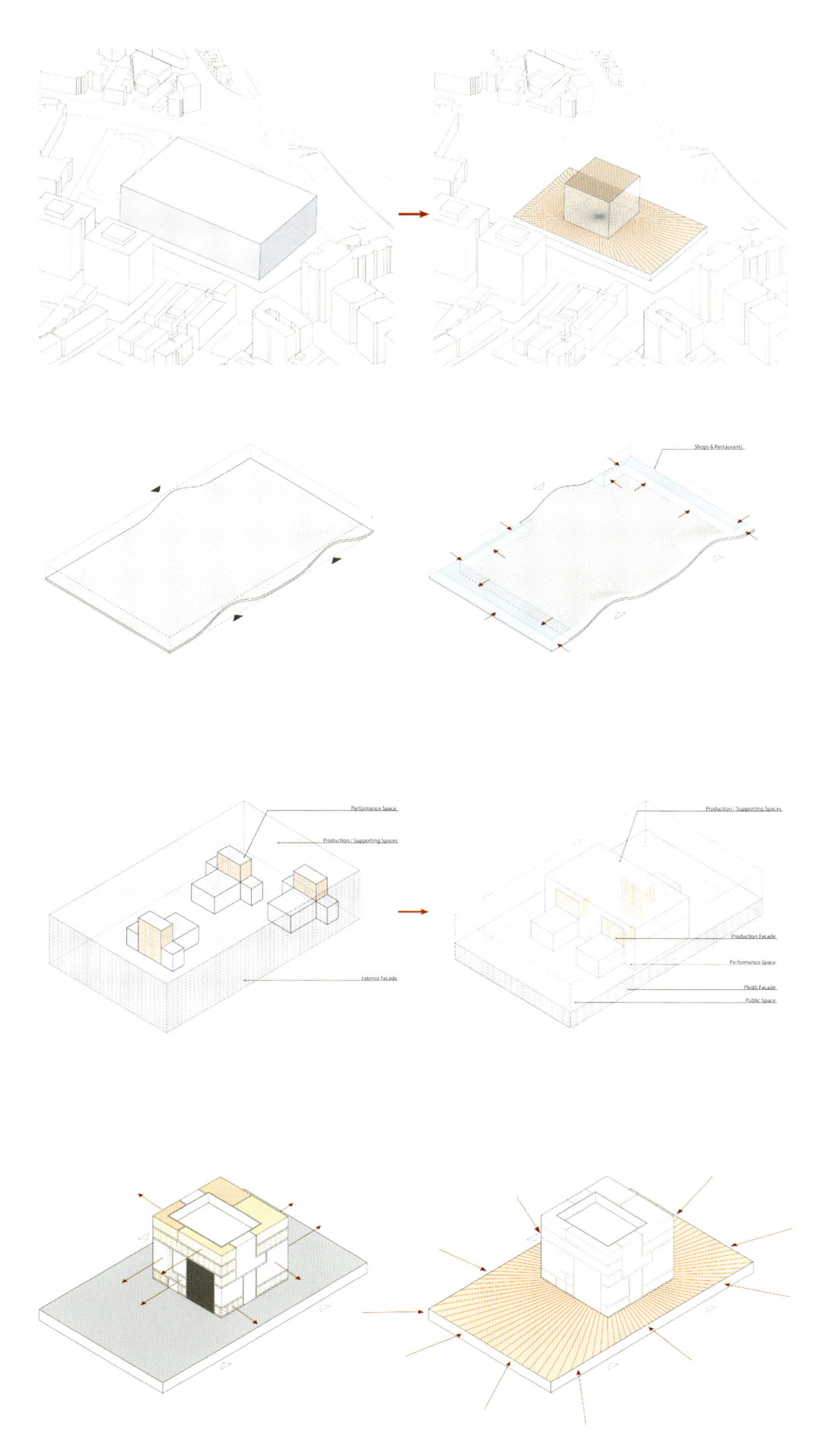

ARCHITECTURAL DIAGRAMS   153

TALLINN TOWN HALL
BIG

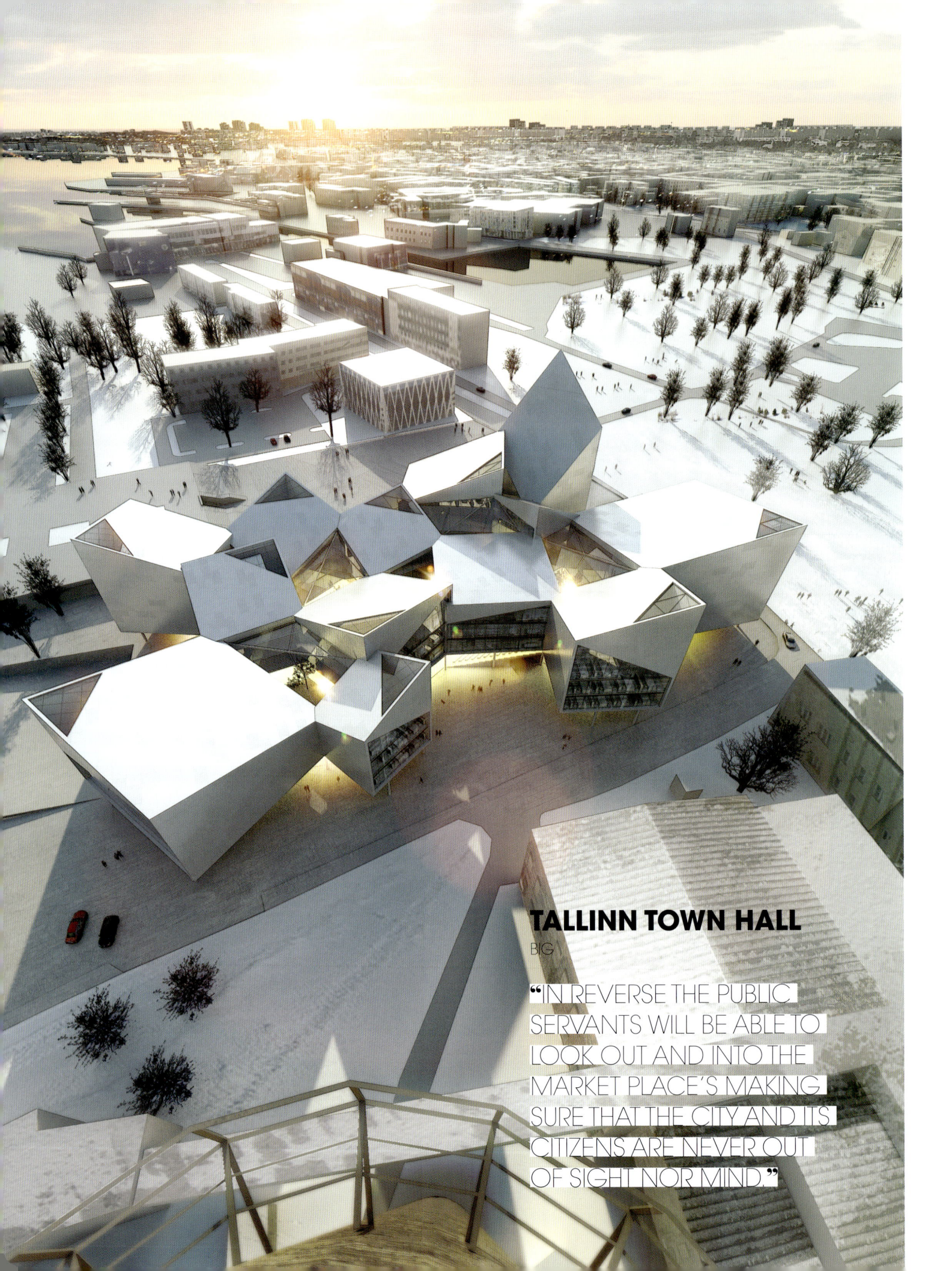

"IN REVERSE THE PUBLIC SERVANTS WILL BE ABLE TO LOOK OUT AND INTO THE MARKET PLACE'S MAKING SURE THAT THE CITY AND ITS CITIZENS ARE NEVER OUT OF SIGHT NOR MIND."

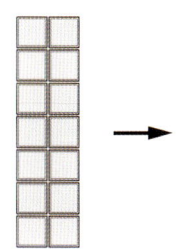

Compact organization
Compact organization and efficient layout at the expense of daylight and views.

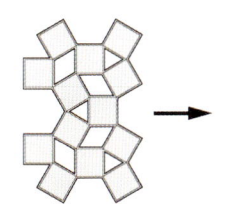

Porous organization
Hinged complex retains compactness and efficiency while maximizing daylight and view.

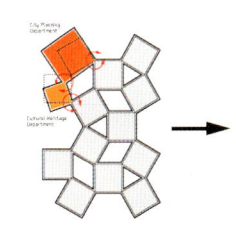

Differentiated program
Programmatic specify transforms generic diagram ie. City planning department and cultural heritage department

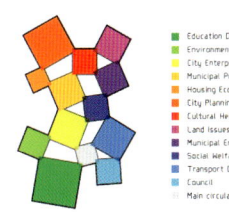

The public village
Specific organization of the public village

- Education Department
- Environment Department
- City Enterprise Department
- Municipal Police Department
- Housing Economy Department
- City Planning Department
- Cultural Heritage Department
- Land Issues Department
- Municipal Engineering Department
- Social Welfare and Healthcare Department
- Transport Department
- Council
- Main circulation

Connections
Each department is rotated in order to create maximum connections between the units and at the same time leave place for internal courtyards

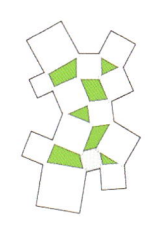

Courtyards
The seven grand light wells allow daylight to enter the market place at the groundfloor.

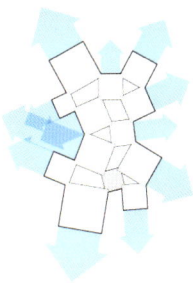

Panoramic views
The large openings offers views of the entire city from within the offices in the town hall.

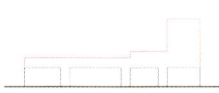

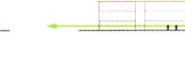

1. DEPARTMENT LAYOUT
The Departments are arranged according to their individual needs.

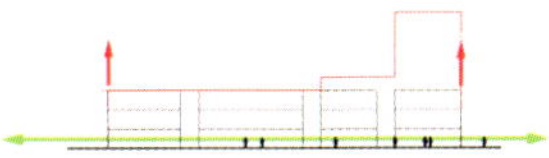

2. MARKETPLACE
The volumes are elevated creating a new public place under the Town Hall.

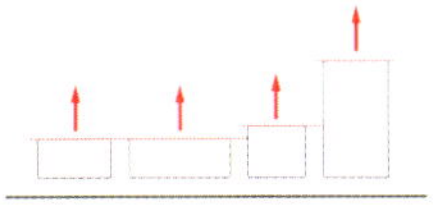

3. HEIGHTS
The main volumes of the building are raised according to the building regulations.

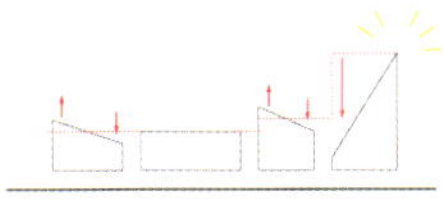

4. DEMOCRATIC TOWER
The roof of the volumes are raised and lowered so only spires breaks the building height limits.

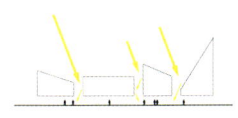

COURTYARDS
The distance between the departments allows natural daylight to enter the marketplace below.

SKYLIGHTS
Windows at the top of each department catches the low sun and reflects diffuse light into the offices.

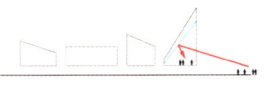

INSIGHT
From outside the Town Hall the citizens can get an insight into the political work.

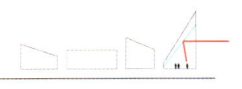

OVERVIEW
A large mirror in the Council Hall above the public servants gives them a periscope view of the city.

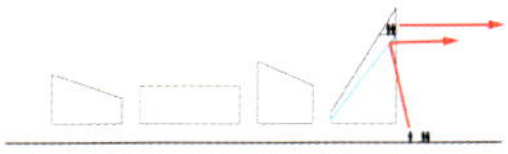

DEMOCRATIC VIEW
From the top of the Town Hall tower the citizens can enjoy the great view of Tallinn. The same view can be experienced via the Council Hall mirror.

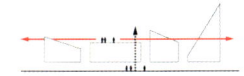

PUBLIC ROOF TERRACE
From the groundfloor restaurant a public elevator brings the citizens to the roof café. From here they can enjoy the 360 degree panorama of Tallinn.

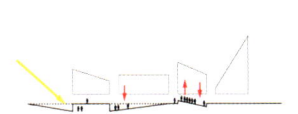

THE CARPET
The groundfloor is manipulated to create access and light for the kitchen. A tilted square becomes the main conference hall.

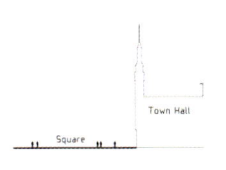

A NEW PUBLIC SPACE
Traditionally the square in front of a town hall has always been the main gathering space for the public in any city.

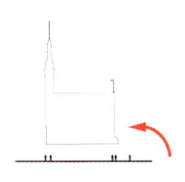

In this new urban context we suggest to elevate the town hall above the public square and create a new urban space where the citizens can interact with the Tallinn officials.

ARCHITECTURAL DIAGRAMS 155

THEATRE AGORA UNStudio

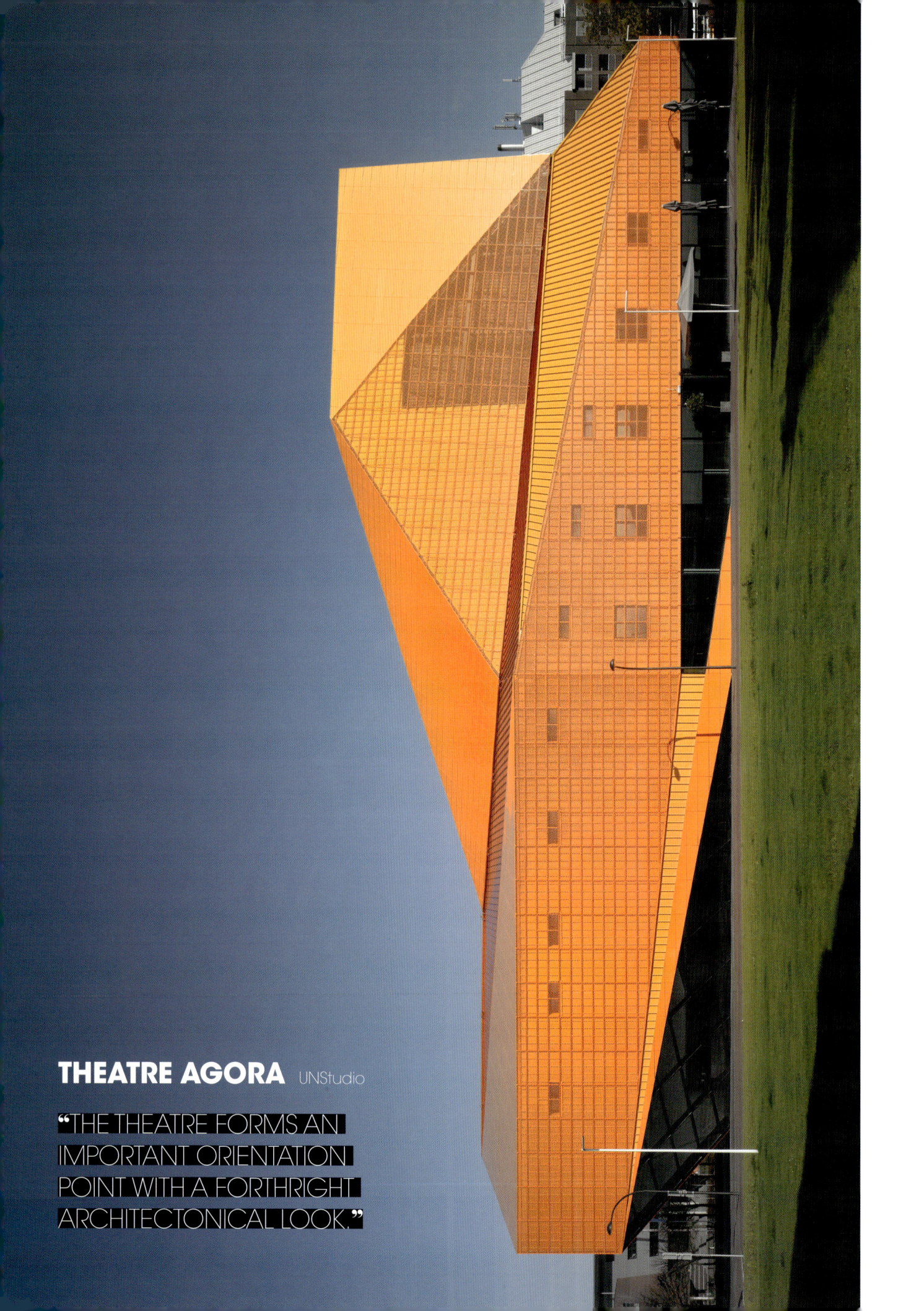

"THE THEATRE FORMS AN IMPORTANT ORIENTATION POINT WITH A FORTHRIGHT ARCHITECTONICAL LOOK."

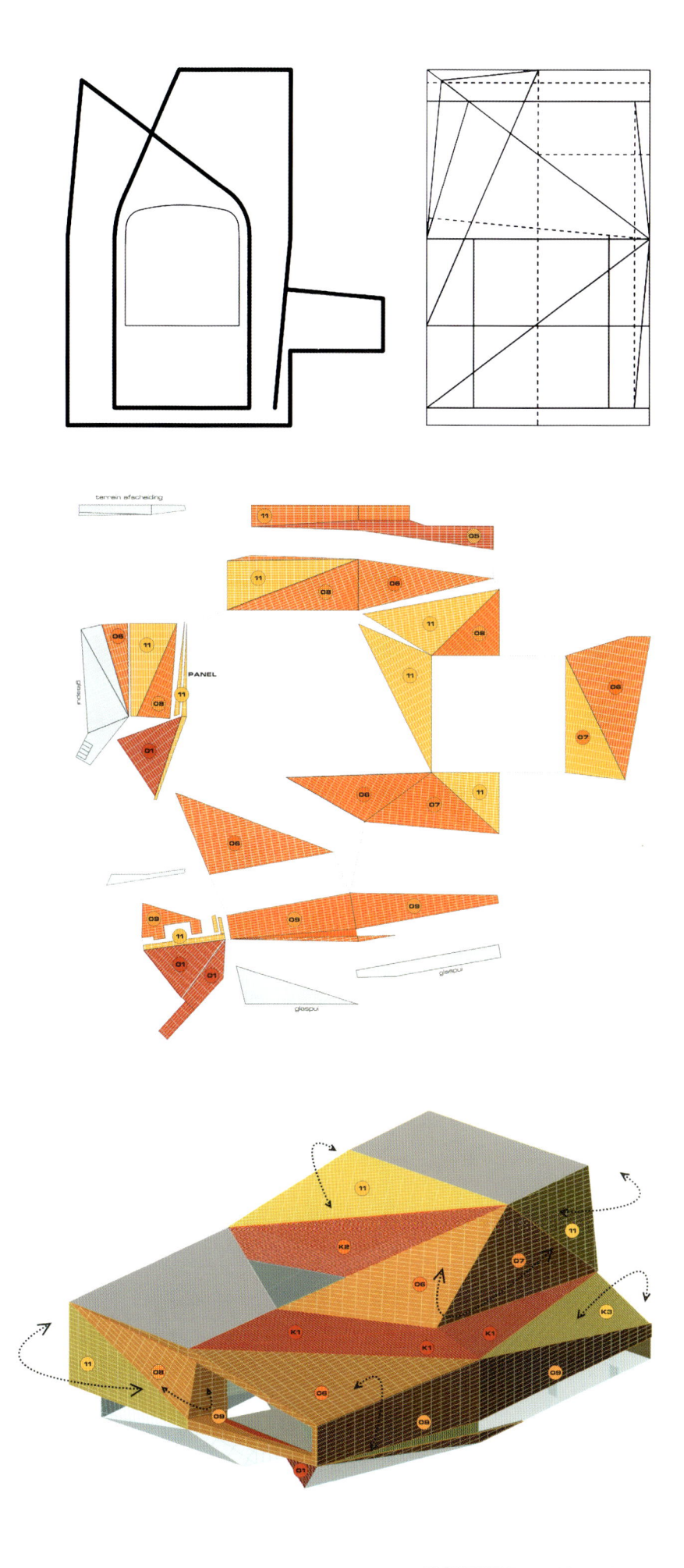

ARCHITECTURAL DIAGRAMS 157

THUNNUS THYNNUS
nodo17 architects

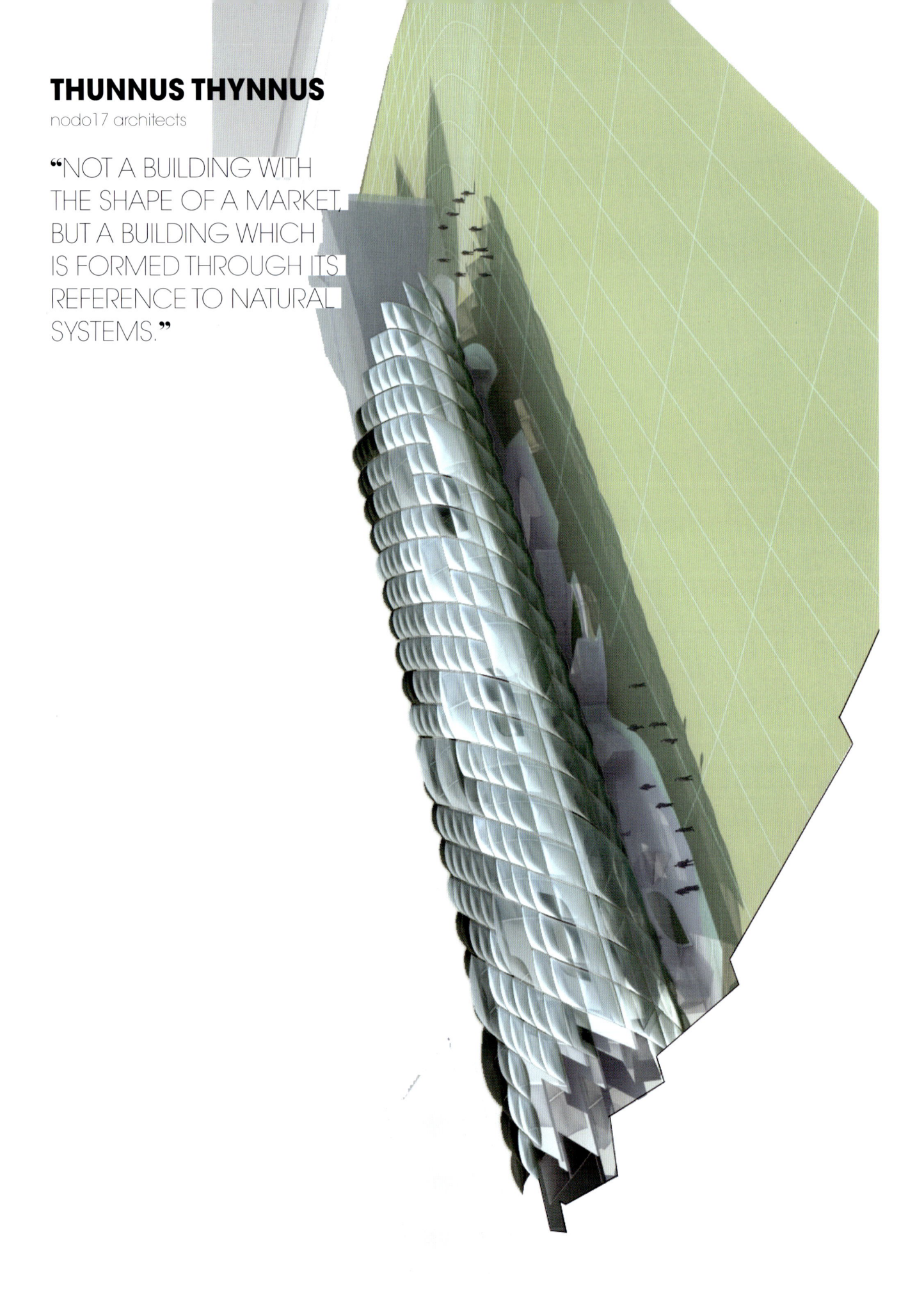

"NOT A BUILDING WITH THE SHAPE OF A MARKET, BUT A BUILDING WHICH IS FORMED THROUGH ITS REFERENCE TO NATURAL SYSTEMS."

fig a

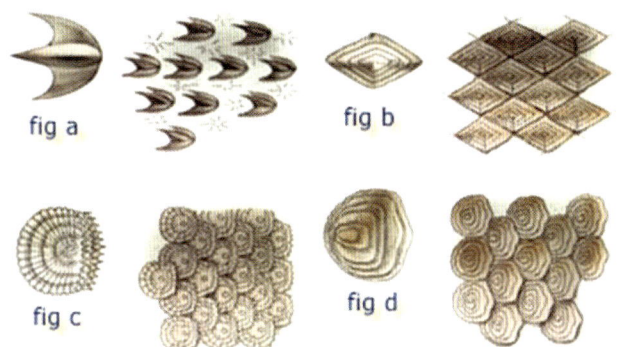

fig b

fig c

fig d

Icon guidelines

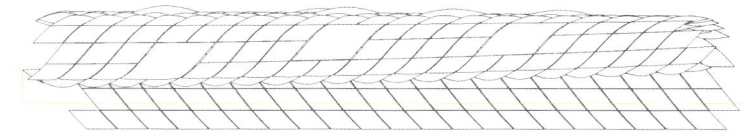

Skin development elevation

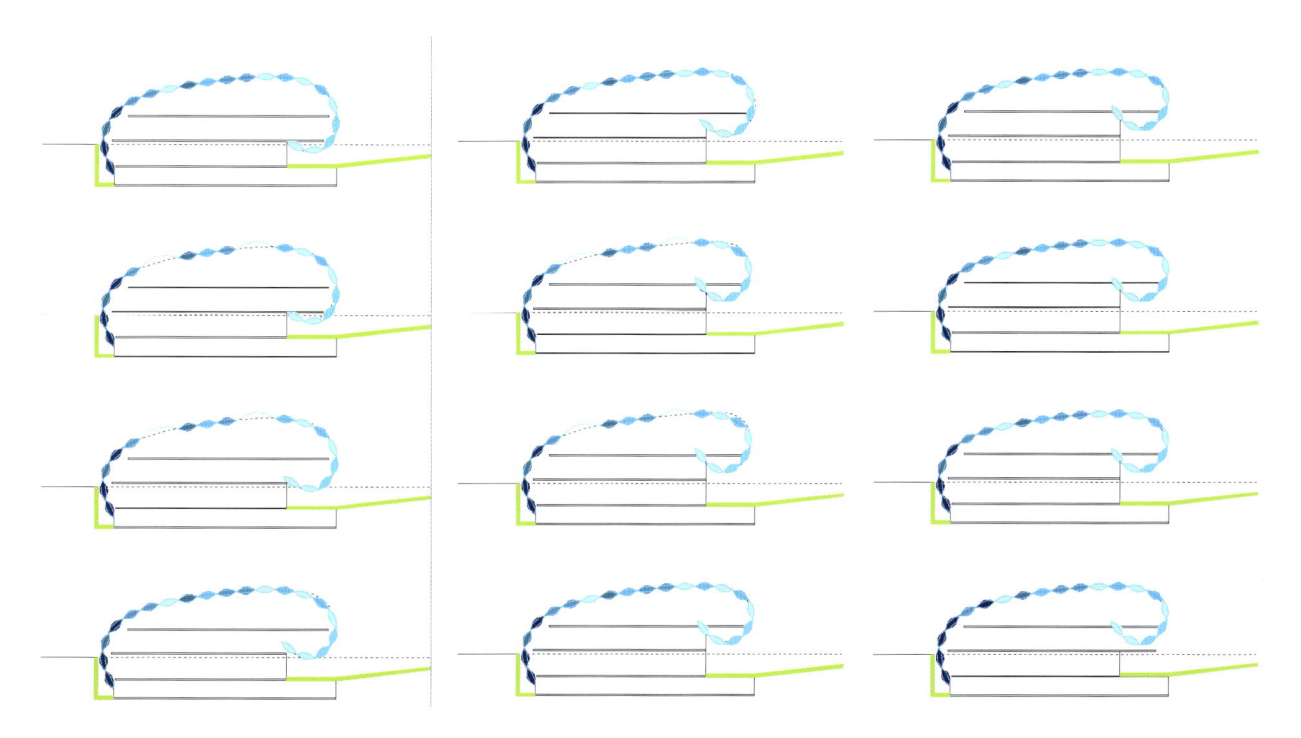

ARCHITECTURAL DIAGRAMS 159

TITTOT GLASS MUSEUM
IaN+

"PLACING THE BUILDING ALONG THE EDGE OF THE LOT, SO TO INTEGRATE THE LANDSCAPE AND TURN IT INTO AN INTERIOR PART OF THE MUSEUM."

Yuan Shan Park

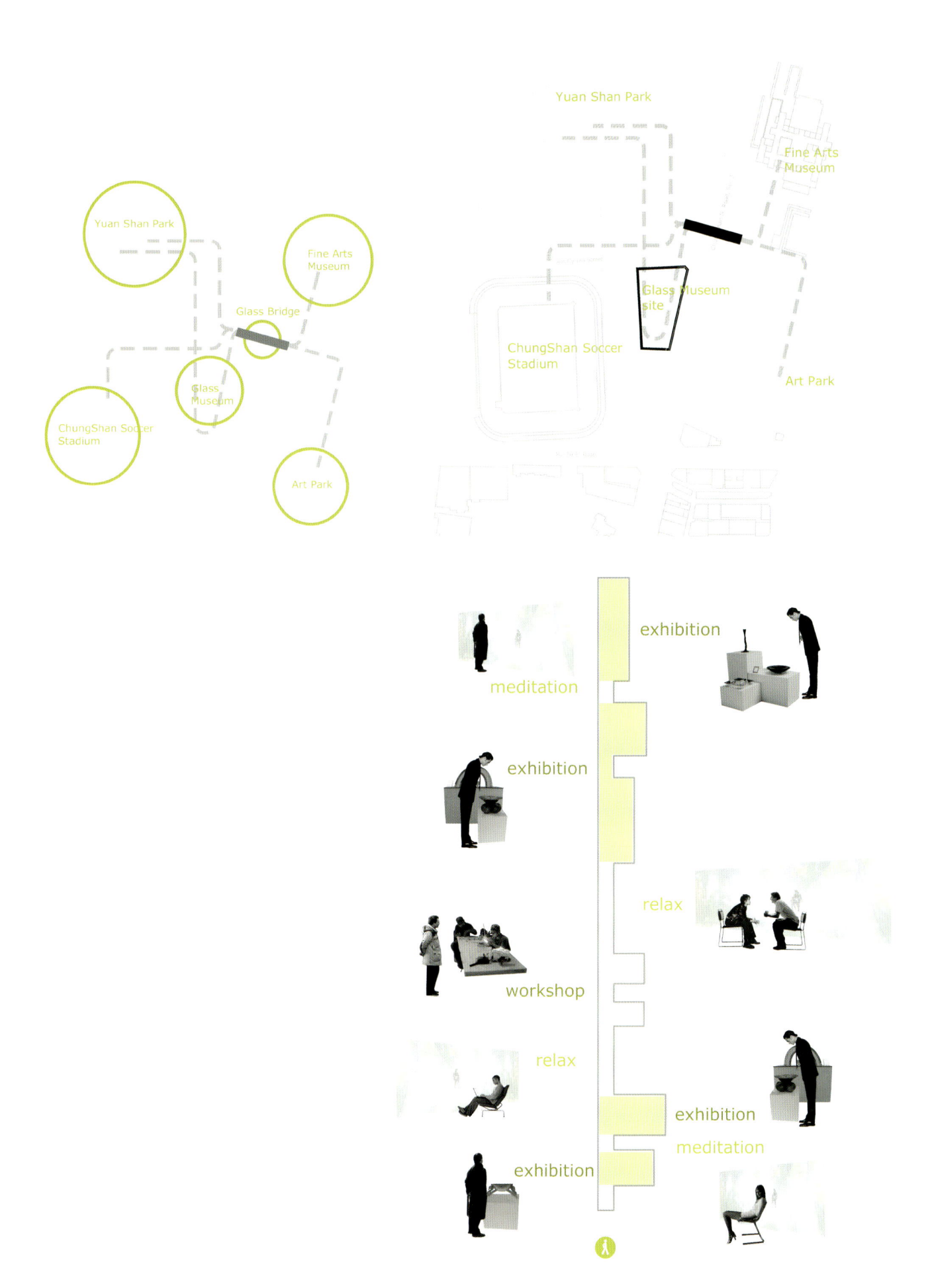

Fine Arts Museum

Glass Bridge

Glass Museum

ChungShan Soccer Stadium

Art Park

Yuan Shan Park

Fine Arts Museum

Glass Museum site

ChungShan Soccer Stadium

Art Park

exhibition
meditation
exhibition
relax
workshop
relax
exhibition
meditation
exhibition

ARCHITECTURAL DIAGRAMS 161

TREVISO CULTURAL CENTRE Re_Load

"RELATING FIGURES EACH OTHER WE CREATE INTERESTING CONFIGURATIONS OF SPACE."

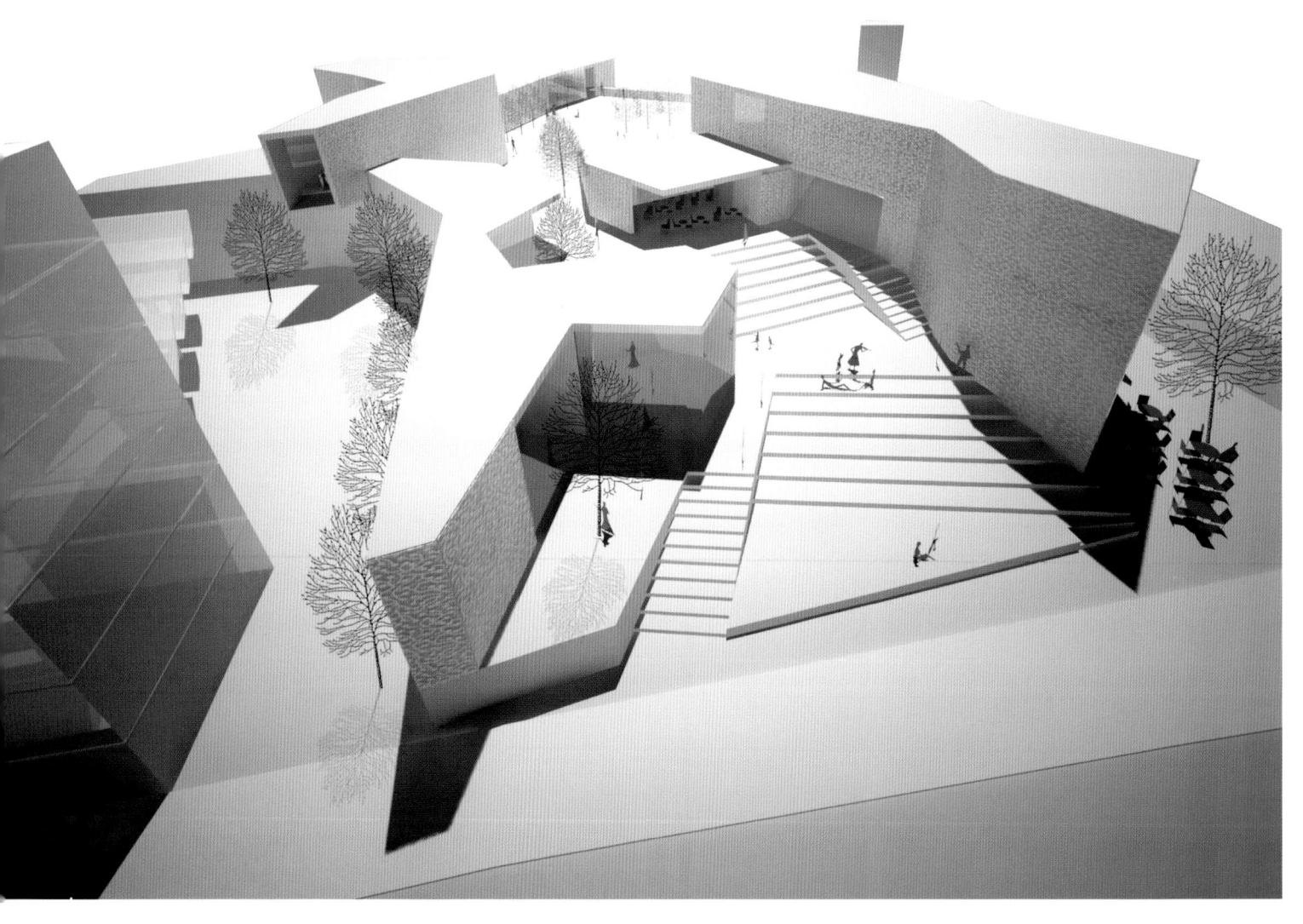

TAN_GRAMMAR

The idea starts from the different configurations of space that the Tangram creates

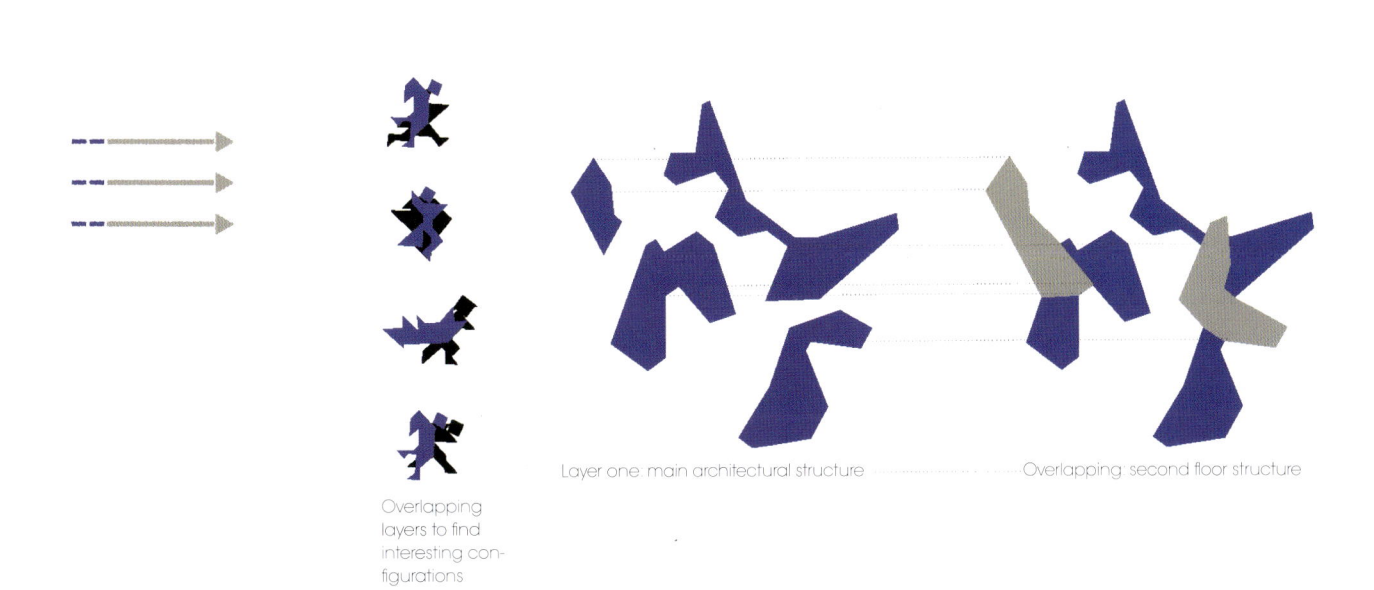

Tasting spatial possibilities

Interstitial spaces created by the figures

Green space

Overlapping layers to find interesting configurations

Layer one: main architectural structure

Overlapping: second floor structure

ARCHITECTURAL DIAGRAMS 163

WELZIJNSCLUSTER ZOETERMEER SeARCH

"THE SCHOOL COMPLEX FORMS A UNITY THROUGH FORMS AND MATERIALS."

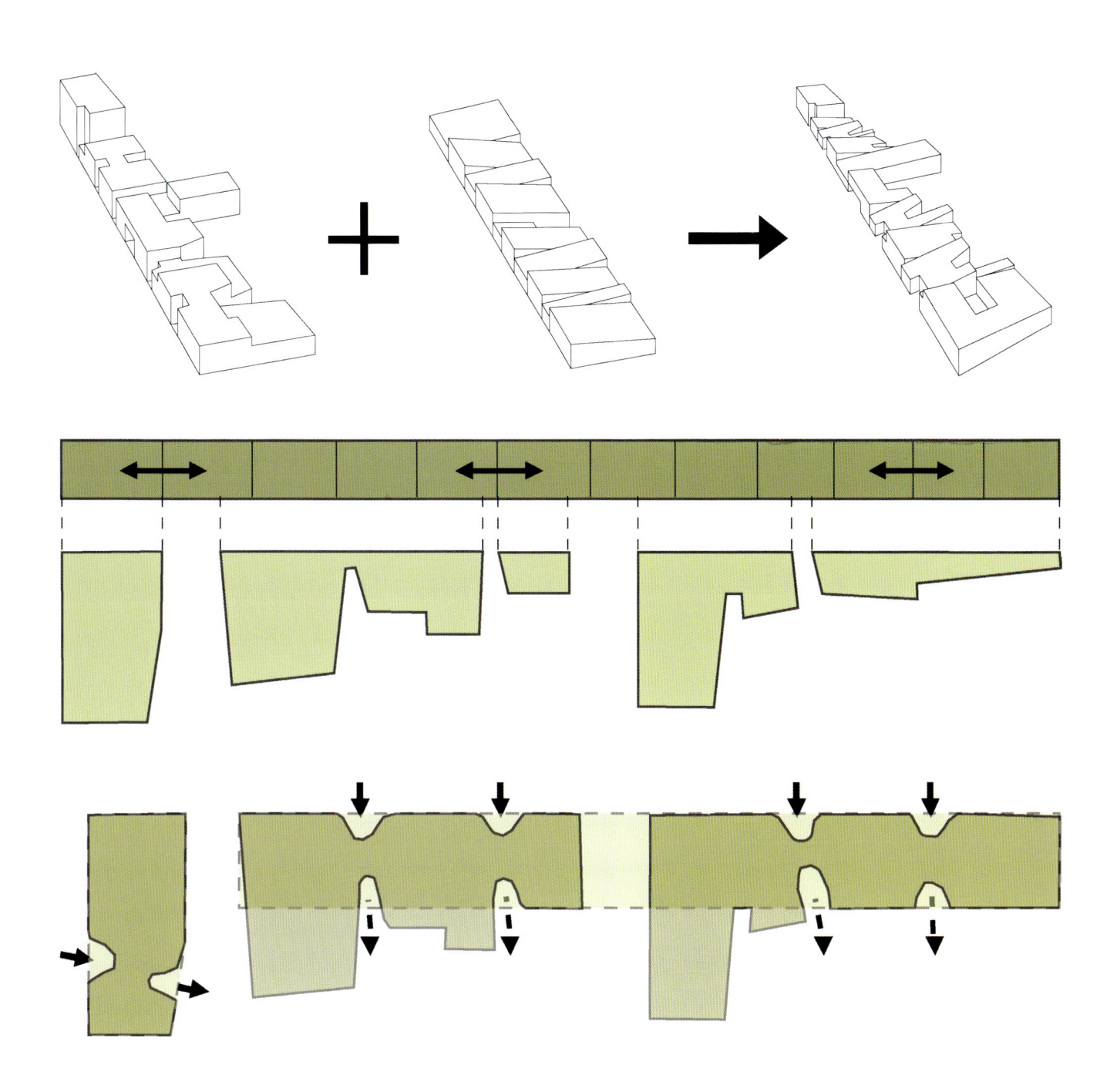

ARCHITECTURAL DIAGRAMS 165

WROCŁAW 2012
Guallart Architects

"THE KEY THEME OF WHICH WILL BE THE CULTURE OF LEISURE IN THE WORLD'S ECONOMIES."

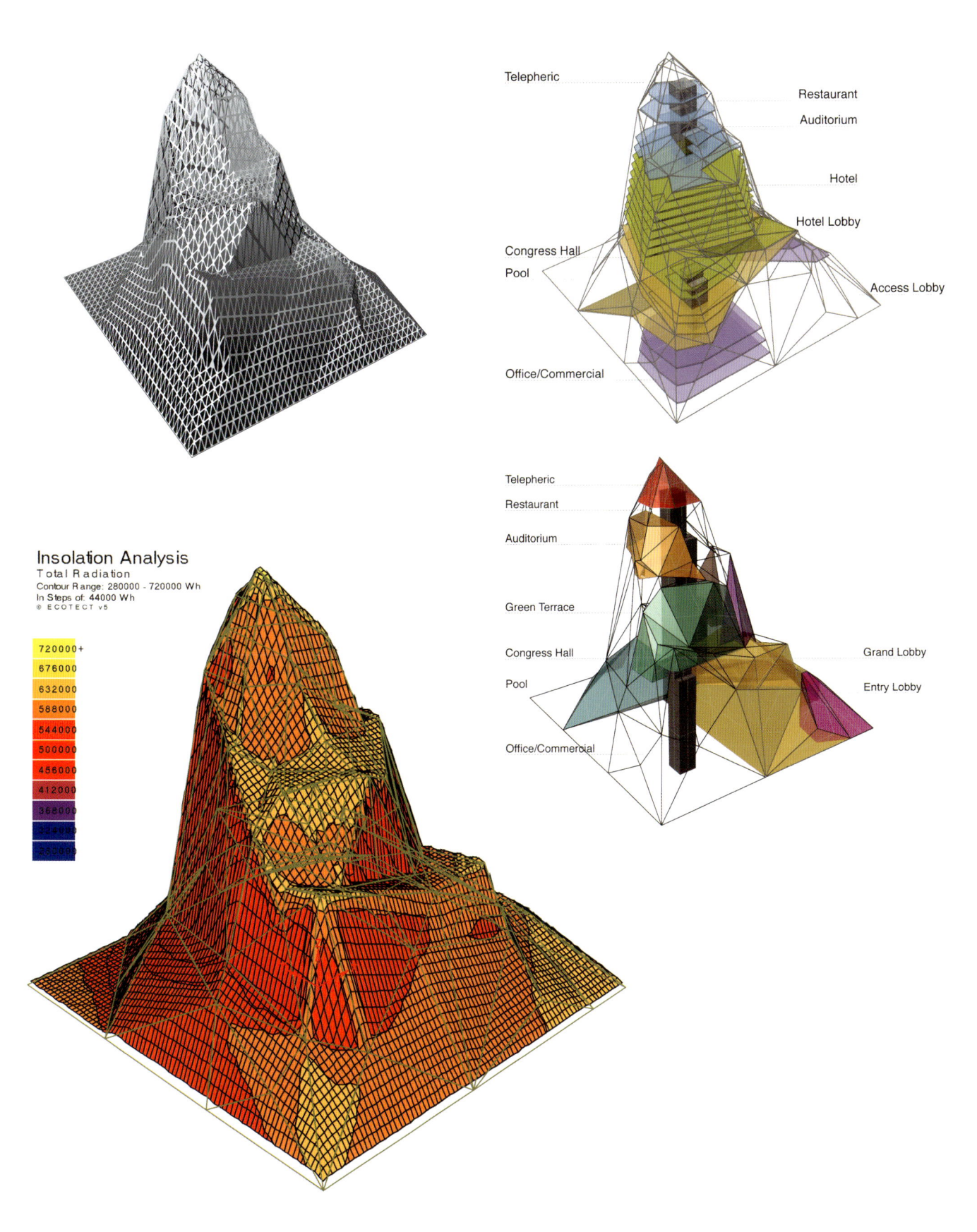

Telepheric
Restaurant
Auditorium
Hotel
Hotel Lobby
Congress Hall
Pool
Access Lobby
Office/Commercial

Telepheric
Restaurant
Auditorium
Green Terrace
Congress Hall
Grand Lobby
Pool
Entry Lobby
Office/Commercial

Insolation Analysis
Total Radiation
Contour Range: 280000 - 720000 Wh
In Steps of: 44000 Wh
© ECOTECT v5

720000+
676000
632000
588000
544000
500000
456000
412000
368000

ARCHITECTURAL DIAGRAMS 167

X SITE NL Architects

"THE TYPOLOGY OF THE STAND COULD BE A SUCCESSFUL TOOL IN THE GAME OF SOCIAL INTERACTION: TO SEE AND BE SEEN."

1,300m² for extra program

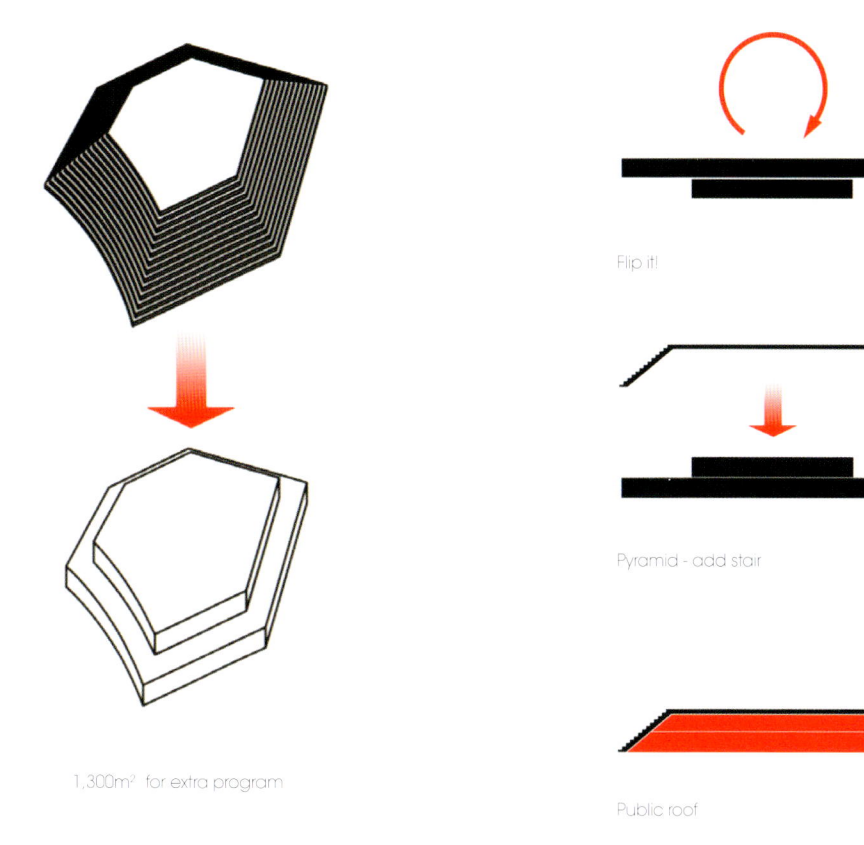

Flip it!

Pyramid - add stair

Public roof

Building is not a border

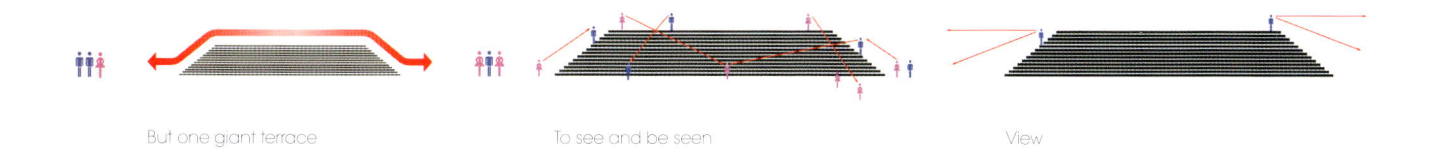

But one giant terrace

To see and be seen

View

ARCHITECTURAL DIAGRAMS 169

ZWALUWEN UTRECHT
1911 NL Architects

"THE ADVANTAGE OF THE DIKE IS THAT THE USUALLY UNATTRACTIVE LOWER PART OF THE BUILDING IS HIDDEN."

Sheme A

0.

The stacking of the more public program on top of the wardrobes creates a terrace that allows for extensive views over the surrounding soccer fields.

1.

The adding of a dike equals the cheapest possible facade. It puts the building on a temple-like pedestal.

2.

By elevating the 4 corners, a difference of spatial opening of the buildings upper level is created for each individual corner.

3.

Tracing and cutting according to scheme B divides the facade into solid walls and semi-transparent, movable flaps.

4.

The 'empty' corners allow for views over the soccer fields and the flaps provide the terrace and interior of the building with cooling shadows. Off-season, the flaps close the corners again and protect the building from any kind of vandalism.

Sheme B

here it is

fold down the 4 walls

move up the 4 corners

move the flaps

close it

ARCHITECTURAL DIAGRAMS 171

LANDSCAPE

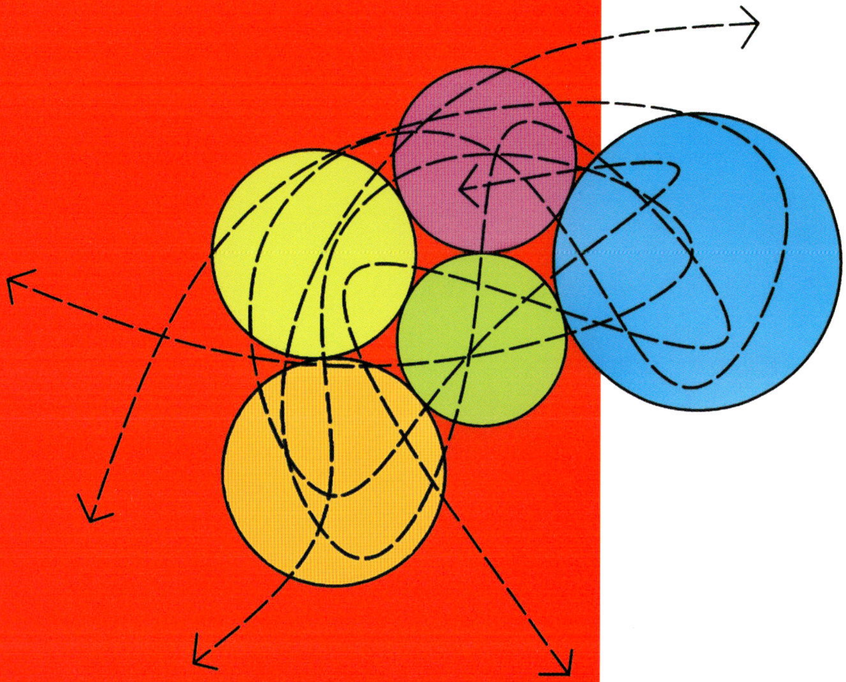

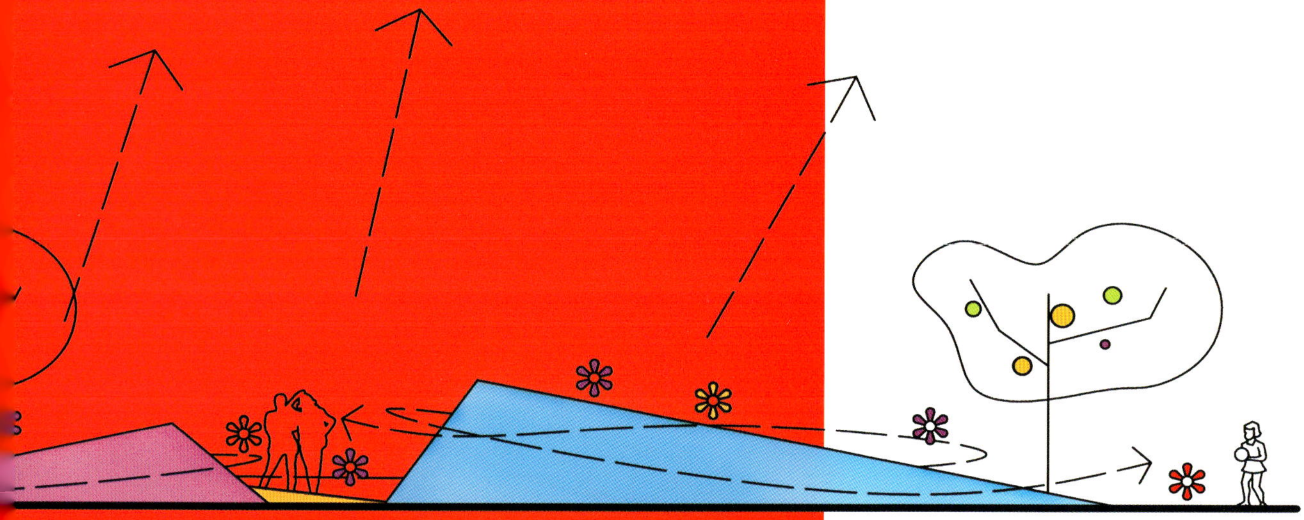

A10 HIGHWAY
kadawittfeldarchitektur

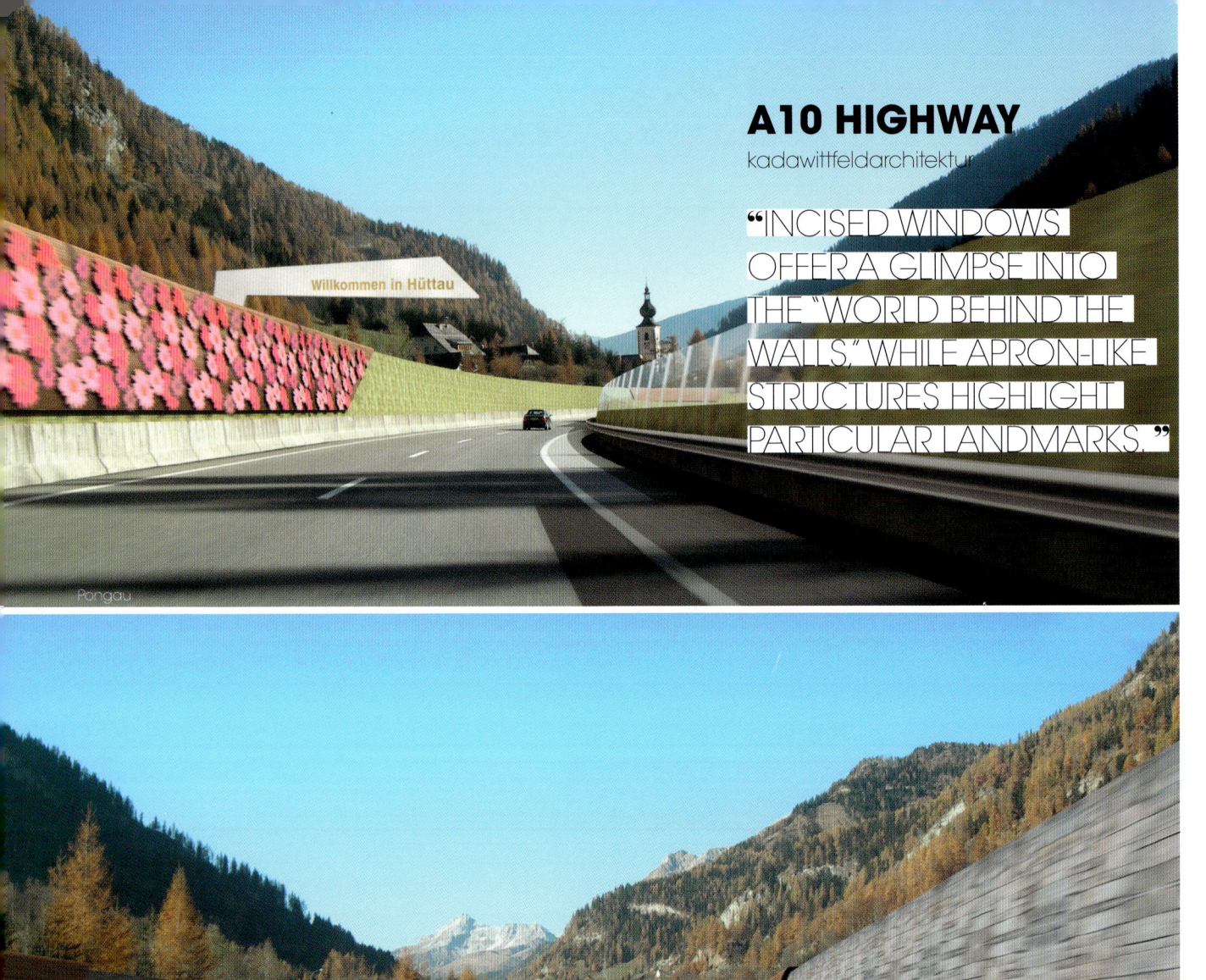

"INCISED WINDOWS OFFER A GLIMPSE INTO THE 'WORLD BEHIND THE WALLS,' WHILE APRON-LIKE STRUCTURES HIGHLIGHT PARTICULAR LANDMARKS."

Catalog types of noise barriers

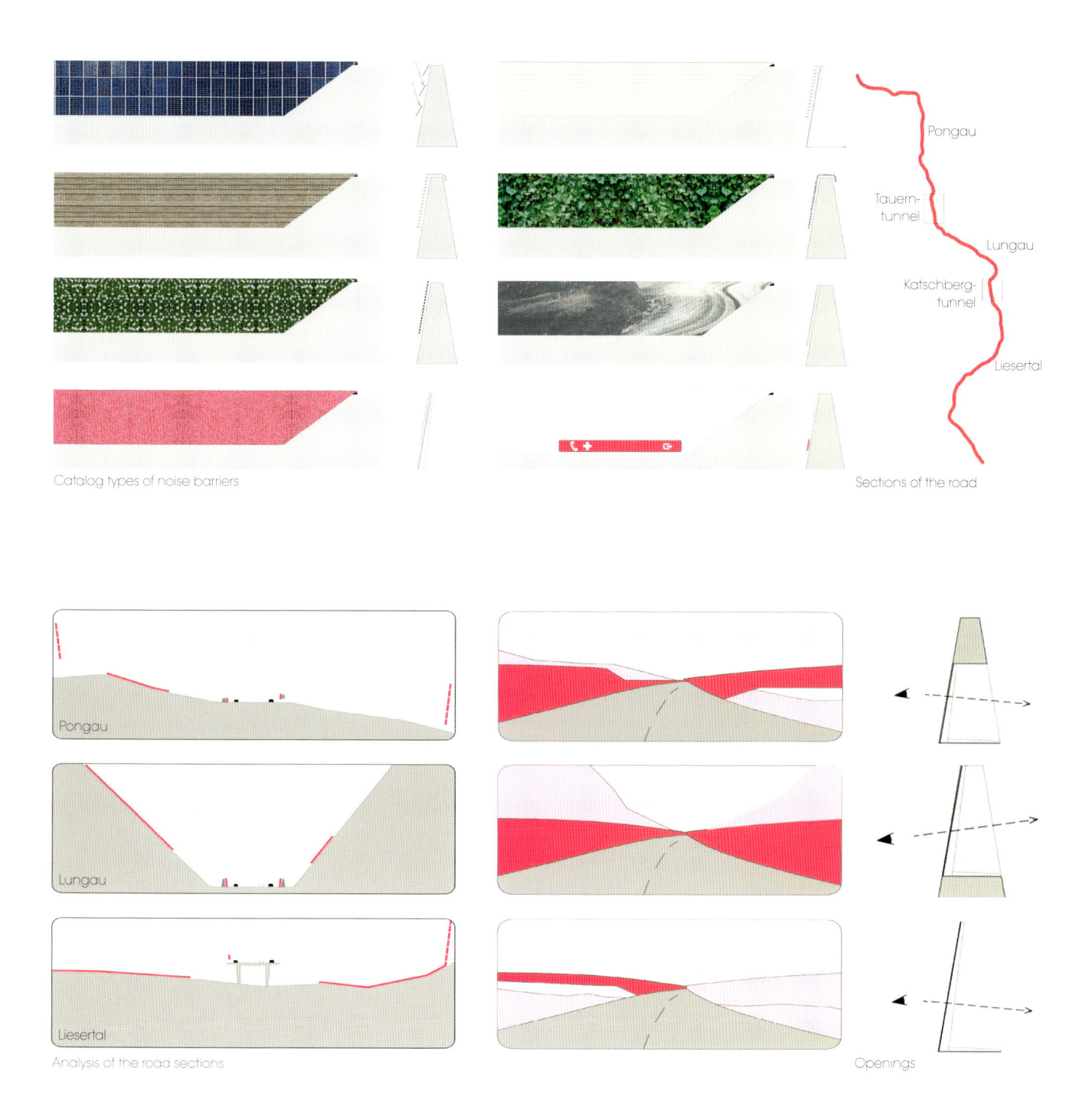

Sections of the road

Pongau

Tauern-
tunnel

Lungau

Katschberg-
tunnel

Liesertal

Pongau

Lungau

Liesertal

Analysis of the road sections

Openings

ARCHITECTURAL DIAGRAMS 175

A8ERNA NL Architects

"THE PROJECT IS AN ATTEMPT TO RESTORE THE CONNECTION BETWEEN BOTH SIDES OF TOWN AND TO ACTIVATE THE SPACE UNDER THE ROAD."

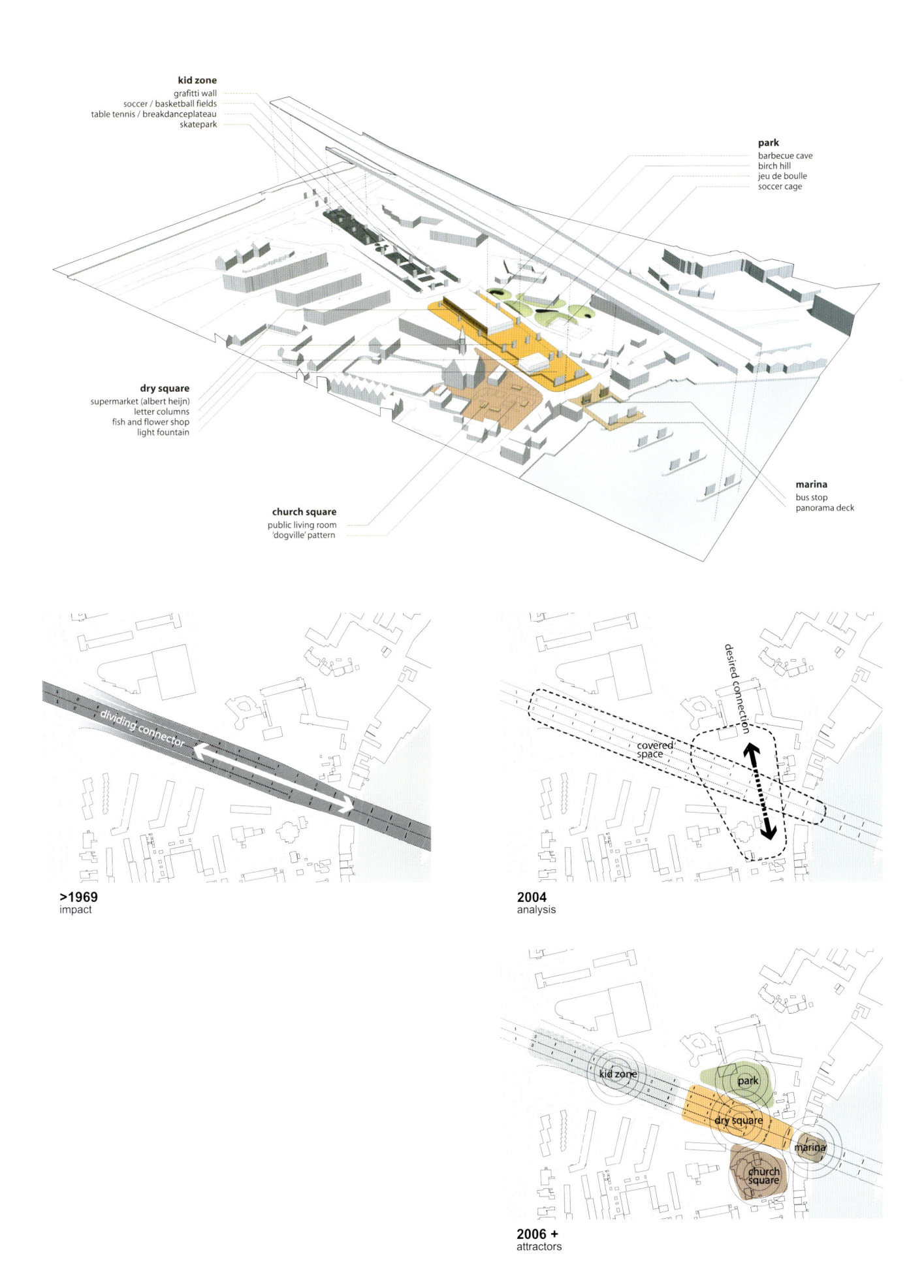

kid zone
grafitti wall
soccer / basketball fields
table tennis / breakdanceplateau
skatepark

park
barbecue cave
birch hill
jeu de boulle
soccer cage

dry square
supermarket (albert heijn)
letter columns
fish and flower shop
light fountain

marina
bus stop
panorama deck

church square
public living room
'dogville' pattern

>1969
impact

2004
analysis

2006 +
attractors

ARCHITECTURAL DIAGRAMS 177

BATOUTZ PORT AND OCEAN PLAZA
Guallart Architects

"OUR PROJECT PROPOSES TO ESTABLISH A LINEAR STRUCTURING SEQUENCE THAT DEFINES A VIBRATION BETWEEN LAND AND SEA TRACING DOZENS OF POSSIBLE COASTLINES."

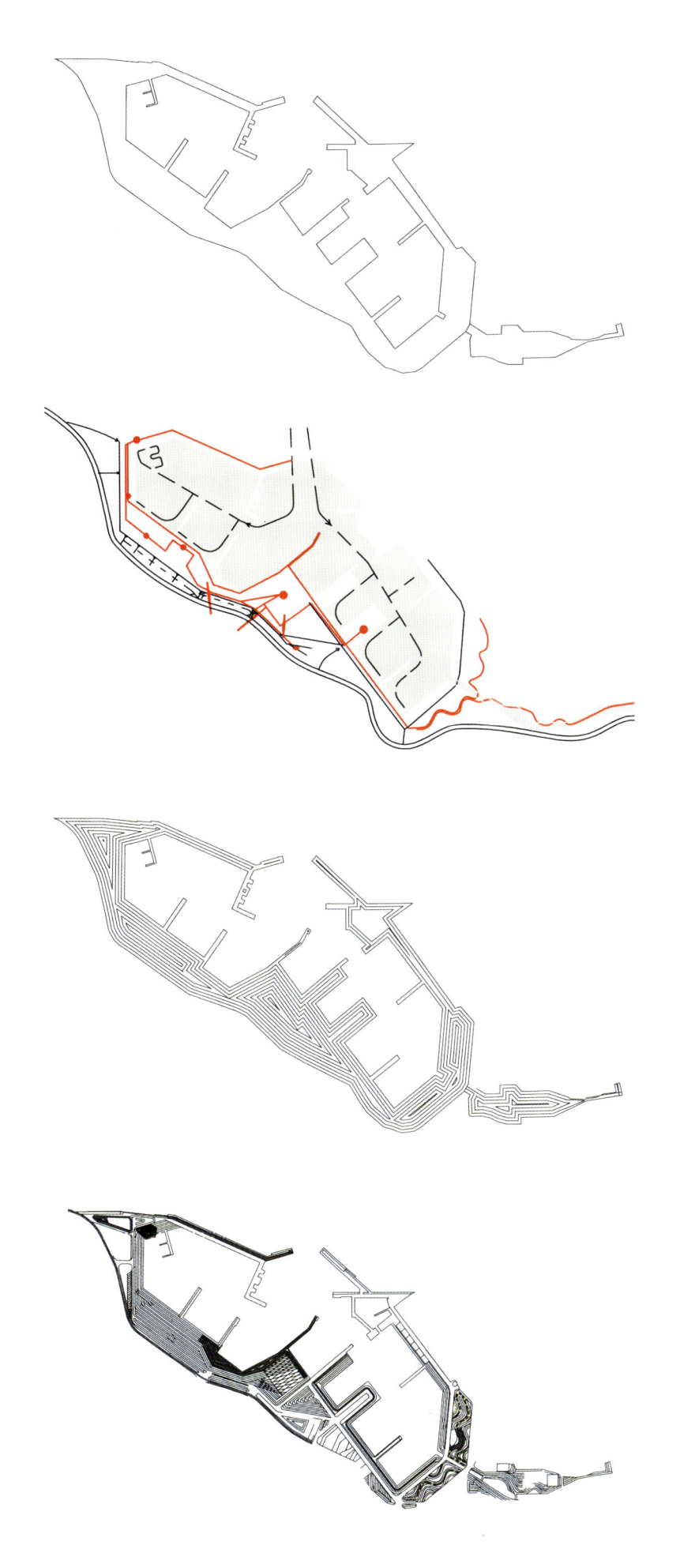

ARCHITECTURAL DIAGRAMS 179

BAYWATCH
PEG office of landscape + architecture

"WE PROPOSE A "WET PARK" A MUTABLE WORKING GROUND FOR THE ENJOYMENT AND AWARENESS OF THE CONNECTIVITY OF HYDROLOGICAL FUNCTIONS."

CUT
ridges and furrows **1**

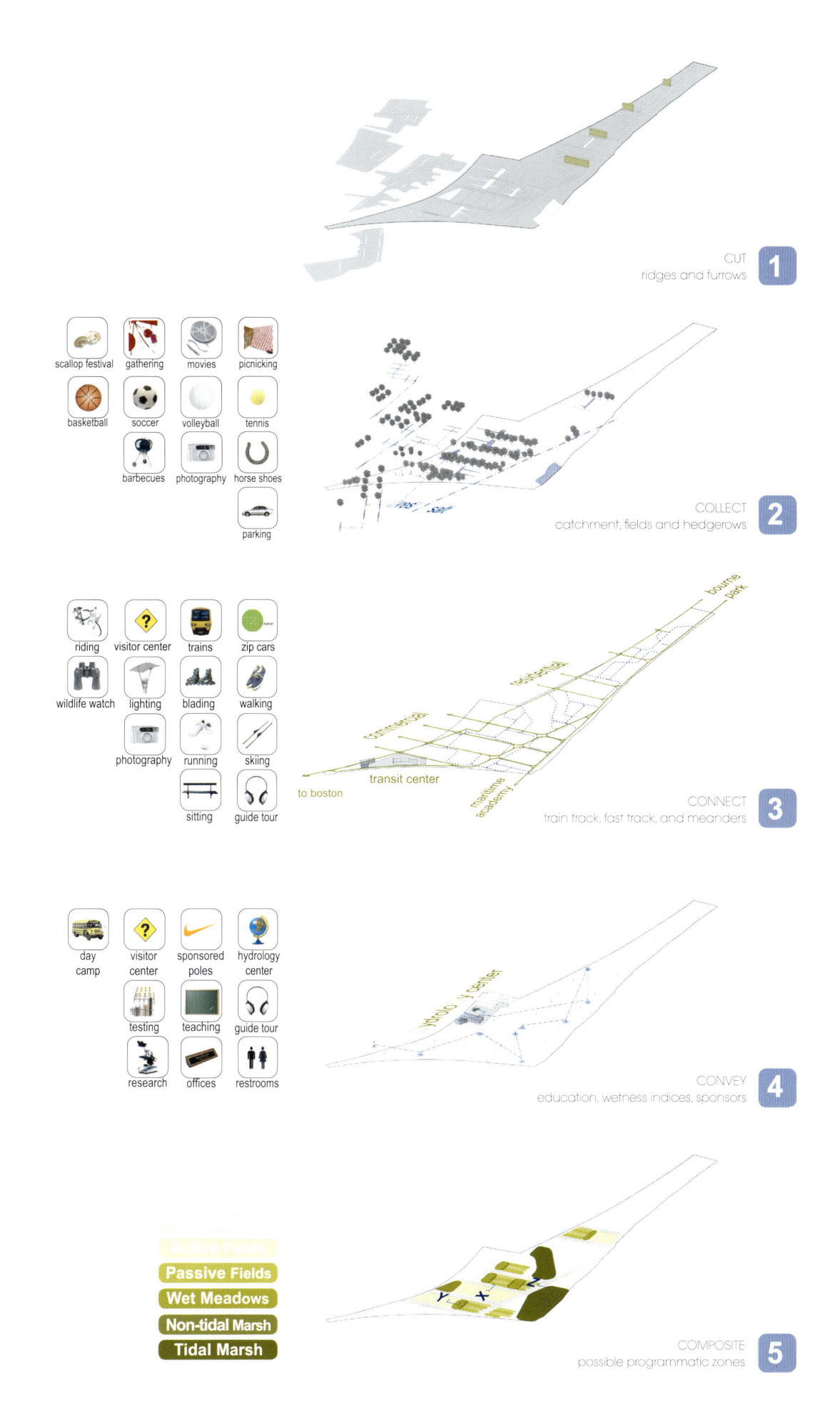

scallop festival | gathering | movies | picnicking
basketball | soccer | volleyball | tennis
barbecues | photography | horse shoes
parking

COLLECT
catchment, fields and hedgerows **2**

riding | visitor center | trains | zip cars
wildlife watch | lighting | blading | walking
photography | running | skiing
sitting | guide tour

CONNECT
train track, fast track, and meanders **3**

day camp | visitor center | sponsored poles | hydrology center
testing | teaching | guide tour
research | offices | restrooms

CONVEY
education, wetness indices, sponsors **4**

Action Fields
Passive Fields
Wet Meadows
Non-tidal Marsh
Tidal Marsh

COMPOSITE
possible programmatic zones **5**

ARCHITECTURAL DIAGRAMS 181

BIOBOX servo

"DIAGRAM ILLUSTRATING VARIOUS FORMS OF FEEDBACK BETWEEN THE SYSTEMS, THEIR INTERNAL USERS, AND A VARIETY OF EXTERNAL ENVIRONMENTAL FORCES."

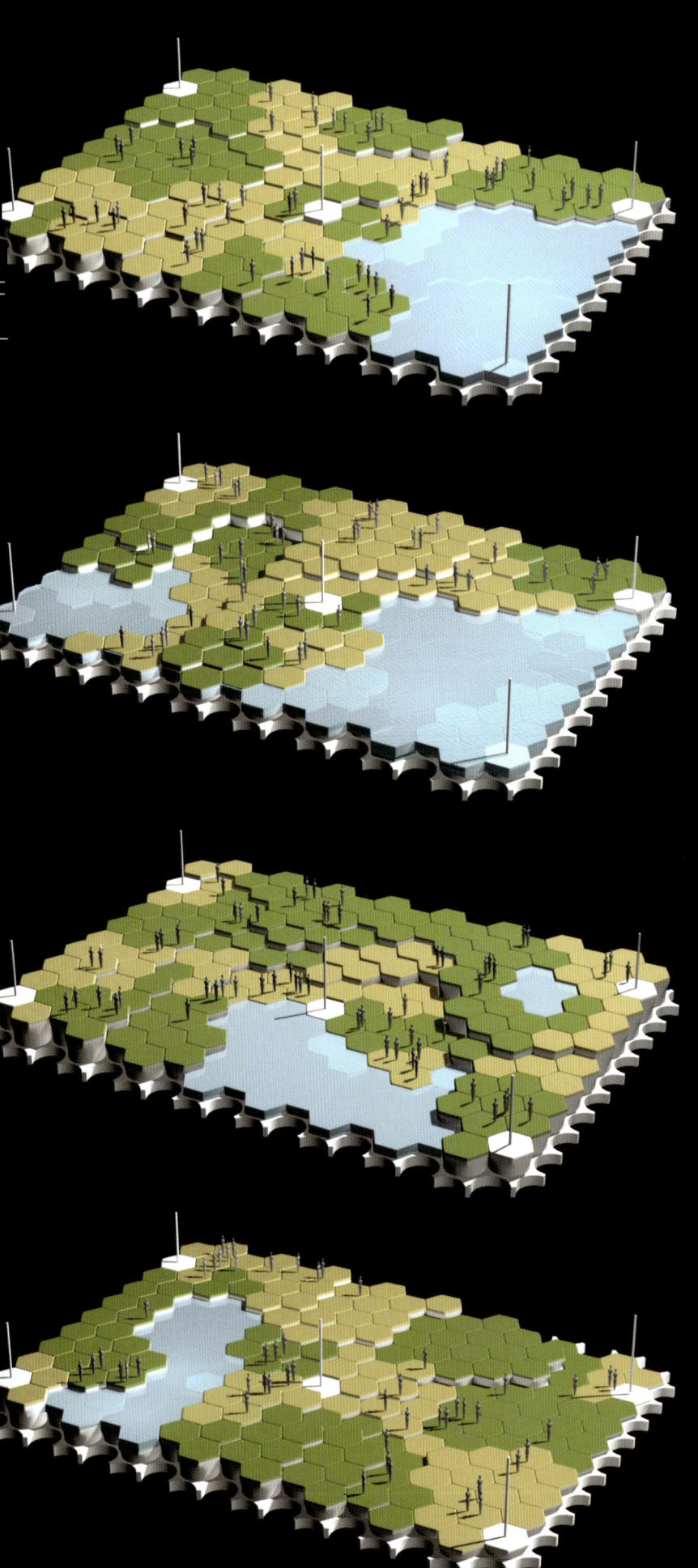

182 LANDSCAPE

Diagram illustrating various forms of feedback between the systems, their internal users, and a variety of external environmental forces.

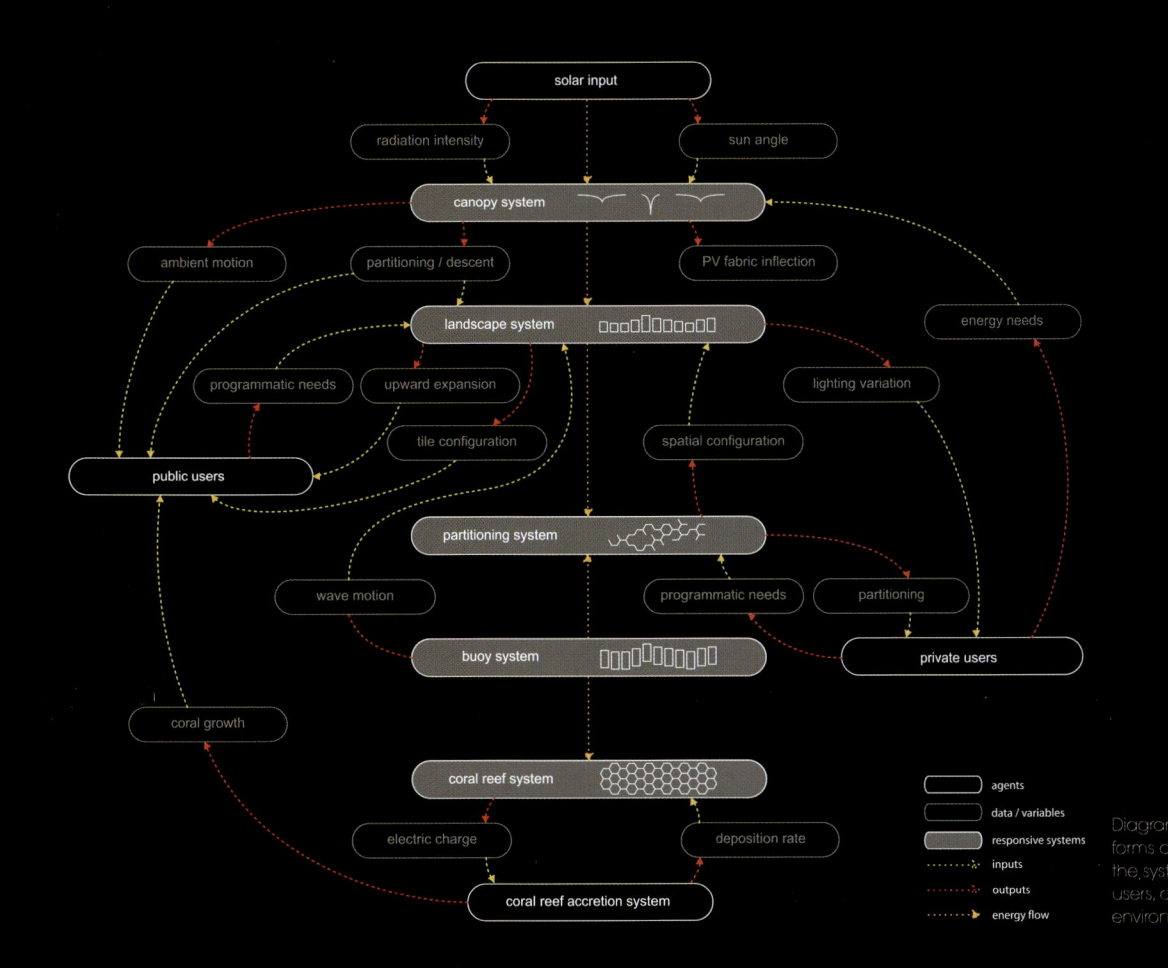

Catalog of material and technological pads whose distribution in the reprogrammable landscape system accommodates a wide range of recreational, agricultural, and infrastructural uses.

ARCHITECTURAL DIAGRAMS 183

BONN SQUARE

CJ Lim | Studio 8 Architects

"A RECONDITIONING OF THE PUBLIC SPACE WITH MINIMUM PHYSICAL INTERVENTION AND NO INTERRUPTION TO ITS EXISTING ARCHAEOLOGY."

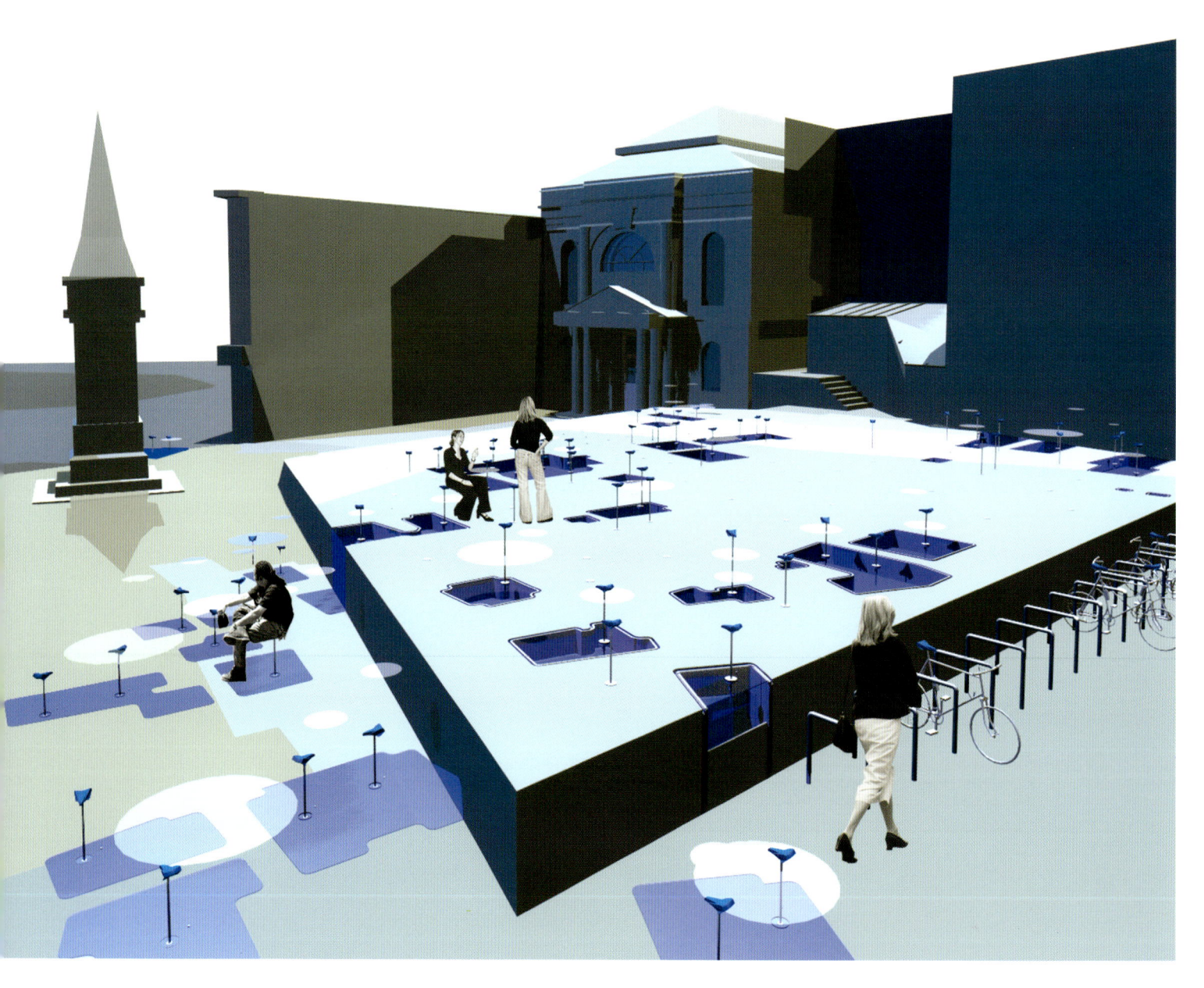

Cycle Routes
24 hours

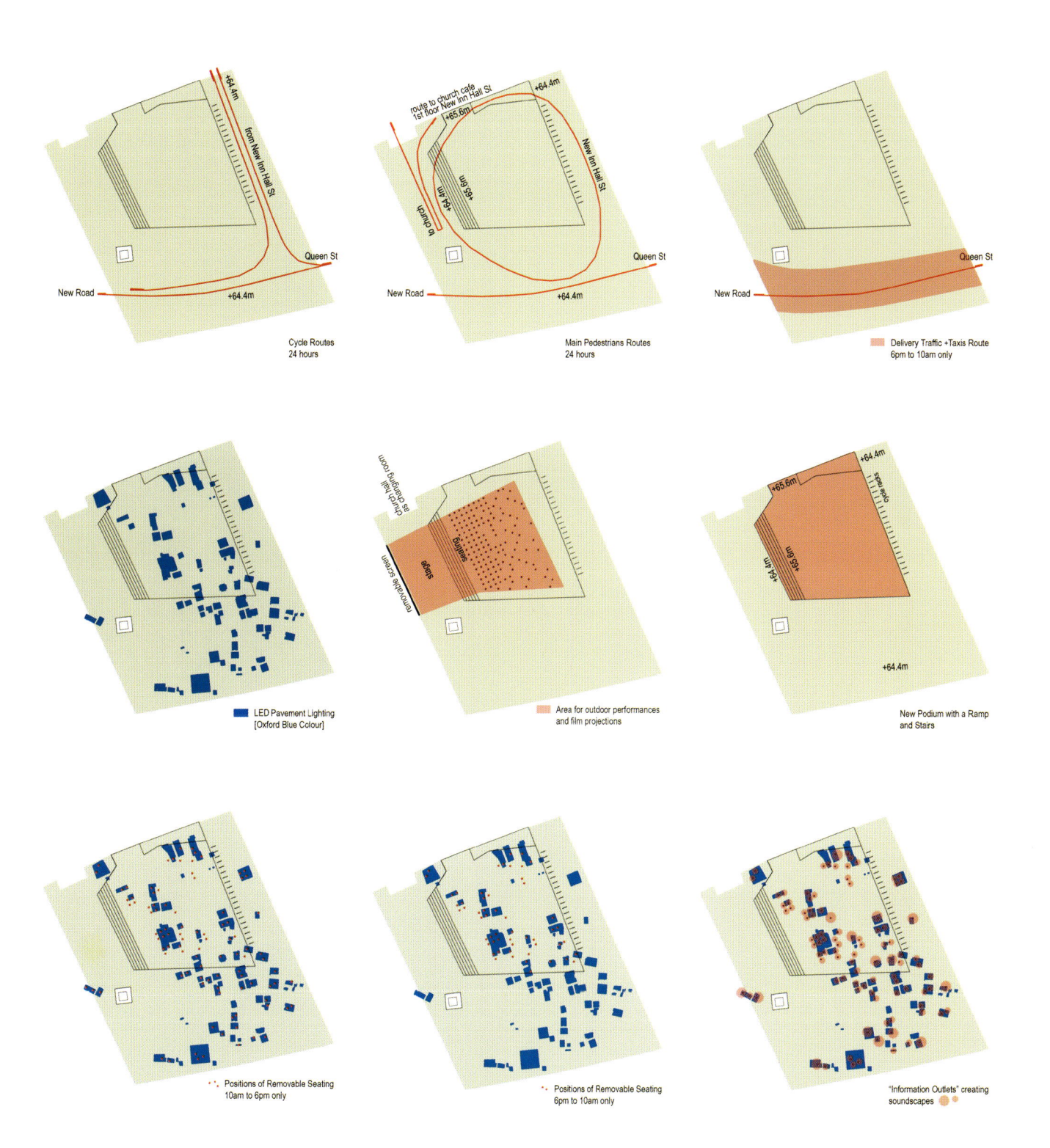

Main Pedestrians Routes
24 hours

Delivery Traffic +Taxis Route
6pm to 10am only

LED Pavement Lighting
[Oxford Blue Colour]

Area for outdoor performances
and film projections

New Podium with a Ramp
and Stairs

Positions of Removable Seating
10am to 6pm only

Positions of Removable Seating
6pm to 10am only

"Information Outlets" creating
soundscapes

ARCHITECTURAL DIAGRAMS 185

COMPOSER TUBIN MONUMENT Zizi&Yoyo

"WITHIN THIS INTERACTIVE LIGHT AND SOUND INSTALLATION, VISITOR CAN HEAR FRAGMENTS OF HIS MUSIC BY KNOCKING ON THE GONGS ON THE BACK WALL"

Composer TUBIN's memorial

186 LANDSCAPE

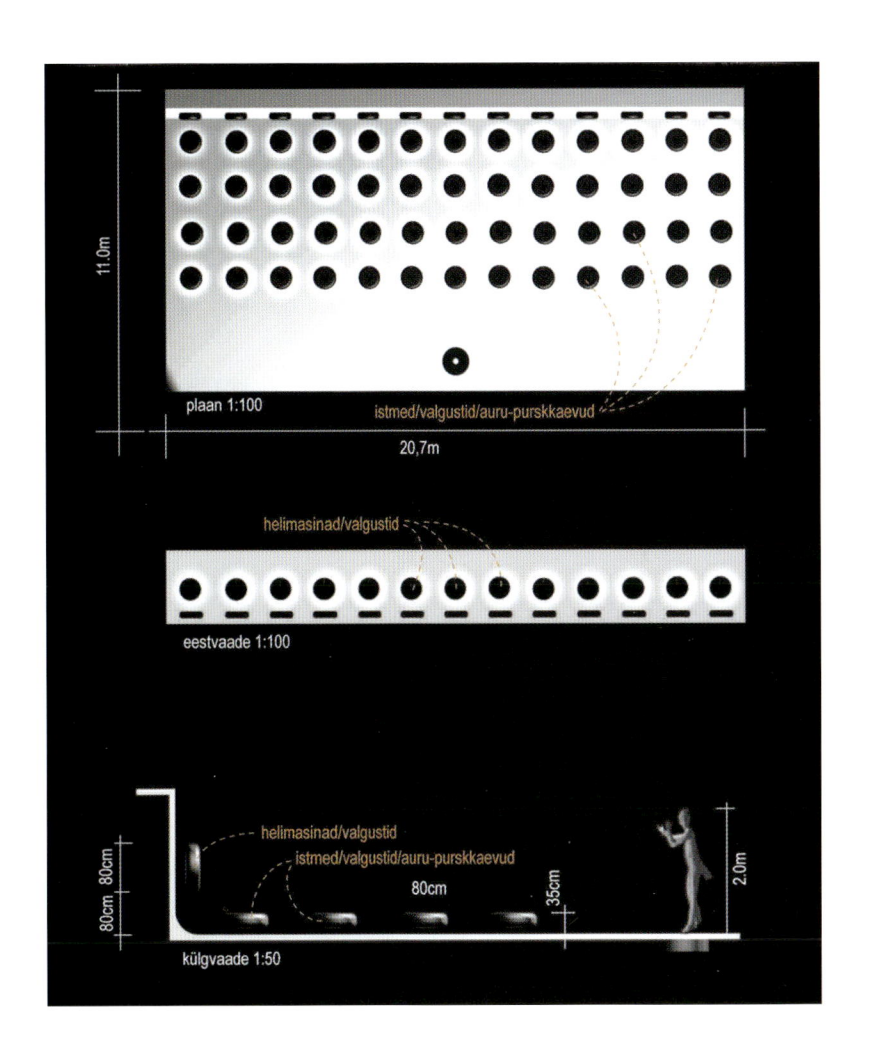

plaan 1:100
istmed/valgustid/auru-purskkaevud
11.0m
20,7m

helimasinad/valgustid
eestvaade 1:100

helimasinad/valgustid
istmed/valgustid/auru-purskkaevud
80cm 80cm
80cm
35cm
2.0m
külgvaade 1:50

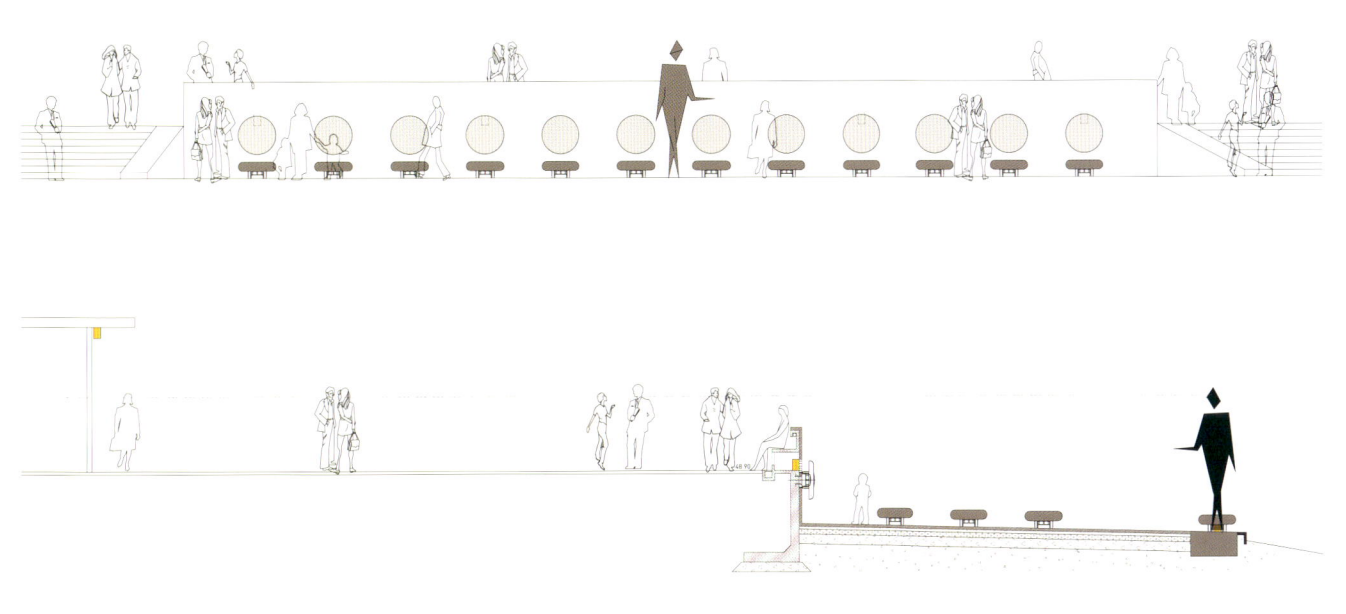

ARCHITECTURAL DIAGRAMS 187

ELEFTHERIA SQUARE

AA + U partnership for Architecture and urbanism

"SYSTEM OF PUBLIC SPACES WHICH FUNCTION AS ONE ENTITY THUS RESPONDING APPROPRIATELY TO THE NEW SCALE OF THE CITY OF NICOSIA."

KEY

Pedestrian movement city level and moat. The platform as a nodal point

Pedestrian movement on city level and through the top of the platform

Vehicle movement

Bicycle movement

P Parking

Pedestrian movement in moat

KEY
- serviced public sitting
- public sitting exposed to flow
- public sitting less exposed to flow
- public sitting not exposed to flow

KEY

Cupressaceae (Κυπαρίσσια)
Pittosporous tobira (Πιτόσπορος)
Thevetia neriifolia (Θηβέτια -μικρό Δένδρο)
Tetraclinis articulate (Καλλιπρίδες- δέντρα)
Ceratonia siliqua (Χαρουπιά)
Phoenix dactylifera (Φοινικιά)
Punica granatum (Ροδιά)
Ficus syricomorus (Φίκυς)
Campsis radicans (Βιγνόνια 14α (κόκκινη))
Jacaranda mimosifolia (Τζακαράντα)
Melia azedarah (Μαυρομμάτα)
Eucalyptus gomphocephala (Ευκάλυπτος)

Juniperus oxycendrus (Αόρατος)
Schinus molle (Αρμαθκιά)
Olea europaea (Ελιά)
Laurus nobillis (Δάφνη)
Pinus canariensis (Πεύκος)
Citrus aurantium (Κιτρομηλιά)
Grevillea robusta (Γρεβιλλέα)
Cercis siliquastrum (Ροζανθή)
Pistacia lentiscus (Σχοινιά)
Amygdalus communis, Prunus dulcis (Αμυγδαλιά)
Viburnum tinus (Βιβούρνο)
Prunus domestica (Πουρνελιά)

- New trees
- Grevillea robusta (Γρεβιλλέα)
- Punica granatum (Ροδιά)
- Jacaranda mimosifolia (Τζακαράντα)
- Eucalyptus gomphocephala (Ευκάλυπτος)
- Removed Trees

ARCHITECTURAL DIAGRAMS 189

ESA STAHLHOF plattformberlin

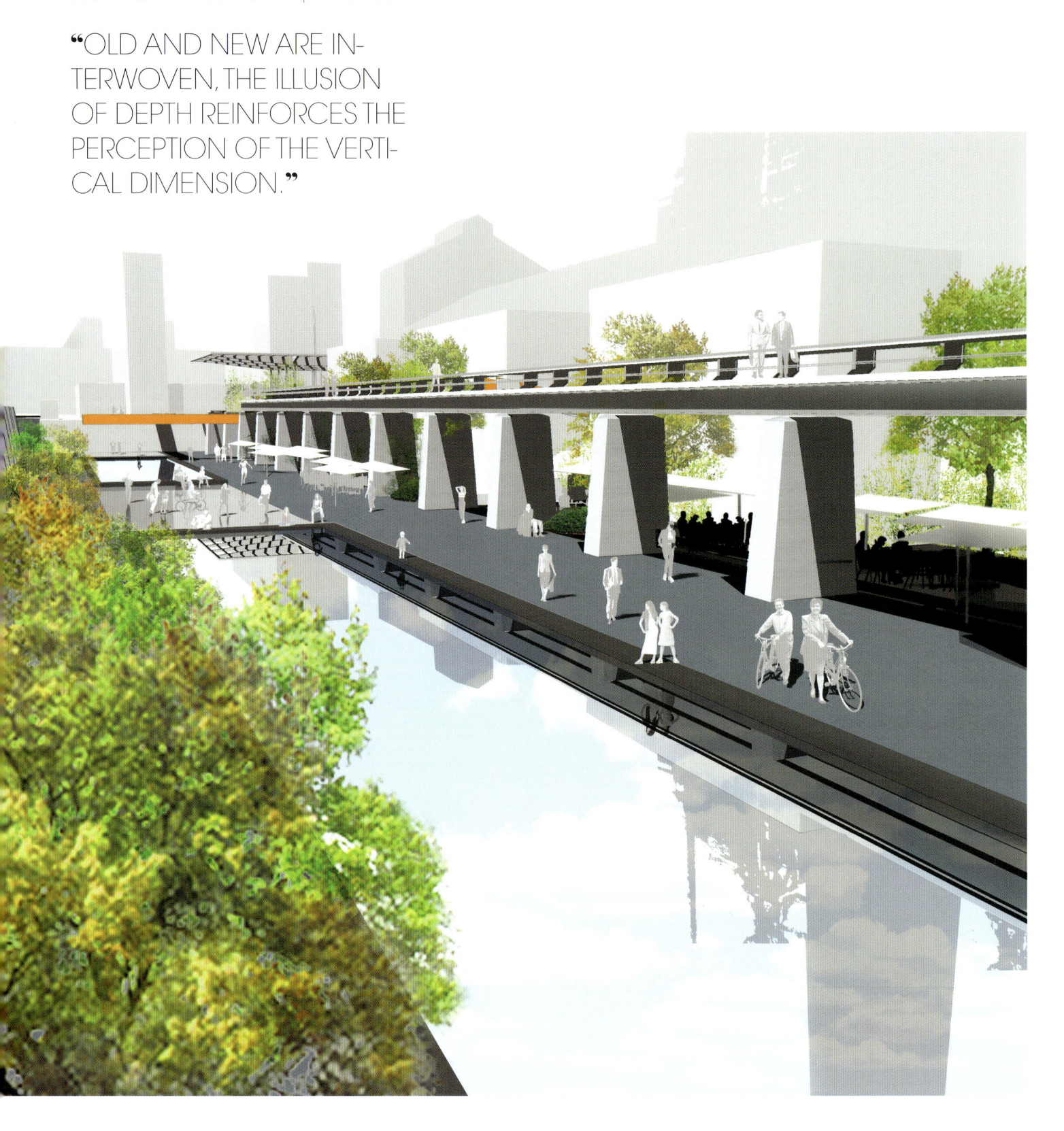

"OLD AND NEW ARE INTERWOVEN, THE ILLUSION OF DEPTH REINFORCES THE PERCEPTION OF THE VERTICAL DIMENSION."

Spaces diagram

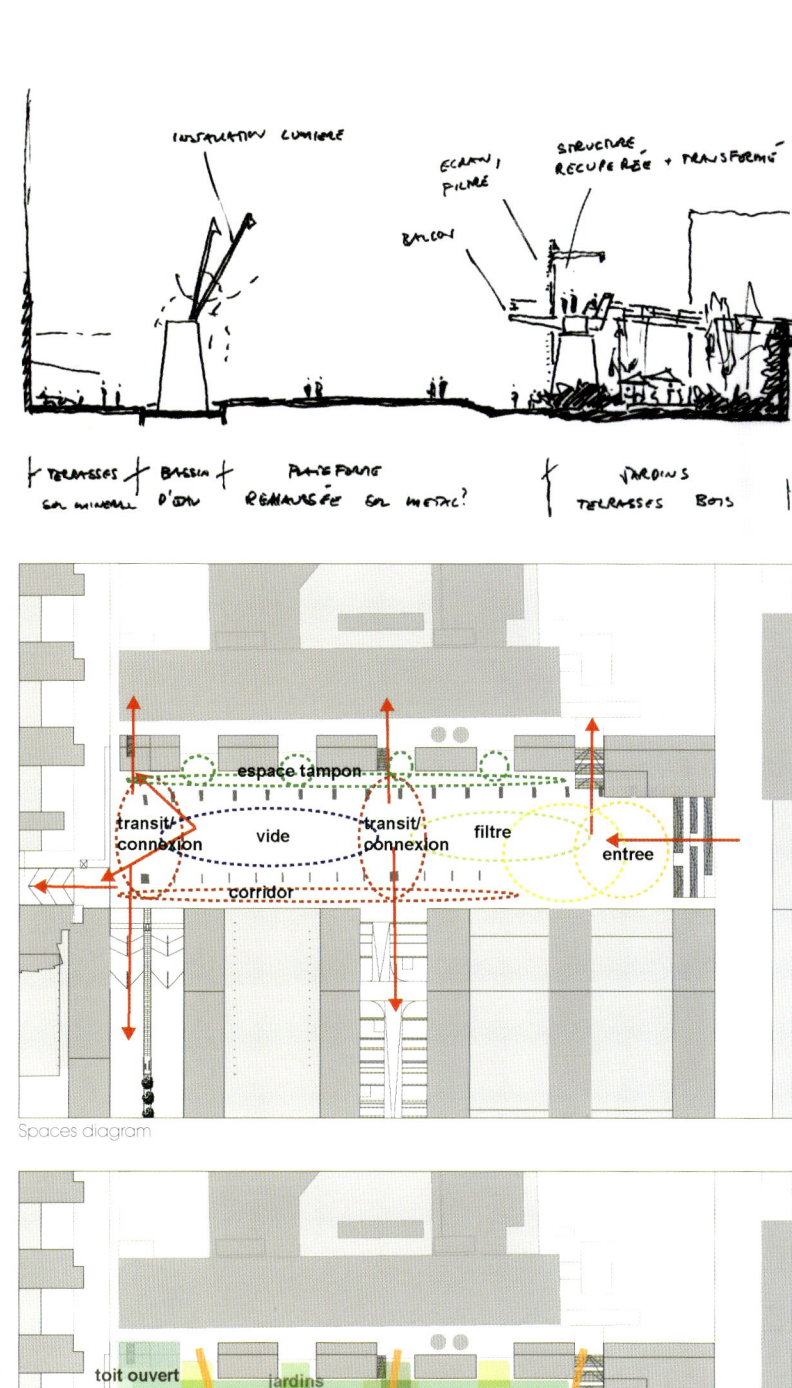

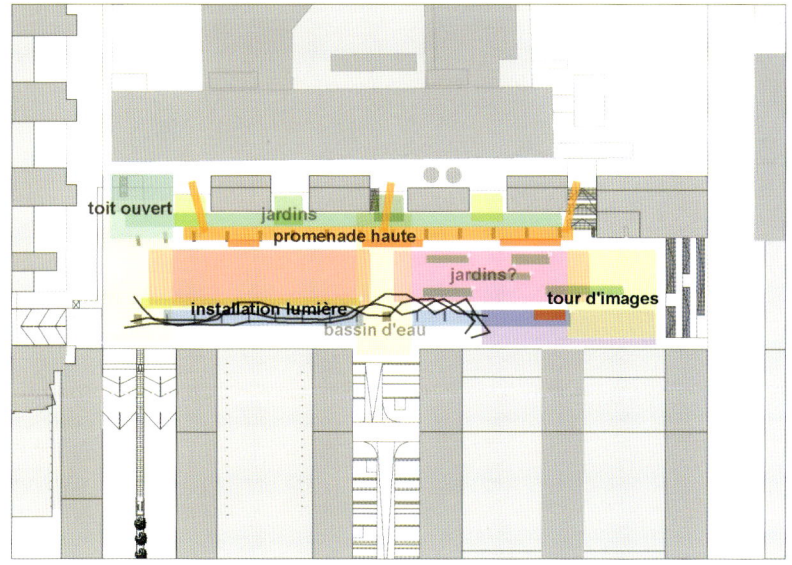

ARCHITECTURAL DIAGRAMS 191

FREGENE SEASIDE
2TR ARCHITETTURA

"AN IDEA OF DUNE WHICH COVERS THE PARKING AND CLIMBS OVER THE EXISTING BUILDINGS ROOF SO TO RE-OFFER TO THE USERS A VIEW OF THE SEA."

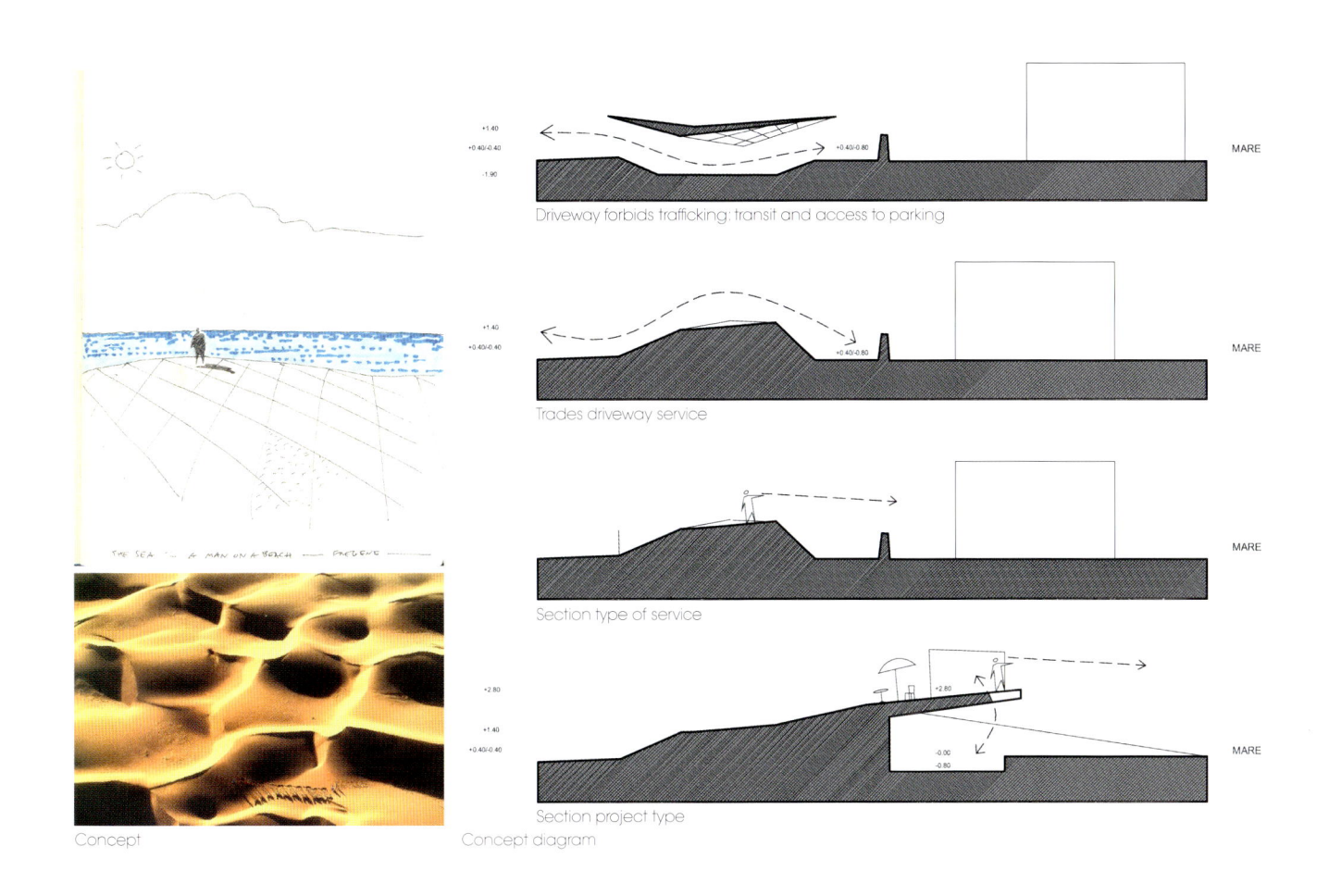

Driveway forbids trafficking: transit and access to parking

Trades driveway service

Section type of service

Section project type

Concept

Concept diagram

ARCHITECTURAL DIAGRAMS 193

FROM FLOWER TO FLOWER nodo17 architects

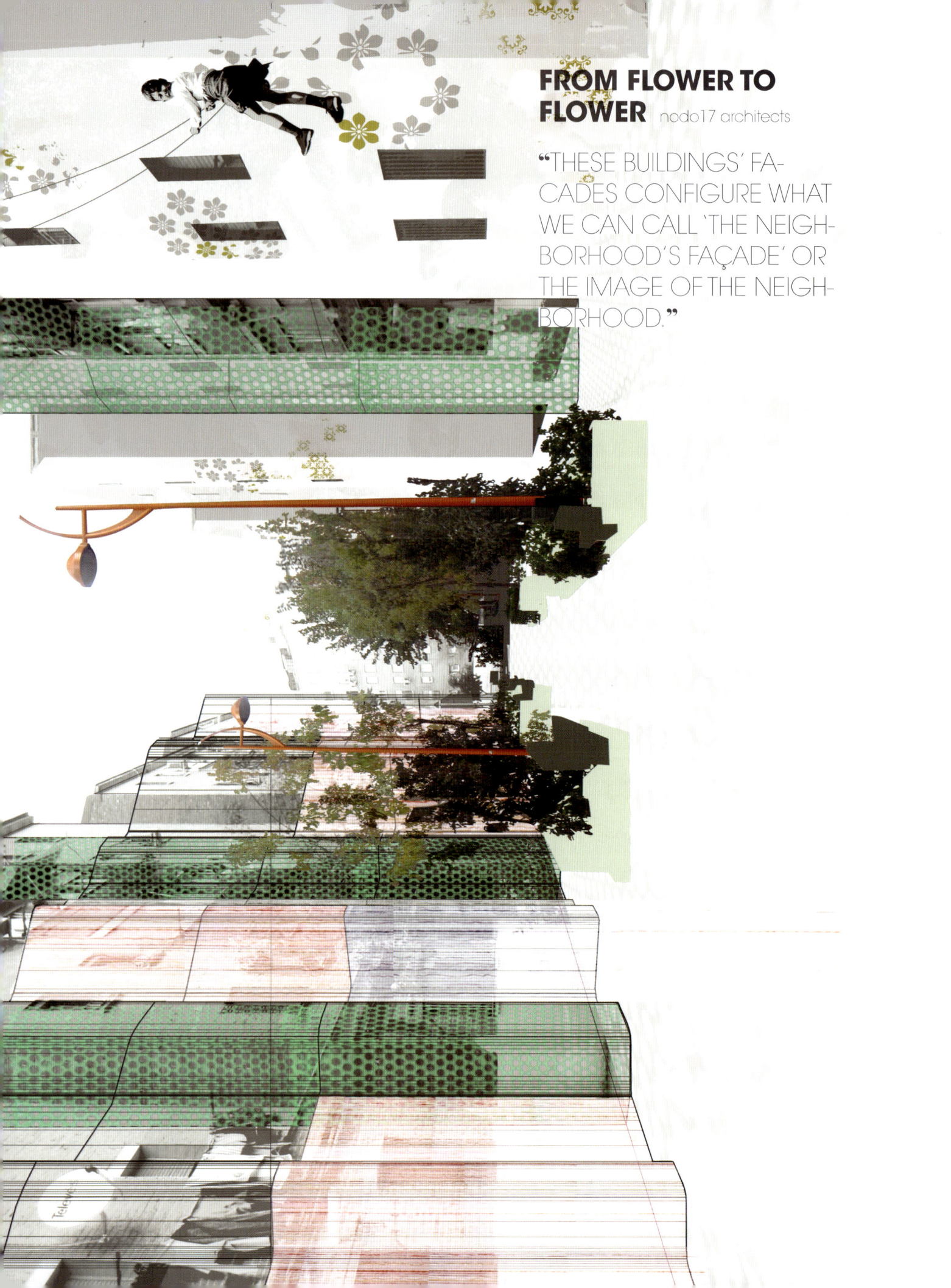

"THESE BUILDINGS' FAÇADES CONFIGURE WHAT WE CAN CALL 'THE NEIGHBORHOOD'S FAÇADE' OR THE IMAGE OF THE NEIGHBORHOOD."

Chrysanthemum

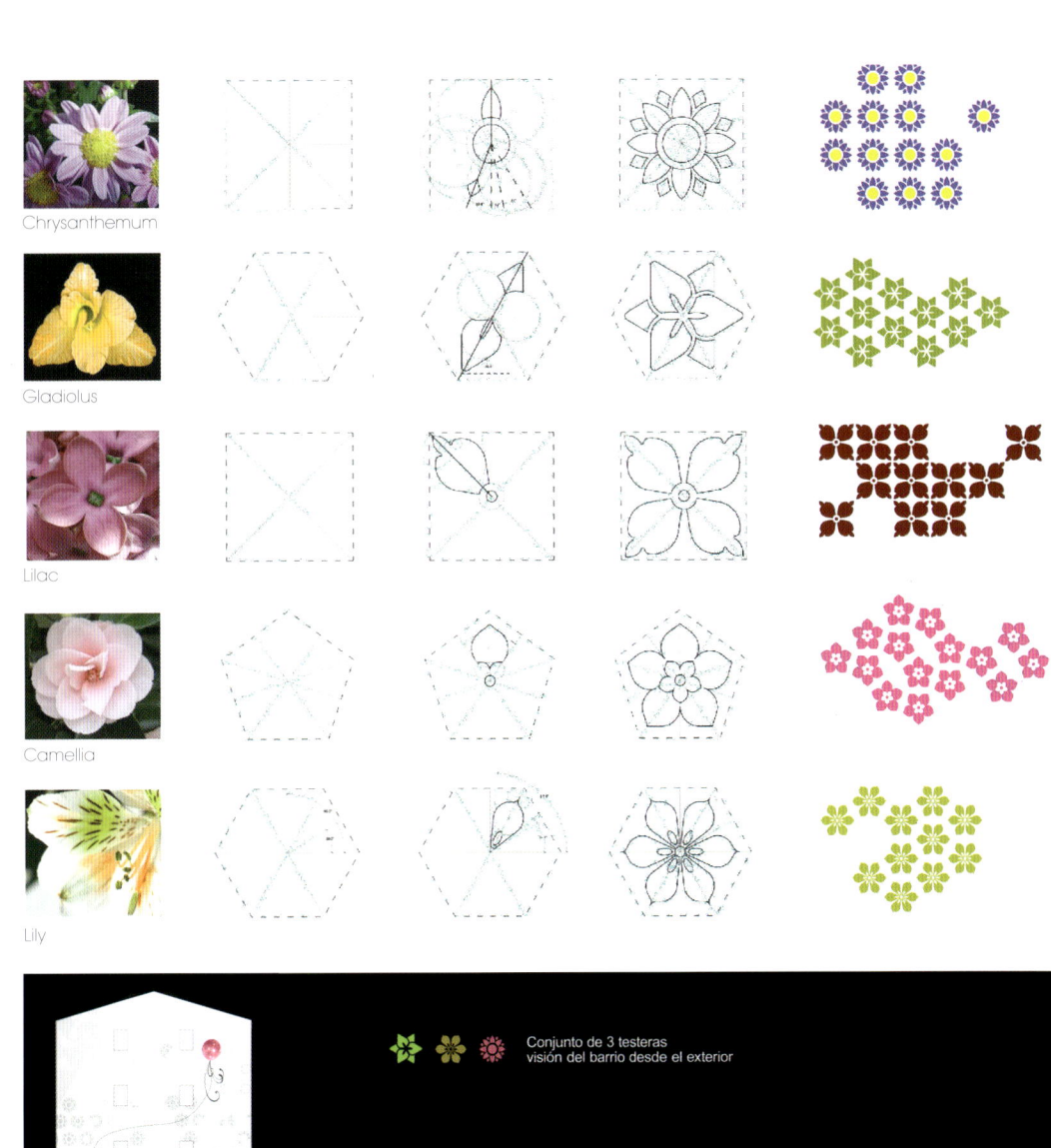

Gladiolus

Lilac

Camellia

Lily

Conjunto de 3 testeras
visión del barrio desde el exterior

ARCHITECTURAL DIAGRAMS 195

FUGEE PORT Guallart Architects

"OUR PROPOSAL ENVISAGES A TOURIST OPERATION DESIGNED TO COMPLEMENT TAIWAN'S PRINCIPAL EXISTING FACILITIES."

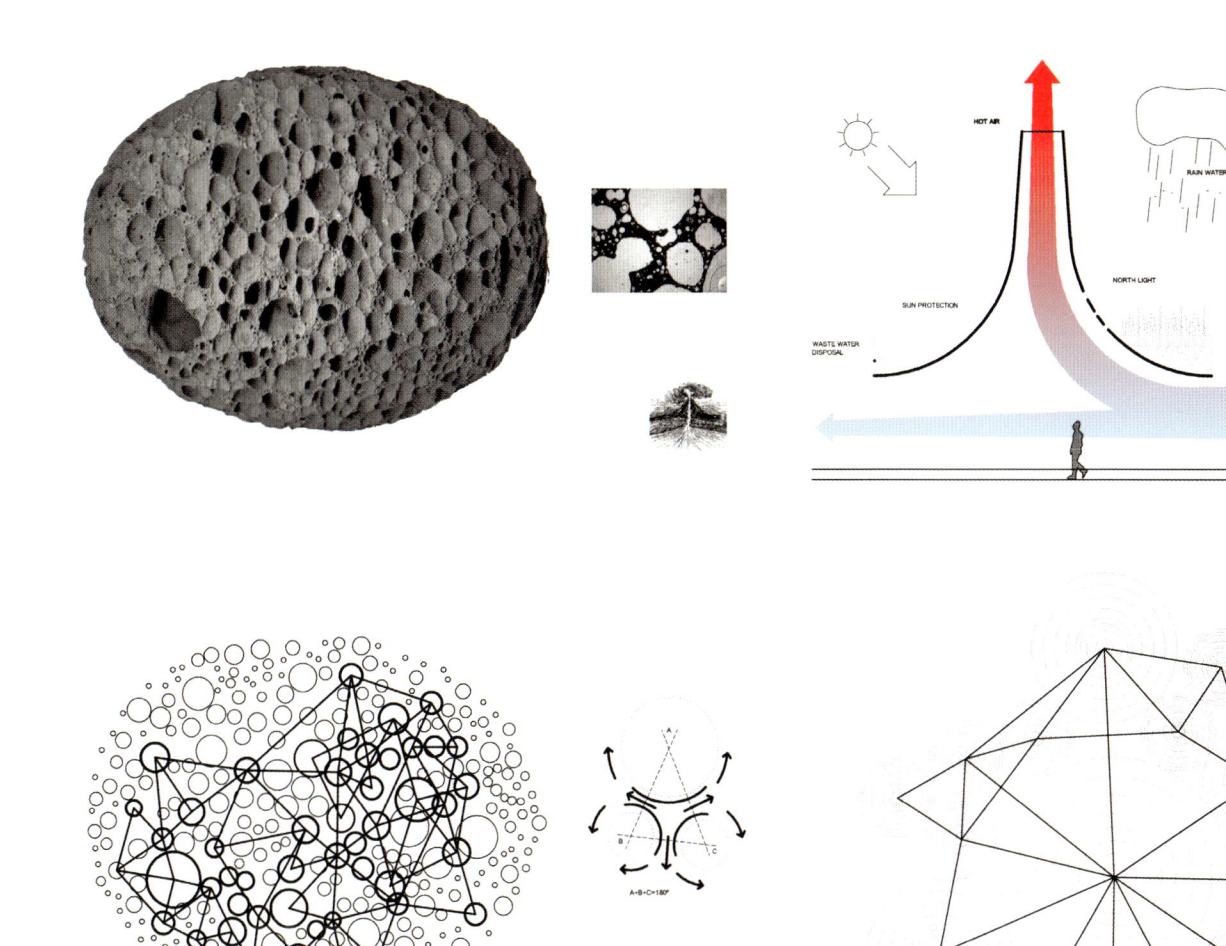

ARCHITECTURAL DIAGRAMS 197

GARDEN IN BARI ma0

"THE CIRCULAR ISLANDS INJECT INTO THE VARIOUS LANDSCAPES AND DISSEMINATE DIVERSE SITUATIONS AMONG THE GARDEN."

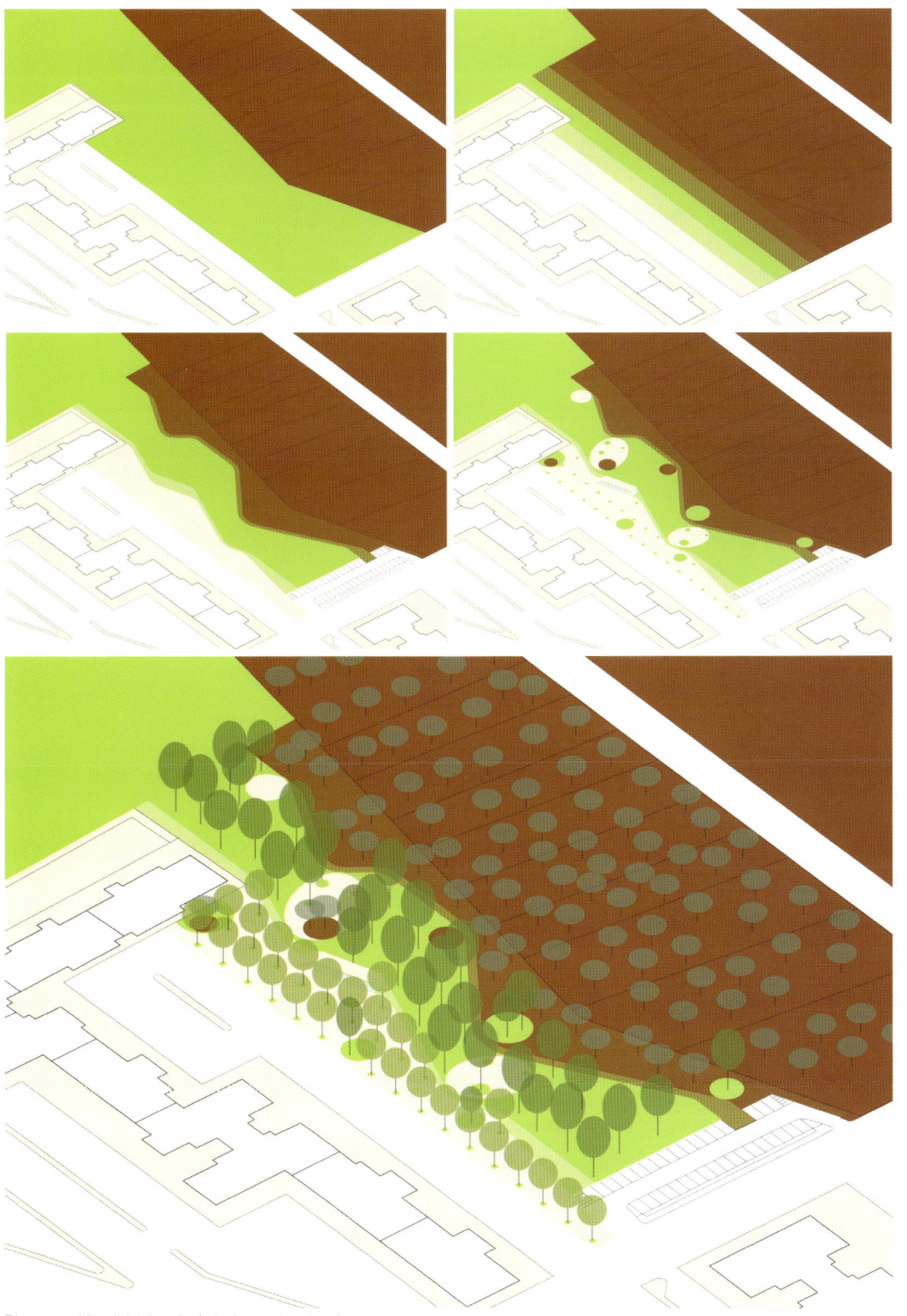

Diagrams / the thick border in between two landscapes

ARCHITECTURAL DIAGRAMS 199

GUANGMING SUSTAINABLE CENTRE PARK

CJ Lim | Studio 8 Architects

"SHENZHEN IS CONCEIVED AS AN "ARABLE-GARDEN + ENERGY PARK". A NEW URBAN LANDSCAPE TYPOLOGY."

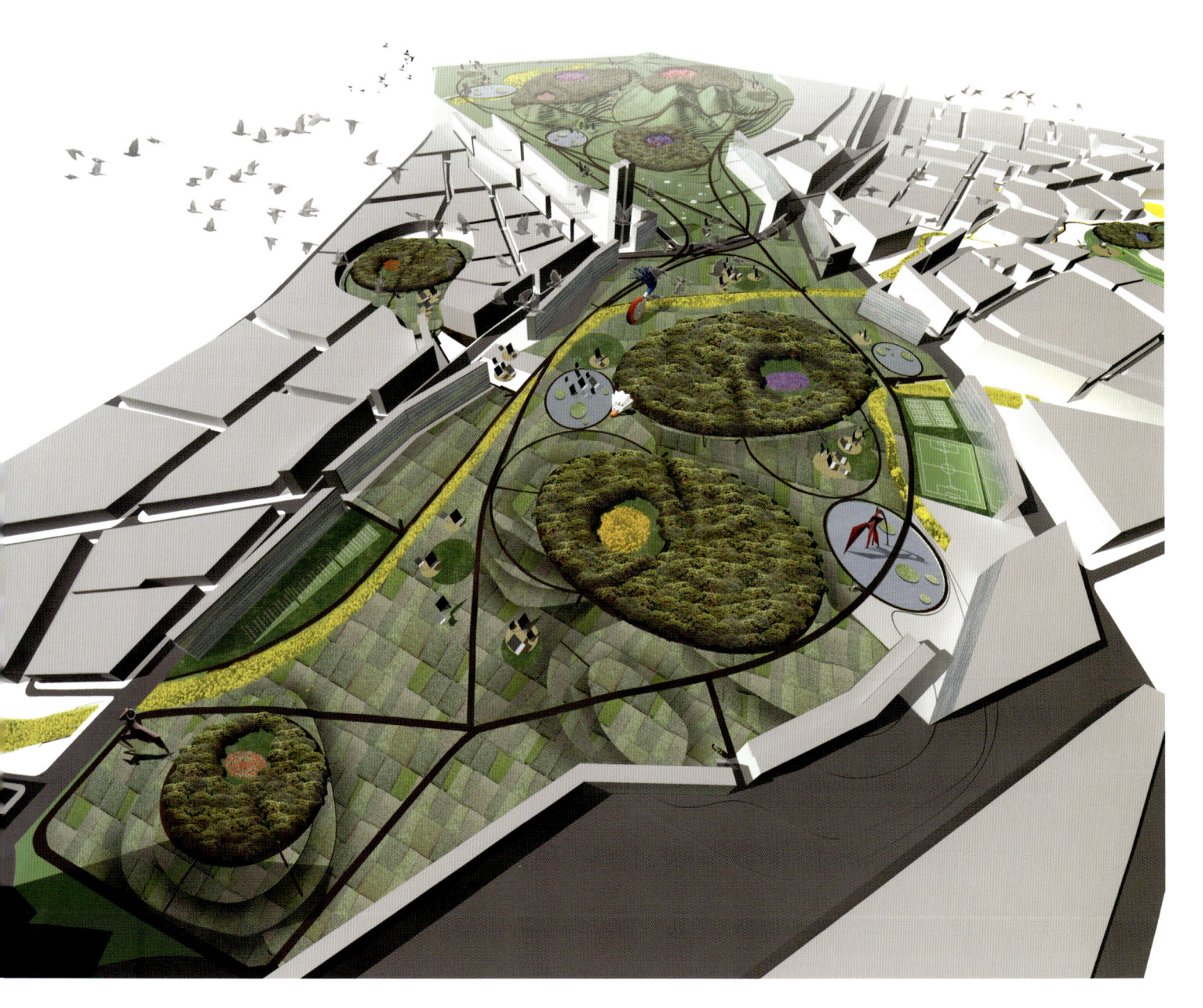

Existing topography

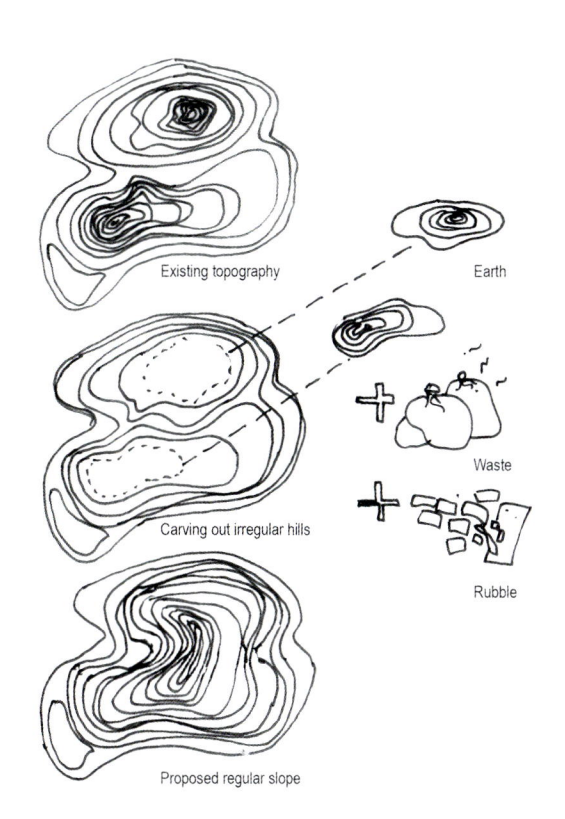

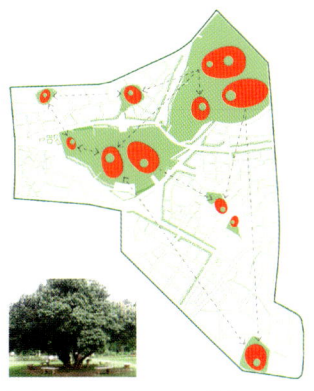

Earth

Carving out irregular hills

Waste

Rubble

Proposed regular slope

Lychee hills making visual links throughout the city

Arable organic gardening fields

Lawn patch

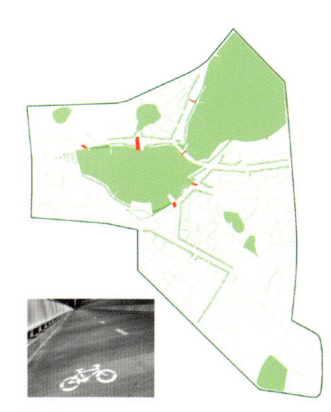

Underpasses

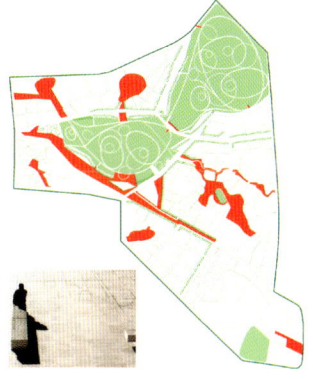

Plazas

Circulation for pedestrians + cyclists

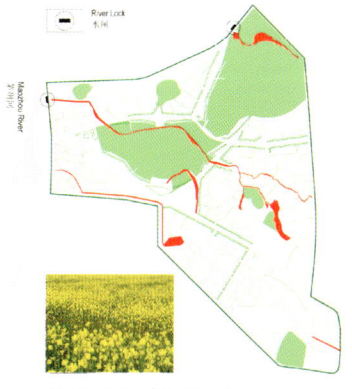

Guangming flower river

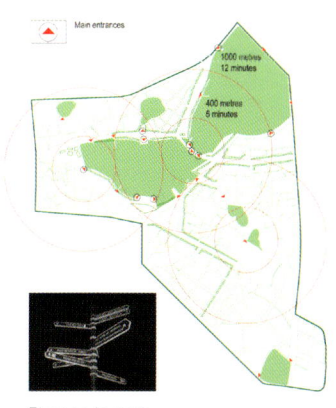

Etrance to park

ARCHITECTURAL DIAGRAMS 201

HAG ST. JOSEPH
plattformberlin

"THE PROJECT IS A PLATFORM OF DIFFERENT ACTIVITIES AND WILL BE GRADUALLY FILLED BY THE RESIDENTS."

Children's workshops

Steering

Group sites

...it crosses the park...

...square...

...and courses

The coil area St. Joseph...

ARCHITECTURAL DIAGRAMS 203

HEART OF MAGOK IS NATURE OF LIVING WATER
Samoo Architects & Engineers

"NEW LAYERS ADDED SECURE THE HYDROPHILE PROPERTY AND PROVIDE MORE OPEN SPACES."

Urban axis Green axis Blue axis

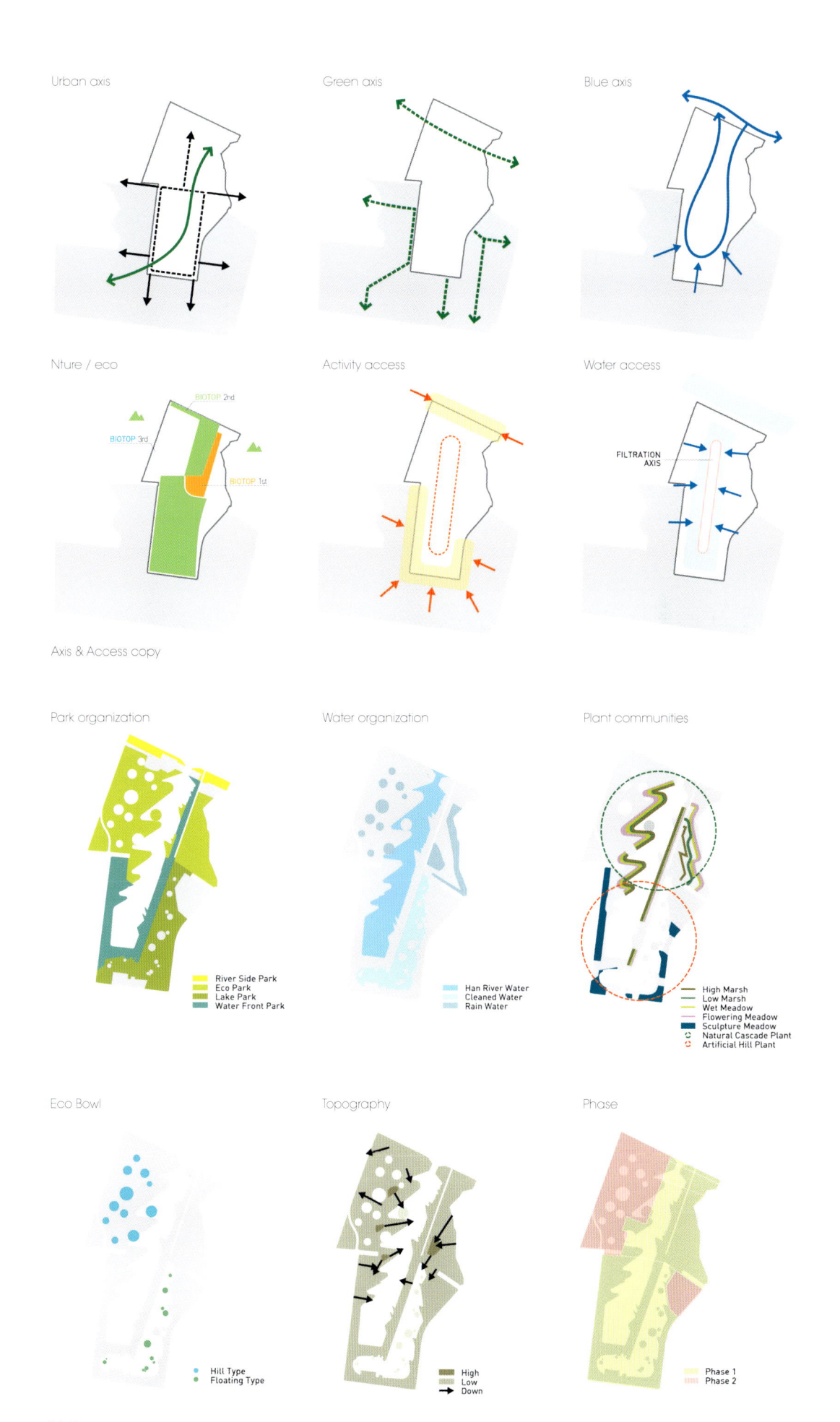

Nture / eco Activity access Water access

BIOTOP 2nd
BIOTOP 3rd
BIOTOP 1st

FILTRATION AXIS

Axis & Access copy

Park organization Water organization Plant communities

River Side Park
Eco Park
Lake Park
Water Front Park

Han River Water
Cleaned Water
Rain Water

High Marsh
Low Marsh
Wet Meadow
Flowering Meadow
Sculpture Meadow
Natural Cascade Plant
Artificial Hill Plant

Eco Bowl Topography Phase

Hill Type
Floating Type

High
Low
Down

Phase 1
Phase 2

Metric sequence

ARCHITECTURAL DIAGRAMS 205

INDRE SOGN ARTS CENTRE IaN+

"THE DESIGN IS CHARACTERISTIC OF OUR APPROACH TO A PROJECT, COMES INTO DIALOGUE WITH A FRAGMENTED FABRIC, FULL OF NATURAL SUGGESTIONS."

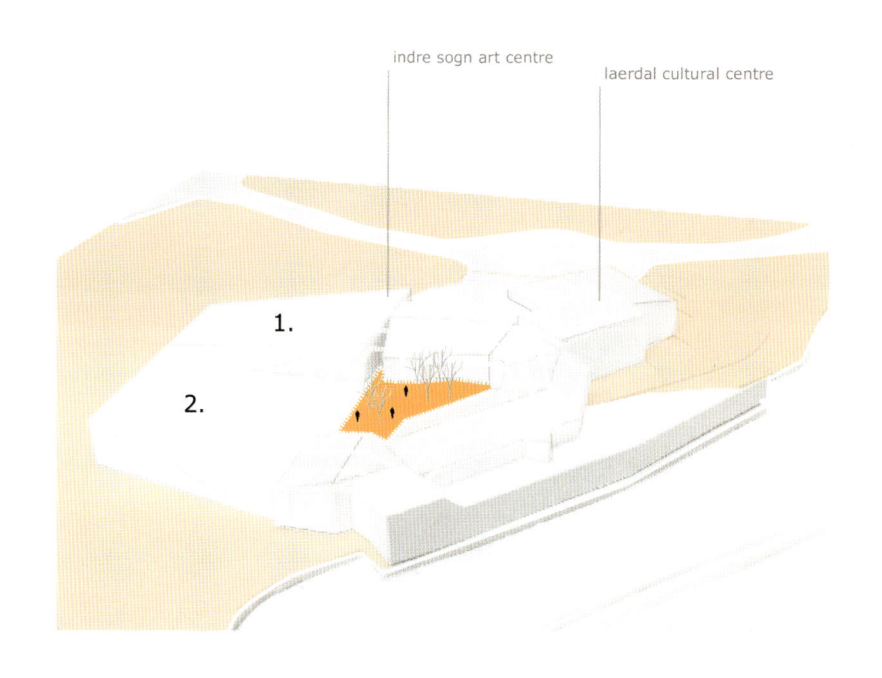

indre sogn art centre laerdal cultural centre

1.
2.

indre sogn art centre laerdal cultural centre

1.
2.

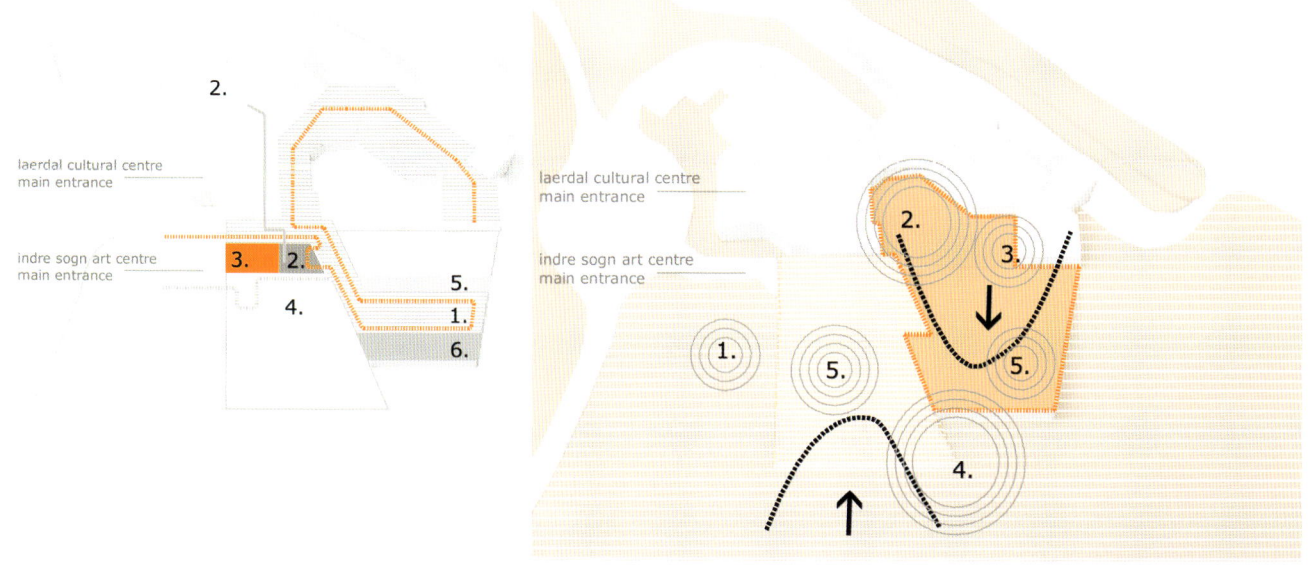

2.
laerdal cultural centre main entrance
indre sogn art centre main entrance
3. 2.
4.
5.
1.
6.

laerdal cultural centre main entrance
indre sogn art centre main entrance
2. 3.
1. 5. 5.
4.

ARCHITECTURAL DIAGRAMS 207

ISOLE D'ACQUA
NL Architects + Bureau B+B

"ISOLE D'ACQUA WILL BE A DIALOGUE BETWEEN NATURE AND MAN."

closed compound → open configuration

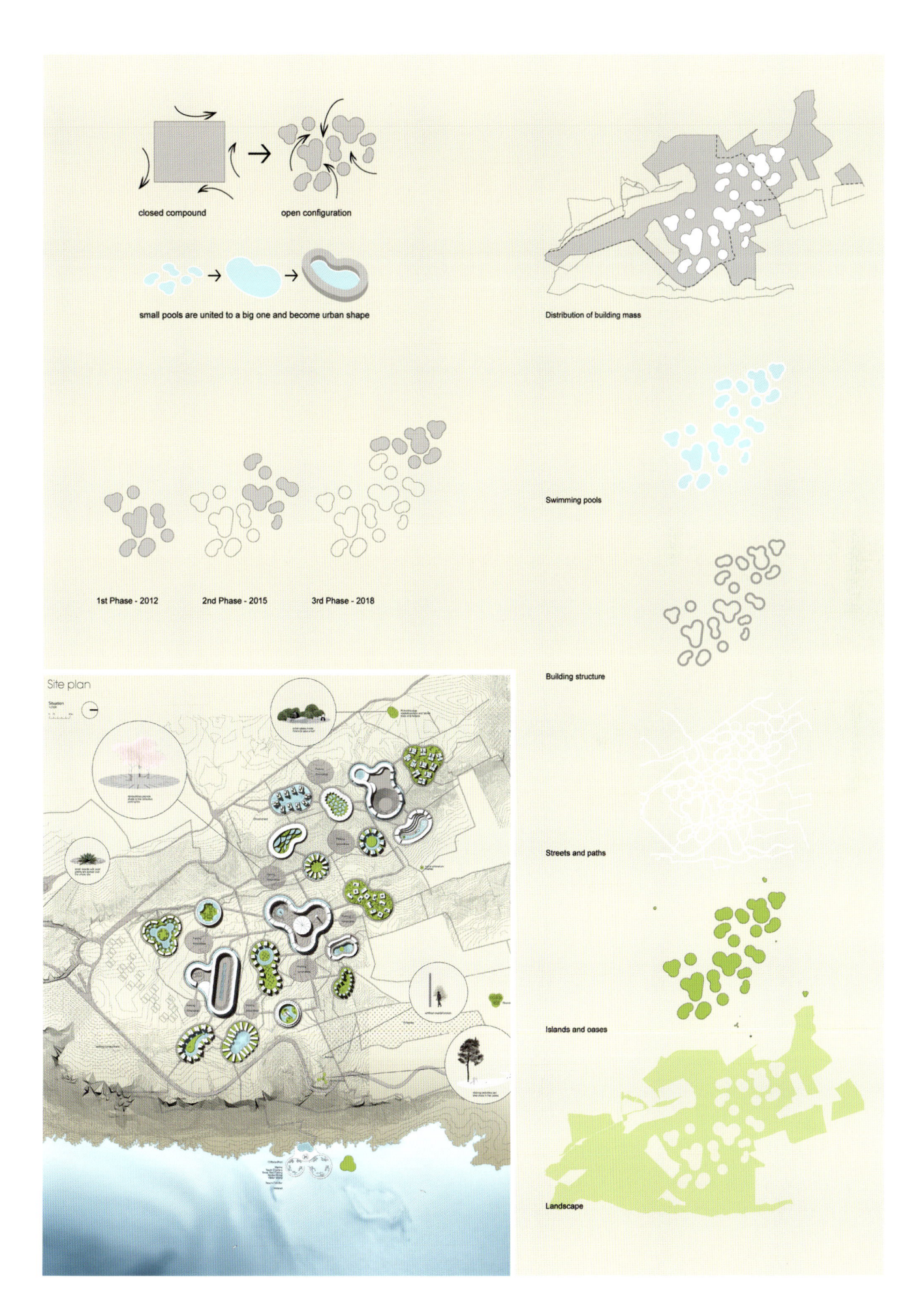

small pools are united to a big one and become urban shape

1st Phase - 2012   2nd Phase - 2015   3rd Phase - 2018

Site plan

Distribution of building mass

Swimming pools

Building structure

Streets and paths

Islands and oases

Landscape

ARCHITECTURAL DIAGRAMS 209

JOIE DE VIE(W)
PEG office of landscape + architecture

"OUR PROPOSAL IS AN EXPLORATION AND EXPANSION OF SOME OF THE FUNDAMENTALS OF GARDEN DESIGN."

210 LANDSCAPE

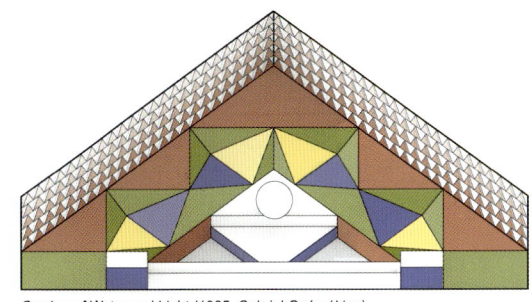

Garden of Water and Light (1925, Gabriel Guévrékian)

Concept

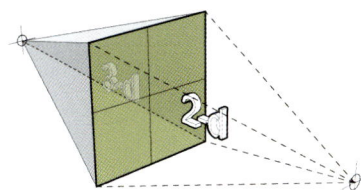

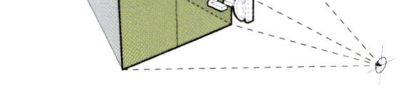

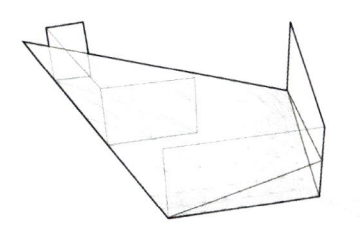

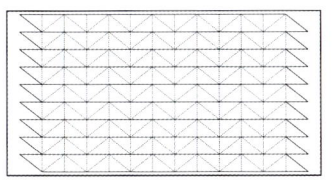

Precedent: 2-d suppresses 3-d

Proposal: 2-d enhances 3-d

Projection diagram

Version 1: The initial version of the wall tile used a maximally-efficient cut pattern to create a continuous band of half-units that fit together with an identical band to create a woven, three dimensional tiling pattern. While this allowed for a seamless connection along one diagonal of the pattern, there was no simple or intuitive way to connect these bands together along the perpendicular axis.

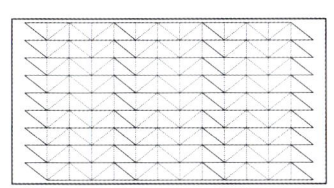

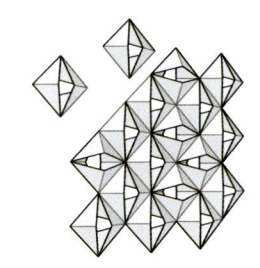

Version 2: The assembly of the original tile required an extremely high degree of precision to fit the half-units together. To simplify the fabrication process, the base unit of the next version was reduced to a single tile rather than a continuos chain. This also allowed for non-uniform arrangement of the tile's apertures. The cut pattern was only slightly altered, so the material efficiency remained very high.

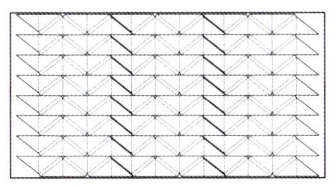

Version 3: The next iteration resolved the issue of connection by adding a 2" flat face around the outside of the tile where the preceding version had only an edge. The assembled tiles could then be easily fastened together along its face.

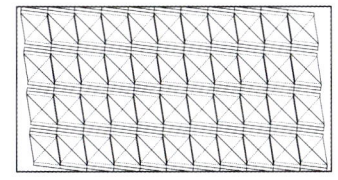

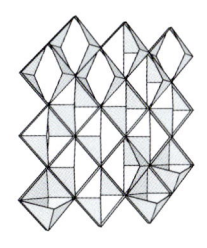

Version 4: The final version was created by removing select faces from the tile to create precise controlled views through the wall. Each tile is cut as two separate pieces and can be assembled to produce four different directional configurations. The overall assembly can then be fine-tuned to create a diversity of views and spatial experience as the visitor moves around the wall.

Fabrication

KALEIDOSCOPE STREET Re_Load

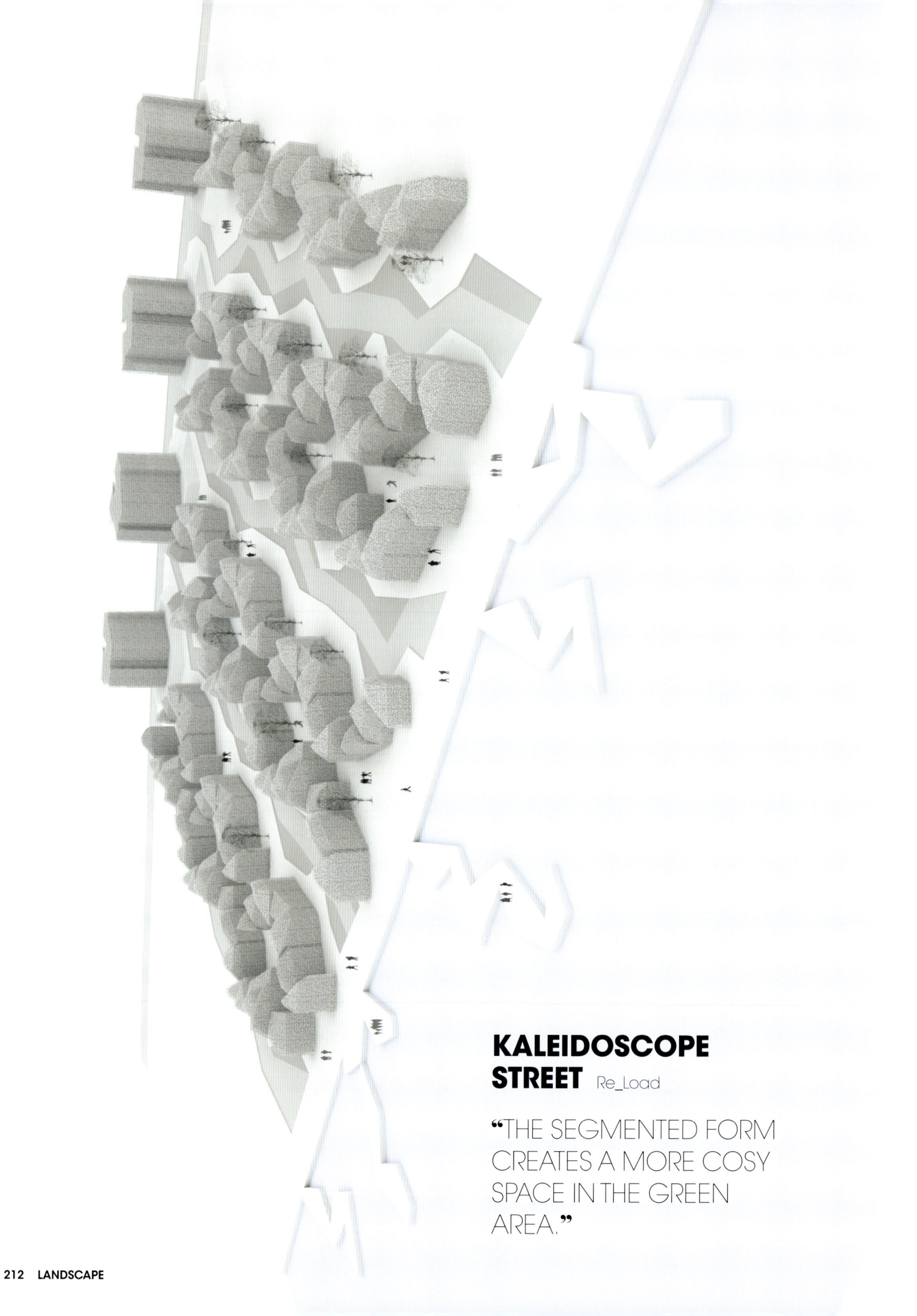

"THE SEGMENTED FORM CREATES A MORE COSY SPACE IN THE GREEN AREA."

• houses access

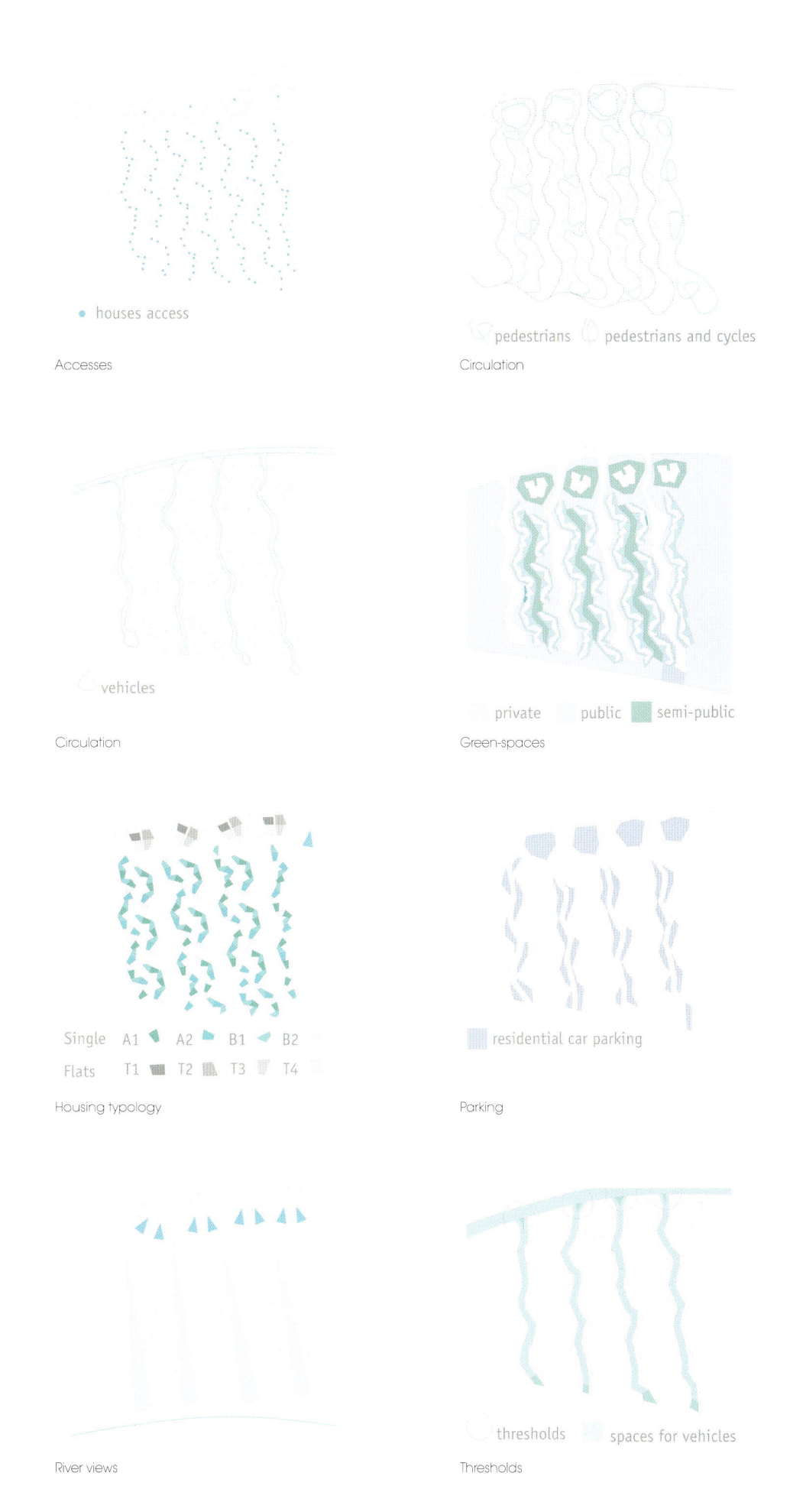

Accesses

pedestrians   pedestrians and cycles

Circulation

vehicles

Circulation

private   public   semi-public

Green-spaces

Single A1 A2 B1 B2
Flats   T1 T2 T3 T4

Housing typology

residential car parking

Parking

River views

thresholds   spaces for vehicles

Thresholds

ARCHITECTURAL DIAGRAMS 213

KEELUNG
Gudart Architects

"A DYNAMIC INSIDE-OUTSIDE RELATIONSHIP THAT HAS GENERATED NUMEROUS INSTANCES OF GREAT URBANITY."

Analysis

ARCHITECTURAL DIAGRAMS 215

LA JOLIETTE plattformberlin

"THE PLAN AND THE FACADES ARE COMPOSED IN LAYERS."

ARCHITECTURAL DIAGRAMS 217

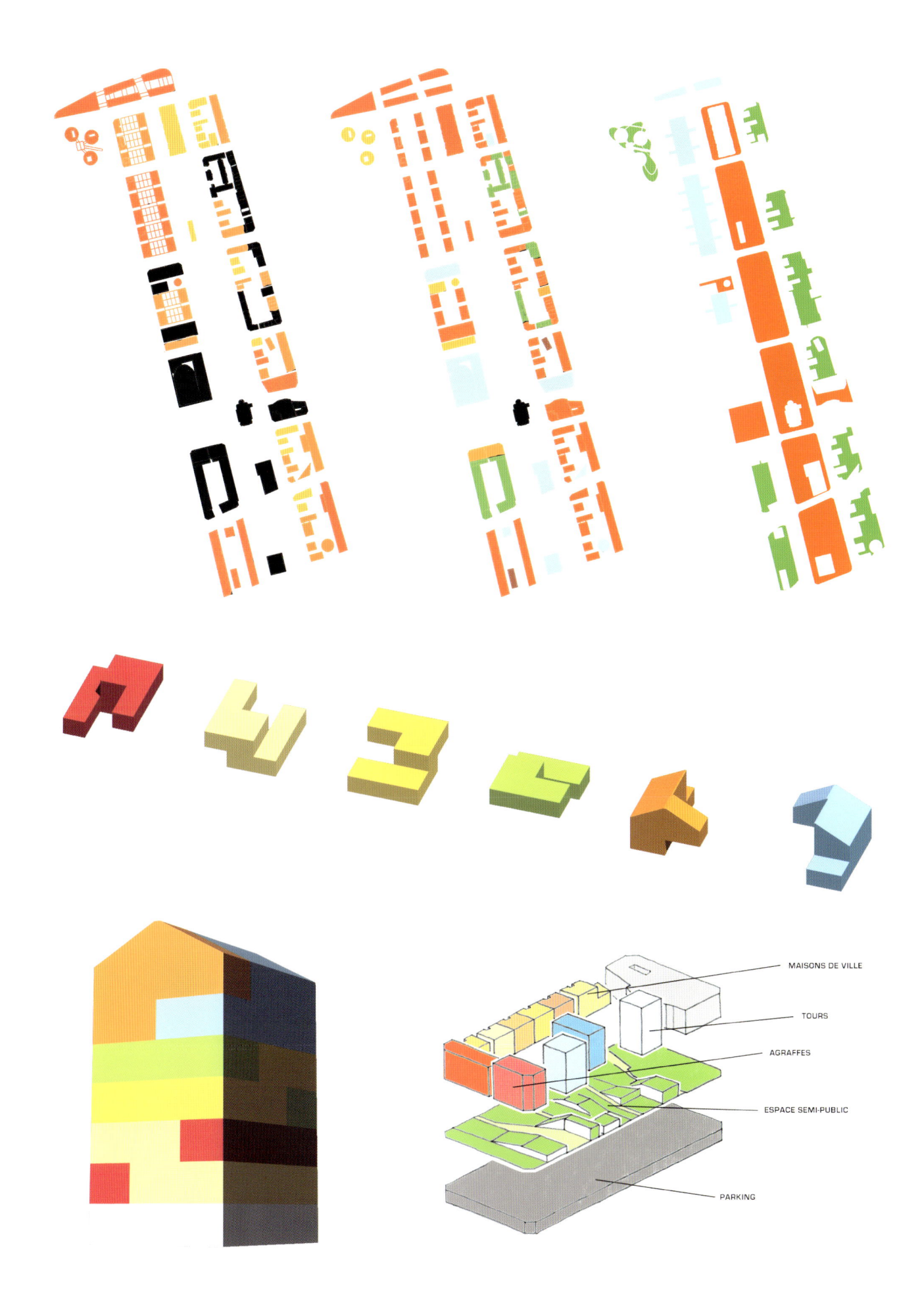

LINEAR PARK
Gálvez + Wieczorek

"THE PROJECT EMERGES FROM THE NEED TO REMOVE THE CURRENT EXISTING BARRIER AS IT PASSES BY THE NORTHERN AREA."

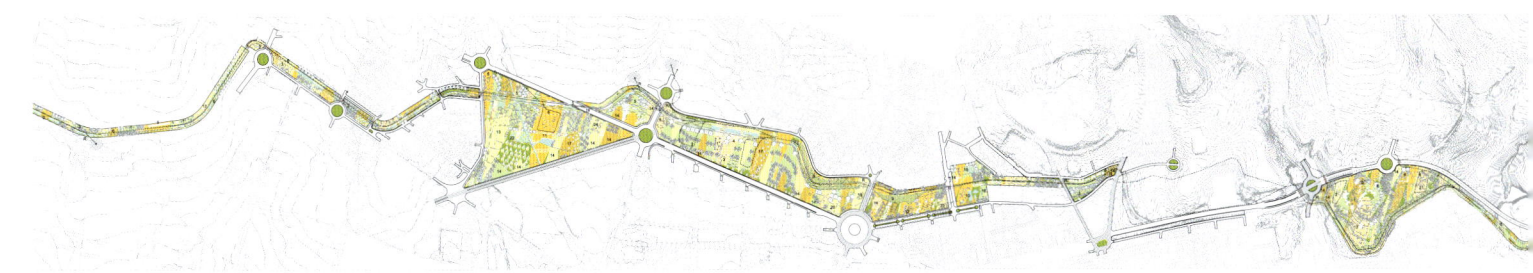

General plan

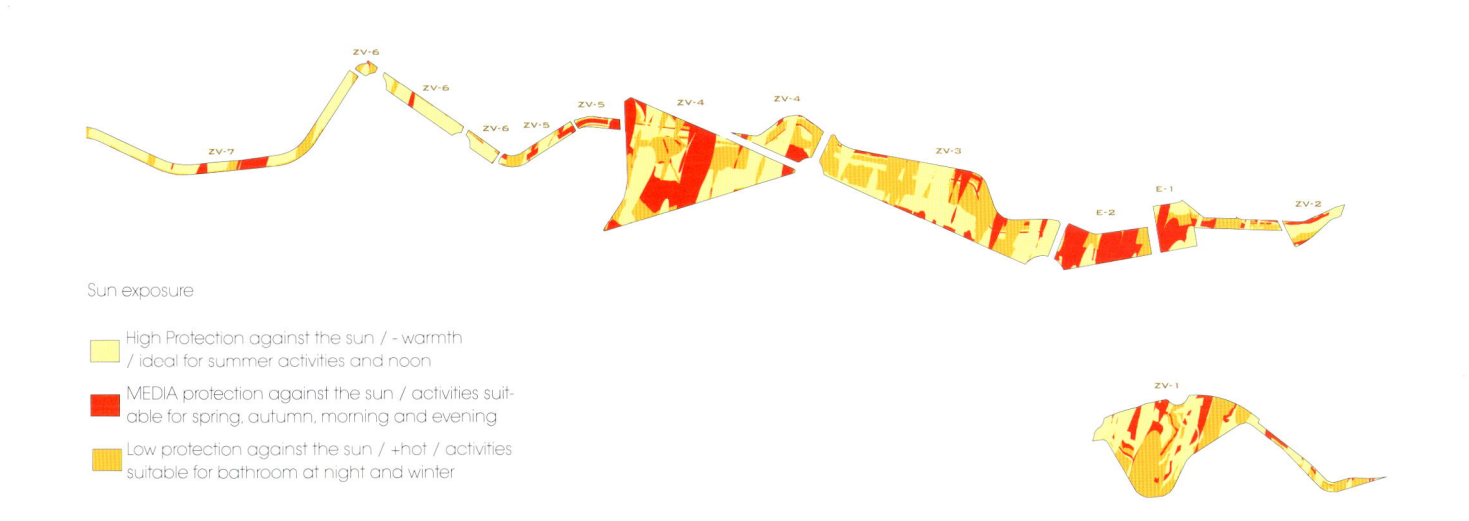

Sun exposure

- High Protection against the sun / - warmth / ideal for summer activities and noon
- MEDIA protection against the sun / activities suitable for spring, autumn, morning and evening
- Low protection against the sun / +hot / activities suitable for bathroom at night and winter

Solar architectural materials

- Color (canopy, flowering..)
- Light (sun visors, trims bright sun..)
- Shadow (branches, trees..)
- Reflection (water, structures stud..)
- Temperature (soil materials, manipulations topographic..)

ARCHITECTURAL DIAGRAMS   219

MASDAR PLAZA, OASIS OF THE FUTURE LAVA

ARCHITECTURAL DIAGRAMS 221

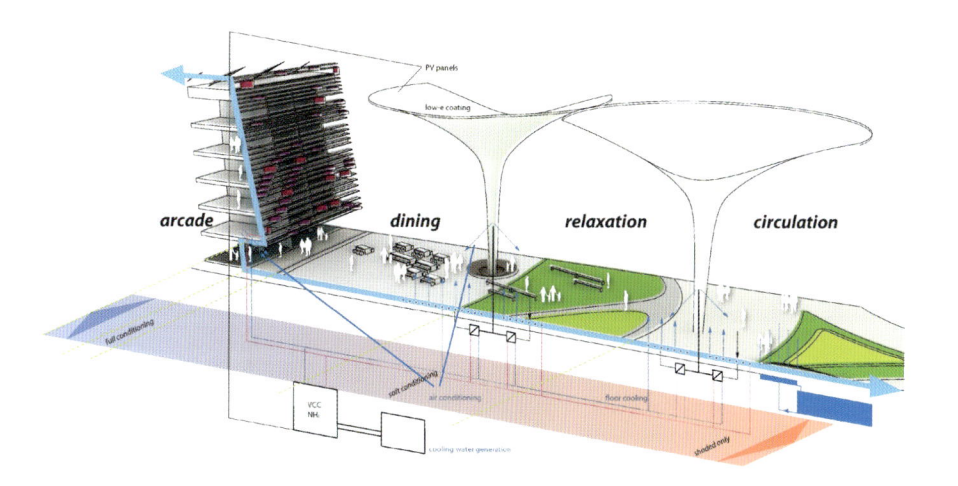

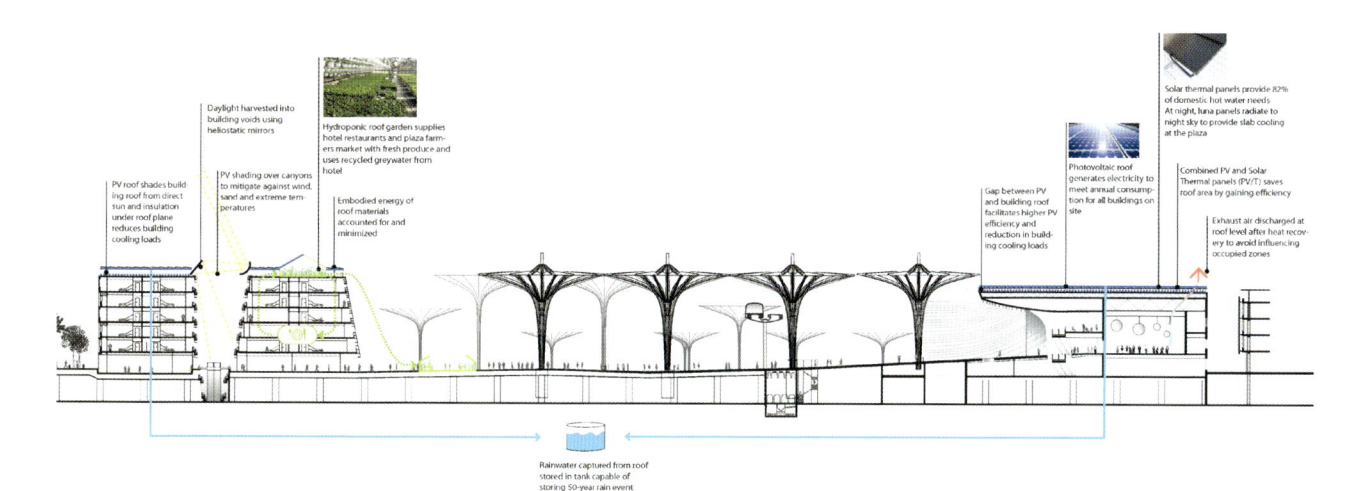

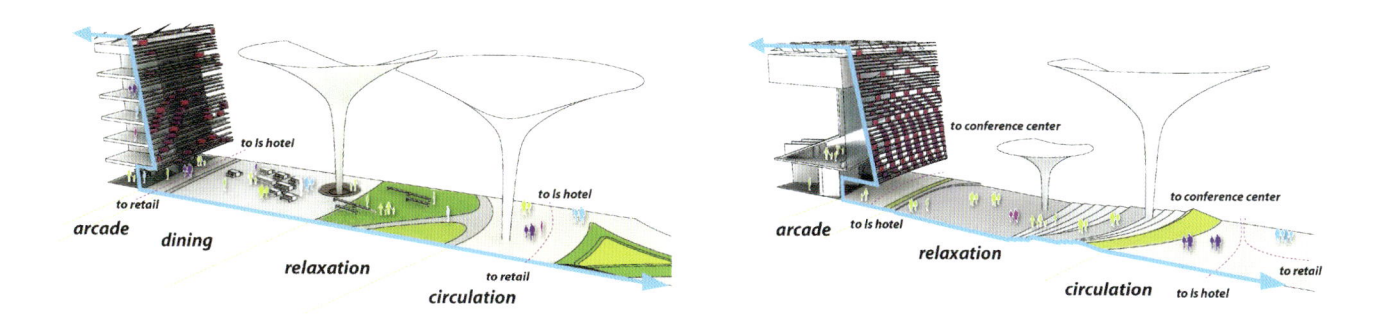

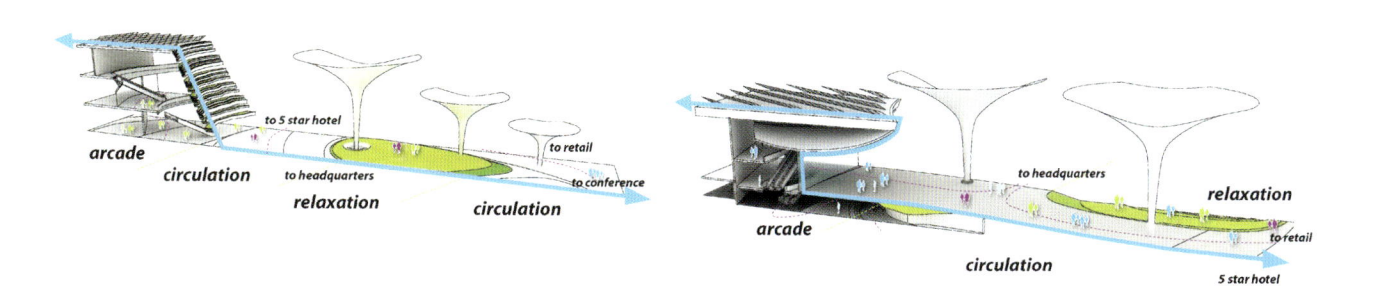

MIES VAN DER ROHE PLAZA
PEG office of landscape + architecture

"DRAWING ON MIES' TRADEMARK OF CUTTING STONE SLABS SYMMETRICALLY ACROSS THEIR DOMINANT PATTERN."

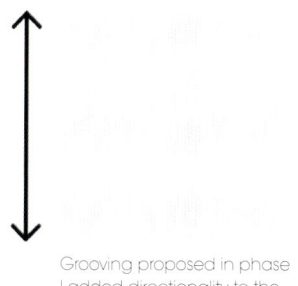

Grooving proposed in phase I added directionality to the tiles and directed water

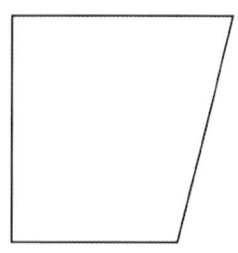

Geometry of the tiles leads to a distortion of the groove patterns

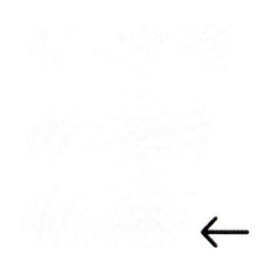

The grooves adjusted

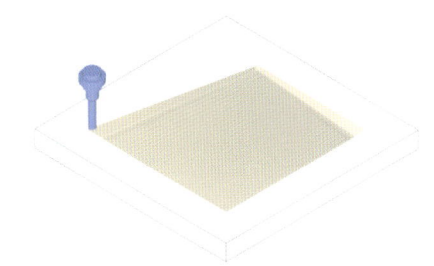

Flat CNC router bit

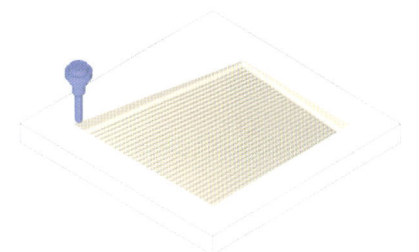

Round CNC router bit

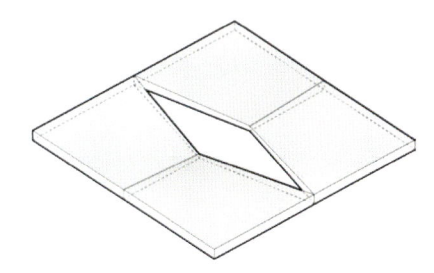

Tile grooves

Tile types/assembly: for configuring our concrete tiles, we borrowed Mies' trademark use of large slabs of stone cut into rectangles and "book-matched" symmetrically about their joints.

TILE 001
6 required
48/36x96
8.22 cubic feet
1233 lbs.

TILE 007
18 required
48/42x48
4.39 cubic feet
659 lbs.

TILE 002
7 required
48/36x96M
8.22 cubic feet
1233 lbs.
(mirror of tile 001)

TILE 008
19 required
48/42x48M
4.39 cubic feet
659 lbs.
(mirror of tile 007)

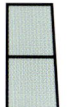

TILE 003
9 required
48/42x96
8.78 cubic feet
1317 lbs.

TILE 009
22 required
48/36x48
4.11 cubic feet
617 lbs.

TILE 004
8 required
48/42x96M
8.78 cubic feet
1317 lbs.
(mirror of tile 003)

TILE 010
21 required
48/36x48M
4.11 cubic feet
617 lbs.
(mirror of tile 009)

TILE 005
26 required
48/45x48
4.52 cubic feet
678 lbs.

TILE 006
26 required
48/45x48M
4.52 cubic feet
678 lbs.
(mirror of tile 005)

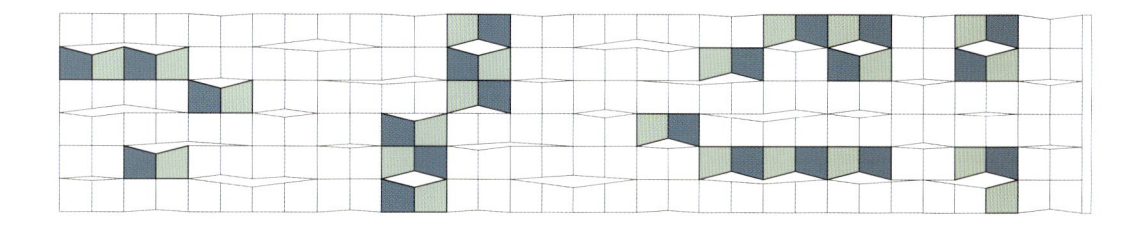

ARCHITECTURAL DIAGRAMS 223

NANYU SHOPPING PARK
CJ Lim | Studio 8 Architects

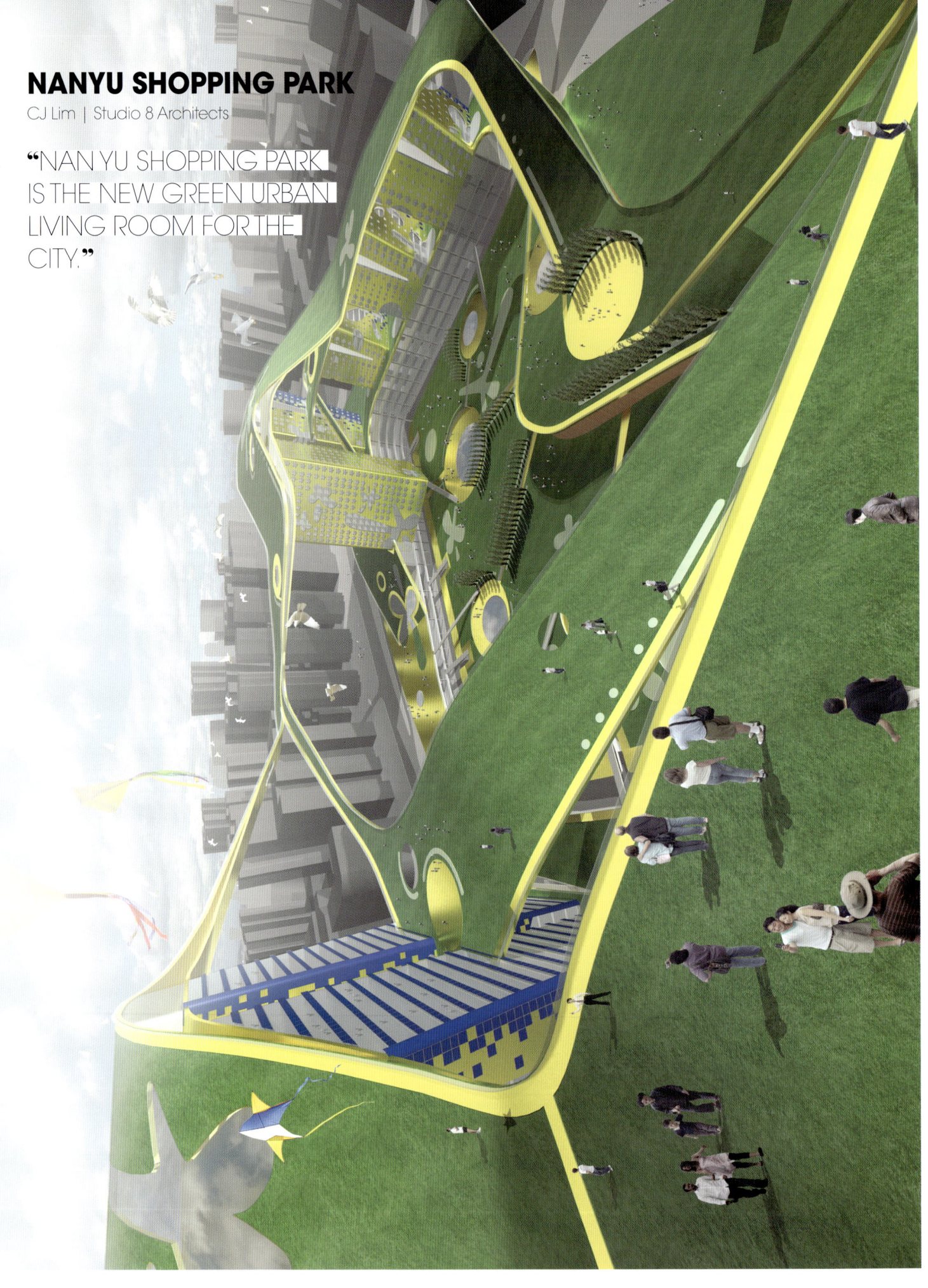

"NAN YU SHOPPING PARK IS THE NEW GREEN URBAN LIVING ROOM FOR THE CITY."

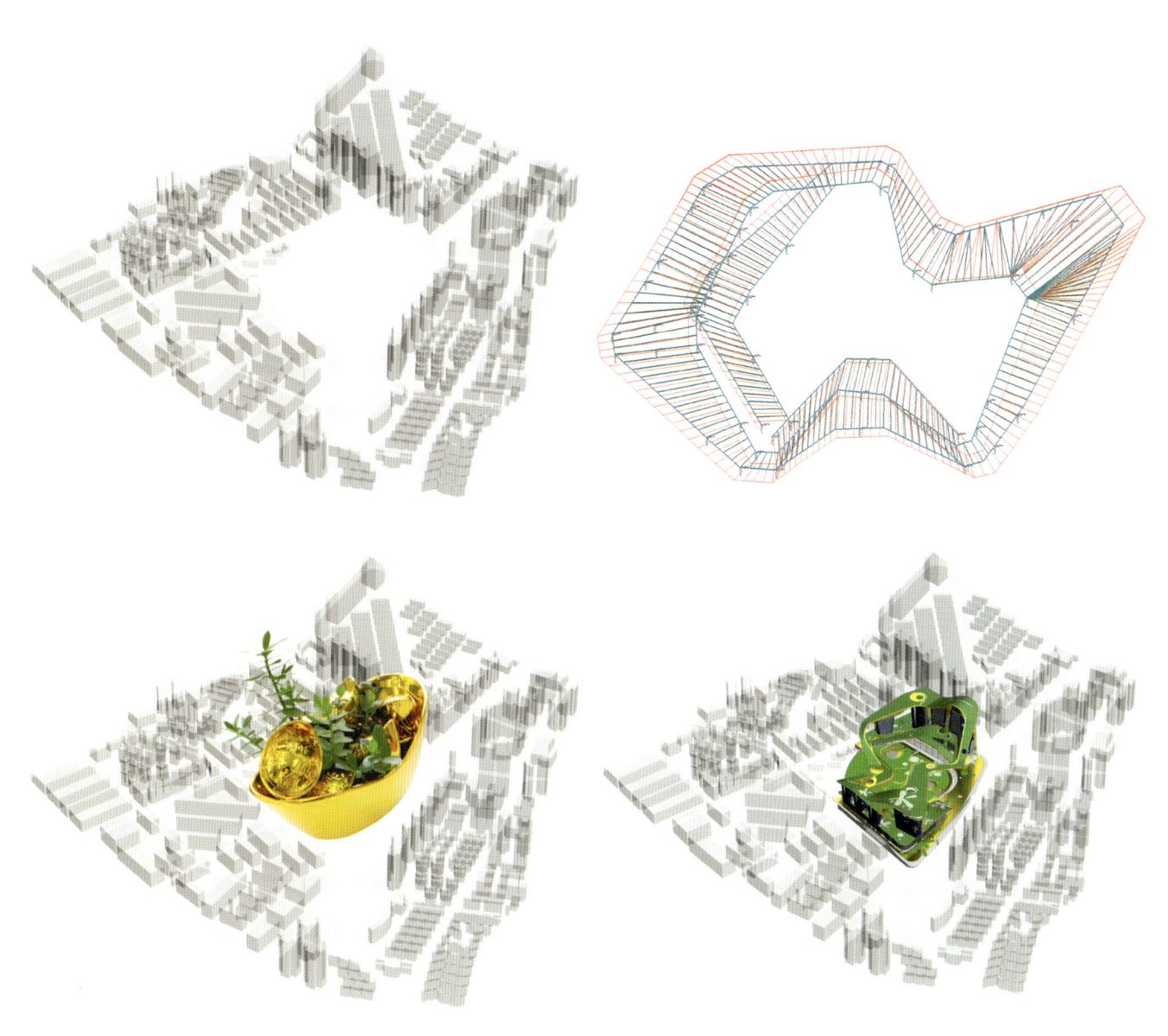

Concept vertical

ARCHITECTURAL DIAGRAMS 225

ON CANAL STREET beva

"THE URBAN GRID OF THE PROJECT INTERACTS WITH SENSITIVITY TO THE EXISTING CONTEXT."

Urban plan principle

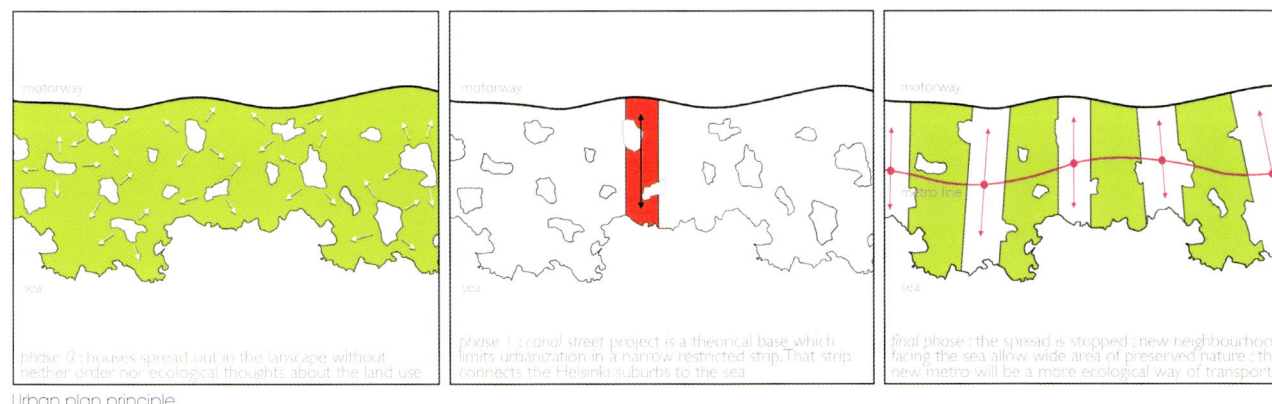

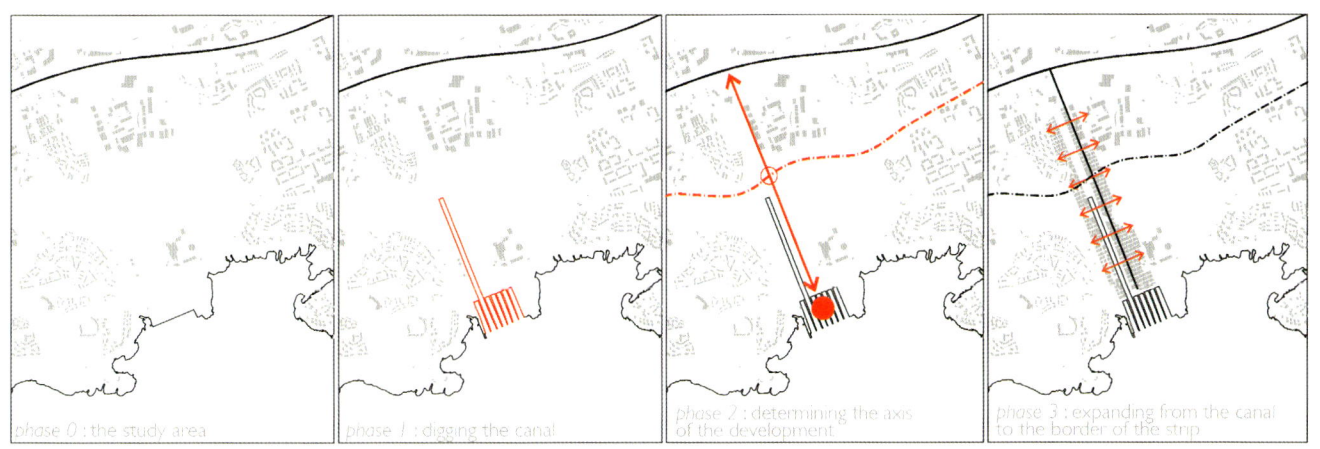

phase 0: houses spread out in the lanscape without neither order nor ecological thoughts about the land use

phase 1: canal street project is a theorical base which limits urbanization in a narrow restricted strip. That strip connects the Helsinki suburbs to the sea

final phase: the spread is stopped ; new neighbourhoods facing the sea allow wide area of preserved nature ; the new metro will be a more ecological way of transportation

Building process involved

phase 0: the study area

phase 1: digging the canal

phase 2: determining the axis of the development

phase 3: expanding from the canal to the border of the strip

ARCHITECTURAL DIAGRAMS 227

OPATIJA NEW SQUARE
PSA

"FLAT SQUARE IN THE COURSE OF THE DAY FOSTER DIFFERENT ZONES OF ACCUMULATION OF VISITORS, WHICH ACTIVATE PROGRAMMES."

09:00

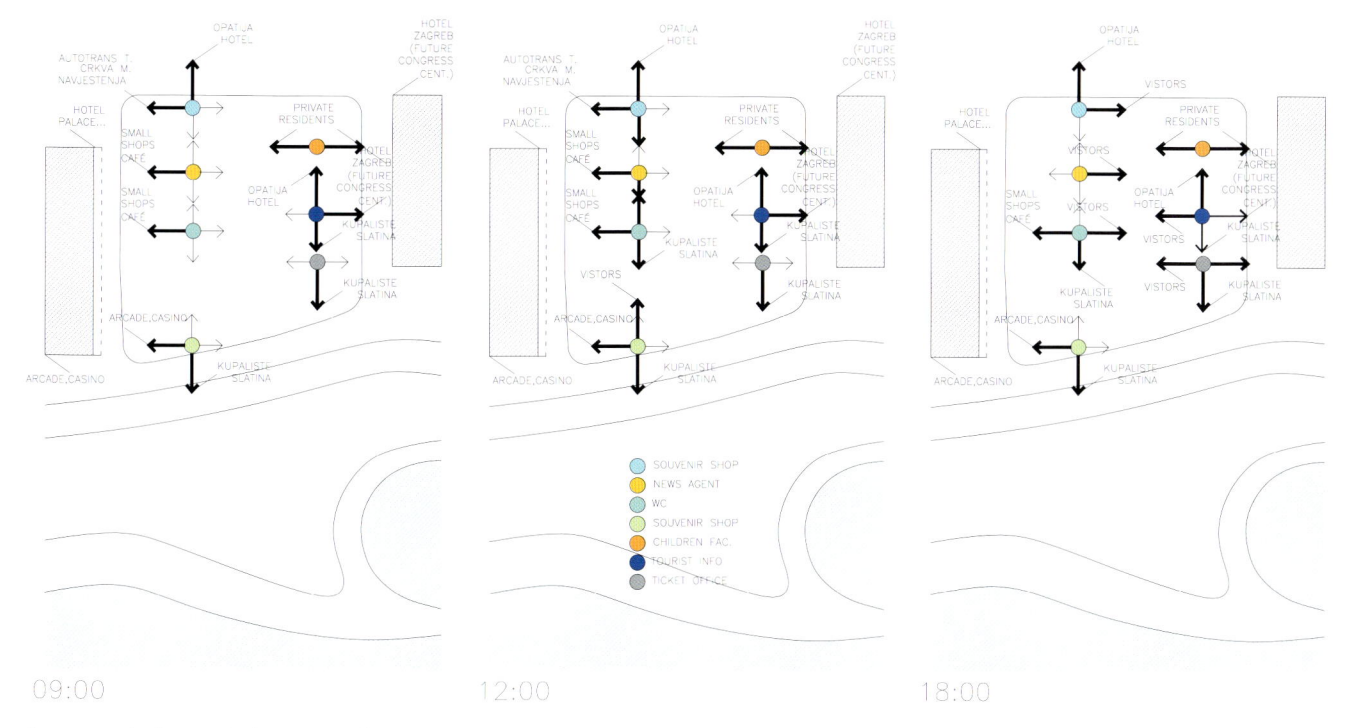

12:00

18:00

○ SOUVENIR SHOP
○ NEWS AGENT
○ WC
○ SOUVENIR SHOP
○ CHILDREN FAC.
○ TOURIST INFO
○ TICKET OFFICE

Program_ activation acc to shading conditions

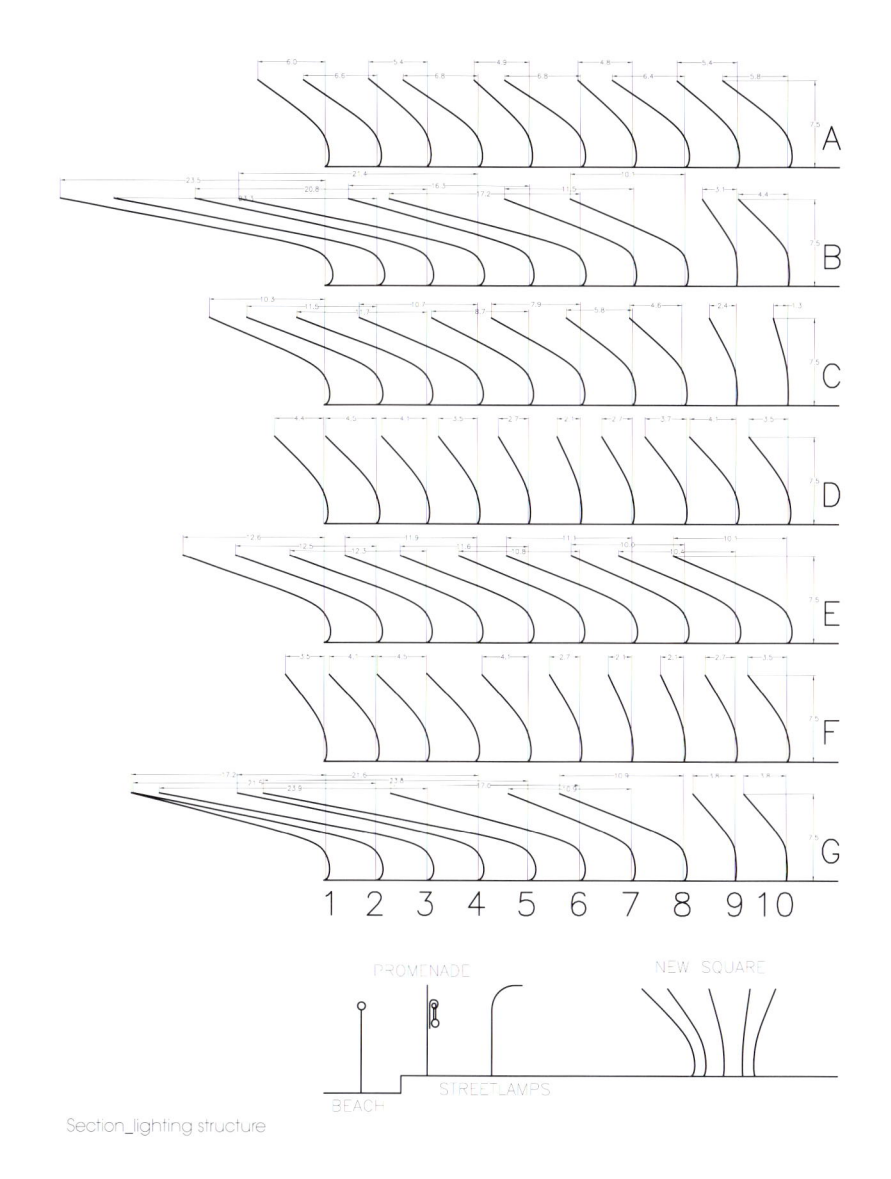

A

B

C

D

E

F

G

1 2 3 4 5 6 7 8 9 10

PROMENADE   NEW SQUARE

BEACH   STREETLAMPS

Section_lighting structure

ARCHITECTURAL DIAGRAMS 229

PLANKEN MANNHEIM
plattformberlin

"THE CITY SPACE IS TIDY, BUT NOT BARE."

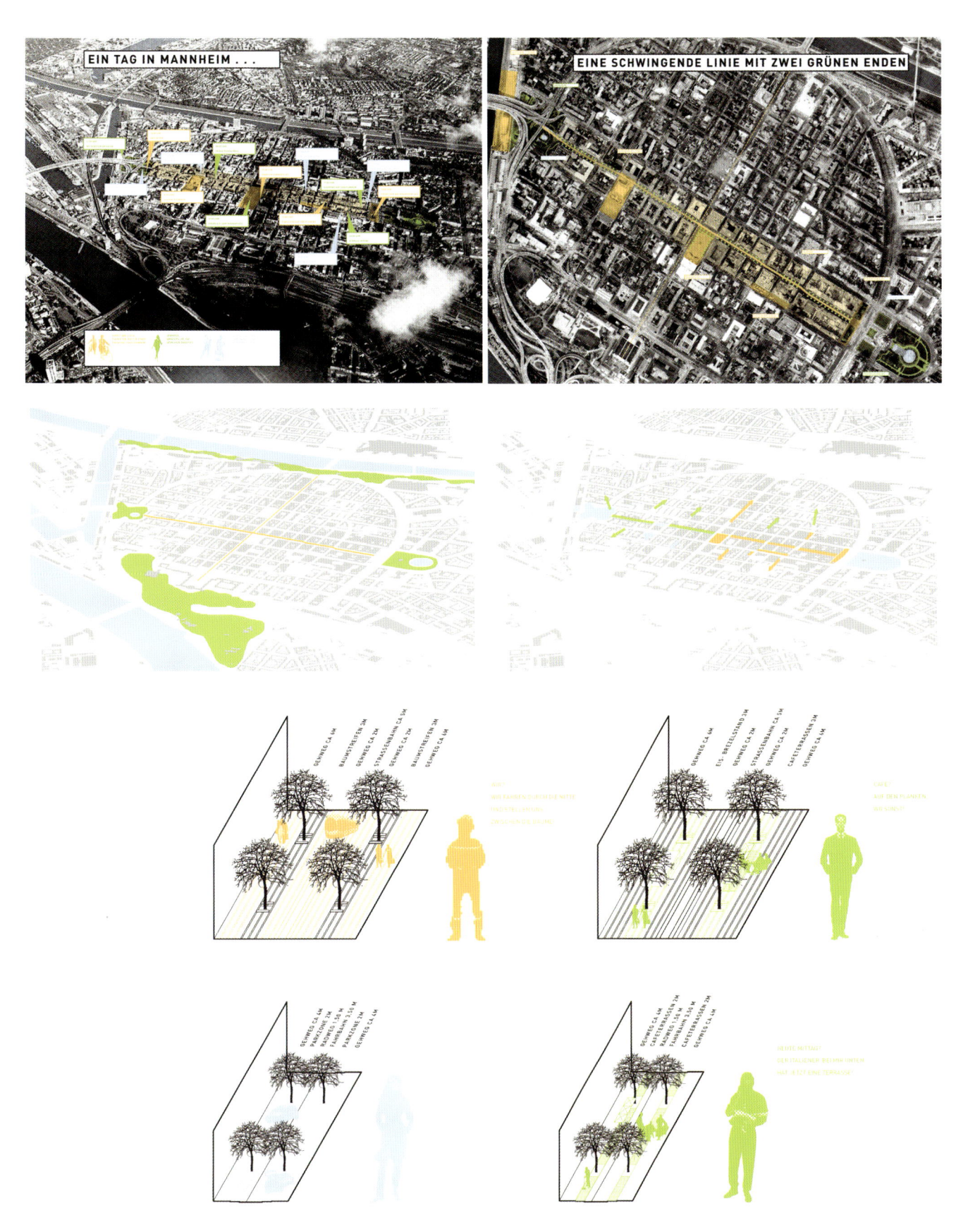

ARCHITECTURAL DIAGRAMS 231

PLAYA LAVA
J. MAYER H. ARCHITECTS

"PLAYA LAVA RETAKES THE NATURAL FORMAL LANGUAGE OF THE SITE TO BLEND ITSELF INTO THE EXISTING LANDSCAPE."

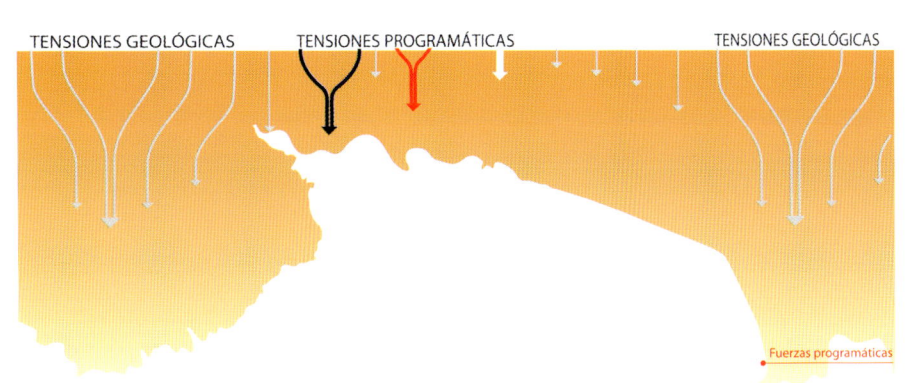

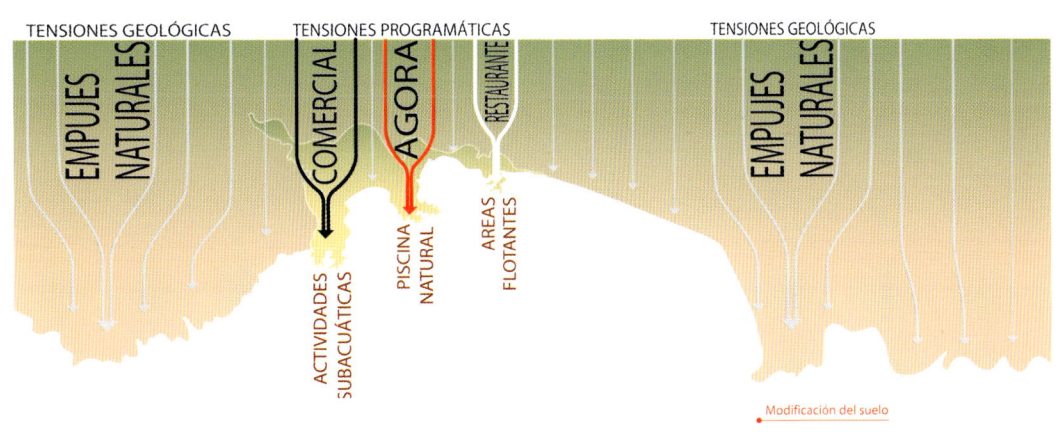

Situación actual

TENSIONES GEOLÓGICAS · TENSIONES PROGRAMÁTICAS · TENSIONES GEOLÓGICAS

Fuerzas programáticas

TENSIONES GEOLÓGICAS · TENSIONES PROGRAMÁTICAS · TENSIONES GEOLÓGICAS

EMPUJES NATURALES · COMERCIAL · AGORA · RESTAURANTE · EMPUJES NATURALES

ACTIVIDADES SUBACUÁTICAS · PISCINA NATURAL · AREAS FLOTANTES

Modificación del suelo

Diagram

P.O.R.T. nARCHITECTS

"P.O.R.T. PROPOSED DIVERSE NORTH/SOUTH CONNECTIONS BETWEEN CITY AND LAKE, AND VARIOUS SCALES OF RESPONSE TO CLIMATE."

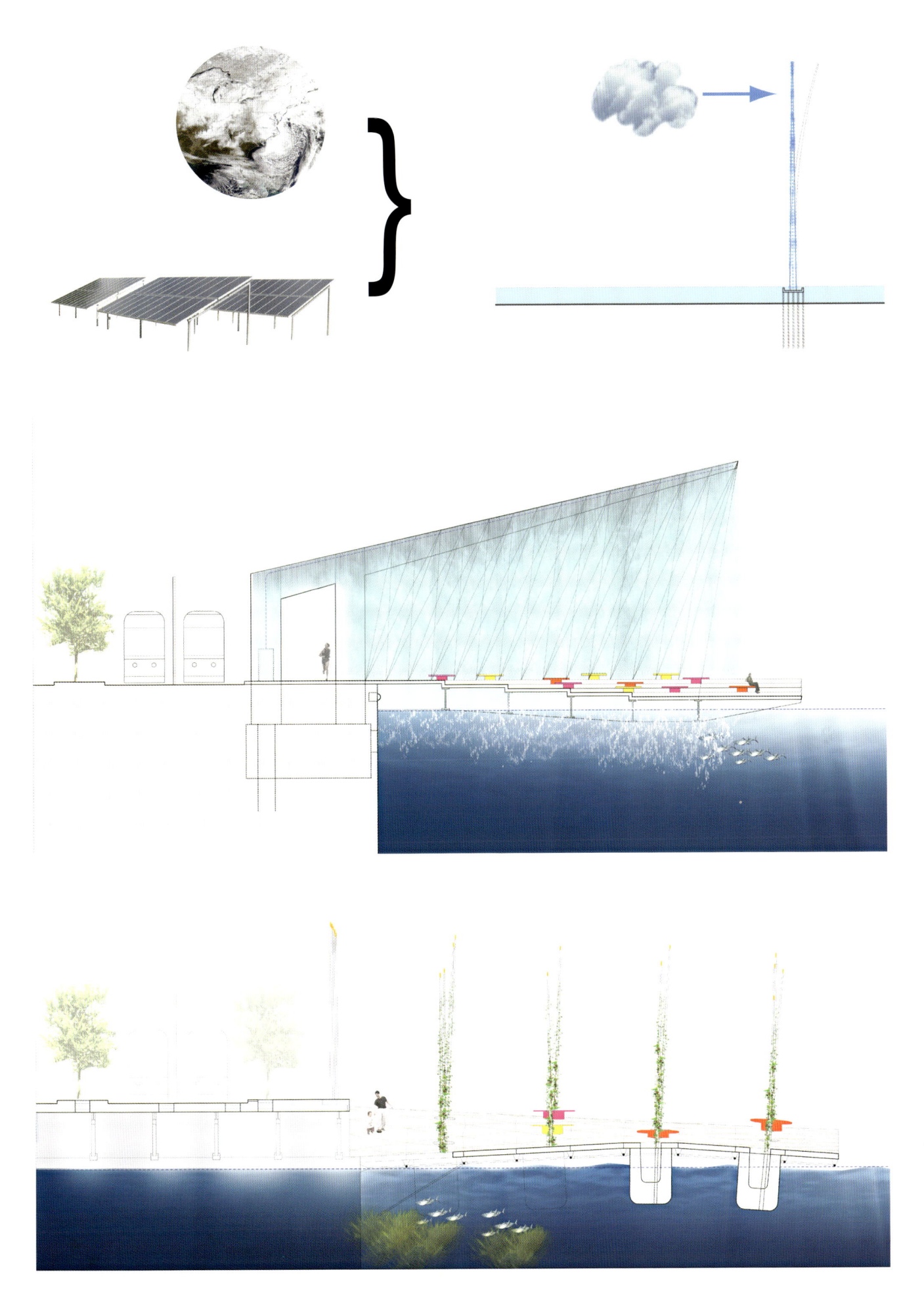

ARCHITECTURAL DIAGRAMS 235

PUBLIC GRADATION ON GREEN ARMED PLAZA
Jungwoo Ji

"THE RIBBON SHAPE WITH SMALL OVAL RINGS PARTICLIZED FROM THE OVAL ICONIC FORM OF ORIGINAL GRAND ARMY PLAZA."

Ground Level View to the Prospect Park

Hardscape + Park = GAP
Ground Army Plaza
Green Armed Plaza

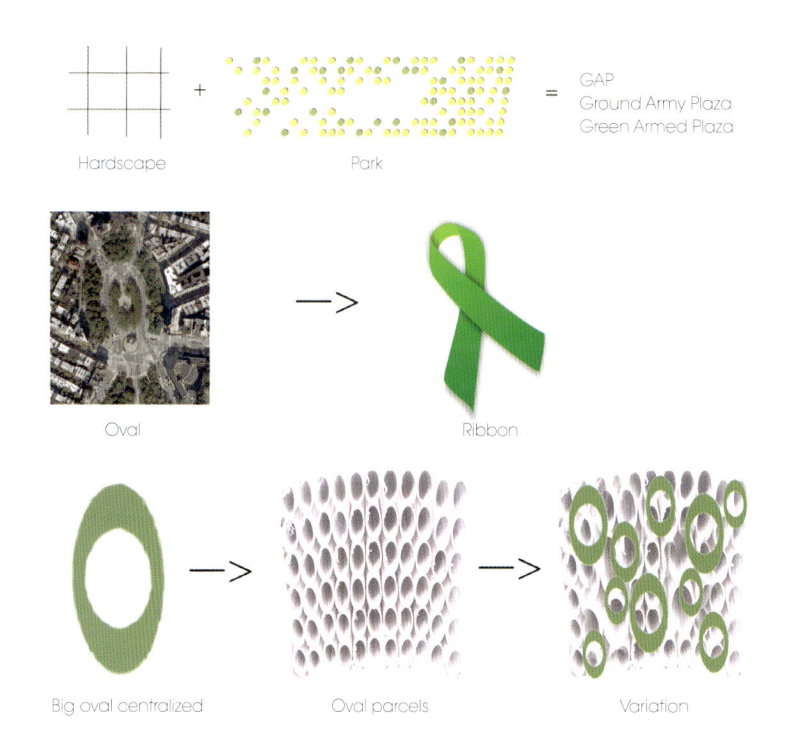

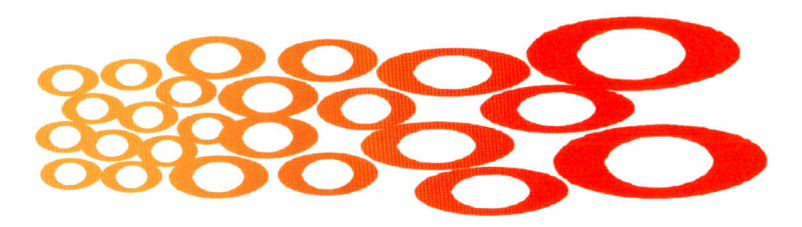

Oval → Ribbon

Big oval centralized → Oval parcels → Variation

Gradation in shape / pattern / color / planting

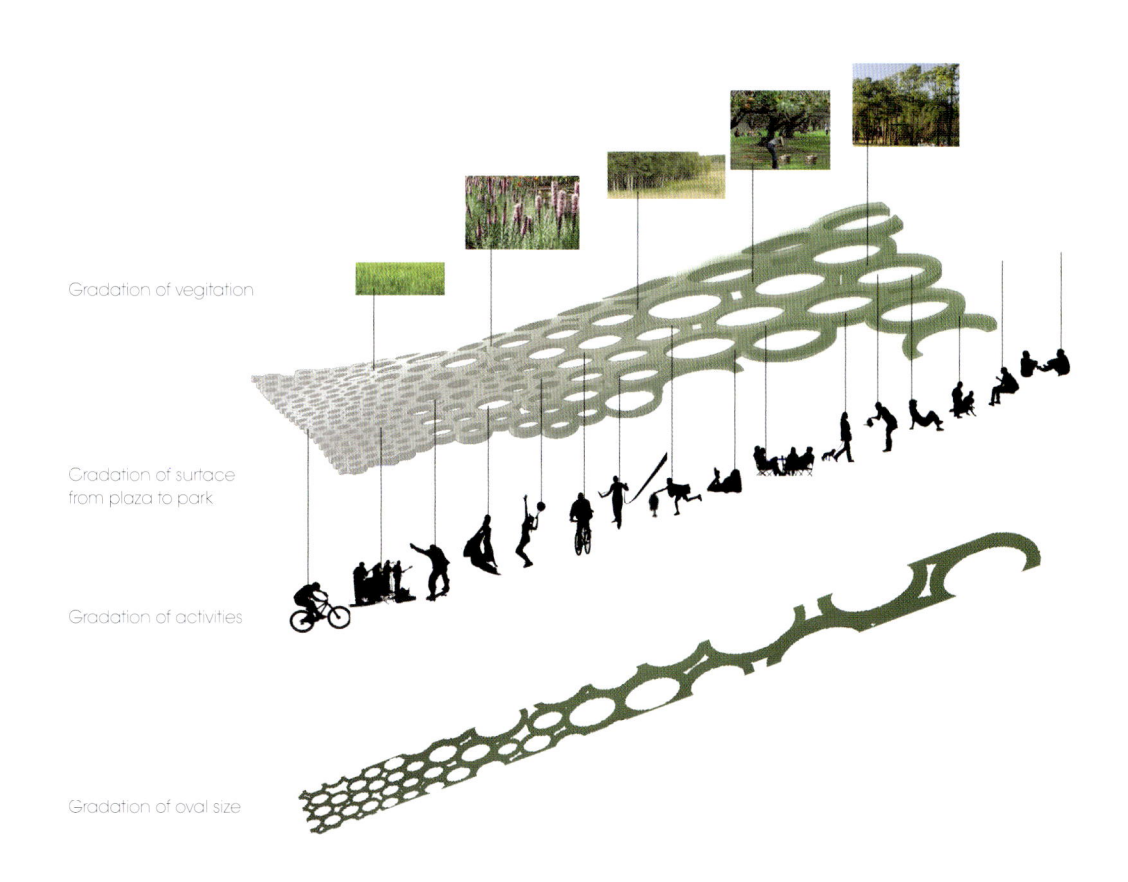

Gradation of vegitation

Gradation of surface from plaza to park

Gradation of activities

Gradation of oval size

ARCHITECTURAL DIAGRAMS 237

ROZZOL MELARA ma0

"THE AIM IS TO LIBERATE MOVEMENT AND CROSSINGS, OVERLAPPING PLANES/LEVELS AND FUNCTIONS."

ARCHITECTURAL DIAGRAMS 239

SCHOOLS ONE ARCHITECTURE

"IN SCHOOLS, THE NEIGH-BORHOOD MEETS. THE SCHOOL HAS COME TO REPLACE THE PUBLIC SQUARE."

outside   inside

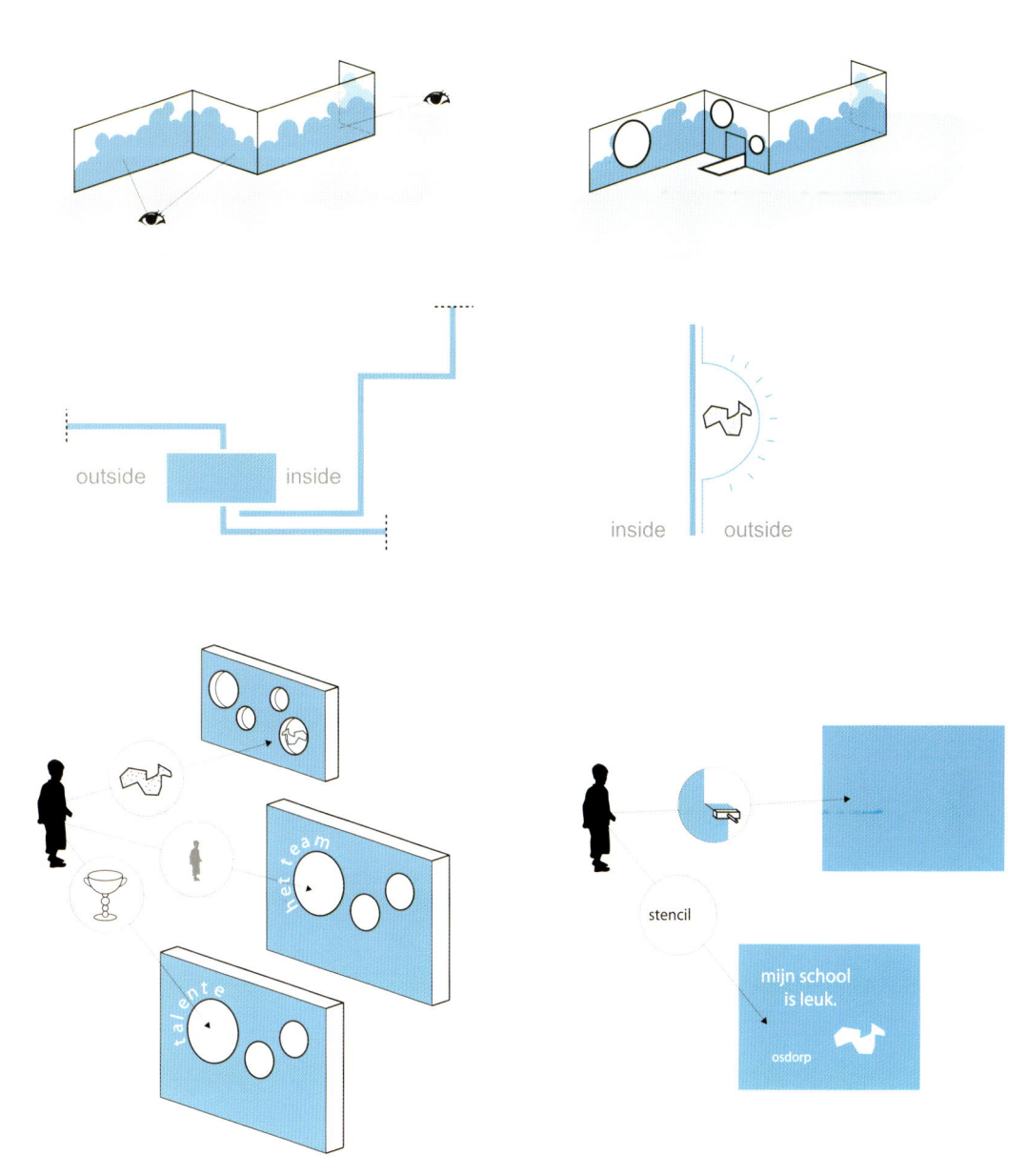

inside   outside

net team

talente

stencil

mijn school
is leuk.

osdorp

Diagram

ARCHITECTURAL DIAGRAMS   241

SENSATIONAL PARK
NABITO ARQUITECTURA S.C.P

"THE PROJECT IS TO INVITE USERS TO A PATH IN WHICH SCENE ARE ALWAYS CHANGING"

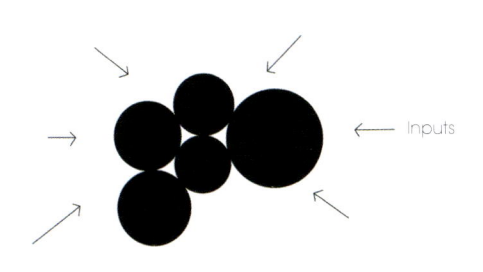

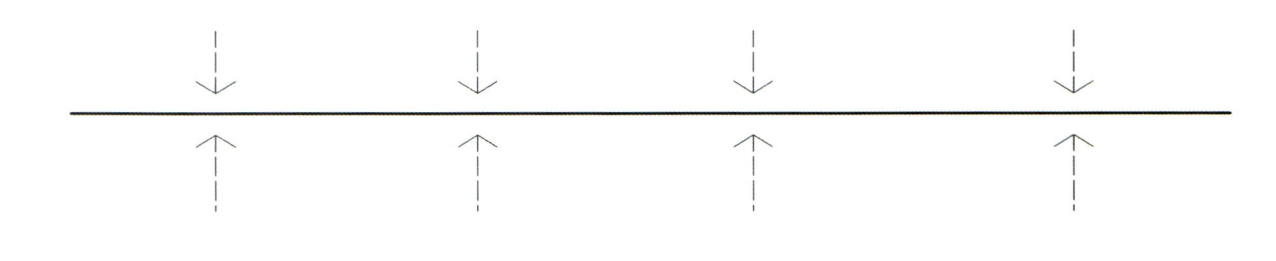

Inputs

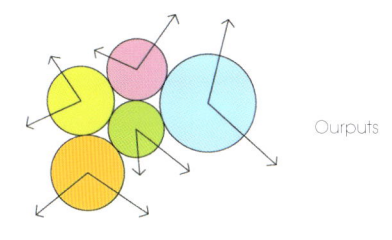

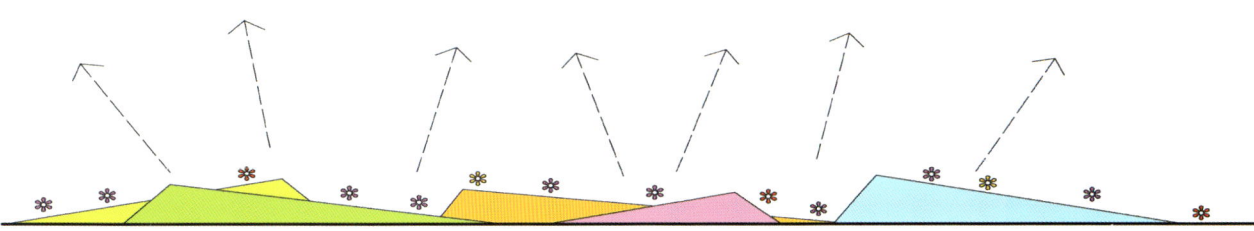

Outputs

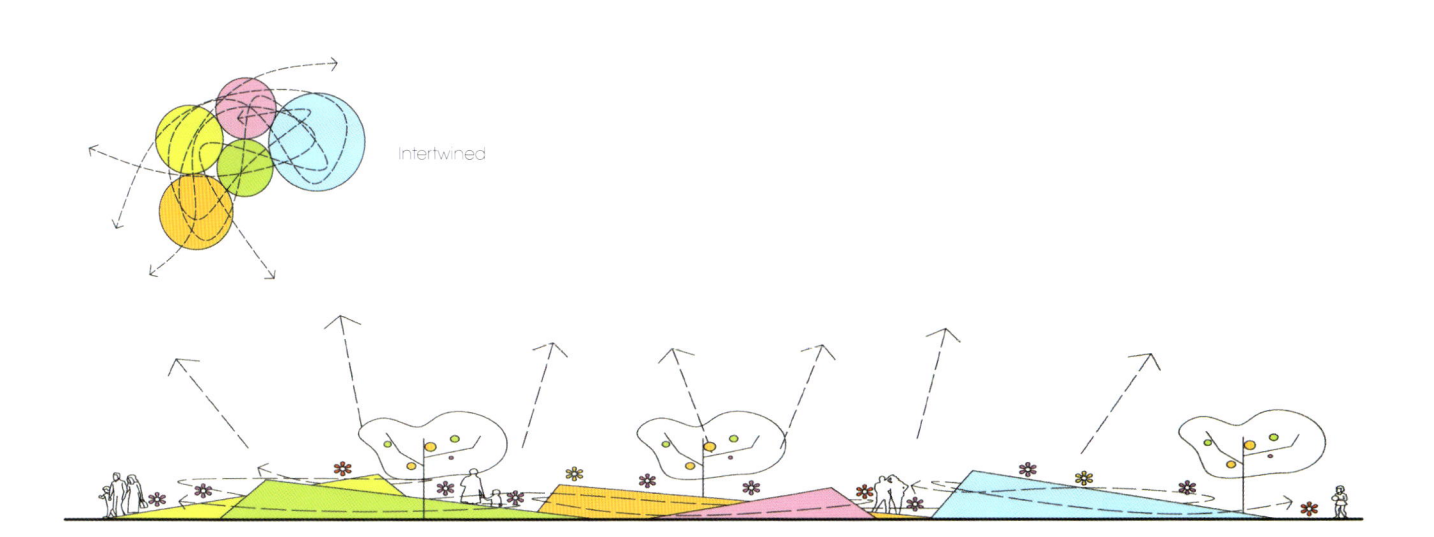

Intertwined

ARCHITECTURAL DIAGRAMS 243

SQUARE IN COPENHAGEN
Leon 11 ARCHITECTS

"THE SQUARE IS A SPACE OF PROGRAMMATIC CULTIVATION AREAS WHERE DIFFERENT ACTIVITIES TAKE PLACE."

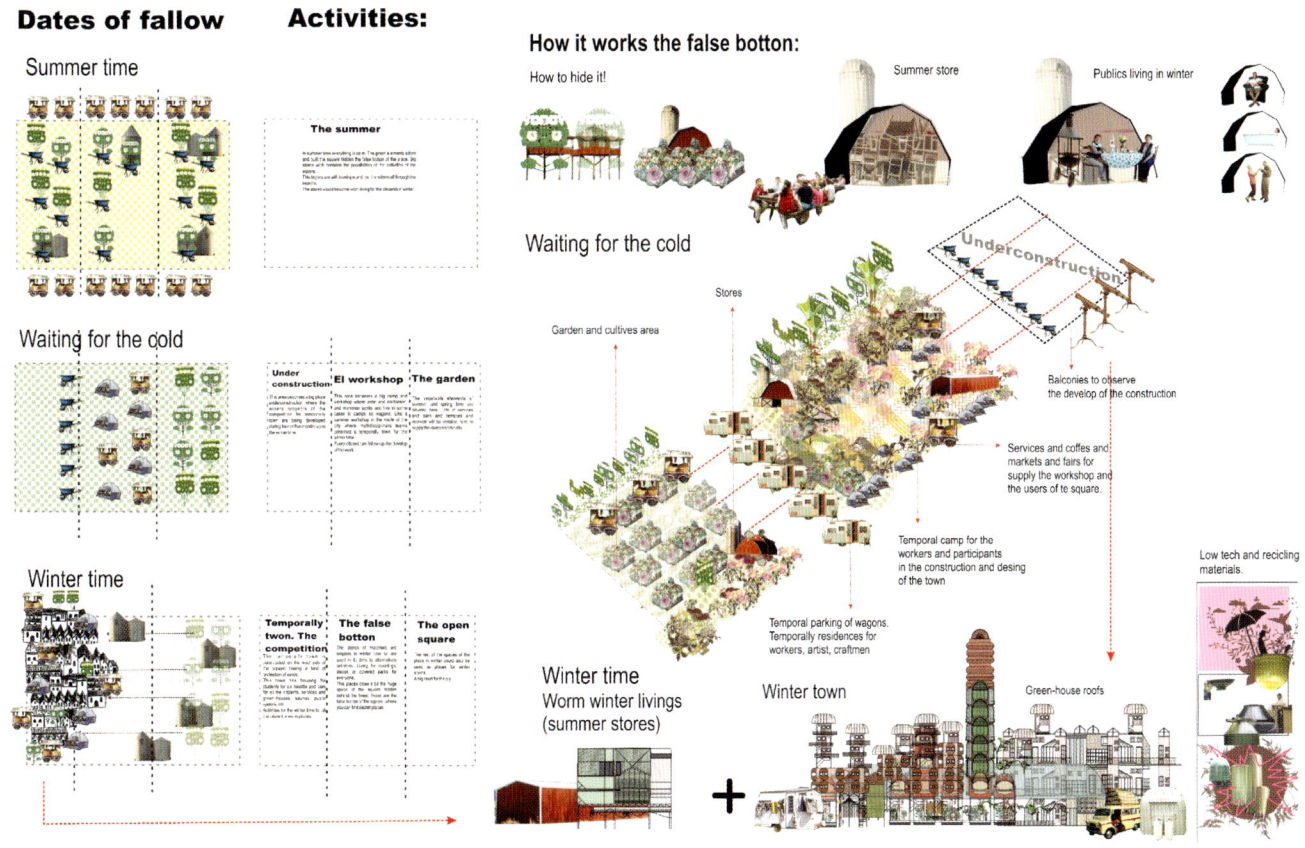

Topography and estructural lines · Pedestrian path · Garden areas · Trees · Fixed pug-ins · Energetic devices

Dates of fallow

Activities:

Summer time

Waiting for the cold

Winter time

Activities

How it works the false botton:

How to hide it! · Summer store · Publics living in winter

Waiting for the cold

Stores

Garden and cultives area

Underconstruction

Balconies to observe the develop of the construction

Services and coffes and markets and fairs for supply the workshop and the users of te square.

Temporal camp for the workers and participants in the construction and desing of the town

Temporal parking of wagons. Temporally residences for workers, artist, craftmen

Winter time
Worm winter livings (summer stores)

Winter town

Green-house roofs

Low tech and recicling materials.

ARCHITECTURAL DIAGRAMS 245

THE NEW ENTRANCE TO TJÖRN gunnarssonpettersson

"TJÖRN BRIDGE REACHES THE ISLAND AND CREATE A NEW STRONG ENTRANCE."

LED-illuminated surface   Warm terrace
Solar

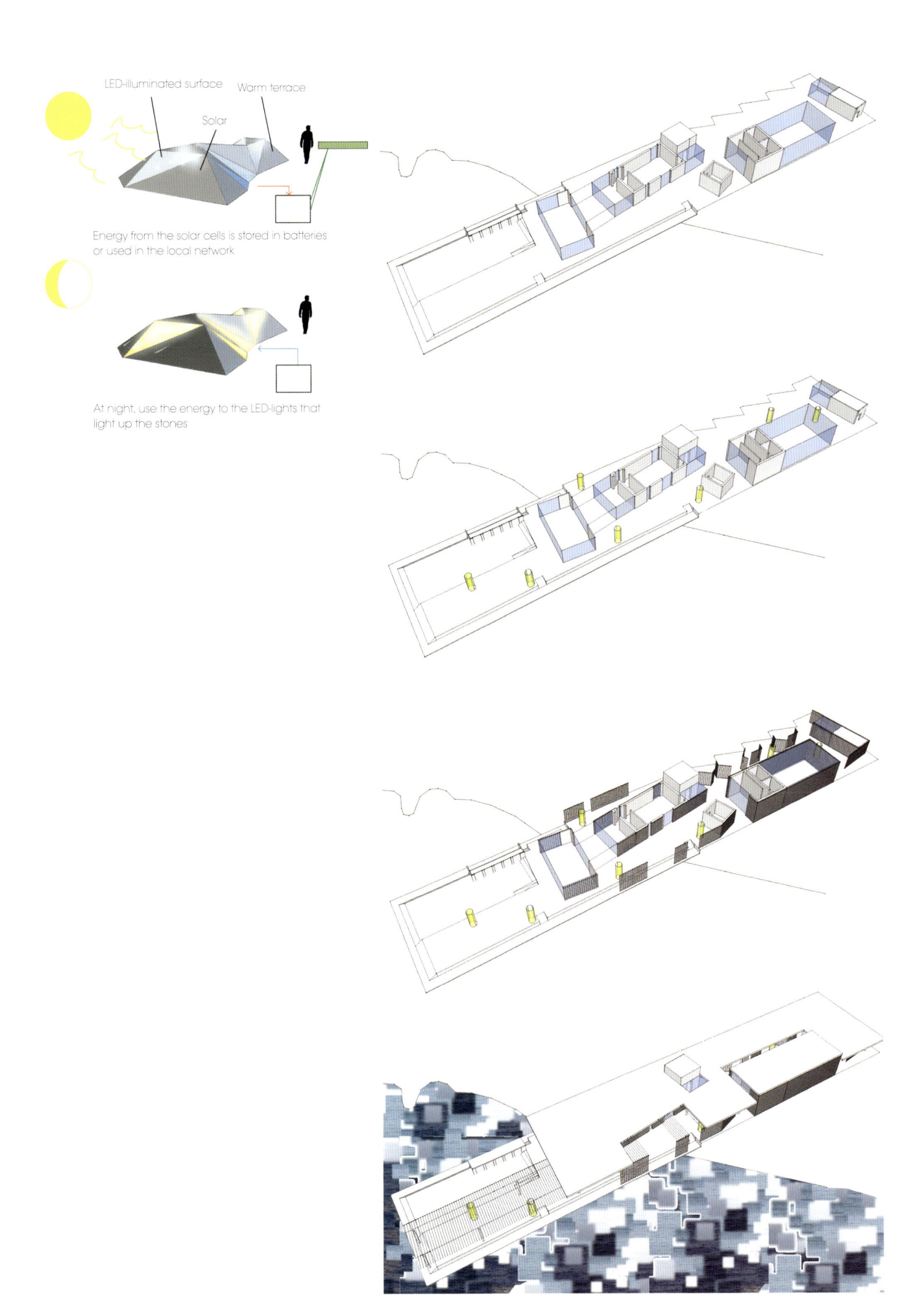

Energy from the solar cells is stored in batteries or used in the local network

At night, use the energy to the LED-lights that light up the stones

ARCHITECTURAL DIAGRAMS 247

TRONDHEIM FJORD-PARK
JDS Architects + KLAR

"IN AREAS WHERE THE SIGHT LINES MEET THE FJORDS, THE NEW COAST PARK PULLS BACK TO THE CITY SO THE RELATIONSHIP BETWEEN THE LAND AND THE CITY BECOMES TIGHTLY KNIT — BOTH VISUALLY AND PHYSICALLY."

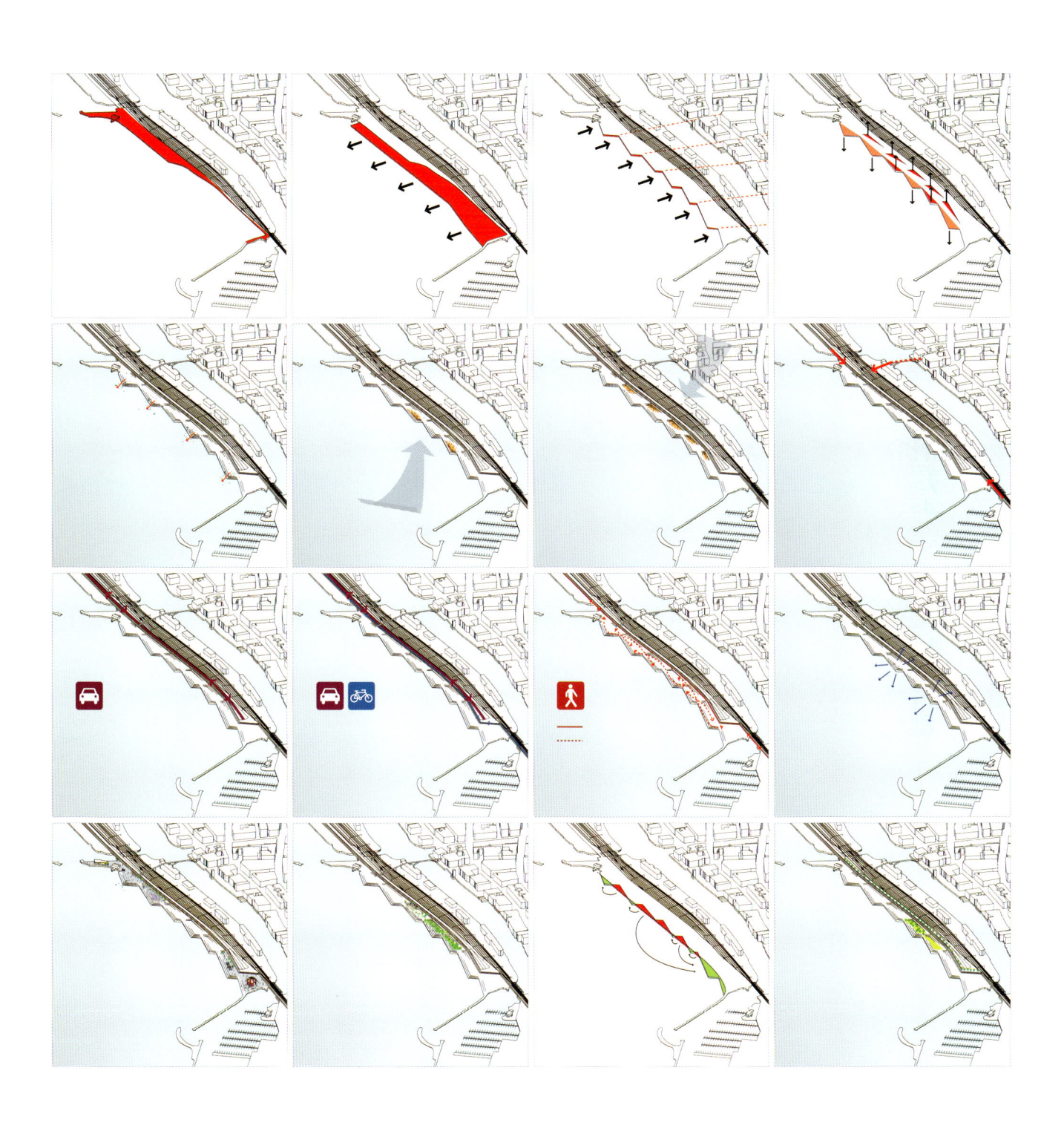

ARCHITECTURAL DIAGRAMS 249

UPGRADE PILONI

NABITO ARQUITECTURA S.C.P

"SQUARE BECOMES A SLOPING URBAN SPACE, STALLS ON THE LANDSCAPE, MEETING POINT BETWEEN SHOWS AND PEOPLE."

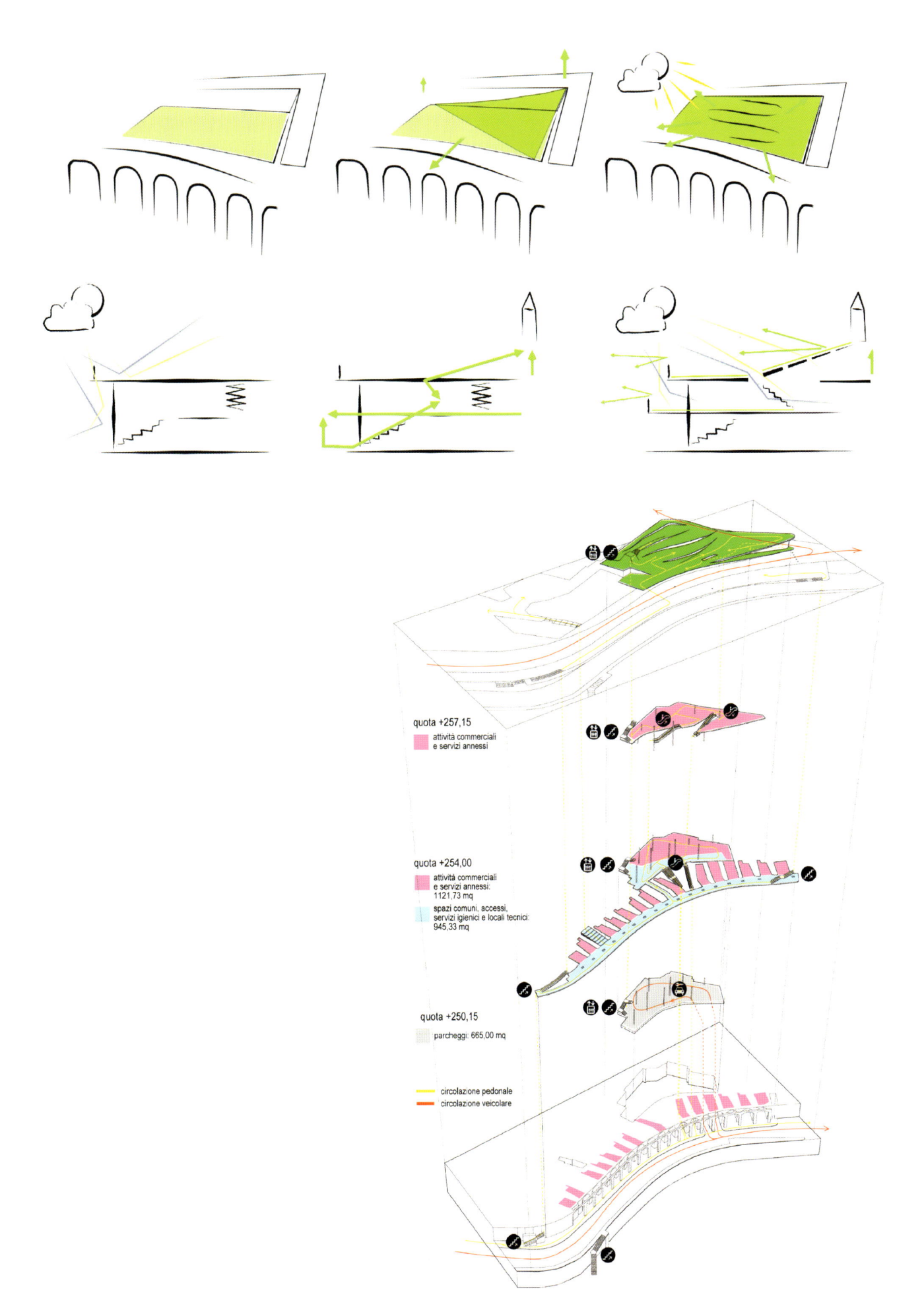

quota +257,15
attività commerciali
e servizi annessi

quota +254,00
attività commerciali
e servizi annessi:
1121,73 mq
spazi comuni, accessi,
servizi igienici e locali tecnici:
945,33 mq

quota +250,15
parcheggi: 665,00 mq

— circolazione pedonale
— circolazione veicolare

ARCHITECTURAL DIAGRAMS 251

URBAN STUDY beva

"REMARKABLE FEATURES WILL BE THE PURPOSE OF A PROJECT BASED ON THE IDENTITY OF THE AREA."

Visual perception sketches

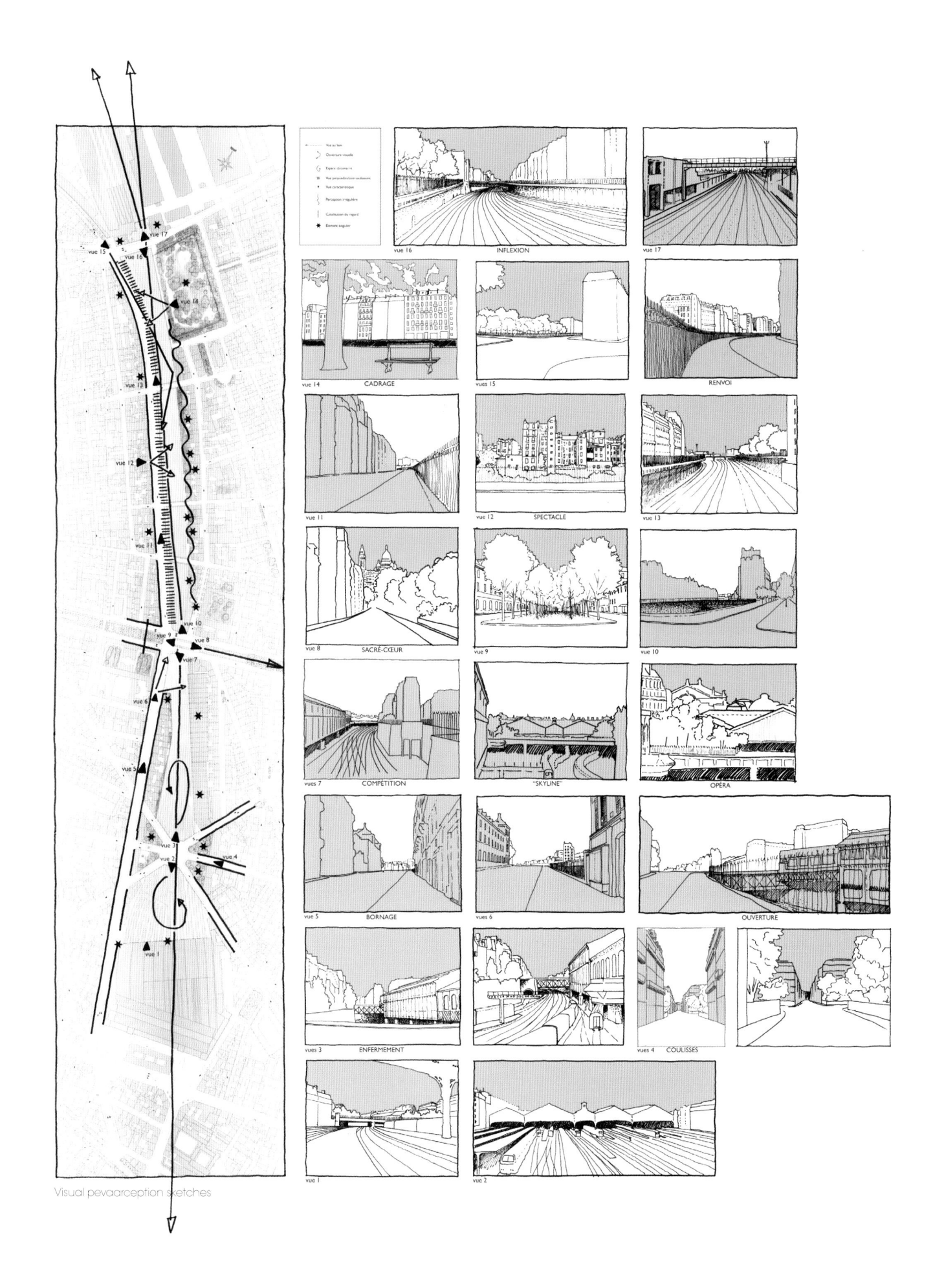

ARCHITECTURAL DIAGRAMS 253

VINARÒS PROJECT
Guallart Architects

"FOLLOWING THEIR INSTALLATION, PEOPLE WERE QUICK TO APPROPRIATE THE NEW MICRO-COASTS AND UTILIZE THEM IN A VARIETY OF WAYS."

ARCHITECTURAL DIAGRAMS 255

VOSSELVELD ONE ARCHITECTURE

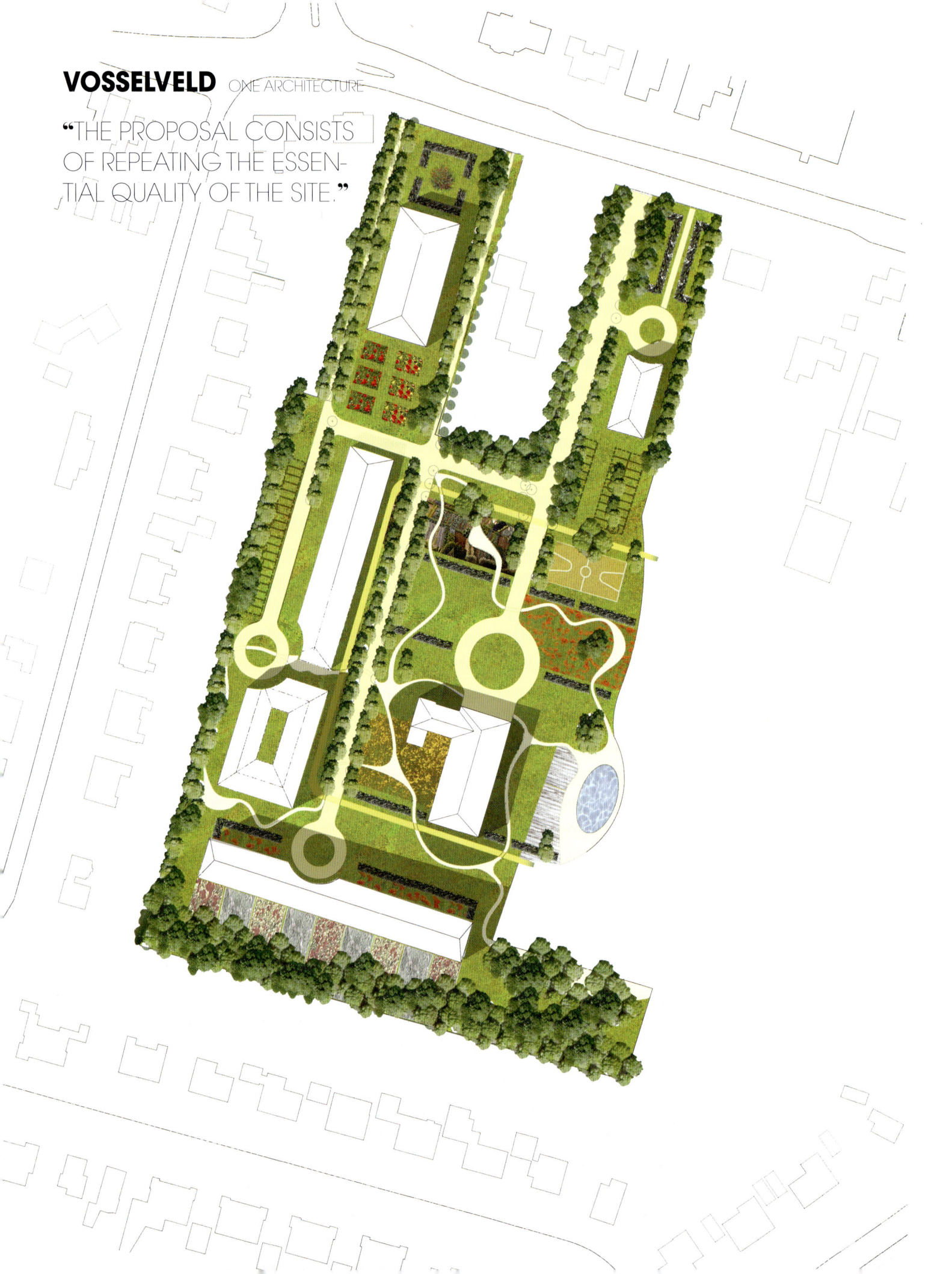

"THE PROPOSAL CONSISTS OF REPEATING THE ESSENTIAL QUALITY OF THE SITE."

existing

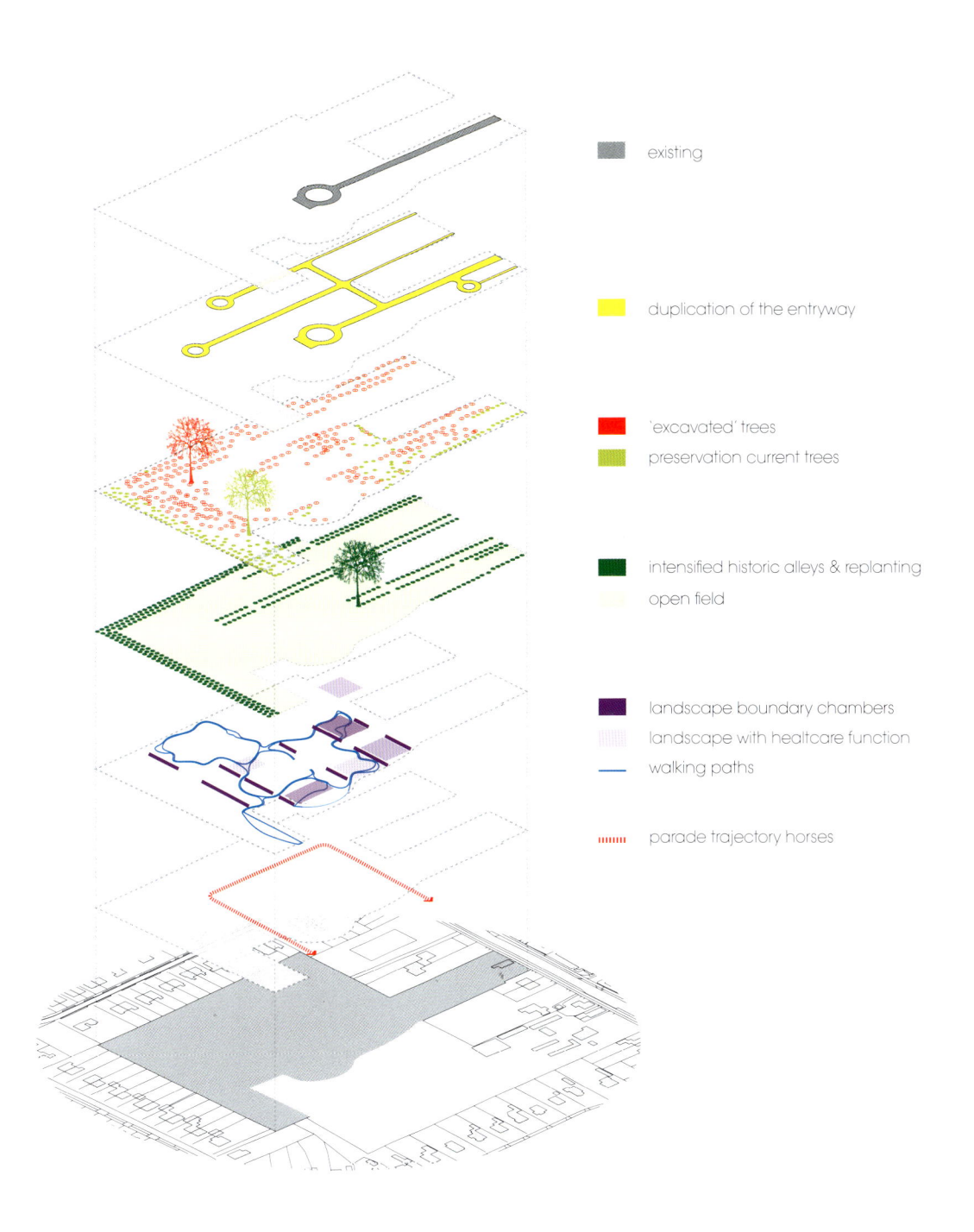

duplication of the entryway

'excavated' trees
preservation current trees

intensified historic alleys & replanting
open field

landscape boundary chambers
landscape with healtcare function
walking paths

parade trajectory horses

ARCHITECTURAL DIAGRAMS 257

WATERCOURSE
PEG office of landscape + architecture

"WE PROPOSE A NEW OPENLY CULTIVATED THIRD LANDSCAPE, SITUATED PHYSICALLY AND PSYCHICALLY BETWEEN THE LAGOON AND LANDFILL."

Step 1: Scale
Scale Venice's St. Mark's Square by Six times to fit the size of the Island of Sacca San Mattia. The conceptual result is a clearly programmed envelope and an indeterminate middle.

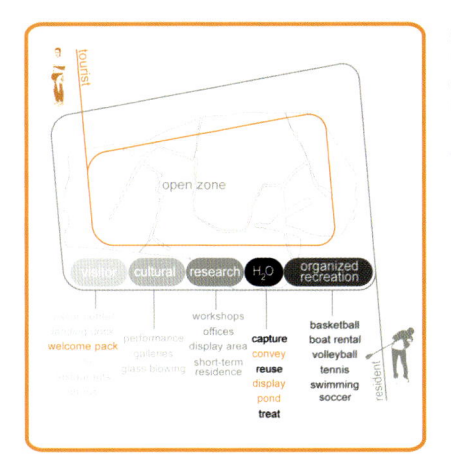

Step 2: Differentiate
Differentiate between the city-park edge and the water-park edge by contextualizing the envelope. Pack the regulated program into a 'channel' at the southern edge to intersect with Murano. Leave an unprogrammed open zone to the north.

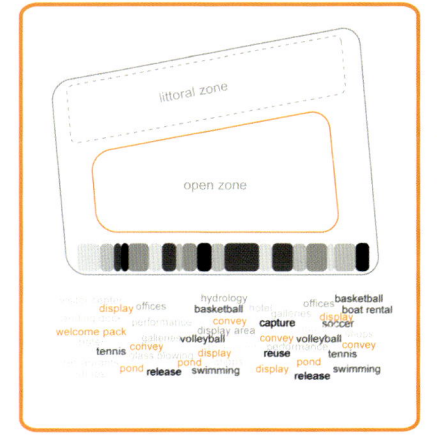

Step 3: Redistribute
Redistribute the program by weaving together resident, researcher and tourist. The new program 'DNA' determines maximum developable area but leaves the specific configuration undetermined.
Redistribute the landfill by re-grading it to a lower elevation, thereby creating an accessible edge and access to the littoral zone.

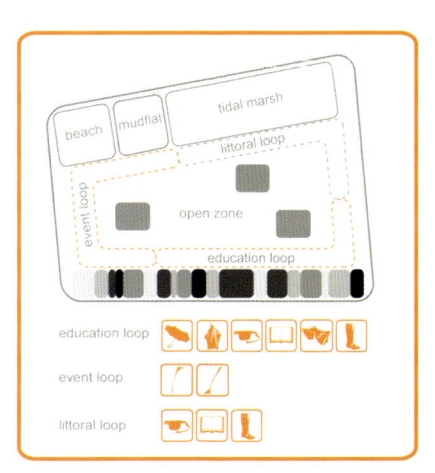

Step 4: Connect
Connect the three programmatic zones through three distinct 1-mile paths that engage the zones differently: the education loop, the event loop and th littoral loop.

ARCHITECTURAL DIAGRAMS 259

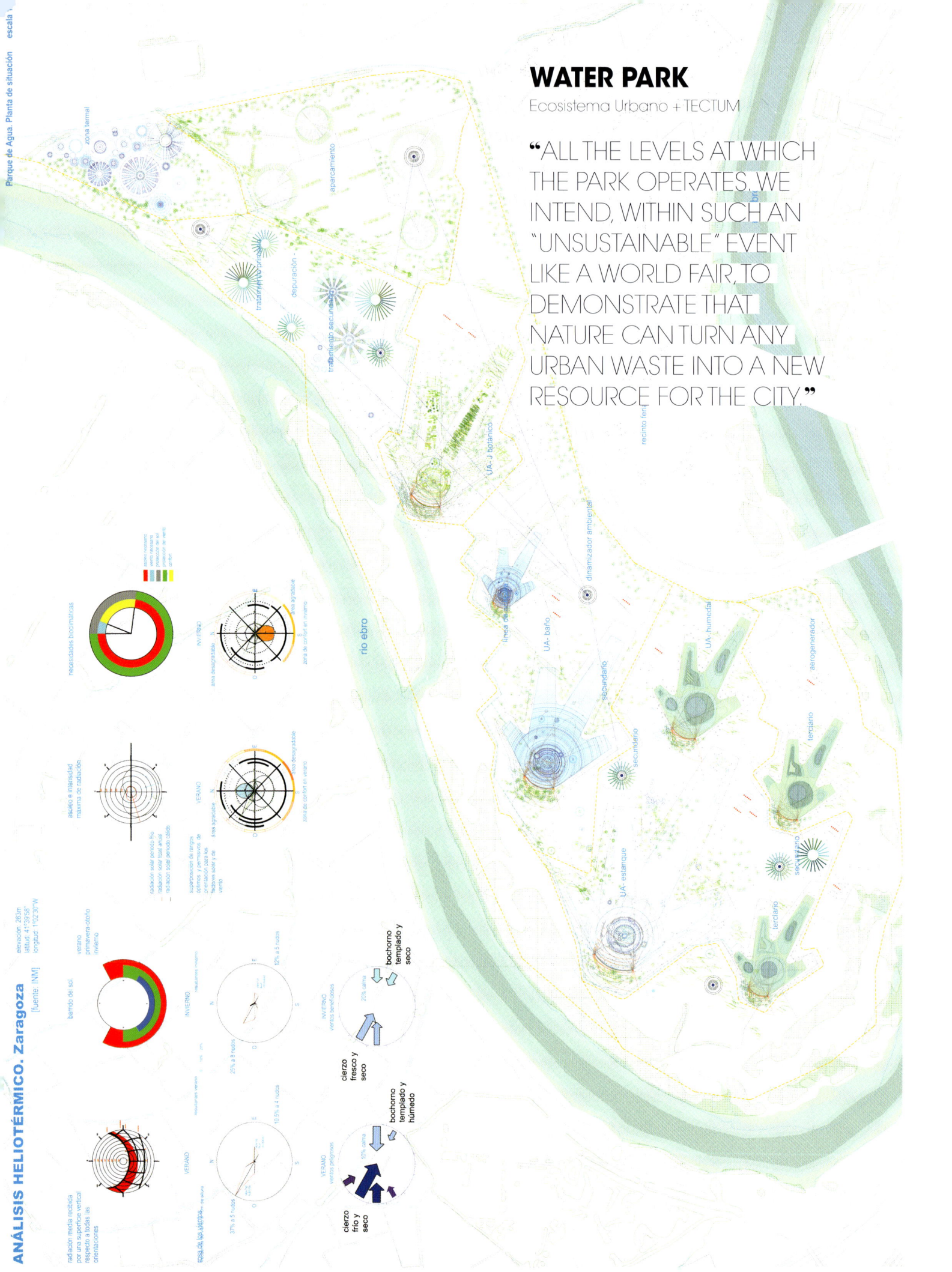

WATER PARK
Ecosistema Urbano + TECTUM

"ALL THE LEVELS AT WHICH THE PARK OPERATES, WE INTEND, WITHIN SUCH AN "UNSUSTAINABLE" EVENT LIKE A WORLD FAIR, TO DEMONSTRATE THAT NATURE CAN TURN ANY URBAN WASTE INTO A NEW RESOURCE FOR THE CITY."

North wind sweeping scale 1/20000

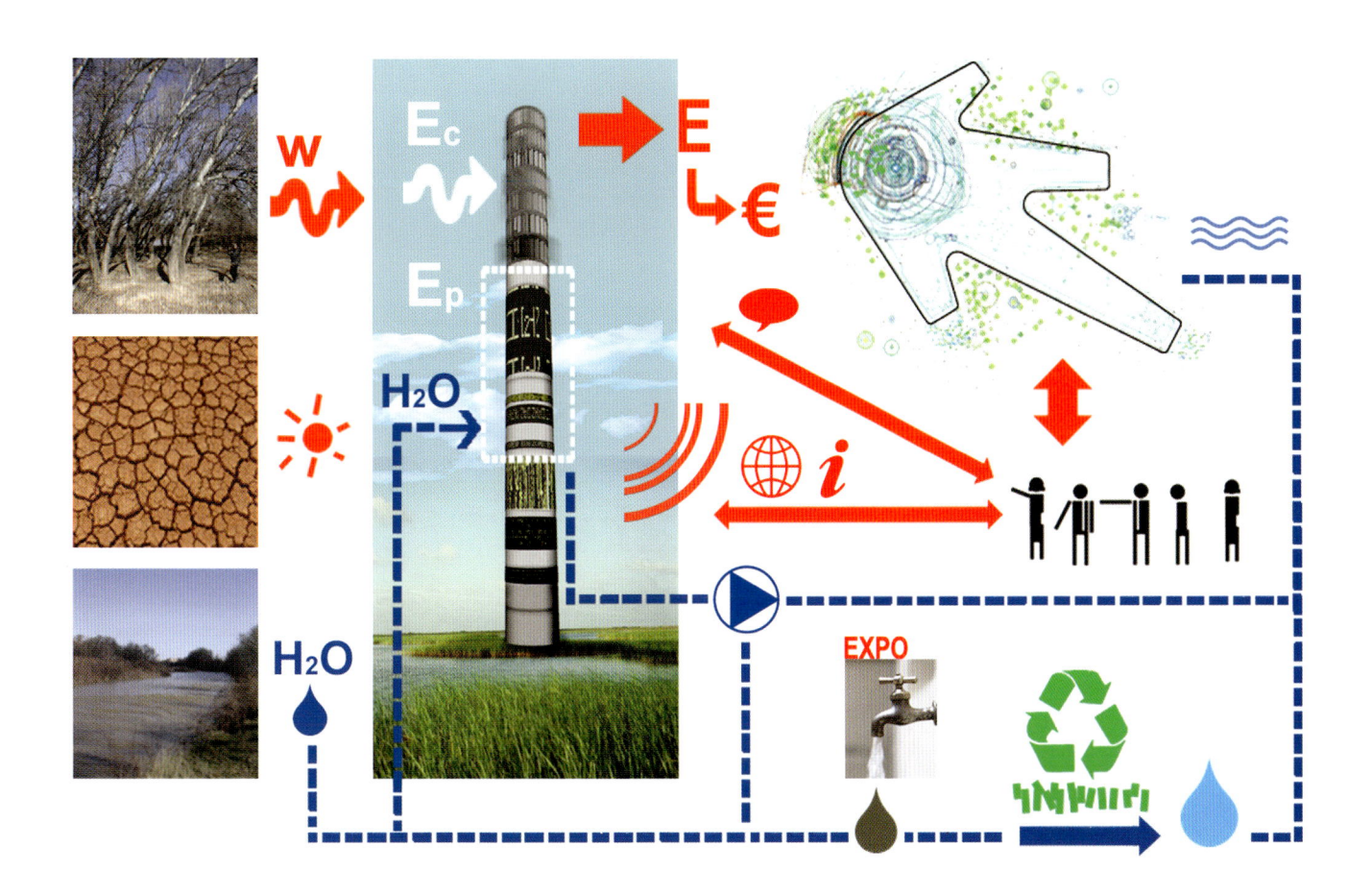

Flooding regimes scale 1/20000
Ebro river flood
Bathing areas
Pond
Botanical garden

ARCHITECTURAL DIAGRAMS 261

URBAN DESIGN

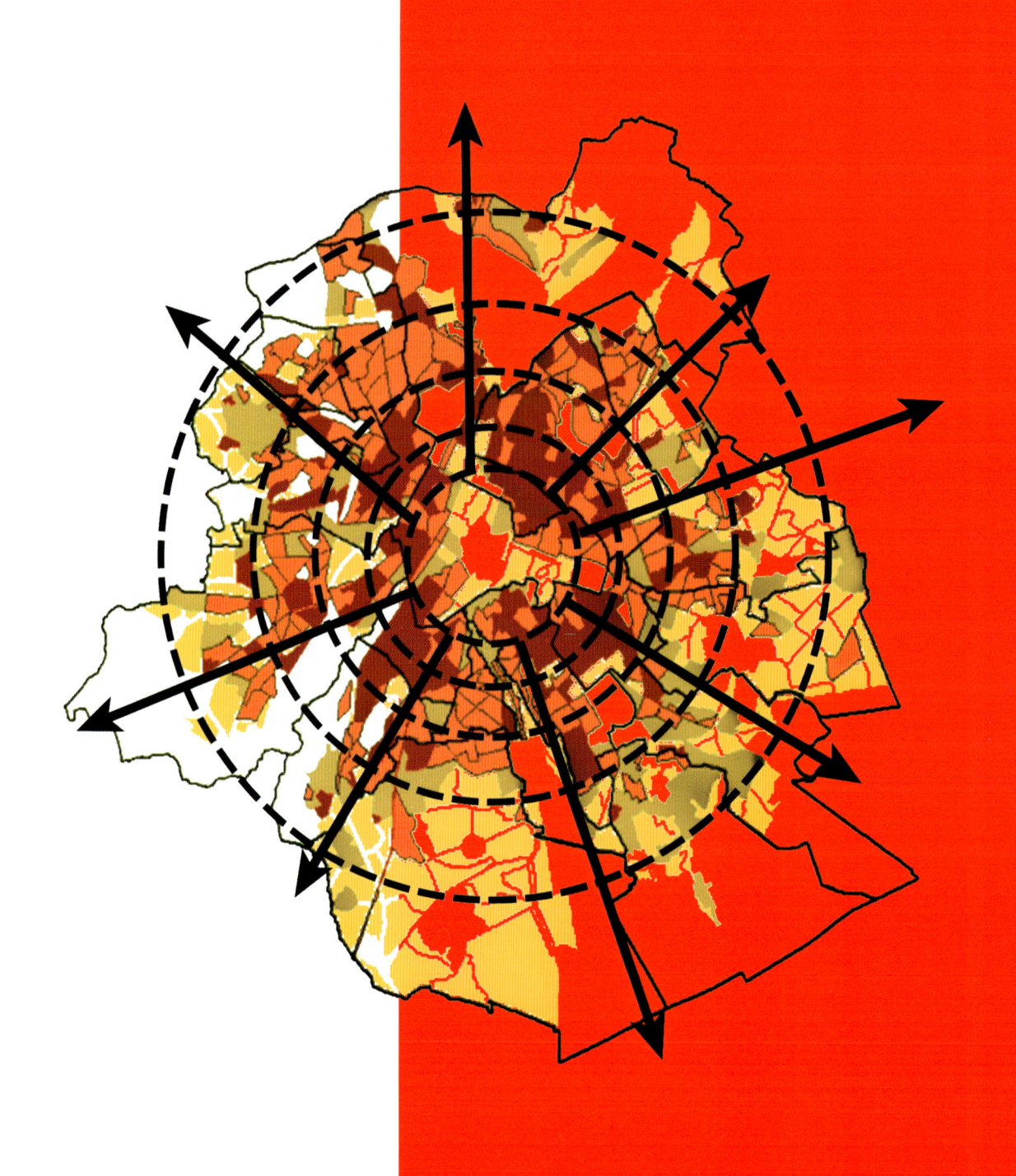

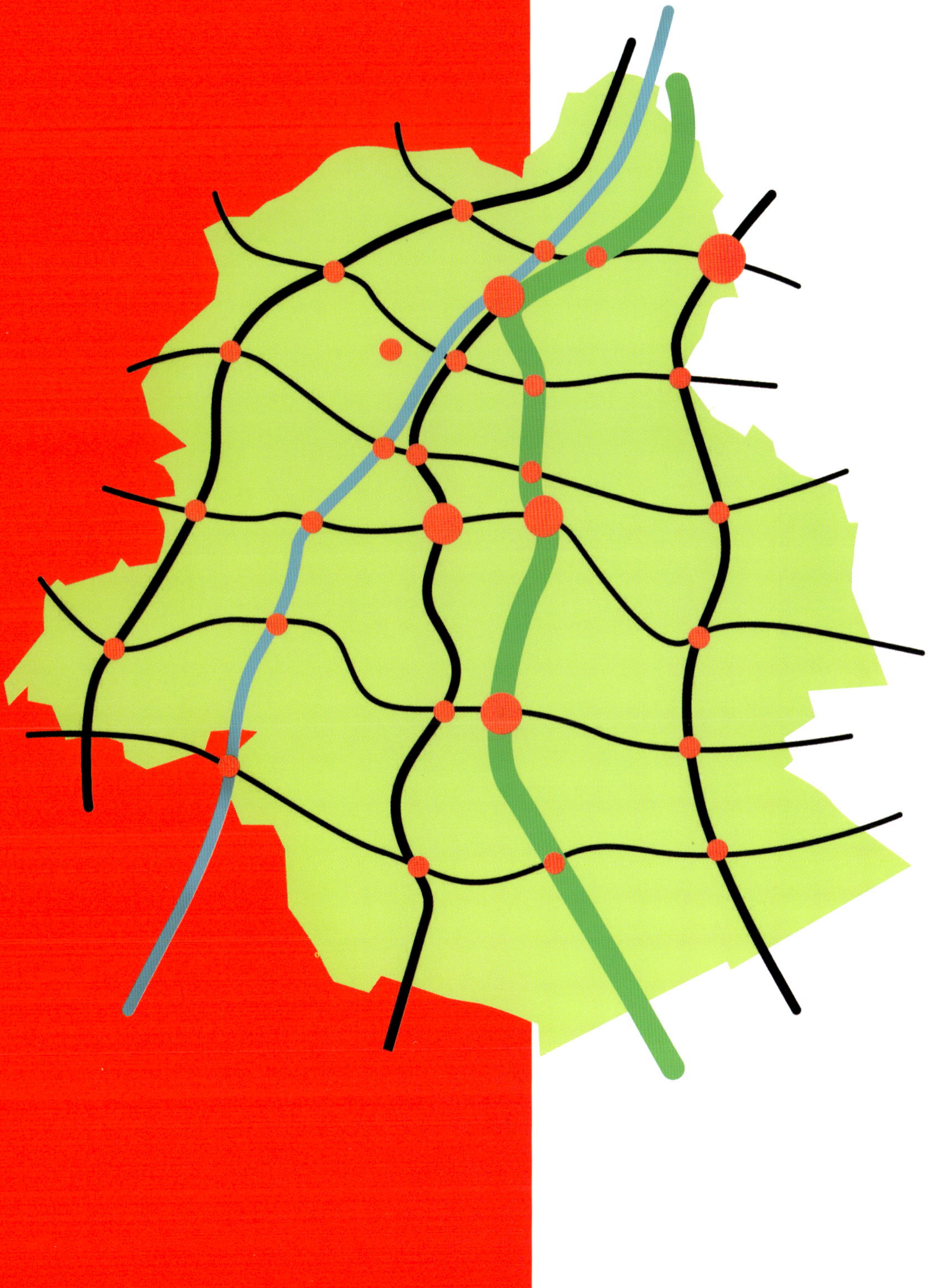

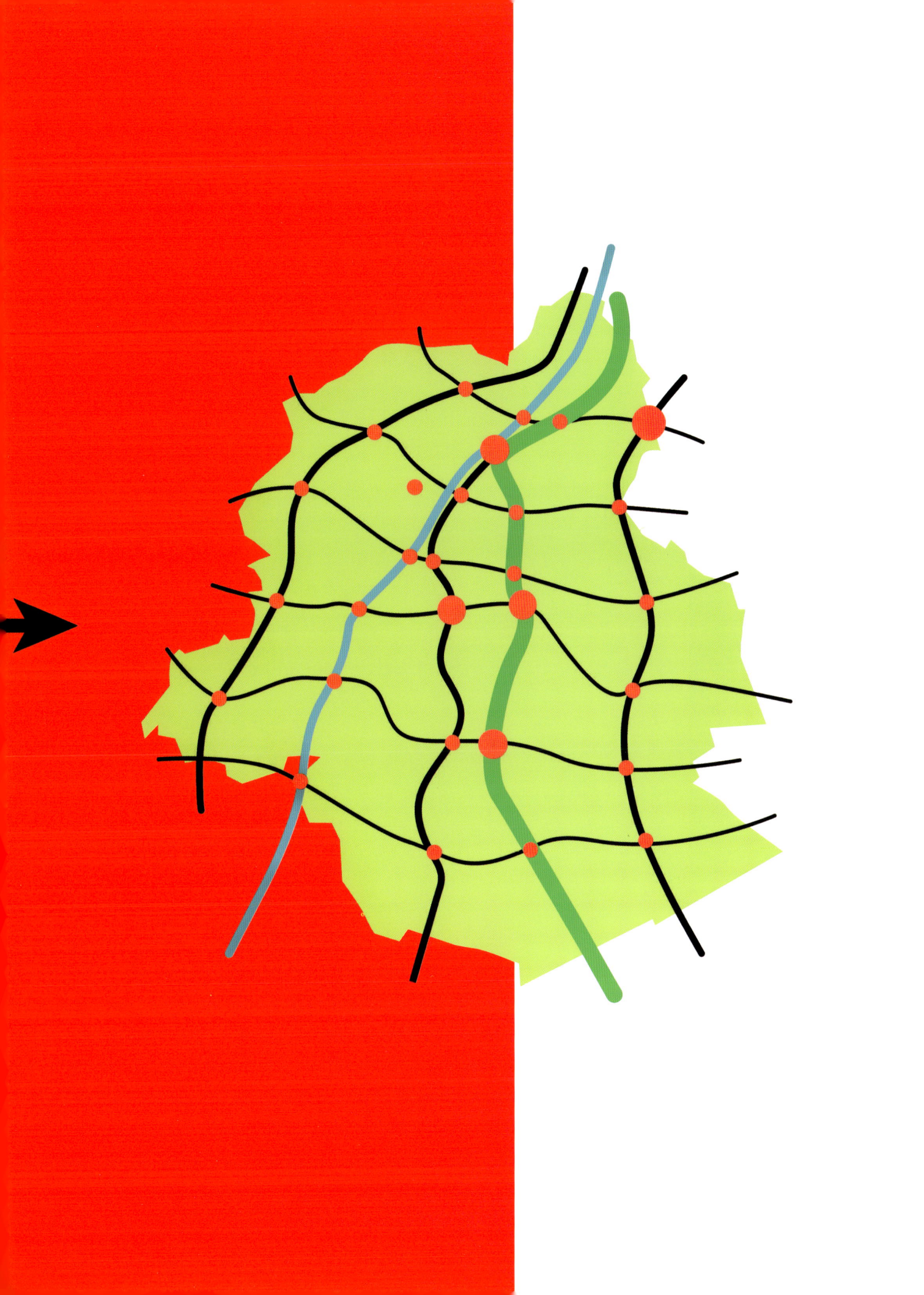

ALMERE HOUT ma0

"THE FOOTPRINT IS BOTH A SPACE THAT SEPARATES AND CONNECTS, BOTH A DENSE BOUNDARY ENCLOSING THE MICRO-CITIES AND A SPACE."

Strategy / proximity and identity

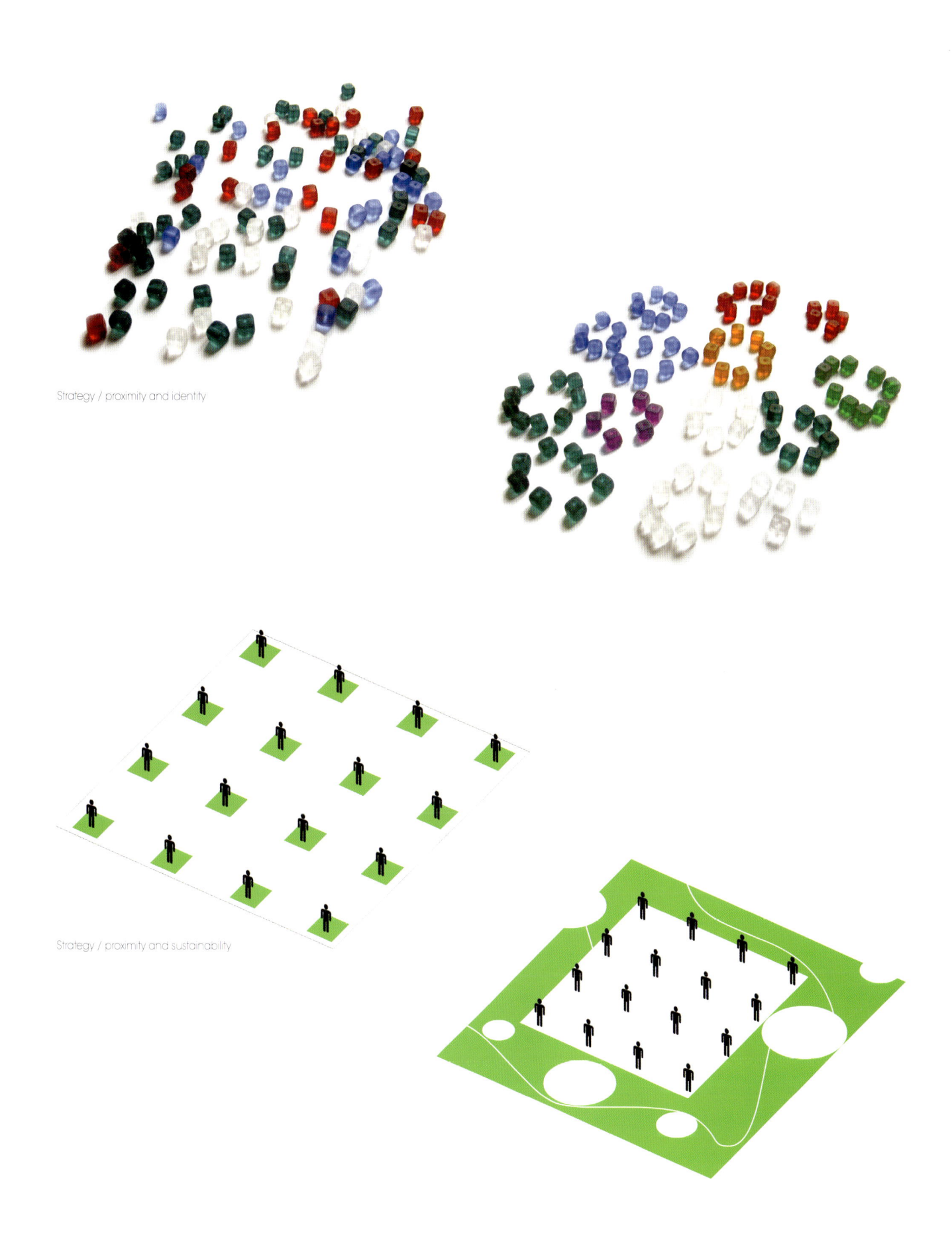

Strategy / proximity and sustainability

ARCHITECTURAL DIAGRAMS 265

BADAJOZ CH 852
Leon 11 ARCHITECTS

"THE PROJECT IS PART OF A TERRITORY MADE UP WITH DISJOINTED URBAN FRAGMENTS WITH SOCIAL PROBLEMS."

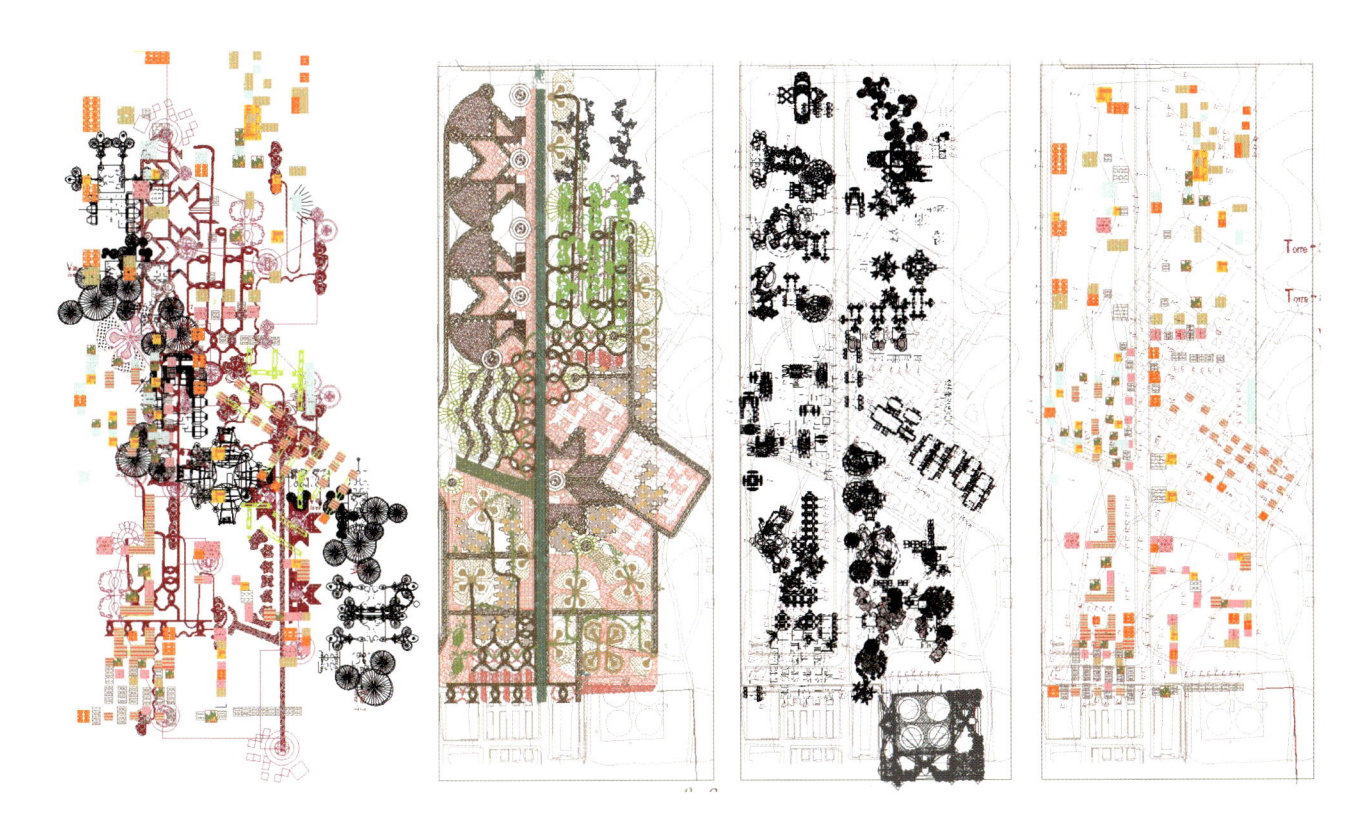

lounge and squares orchards parkin plastic park

tab elevations and floors of the artificial topographies

ARCHITECTURAL DIAGRAMS 267

BRUSSELS ADMINISTRATIVE CITY JDS Architects

"THE TASK ON THIS PROJECT WILL BE TO EMBRACE AND NOURISH A MODERN LIFE BASED ON DIVERSITY, INDIVIDUALITY AND IDENTITY."

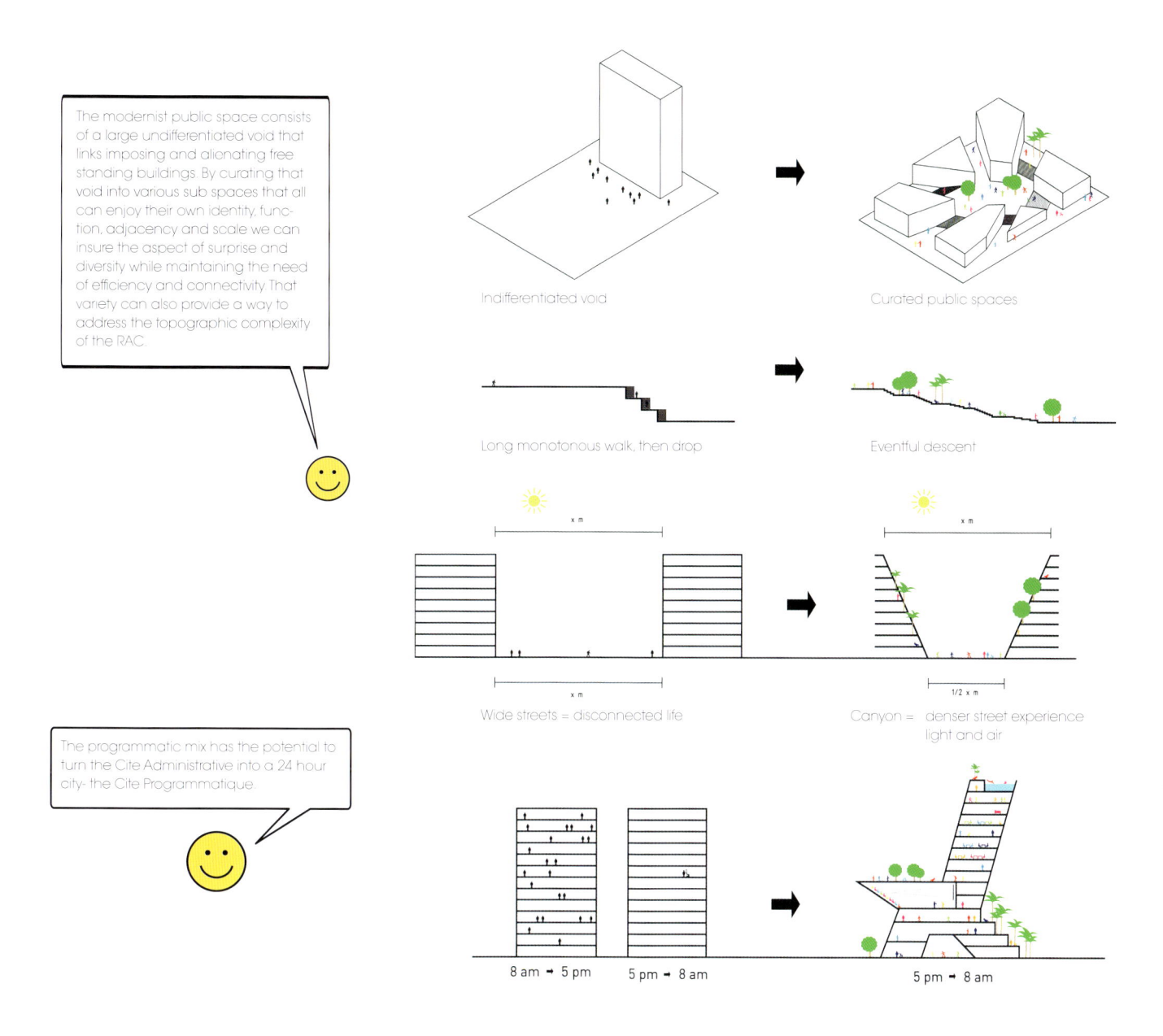

The modernist public space consists of a large undifferentiated void that links imposing and alienating free standing buildings. By curating that void into various sub spaces that all can enjoy their own identity, function, adjacency and scale we can insure the aspect of surprise and diversity while maintaining the need of efficiency and connectivity. That variety can also provide a way to address the topographic complexity of the RAC.

Indifferentiated void → Curated public spaces

Long monotonous walk, then drop → Eventful descent

Wide streets = disconnected life → Canyon = denser street experience light and air

The programmatic mix has the potential to turn the Cite Administrative into a 24 hour city- the Cite Programmatique.

8 am → 5 pm   5 pm → 8 am   5 pm → 8 am

ARCHITECTURAL DIAGRAMS 269

BRUXELLES LANDS-FLOW
Actar Arquitectura

"HOT POINTS AS NODAL ELEMENTS OF THE SYSTEM. THEY FOCUS THE ACTIVITY AND FLOWS THAT INTENSIFY URBAN RELATIONS."

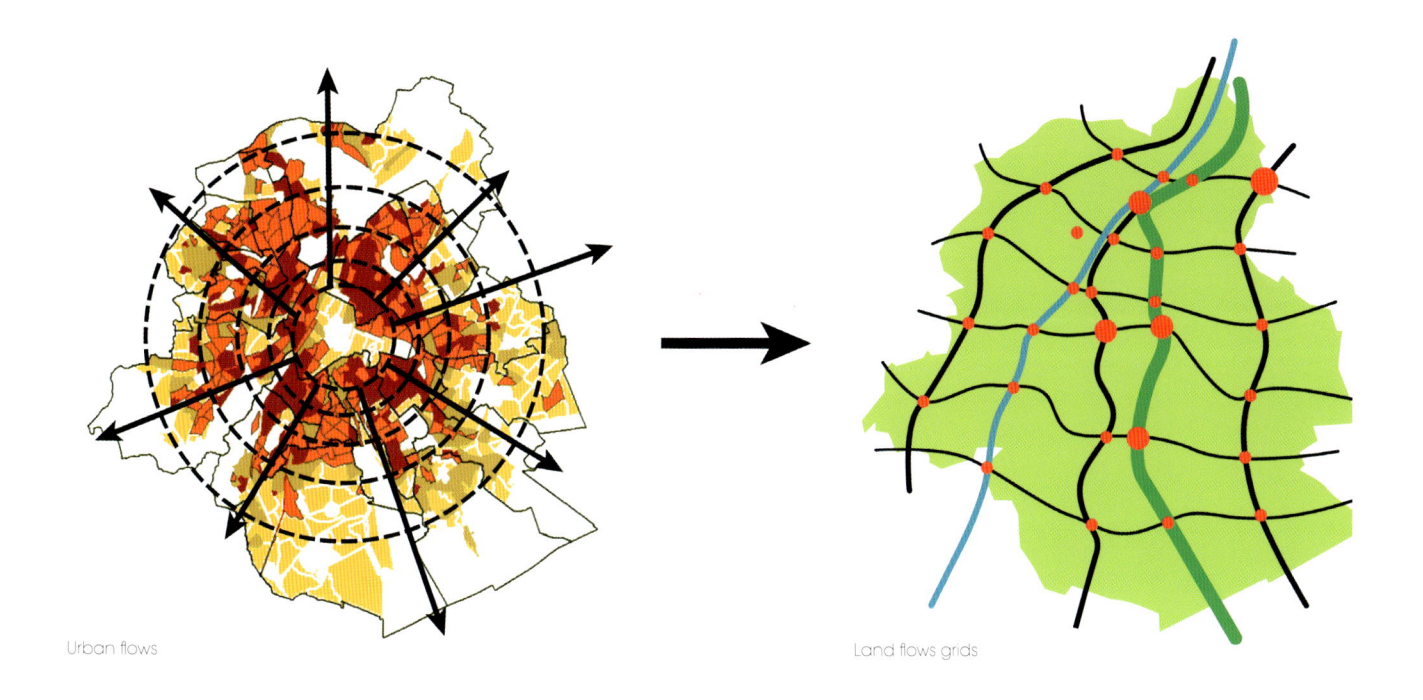

Urban flows

Land flows grids

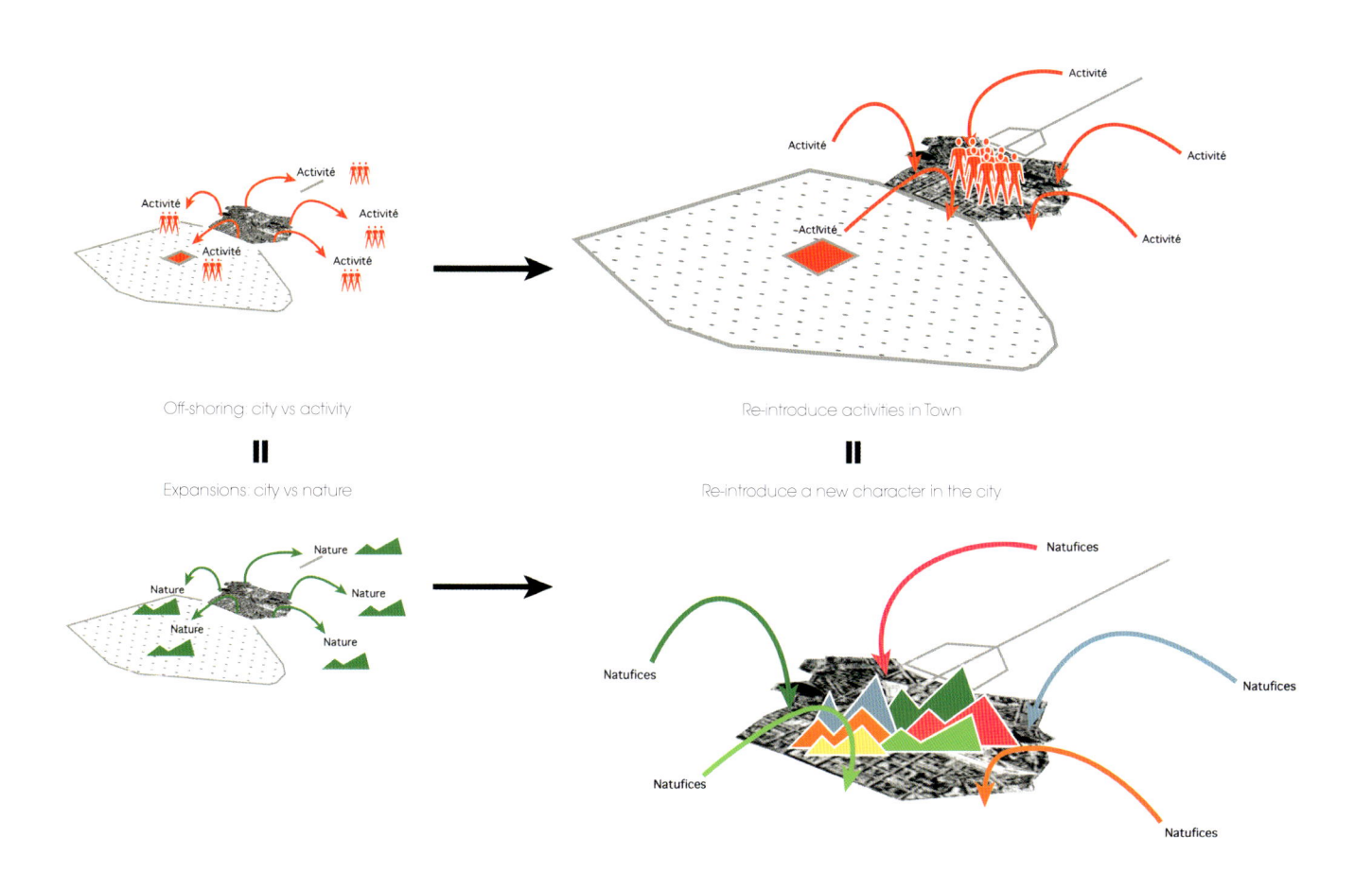

Off-shoring: city vs activity

=

Expansions: city vs nature

Re-introduce activities in Town

=

Re-introduce a new character in the city

ARCHITECTURAL DIAGRAMS 271

CAMPUS BORDEAUX
Tania Concko Architects

"TO OPEN UP, DIVERSITY, DENSITY, ENHANCE THE WHOLE AREA."

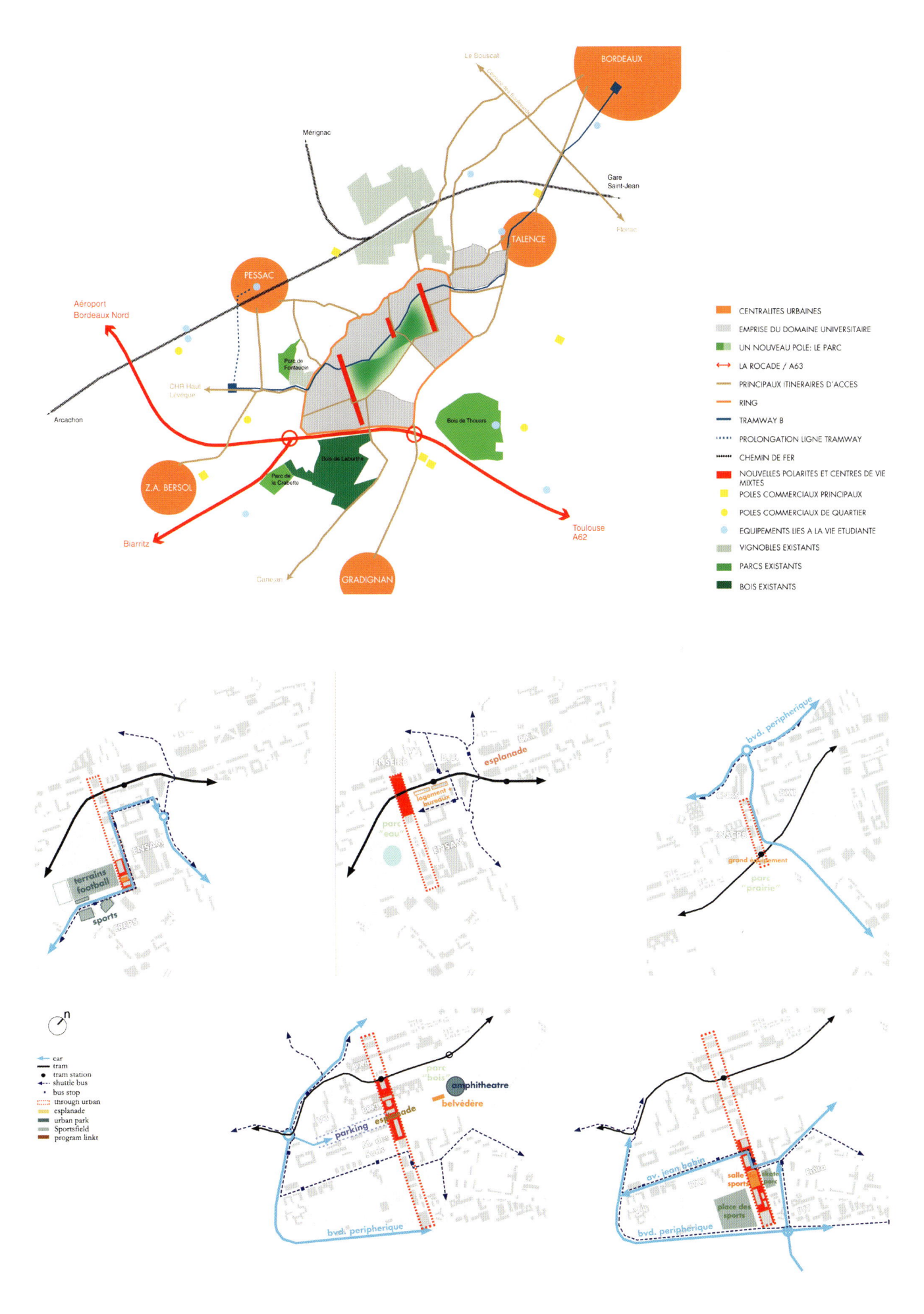

ARCHITECTURAL DIAGRAMS 273

CARLSBERG VORES BY

Leon 11 ARCHITECTS

"AN OPEN URBANISM IN WHICH THE CITY AND THE CITIZIENS COULD DE-TERMINATE STEP BY STEP, THEIR OWN DEVELOPING PARAMETERS."

GRADIENT 02 »   · technology ·

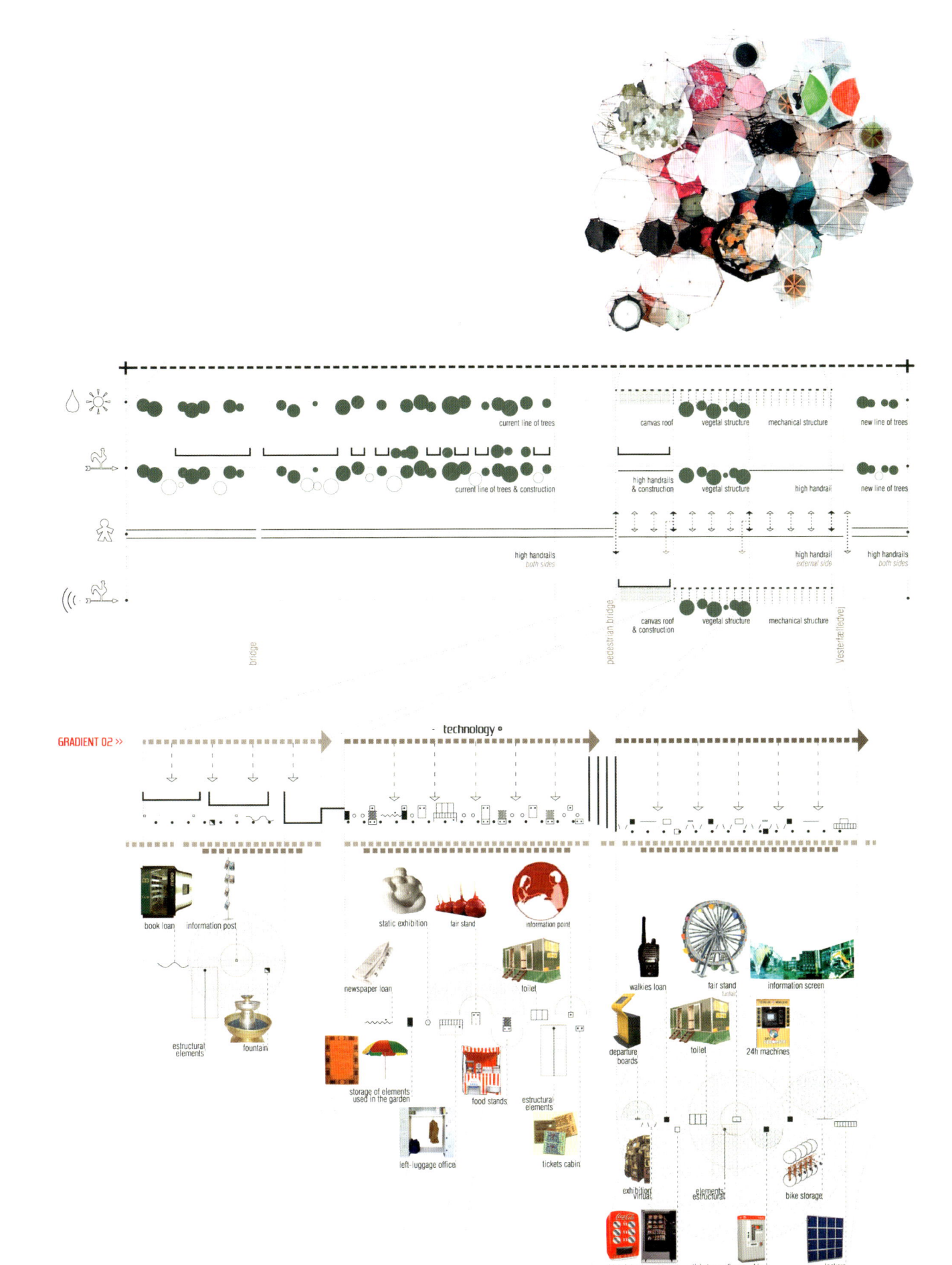

| book loan | information post | | static exhibition | fair stand | information point | | walkies loan | fair stand | information screen |

newspaper loan | toilet | departure boards | toilet | 24h machines

estructural elements | fountain | storage of elements used in the garden | food stands | estructural elements

left-luggage office | tickets cabin | exhibition virtual | elements estructural | bike storage

drink & food machines | tickets vending machine | lockers

ARCHITECTURAL DIAGRAMS 275

CBO COTTBUS plattformberlin

"THE DEVELOPMENT OF THE EXISTING INDUSTRIAL FACILITIES OFFERS THE POTENTIAL OF A CONTROLLED MUTATION."

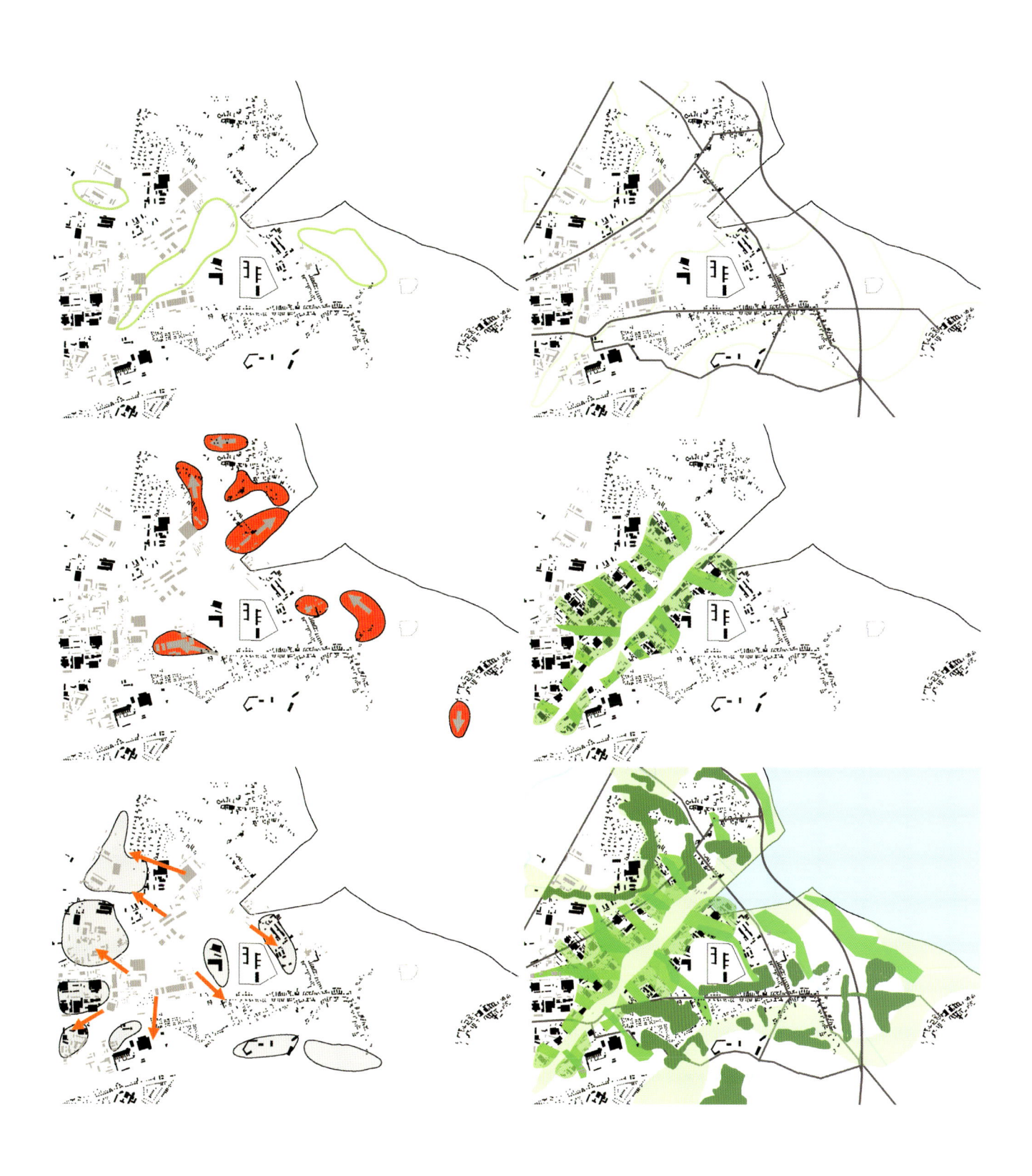

ARCHITECTURAL DIAGRAMS 277

CIPPS 2TR ARCHITETTURA

"IT AIMS TO IDENTIFY AN INNOVATIVE CONCEPT FOR WHAT IS TO BECOME A HUB OF ECONOMIC DEVELOPMENT."

COMPARTO A
COMPARTO B
COMPARTO C
COMPARTO D
COMPARTO E

278 URBAN DESIGN

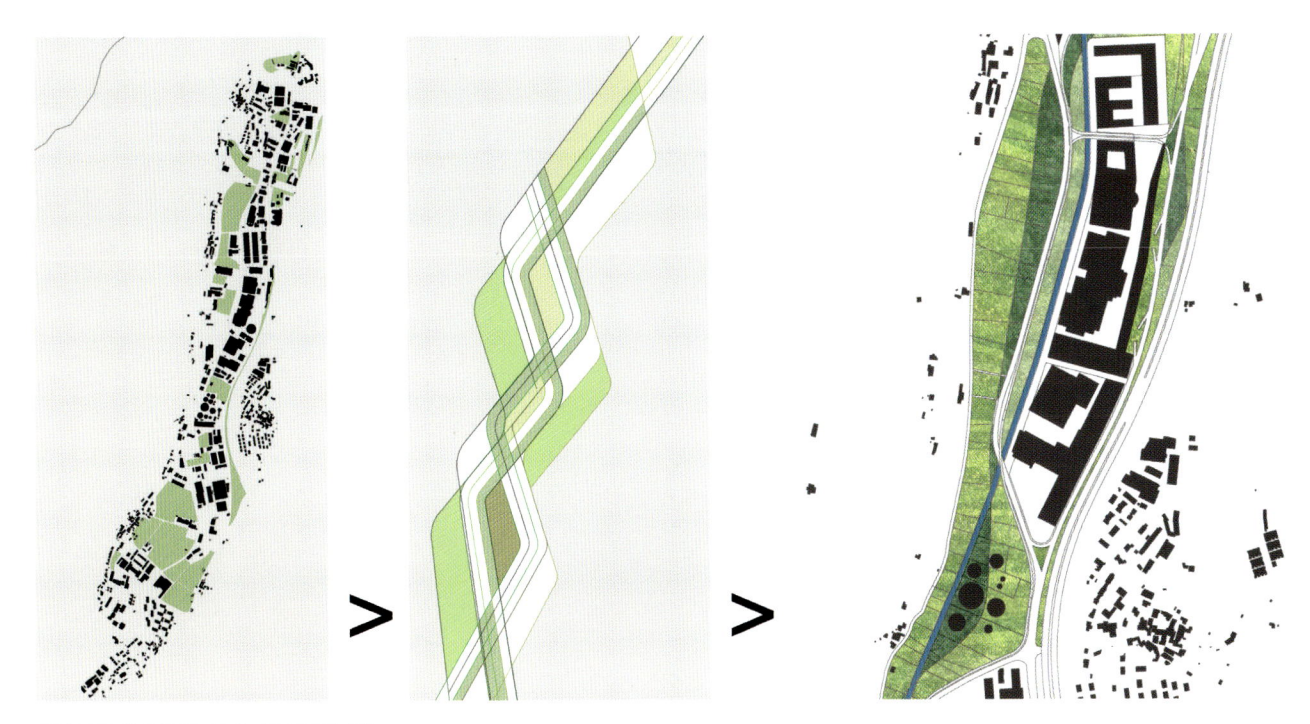

Concept - Green structure - Road network

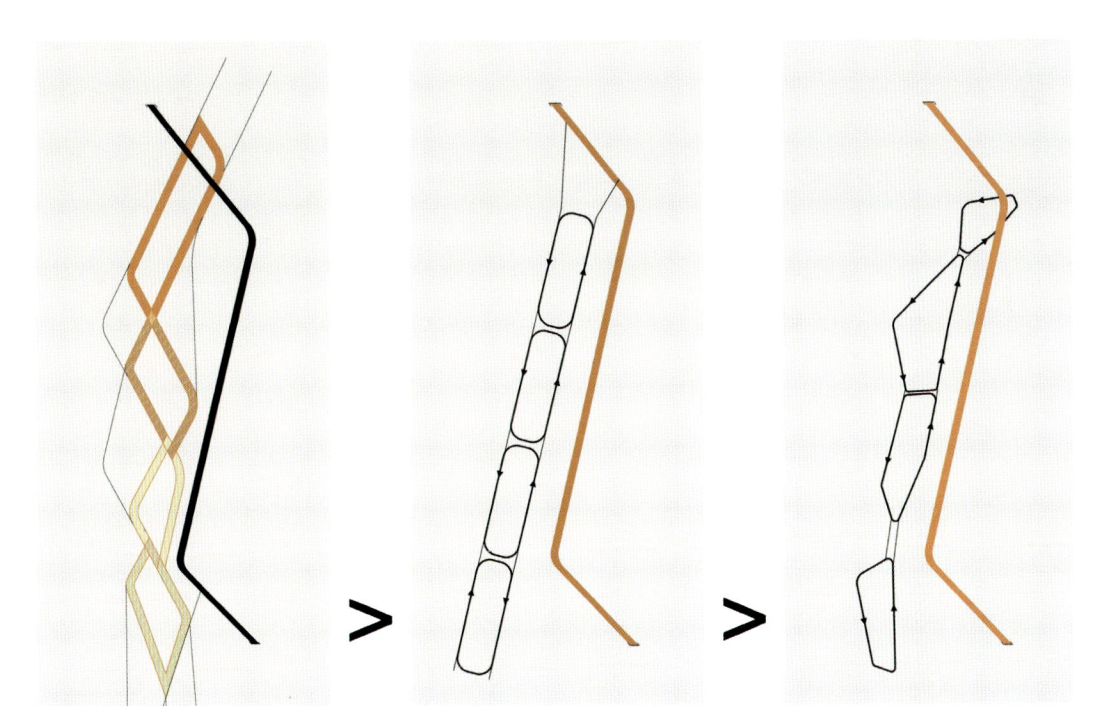

ARCHITECTURAL DIAGRAMS 279

CONTEMPORARY RAUMPLAN EBPC

"PECULIARITY OF THE PROJECT IS TO CONSIDER THE SURROUNDING LANDSCAPE MATERIAL COMPOSITION AS A NEW LAYER TO BASE THE MAIN STRUCTURE ON."

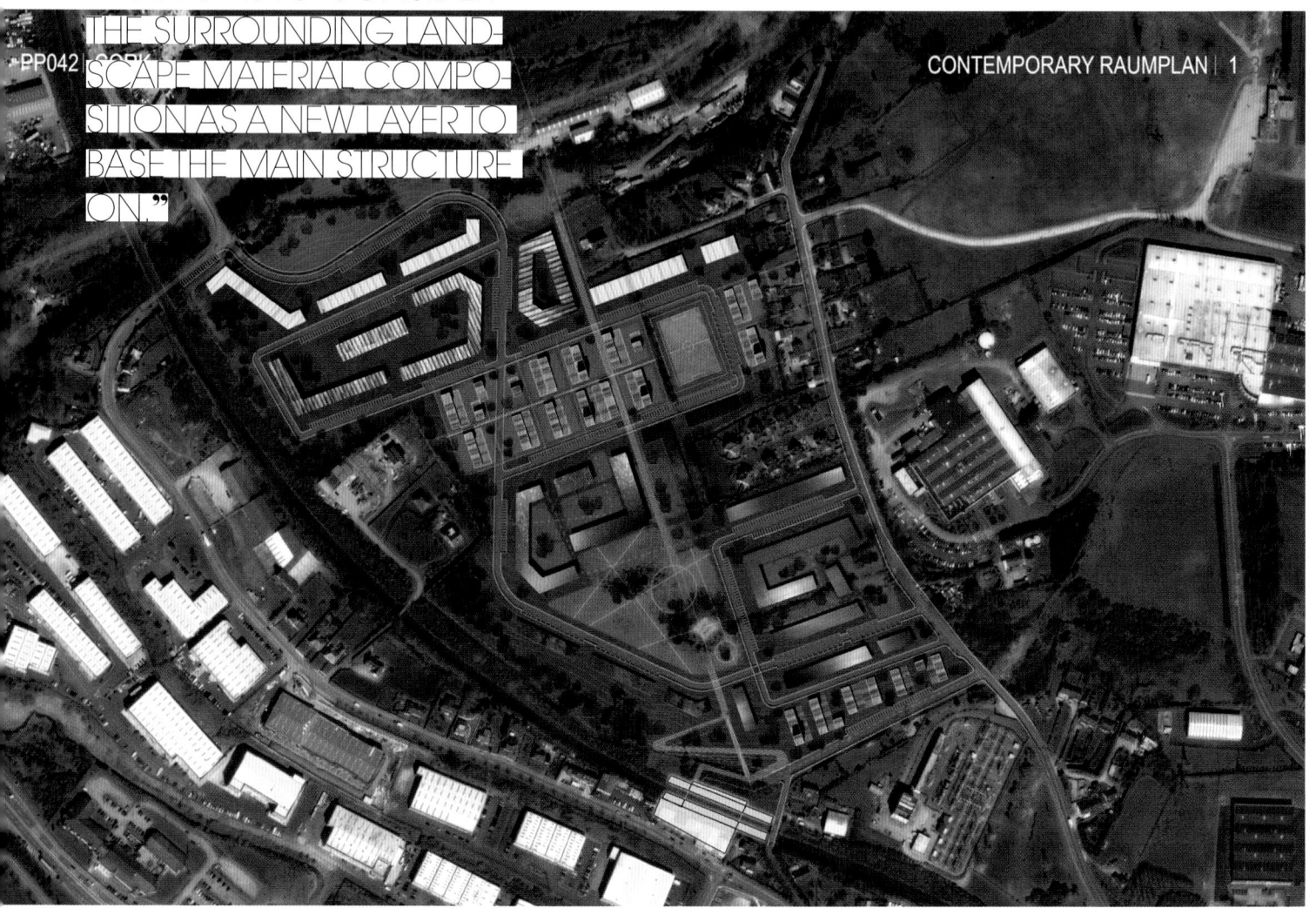

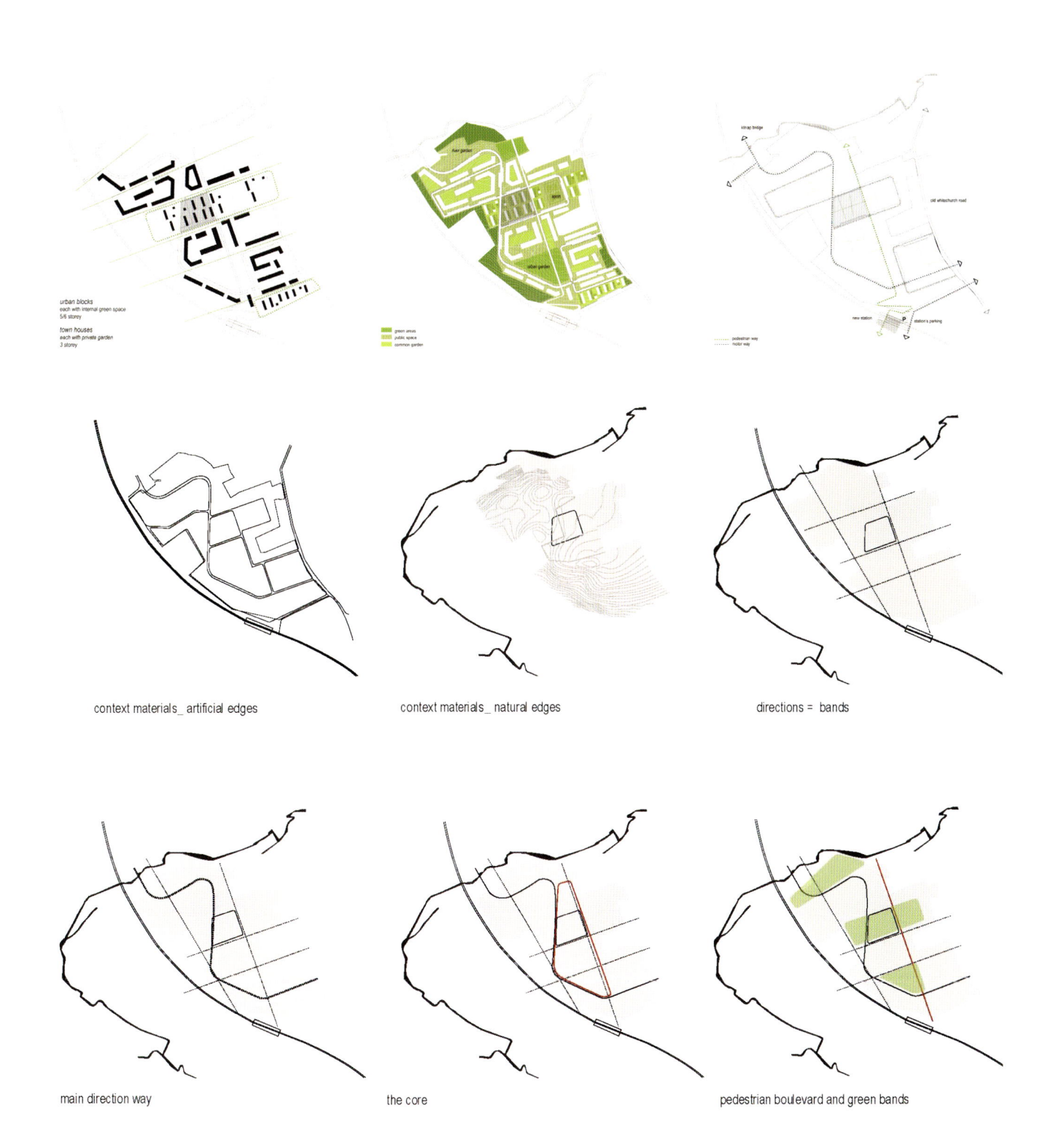

urban blocks
each with internal green space
5/6 storey

town houses
each with private garden
3 storey

green areas
public space
common garden

pedestrian way
motor way

context materials_ artificial edges

context materials_ natural edges

directions = bands

main direction way

the core

pedestrian boulevard and green bands

ARCHITECTURAL DIAGRAMS

CUMULUS
SMAQ

"AN URBAN STRATEGY THAT CONCEIVES PUBLIC SPACES AS RELATED TO THE ENVIRONMENTAL DYNAMICS OF NORTHERN LIVING."

Modernist + Old Town Diagram
Modernist dwelling and/or inhabiting the sky

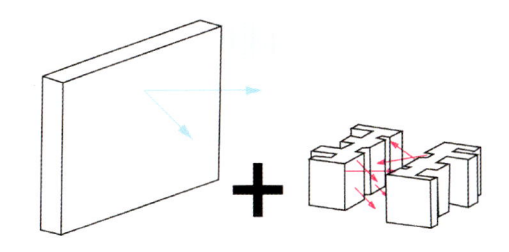

Combining modernist panoramic view and old town intimate relationship

Inventory | it's all there
Urban Programatic Diagrams

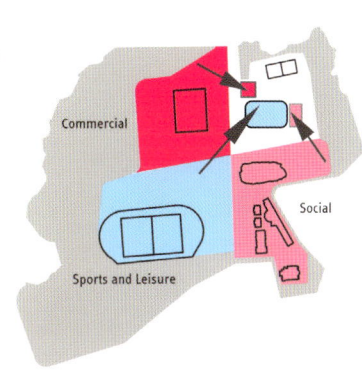

4 programmatic fields and crossover as initial

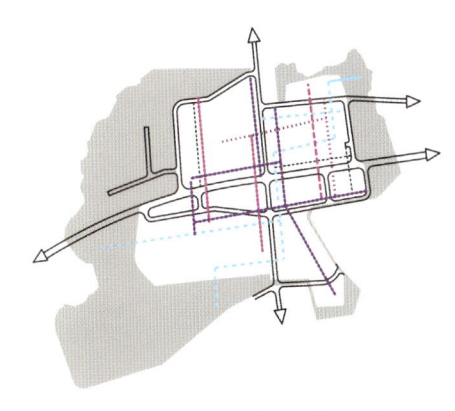

Web of urban roads and pedestrian path supports horizontallity of movements

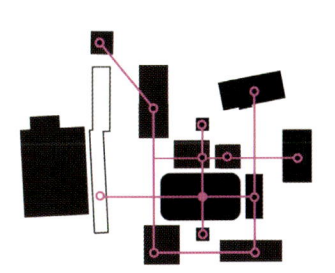

Connections and relations of programmes

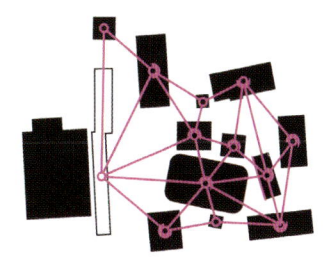

Adjustments of programmes
to site boundaries and through rotation of the central ice skating rink for better connectivity

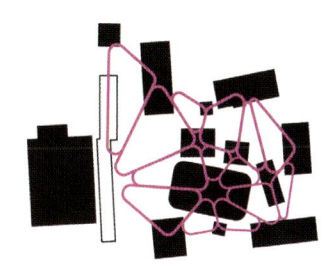

Resulting spaces of interaction

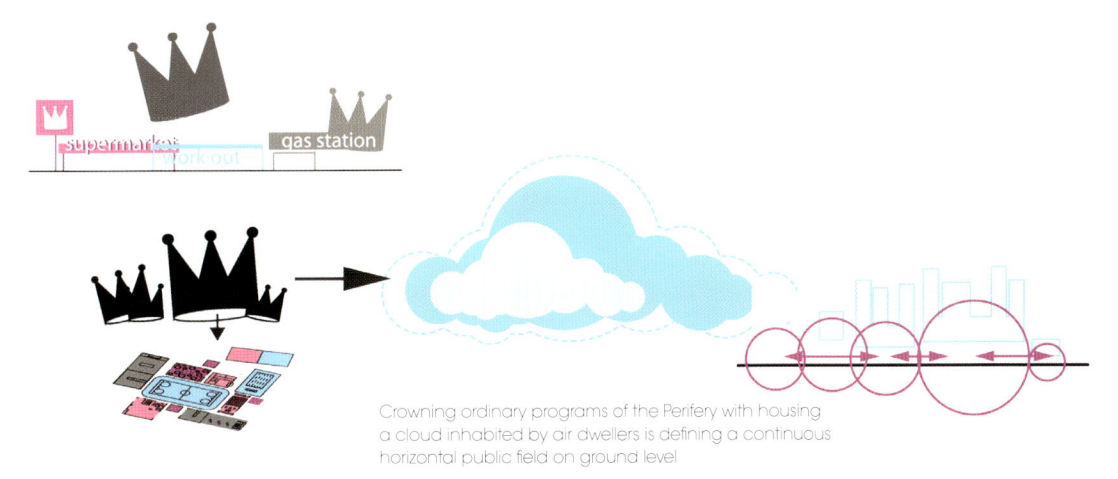

Crowning ordinary programs of the Perifery with housing a cloud inhabited by air dwellers is defining a continuous horizontal public field on ground level.

Urban Programatic Diagrams

ARCHITECTURAL DIAGRAMS 283

CRYSTAL PALACE
mxg architects

competition area

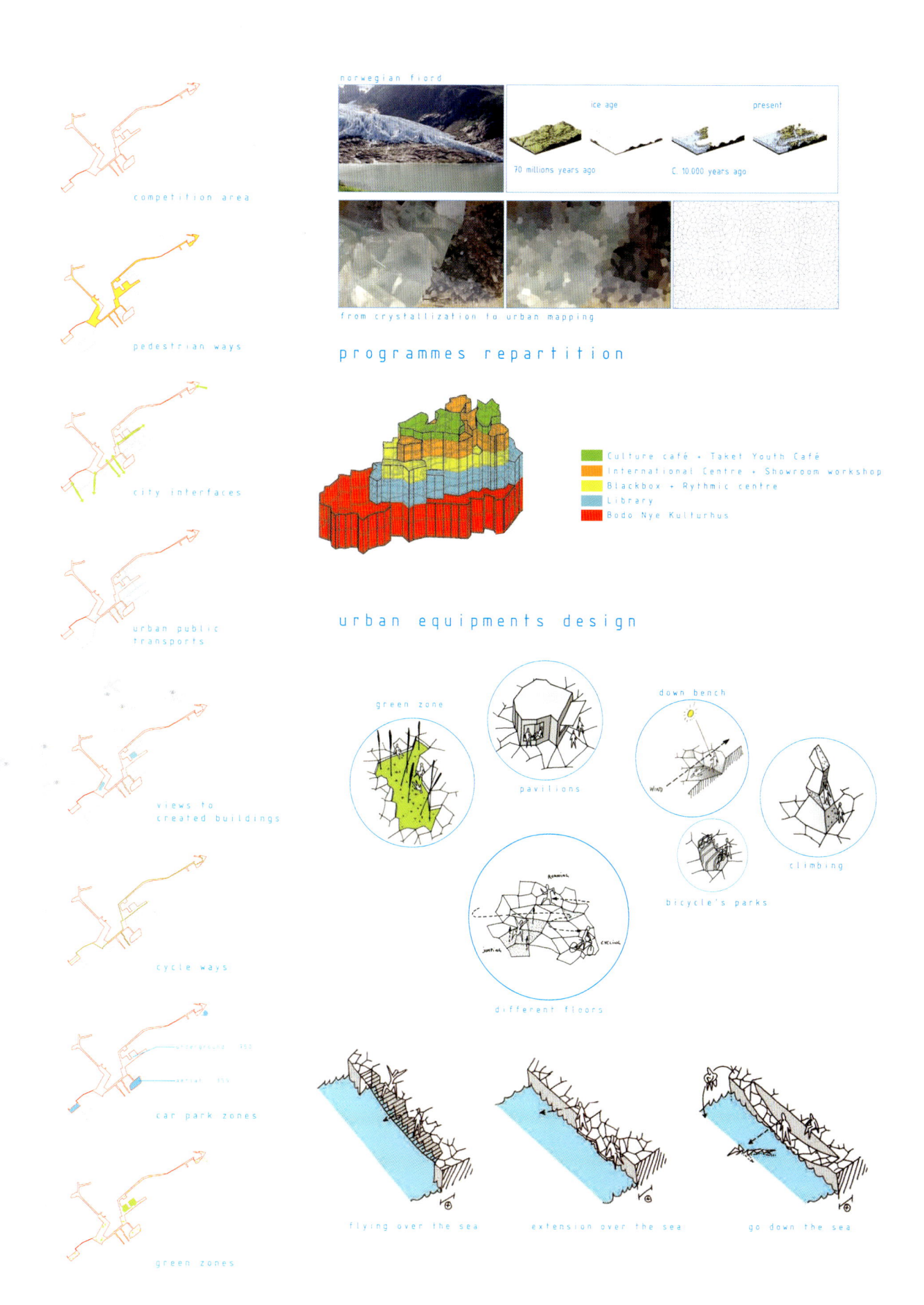

pedestrian ways

city interfaces

urban public transports

views to created buildings

cycle ways

car park zones

green zones

norwegian fiord

ice age | present
70 millions years ago | C. 10.000 years ago

from crystallization to urban mapping

programmes repartition

- Culture café + Taket Youth Café
- International Centre + Showroom workshop
- Blackbox + Rythmic centre
- Library
- Bodo Nye Kulturhus

urban equipments design

green zone

pavilions

down bench

climbing

bicycle's parks

different floors

flying over the sea

extension over the sea

go down the sea

ARCHITECTURAL DIAGRAMS 285

DOTSANDLOOPS SMAQ

"THE APARTMENT ACTS AS THE ARRIVING BY CAR AND THE GOING OUTDOORS INTO THE LANDSCAPE."

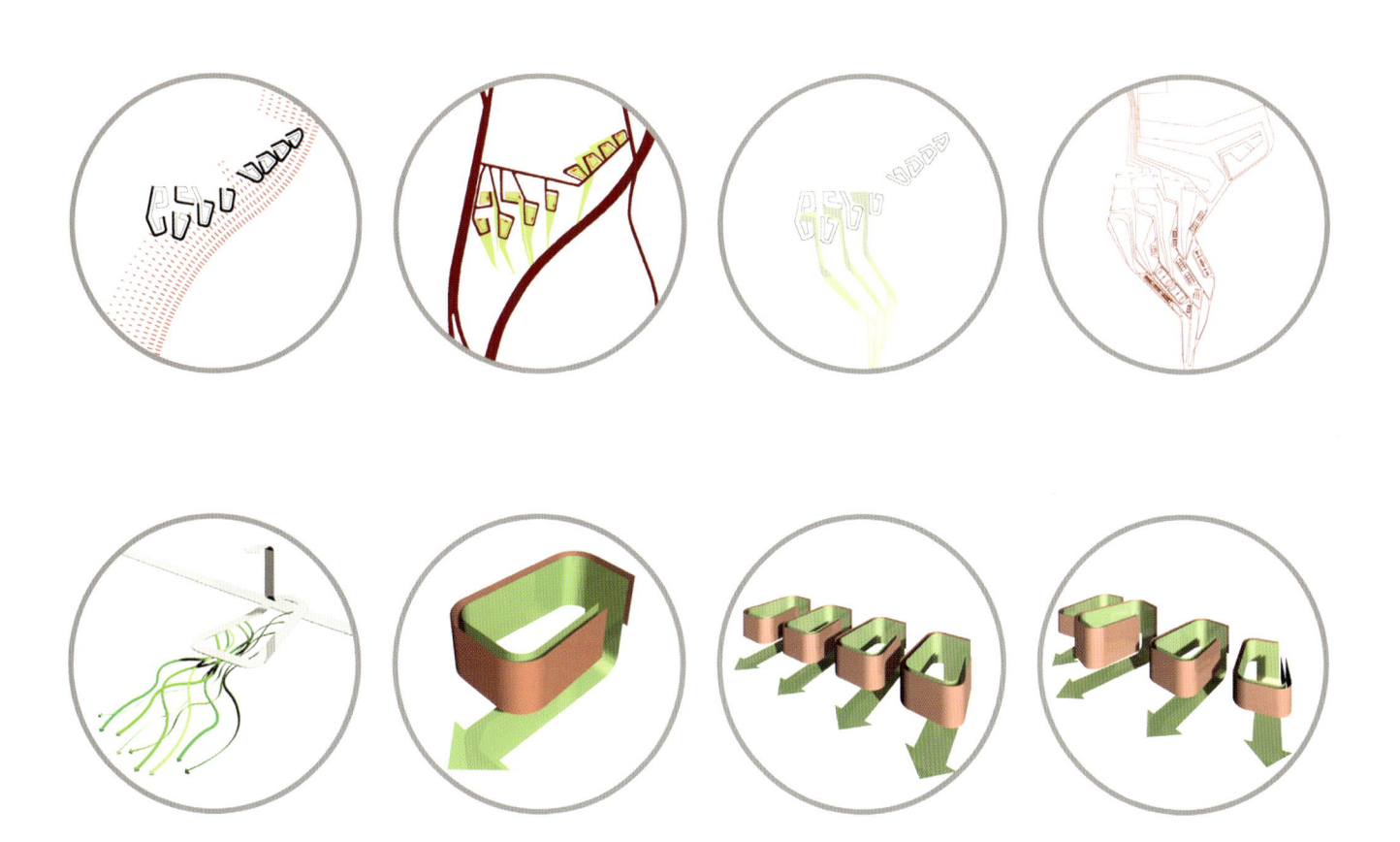

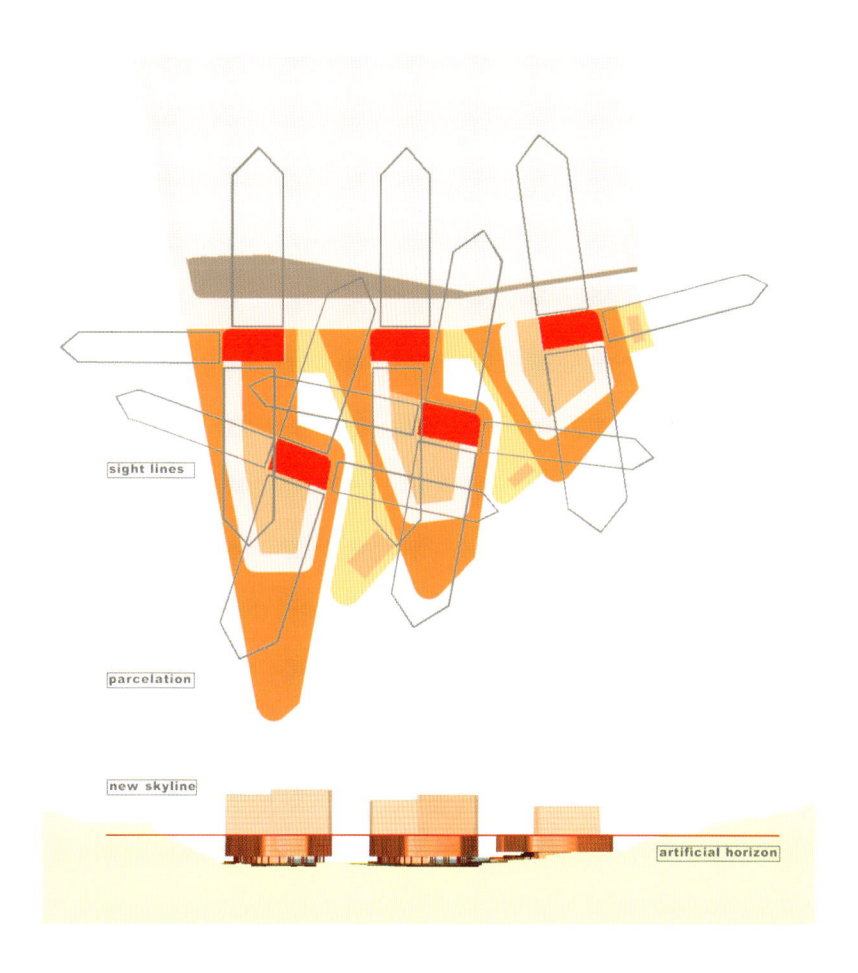

sight lines

parcelation

new skyline

artificial horizon

ARCHITECTURAL DIAGRAMS 287

DUTCH MOUNTAINS
ONE ARCHITECTURE

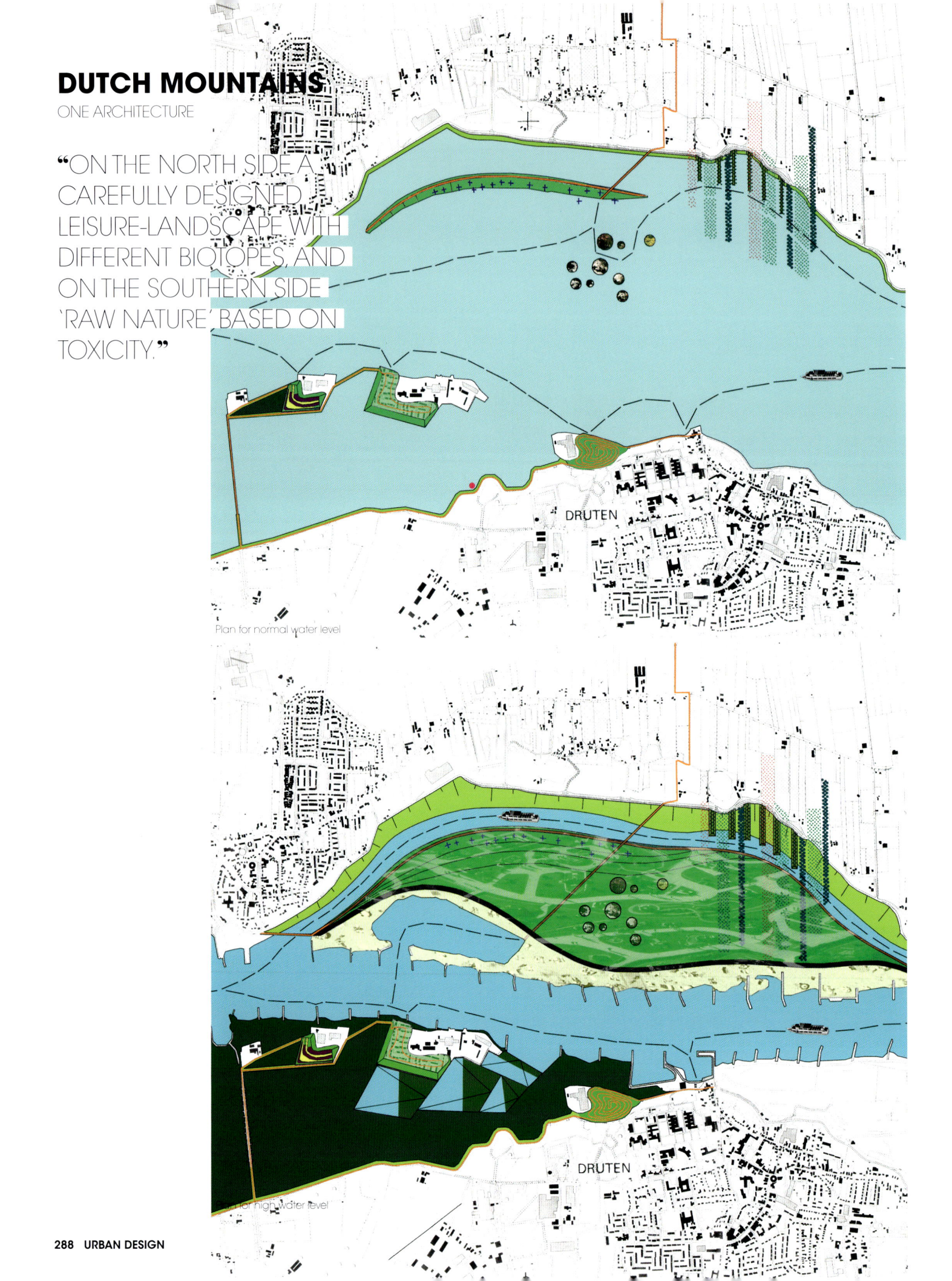

"ON THE NORTH SIDE A CAREFULLY DESIGNED LEISURE-LANDSCAPE WITH DIFFERENT BIOTOPES, AND ON THE SOUTHERN SIDE 'RAW NATURE' BASED ON TOXICITY."

Plan for normal water level

Plan for high water level

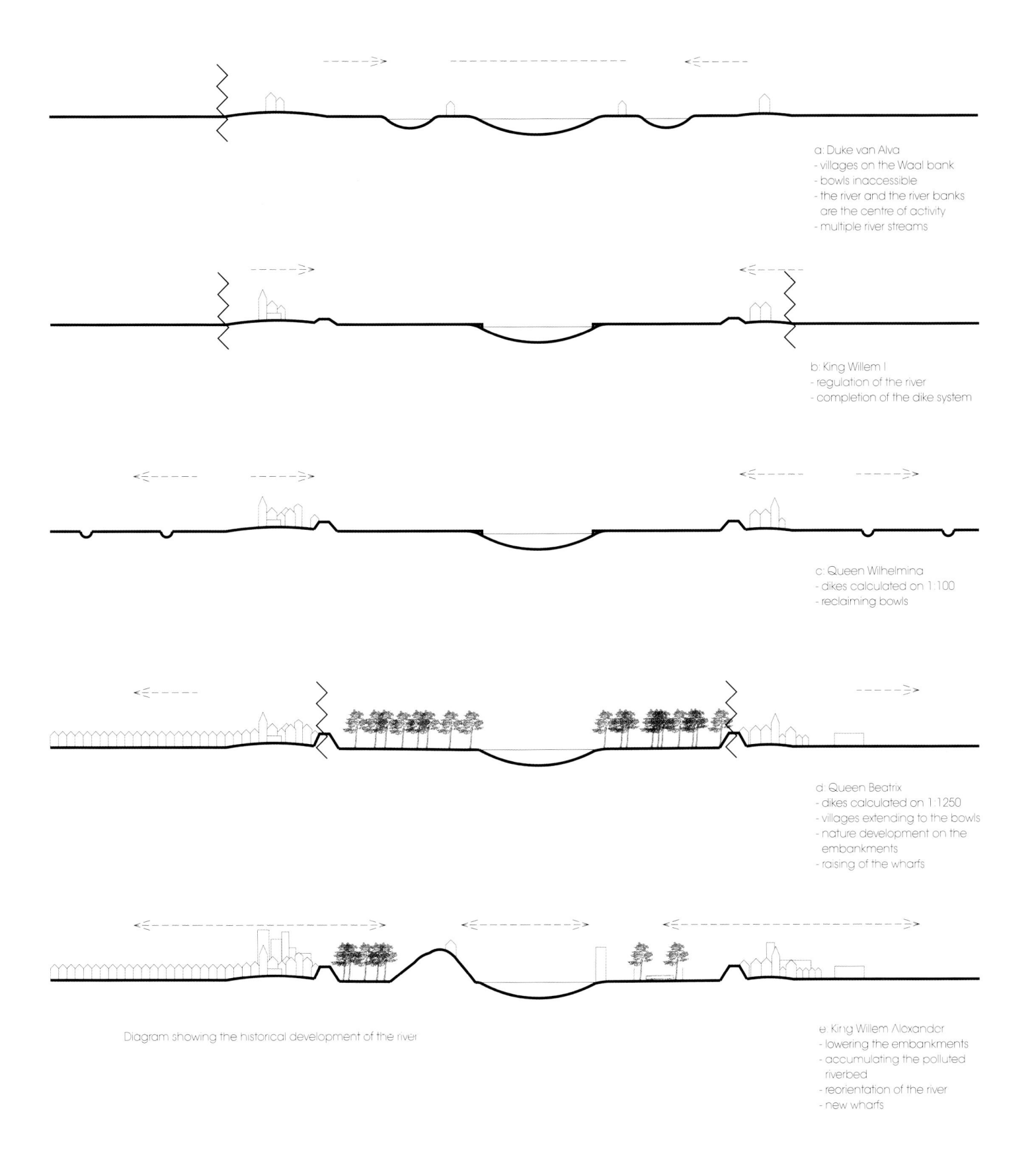

a: Duke van Alva
- villages on the Waal bank
- bowls inaccessible
- the river and the river banks are the centre of activity
- multiple river streams

b: King Willem I
- regulation of the river
- completion of the dike system

c: Queen Wilhelmina
- dikes calculated on 1:100
- reclaiming bowls

d: Queen Beatrix
- dikes calculated on 1:1250
- villages extending to the bowls
- nature development on the embankments
- raising of the wharfs

Diagram showing the historical development of the river

e: King Willem Alexander
- lowering the embankments
- accumulating the polluted riverbed
- reorientation of the river
- new wharfs

ARCHITECTURAL DIAGRAMS 289

ECO VILLAGE RIGA
Iotti+Pavarani Architetti

"THE CONCEPT OF A MONO-FUNCTIONAL AND DISCONNECTED RESIDENTIAL DEVELOPMENT INTO A VIBRANT OPEN ENVIRONMENT."

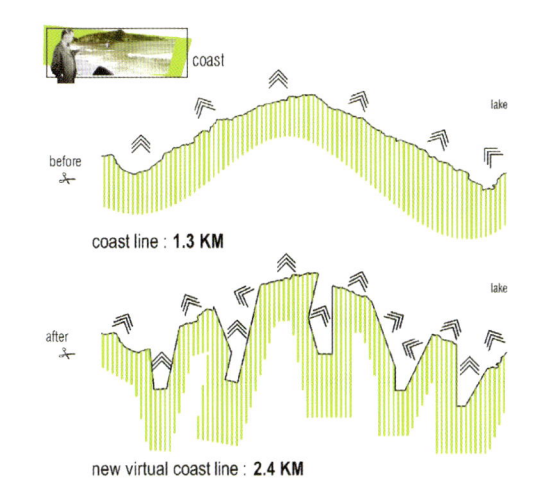

New 'virtual' coast-line

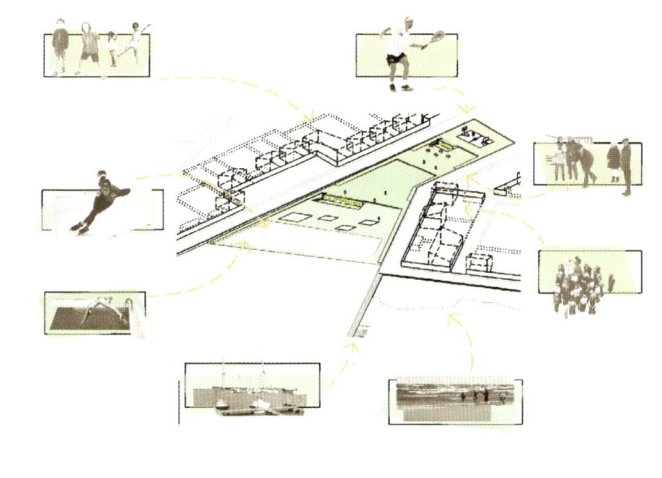

The creation of public spaces

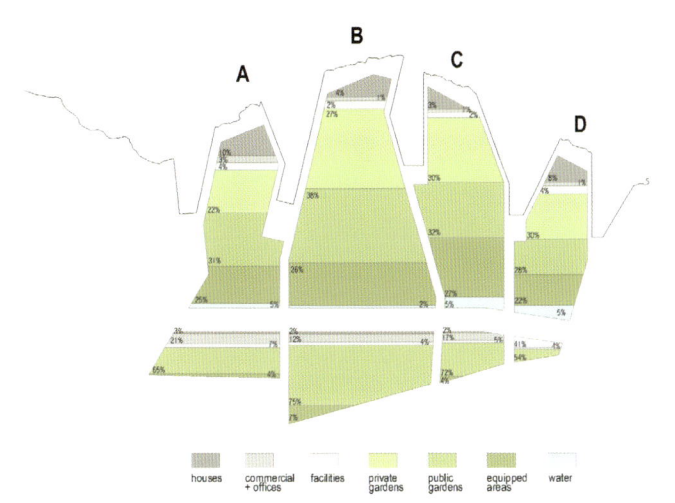

States of construction

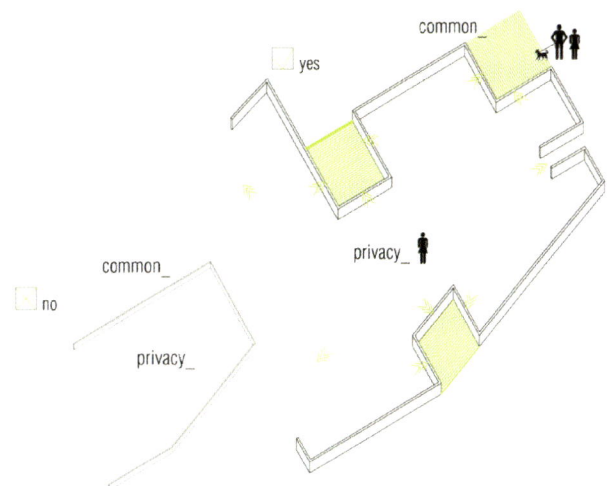

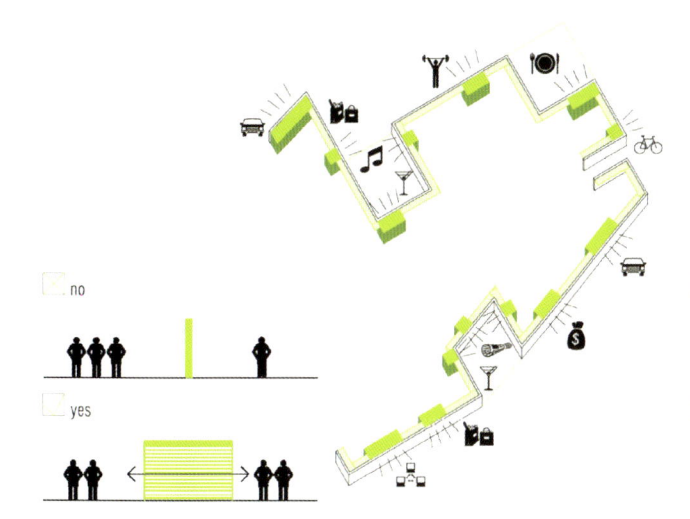

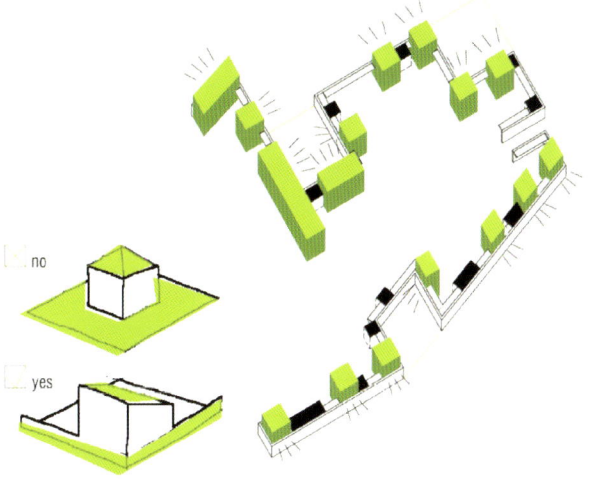

Privacy – social spaces

The active boundary

Building on the boundary

ARCHITECTURAL DIAGRAMS 291

FBM PERUGIA EBPC

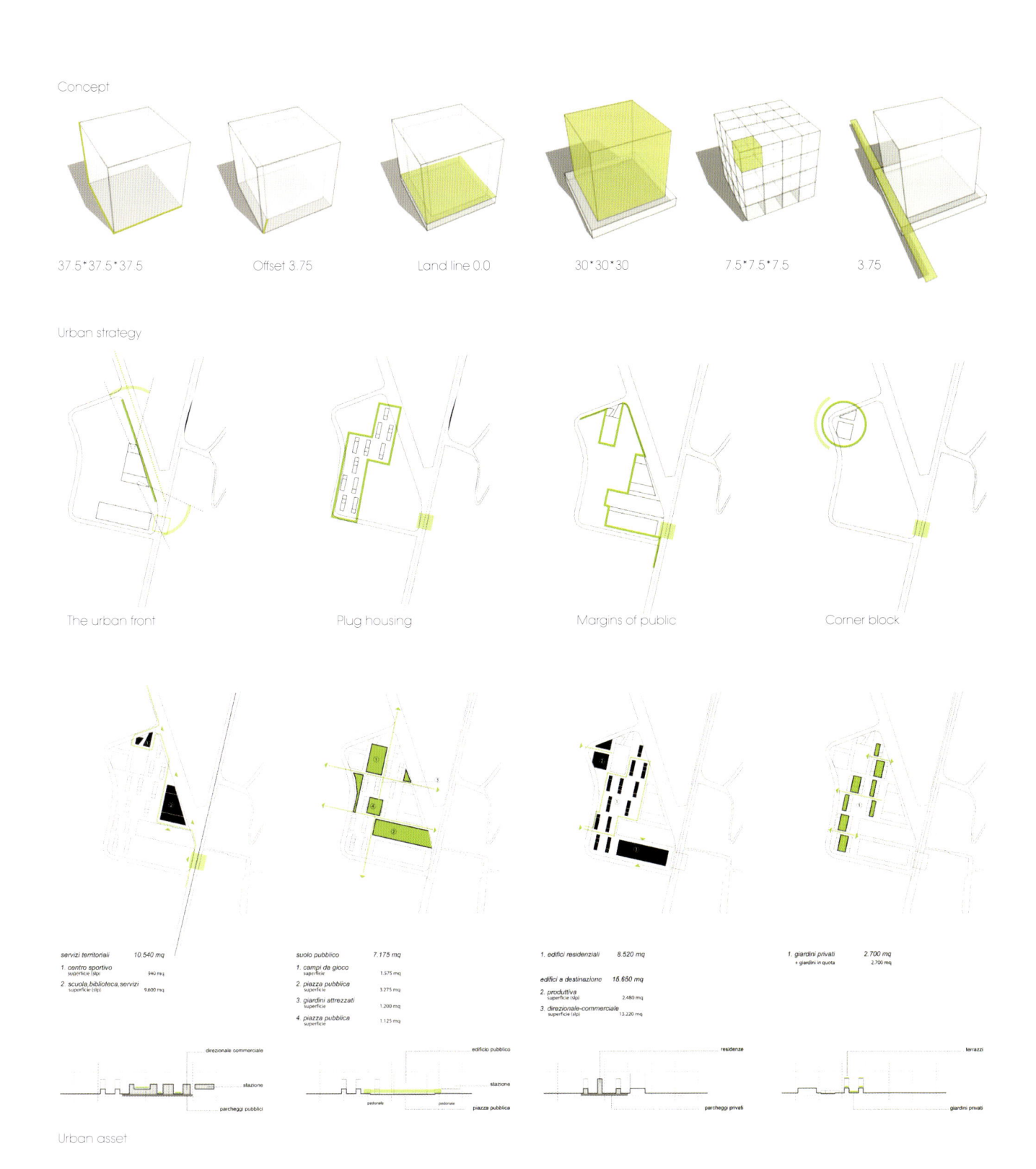

Concept

37.5*37.5*37.5   Offset 3.75   Land line 0.0   30*30*30   7.5*7.5*7.5   3.75

Urban strategy

The urban front   Plug housing   Margins of public   Corner block

servizi territoriali   10.540 mq
1. centro sportivo
   superficie (slp)   940 mq
2. scuola, biblioteca, servizi
   superficie (slp)   9.600 mq

suolo pubblico   7.175 mq
1. campi da gioco
   superficie   1.575 mq
2. piazza pubblica
   superficie   3.275 mq
3. giardini attrezzati
   superficie   1.200 mq
4. piazza pubblica
   superficie   1.125 mq

1. edifici residenziali   8.520 mq

edifici a destinazione   15.650 mq
2. produttiva
   superficie (slp)   2.480 mq
3. direzionale-commerciale
   superficie (slp)   13.220 mq

1. giardini privati   2.700 mq
   + giardini in quota   2.700 mq

Urban asset

ARCHITECTURAL DIAGRAMS

FILIPSTAD SPACEGROUP

"THE CITY NEEDS DIVERSITY AND SPACE TO EVOLVE."

Oslo OUT

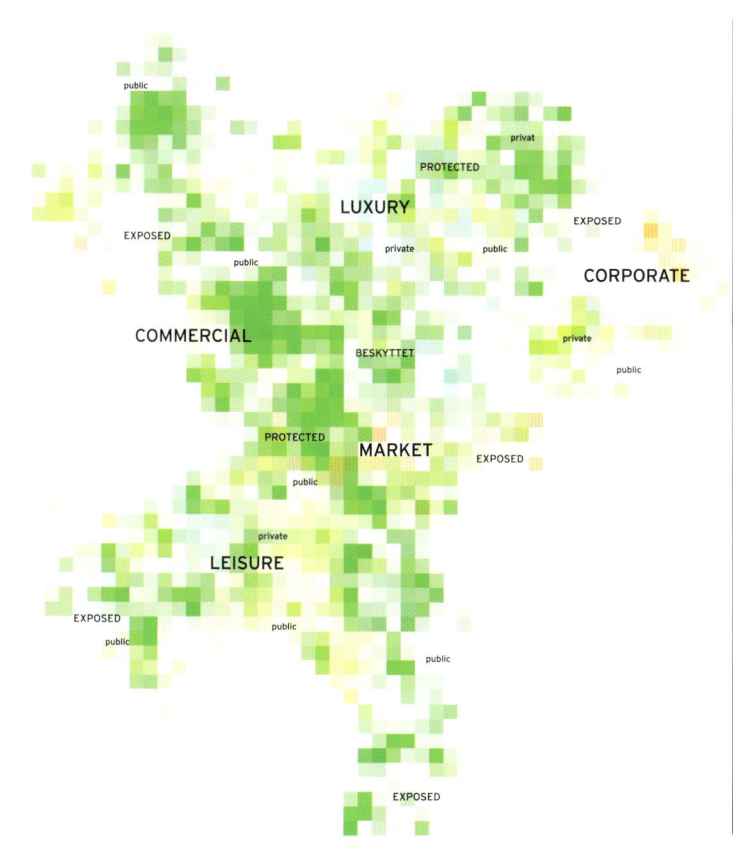

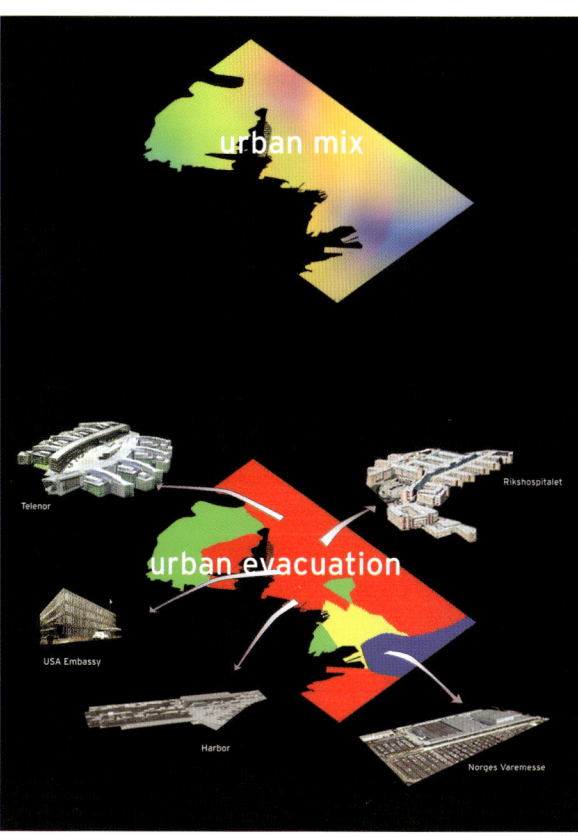

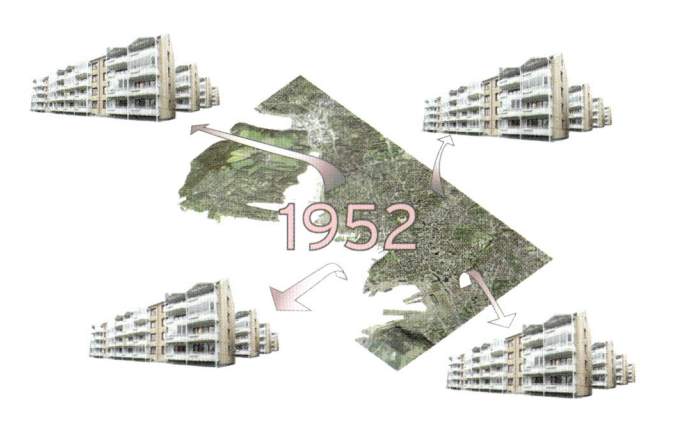

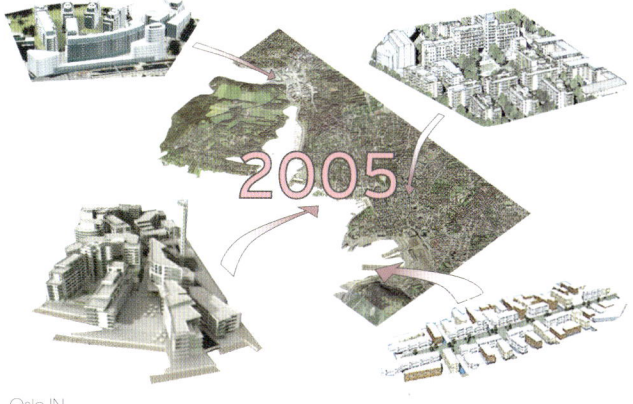

Oslo IN

ARCHITECTURAL DIAGRAMS 295

FOSHAN SANSUI URBAN PLAN
Reiser+Umemoto RUR Architecture PC

Highrise towers

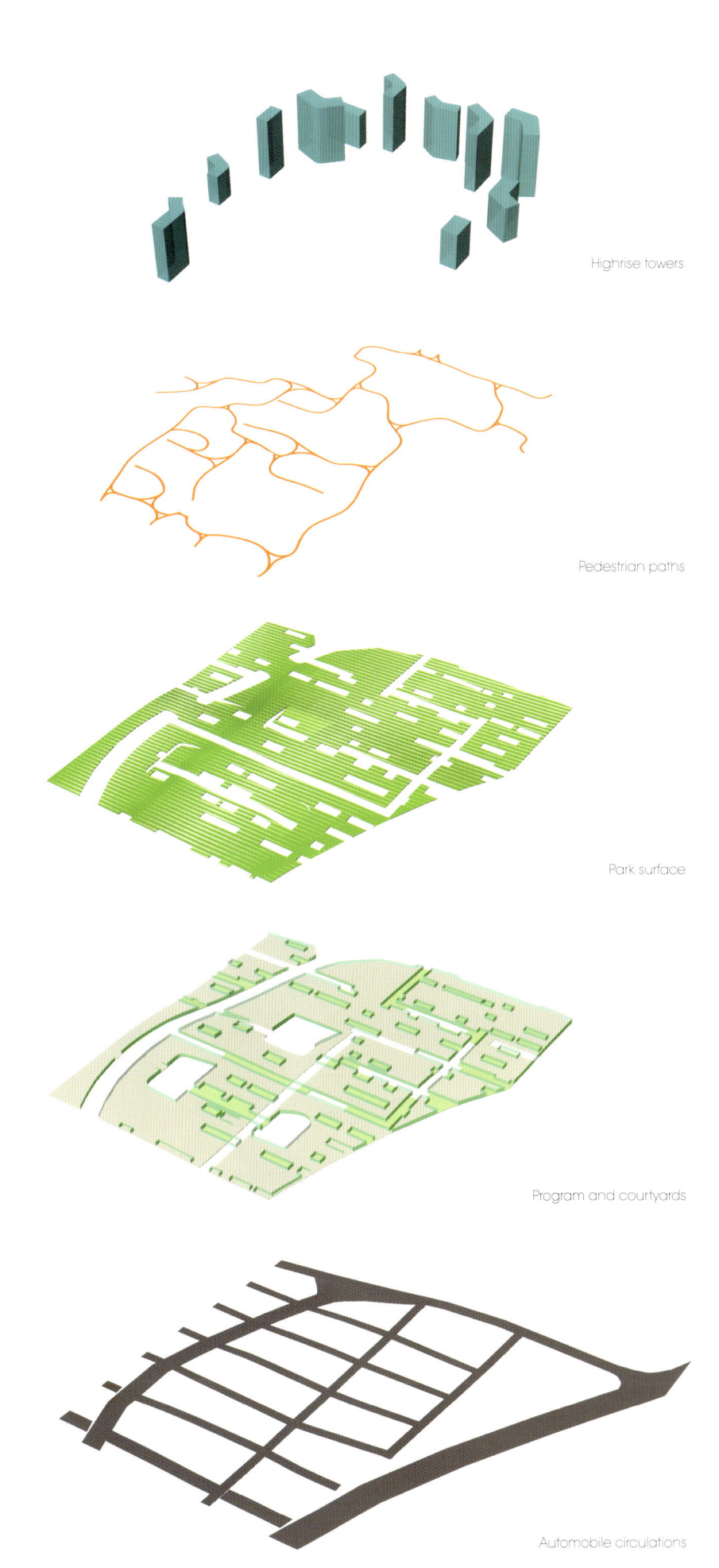

Pedestrian paths

Park surface

Program and courtyards

Automobile circulations

ARCHITECTURAL DIAGRAMS 297

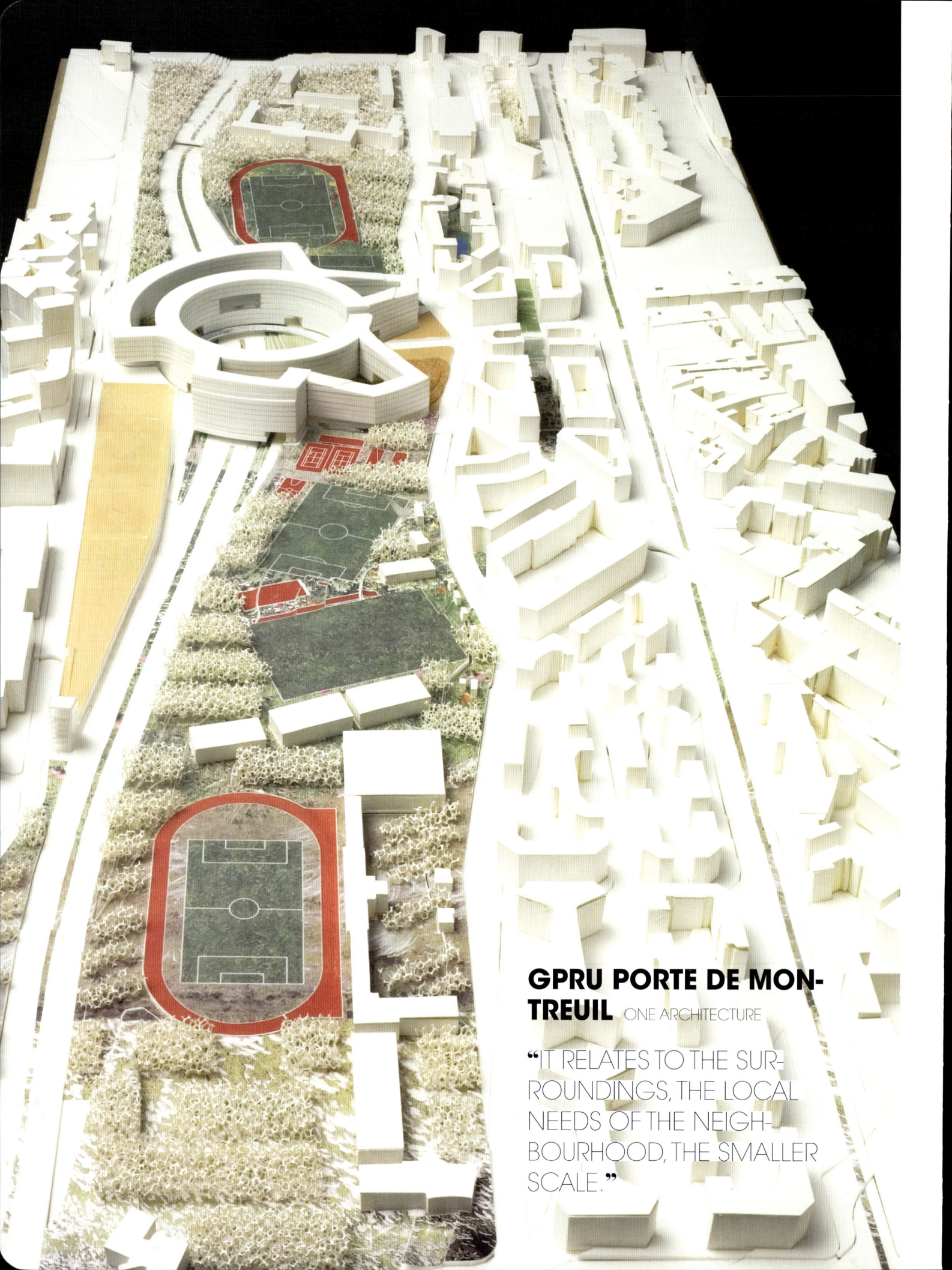

**GPRU PORTE DE MON-
TREUIL** ONE ARCHITECTURE

"IT RELATES TO THE SUR-
ROUNDINGS, THE LOCAL
NEEDS OF THE NEIGH-
BOURHOOD, THE SMALLER
SCALE."

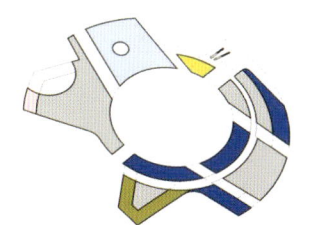

GPRU Porte de Montreuil, roundabout building, programmatic diagram, level 0

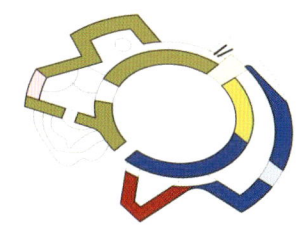

GPRU Porte de Montreuil, roundabout building, programmatic diagram, level 1

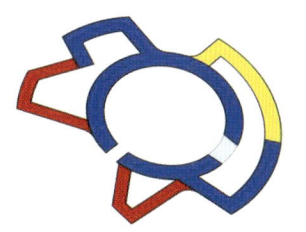

GPRU Porte de Montreuil, roundabout building, programmatic diagram, level 2

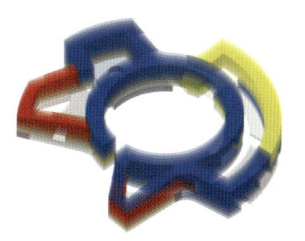

GPRU Porte de Montreuil, roundabout building, programmatic diagram

Current site with the extremely wide roundabout

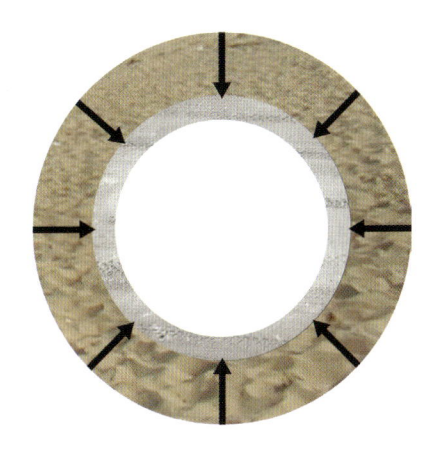

GPRU Porte de Montreuil, concept diagram

Step 1: reduce the size of the roundabout to three lanes and thus free up space

Step 2: a new building on the freed-up space contains the car noise

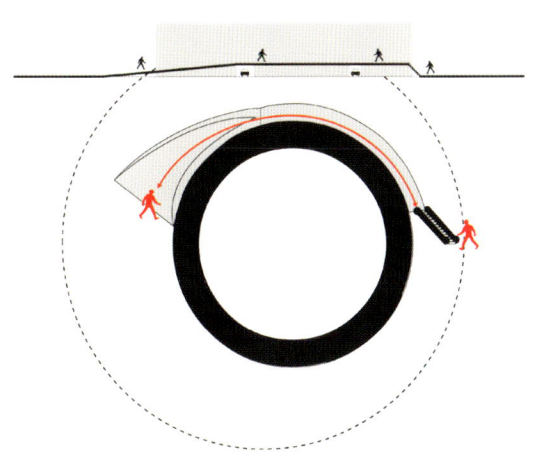

Step 3: make a pedestrian connection between Paris and Montreuil on the quiet side

Step 4: a second circle adapts itself to the neighbourhood

ARCHITECTURAL DIAGRAMS 299

HICAT: NEW PORT, NEW CITY
Willy Müller Architects

> "COULD WE THINK, THAT IN THIS CENTURY IT WOULDN'T BE NECESSARY TO HAVE THE PORTS ON CONTINENTAL PLATFORMS."

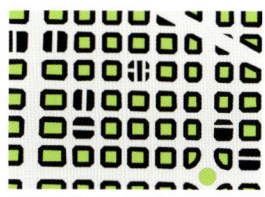

ACTUAL "ENSANCHE"
STREET=SPACES=BUILDINGS

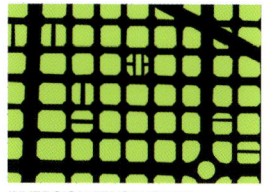

INVERSION "ENSANCHE"
STREET=BUILDINGS=SPACES

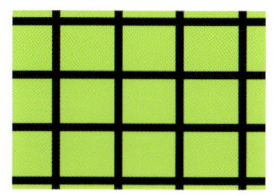

SUPER MESH ENSANCHE
[STREET=BUILDINGS]/SPACES=X

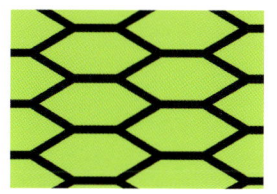

HEXAGONAL MESH
HIGH SURROUNDING ADAPTABILIT

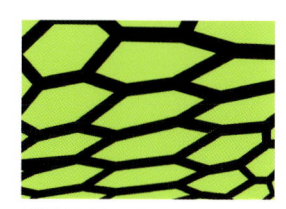

DEFORMED MESH
ADAPTATION PROCESS

NEW URBAN STRUCTURE
SUPER BLOCKS ORGANIZATION

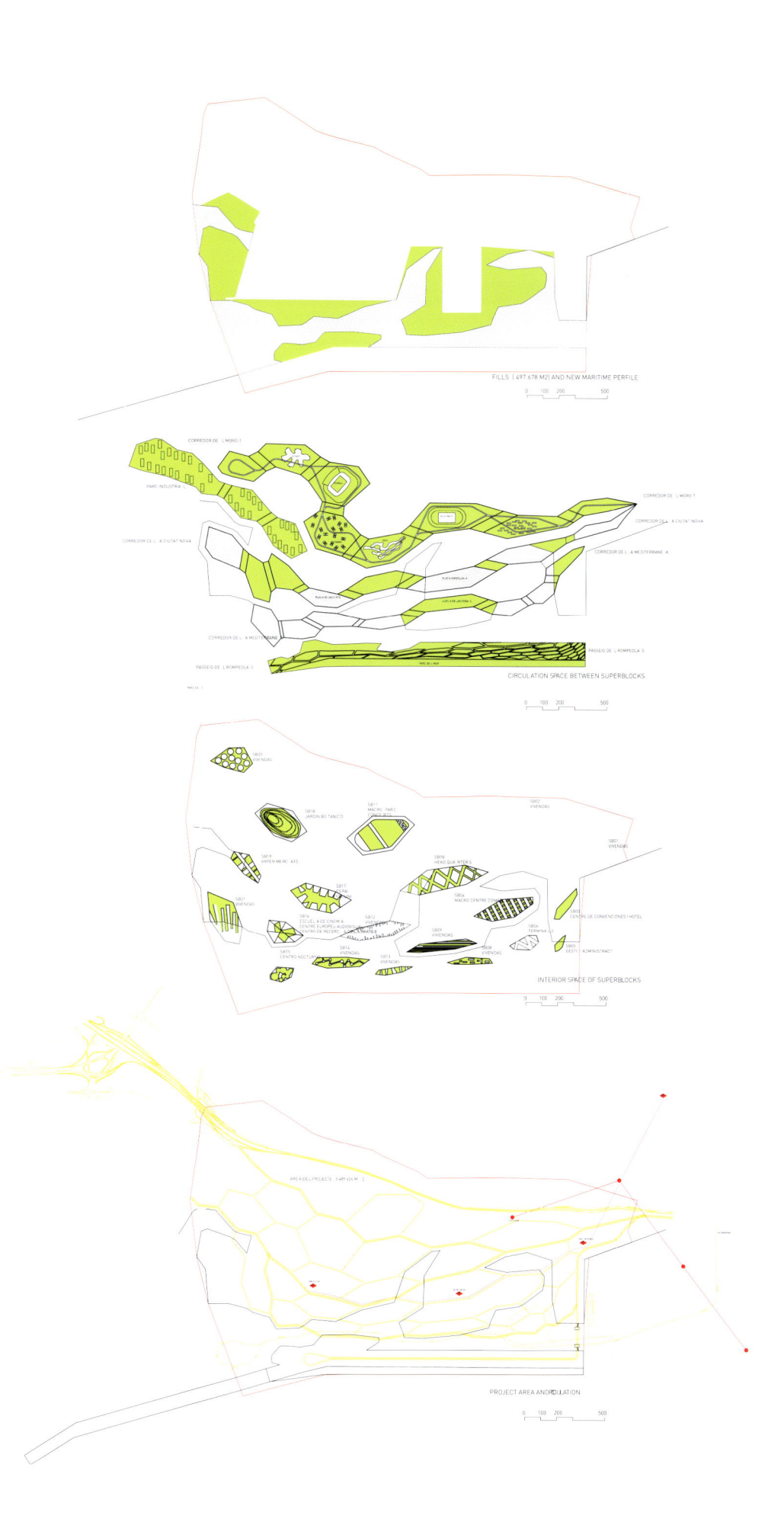

FILLS (497.678 M2) AND NEW MARITIME PERFILE

CIRCULATION SPACE BETWEEN SUPERBLOCKS

INTERIOR SPACE OF SUPERBLOCKS

PROJECT AREA AND POPULATION

ARCHITECTURAL DIAGRAMS 301

**IFCCA 42ND-23RD
STREET** UNStudio

"ITS HISTORICAL DEVELOP-
MENT, TO THE GREATER
METROPOLITAN AREA OF
NEW YORK CITY AND ESPE-
CIALLY TO ITS IMMEDIATE
SURROUNDINGS."

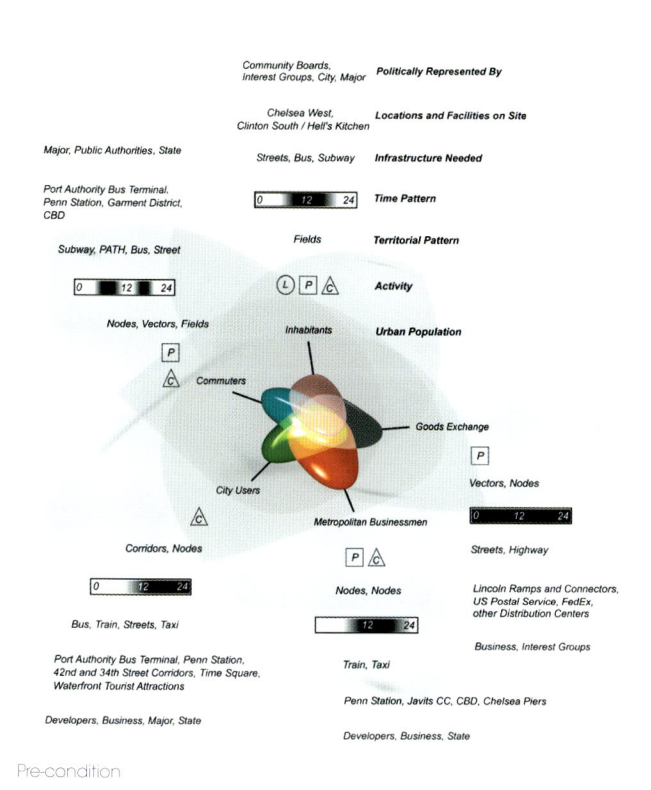

Pre-condition

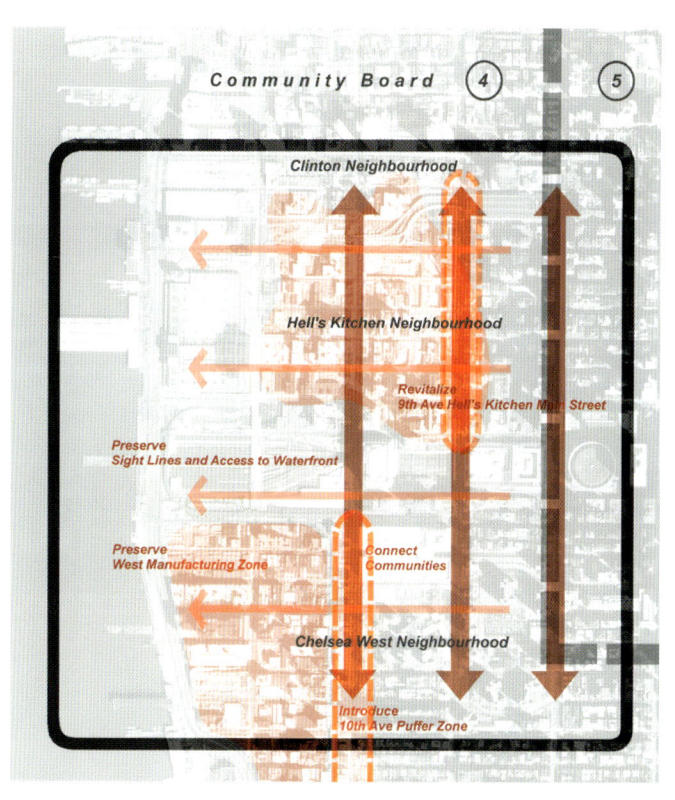

Community Boards, Interest Groups, City, Major		Politically Represented By
Chelsea West, Clinton South / Hell's Kitchen		Locations and Facilities on Site
Major, Public Authorities, State	Streets, Bus, Subway	Infrastructure Needed
Port Authority Bus Terminal, Penn Station, Garment District, CBD	0 12 24	Time Pattern
Subway, PATH, Bus, Street	Fields	Territorial Pattern
0 12 24	L P C	Activity
Nodes, Vectors, Fields	Inhabitants	Urban Population
	Commuters	Goods Exchange
	City Users	Vectors, Nodes
Corridors, Nodes	Metropolitan Businessmen	Streets, Highway
0 12 24	P C	
Bus, Train, Streets, Taxi	Nodes, Nodes	Lincoln Ramps and Connectors, US Postal Service, FedEx, other Distribution Centers
	12 24	Business, Interest Groups
Port Authority Bus Terminal, Penn Station, 42nd and 34th Street Corridors, Time Square, Waterfront Tourist Attractions	Train, Taxi	Penn Station, Javits CC, CBD, Chelsea Piers
Developers, Business, Major, State		Developers, Business, State

Community Board 4 5

- Clinton Neighbourhood
- Hell's Kitchen Neighbourhood
  - Revitalize 9th Ave Hell's Kitchen Main Street
- Preserve Sight Lines and Access to Waterfront
- Preserve West Manufacturing Zone
- Connect Communities
- Chelsea West Neighbourhood
- Introduce 10th Ave Puffer Zone

Five movement patterns

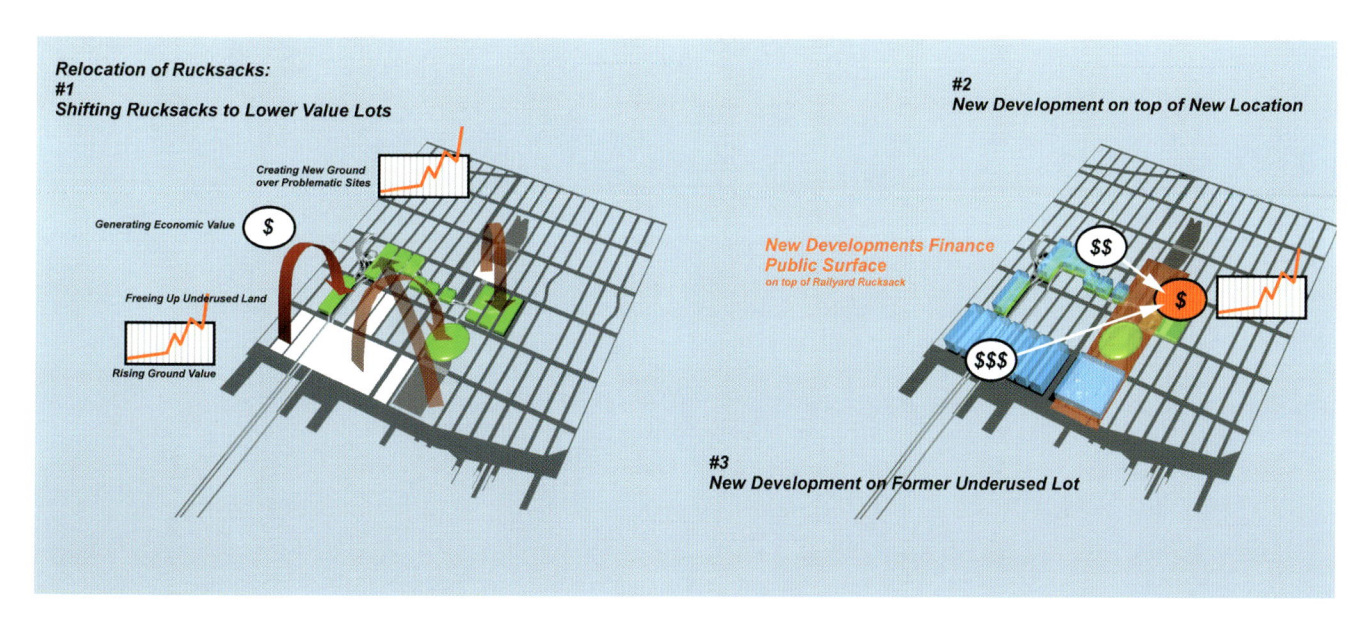

Relocation of Rucksacks:

#1 Shifting Rucksacks to Lower Value Lots
- Creating New Ground over Problematic Sites
- Generating Economic Value $
- Freeing Up Underused Land
- Rising Ground Value

#2 New Development on top of New Location
- New Developments Finance Public Surface on top of Railyard Rucksack

#3 New Development on Former Underused Lot

ARCHITECTURAL DIAGRAMS 303

KLM BIG

"THE DESIGN OF THE DIFFERENTIATED HEIGHTS AND SEQUENCE PROVIDES A HIGH LEVEL OF ACCESSIBILITY TO THE SURROUNDING CITY."

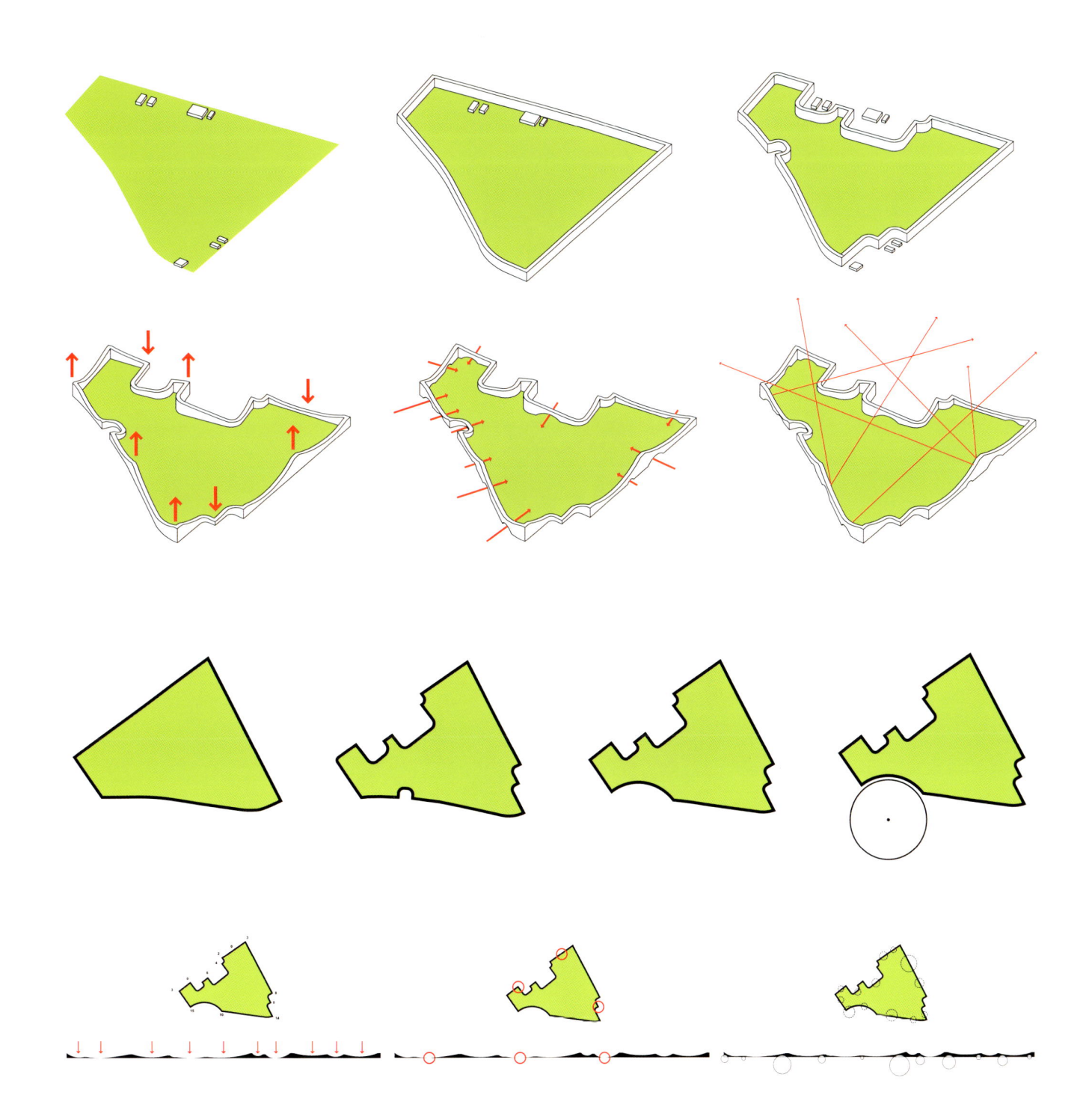

ARCHITECTURAL DIAGRAMS 305

L.A.R.S. SMAQ

"AS FLEXIBLE AND ELASTIC, THE LAYERS AND VOLUMES REACT TO LANDSCAPE CAPITAL OF THE SITUATION."

A. LANDSCAPE LINKING & INTERTWINING STRATEGY

1 LANDSCAPE SWIRL

SPECIFIC GREEN FACETS

2 SOCIAL PROGRAM

DWELLING

3 INTEGRATION - MERGED CONNECTIONS

CONNECTED AND INTERCONNECTED

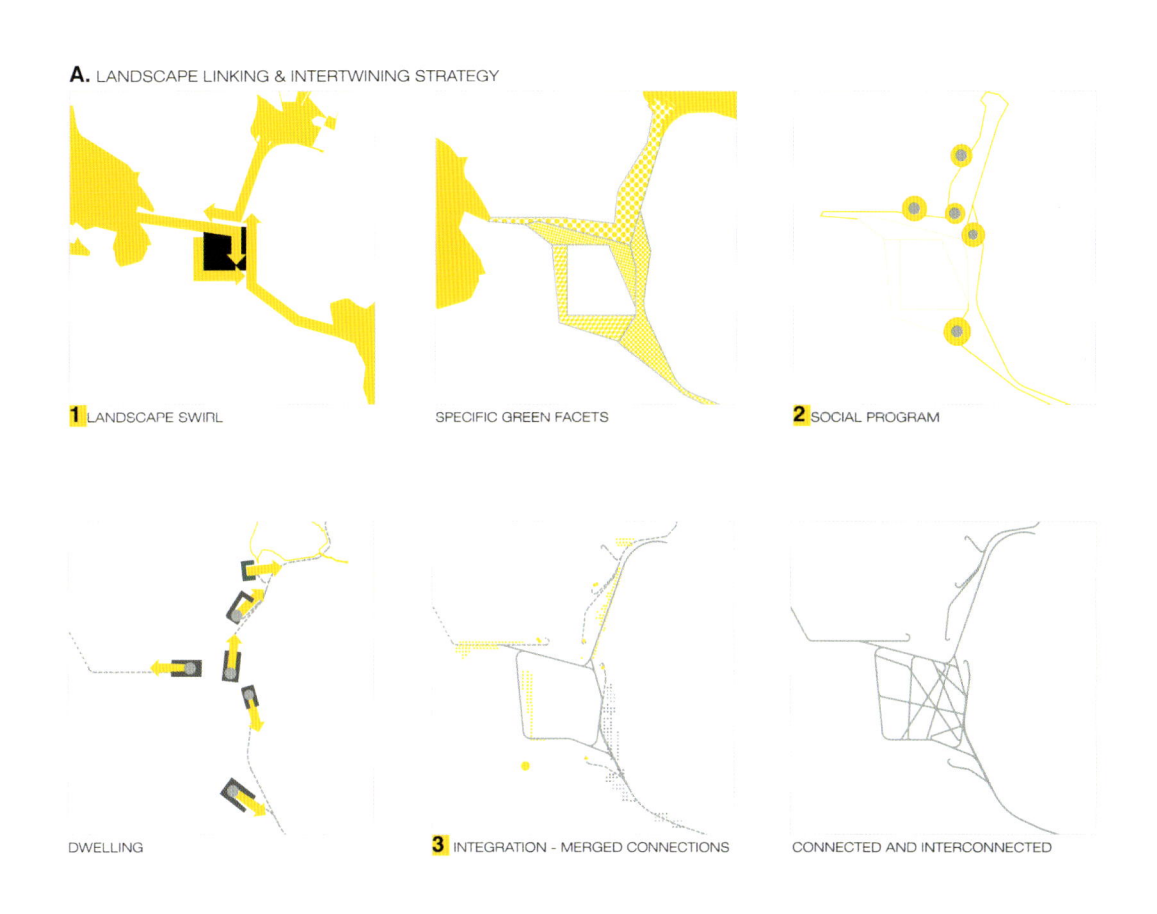

B. EXTENSION STRATEGY

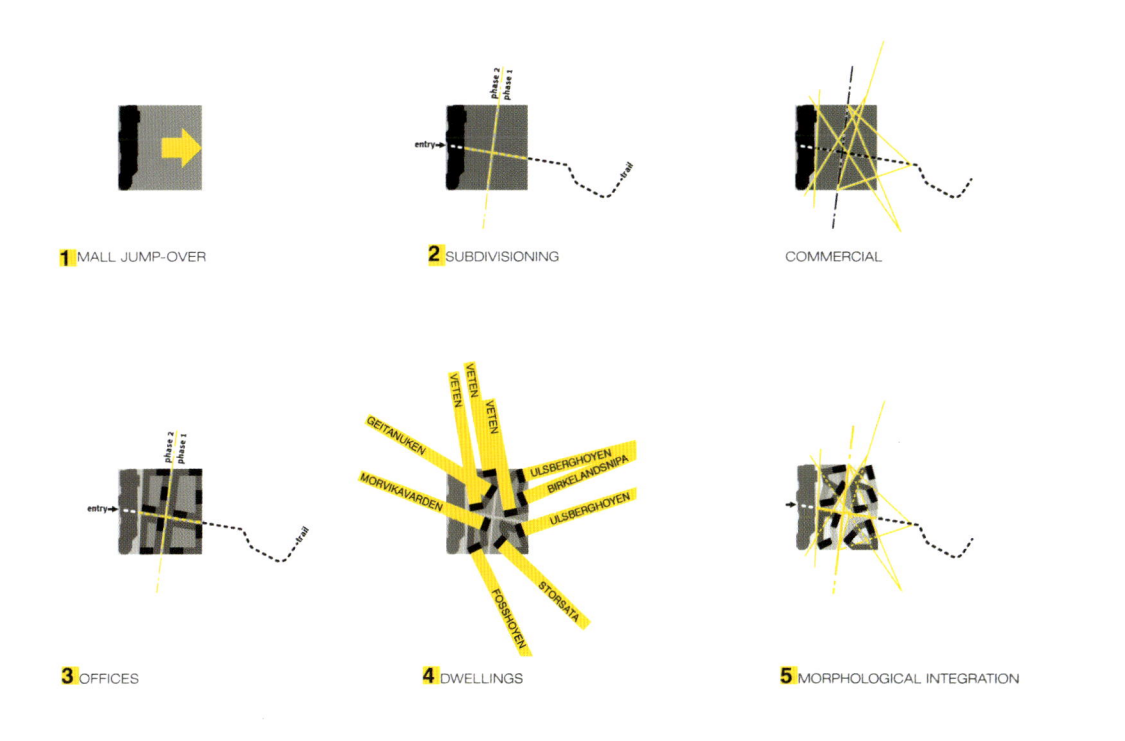

1 MALL JUMP-OVER

2 SUBDIVISIONING

COMMERCIAL

3 OFFICES

4 DWELLINGS

5 MORPHOLOGICAL INTEGRATION

ARCHITECTURAL DIAGRAMS 307

LA PIROTTERIE
PERIPHERIQUES architectes

"THIS OPERATION WAS TO OFFER A VARIETY OF MODELS OF HOMES IN AN ARCHITECTURAL STYLE OPEN TO NEW SPATIAL PRACTICES."

Urban diagrams

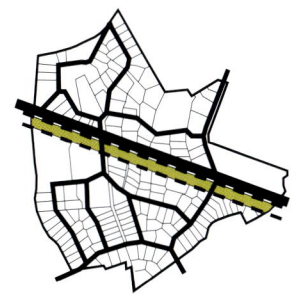

Field Peru
Online - High Voltage = area of land not buildable = green surface imposed

Gaining ground
Displacement Boulevard City = distribution of public spaces = Liasons public inter-city

State of play
parcels, roads, timber

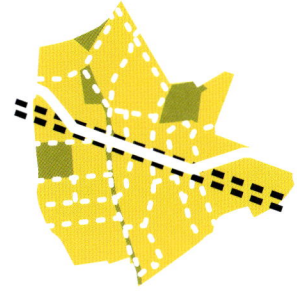

Public infrastructure
Main road, high voltage line

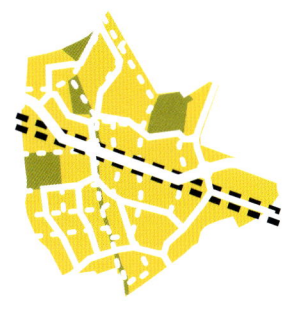

Networks of even

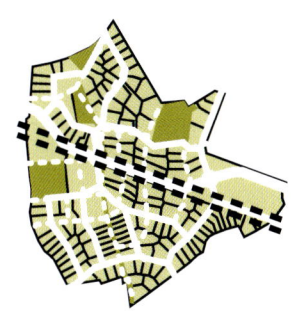

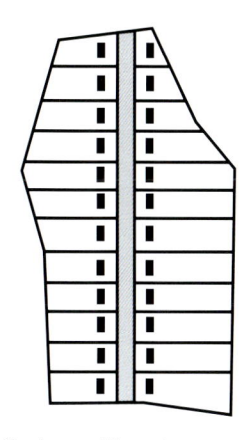

Tracts

Studies for parcel

Tracts on evil through common

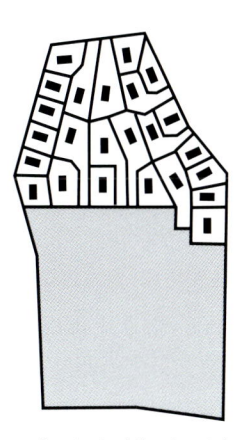

Remix of existing hamlet

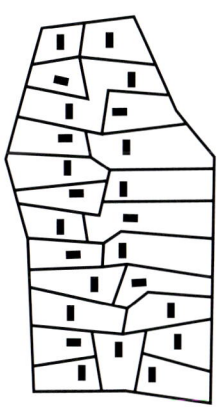

Random tracts

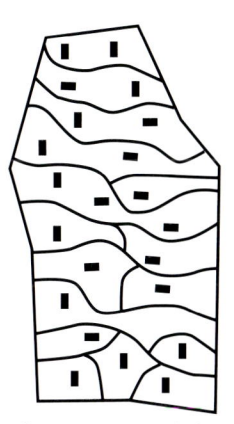

Opportunistic plots for forests

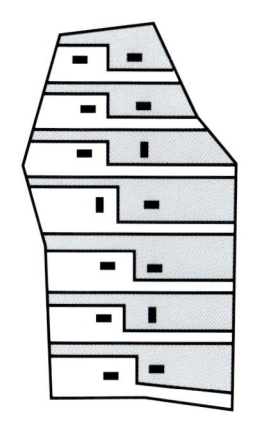

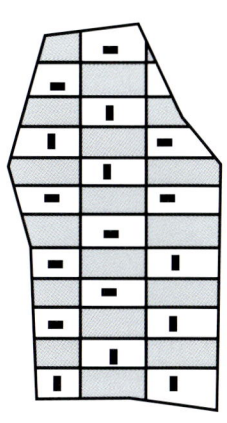

Through tracts

Alternate occupation

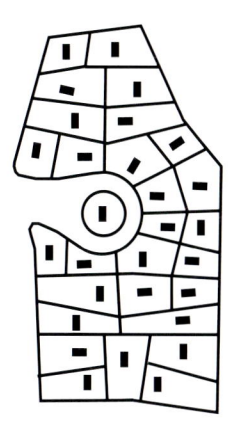

Random tracts

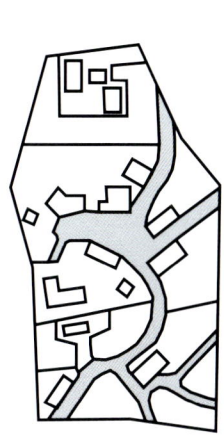

Remix of hamlets existing

ARCHITECTURAL DIAGRAMS 309

LACTARIUS nodo17 architects

"OUR PROPOSAL FOR 'THE EXTENSION OF AGUAS VIVAS' IS NOT AN EXTENSION OF THE EXISTING CITY."

Camino
Plaza
Patio interior
Fachada borde

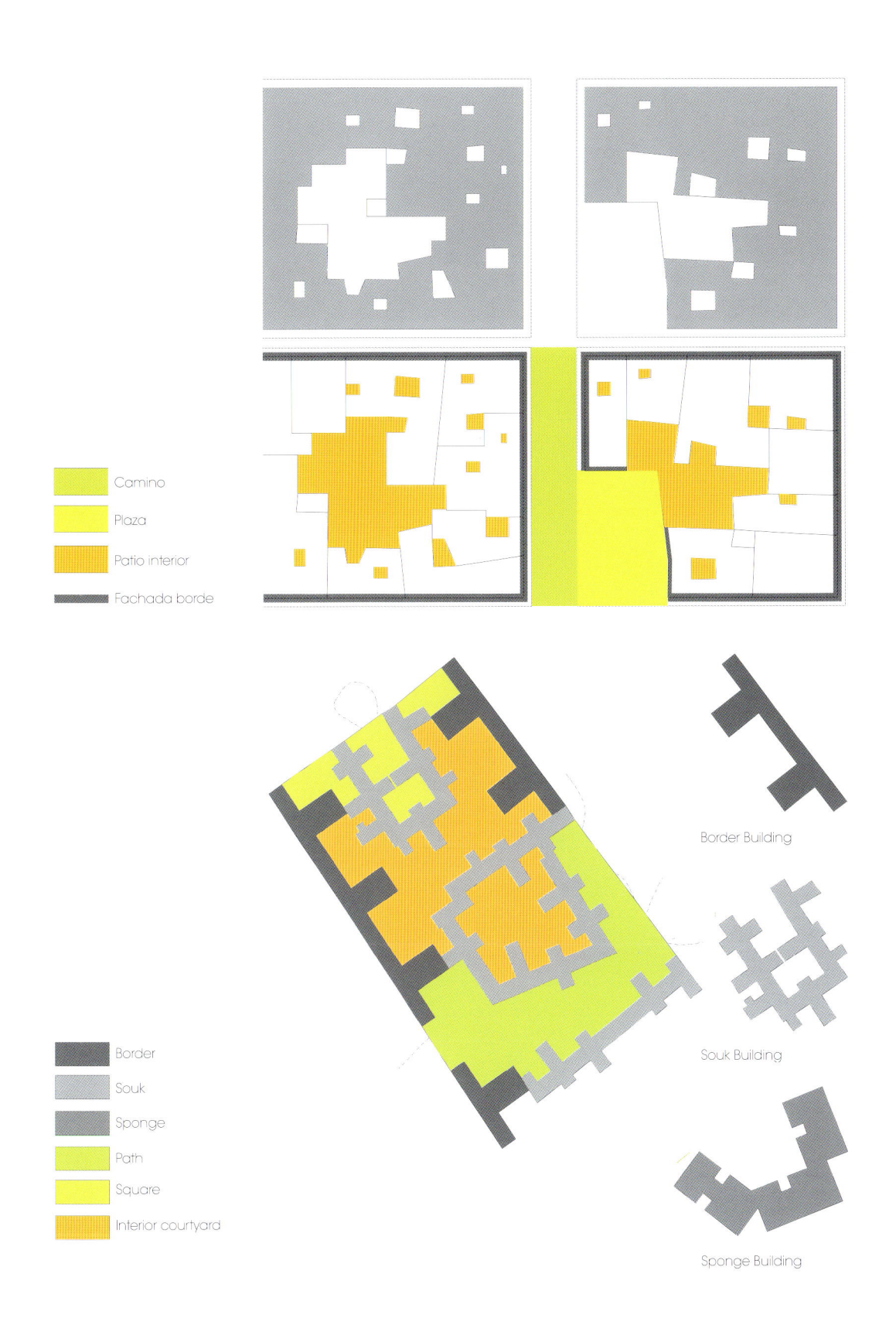

Border
Souk
Sponge
Path
Square
Interior courtyard

Border Building

Souk Building

Sponge Building

ARCHITECTURAL DIAGRAMS 311

LES HALLES ONE ARCHITECTURE

"WE PROPOSED BRINGING THE DYNAMICISM AND THE YOUTH OF THE ENTIRE ILE-DE-FRANCE INTO THE HEART OF PARIS."

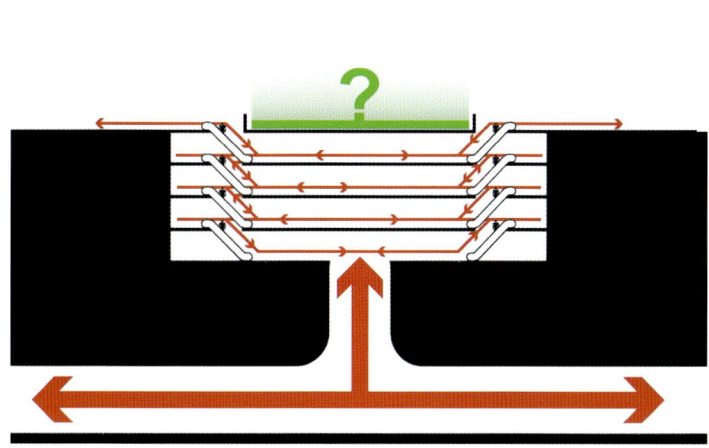

Les Halles, diagram showing how people have to cross the mall in order to exit the train station

Like an iceberg, Les Halles' mix of different cultures is not visible on the surface

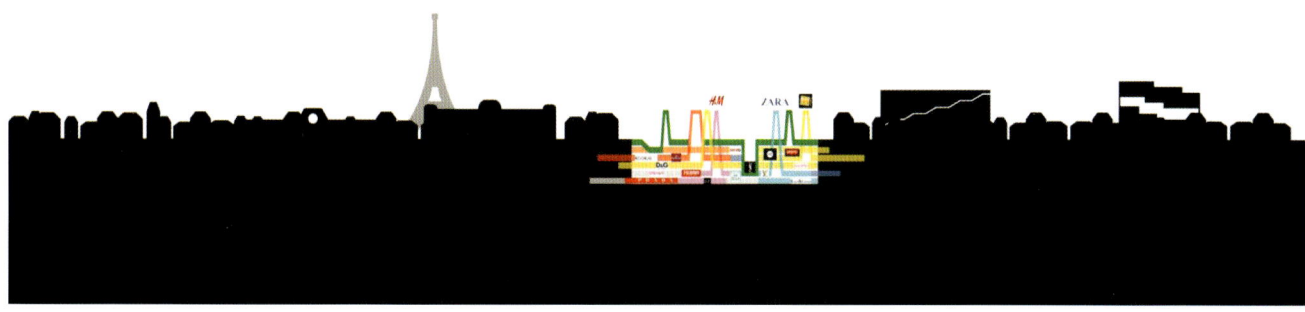

Les Halles, diagram of future situation

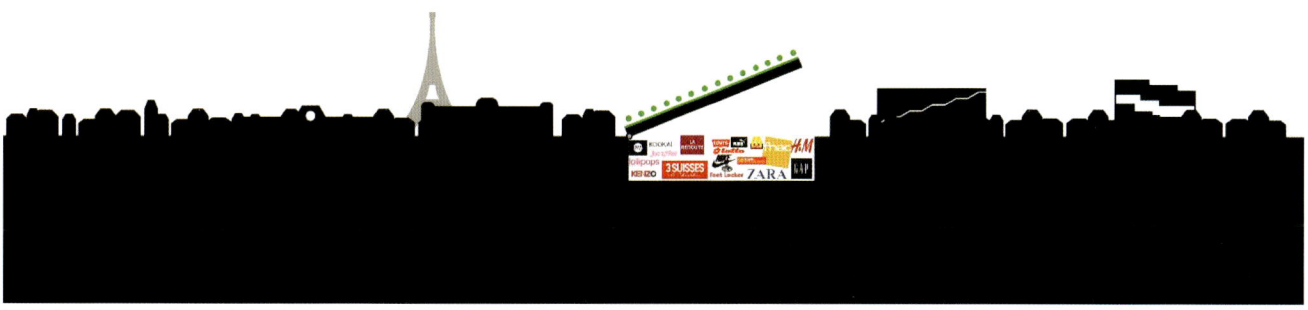

Les Halles, diagram of current situation

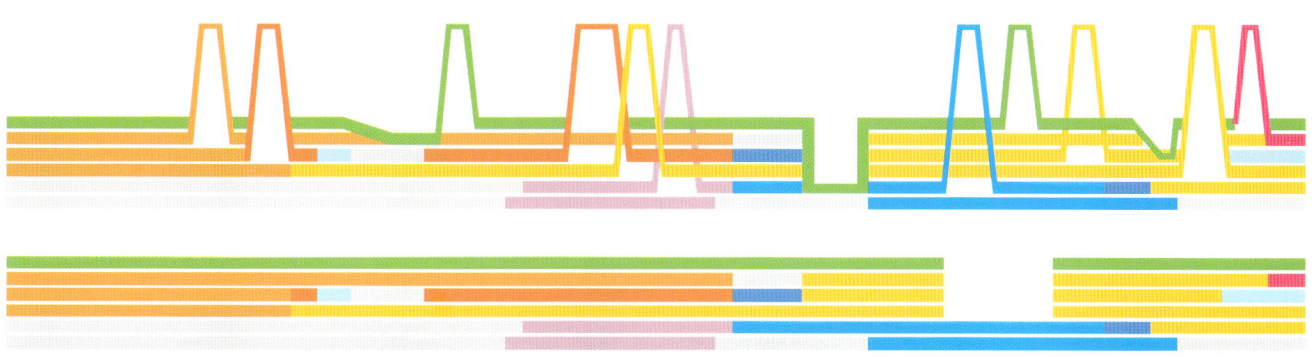

Les Halles, principal idea with the new section on top, the current below

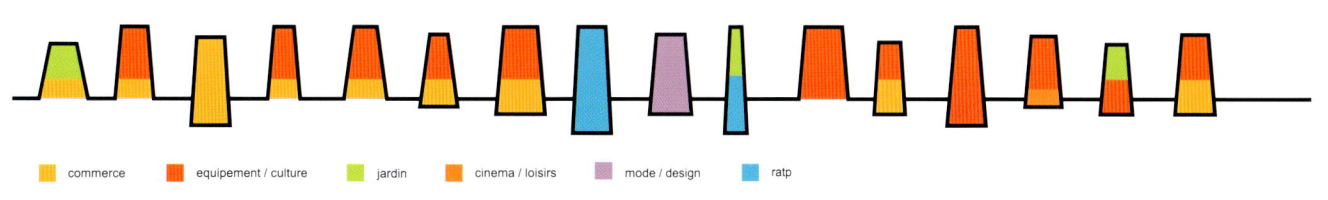

commerce   equipement / culture   jardin   cinema / loisirs   mode / design   ratp

Diagram showing the different programs

ARCHITECTURAL DIAGRAMS   313

LJ:SONIC POLDER
Bernd Kniess Architects Urban Planners

"REDISTRIBUTION AND LANDSCAPING OF THE GROUND IN QUESTION REDUCE NOISE EMISSION TO A LEVEL THAT MAKES RESIDENTIAL USE POSSIBLE."

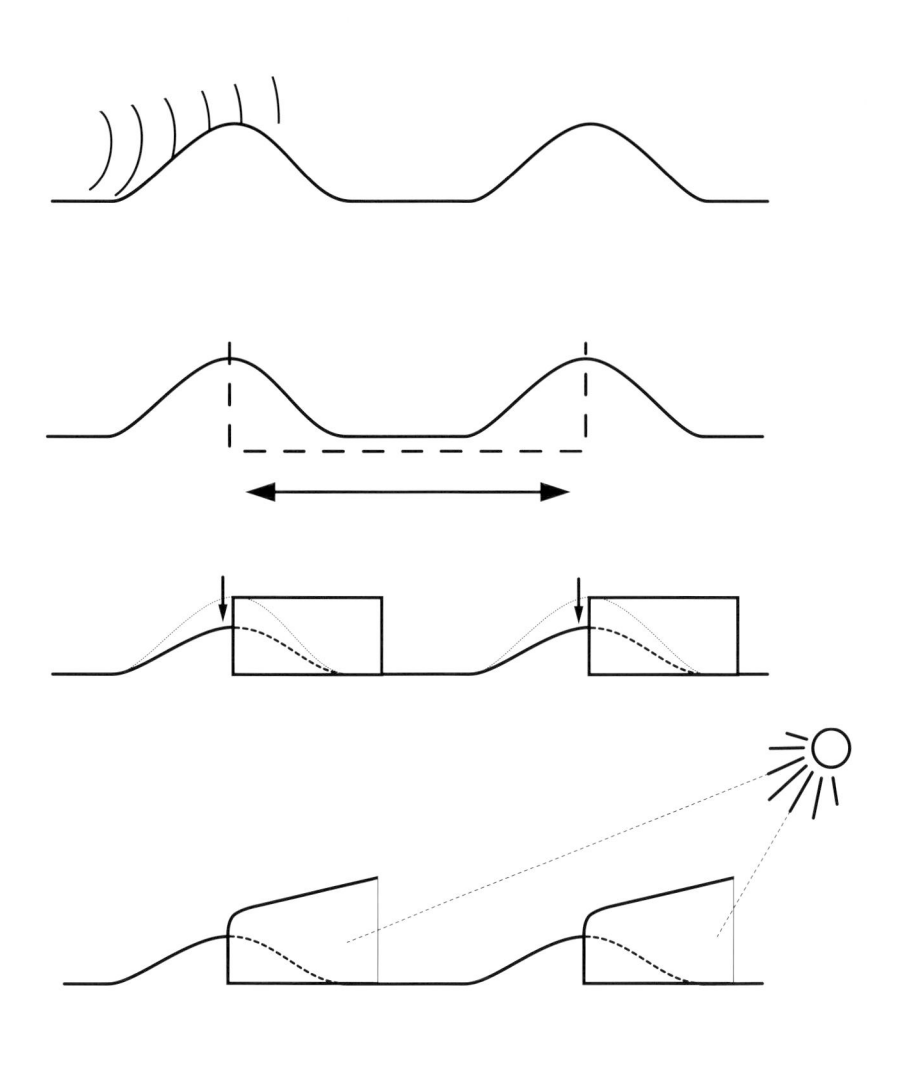

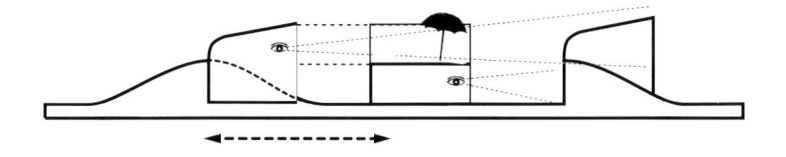

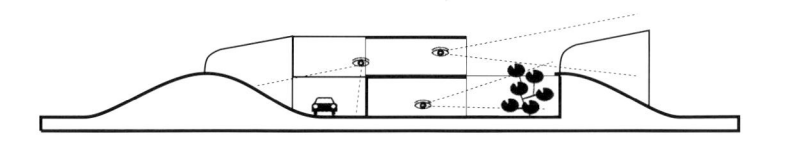

ARCHITECTURAL DIAGRAMS 315

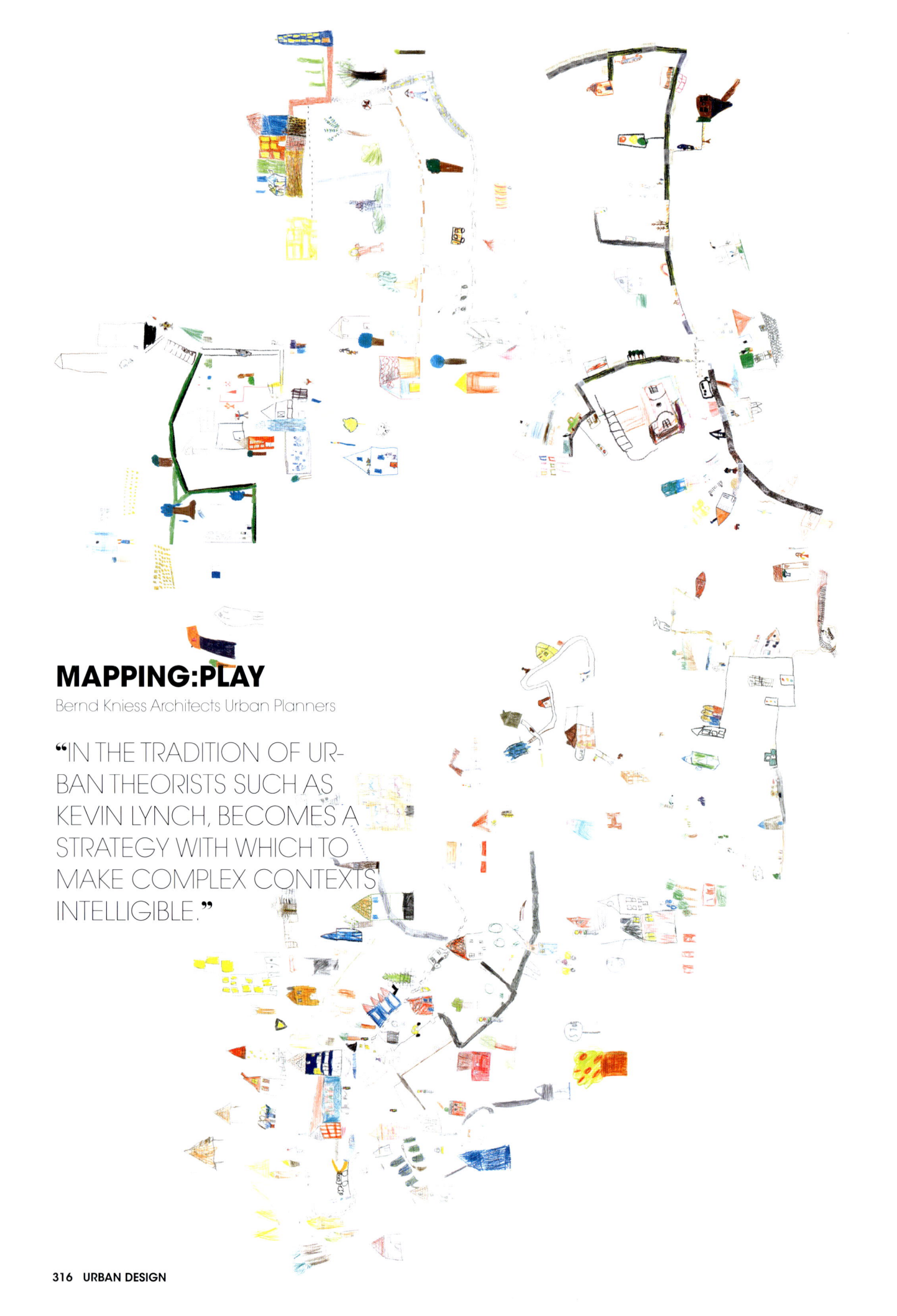

MAPPING:PLAY
Bernd Kniess Architects Urban Planners

"IN THE TRADITION OF UR-
BAN THEORISTS SUCH AS
KEVIN LYNCH, BECOMES A
STRATEGY WITH WHICH TO
MAKE COMPLEX CONTEXTS
INTELLIGIBLE."

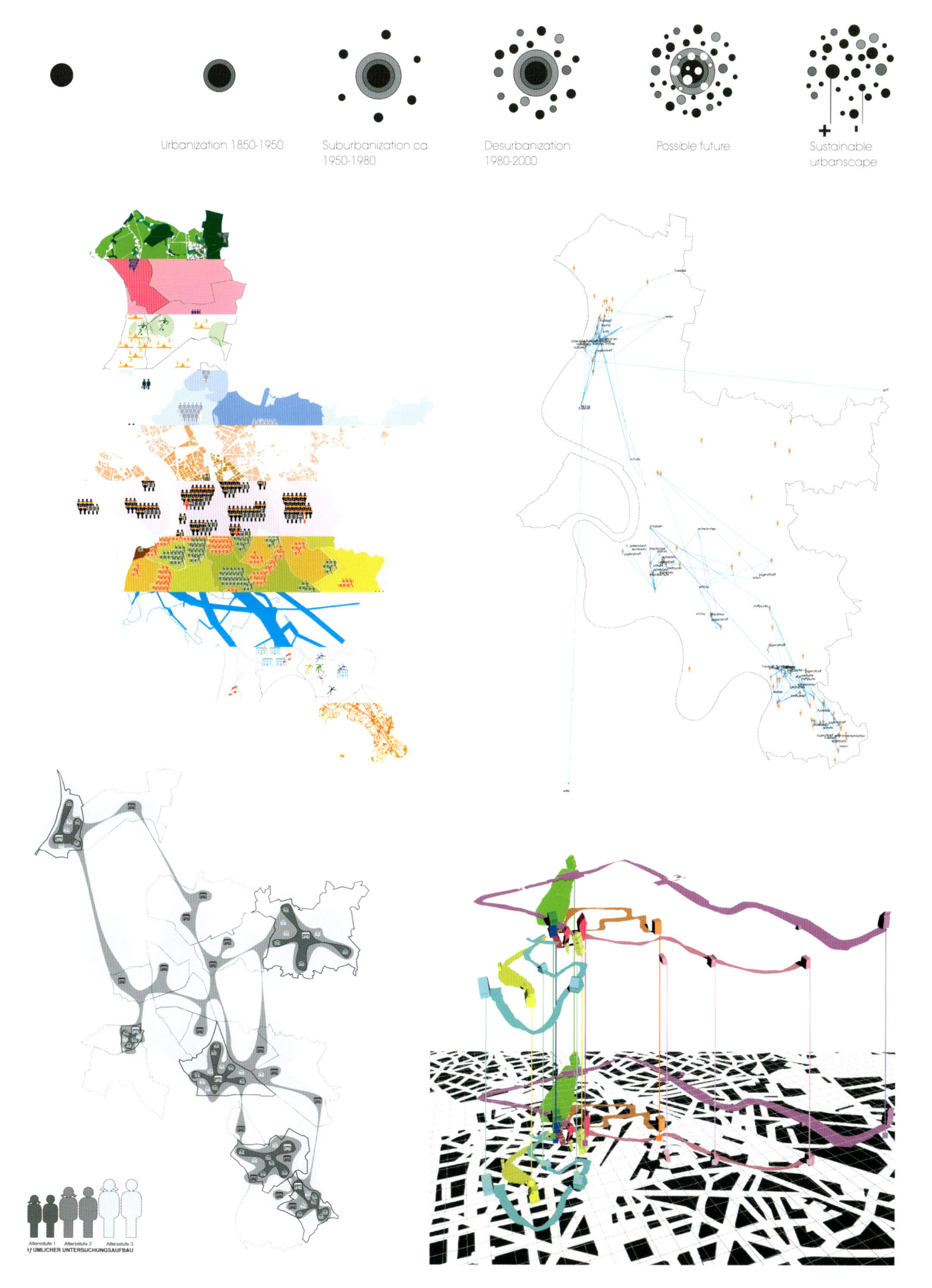

Urbanization 1850-1950   Suburbanization ca 1950-1980   Desurbanization 1980-2000   Possible future   Sustainable urbanscape

ARCHITECTURAL DIAGRAMS 317

MARITIME FRONT OF ALMERIA Willy Müller Architects

"EXTENDING THIS LIMIT TOWARDS THE SEA COULD BE SEEN FROM THE CONCEPT LIKE AN OPPORTUNITY OF DEVELOPMENT, RATHER THAN A THREAT."

NUEVO DISTRIBUIDOR

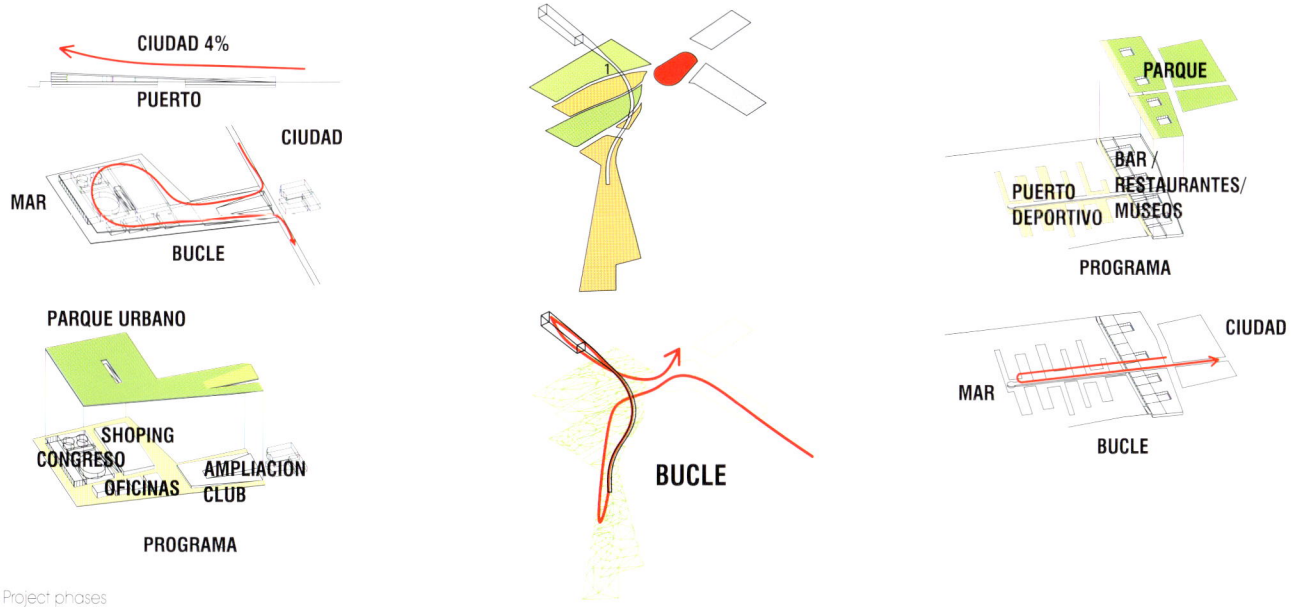

PASARELA ELEVADA

MUSEO DEL ALQUIFE

0 25 50 100m

CIUDAD 4%
PUERTO
MAR CIUDAD
BUCLE

PARQUE URBANO

SHOPING
CONGRESO   AMPLIACIÓN
OFICINAS   CLUB

PROGRAMA

BUCLE

PARQUE
BAR/
RESTAURANTES/
PUERTO MUSEOS
DEPORTIVO

PROGRAMA

MAR CIUDAD
BUCLE

Project phases

ARCHITECTURAL DIAGRAMS   319

MAYDAY data architects

"ON THE LA LAGUNA SITE, THE ADAPTATION OF THIS MESH GENERATES AN OCCUPATION SYSTEM FOR THE ORGANISATIONAL CELLS."

Geometry of the cell, tissue definition of landscape

Generation of local gradients landscape fabric

Social stimuli station cell
Receptor cells of stimuli

Gradient processing and generation of inter-nal response
Modification behavior of internal response generation

Precedence cell | Gradient cell | Filament 1 Filament 2 | Tensions between filaments | Adaptability to local gradients

Transmutation of the cell geometry and spatial adaptability

Geometry of cell transmutation and programmatic adaptability

Cell geometry | System occupancy of the cell | Filamentous occupancy housing program

Generation of landscape fabric

Related = tissue cells | X-axis transformation | Axis transformation

Degrees of freedom pattern of urban fabric

Concept and source

ARCHITECTURAL DIAGRAMS 321

NETWORKING FOR THE MULTI-FUNCTIONAL ADMINISTRATIVE CITY
Jungwoo Ji

"THE NATURAL TOPOGRAPHY CONVEYS A RATIONALE OF APPROPRIATE LOCATIONS FOR THE ADMINISTRATION BUILDINGS."

Network　　　　　　　Pattern　　　　　　　Landscape

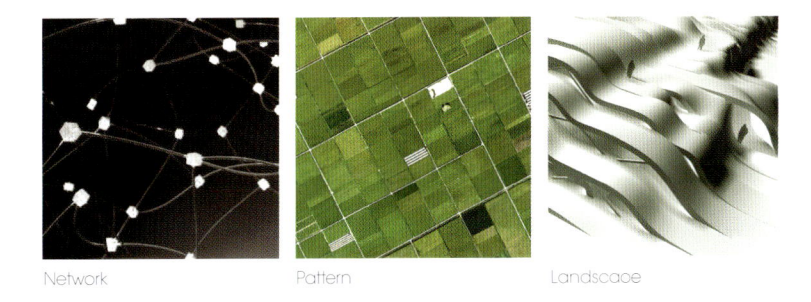

Two layers – admin carpet and building network
Network is comprised of two systems; one is landscape network and the other is building network.

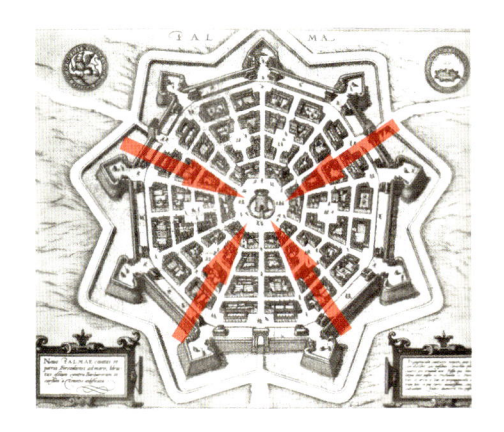

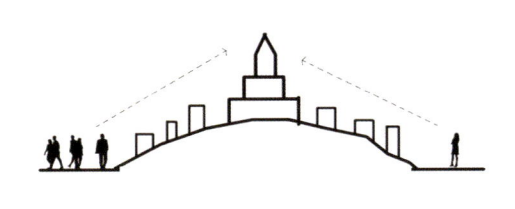

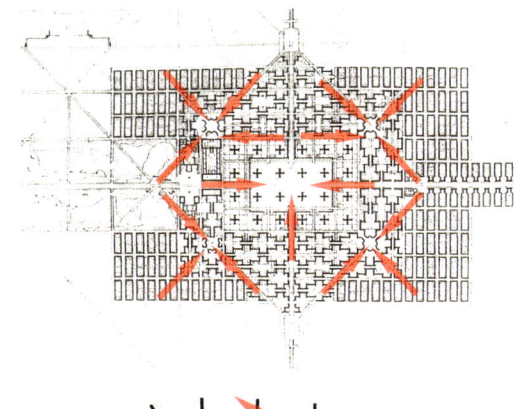

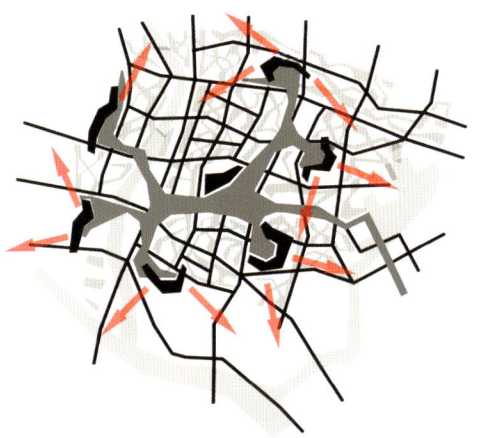

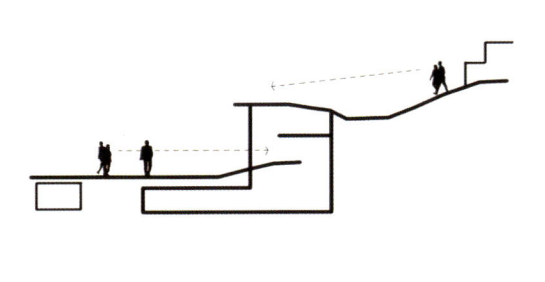

Building network + landscape = cityscape

ARCHITECTURAL DIAGRAMS 323

NEW TAINAN TAIWAN BY DESIGN
Willy Müller Architects

"PARTICULAR EMPHASIS IS GIVEN TO THE WEB THAT LINKS PUBLIC AND GREEN SPACES- BOTH ON A FUNCTIONAL AND VISUAL LEVEL."

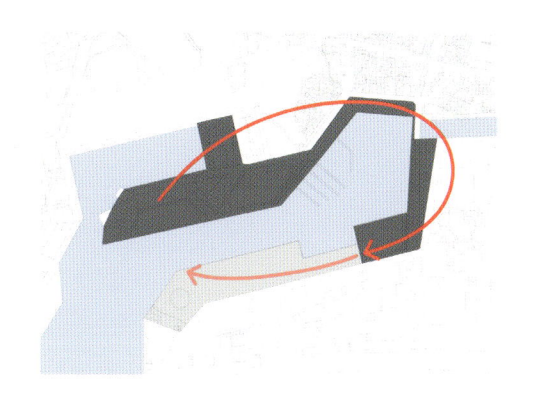

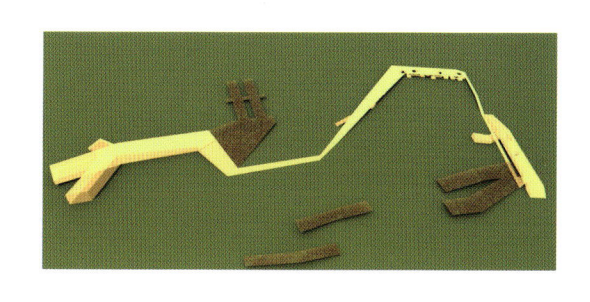

GREEN AXIS
URBAN STRIP

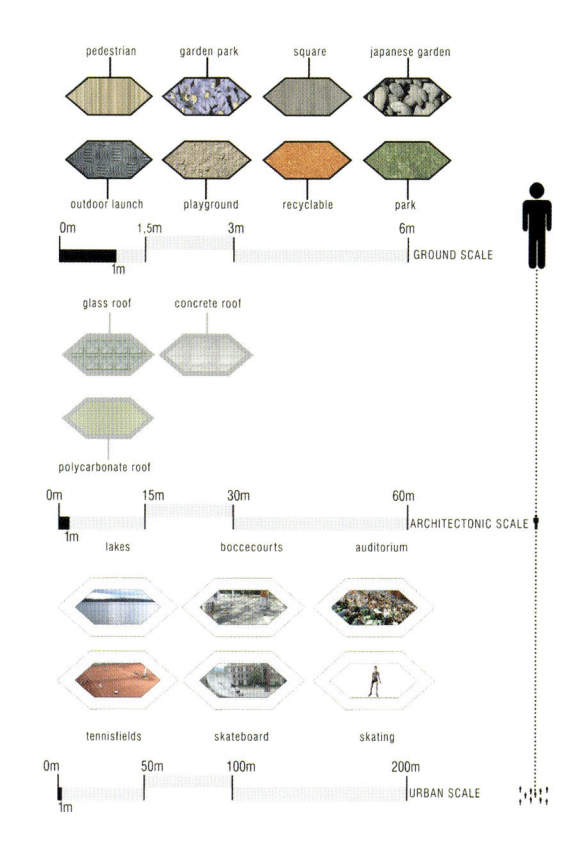

1. ESPLANADE
2. PLAZA
3. COVERED TERRACE
4. PARKING
5. PARKING
VEHICULAR CIRCULATION
PEDESTRIAN CIRCULATION

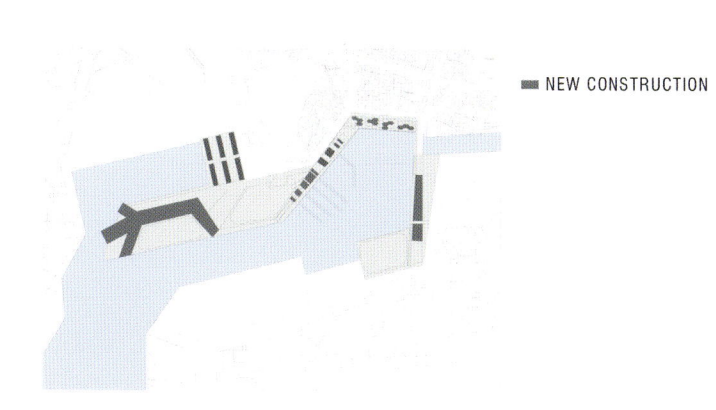

NEW CONSTRUCTION

pedestrian — garden park — square — japanese garden
outdoor launch — playground — recyclable — park

0m 1m 1,5m 3m 6m
GROUND SCALE

glass roof — concrete roof
polycarbonate roof

0m 1m 15m 30m 60m
ARCHITECTONIC SCALE
lakes — boccecourts — auditorium

tennisfields — skateboard — skating

0m 1m 50m 100m 200m
URBAN SCALE

PEDESTRIAN SCALE : MARITIME PLAZA   ARCHITECTONIC SCALE : FERRY STATION   URBAN SCALE : HARBOR PARK

Scales

ARCHITECTURAL DIAGRAMS 325

NOUVEAU BASSIN ECDM

"BALCONIES ARE DESIGNED AS SINE CURVES IN INVERSION OF PHASE FROM A LEVEL TO THE OTHER ONE, IN ORDER TO PROPOSE OUTSIDE SPACES IN DOUBLE HEIGHT."

1 apartment = 1 balcony

x 4

=

Volume + External Insulation + Consoles + Balconies

SITE

sculpture

< city centre

buildings
tramway
street
buildings
gardens
buildings
green promenade
"Nouveau Bassin" canal
street
scattered buildings

motorway >

ARCHITECTURAL DIAGRAMS 327

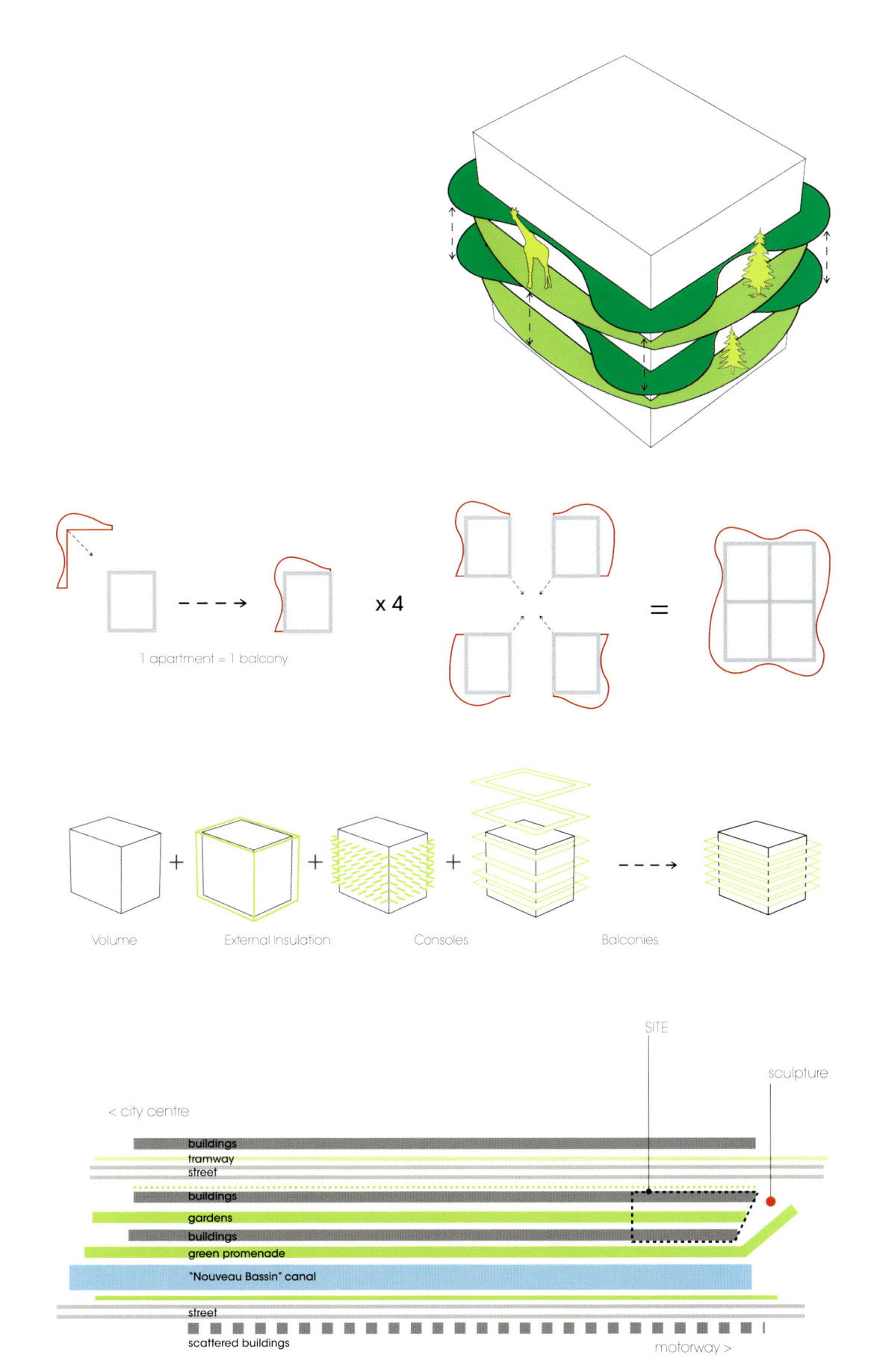

OSAKA CENTRAL STATION AREA IaN+

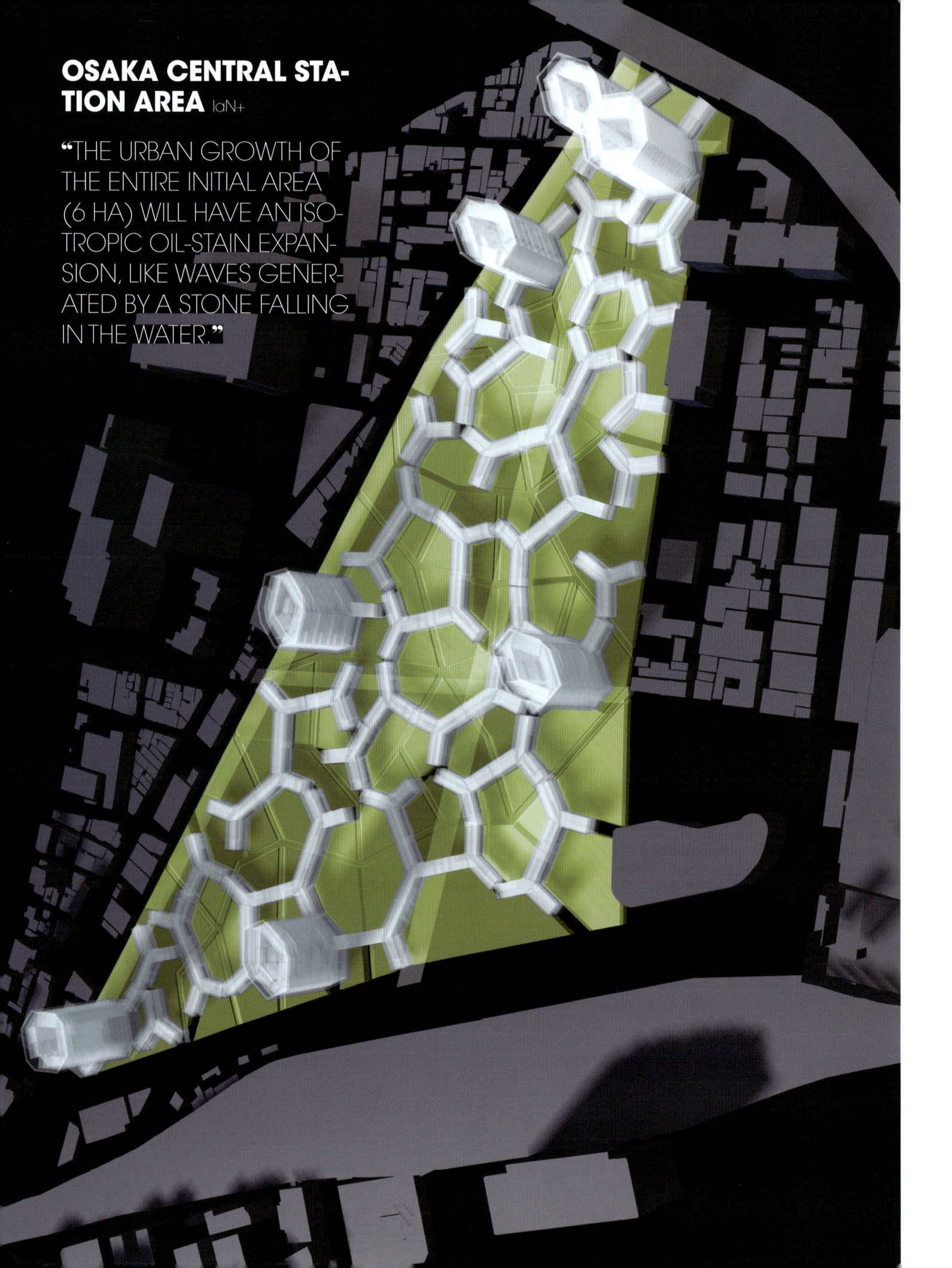

"THE URBAN GROWTH OF THE ENTIRE INITIAL AREA (6 HA) WILL HAVE AN ISOTROPIC OIL-STAIN EXPANSION, LIKE WAVES GENERATED BY A STONE FALLING IN THE WATER."

Concept: city of void

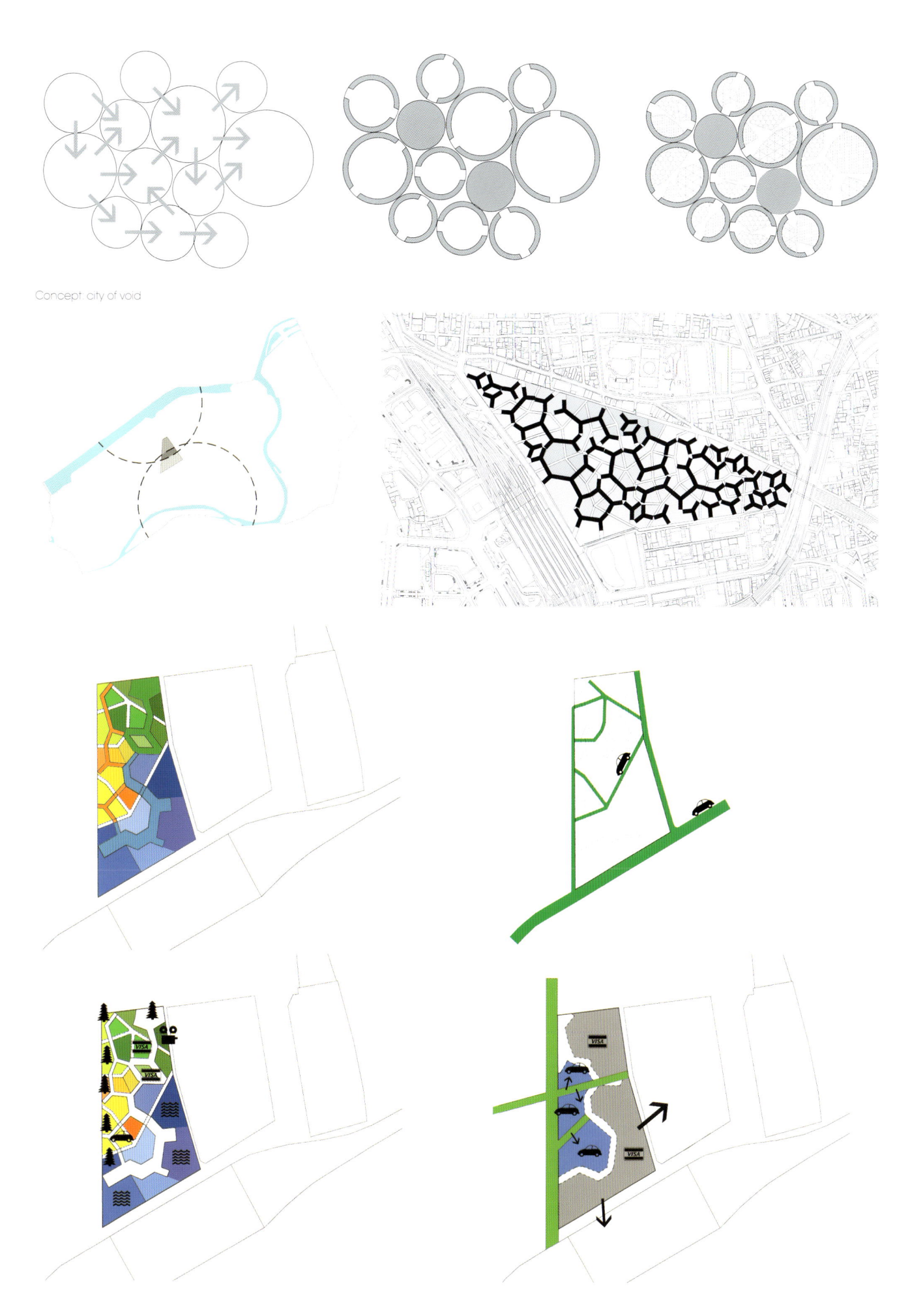

ARCHITECTURAL DIAGRAMS 329

PANIC & PLANTING

Bernd Kniess Architects Urban Planners

"THE URBAN FABRIC HAS BEEN OCCUPIED BY A MIXTURE OF SMALL RESIDENTIAL BUILDINGS AND THE REMAINING PARTS OF THE LOTS."

- House for a Family

- House for 2 Families

  In many cases, house for 2 families has two different name plates and mail boxes.

- Appartment for Single (number means households)

- Appartment for 2~people (number means households)

- Building with a office or the other function

Ookayama 1st district

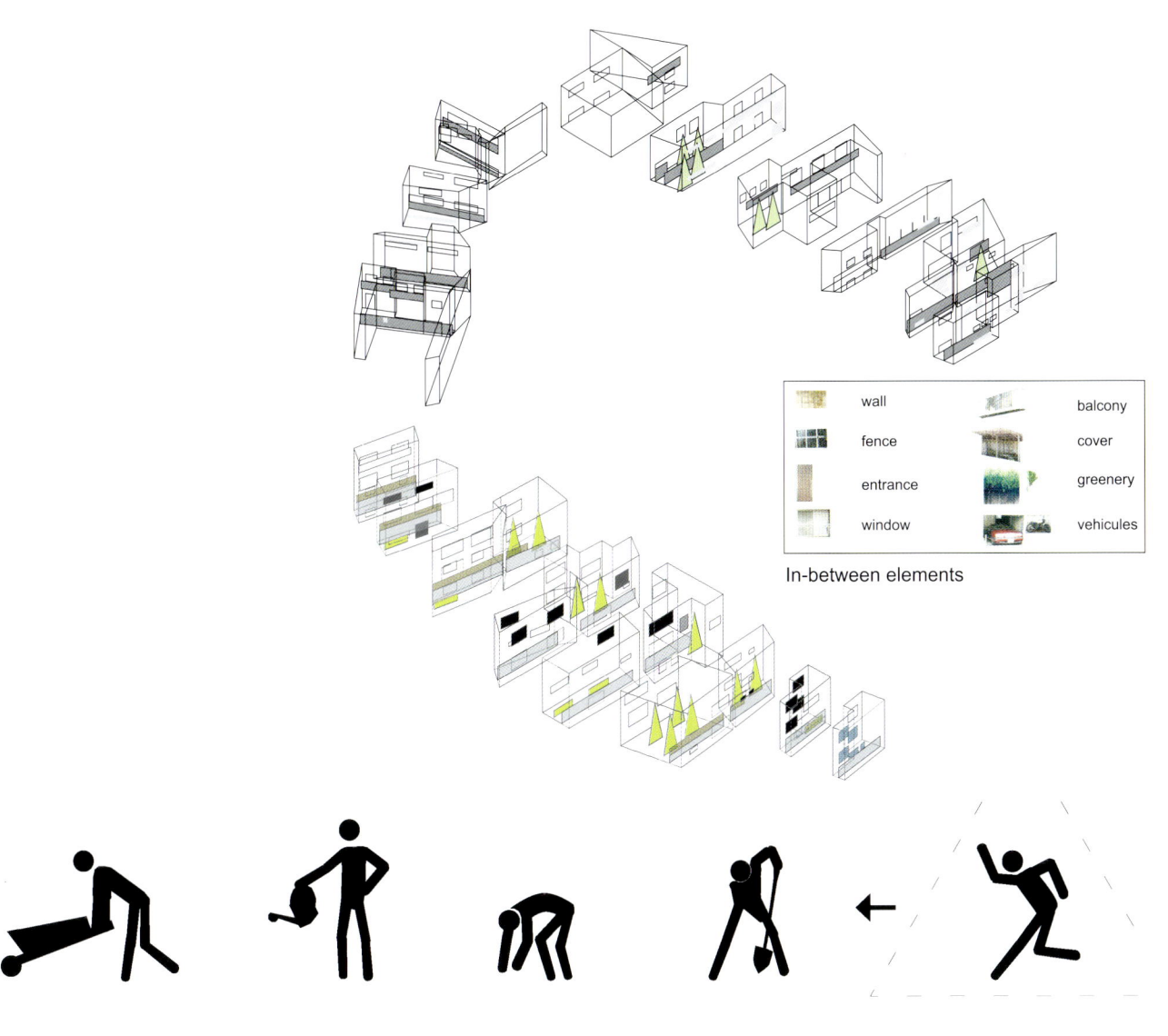

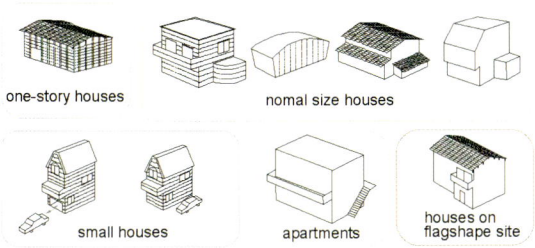

	wall		balcony
	fence		cover
	entrance		greenery
	window		vehicles

In-between elements

types of building with greenery

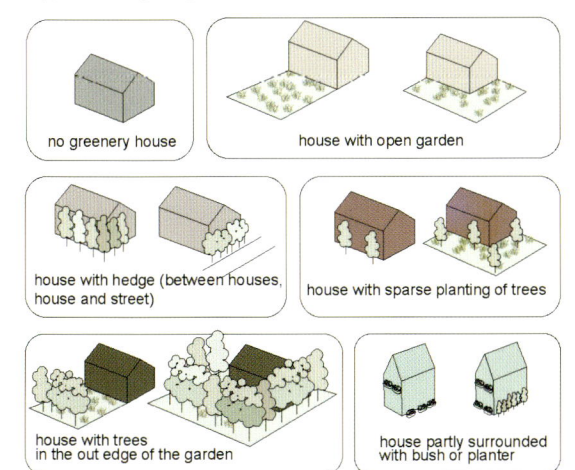

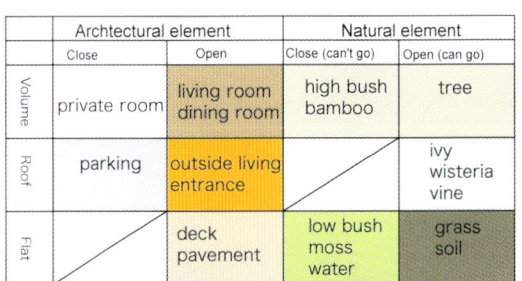

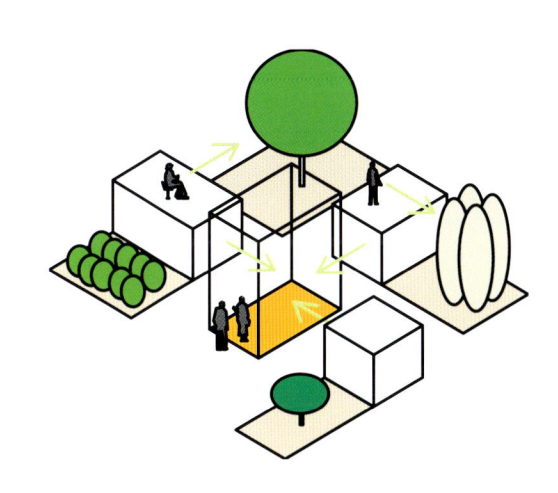

one-story houses
nomal size houses
small houses
apartments
houses on flagshape site

		Archtectural element		Natural element	
		Close	Open	Close (can't go)	Open (can go)
Volume		private room	living room dining room	high bush bamboo	tree
Roof		parking	outside living entrance		ivy wisteria vine
Flat			deck pavement	low bush moss water	grass soil

no greenery house
house with open garden
house with hedge (between houses, house and street)
house with sparse planting of trees
house with trees in the out edge of the garden
house partly surrounded with bush or planter

ARCHITECTURAL DIAGRAMS 331

PERFUMED JUNGLE Vincent Callebaut Architectures

"THE ARBORESCENT TOWERS LINKED TOGETHER BY A ROAD AND PEDESTRIAN NETWORK CHANGES THUS INTO TRUE VERTICAL GARDENS."

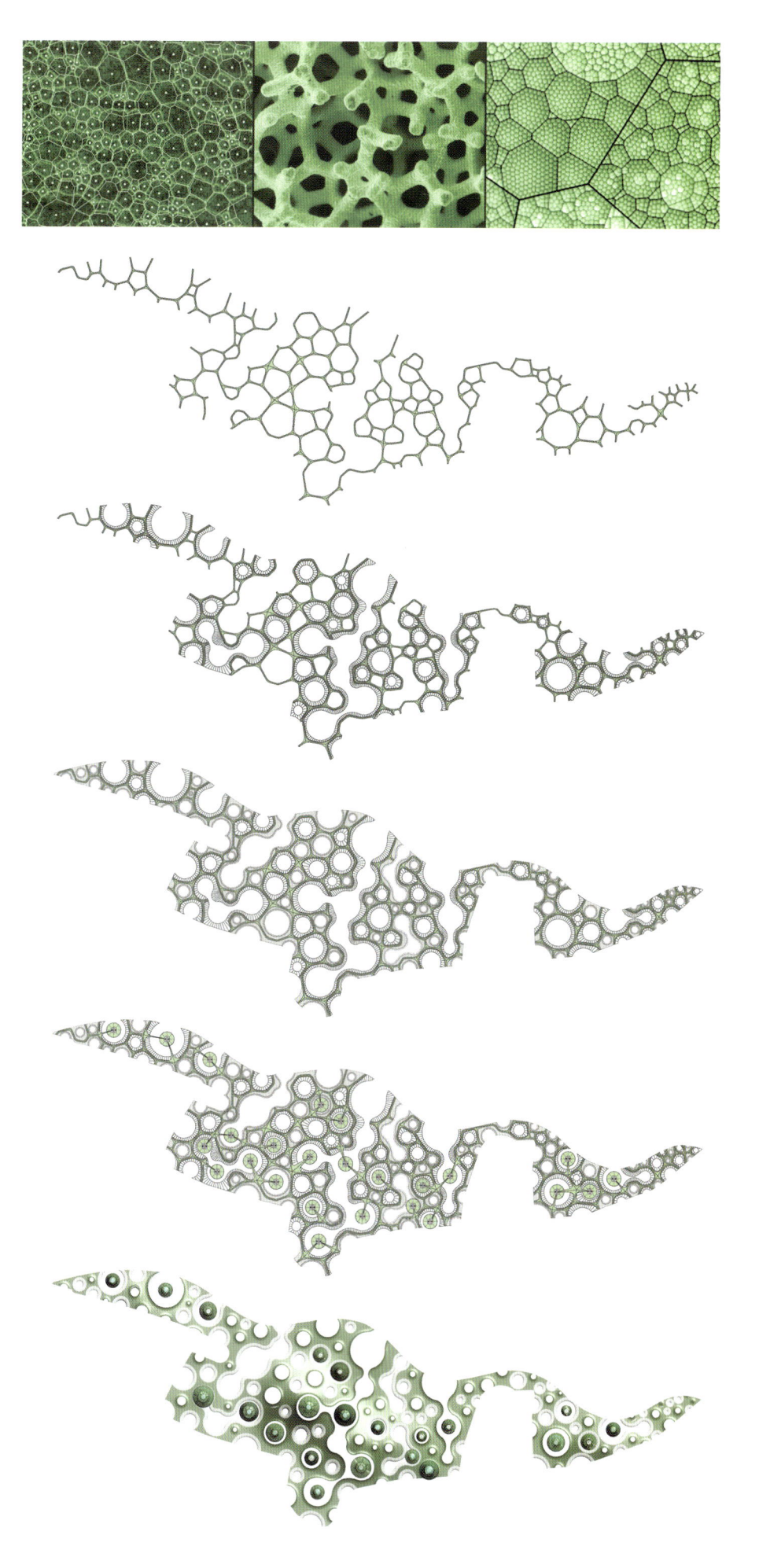

ARCHITECTURAL DIAGRAMS

REFILLING GREEN Re_Load

"THESE COURTYARDS ARE EVEN LINKED BY SMALL FOOTBRIDGES THAT CROSS THE MAIN STREET TO THE WALKWAY AND TO THE PARKS."

Method of aligning: scretching

From walkway: green public spaces

From housing: view on green

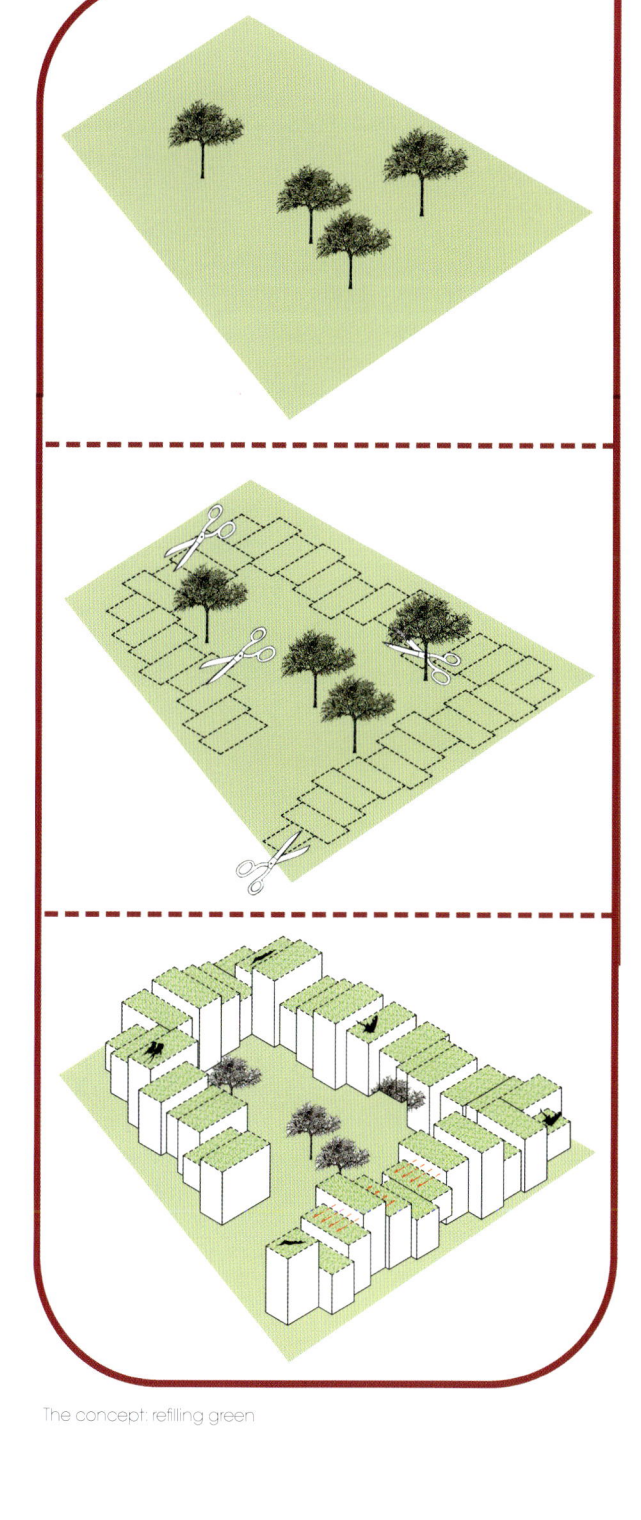

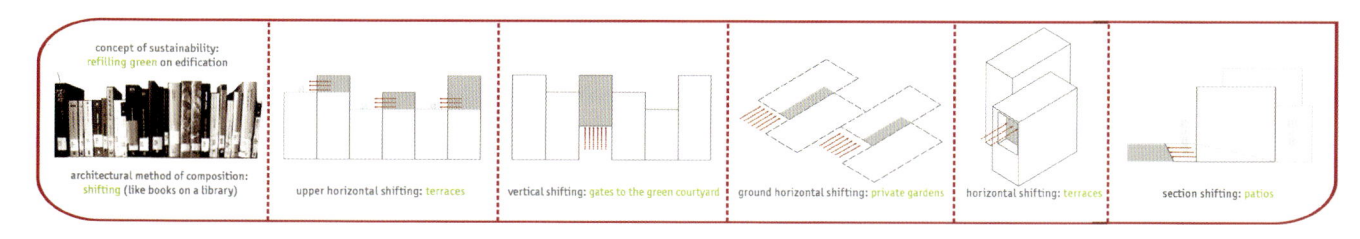

The concept: refilling green

concept of sustainability: refilling green on edification					
architectural method of composition: shifting (like books on a library)	upper horizontal shifting: terraces	vertical shifting: gates to the green courtyard	ground horizontal shifting: private gardens	horizontal shifting: terraces	section shifting: patios

ARCHITECTURAL DIAGRAMS 335

SEEDS AND VECTOR

Enrique Arenas Laorga & Luis Basabe Montalvo

"A LIQUID CITY IS PROPOSED, ANYTIME ADAPTABLE TO ITS SOCIAL CONTENTS."

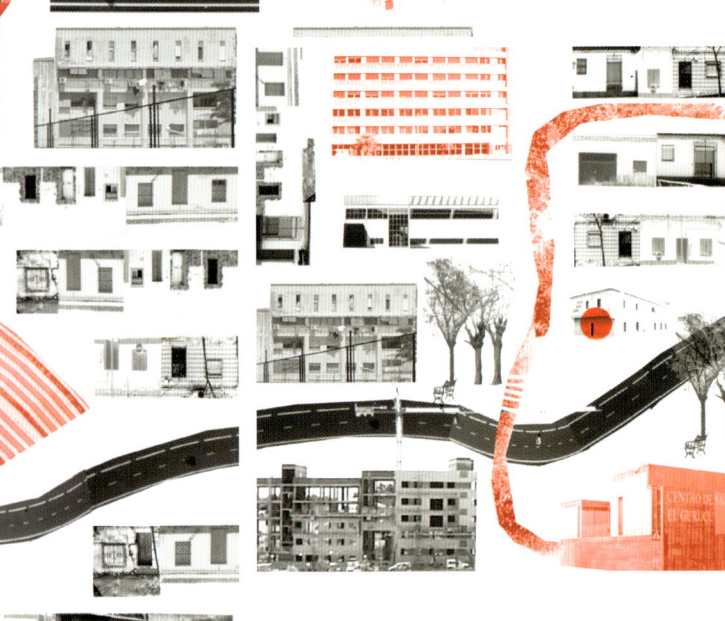

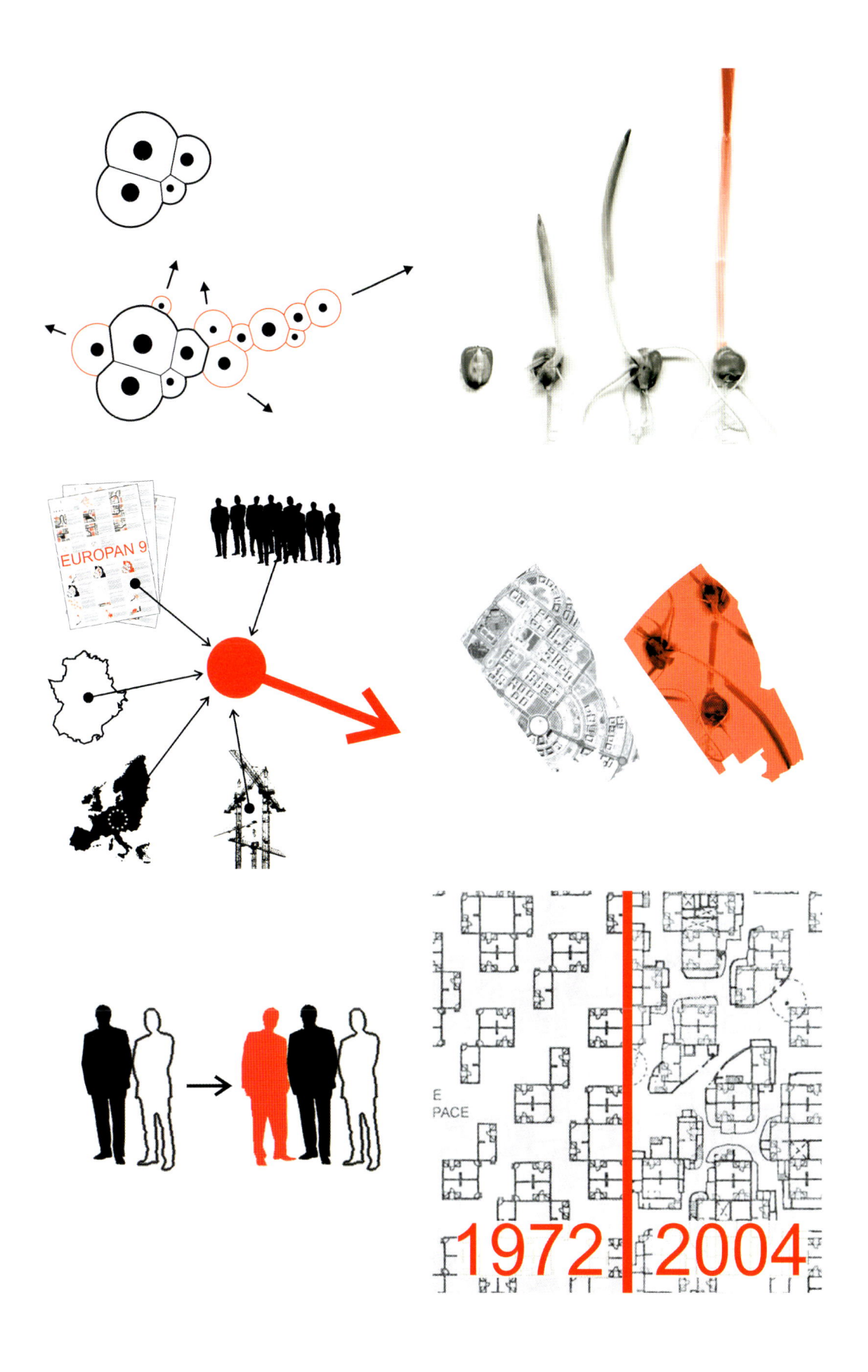

ARCHITECTURAL DIAGRAMS 337

SLOW TOWN VEMA
Iotti + Pavarani Architetti

"THE ROLE OF ARCHITECTURE IS TO REMAIN IN THE BACKGROUND, AS ENRICHING AS IT IS DISCREET."

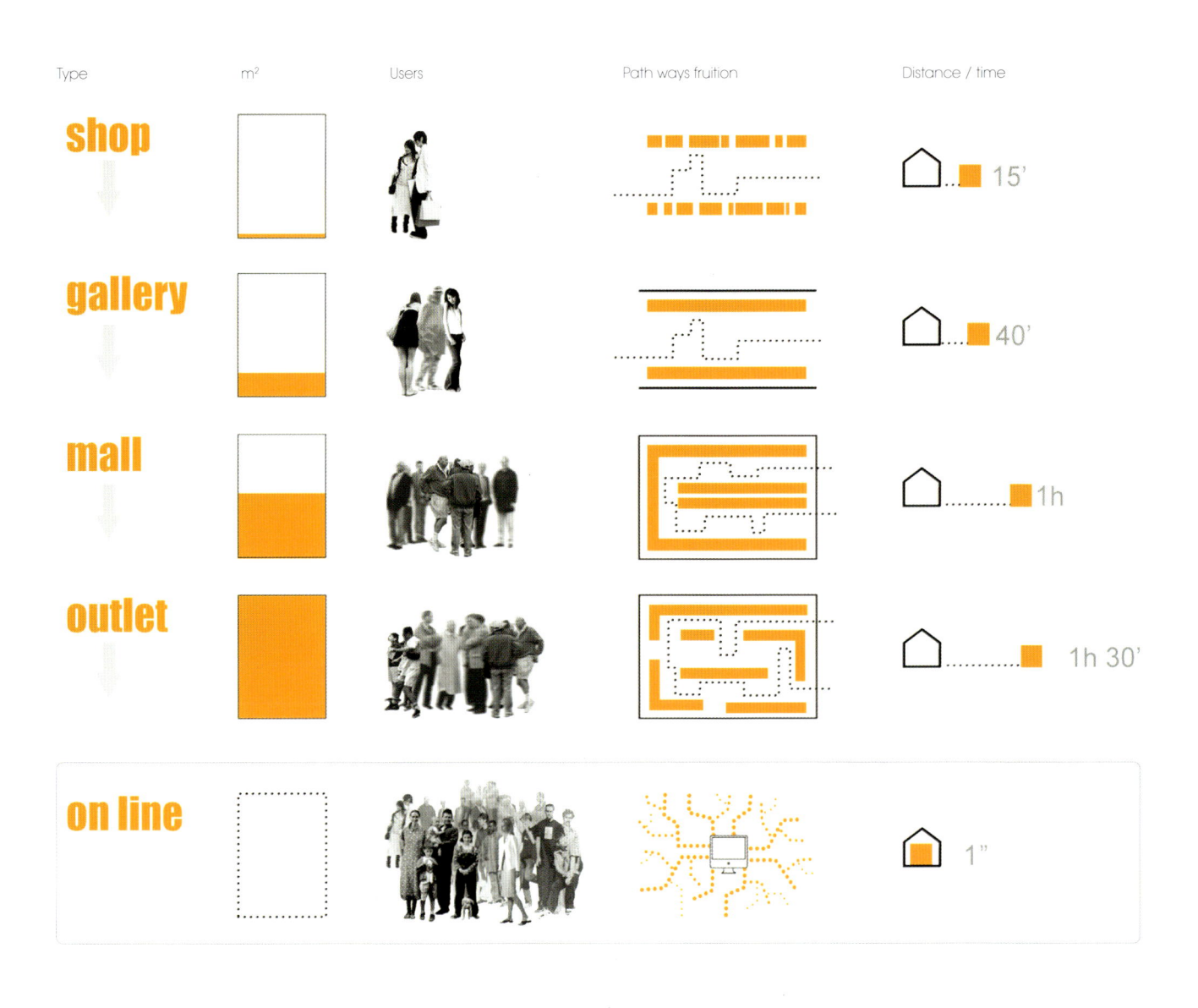

Type	m²	Users	Path ways fruition	Distance / time
shop				15'
gallery				40'
mall				1h
outlet				1h 30'
on line				1"

ARCHITECTURAL DIAGRAMS 339

STEPSCAPE – GREENSCAPE - WATERSCAPE

Florian Krieger

"LESS HIGHT ALLOWS MORE DEPTH WITHOUT AFFECTING THE NEIGHBOURING STRUCTURE."

Inner city

New quarter

Green spaces   Water

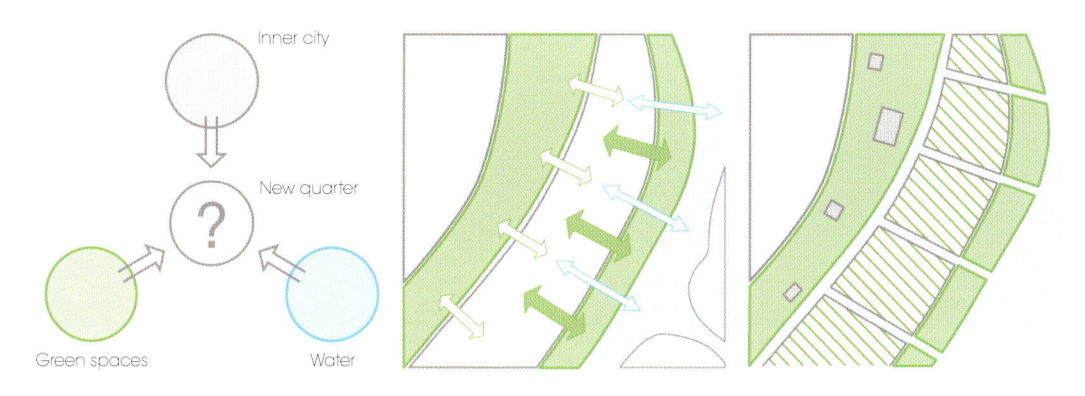

Stay between the town and water

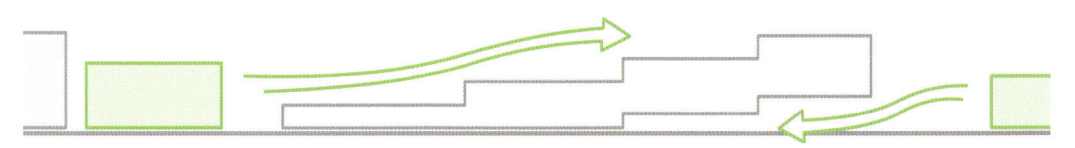

Building on green spaces

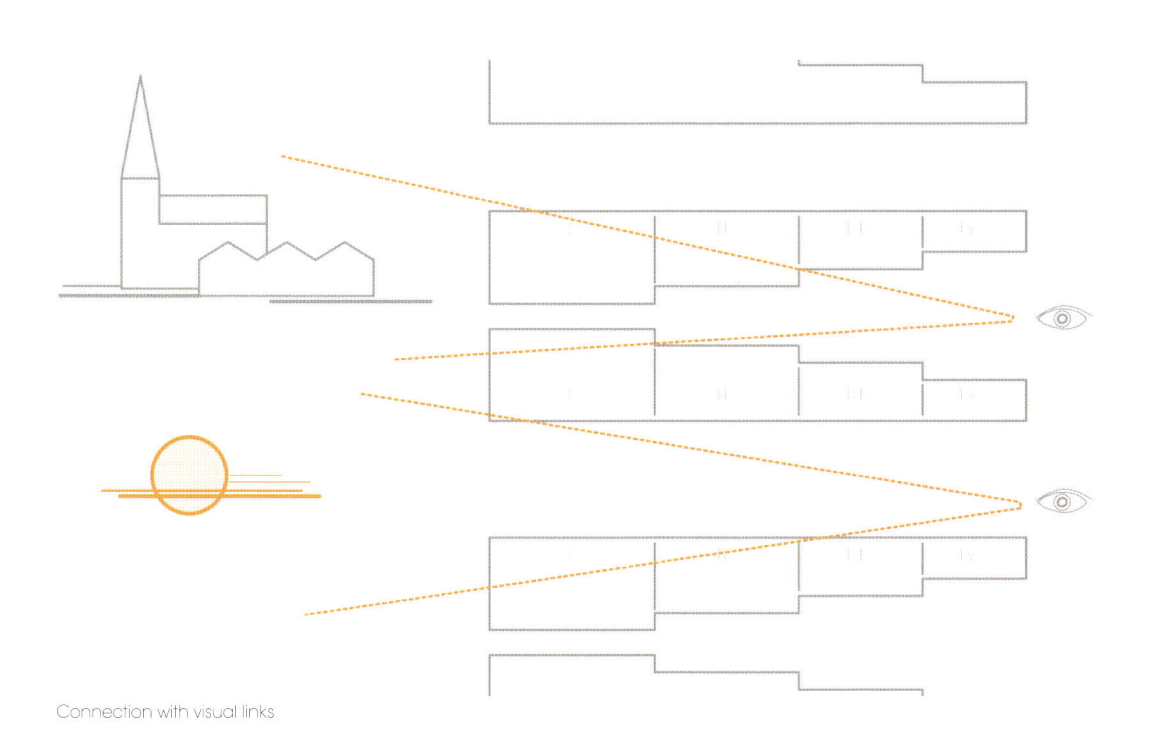

Connection with visual links

ARCHITECTURAL DIAGRAMS 341

STU CAMPUS
CJ Lim | Studio 8 Architects

"GRADUALLY BUILDING UP THE CAMPUS'S MASS INTO A FLEXIBLE PATCHWORK OF BUILT CLUSTERS SEPARATED BY OPEN LANDSCAPE."

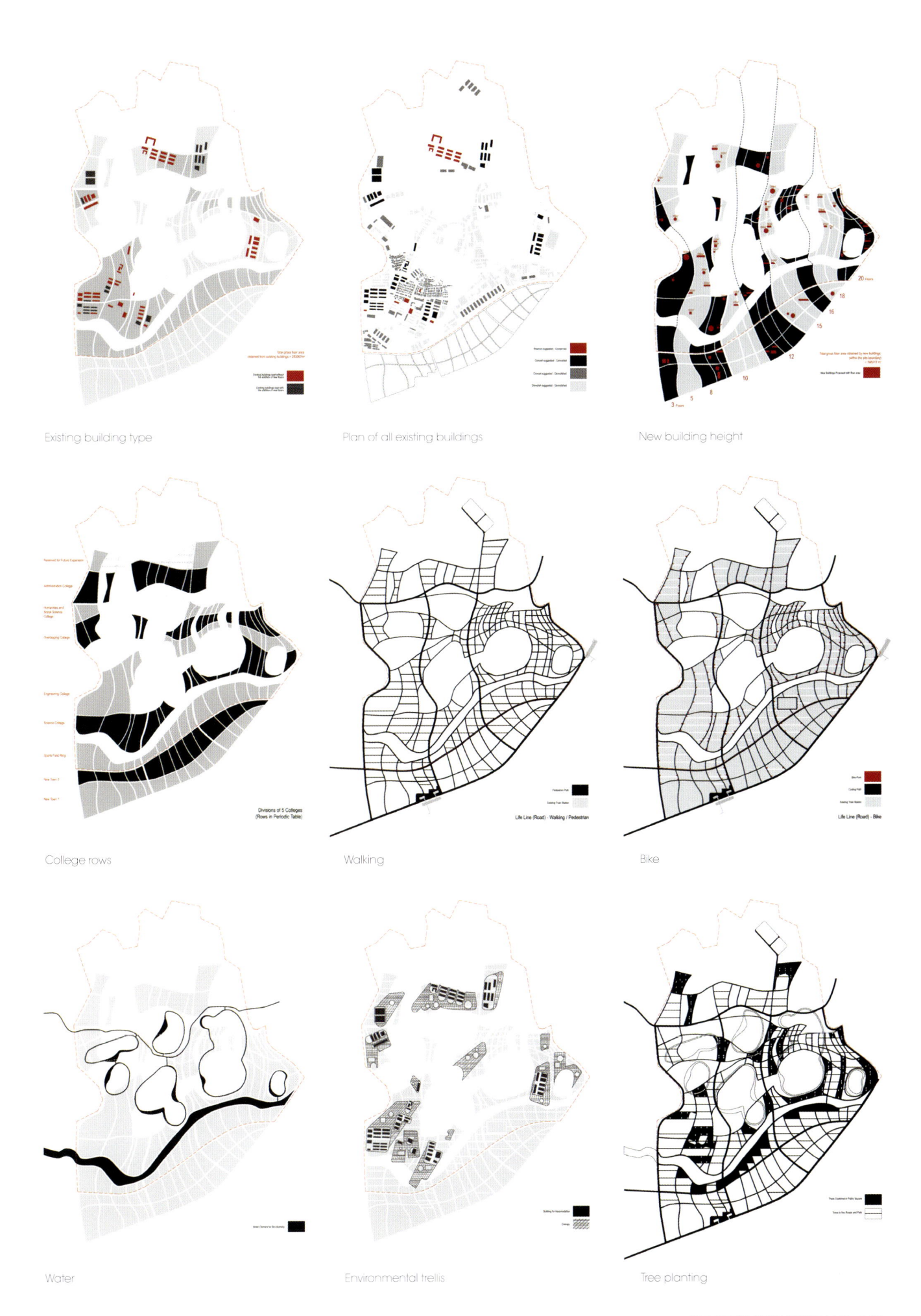

Existing building type

Plan of all existing buildings

New building height

College rows

Walking

Bike

Water

Environmental trellis

Tree planting

ARCHITECTURAL DIAGRAMS 343

SUBURBAN FRAMES
Florian Krieger

"THE AMBIVALENT SUBURBAN STRUCTURE OSCILLATES BETWEEN SPATIAL DEFINITION AND THE CONTINUOUS SPATIAL CHANGE."

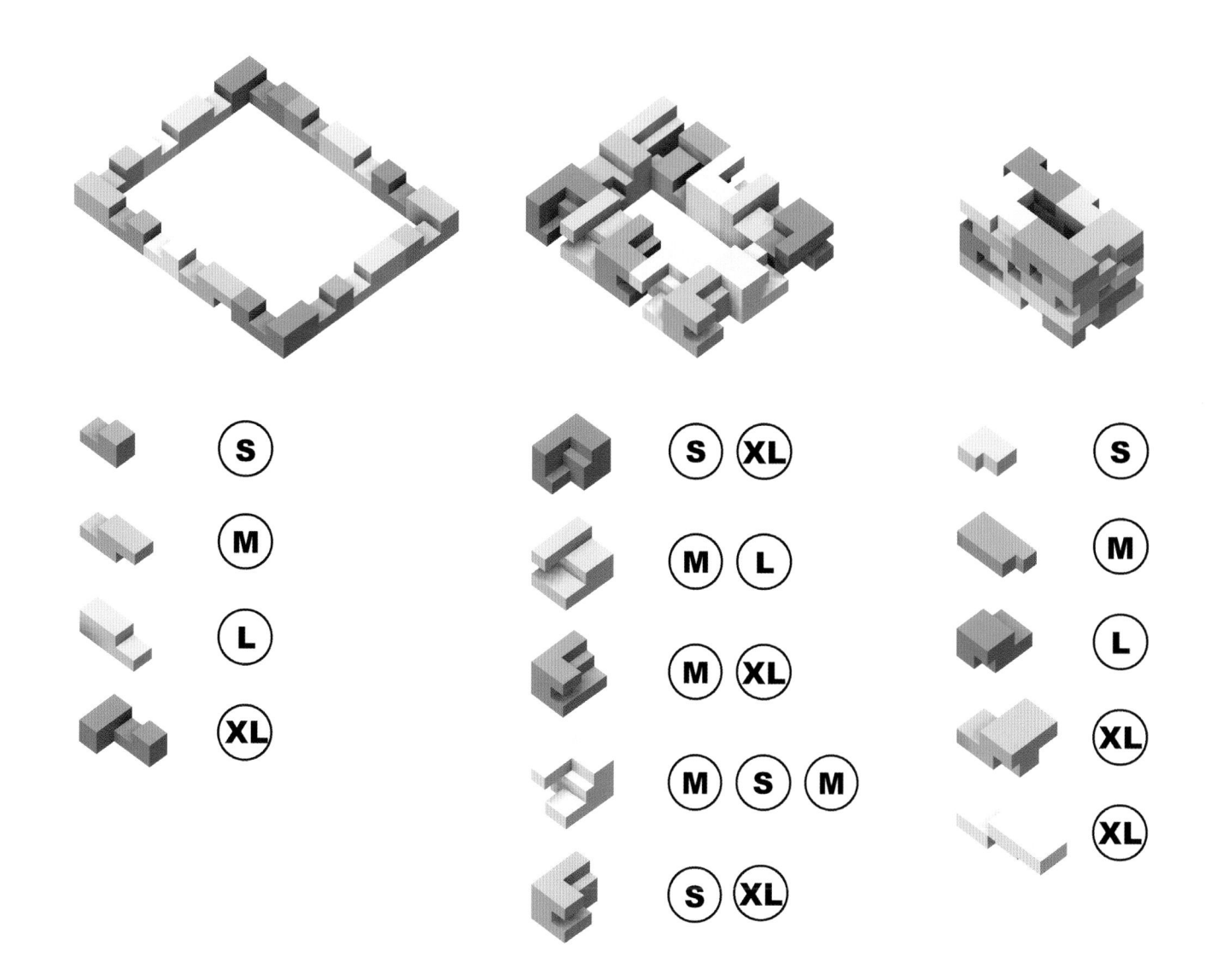

ARCHITECTURAL DIAGRAMS 345

SUN-FIELDS Florian Krieger

"THE SIMPLE AND CLEAR URBAN LAYOUT OFFERS A MIX OF DIFFERENT BUILDING TYPES."

The slider: more flexibility

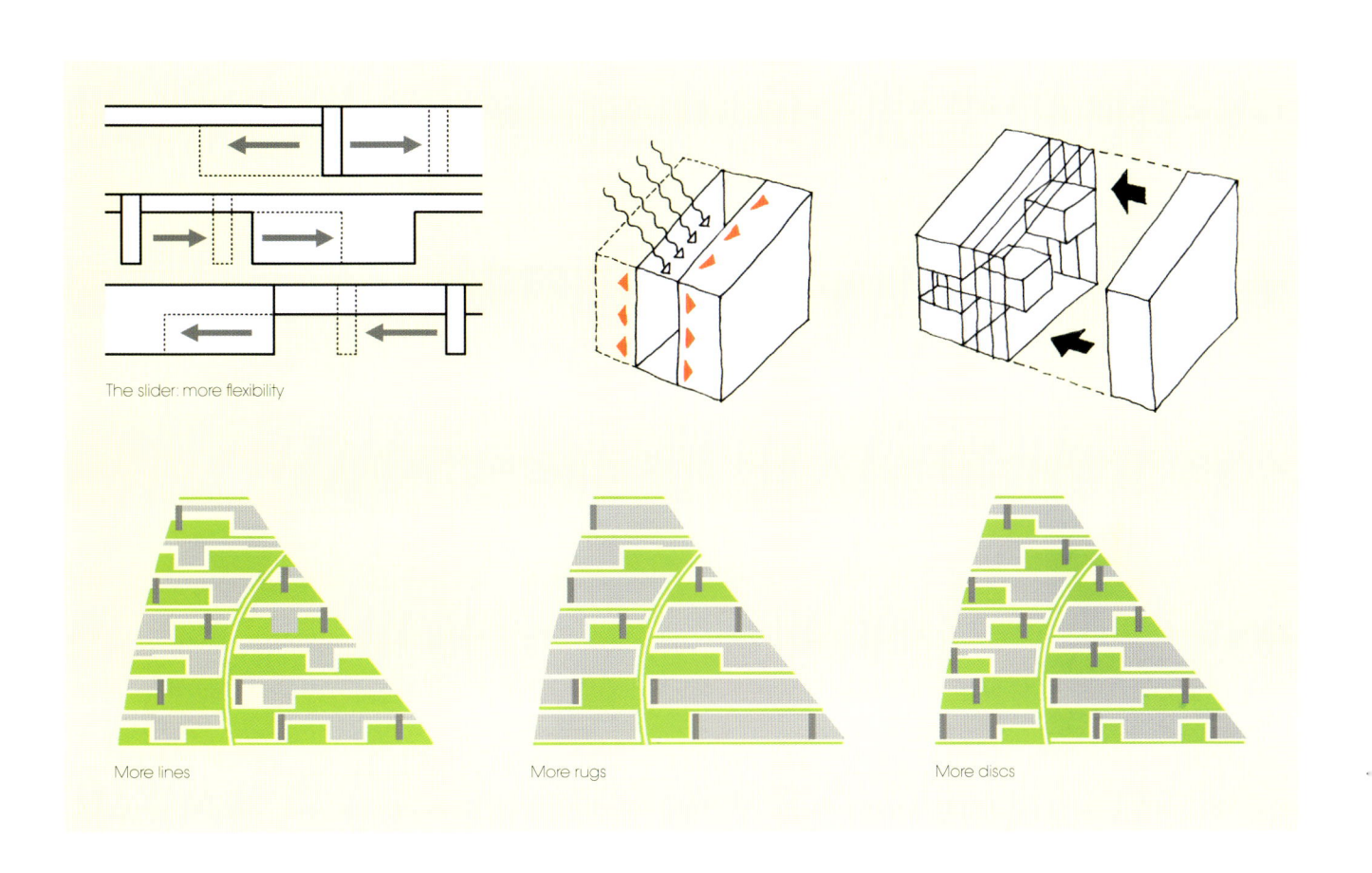

More lines

More rugs

More discs

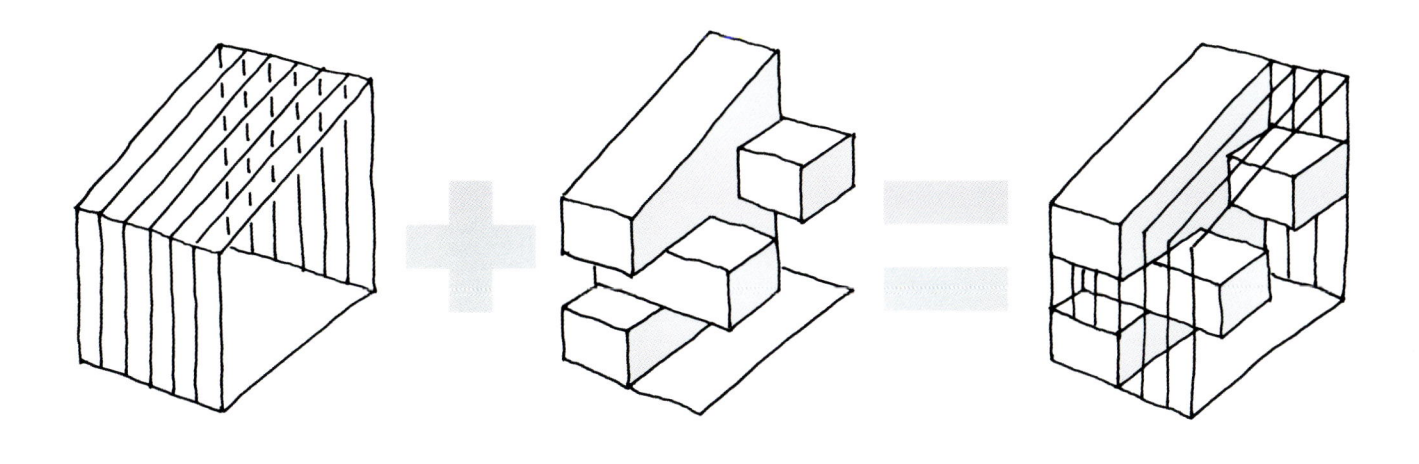

ARCHITECTURAL DIAGRAMS 347

THE URBAN CORSET, A HYBRID INTERMEDIARY
Vincent Callebaut Architectures

"THE CITY MUST FORGET ITS BOUNDARIES AND ACCEPT THE NEW PARADIGMS OF NOMADIC URBANITY."

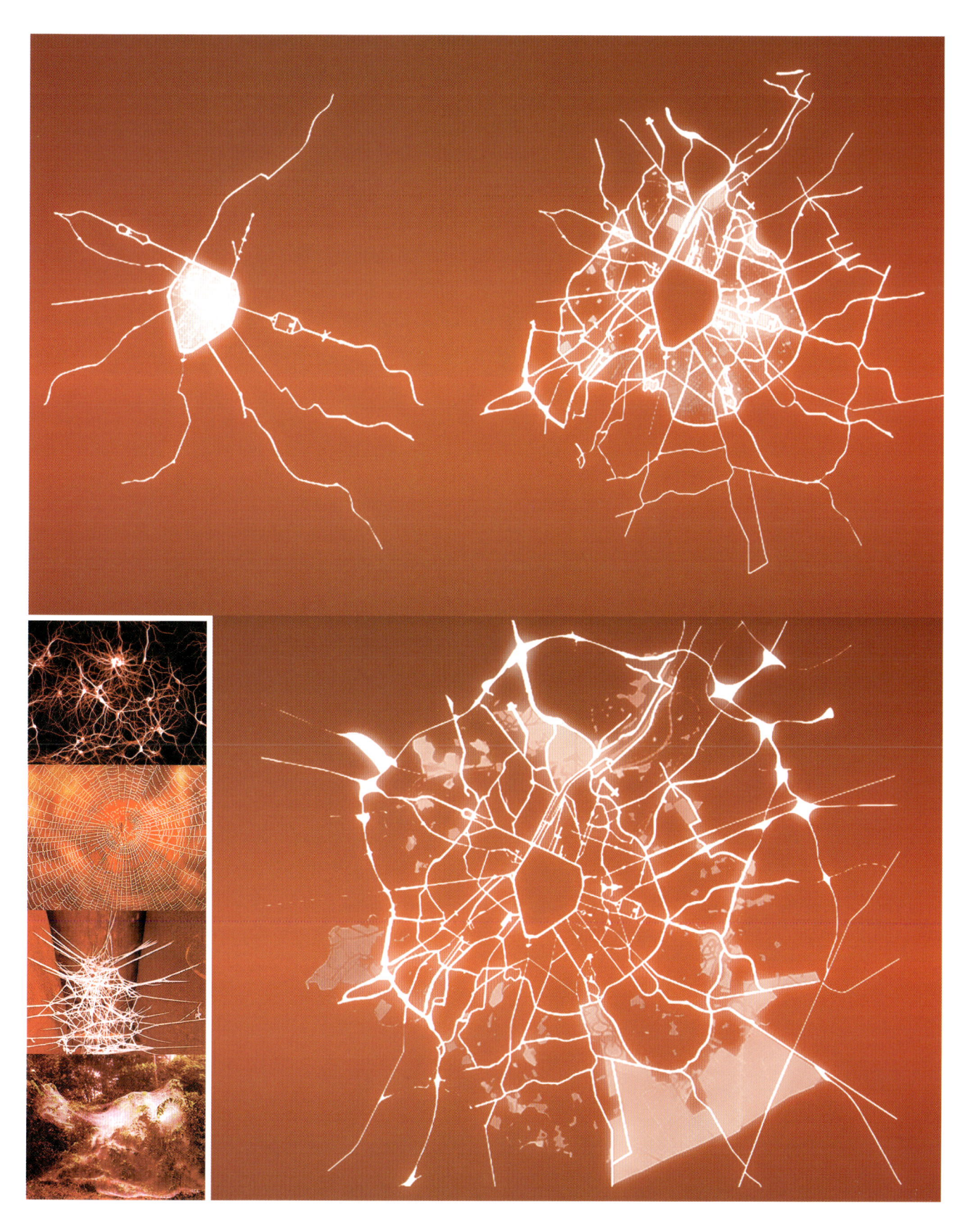

ARCHITECTURAL DIAGRAMS 349

TOUCHING WATER
b4architects

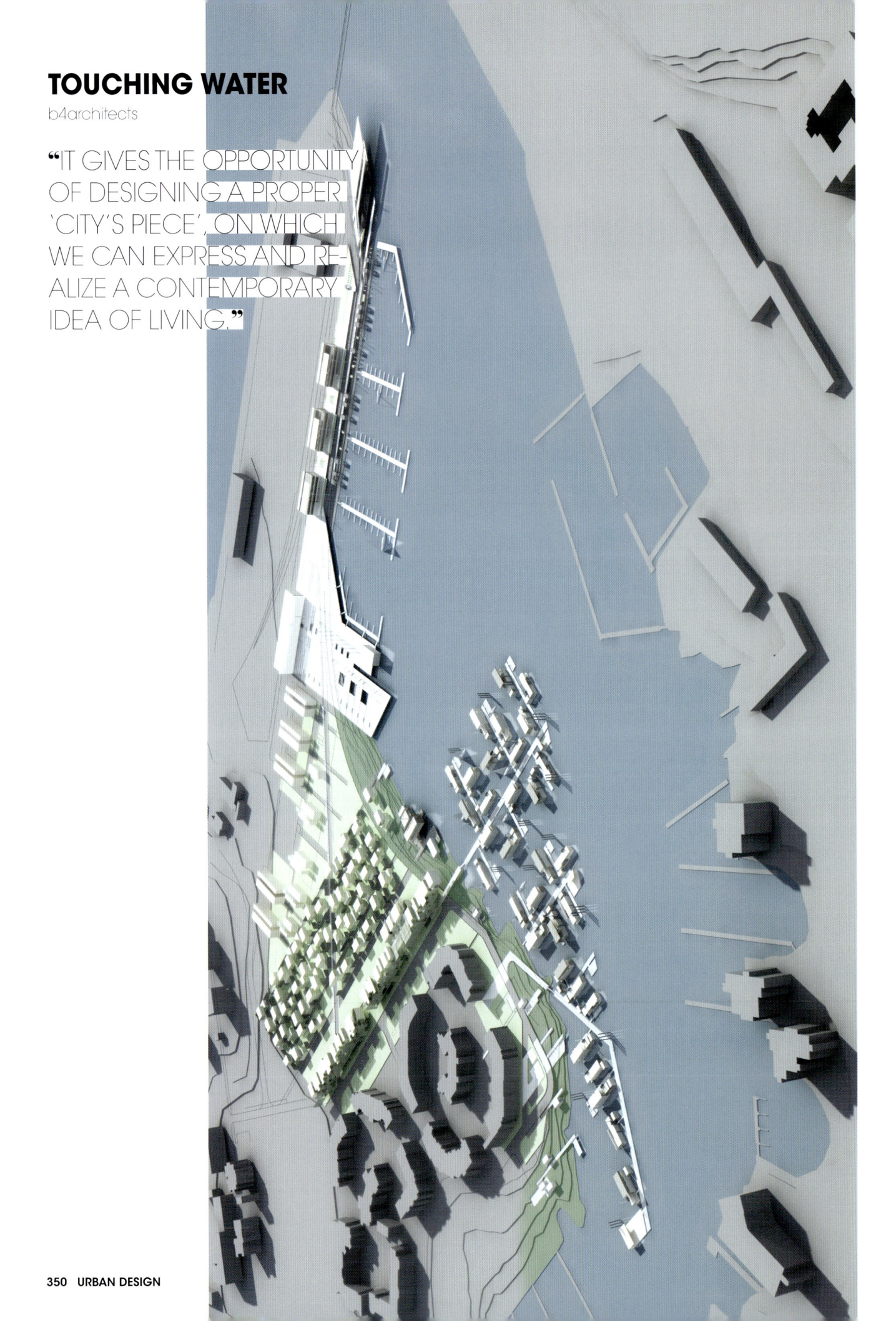

"IT GIVES THE OPPORTUNITY OF DESIGNING A PROPER 'CITY'S PIECE', ON WHICH WE CAN EXPRESS AND REALIZE A CONTEMPORARY IDEA OF LIVING."

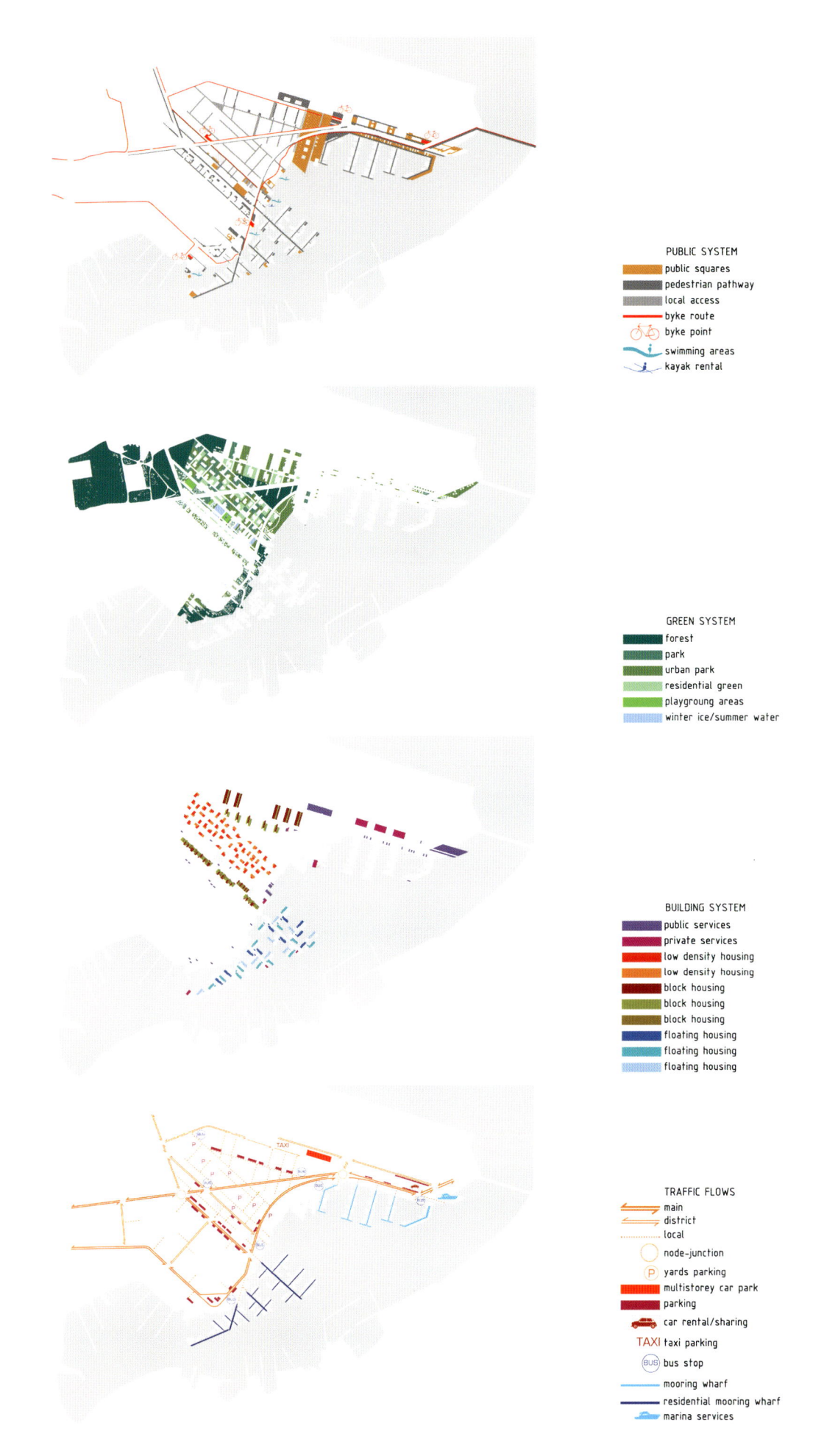

PUBLIC SYSTEM
- public squares
- pedestrian pathway
- local access
- byke route
- byke point
- swimming areas
- kayak rental

GREEN SYSTEM
- forest
- park
- urban park
- residential green
- playgroung areas
- winter ice/summer water

BUILDING SYSTEM
- public services
- private services
- low density housing
- low density housing
- block housing
- block housing
- block housing
- floating housing
- floating housing
- floating housing

TRAFFIC FLOWS
- main
- district
- local
- node-junction
- yards parking
- multistorey car park
- parking
- car rental/sharing
- TAXI taxi parking
- bus stop
- mooring wharf
- residential mooring wharf
- marina services

ARCHITECTURAL DIAGRAMS 351

URBAN LIVING ROOMS
Iotti+Pavarani Architetti

"NEW LANDSCAPE GENERATES A STRONG IDENTITY FROM THE INTERVENTION AND THE PLACE SO AS TO BECOME THE VERY LANDMARK OF THE TERRITORY."

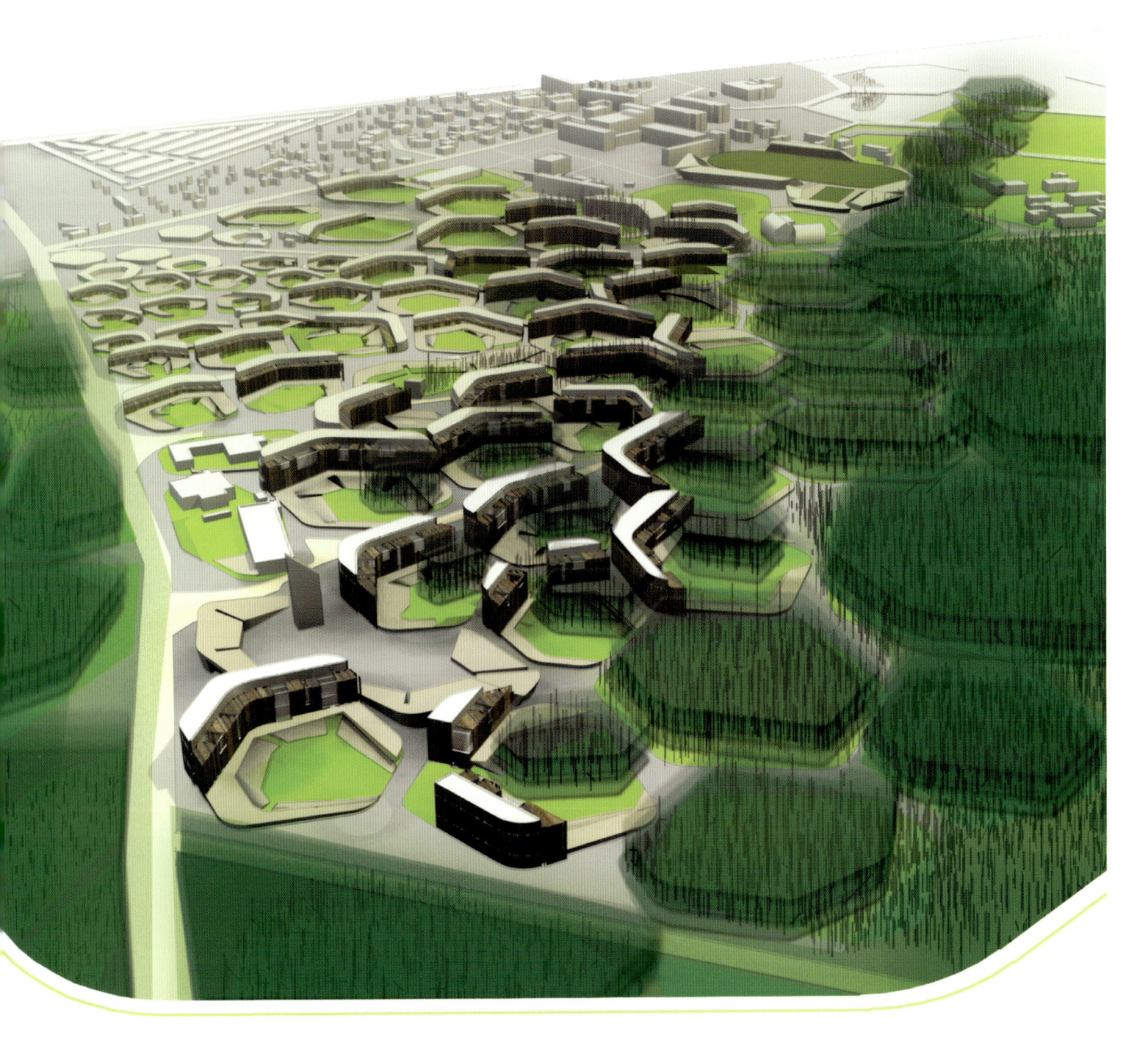

1 site

the extraordinary position of the site, surrounded by the forest, extending towards the lake and directly connected with the city centre of attraction for many different types of users

3 gradients

U1 G1
urban**gradient** green**gradient**

W1
water**gradient**

Accordingly, URBAN LIVING ROOMS consists of a sequence of gathered spaces, generated by the polygonal matrix which arrange and interrelate public and private areas, accommodating activities and functions which change according to their position in the respect of the distinctive features of the area: Jugjas Isla west urban fringe, the forest-screened south-east fringe and the east fringe facing the lake. Under the impulse of similar forces, the net loses its shape and the built-up area adapts to the circumstances, maintaining a profile towards the urban front, while raising progressively and setting on the border of the rings towards the forest.

2 focal points

sports centre — bathing area
commercial service activities — sports centre — beach — pier — restaurants

RESIDENTIAL PARK

facilities in the wood
kindergarten
firestation

firestation   kindergarten   facilities in the wood
commercial activities   sports centre   bathing area   beach
pier   restaurants

the project area, thus, turns into a continuous equipped park, where recreational and cultural activities, for leisure time, coexist with the residential function

4 fluxes.users.use

parking — sports centre
courtyard
house
                             sports centre
                             sports centre
                             beach
                             bathing area
                             restaurants
                             pier
                                                beach
                                                bathing area
                                                restaurants
                                                facilities
facilities
         house   beach
kindergarten   **tourists.circuit**

residents.points

facilities

weekenders.net

residents.points | fruition of the site through concentrated points (dwellings, courtyards, facilities etc.) connected by irregular and unordered movements

weekenders.net | use of the public spaces of the site through regular movements towards the natural attractions of the site and towards the sports centre offered with some little breaks in the semi-public courtyards

tourists.circuit | guided paths towards the strategic natural points of the site

5 net

An irregular, polygonal matrix is taken as a mediation system between the organic, fractioned places of natural evidences and a more rational, necessary frame of a urban settlement. That matrix becomes a net of routes and crossings capable to arrange the movements and the activities inside the project area, while it spreads as a net over the closest areas (i.e. the forest, the lakefront, the present fringe of deteriorated zones), putting them into a system. A similar net can either narrow or spread, following the features of the place, absorbing the pre-existing elements (of which a gradual dismission or reconversion is expected), so making possible the flexibility of a long-term design

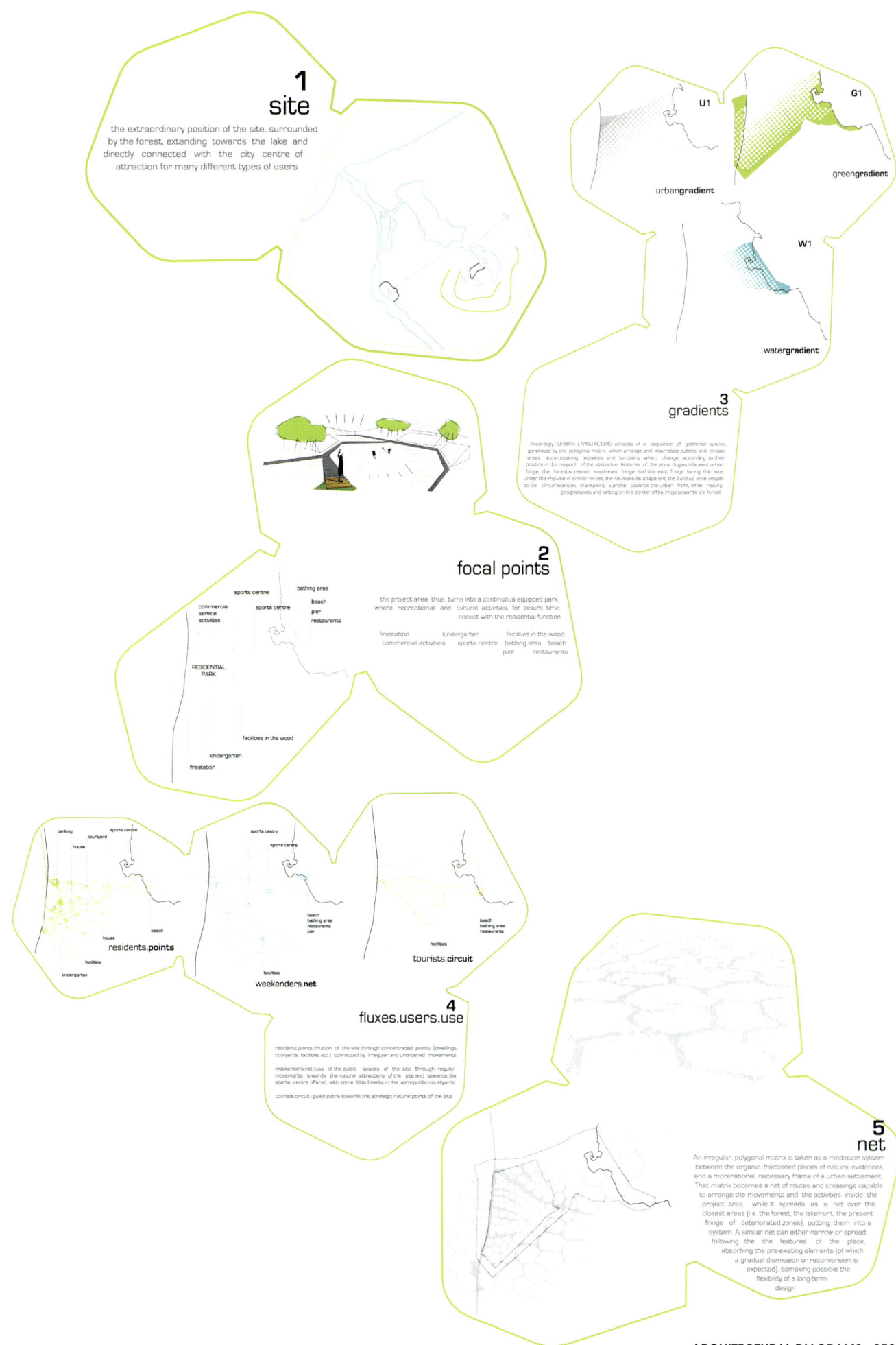

URBAN VOIDS
Ecosistema Urbano + TECTUM

354 URBAN DESIGN

New Ecological Mobility

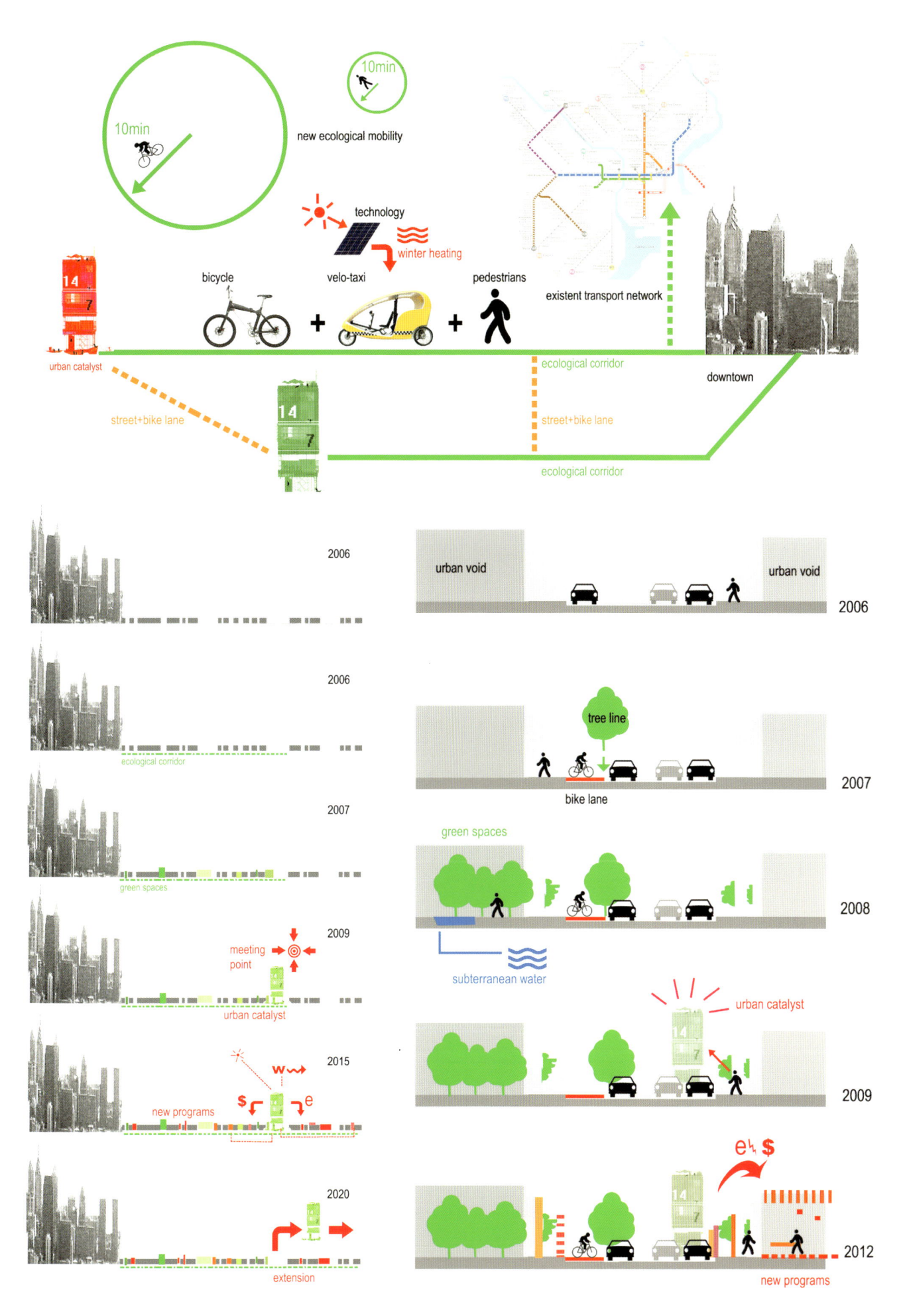

10min (bicycle) — **10min** (pedestrian) — new ecological mobility

bicycle + velo-taxi + pedestrians

technology → winter heating

existent transport network

urban catalyst — ecological corridor — downtown

street+bike lane — street+bike lane — ecological corridor

Timeline (left)

- 2006
- 2006 — ecological corridor
- 2007 — green spaces
- 2009 — meeting point / urban catalyst
- 2015 — new programs ($, w, e)
- 2020 — extension

Section Evolution (right)

- **2006** — urban void | urban void
- **2007** — tree line / bike lane
- **2008** — green spaces / subterranean water
- **2009** — urban catalyst
- **2012** — new programs (e, $)

ARCHITECTURAL DIAGRAMS 355

VELIKA PLAZA
SPACEGROUP & JDS Architects

"ACCESSIBLE FOR ALL, CREATING AN ACTIVE RATHER THAN PASSIVE OR REPRESENTATIONAL INTERFACE WITH NATURE."

| Velika plaza Marina | Radial village | Eco village | Luxury village | Sporting village | Lake district |

Strong programmatic, thematic and typological identity for each area
Diagram 6 villages

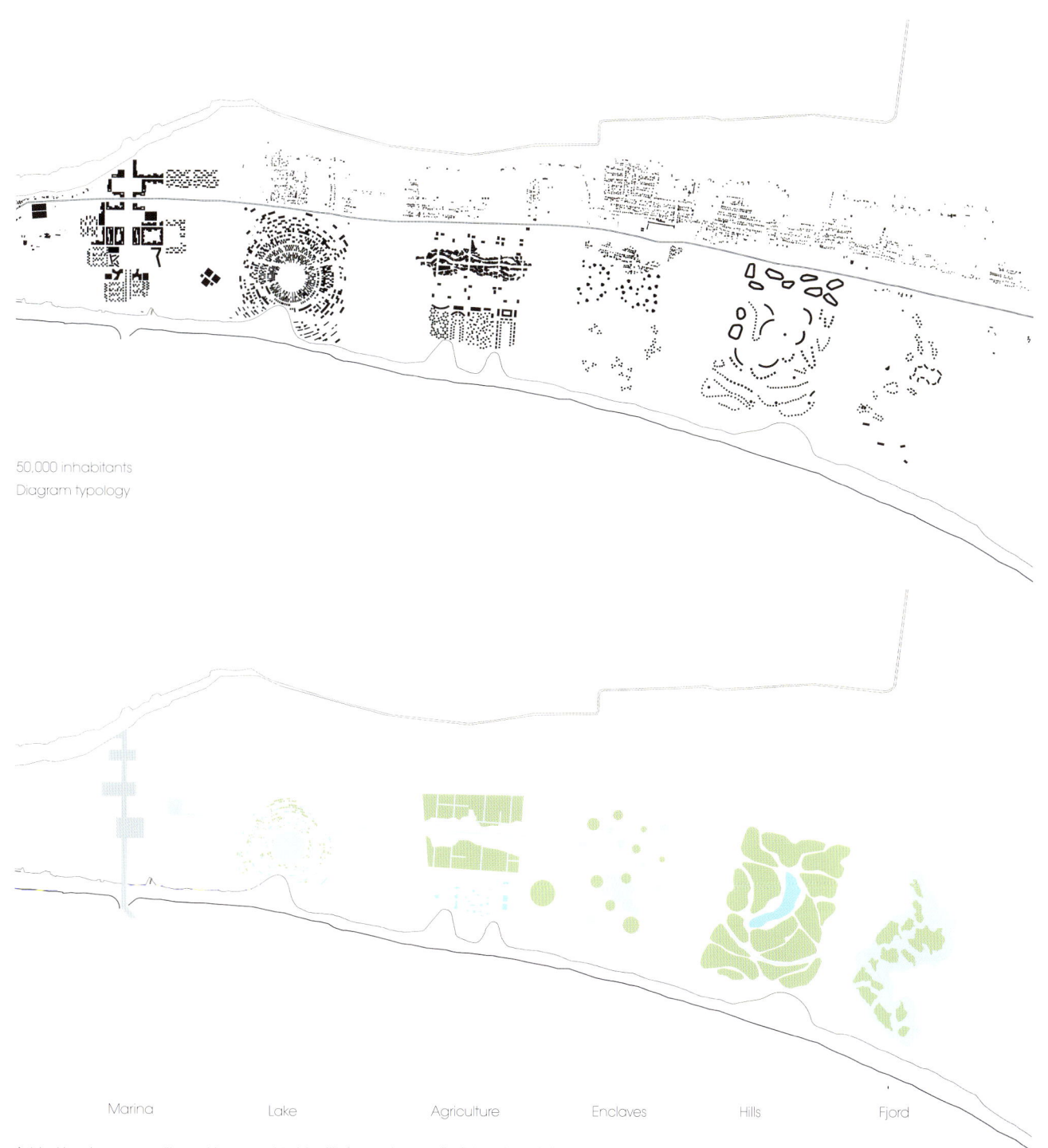

50,000 inhabitants
Diagram typology

| Marina | Lake | Agriculture | Enclaves | Hills | Fjord |

Added landscape quality and topographic identity for each area (build on the existing natural qualities and / or context of each village)
Added Landscape

ARCHITECTURAL DIAGRAMS 357

VEMA ma0

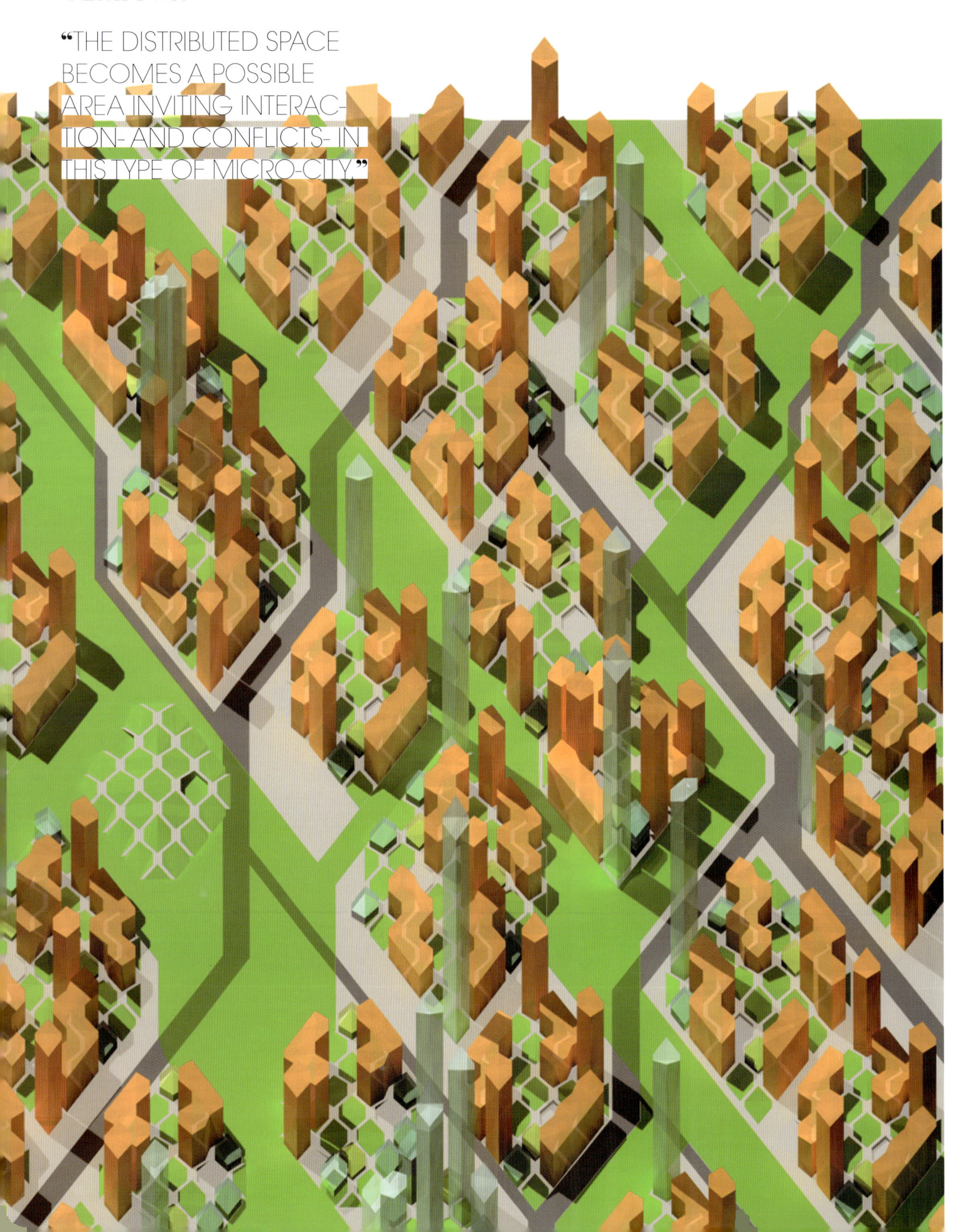

"THE DISTRIBUTED SPACE BECOMES A POSSIBLE AREA INVITING INTERACTION- AND CONFLICTS- IN THIS TYPE OF MICRO-CITY."

Public / green Public / paved Public / cars

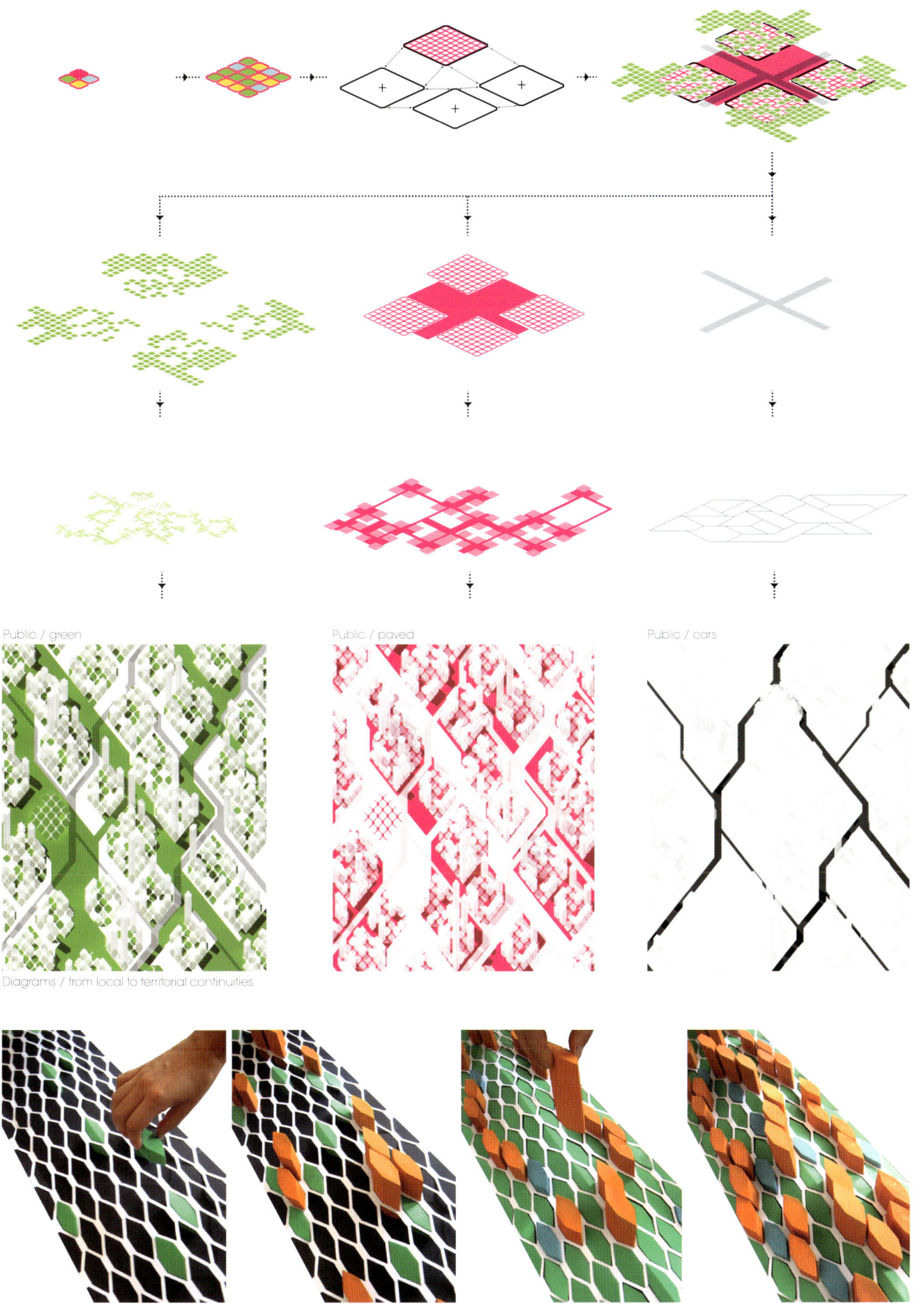

Diagrams / from local to territorial continuities

Study model / the game

ARCHITECTURAL DIAGRAMS 359

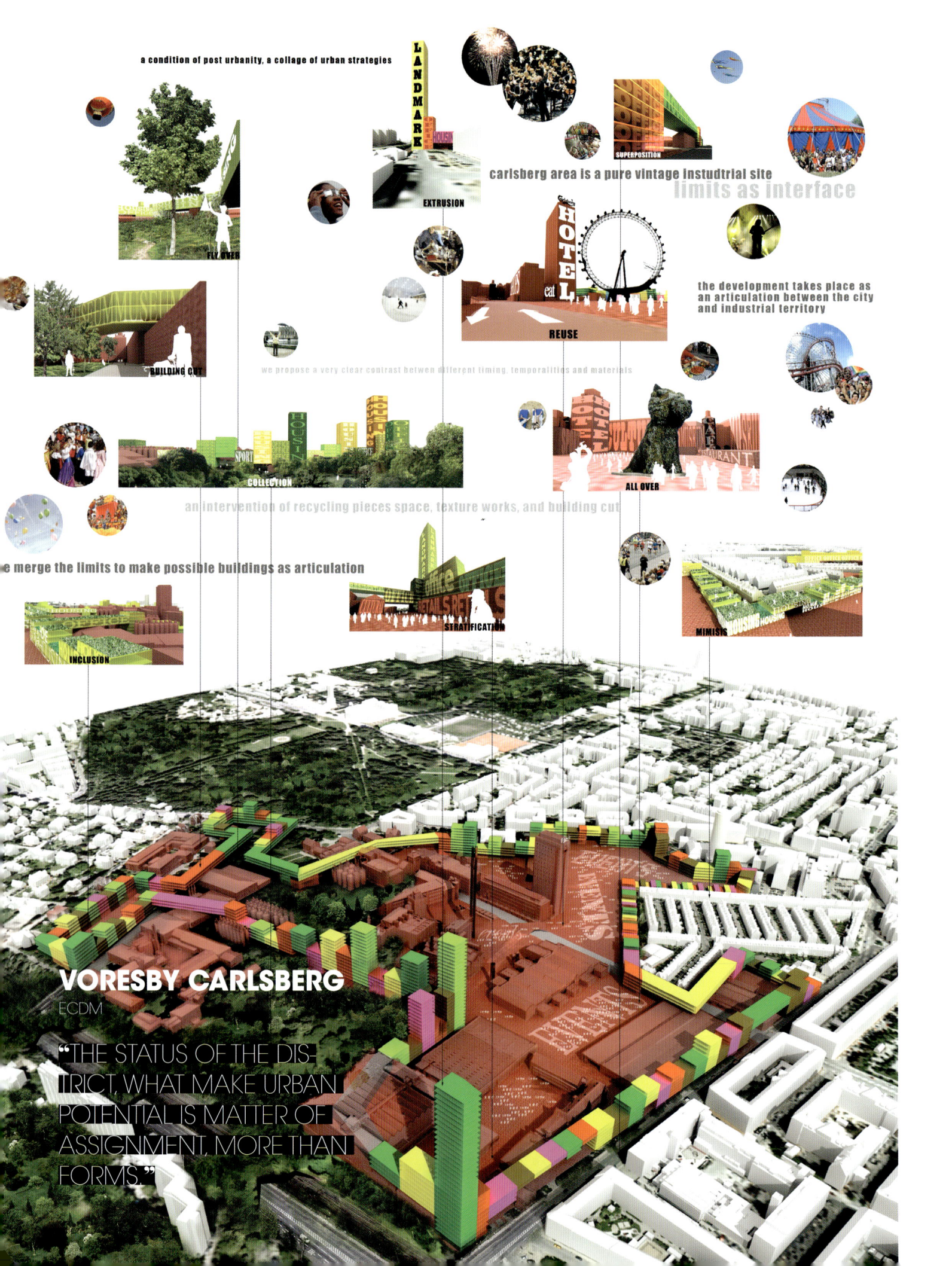

a condition of post urbanity, a collage of urban strategies

LANDMARK
EXTRUSION

SUPERPOSITION

carlsberg area is a pure vintage instudtrial site

limits as interface

FLY OVER

REUSE

the development takes place as an articulation between the city and industrial territory

BUILDING CUT

we propose a very clear contrast between different timing, temporalities and materials

COLLECTION

ALL OVER

an intervention of recycling pieces space, texture works, and building cut

we merge the limits to make possible buildings as articulation

INCLUSION

STRATIFICATION

MIMISIS

VORESBY CARLSBERG
ECDM

"THE STATUS OF THE DISTRICT, WHAT MAKE URBAN POTENTIAL IS MATTER OF ASSIGNMENT, MORE THAN FORMS."

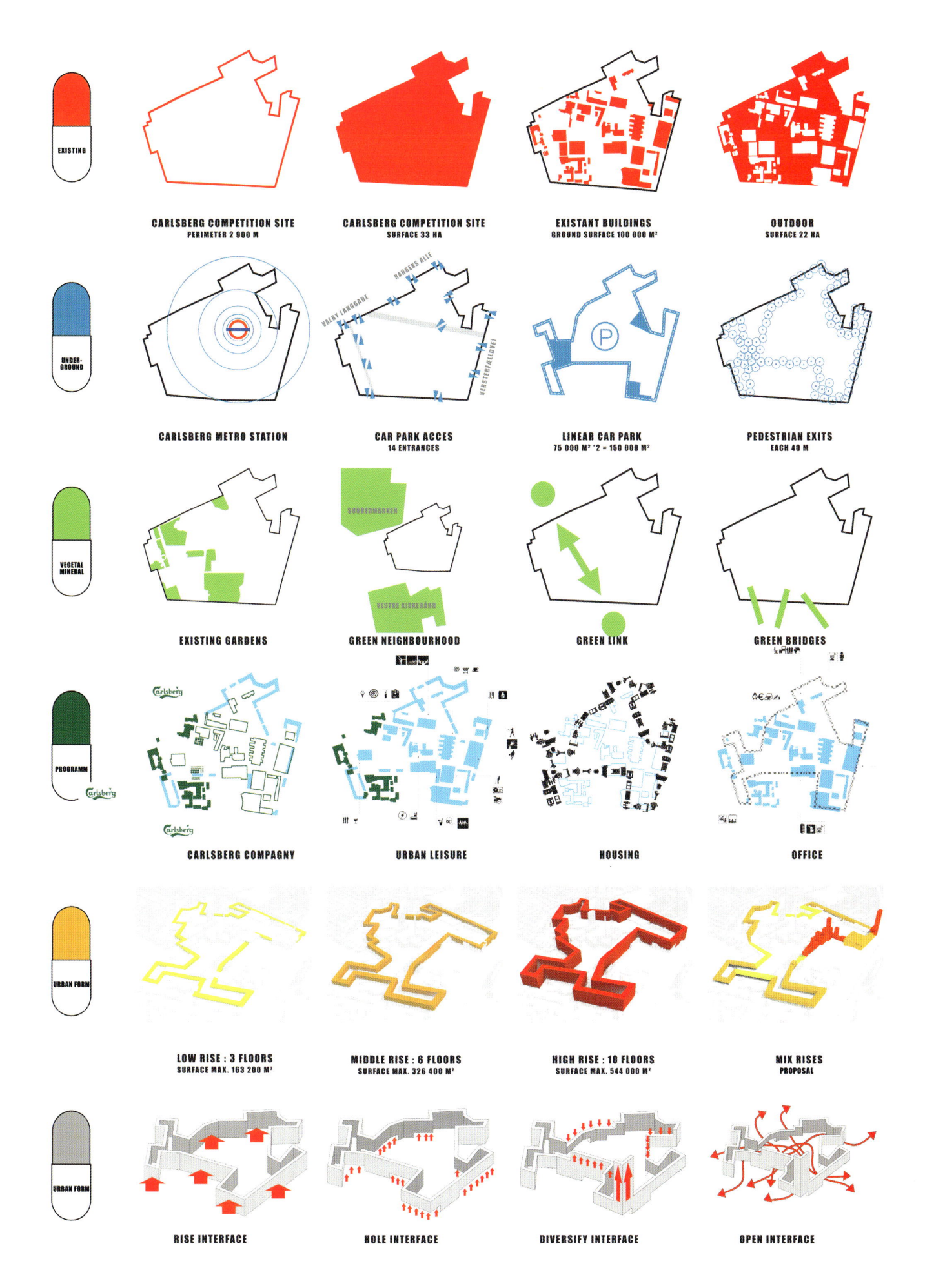

EXISTING				
	CARLSBERG COMPETITION SITE PERIMETER 2 900 M	**CARLSBERG COMPETITION SITE** SURFACE 33 HA	**EXISTANT BUILDINGS** GROUND SURFACE 100 000 M²	**OUTDOOR** SURFACE 22 HA
UNDER-GROUND	**CARLSBERG METRO STATION**	**CAR PARK ACCES** 14 ENTRANCES	**LINEAR CAR PARK** 75 000 M² *2 = 150 000 M²	**PEDESTRIAN EXITS** EACH 40 M
VEGETAL MINERAL	**EXISTING GARDENS**	**GREEN NEIGHBOURHOOD**	**GREEN LINK**	**GREEN BRIDGES**
PROGRAMM	**CARLSBERG COMPAGNY**	**URBAN LEISURE**	**HOUSING**	**OFFICE**
URBAN FORM	**LOW RISE : 3 FLOORS** SURFACE MAX. 163 200 M²	**MIDDLE RISE : 6 FLOORS** SURFACE MAX. 326 400 M²	**HIGH RISE : 10 FLOORS** SURFACE MAX. 544 000 M²	**MIX RISES** PROPOSAL
URBAN FORM	**RISE INTERFACE**	**HOLE INTERFACE**	**DIVERSIFY INTERFACE**	**OPEN INTERFACE**

ARCHITECTURAL DIAGRAMS 361

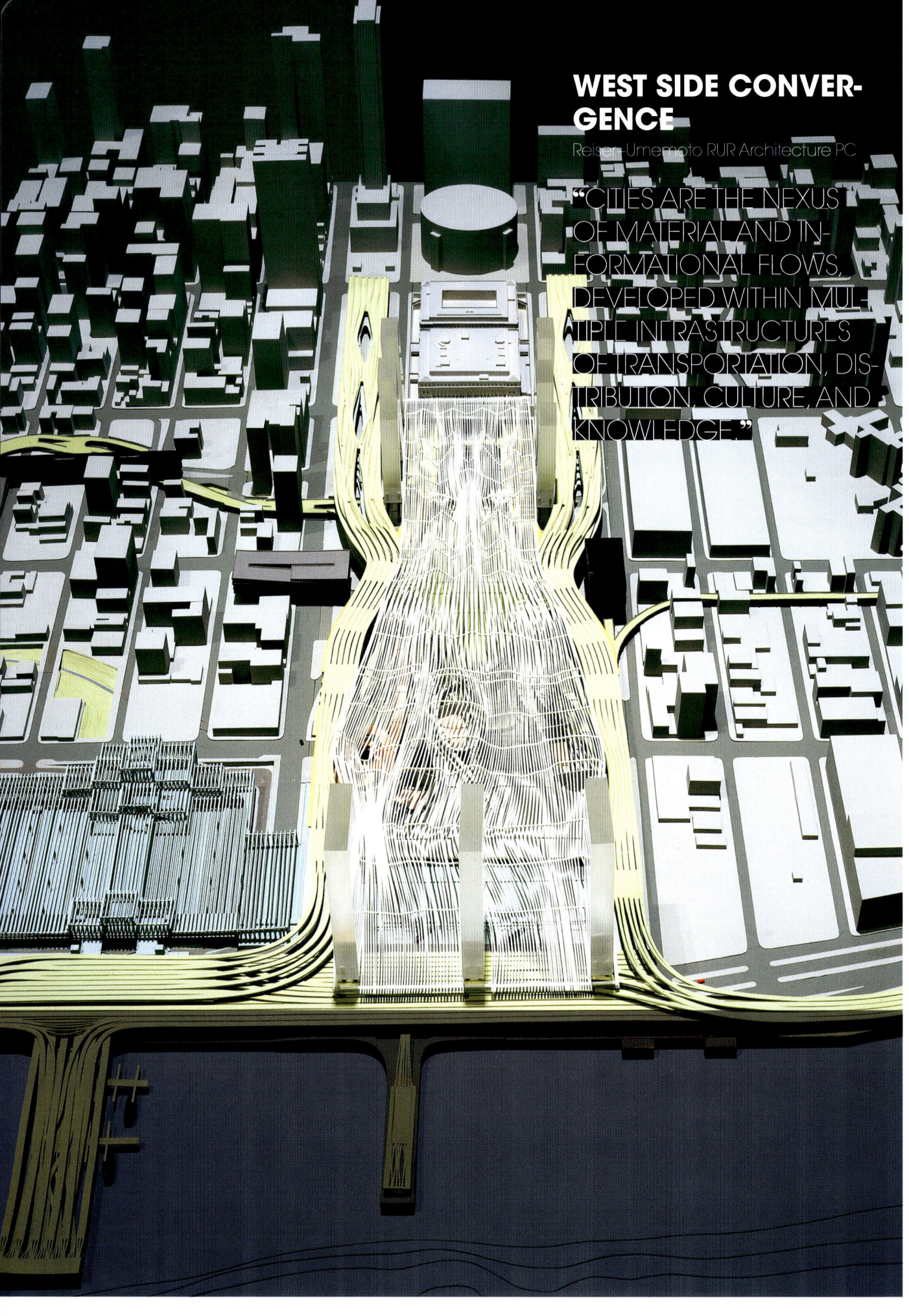

WEST SIDE CONVERGENCE
Reiser+Umemoto RUR Architecture PC

"CITIES ARE THE NEXUS OF MATERIAL AND INFORMATIONAL FLOWS, DEVELOPED WITHIN MULTIPLE INFRASTRUCTURES OF TRANSPORTATION, DISTRIBUTION, CULTURE, AND KNOWLEDGE."

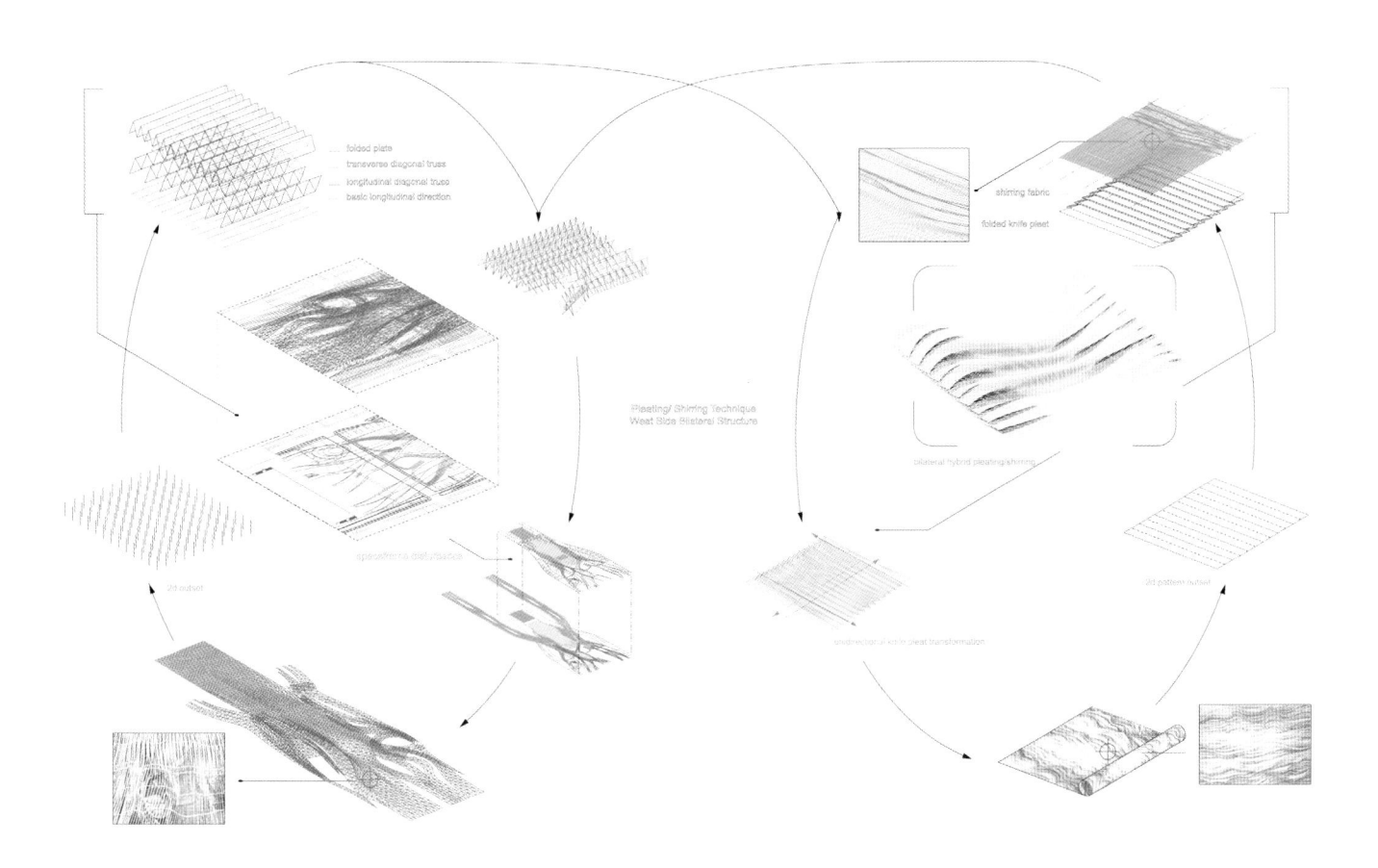

ARCHITECTURAL DIAGRAMS 363

WID

Bernd Kniess Architects Urban Planners

"THE SUBJECT MATTER OF THIS PROJECT IS THE PROBLEMS THAT GO HAND IN HAND WITH THE DESIRE TO OWN A HOUSE IN THE COUNTRY."

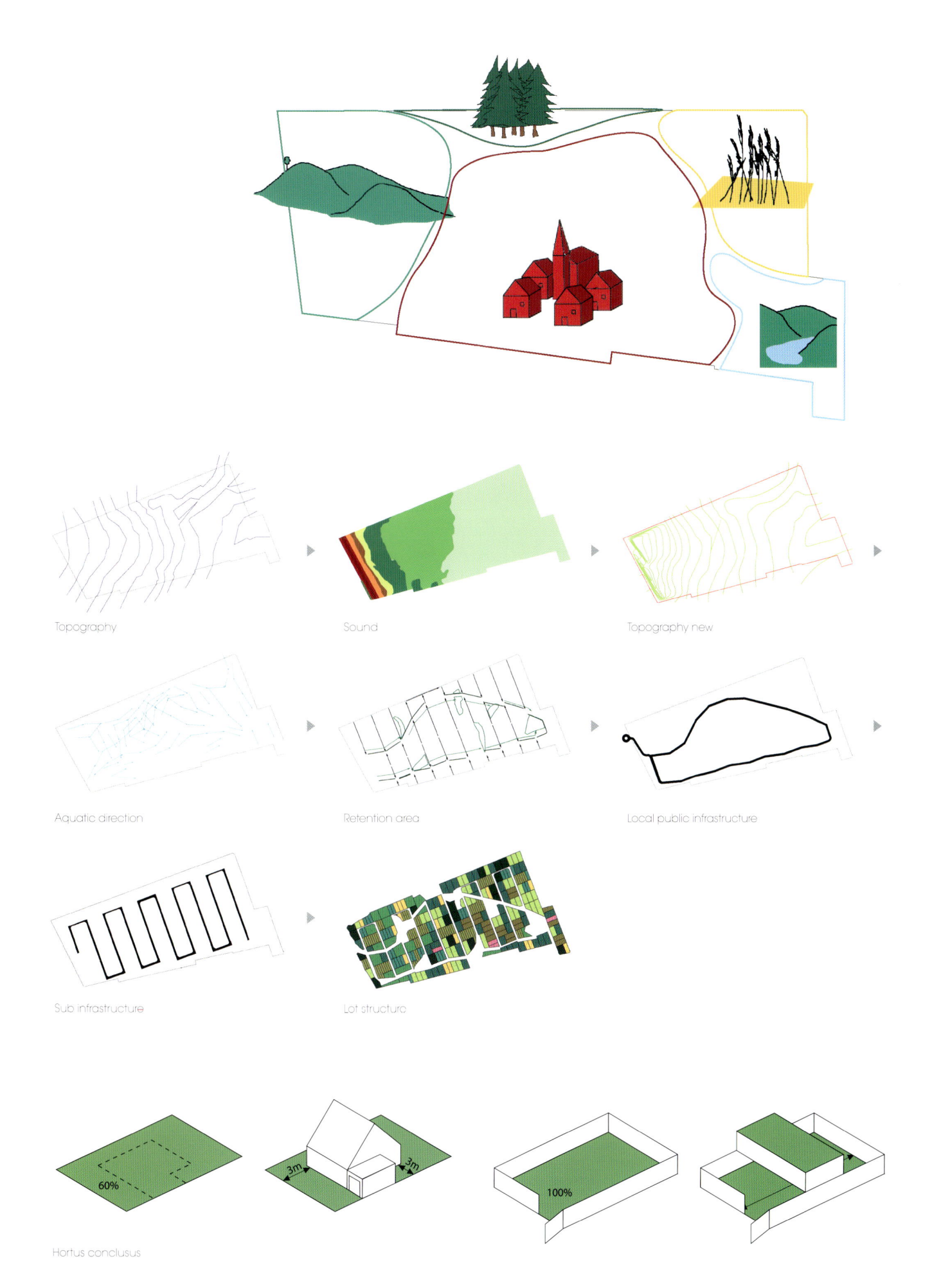

Topography

Sound

Topography new

Aquatic direction

Retention area

Local public infrastructure

Sub infrastructure

Lot structure

Hortus conclusus

ARCHITECTURAL DIAGRAMS 365

WIESENFELD
Florian Krieger

"THE ARCHITECTONIC STRUCTURE IS A HYBRID OF CLASSIC URBAN BLOCK, PUNCTUAL BUILDING AND SLAB-STRUCTURE."

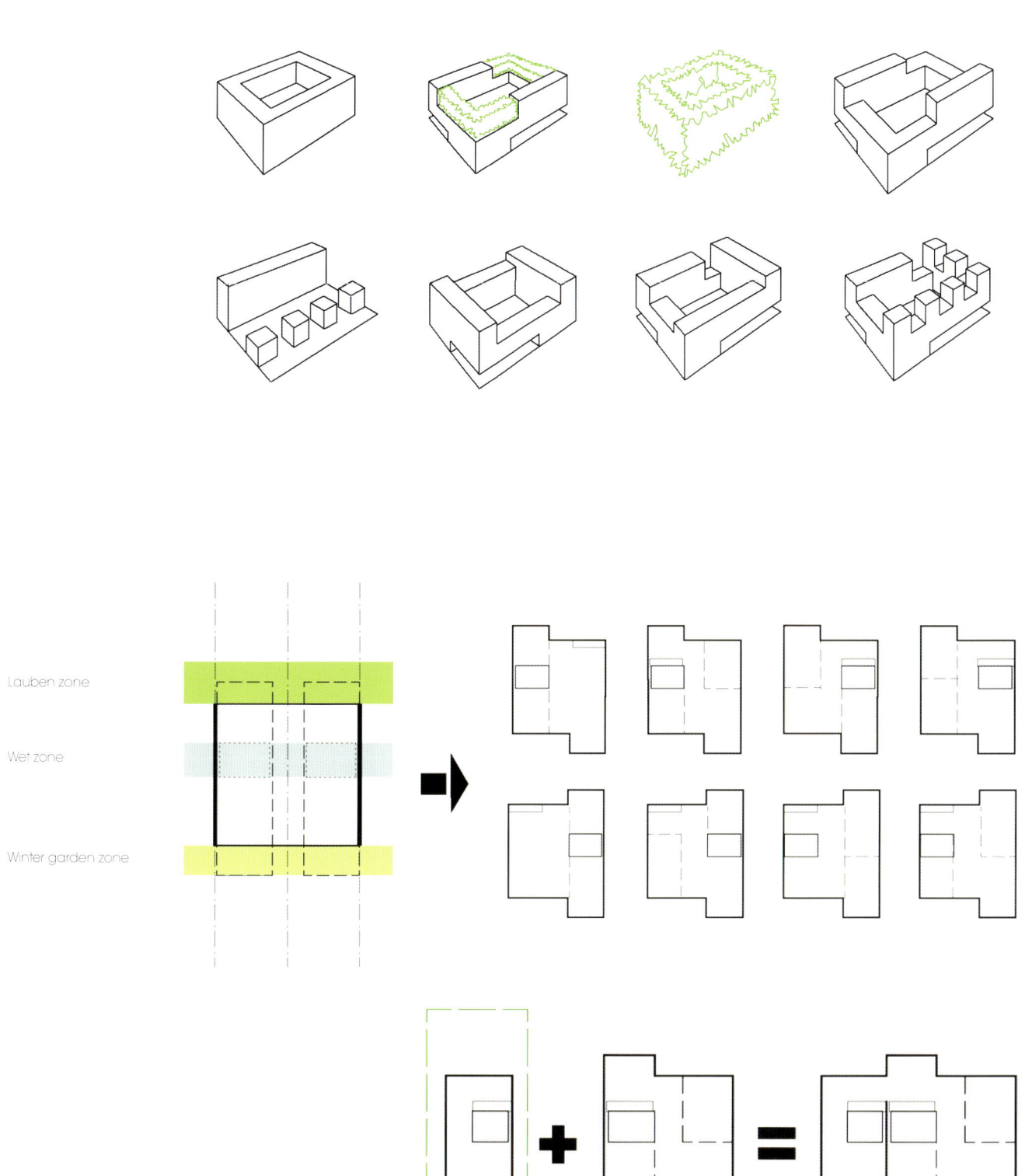

Lauben zone

Wet zone

Winter garden zone

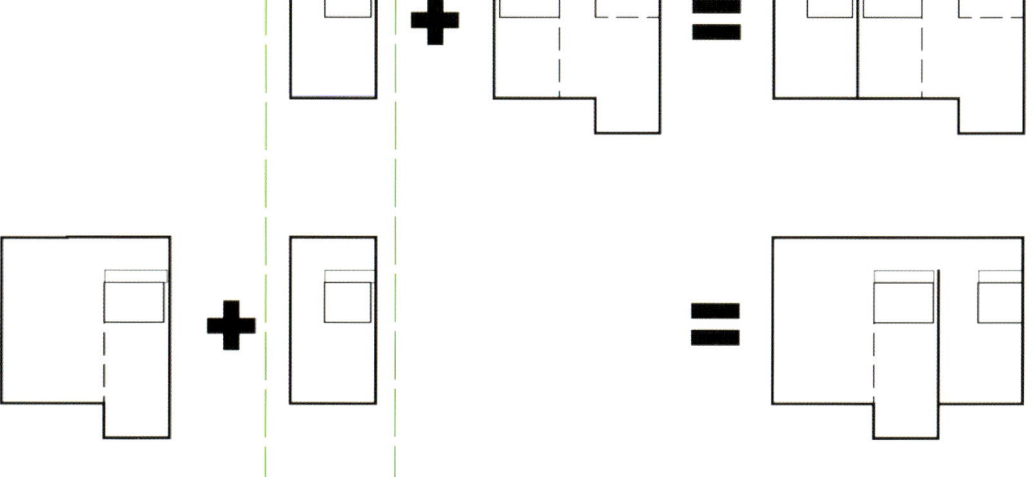

ARCHITECTURAL DIAGRAMS 367

WORLD VILLAGE OF WOMEN SPORTS

"THE STREETS ANIMATED BY PUBLICLY ORIENTED FUNCTIONS FOR EDUCATION, NEWS, CULTURE AND COMMERCE RESEMBLE THE FUNCTIONAL DIVERSITY OF A MEDIEVAL DOWNTOWN."

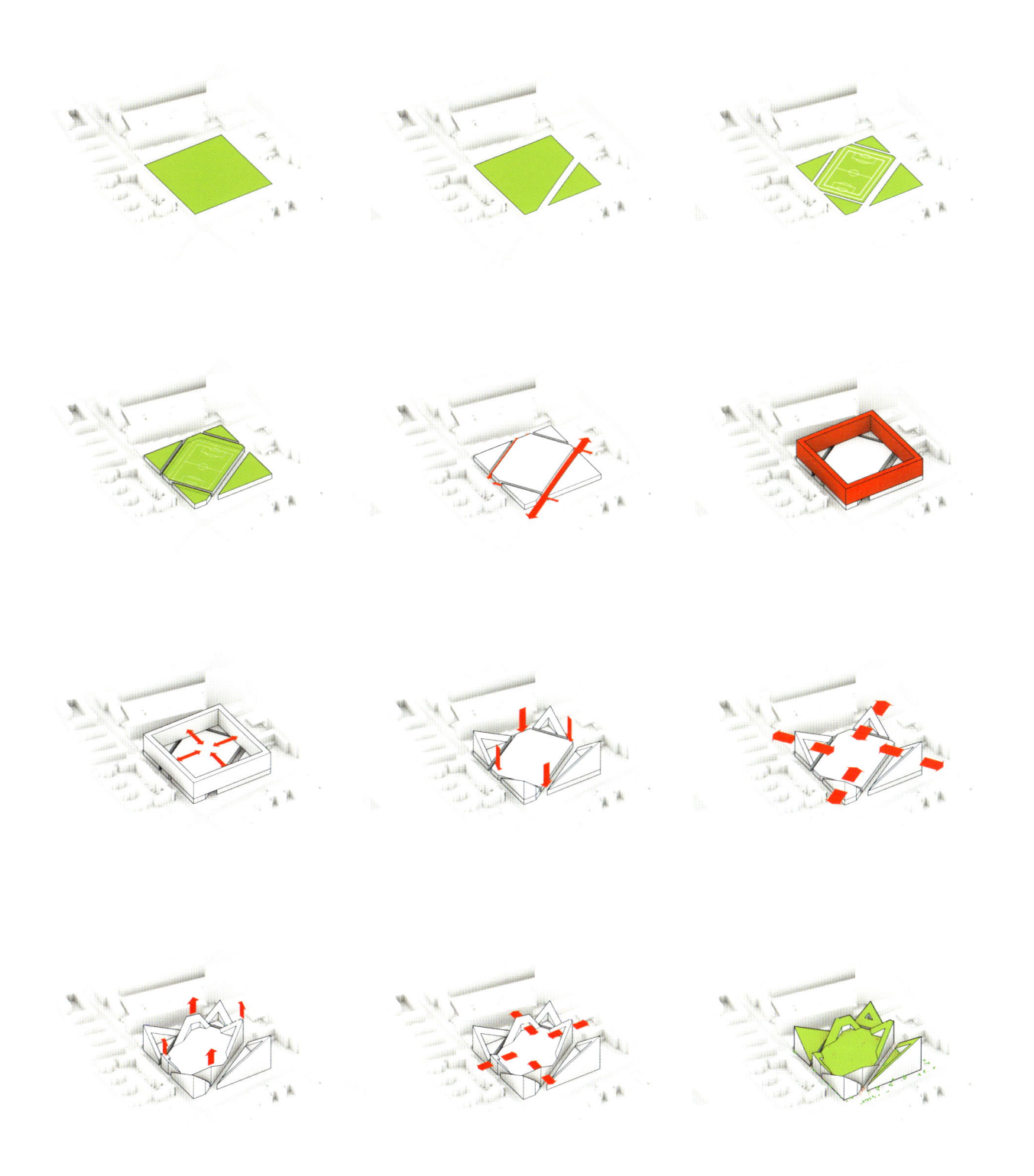

ARCHITECTURAL DIAGRAMS 369

XERITOWN
SMAQ and X Architects

"THE DEVELOPMENT APPEARS AS DUNESCAPE WHERE THE URBAN ISLANDS COULD BE INTERPRETED AS A CONSOLIDATION OF THE DESERT DUNES."

Concept sketch

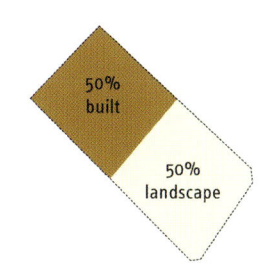

Giving shade
compact urban form

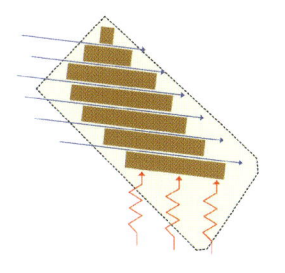

Ventilation by cool winds
built cut into strips for cool wind
channelling

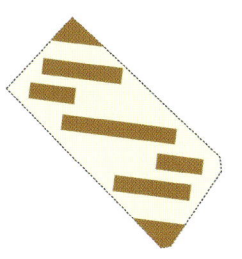

Benefiting from existing humidity
strips positioned to preserve existing
water

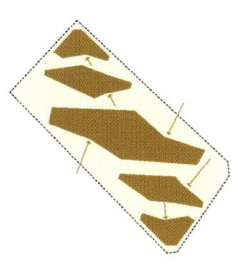

Integraton in the dunescape
strips shaped to recall a
dunescape

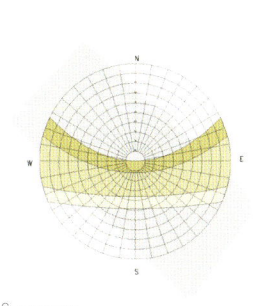

Sun map
Concept diagrams

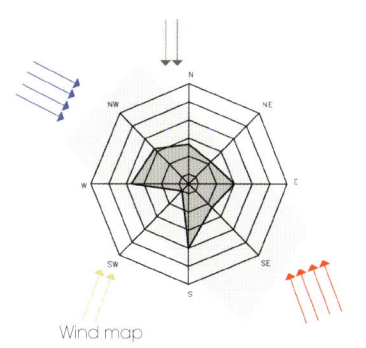

Wind map

Humidity map

Dune map

ARCHITECTURAL DIAGRAMS 371

ZAKUSALA SPACEGROUP

"ZAKUSALA OFFERS THE POSSIBILITY TO START FROM SCRATCH AND TO CREATE A NEW TYPE OF WATERFRONT DEVELOPMENT."

Location aspect

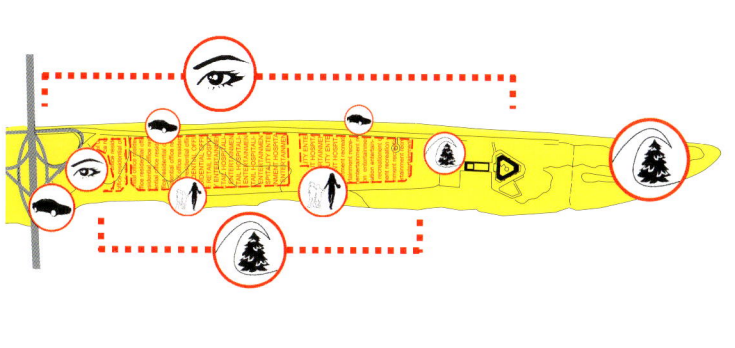

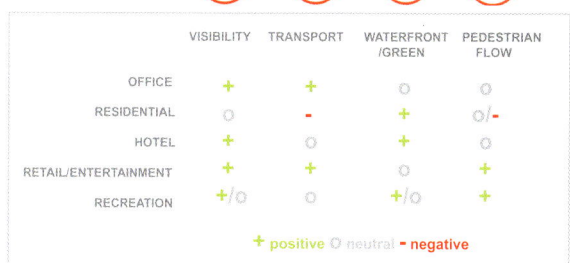

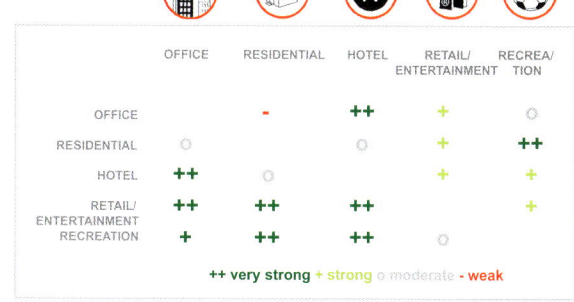

	VISIBILITY	TRANSPORT	WATERFRONT /GREEN	PEDESTRIAN FLOW
OFFICE	+	+	o	o
RESIDENTIAL	o	-	+	o/-
HOTEL	+	o	+	o
RETAIL/ENTERTAINMENT	+	+	o	+
RECREATION	+/o	o	+/o	+

+ positive   o neutral   - negative

Functional zoning

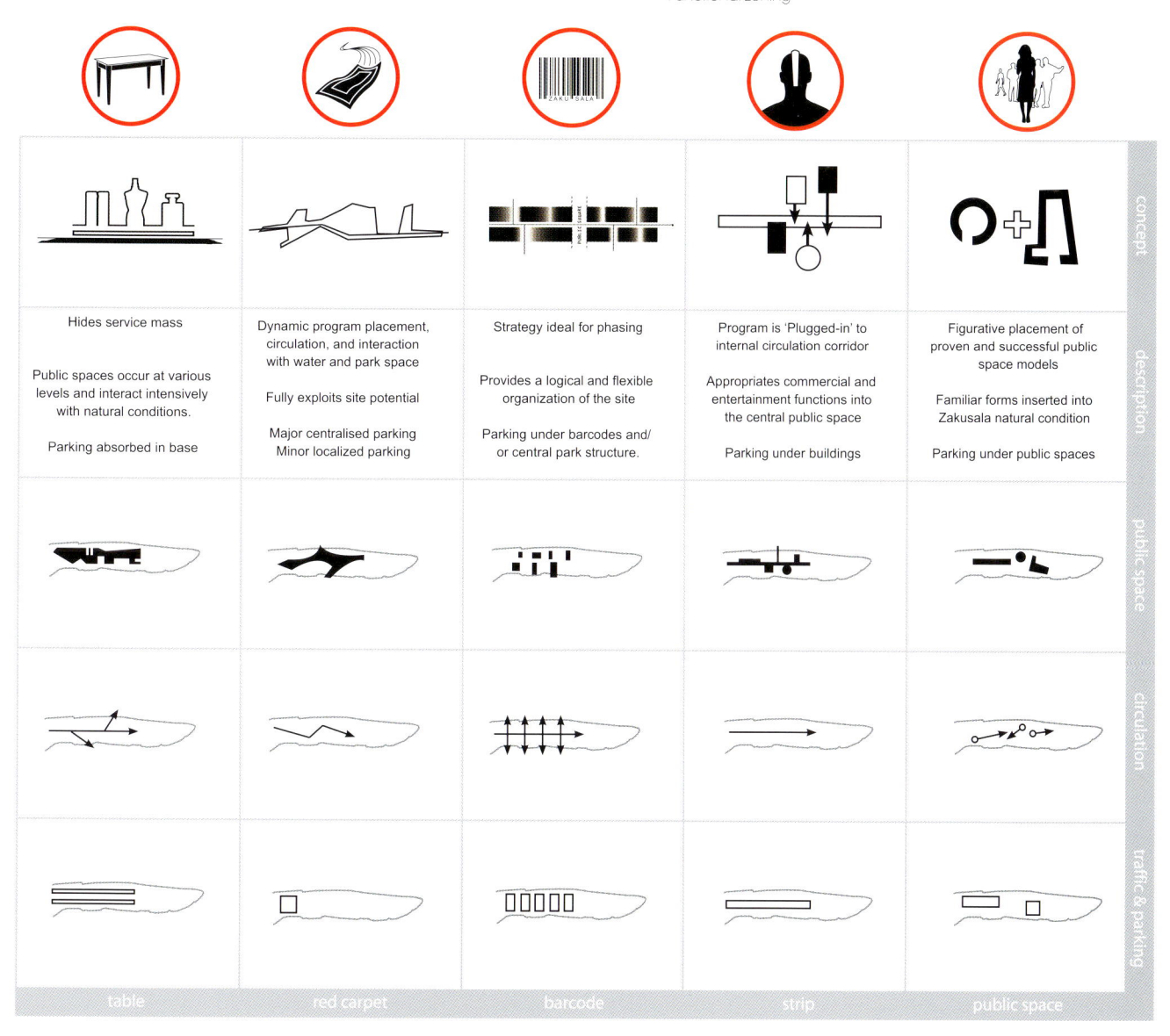

	OFFICE	RESIDENTIAL	HOTEL	RETAIL/ ENTERTAINMENT	RECREATION
OFFICE		-	++	+	o
RESIDENTIAL	o		o	+	++
HOTEL	++	o		++	+
RETAIL/ ENTERTAINMENT	++	++	++		+
RECREATION	+	++	++	o	

++ very strong   + strong   o moderate   - weak

Concept matrix

---

table
Concept description: Hides service mass

Public spaces occur at various levels and interact intensively with natural conditions.

Parking absorbed in base

red carpet
Dynamic program placement, circulation, and interaction with water and park space

Fully exploits site potential

Major centralised parking
Minor localized parking

barcode
Strategy ideal for phasing

Provides a logical and flexible organization of the site

Parking under barcodes and/ or central park structure.

strip
Program is 'Plugged-in' to internal circulation corridor

Appropriates commercial and entertainment functions into the central public space

Parking under buildings

public space
Figurative placement of proven and successful public space models

Familiar forms inserted into Zakusala natural condition

Parking under public spaces

ARCHITECTURAL DIAGRAMS 373

ZIRA ISLAND MASTERPLAN BIG

"THE MOUNTAINS FORM AN ORGANIC SKYLINE MERGING WITH THE NATURAL TOPOGRAPHY OF THE ISLAND."

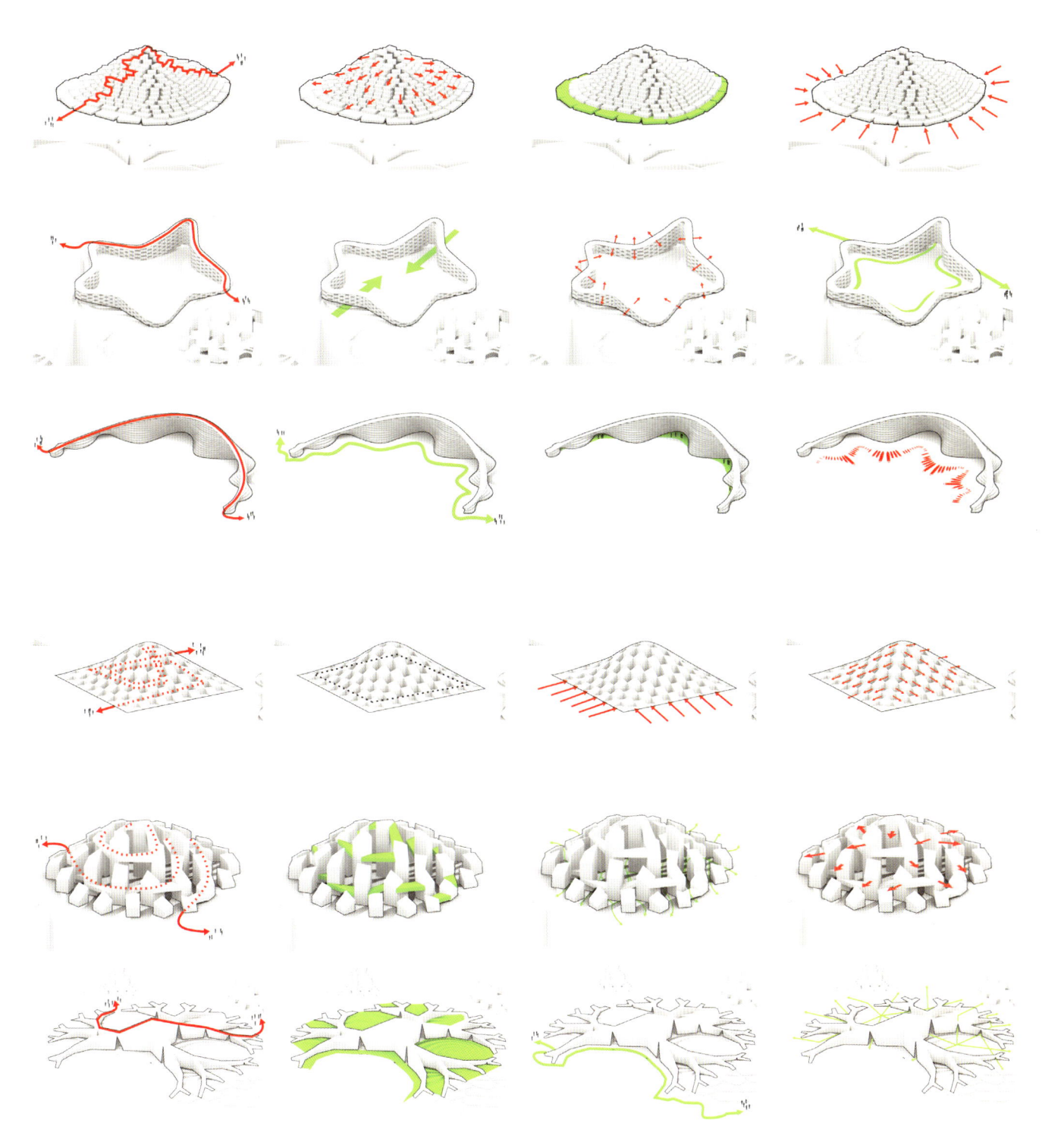

Mountain concepts

ARCHITECTURAL DIAGRAMS 375

ZOETERMEER AFRI-KAWEG ONE ARCHITECTURE

"THE ZIGZAG SHAPE, WITH ALMOST STALINIST LAWNS IN FRONT, ALLOWS FOR THE GREATEST NUMBER OF OFFICES TO BE VISIBLE FROM THE MAIN ROAD."

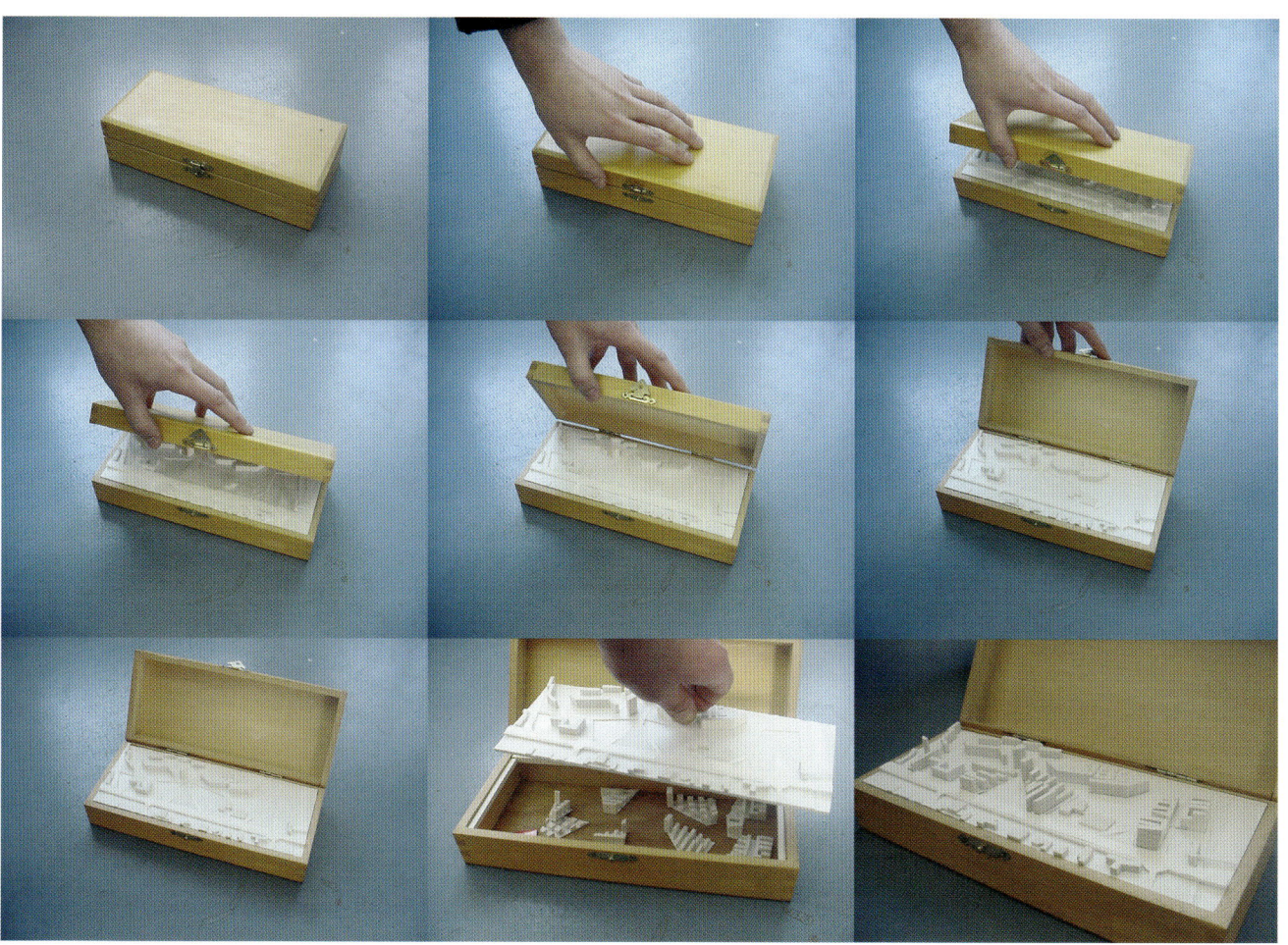

Model showing the development options

Diagram current situation: single plots separated by socialist green, reached via a back road

Diagram showing normal intensification

Diagram showing proposal to have as much front towards the main road as possible

Diagram showing possibility to connect the different areas and to make green zones

ARCHITECTURAL DIAGRAMS 377

3X2 - ELEMENTS FOR THE URBAN LANDSCAPE
Florian Krieger

"THE PROPOSAL IS BASED ON A CATALOGUE OF RULES AND PRINCIPLES OF SPATIAL ORGANISATION."

Villenblock

Density scenarios

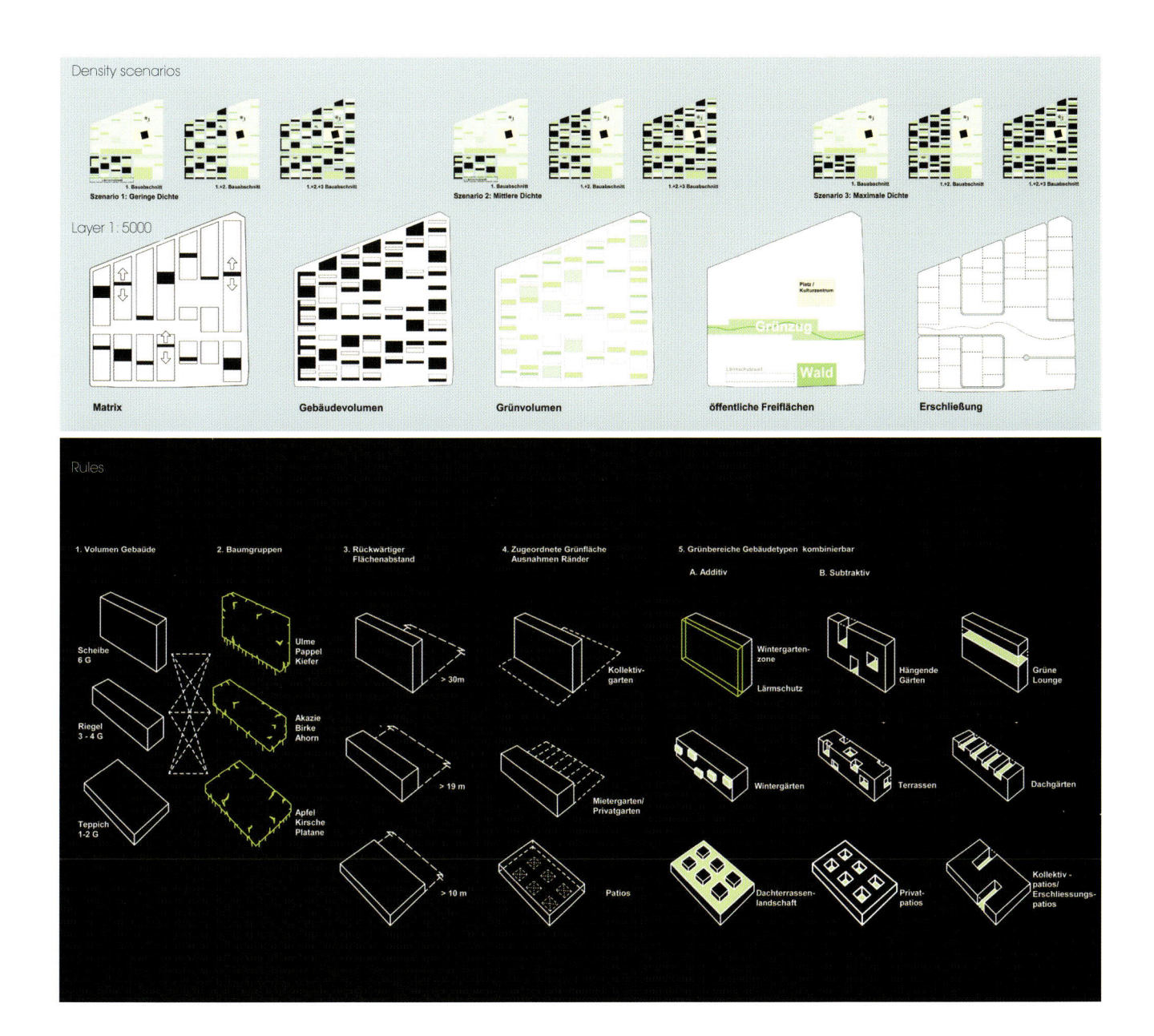

Szenario 1: Geringe Dichte
- 1. Bauabschnitt
- 1.+2. Bauabschnitt
- 1.+2.+3 Bauabschnitt

Szenario 2: Mittlere Dichte
- 1. Bauabschnitt
- 1.+2. Bauabschnitt
- 1.+2.+3 Bauabschnitt

Szenario 3: Maximale Dichte
- 1. Bauabschnitt
- 1.+2. Bauabschnitt
- 1.+2.+3 Bauabschnitt

Layer 1 : 5000

Matrix | Gebäudevolumen | Grünvolumen | öffentliche Freiflächen | Erschließung

Platz / Kulturzentrum — Grünzug — Lärmschutzwall — Wald

Rules

1. Volumen Gebäude
- Scheibe 6 G
- Riegel 3 - 4 G
- Teppich 1-2 G

2. Baumgruppen
- Ulme, Pappel, Kiefer
- Akazie, Birke, Ahorn
- Apfel, Kirsche, Platane

3. Rückwärtiger Flächenabstand
- > 30 m
- > 19 m
- > 10 m

4. Zugeordnete Grünfläche Ausnahmen Ränder
- Kollektivgarten
- Mietergarten/Privatgarten
- Patios

5. Grünbereiche Gebäudetypen kombinierbar

A. Additiv
- Wintergartenzone / Lärmschutz
- Wintergärten
- Dachterrassenlandschaft

B. Subtraktiv
- Hängende Gärten
- Terrassen
- Privatpatios

- Grüne Lounge
- Dachgärten
- Kollektivpatios/ Erschliessungspatios

ARCHITECTURAL DIAGRAMS 379

16 DWELLINGS CHER-LEVILLE-MÉZIÈRES

mxg architects

380 URBAN DESIGN

ARCHITECTURAL DIAGRAMS 381

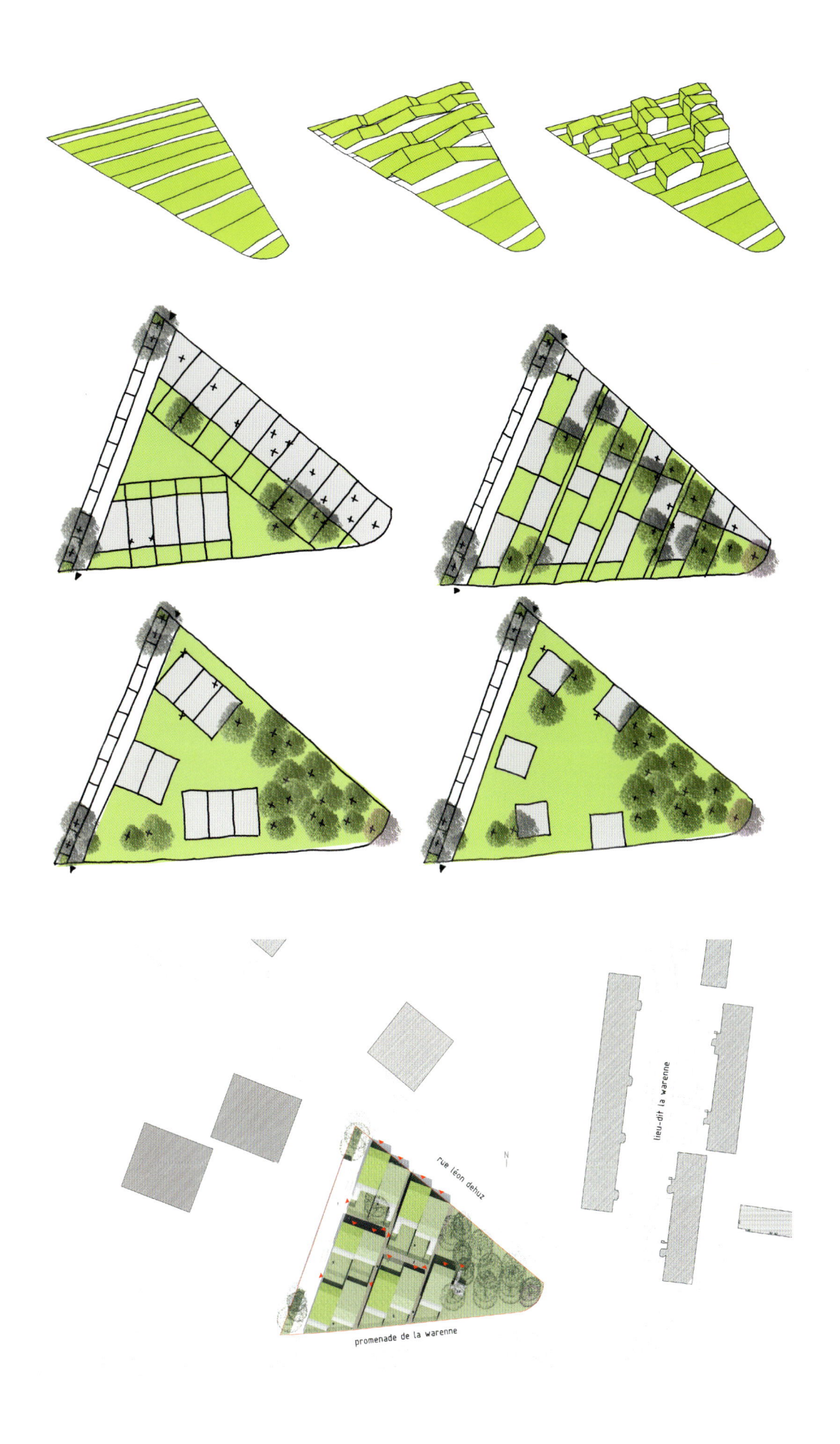

288 DWELLINGS
mxg architects

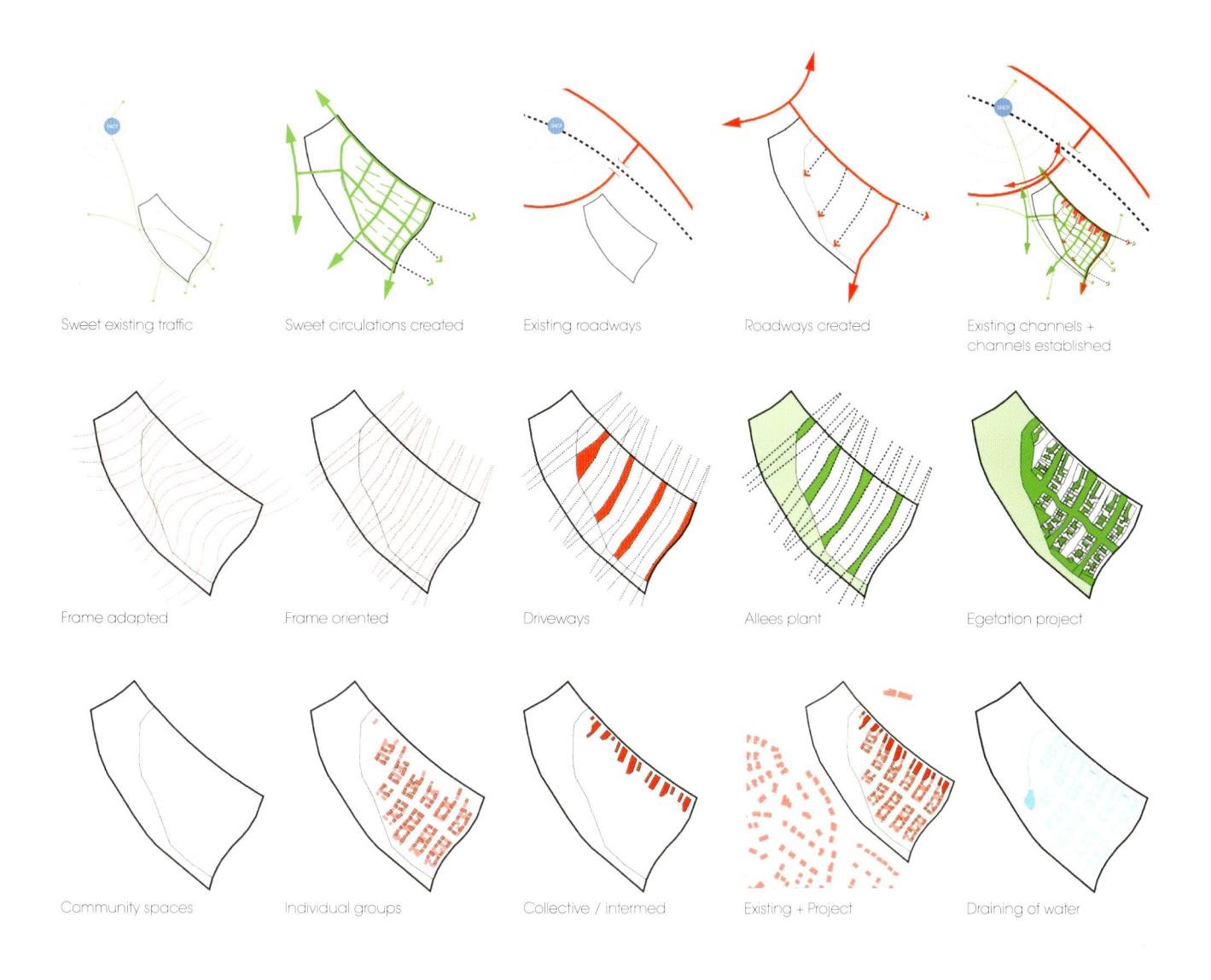

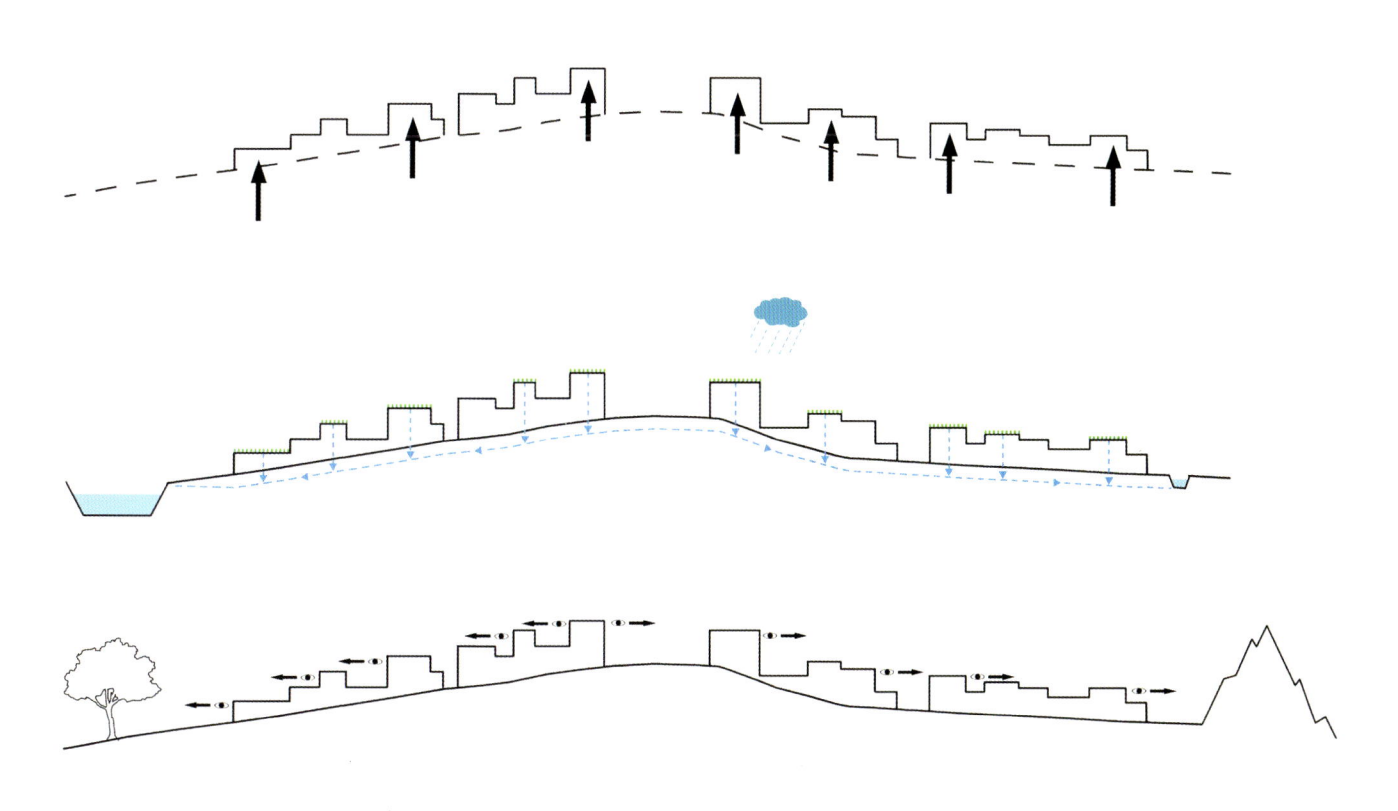

Sweet existing traffic	Sweet circulations created	Existing roadways	Roadways created	Existing channels + channels established
Frame adapted	Frame oriented	Driveways	Allees plant	Egetation project
Community spaces	Individual groups	Collective / intermed	Existing + Project	Draining of water

ARCHITECTURAL DIAGRAMS 383

TO BE CONTINUED